Kristi,

with lots of love

and hugs,

Mummy

Christmas 1990.

The Children's Treasury of Verse

Edited by Eleanor Doan
Illustrated by Nancy Munger
Colour adaptation by George Chrichard

TREASURE PRESS

First published in Great Britain in 1980 by
Hodder & Stoughton under the title
A Child's Treasury of Verse

This edition with colour illustrations first published
in Great Britain in 1981 by Hodder & Stoughton Children's Books

This edition published in 1986 by
Treasure Press
59 Grosvenor Street
London W1

Copyright © 1977 by The Zondervan Corporation, Grand Rapids, Michigan.

ISBN 1 85051 153 5

Printed in Czechoslovakia
50634

The Children's Treasury of Verse

Contents

DEAR YOUNG FRIENDS:

This book has been prepared just for you. It will make your life happier and more meaningful as you grow up. Each selection has been chosen with you in mind — your interests, your sense of rhythm, your growth and development, your imagination, and your love of fun.

This book spans the years of your childhood. Each year it will interest you in a new way as you read it again and again. As you do, you will

> enjoy adventure,
> develop character and Christian graces,
> laugh,
> think about happy times,
> gain wisdom,
> become a better person,
> and
> respond to God's love.

All the selections in this book are favorites of my many young friends across the land, and I am sure they will become your favorites too. I wish you many happy hours of enjoyment.

Your friend,
ELEANOR DOAN

Adventure

There's a place I've dreamed about
    far away
Where a tropical town crowds down
    to a bay
Busy with noise on a blowy day.

A warm mysterious coffee smell
Drifts on the air, and a singing bell
Dins and hums on a windy swell.

I've voyaged over the seven seas
In a ship that scuds before a breeze
That sounds almost like leafy trees.

When the morning is wide and
    windy and warm,
I watch that town from the tall
    yardarm
Of a poplar tree on my uncle's farm.

(Adventure)
Harry Behn

Sea-Fever

I must go down to the seas again, to
    the lonely sea and the sky,
And all I ask is a tall ship and a star to
    steer her by,
And the wheel's kick and the wind's
    song and the white sail's
    shaking
And a gray mist on the sea's face and
    a gray dawn breaking.

I must go down to the seas again, for
    the call of the running tide
Is a wild call and a clear call that may
    not be denied;
And all I ask is a windy day with the
    white clouds flying,
And the flung spray and the blown
    spume and the sea-gulls crying.

I must go down to the seas again, to
    the vagrant gypsy life,
To the gull's way and the whale's
    way where the wind's like a
    whetted knife;
And all I ask is a merry yarn from a
    laughing fellow-rover,
And quiet sleep and a sweet dream
    when the long trick's over.

John Masefield

Not of the sunlight,
Not of the moonlight,
Not of the starlight!
O young Mariner,
Down to the haven,
Call your companions,
Launch your vessel,
And crowd your canvas,
And, ere it vanishes
Over the margin,
After it, follow it,
Follow The Gleam.

Alfred Lord Tennyson
(from Merlin and the
Gleam (IX)

Travel

I should like to rise and go
Where the golden apples grow; —
Where below another sky
Parrot islands anchored lie,
And, watched by cockatoos and
    goats,
Lonely Crusoes building boats; —
Where in sunshine reaching out
Eastern cities, miles about,
Are with mosque and minaret
Among sandy gardens set,
And the rich goods from near and far
Hang for sale in the bazaar; —
Where the Great Wall round China
    goes,
And on one side the desert blows,
And with bell and voice and drum,
Cities on the other hum; —
Where are forests, hot as fire,
Wide as England, tall as a spire,
Full of apes and cocoa-nuts
And the Negro hunters' huts; —
Where the knotty crocodile
Lies and blinks in the Nile,
And the red flamingo flies
Hunting fish before his eyes; —
Where in jungles, near and far,
Man-devouring tigers are,
Lying close and giving ear
Lest the hunt be drawing near,
Or a comer-by be seen
Swinging in a palanquin; —
Where among the desert sands
Some deserted city stands,
All its children, sweep and prince,
Grown to manhood ages since,
Not a foot in street or house,
Not a stir of child or mouse,
And when kindly falls the night,
In all the town no spark of light.
There I'll come when I'm a man
With a camel caravan;
Light a fire in the gloom
Of some dusty dining-room;
See the pictures on the walls,
Heroes, fights, and festivals;
And in a corner find the toys
Of the old Egyptian boys.

Robert Louis Stevenson

Which Is the Way to Somewhere Town?

Which is the way to Somewhere
Town?
Oh, up in the morning early;
Over the tiles and the chimney pots,
That is the way, quite clearly.

And which is the door to
Somewhere Town?
Oh, up in the morning early;
The round red sun is the door to go
through,
That is the way, quite clearly.

Kate Greenaway

Pussy Cat, Pussy Cat

"Pussy cat, Pussy cat,
Where have you been?"
"I've been to London
To look at the Queen."

"Pussy cat, Pussy cat,
What did you there?"
"I frightened a little mouse
Under a chair."

Christina Rossetti

The Wreck of the Hesperus

It was the schooner Hesperus,
    That sailed the wintry sea;
And the skipper had taken his little
    daughter,
    To bear him company.

Blue were her eyes, as the fairy-flax,
    Her cheeks like the dawn of day,
And her bosom white as the
        hawthorn buds,
    That ope in the month of May.

The skipper he stood beside the
    helm,
    His pipe was in his mouth;
And he watched how the veering
    flaw did blow
    The smoke now West, now South.

Then up spake an old Sailor,
    Had sailed to the Spanish Main:
"I pray thee, put into yonder port,
    For I fear a hurricane.

"Last night, the moon had a golden
    ring,
    And tonight no moon we see!"
The skipper, he blew a whiff from
    his pipe,
    And a scornful laugh laughed he.

Colder and louder blew the wind,
    A gale from the Northeast;
The snow fell hissing in the brine,
    And the billows frothed like yeast.

11

Down came the storm, and smote
  amain
  The vessel in its strength;
She shuddered and paused, like a
  frightened steed,
  Then leaped her cable's length.

"Come hither! come hither! my little
  daughter,
  And do not tremble so;
For I can weather the roughest gale,
  That ever wind did blow."

He wrapped her warm in his
  seaman's coat,
  Against the stinging blast;
He cut a rope from a broken spar
  And bound her to the mast.

"O father! I hear the church-bells
  ring,
  O say, what may it be?"
"'Tis a fog-bell on a rock-bound
  coast!" —
  And he steered for the open sea.

"O father! I hear the sound of guns,
  O say, what may it be?"
"Some ship in distress, that cannot
  live
  In such an angry sea!"

"O father! I see a gleaming light,
  O say, what may it be?"
But the father answered never a
  word,
  A frozen corpse was he.

Lashed to the helm, all stiff and
  stark,
  With his face turned to the skies,
The lantern gleamed through the
  gleaming snow
  On his fixed and glassy eyes.

Then the maiden clasped her hands
  and prayed
  That saved she might be;
And she thought of Christ, who
  stilled the waves,
  On the Lake of Galilee.

And fast through the midnight dark
  and drear,
  Through the whistling sleet and
  snow,
Like a sheeted ghost, the vessel
  swept
  Towards the reef of Norman's
  Woe.

And ever the fitful gusts between
  A sound came from the land;
It was the sound of the trampling
  surf,
  On the rocks and the hard
  sea-sand.

The breakers were right beneath her
  bows,
  She drifted a dreary wreck,
And a whooping billow swept the
  crew
  Like icicles from her deck.

She struck where the white and
  fleecy waves
  Looked soft as carded wool,
But the cruel rocks, they gored her
  side
  Like the horns of an angry bull.

Her rattling shrouds, all sheathed in
  ice,
  With the masts went by the board;
Like a vessel of glass, she stove and
  sank,
  Ho! ho! the breakers roared!

At daybreak, on the bleak
  sea beach,
  A fisherman stood aghast,
To see the form of a maiden fair,
  Lashed close to a drifting mast.

The salt sea was frozen on her breast,
  The salt tears in her eyes;
And he saw her hair, like the brown
  seaweed,
  On the billows fall and rise.

Such was the wreck of the Hesperus,
  In the midnight and the snow!
Christ save us all from a death like
  this,
  On the reef of Norman's Woe!

Henry Wadsworth Longfellow

Grandpa Dropped His Glasses

Grandpa dropped his glasses once
In a pot of dye,
And when he put them on again
He saw a purple sky.
Purple fires were rising up
From a purple hill,
Men were grinding purple cider
At a purple mill.
Purple Adeline was playing
With a purple doll;
Little purple dragonflies
Were crawling up the wall.
And at the supper-table
He got a crazy loon
From eating purple apple dumplings
With a purple spoon.

Leroy F. Jackson

The Little Turtle

There was a little turtle,
He lived in a box,
He swam in a puddle,
He climbed on the rocks.

He snapped at a mosquito.
He snapped at a flea.
He snapped at a minnow,
And he snapped at me.

He caught the mosquito.
He caught the flea.
He caught the minnow,
But he didn't catch me.

Vachel Lindsay

The Leak in the Dike

The good dame looked from her
    cottage
  At the close of the pleasant day,
And cheerily called to her little son
  Outside the door at play:
"Come, Peter! Come! I want you to
    go,
  While there is light to see,
To the hut of the blind old man who
    lives
  Across the dike, for me;
And take these cakes I made for
    him —
  They are hot and smoking yet;
You have time enough to go and
    come
  Before the sun is set."

Then the good wife turned to her
    labor,
  Humming a simple song,
And thought of her husband
    working hard
  At the sluices all day long;
And set the turf a-blazing,
  And brought the coarse black
    bread:
That he might find a fire at night,
  And find the table spread.

And Peter left the brother,
  With whom all day he had played,
And the sister who had watched
    their sports
  In the willow's tender shade;
And told them they'd see him back
    before
  They saw a star in sight,
Though he wouldn't be afraid to go
  In the very darkest night!
For he was a brave, bright fellow,
  With eye and conscience clear;
He could do whatever a boy might
    do,
  And he had not learned to fear.
Why, he wouldn't have robbed a
    bird's nest
  Nor brought a stork to harm,
Though never a law in Holland
  Had stood to stay his arm!

And now with his face all glowing,
  And eyes as bright as the day
With the thoughts of his pleasant
    errand,
  He trudged along the way;
And soon his joyous prattle
  Made glad a lonesome place —
Alas! if only the blind old man
  Could have seen that happy face!
Yet he somehow caught the
    brightness
  Which his voice and presence lent
And he felt the sunshine come and
    go
  As Peter came and went.

And now, as the day was sinking,
  And the winds began to rise,
The mother looked from her door
    again,
  Shading her anxious eyes,
And saw the shadows deepen
  And birds to their home come
    back,
But never a sign of Peter
  Along the level track.
But she said: "He will come at
    morning,
  So I need not fret or grieve —
Though it isn't like my boy at all
  To stay without my leave."

But where was the child delaying?
  On the homeward way was he,
And across the dike while the sun
    was up
  An hour above the sea.
He was stopping to gather flowers,
  Now listening to the sound,
As the angry waters dashed
    themselves
  Against their narrow bound.
"Ah! well for us," said Peter,
  "That the gates are good and
    strong,
And my father tends them carefully,
  Or they would not hold you long!
You're a wicked sea," said Peter;
  "I know why you fret and chafe;
You would like to spoil our lands
    and homes;

But our sluices keep you safe."
But hark! through the noise
    of waters
Comes a low, clear, trickling
    sound;
And the child's face pales with
    terror,
  And his blossoms drop to the
    ground.
He is up the bank in a moment,
  And, stealing through the sand,
He sees a stream not yet so large
  As his slender, childish hand.

"Tis a leak in the dike!" — He is but a
    boy,
  Unused to fearful scenes;
But, young as he is, he has learned to
    know
  The dreadful thing that means.
"A leak in the dike!" The stoutest
    heart
  Grows faint that cry to hear,
And the bravest man in all the land
  Turns white with mortal fear.
For he knows the smallest leak may
    grow
  To a flood in a single night;
And he knows the strength of the
    cruel sea
  When loosed in its angry might.

And the boy! He has seen the danger
  And, shouting a wild alarm,
He forces back the weight of the sea
  With the strength of his single
    arm!
He listens for the joyful sound
  Of a footstep passing nigh;
And lays his ear to the ground to
    catch
  The answers to his cry.
And he hears the rough winds
    blowing,
  And the waters rise and fall,
But never an answer comes to him
  Save the echo of his call.
He sees no hope, no succor,
  His feeble voice is lost;
Yet what shall he do but watch and
    wait
  Though he perish at his post!

14

So, faintly calling and crying
  Till the sun is under the sea;
Crying and moaning till the stars
  Come out for company;
He thinks of his brother and sister,
  Asleep in their safe warm bed;
He thinks of his father and mother,
  Of himself as dying — and dead;
And of how, when the night is over,
  They must come and find him at
    last;
But he never thinks he can leave the
  place
  Where duty holds him fast.

The good dame in the cottage
  Is up and astir with the light,
For the thought of her little Peter
  Has been with her all the night.
And now she watches the pathway,
  As yester-eve she had done;
But what does she see so strange and
  black
  Against the rising sun?
Her neighbors are bearing between
  them
  Something straight to her door;
Her child is coming home, but not
  As he ever came before!

"He is dead!" she cries. "My
  darling!"
  And the startled father hears,
And comes and looks the way she
  looks,
  And fears the thing she fears;
Till a glad shout from the bearers
  Thrills the stricken man and
    wife —
"Give thanks, for your son has saved
  our land,
  And God has saved his life!"
So there in the morning sunshine
  They knelt about the boy;
And every head was bared and bent
  In tearful, reverent joy.

'Tis many a year since then; but still
  When the sea roars like a flood,
The boys are taught what a boy can
  do
  Who is brave and true and good;
For every man in that country
  Takes his son by the hand
And tells him of little Peter,
  Whose courage saved the land.
They may have a valiant hero,
  Remembered through the years;
But never one whose name so oft
  Is named with loving tears.
And his deed shall be sung by the
  cradle,
  And told to the child on the knee,
So long as the dikes of Holland
  Divide the land from the sea!

Phoebe Cary.

The Travelers

The moon and the satellite orbit
    together,
Tracing trackless circles in an end-
    less sky,
The satellite turns to the moon in
    wonder
As they sail over continent, ocean,
    and sea,
Muses over Africa, Afghanistan,
    Alaska,
"Can it be that I'll become ancient as
    she?"
Sailing South America the moon
    looks backward,
Skims the towering Andes with
    scarcely a sigh,
    "Wait, wait,
    Wait," she whispers,
    "Time is nothing
    In the endless sky."

Patricia Hubbell

A Kite

I often sit and wish that I
Could be a kite up in the sky,
And ride upon the breeze and go
Whichever way I chanced to blow.
Then I could look beyond the town,
And see the river winding down,
And follow all the ships that sail
Like me before the merry gale,
Until at last with them I came
To some place with a foreign name.

Frank Dempster Sherman

The Nightingale and the Glowworm

A nightingale that all day long
Had cheer'd the village with his
    song,
Nor yet at eve his note suspended,
Nor yet when eventide was ended,
Began to feel, as well he might,
The keen demands of appetite;
When looking early around,
He spied far off, upon the ground,
A something shining in the dark,
And knew the Glowworm by his
    spark;
So, stooping down from hawthorn
    top,
He thought to put him in his crop.
The worm, aware of his intent,
Harangued him thus, right
    eloquent —:
"Did you admire my lamp," quoth
    he,
"As much as I your minstrelsy,
You would abhor to do me wrong,
As much as I to spoil your song:
For 'twas the self-same Power
    Divine
Taught you to sing, and me to shine;
That you with music, I with light,
Might beautify and cheer the night."
The songster heard this short
    oration,
And warbling out his approbation,
Released him, as my story tells,
And found a supper somewhere
    else.

William Cowper

I Meant to Do My Work Today

I meant to do my work today,
But a brown bird sang in the apple-
    tree,
And a butterfly flitted across the
    field,
And all the leaves were calling me.

And the wind went sighing over the
    land,
Tossing the grasses to and fro,
And a rainbow held out its shining
    hand —
So what could I do but laugh and go?

Richard Le Gallienne

When You and I Grow Up

When you and I
Grow up — Polly —
    I mean that you and me
Shall go sailing in a big ship
    Right over all the sea.
We'll wait till we are older,
    For if we went today,
You know that we might lose
        ourselves,
    And never find the way.

Kate Greenaway

It's such a shock, I almost screech,
When I find a worm inside my
        peach!
But then, what really makes me blue,
Is to find a worm who's bit in two!

William Cole

The Mountain and the Squirrel

The mountain and the squirrel
Had a quarrel,
And the former called the latter
    "Little prig":
Bun replied,
"You are doubtless very big;
But all sorts of things and weather
Must be taken in together
To make up a year,
And a sphere.
And I think it no disgrace
To occupy my place.
If I'm not so large as you,
You are not so small as I,
And not half so spry.
I'll not deny you make
A very pretty squirrel track.
Talents differ; all is well and wisely
    put,
If I cannot carry forests on my back,
Neither can you crack a nut."

Ralph Waldo Emerson

Algy Met a Bear

Algy met a bear,
The bear was bulgy,
The bulge was Algy.

The Skeleton in Armor

"Speak! speak! thou fearful guest!
Who, with thy hollow breast
Still in rude armor drest,
   Comest to daunt me!
Wrapt not in Eastern balms,
But with thy fleshless palms
Stretched, as if asking alms,
   Why does thou haunt me?"

Then, from those cavernous eyes
Pale flashes seemed to rise,
As when the Northern skies
   Gleam in December;
And, like the water's flow
Under December's snow,
Came a dull voice of woe
   From the heart's chamber.

"I was a Viking old!
My deeds, though manifold,
No Skald in song has told
   No Saga taught thee!
Take heed, that in thy verse
Thou dost the tale rehearse,
Else dread a dead man's curse;
   For this I sought thee.

"Far in the Northern Land,
By the wild Baltic's strand,
I, with my childish hand,
   Tames the ger-falcon;
And, with my skates fast-bound,
Skimmed the half-frozen Sound,
That the poor whimpering hound
   Trembled to walk on.

"Oft to his frozen lair
Tracked I the grisly bear,
While from my path the hare
   Fled like a shadow;
Oft through the forest dark
Followed the were-wolf's bark,
Until the soaring lark
   Sang from the meadow.

"But when I older grew,
Joining a corsair's crew,
O'er the dark sea I flew
   With the marauders.
Wild was the life we led;
Many the souls that sped,
Many the hearts that bled,
   By our stern orders.

"Many a wassil-bout
Wore the long Winter out;
Often our midnight shout
   Set the cocks crowing,
As we the Berserk's tale
Measured in cups of ale,
Draining the oaken pail,
   Filled to o'erflowing.

"Once as I told in glee
Tales of the stormy sea,
Soft eyes did gaze on me,
   Burning yet tender;
And as the white stars shine
On the dark Norway pine,
On that dark heart of mine
   Fell their soft splendor.

"I wooed the blue-eyed maid,
Yielding, yet half afraid,
And in the forest's shade
   Our vows were plighted.
Under its loosened vest
Fluttered her little breast,
Like birds within their nest
   By the hawk frighted.

"Bright in her father's hall
Shields gleamed upon the wall,
Loud sang the minstrels all,
   Chanting his glory;
When of old Hildebrand
I asked his daughter's hand,
Mute did the minstrels stand
   To hear my story.

"While the brown ale he quaffed,
Loud then the champion laughed,
And as the wind-gusts waft
   The sea-foam brightly,
So the loud laugh of scorn,
Out of those lips unshorn,
From the deep drinking horn
   Blew the foam lightly.

"She was a Prince's child,
I but a Viking wild,
And though she blushed and
   smiled,
   I was discarded!
Should not the dove so white
Follow the sea-mew's flight,
Why did they leave that night
   Her nest unguarded?

"Scarce had I put to sea,
Bearing the maid with me,
Fairest of all was she
    Among the Norsemen!
When on the white sea-strand,
Waving his armed hand,
Saw we old Hildebrand,
    With twenty horsemen.

"Then launched they to the blast,
Bent like a reed each mast,
Yet we were gaining fast,
    When the wind failed us;
And with a sudden flaw
Came round the gusty Skaw,
So that our foe we saw
    Laugh as he failed us.

"And as to catch the gale
Round veered the flapping sail,
Death! was the helmsman's hail,
    Death without quarter!
Mid-ships with iron keel
Struck we her ribs of steel;
Down her black hulk did reel
    Through the black water!

"As with his wings aslant,
Sails the fierce cormorant,
Seeking some rocky haunt,
    With his prey laden,
So toward the open main,
Beating to sea again,
Through the wild hurricane,
    Bore I the maiden.

"Three weeks we westward bore,
And when the storm was o'er,
Cloud-like we saw the shore
    Stretching to leeward;
There for my lady's bower
    Built I the lofty tower,
Which, to this very hour,
    Stands looking sea-ward.

"There lived we many years;
Time dried the maiden's tears;
She had forgot her fears,
    She was a mother;
Death closed her mild blue eyes,
Under that tower she lies!
Ne'er shall the sun arise
    On such another!

"Still grew my bosom then,
Still as a stagnant fen!
Hateful to me were men,
    The sunlight hateful!
In the vast forest here,
Clad in my warlike gear,
Fell I upon my spear,
    O, death was grateful!

"Thus, seamed with many scars,
Bursting these prisons bars,
Up to its native stars
    My soul ascended!
There from the flowing bowl
Deep drinks the warrior's soul,
Skoal! to the Northland! *Skoal!*"
    — Thus the tale ended.

Henry Wadsworth Longfellow

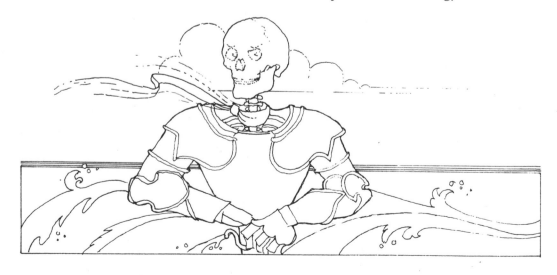

19

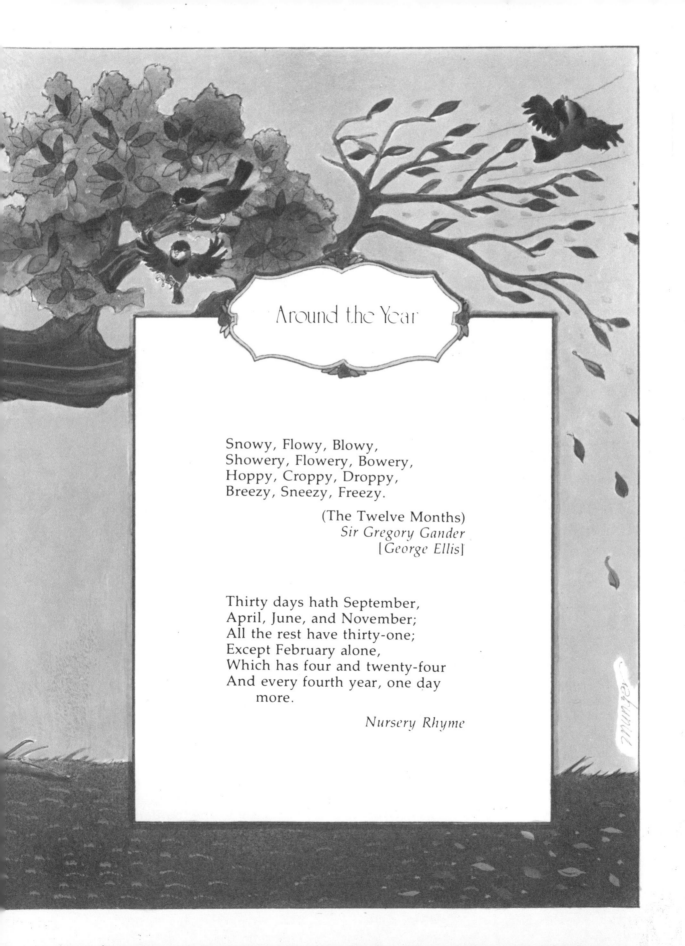

Around the Year

Snowy, Flowy, Blowy,
Showery, Flowery, Bowery,
Hoppy, Croppy, Droppy,
Breezy, Sneezy, Freezy.

       (The Twelve Months)
         Sir Gregory Gander
          [George Ellis]

Thirty days hath September,
April, June, and November;
All the rest have thirty-one;
Except February alone,
Which has four and twenty-four
And every fourth year, one day
    more.

         Nursery Rhyme

The New Year

Farewell old year,
With goodness crowned,
A hand divine hath set thy bound.

Welcome New Year,
Which shall bring
Fresh blessings from
Our Lord and King.

The old we leave without a tear,
The new we enter without fear.

Spring is showery, flowery, bowery;
Summer: hoppy, croppy, poppy;
Autumn: wheezy, sneezy, freezy;
Winter: slippy, drippy, nippy.

Mother Goose

Thirty days hath September,
April, June, and November,
Save February; the rest have thirty-
one
Unless you hear from Washington.

To My Valentine

If apples were pears,
And peaches were plums,
And the rose had a different name;
If tigers were bears,
And fingers were thumbs,
I'd love you just the same!

For, lo, the winter is past,
The rain is over and gone;
The flowers appear on the earth;
The time of the singing of birds is
come,
And the voice of the turtle is heard in
our land.

The Bible, Song of Solomon 2:11,12

Tomorrow is Saint Valentine's Day,
All in the morning betime,
And I a maid at your window,
To be your Valentine.

William Shakespeare

Written in March

The cock is crowing,
The stream is flowing,
The small birds twitter,
The lake doth glitter,
The green field sleeps in the sun;
The oldest and youngest
Are at work with the strongest;
The cattle are grazing,
Their heads never raising;
There are forty feeding like one!

Like an army defeated
The snow hath retreated,
And now doth fare ill
On the top of the bare hill;
The ploughboy is whooping —
anon-anon:
There's joy in the mountains;
There's life in the fountains;
Small clouds are sailing,
Blue sky prevailing;
The rain is over and gone!

William Wordsworth

God's Plan for Spring

It never has failed, and it never will,
The wind swings around and the
violets come;
There's a touch of green on a bare
gray hill,
And the robin is building himself a
home.

Year after year, year after year —
That is the way that God has
planned —
We feel a loveliness somewhere
near,
And spring comes moving across
the land.

Boughs grow heavy with leaf and
bud,
The sky is a sea with drifting sails;
And spring comes back, as we knew
she would,
That is God's plan, and it never fails.

Nancy Byrd Turner

On Easter Day

Easter lilies! Can you hear
What they whisper, low and clear?
In dewy fragrance they unfold
Their splendor sweet, their snow
and gold.
Every beauty-breathing bell
News of heaven has to tell.
Listen to their mystic voice,
Hear, oh mortal, and rejoice!
Hark, their soft and heavenly chime!
Christ is risen for all time!

Celia Laighton Thaxter

In the bonds of Death He lay
Who for our offense was slain;
But the Lord is risen to-day,
Christ hath brought us life again,
Wherefore let us all rejoice,
Singing loud, with cheerful voice,
Hallelujah!

Martin Luther

We have tulips in our flower bed.
This spring they looked so pretty —
pink and white.
Now they've gone to sleep in small
brown bulbs.
Next spring they'll bloom again —
still pink and white.
All winter God remembers who they
are,
And never gets them mixed with
other things.
I'm sure he'll always know that I am
me.

Jessie Orton Jones
(VII from Secrets)

I am the resurrection, and the life:
he that believeth in me, though he
were dead, yet shall he live:
And whosoever liveth and believeth
in me shall never die.
Believest thou this?

The Bible, John 11:25,26

Wise Johnny

Little Johnny-jump-up said,
"It must be spring,
I just saw a lady-bug
And heard a robin sing."

Edwina Fallis

April Fool's Day

The first of April, some do say,
Is set apart for All Fools' Day,
But why the people call it so,
Nor I, nor they themselves, do
   know.

Old English Almanac

May Day

Spring is coming, spring is coming,
  Birdies, build your nest;
Weave together straw and feather,
  Doing each your best.

Spring is coming, spring is coming,
  Flowers are coming too:
Pansies, lilies, daffodillies,
  Now are coming through.

Spring is coming, spring is coming,
  All around is fair;
Shimmer and quiver on the river,
  Joy is everywhere.
We wish you a happy May.

Remembering Day

All the soldiers marching along;
All the children singing a song;
All the flowers dewy and sweet;
All the flags hung out in the street;
Hearts that throb in a grateful way —
For this is our Remembering Day.*

Mary Wright Saunders

*Memorial Day

A Day in June

And what is so rare as a day in June?
  Then, if ever, come perfect days;
Then Heaven tries earth if it be in
   tune,
  And over it softly her warm ear
    lays;
Whether we look, or whether we
   listen,
  We hear life murmur, or see it
    glisten;
Every clod feels a stir of might,
  An instinct within it that reaches
    and towers,
And, groping blindly above it for
   light,
  Climbs to a soul in grass and
    flowers.

James Russell Lowell
(from The Vision of Sir Launfal)

Fourth of July

Fat torpedoes in bursting jackets,
Firecrackers in scarlet packets.
We'll be up at crack o' day,
Fourth of July — Hurrah! Hooray!

Rachel Field

The Fourth of July

Day of glory! Welcome day!
Freedom's banners greet thy ray;
See! how cheerfully they play
  With thy morning breeze,
On the rocks where pilgrims
   kneeled,
On the heights where squadrons
   wheeled,
When a tyrant's thunder pealed
  O'er the trembling seas.

God of armies! did thy stars
On their courses smite his oars,
Blast his arm, and wrest his bars
  From the heaving tide?
On our standard, lo! they burn,
And, when days like this return,
Sparkle o'er the soldier's urn
  Who for freedom died.

God of peace! whose spirit fills
All the echoes of our hills,
All the murmur of our rills,
  Now the storm is o'er,
O let free men be our sons,
And let future Washingtons
Rise to lead their valiant ones
  Till there's war no more!

John Pierpont

Benjamin Jones Goes Swimming

Benjamin Jones in confident tones
  Told his wife, ''On the Fourth of
    July
I think I'll compete in the free-for-all
  meet,
  I bet I can win, if I try.''

But his wife said, ''My word! How
    very absurd!
  You haven't gone swimming for
    years.
With others so fast, you're sure to be
    LAST,
  And I'll blush to the tips of my
    ears.''

Well, the Fourth quickly came, and
    waiting acclaim
  Were wonderful swimmers
    galore,
Each poised in his place for the start
    of the race,
  While spectators crowded the
    shore.

The contest began, and Benjy, poor
    man,
  Was passed on the left and the
    right.
His pace was so slow that a crab saw
    his toe
  And thought it would venture a
    bite.

Ben noticed the crab as it started to
    grab
  And — perhaps the result can be
    guessed;
The thought of his toe in the claws of
    his foe
  Made him swim like a swimmer
    possessed!

And the crowd on the shore sent up a
    great roar
  As Ben took the lead in the dash,
While his wife on the dock received
    such a shock
  She fell in the lake with a splash.

Aileen Fisher

25

August

Buttercup nodded and said
　　good-by,
　　Clover and daisy went off
　　　　together,
But the fragrant water lilies lie
　　Yet moored in the golden August
　　　　weather.
The swallows chatter about their
　　flight,
　　The cricket chirps like a rare good
　　　　fellow,
The asters twinkle in clusters bright,
　　While the corn grows ripe and the
　　　　apples mellow.

Celia Laighton Thaxter

The Mist and All

I like the fall,
The mist and all.
I like the night owl's
Lonely call —
And wailing sound
Of wind around.

I like the gray
November day,
And bare, dead boughs
That coldly sway
Against my pane.
I like the rain.

I like to sit
And laugh at it —
And tend
My cozy fire a bit.
I like the fall —
The mist and all.

Dixie Willson

Summer Days

Winter is cold-hearted;
　　Spring is yea and nay;
Autumn is a weathercock,
　　Blown every way:
Summer days for me,
When every leaf is on its tree,

When Robin's not a beggar,
　　And Jenny Wren's a bride,
And larks hang, singing, singing,
　　　　singing,
　　Over the wheat-fields wide,
　　And anchored lilies ride,
And the pendulum spider
　　Swings from side to side,

And blue-black beetles transact
　　　　business,
　　And gnats fly in a host,
And furry caterpillars hasten
　　That no time be lost,
And moths grow fat and thrive,
And ladybirds arrive.

Before green apples blush,
　　Before green nuts embrown,
Why, one day in the country
　　Is worth a month in town —
Is worth a day and a year
　　Of the dusty, musty, lag-last
　　　　fashion
That days drone elsewhere.

Christina Rossetti

Black and Gold

Everything is black and gold,
　　Black and gold, tonight;
Yellow pumpkins, yellow moon,
　　Yellow candlelight.

Jet-black cat with golden eyes,
　　Shadows black as ink,
Firelight blinking in the dark
　　With a yellow blink.

Black and gold, black and gold,
  Nothing in between —
When the world turns black and
    gold,
  Then it's Halloween!

Nancy Byrd Turner

Something Told the Wild Geese

Something told the wild geese
  It was time to go.
Though the fields lay golden,
  Something whispered — "Snow."
Leaves were green and stirring,
  Berries, luster-glossed,
But beneath warm feathers,
  Something cautioned — "Frost."
All the sagging orchards
  Steamed with amber spice,
But each wild breast stiffened
  At remembered ice.
Something told the wild geese
  It was time to fly —
Summer sun was on their wings,
  Winter in their cry.

Rachel Field

Thanksgiving

I thank you, God,
That swallows know their way
In the great sky;
That grass, all brown today,
And dead and dry,
Will quiver in the sun
All green and gay
When winter's done.

Louise Driscoll

Thanksgiving Day

Over the river and through the
    wood,
  To grandfather's house we'll go;
    The horse knows the way
    To carry the sleigh,
Through the white and drifted
    snow.

Over the river and through the
    wood —
  Oh, how the wind does blow!
    It stings the toes
    And bites the nose,
As over the ground we go.

Over the river and through the
    wood,
  To have a first-rate play.
    Hear the bells ring!
    "Ting-ling-ding!"
Hurrah for Thanksgiving Day!

Over the river and through the
    wood,
  Trot fast, my dapple-gray!
    Spring over the ground,
    Like a hunting-hound:
For this is Thanksgiving Day.

Over the river and through the
    wood,
  And straight through the
    barnyard gate.
    We seem to go
    Extremely slow —
It is so hard to wait!

Over the river and through the
    wood,
  Now grandmother's cap I spy!
    Hurrah for the fun!
    Is the pudding done?
Hurrah for the pumpkin pie!

Lydia Maria Child

27

November

No sun — no moon!
No morn — no noon —
No dawn — no dusk — no proper
    time of day —
No sky — no earthly view —
No distance looking blue —
No road — no street — no "t'other
    side the way" —
No end to any row —
No indications where the crescents
    go —
No top to any steeple —
No recognitions of familiar
    people —
No courtesies for showing 'em —
No knowing 'em!
No traveling at all — no
    locomotion —
No inkling of the way — no notion
"No go" — by land or ocean —
No mail — no post —
No news from any foreign coast —
No park — no ring — no afternoon
    gentility —
No company — no nobility —
No warmth, no cheerfulness, no
    healthful ease,
No comfortable feel in any
    member —
No shade, no shine, no butterflies,
    no bees,
No fruits, no flowers, no leaves, no
    birds —
November!

Thomas Hood

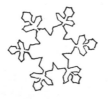

Snow-Stars

The air is full of flying stars,
    The sky is shaking down
A million silver stars of snow
    On wood and field and town.

Frances Frost

Come, Ye Thankful People

Come, ye thankful people, come
Raise the song of harvest home;
    All is safely gathered in,
    Ere the winter storms begin;
God our Maker doth provide
For our wants to be supplied;
    Come to God's own temple, come,
    Raise the song of harvest home.

All the world is God's own field
Fruit unto his praise to yield;
    Wheat and tares together sown,
    Unto joy or sorrow grown;
First the blade, and then the ear,
Then the full corn shall appear;
    Lord of harvest, grant that we
    Wholesome grain and pure may
    be.

Henry Alford

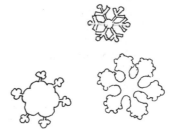

Falling Snow

See the pretty snowflakes
    Falling from the sky;
On the walk and housetop
    Soft and thick they lie.

On the window-ledges
    On the branches bare;
Now how fast they gather,
    Filling all the air.

Look into the garden,
    Where the grass was green;
Covered by the snowflakes,
    Not a blade is seen.

Now the bare black bushes
    All look soft and white,
Every twig is laden —
    What a pretty sight!

There were some shepherds living in the same part of the country, keeping guard throughout the night over their flock in the open fields. Suddenly an angel of the Lord stood before them, the splendour of the Lord blazed around them, and they were terror-stricken. But the angel said to them,

"Do not be afraid! Listen, I bring you glorious news of great joy which is for all the people. This very day, in David's town, a Saviour has been born for you. He is Christ, the Lord. Let this prove it to you: you will find a baby, wrapped up and lying in a manger."

And in a flash there appeared with the angel a vast host of the armies of Heaven, praising God, saying,

"Glory to God in the highest Heaven! Peace upon earth among men of goodwill!"

When the angels left them and went back into Heaven, the shepherds said to each other,

"Now let us go straight to Bethlehem and see this thing which the Lord has made known to us."

So they went as fast as they could and they found Mary and Joseph — and the baby lying in the manger. And when they had seen this sight, they told everybody what had been said to them about the little child. And all those who heard them were amazed at what the shepherds said. But Mary treasured all these things and turned them over in her mind. The shepherds went back to work, glorifying and praising God for everything that they had heard and seen, which had happened just as they had been told.

The Bible, Luke 2:8-20, Phillips

Long, Long Ago

Winds through the olive trees
  Softly did blow,
Round little Bethlehem,
  Long, long ago.

Sheep on the hillside lay
  Whiter than snow;
Shepherds were watching them,
  Long, long ago.

Then from the happy skies,
  Angels bent low,
Singing their songs of joy,
  Long, long ago.

For in a manger bed,
  Cradled we know,
Christ came to Bethlehem,
  Long, long ago.

Katherine Parker

Cradle Hymn

Away in a manger,
  No crib for a bed,
The little Lord Jesus
  Lay down his sweet head;
The stars in the heavens
  Looked down where he lay,
The little Lord Jesus
  Asleep in the hay.

The cattle are lowing,
  The poor baby wakes,
But little Lord Jesus
  No crying he makes.
I love thee, Lord Jesus,
  Look down from the sky,
And stay by my cradle
  Till morning is nigh.

Martin Luther

I Heard the Bells on Christmas Day

I heard the bells on Christmas day
Their old familiar carols play,
And wild and sweet the words
  repeat
Of peace on earth, good-will to men.

I thought how, as the day had come,
The belfries of all Christendom
Had rolled along the unbroken song
Of peace on earth, good-will to men.

And in despair I bowed my head:
"There is no peace on earth," I said:
"For hate is strong and mocks the
  song
Of peace on earth, good-will to
  men."

Then pealed the bells more loud and
  deep:
"God is not dead, no doth he sleep:
The wrong shall fail, the right
  prevail,
With peace on earth, good-will to
  men."

Till ringing, singing on its way
The world revolved from night to
  day,
A voice, a chime, a chant sublime,
Of peace on earth, good-will to men.

Henry Wadsworth Longfellow

Song

Why do bells for Christmas ring?
Why do little children sing?

Once a lovely, shining star,
Seen by shepherds from afar,
Gently moved until its light
Made a manger's cradle bright.

There a darling baby lay,
Pillowed soft upon the hay;
And its mother sang and smiled,
"This is Christ, the holy child!"

Therefore bells for Christmas ring,
Therefore little children sing.

Eugene Field

The Christmas Exchange

When Bill gives me a book, I know
It's just the book he wanted, so
When I give him a Ping-Pong set,
He's sure it's what I hoped to get.

Then after Christmas we arrange
A little Christmas gift exchange;
I give the book to him, and he
Gives back the Ping-Pong set to me.

So each gives twice — and that is
    pleasant —
To get the truly wanted present.

Arthur Guiterman

Christmas Everywhere

Everywhere, everywhere, Christmas
    to-night!
Christmas in lands of the fir-tree and
    pine,
Christmas in lands of the palm-tree
    and vine,
Christmas where snow-peaks stand
    solemn and white,
Christmas where cornfields lie
    sunny and bright,
    Everywhere, everywhere,
        Christmas to-night!

Christmas where children are
    hopeful and gay,
Christmas where old men are
    patient and gray,
Christmas where peace, like a dove
    in its flight,
Broods o'er brave men in the thick of
    the fight.
    Everywhere, everywhere,
        Christmas to-night!

For the Christ-child who comes is
    the Master of all,
No palace too great and no cottage
    too small;

The angels who welcome Him sing
    from the height,
"In the City of David, a King in His
    might."
    Everywhere, everywhere,
        Christmas to-night!

Then let every heart keep its
    Christmas within,
Christ's pity for sorrow, Christ's
    hatred for sin,
Christ's care for the weakest,
    Christ's courage for right,
Christ's dread of the darkness,
    Christ's love of the light,
    Everywhere, everywhere,
        Christmas to-night!

So the stars of the midnight which
    compass us round
Shall see a strange glory and hear a
    sweet sound,
And cry, "Look! the earth is aflame
    with delight,
O sons of the morning, rejoice at the
    sight."
    Everywhere, everywhere,
        Christmas to-night!

Phillips Brooks

Christmas Carol

God bless the master of this house,
    The mistress also,
And all the little children,
    That round the table go,
And all your kin and kinsmen
    That dwell both far and near;
I wish you a Merry Christmas
    And a Happy New Year.

A Visit from St. Nicholas

'Twas the night before Christmas,
    when all through the house
Not a creature was stirring, not even
    a mouse;
The stockings were hung by the
    chimney with care,
In hopes that St. Nicholas soon
    would be there;
The children were nestled all snug in
    their beds
While visions of sugar-plums
    danced in their heads;
And mamma in her kerchief, and I in
    my cap,
Had just settled our brains for a long
    winter's nap, —
When out on the lawn there arose
    such a clatter,
I sprang from my bed to see what
    was the matter.
Away to the window I flew like a
    flash,
Tore open the shutters and threw up
    the sash.
The moon on the breast of the new-
    fallen snow
Gave a lustre of midday to objects
    below;
When what to my wondering eyes
    should appear,

But a miniature sleigh and eight tiny
    reindeer,
With a little old driver, so lively and
    quick,
I knew in a moment it must be St.
    Nick.
More rapid than eagles his coursers
    they came,
And he whistled and shouted, and
    called them by name:
"Now, Dasher! now, Dancer! now,
    Prancer and Vixen!
On, Comet! on, Cupid! on, Donder
    and Blitzen!
To the top of the porch, to the top of
    the wall!
Now dash away, dash away, dash
    away, all!"
As dry leaves that before the wild
    hurricane fly,
When they meet with an obstacle,
    mount to the sky,
So up to the housetop the coursers
    they flew,
With the sleigh full of toys, and St.
    Nicholas too.
And then in a twinkling I heard on
    the roof
The prancing and pawing of each
    little hoof.
As I drew in my head, and was
    turning around,

Down the chimney St. Nicholas
   came with a bound.
He was dressed all in fur from his
   head to his foot,
And his clothes were all tarnished
   with ashes and soot;
A bundle of toys he had flung on his
   back,
And he looked like a peddler just
   opening his pack.
His eyes — how they twinkled! his
   dimples, how merry!
His cheeks were like roses, his nose
   like a cherry!
His droll little mouth was drawn up
   like a bow,
And the beard on his chin was as
   white as the snow.
The stump of a pipe he held tight in
   his teeth,
And the smoke it encircled his head
   like a wreath.
He had a broad face and a little
   round belly
That shook, when he laughed, like a
   bowl full of jelly.
He was chubby and plump, a right
   jolly old elf;
And I laughed when I saw him, in
   spite of myself.
A wink of his eye and a twist of his
   head
Soon gave me to know I had nothing
   to dread.
He spoke not a word, but went
   straight to his work,
And filled all the stockings; then
   turned with a jerk,
And laying his finger aside of his
   nose,
And giving a nod, up the chimney
   he rose.
He sprang to his sleigh, to his team
   gave a whistle,
And away they all flew like the down
   of a thistle;
But I heard him exclaim, ere he
   drove out of sight,
"Happy Christmas to all, and to all a
   good-night!"

Clement C. Moore

Mister Snow Man

A cranberry nose and a tin-can hat
Belong to a snow man, jolly and fat.
We rolled him up by the fence today.
Please, Mr. Sun, don't melt him
   away!

Bertha Wilcox Smith

Around the Year

January brings the snow,
   Makes our feet and fingers glow,
February brings the rain,
   Thaws the frozen lake again,
March brings breezes loud and
   shrill,
   Stirs the dancing daffodil.

April brings the primrose sweet,
   Scatters daisies at our feet,
May brings flocks of pretty lambs,
   Skipping by their fleecy dams,
June brings tulips, lilies, roses,
   Fills the children's hands with
   posies.

Hot July brings cooling showers,
   Apricots and gillyflowers,
August brings the sheaves of corn,
   Then the harvest home is borne.
Warm September brings the fruit,
   Sportsmen then begin to shoot.

Fresh October brings the pheasant,
   Then to gather nuts is pleasant,
Dull November brings the blast,
   Then the leaves are whirling fast.
Chill December brings the sleet,
   Blazing fire and Christmas treat.

Sara Coleridge

Beauty and Discovery

It is not raining rain to me,
   It's raining daffodils;
In every dimpled drop I see
   Wildflowers on the hills.
The clouds of gray engulf the day,
   And overwhelm the town;
It is not raining rain to me,
   It's raining roses down.

It is not raining rain to me,
   But fields of clover bloom,
Where every buccaneering bee
   May find a bed and room.
A health unto the happy!
   A fig for him who frets!
It is not raining rain to me,
   It's raining violets.

(April Rain)
Robert Loveman

The Rainbow

I saw the lovely arch
Of Rainbow span the sky,
The gold sun burning
As the rain swept by.

In bright-ringed solitude
The showery foliage shone
One lovely moment,
And the Bow was gone.

Walter de la Mare

A Thing of Beauty

A thing of beauty is a joy for ever:
Its loveliness increases; it will never
Pass into nothingness; but still will
    keep
A bower quiet for us, and a sleep
Full of sweet dreams, and health,
    and quiet breathing.
Therefore, on every morrow, we are
    wreathing
A flowery band to bind us to the
    earth,
Spite of despondence, of the
    inhuman dearth
Of noble natures, of the gloomy
    days,
Of all the unhealthy and o'er-
    darkened ways
Made for our searching: yes, in spite
    of all,
Some shape of beauty moves away
    the pall
From our dark spirits. Such the sun,
    the moon,
Trees old and young, sprouting a
    shady boon
For simple sheep; and such are
    daffodils
With the green world they live in;
    and clear rills
That for themselves a cooling covert
    make
'Gainst the hot season; the
    mid-forest brake,

Rich with a sprinkling of fair
    musk-rose blooms:
And such too is the grandeur of the
    dooms
We have imagined for the mighty
    dead;
All lovely tales that we have heard or
    read:
An endless fountain of immortal
    drink,
Pouring unto us from the heaven's
    brink.

John Keats

Music

Let me go where'er I will,
I hear a sky-born music still:
It sounds from all things old,
It sounds from all things young;
From all that's fair, from all that's
    foul,
Peals out a cheerful song.
It is not only in the rose,
It is not only in the bird,
Not only where the rainbow glows,
Nor in the song of woman heard,
But in the darkest, meanest things
There always, always something
    sings.
'Tis not in the high stars alone,
Nor in the cups of budding flowers,
Nor in the redbreast's mellow tone,
Nor in the bow that smiles in
    showers,
But in the mud and scum of things
There always, always something
    sings.

Ralph Waldo Emerson

Holy, holy, holy,
is the Lord of hosts:
the whole earth
is full of his glory.

The Bible, Isaiah 6:3

36

The Waterfall

Tinkle, tinkle!
Listen well!
Like a fairy silver bell
  In the distance ringing,
   Lightly swinging
    In the air;
'Tis the water in the dell
Where the elfin minstrels dwell,
  Falling in a rainbow sprinkle,
  Dropping stars that brightly
     twinkle,
   Bright and fair,
On the darkling pool below,
Making music so;
  'Tis the water elves who play
  On their lutes of spray.
Tinkle, tinkle!
Like a fairy silver bell;
Like a pebble in a shell;
Tinkle, tinkle!
Listen well!

         Frank Dempster Sherman

  I can climb our apple tree,
If I put my feet carefully in the right
    places,
  And pull myself up by my hands.
Then I come to my little seat in the
    arms of the tree.
  I can sit there and see everything.
I can see a measuring worm, light
    green,
  Climbing our apple tree.
  At every step
He has to make his whole body into
    a hump,
While his back feet catch up with his
    front feet.
That is a hard way to climb a tree,
  But it's his way
  And he doesn't seem to mind.

         Jessie Orton Jones
         (IX from Secrets)

What Do We Plant?

What do we plant when we plant the
    tree?
We plant the ship which will cross
    the sea.
We plant the mast to carry the sails;
We plant the planks to withstand the
    gales —
The keel, the keelson, the beam, the
    knee;
We plant the ship when we plant the
    tree.

What do we plant when we plant the
    tree?
We plant the houses for you and me.
We plant the rafters, the shingles,
    the floors,
We plant the studding, the lath, the
    doors,
The beams and siding, all parts that
    be;
We plant the house when we plant
    the tree.

What do we plant when we plant the
    tree?
A thousand things that we daily see;
We plant the spire that out-towers
    the crag,
We plant the staff for our country's
    flag,
We plant the shade, from the hot sun
    free;
We plant all these when we plant the
    tree.

Henry Abbey

God Is Everywhere

There's not a tint that paints the rose
    Or decks the lily fair,
Or marks the humblest flower that
    grows,
    But God has placed it there.

There's not a star whose twinkling
    light
    Illumes the spreading earth;
There's not a cloud, so dark or
    bright,
    But wisdom gave it birth.

There's not a place on earth's vast
    round,
    In ocean's deep or air,
Where love and beauty are not
    found,
    For God is everywhere.

I Never Saw a Moor

I never saw a moor;
I never saw the sea,
Yet know I how the heather looks
And what a billow be.

I never spoke with God
Nor visited in heaven,
Yet certain am I of the spot
As if the checks were given.

Emily Dickinson

Boats sail on the rivers,
    And ships sail on the seas;
But clouds that sail across the sky
    Are prettier far than these.

There are bridges on the rivers,
    As pretty as you please;
But the bow that bridges heaven,
    And overtops the trees,
And builds a road from earth to sky,
    Is prettier far than these.

Christina Rossetti

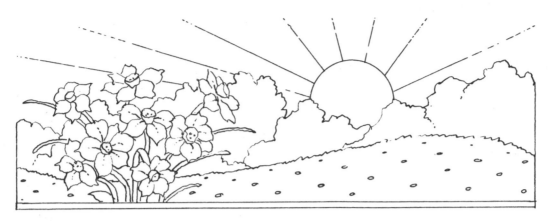

Covering the Subject

The turtle, clam and crab as well
Are covered with a sturdy shell,
While fish, excepting maybe whales,
Are shingled fore and aft with
    scales.

Though most, perhaps, have not the
    plating
Of armadillos, it's worth stating
That animals at least have hides
That give them fairly firm outsides.

And yet that upright mammal, man,
Must get along as best he can
With nothing but a little skin
To keep his precious insides in.

Richard Armour

Flowers always know what they
    should do.
The buttercup grows always shining
    yellow
  And the larkspur blue.
The lily always smells like lily,
  And the rose like rose.
Do you suppose the yellow
    buttercup
  Would like to be a rose?
Or the rose have the perfume of a
    lily?
  I think each one looks happy
  Being its very own self!

Jessie Orton Jones
(VI from Secrets)

Spring Song

The year's at the spring
And day's at the morn;
Morning's at seven;
The hillside's dew-pearled;
The lark's on the wing;
The snail's on the thorn;
God's in his heaven —
All's right with the world!

Robert Browning
(from Pippa Passes)

I Like to See It Lap the Miles

I like to see it lap the miles —
And lick the valleys up —
And stop to feed itself at banks;
And then, prodigious, step

Around a pile of mountains
And, supercilious, peer
In shanties by the sides of roads;
And then a quarry pace,

To fit its sides, and crowd between,
Complaining all the while
In horrid, hooting stanza;
Then chase itself down hill

And neigh like Boanerges —
Then punctual as a star
Stop — docile and omnipotent
At its own stable door.

Emily Dickinson

Leisure

What is this life if, full of care,
We have no time to stand and stare.

No time to stand beneath the boughs
And stare as long as sheep or cows.

No time to see, when woods we
    pass,
Where squirrels hide their nuts in
    grass.

No time to see, in broad daylight,
Streams full of stars, like stars at
    night.

No time to turn at Beauty's glance,
And watch her feet, how they can
    dance.

No time to wait till her mouth can
Enrich that smile her eyes began.

A poor life this if, full of care,
We have no time to stand and stare.

William Henry Davies

Sometimes I hear God's whisper in
    the night.
The birds do, too, because they
    answer him
    In small bird voices.
I think he's telling them just what to
    do.
I think he tells them how to build
    their nests,
    And make them safe for eggs.
He tells them how to feed the baby
    birds.
He tells them when to fly away from
    cold,
And where to find a warmer place to
    live.
    So many things for birds to know!
    So many things to do!

Jessie Orton Jones
(V from Secrets)

Night

My kitten walks on velvet feet
And makes no sound at all;
And in the doorway nightly sits
To watch the darkness fall.

I think he loves the lady, Night,
And feels akin to her
Whose footsteps are as still as his,
Whose touch as soft as fur.

Lois Weakley McKay

The best portion of a good man's
life is his little, nameless, unremem-
bered acts of kindness and of love.

William Wordsworth

If you wisely invest in beauty, it
will remain with you all the days of
your life.

Frank Lloyd Wright

40

The Legend of the Raindrop

The legend of the raindrop
Has a lesson for us all,
As it trembled in the heavens . . .
Questioning whether it should fall
For the glistening raindrop argued
To the genie of the sky,
"I am beautiful and lovely
As I sparkle here on high,
And hanging here I will become
Part of the rainbow's hue
And I'll shimmer like a diamond
For all the world to view." . . .
But the genie told the raindrop,
"Do not hesitate to go,
For you will be more beautiful
If you fall to earth below,
For you will sink into the soil
And be lost a while from sight,
But when you reappear on earth,
You'll be looked on with delight;
For you will be the raindrop
That quenched the thirsty ground
And helped the lovely flowers
To blossom all around,
And in your resurrection
You'll appear in queenly clothes
With the beauty of the lily
And the fragrance of the rose;
Then, when you wilt and wither,
You'll become part of the earth
And make the soil more fertile
And give new flowers birth." . . .
For there is nothing ever lost
Or *eternally neglected*
For *everything God ever made*
Is always resurrected;
So trust God's all-wise wisdom
And doubt the Father never,
For in *His heavenly kingdom*
There is nothing lost forever.

Helen Steiner Rice

She Was a Phantom of Delight

She was a Phantom of delight
When first she gleamed upon my
     sight;
A lovely Apparition, sent
To be a moment's ornament;
Her eyes as stars of Twilight fair;
Like Twilight's, too, her dusky hair;
But all things else about her drawn
From May-time and the cheerful
     Dawn;
A dancing Shape, an Image gay,
To haunt, to startle, and way-lay.

I saw her upon nearer view,
A Spirit, yet a Woman too!
Her household motions light and
     free,
And steps of virgin-liberty;
A countenance in which did meet
Sweet records, promises as sweet;
A Creature not too bright or good
For human nature's daily food;
For transient sorrows, simple wiles,
Praise, blame, love, kisses, tears,
     and smiles.

And now I see with eye serene
The very pulse of the machine;
A Being breathing thoughtful
     breath,
A Traveller between life and death;
The reason firm, the temperate will,
Endurance, foresight, strength, and
     skill;
A perfect Woman, nobly planned,
To warn, to comfort, and command;
And yet a Spirit still, and bright,
With something of angelic light.

William Wordsworth

Bits of Wisdom

Little drops of water,
   Little grains of sand,
Make the mighty ocean
   And the pleasant land.

So the little moments,
   Humble though they be,
Make the mighty ages
   Of eternity.

So our little errors
   Lead the soul away
From the path of virtue,
   Far in sin to stray.

Little deeds of kindness,
   Little words of love,
Help make earth happy
   Like the heaven above.

(Little Things)
Julia Carney

A Wise Old Owl

A wise old owl lived in an oak;
The more he saw the less he spoke;
The less he spoke the more he heard:
Why can't we all be like that bird?

Edward Hersey Richards

Bits of Wisdom

Keep conscience clear,
Then never fear.

From a slip of the foot you may soon
    recover,
But a slip of the tongue you may
    never get over.

Tomorrow I'll reform,
The fool does say.
Today's too late,
The wise did yesterday.

Haste
Makes waste.

Benjamin Franklin

He Who Knows

He who knows not, and knows not
    that he knows not, is a fool.
Shun him.
He who knows not, and knows that
    he knows not, is a child.
Teach him.
He who knows, and knows not that
    he knows, is asleep.
Wake him.
He who knows, and knows that he
    knows, is wise.
Follow him.

From the Persian

One, two, whatever you do,
Start it well and carry it through.

From the Sermon on the Mount

Blessed are the poor in spirit:
For theirs is the kingdom of heaven.

Blessed are they that mourn:
For they shall be comforted.

Blessed are the meek:
For they shall inherit the earth.

Blessed are they which do hunger
    and thirst after righteousness:
For they shall be filled.

Blessed are the merciful:
For they shall obtain mercy.

Blessed are the pure in heart:
For they shall see God.

Blessed are the peacemakers:
For they shall be called the children
    of God.

Blessed are they which are
    persecuted for righteousness'
    sake:
For theirs is the kingdom of heaven.

The Bible, Matthew 5:3-10

Four Things

There be four things which are little
    upon the earth,
but they are exceeding wise:

The ants are a people not strong,
yet they prepare their meat in the
    summer;

The conies are but a feeble folk,
yet make they their houses in the
    rocks;

The locusts have no king,
yet go they forth all of them by
    bands;

The spider taketh hold with her
    hands,
and is in kings' palaces.

The Bible, Proverbs 30:24-28

Overheard in an Orchard

Said the Robin to the Sparrow:
  "I should really like to know
Why these anxious human beings
  Rush about and worry so."

Said the Sparrow to the Robin:
  "Friend, I think that it must be
That they have no heavenly Father
  Such as cares for you and me."

Elizabeth Cheney

Good Advice

  Don't shirk
  Your work
For the sake of a dream;
  A fish
  In the dish
Is worth ten in the stream.

*Adapted from the German by
Louis Untermeyer*

The Best Thing to Give

The best thing to give:
  to your enemy is forgiveness;
  to an opponent, tolerance;
  to a friend, your heart;
  to your child, a good example;
  to a father, deference;
  to your mother, conduct that will
     make her proud of you; ·
  to yourself, respect;
  to all men, charity.

Lord Balfour

Circles

The things to draw with compasses
Are suns and moons and circlesses
And rows of humptydumpasses
Or anything in circuses
Like hippopotamusseses
And hoops and camels' humpasses
And wheels on clowneses busseses
And fat old elephumpasses.

Harry Behn

Four Things

Four things in any land must dwell,
If it endures and prospers well:
One is manhood true and good;
One is noble womanhood;
One is child life, clean and bright;
And one an altar kept alight.

The Frog

Be kind and tender to the Frog,
And do not call him names,
As "Slimey-skin," or "Pollywog,"
Or likewise "Ugly James,"
Or "Gape-a-grin," or "Toad-gone-
    wrong,"
Or "Billy Bandy-knees";
The frog is justly sensitive
To epithets like these.

No animal will more repay
A treatment kind and fair,
At least so lonely people say
Who keep a frog (and, by the way,
They are extremely rare).

Hilaire Belloc

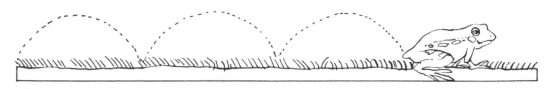

The Blind Men and the Elephant

It was six men of Indostan
  To learning much inclined,
Who went to see the elephant
  (Though all of them were blind),
That each by observation
  Might satisfy his mind.

The *First* approached the elephant,
  And, happening to fall
Against his broad and sturdy side,
  At once began to bawl:
"God bless me! but the elephant
  Is very like a wall!"

The *Second*, feeling of the tusk,
  Cried, "Ho! what have we here
So very round and smooth and
    sharp?
  To me 'tis mighty clear
This wonder of an elephant
  Is very like a spear!"

The *Third* approached the animal,
  And happening to take
The squirming trunk within his
    hands,
  Thus boldly up and spake:
"I see," quoth he, "the elephant
  Is very like a snake!"

The *Fourth* reached out an eager
    hand,
  And felt about the knee.

"What most this wondrous beast is
    like
  Is mighty plain," quoth he;
" 'Tis clear enough the elephant
  Is very like a tree!"

The *Fifth*, who chanced to touch the
    ear,
  Said: "E'en the blindest man
Can tell what this resembles most;
  Deny the fact who can,
This marvel of an elephant
  Is very like a fan!"

The *Sixth* no sooner had begun
  About the beast to grope,
Then, seizing on the swinging tail
  That fell within his scope,
"I see," quoth he, "the elephant
  Is very like a rope!"

And so these men of Indostan
  Disputed loud and long,
Each in his own opinion
  Exceeding stiff and strong,
Though each was partly in the right,
  And all were in the wrong!

The Moral:
So, oft in theologic wars,
  The disputants, I ween,
Rail on in utter ignorance
  Of what each other mean,
And prate about an elephant
  Not one of them has seen!

John Godfrey Saxe

The Difference

'Twixt optimist and pessimist
The difference is droll:
The optimist sees the doughnut;
The pessimist sees the hole.

However they talk, whatever they
    say,
Look straight at the task without
    dismay —
And if you can do it, do it today.

*Adapted from the German by
Louis Untermeyer*

Tremendous Trifles

For want of a nail, the shoe was lost;
For want of the shoe, the horse was
    lost;
For want of the horse, the rider was
    lost;
For want of the rider, the battle was
    lost;
For want of the battle, the kingdom
    was lost;
And all from the want of a horseshoe
    nail.

The words of a wise man's mouth are
gracious.

The Bible, Ecclesiastes 10:12

It is a good thing to give thanks
unto the Lord, and to sing praises
unto thy name, O most High.

The Bible, Psalm 92:1

One reason a dog is such a lovable
creature is that his tail wags instead
of his tongue.

Waste not, want not, is a maxim I
    would teach.
Let your watchword be dispatch,
    and practice what you preach;
Do not let your chances like
    sunbeams pass you by,
For you never miss the water till the
    well runs dry.

Rowland Howard

Willful waste brings woeful want
And you may live to pay.
How I wish I had that crust
That once I threw away.

Mother Goose

He that heareth my word,
and believeth on him that sent me,
    hath everlasting life,
and shall not come into
    condemnation;
but is passed from death unto life.

The Bible, John 5:24

To sleep easy at night,
Let your supper be light,
Or else you'll complain
Of a stomach in pain.

Mother Goose

Be sure your sin will find you out.

The Bible, Numbers 32:23

Character

Let me be a little kinder,
Let me be a little blinder
   To the faults of those about me;
   Let me praise a little more.
Let me be, when I am weary,
Just a little bit more cheery;
   Let me serve a little better
   Those that I am striving for.

Let me be a little braver
When temptation bids me waver;
   Let me strive a little harder
   To be all that I should be.
Let me be a little meeker
With the brother that is weaker;
   Let me think more of my neighbor
   And a little less of me.

(My Daily Creed)

A Psalm of Life

Tell me not, in mournful numbers,
  "Life is but an empty dream!"
For the soul is dead that slumbers,
  And things are not what they
    seem.

Life is real! Life is earnest!
  And the grave is not its goal;
"Dust thou art, to dust returnest,"
  Was not spoken of the soul.

Not enjoyment, and not sorrow,
  Is our destined end or way;
But to act, that each to-morrow
  Find us farther than to-day.

Art is long, and Time is fleeting,
  And our hearts, though stout and
    brave,
Still, like muffled drums are beating
  Funeral marches to the grave.

In the world's broad field of battle,
  In the bivouac of Life,
Be not like dumb, driven cattle;
  Be a hero in the strife!

Trust no Future, howe'er pleasant!
  Let the dead Past bury its dead!
Act, — act in the living Present!
  Heart within, and God o'erhead!

Lives of great men all remind us
  We can make our lives sublime,
And, departing, leave behind us
  Footprints on the sands of time!

Footprints, that perhaps another,
  Sailing o'er life's solemn main,
A forlorn and shipwrecked brother,
  Seeing, shall take heart again.

Let us, then, be up and doing,
  With a heart for any fate;
Still achieving, still pursuing,
  Learn to labor and to wait.

Henry Wadsworth Longfellow

I Would Be True

I would be true, for there are those
  who trust me;
I would be pure, for there are those
  who care;
I would be strong, for there is much
  to suffer;
I would be brave, for there is much
  to dare.

I would be friend of all — the foe, the
  friendless;
I would be giving, and forget the
  gift;
I would be humble, for I know my
  weakness;
I would look up, and laugh, and
  love, and lift.

I would be learning, day by day, the
  lessons
My heavenly Father gives me in His
  Word;
I would be quick to hear His lightest
  whisper,
And prompt and glad to do the
  things I've heard.

Howard Arnold Walter

An Ancient Prayer

Give me a good digestion, Lord,
  and also something to digest.
Give me a healthy body, Lord,
  and sense to keep it at its best.
Give me a healthy mind, good Lord,
  to keep the good and pure in sight,
Which, seeing sin, is not appalled,
  but finds a way to set it right.

Give me a mind that is not bound,
  that does not whimper, whine,
    or sigh.
Don't let me worry overmuch about
  the fussy thing called I.
Give me a sense of humor, Lord;
  give me the grace to see a joke,
To get some happiness from life
  and pass it on to other folk.

Thomas H. B. Webb

Young men! let the nobleness of your mind impel you to its improvement. You are too strong to be defeated, save by yourselves.

Refuse to live merely to eat and sleep. Brutes can do these, but you are men. Act the part of men.

Prepare yourselves to endure toil. Resolve to rise; you have but to resolve. Nothing can hinder your success if you determine to succeed.

Do not waste your time by wishing and dreaming, but go earnestly to work.

Let nothing discourage you. If you have but little time, improve that little; if you have no books, borrow them; if you have no teachers, teach yourself; if your early education has been neglected, by the greater diligence repair the defect.

Let not a craven heart or a love of ease rob you of the inestimable benefit of self-culture.

Labor faithfully, labor fearlessly, and look to God, who giveth wisdom and upbraideth not, and you shall reap a harvest more valuable than gold or jewels.

W. D. Howard

A man of words and not of deeds
Is like a garden full of weeds;
And when the weeds begin to grow
It's like a garden full of snow;
And when the snow begins to fall
It's like a bird upon the wall;
And when the bird begins to fly
It's like an eagle in the sky;
And when the sky begins to roar
It's like a lion at the door;
And when the door begins to crack
It's like a stick across your back;
And when your back begins to smart
It's like a penknife in your heart;
And when your heart begins to bleed
You're dead, and dead, and dead indeed.

Be Strong

Be strong!
We are not here to play, to dream, to drift;
We have hard work to do and loads to lift;
Shun not the struggle — face it; 'tis God's gift.

Be strong!
Say not, "The days are evil. Who's to blame?"
And fold the hands and acquiesce — oh, shame!
Stand up, speak out, and bravely, in God's name.

Be strong!
It matters not how deep entrenched the wrong,
How hard the battle goes, the day how long;
Faint not — fight on! Tomorrow comes the song.

Maltbie D. Babcock

A Child's Creed

I believe in God above;
I believe in Jesus' love;
I believe His Spirit, too,
Comes to teach me what to do;
I believe that I must be
True and good, dear Lord, like Thee.

Courage

Dare to be true;
    Nothing can need a lie;
The fault that needs one most
    Grows two thereby.

George Herbert

Today

The best thing you have in this world is Today. Today is your savior; it is often crucified between two thieves, Yesterday and Tomorrow.

Today you can be happy, not Yesterday or borrowed from Tomorrow. There is no happiness except Today's.

Most of our misery is left over from Yesterday or borrowed from Tomorrow. Keep Today clean. Make up your mind to enjoy your food, your work, your play Today anyhow. . . .

Today is yours. God has given it to you. All your Yesterdays He has taken back. All your Tomorrows are still in His hands.

Today is yours. Take its pleasures and be glad. Take its pains and play the man. . . .

Today is yours. Use it so that at its close you can say:

I have lived, and loved, Today!

Frank Crane

How Did You Die?

Did you tackle that trouble that came
    your way
  With a resolute heart and
    cheerful?
Or hide your face from the light of
    day
  With a craven soul and fearful?
Oh, a trouble's a ton, or a trouble's
    an ounce,
  Or a trouble is what you make it,
And it isn't the fact that you're hurt
    that counts,
  But only how did you take it?

You are beaten to earth? Well, well,
    what's that?
  Come up with a smiling face.
It's nothing against you to fall down
    flat,
  But to lie there — that's disgrace.
The harder you're thrown, why the
    higher you bounce;
  Be proud of your blackened eye!
It isn't the fact that you're licked that
    counts;
  It's how did you fight — and why?

And though you be done to the
    death, what then?
  If you battled the best you could;
If you played your part in the world
    of men,
  Why, the Critic will call it good.
Death comes with a crawl, or comes
    with a pounce,
  And whether he's slow or spry,
It isn't the fact that you're dead that
    counts,
  But only, how did you die?

Edmund Vance Cooke

Question not, but live and labour
  Till your goal be won,
Helping every feeble neighbour,
  Seeking help from none;
Life is mostly froth and bubble,
  Two things stand like stone —
Kindness in another's trouble,
  Courage in our own.

Adam Lindsay Gordon

I am not bound to win,
But I am bound to be true.
I am not bound to succeed,
But I am bound to live up to what
    light I have.
I must stand with anybody that
    stands right
And part with him when he goes
    wrong.

Abraham Lincoln

Eldorado

Gaily bedight,
  A gallant knight,
In sunshine and in shadow,
  Had journeyed long,
  Singing a song,
In search of Eldorado.

  But he grew old —
  This knight so bold —
And o'er his heart a shadow
  Fell as he found
  No spot of ground
That looked like Eldorado.

  And, as his strength
  Failed him at length,
He met a pilgrim shadow —
  "Shadow," said he,
  "Where can it be —
This land of Eldorado?"

  "Over the Mountains
  Of the Moon,
Down the Valley of the Shadow,
  Ride, boldly ride,"
  The shade replied —
"If you seek for Eldorado!"

Edgar Allen Poe

Oh, Adam was a gardener, and God
  who made him sees
That half a proper gardener's work
  is done upon his knees.
So when your work is finished,
  you can wash your hands
    and pray
For the glory of that garden,
  that it may not pass away.

Rudyard Kipling
(from The Glory of the Garden)

My heart leaps up when I behold
  A rainbow in the sky:
So was it when my life began;
So is it now I am a man;
So be it when I shall grow old,
  Or let me die!

William Wordsworth

Dear God,
When someone tries to make me do
What I am sure would not please
    You,
Do help me then to be so strong
That I just couldn't do the wrong.

Garry Cleveland Myers

Make a joyful noise unto the Lord,
  all ye lands.
Serve the Lord with gladness:
Come before his presence
  with singing.
Know ye that the Lord he is God:
It is he that hath made us,
  and not we ourselves;
We are his people, and the sheep
  of his pasture.
Enter into his gates with thanks-
  giving,
And into his courts with praise:
Be thankful unto him, and bless his
  name.
For the Lord is good;
  his mercy is everlasting;
And his truth endureth to all
  generations.

The Bible, Psalm 100

Courtesy and Graces

I'll be polite in many ways
And kindness show to others,
My parents, friends, and neighbors
    too,
My sister and my brother.

I'll run on errands when I can,
Sweep the walk, rake the leaves;
I'll carry groceries from the car,
Say "Thanks" and "If you please."

When company comes I'll gladly
    share
My books and all my toys;
And if there's grownup visitors
I'll not make too much noise.

At mealtime I will bow my head
And wait till prayer is said;
Sometimes I'll say the prayer myself:
"Thanks, dear God, for our bread."

(I'll Be Polite)
Lloyd E. Werth

Courtesy

Courtesy is a quality of soul refinement impossible to purchase, impossible to acquire at easy cost.

Politeness is but the shallow imitation of courtesy, and often masquerades as a refining quality in life when it is courtesy that truly refines mankind. Politeness can be assumed, courtesy never. One can be trained upon the surface of the mind, the other must be born in the soul.

Noble natures are often impolite, often lack surface politeness, but have real courtesy in the soul, where great and good men really live. They would not stoop to low cunning or contemptible meanness.

Polite people may be the very quintessence of cunning, so artful that the world regards them as delightful people until their shallow souls are uncovered. The difference between the polite person and the courteous soul is as wide as the gulf that separates evil from good.

F. E. Elwell

Hurt No Living Thing

Hurt no living thing:
  Ladybird, nor butterfly,
Nor moth with dusty wing,
  Nor cricket chirping cheerily,
Nor grasshopper so light of leap,
  Nor dancing gnat, nor beetle fat,
Nor harmless worms that creep.

Christina Rossetti

Don't look for the flaws as you go
    through life,
And even if you find them,
Be wise and kind and somewhat
    blind
And look for the good behind them.

Kindness is a language which the blind can see and the deaf can hear.

Important Words

The Four Most Important Words:
  "It was my fault."
The Three Most Important Words:
  "If you please."
The Two Most Important Words:
  "Thank you."
The One Most Important Word:
  "We."
The Least Important Word:
  "I."

Politeness is to do and say
The kindest thing in the kindest
  way.

Kindness to Animals

Little children, never give
Pain to things that feel and live;
Let the gentle robin come
For the crumbs you save at home, —
As his meat you throw along
He'll repay you with a song;
Never hurt the timid hare
Peeping from her green grass lair,
Let her come and sport and play
On the lawn at close of day;
The little lark goes soaring high
To the bright windows of the sky,
Singing as if 'twere always spring,
And fluttering on an untired
    wing, —
Oh! let him sing his happy song,
Nor do these gentle creatures wrong.

Table Manners I

The Goops they lick their fingers,
  And the Goops they lick their
    knives;
They spill their broth on the
    tablecloth —
  Oh, they lead disgusting lives!
The Goops they talk while eating,
  And loud and fast they chew;
And that is why I'm glad that I
  Am not a Goop — are you?

Table Manners II

The Goops are gluttonous and rude,
  They gug and gumble with their
    food;
They throw their crumbs upon the
    floor,
  And at dessert they tease for more;
They will not eat their soup and
    bread
  But like to gobble sweets, instead;
And this is why I oft decline,
  When I am asked to stay and dine!

Gelett Burgess

Courtesy Hints

Use good table manners.
Don't interrupt your parents when
        they are talking.
Say "please" and "thank you."
Say "excuse me" when you bump
        into someone.

Beautiful faces are they that wear
The light of a pleasant spirit there;
Beautiful hands are they that do
Deeds that are noble, good, and
        true;
Beautiful feet are they that go
Swiftly to lighten another's woe.

Keep this in mind, and all will go
        right
As on your way you go;
Be sure you know about all you tell
But don't tell all you know.

If you must yawn, just turn aside
And with your hand the motion
        hide.
And when you blow your nose, be
        brief;
And neatly use your handkerchief.

Of Courtesy

Good Manners may in Seven Words
        be found:
Forget Yourself and Think of Those
        Around.

                        Arthur Guiterman

Manners are the happy way of doing
        things.
Your manners are always under
        examination.

                        Ralph Waldo Emerson

Courtesy Tips

Be helpful
Be nice
Talk proper
Smile

Talking to God

I close my eyes and bow my head
When a grace or prayer is said.
I wouldn't stir or even nod
When other persons talk to God.

Garry Cleveland Myers

Hearts, Like Doors

Hearts, like doors,
        will open with ease
To very very little
        keys,
And don't forget that
        two of these
Are "Thank you, Sir,"
        and "If you please."

Robert Louis Stevenson

Golden Keys

A bunch of golden keys is mine
To make each day with gladness
    shine.
"Good Morning!" that's the golden
    key
That unlocks every day for me.
When evening comes, "Good
    Night!" I say
And close the door of each glad day.
When at the table "If you please,"
I take from off my bunch of keys.
When friends give anything to me,
I'll use my little "Thank you" key.
"Excuse me," "Beg your pardon,"
    too,
If by mistake some harm I do.
Or if unkindly harm I've given
With "Forgive me" key I'll be
    forgiven.
On a golden ring these keys I'll bind;
This is its motto: "Be ye kind."
I'll often use each golden key,
And so a happy child, polite I'll be.

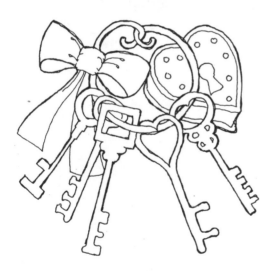

Whole Duty of Children

A child should always say what's
    true,
And speak when he is spoken to,
And behave mannerly at table —
At least as far as he is able.

Robert Louis Stevenson

Creatures of Every Kind

I think mice
Are rather nice.

Their tails are long,
Their faces small,
They haven't any
Chins at all.
Their ears are pink,
Their teeth are white,
They run about
The house at night.
They nibble things
They shouldn't touch
And no one seems
To like them much.

But *I* think mice
Are nice.

(Mice)
Rose Fyleman

Mary's Lamb

Mary had a little lamb,
 Its fleece was white as snow,
And every where that Mary went
 The lamb was sure to go;
He followed her to school one day —
 That was against the rule,
It made the children laugh and play,
 To see a lamb at school.

And so the Teacher turned him out,
 But still he lingered near,
And waited patiently about,
 Till Mary did appear;
And then he ran to her, and laid
 His head upon her arm,
As if he said — "I'm not afraid —
 You'll keep me from all harm."

"What makes the lamb love Mary
 so?"
 The eager children cry —
"O, Mary loves the lamb, you
 know,"
 The Teacher did reply —
"And you each gentle animal
 In confidence may bind,
And make them follow at your call,
 If you are always kind."

Sarah Josepha Hale

The Cow

The friendly cow all red and white,
 I love with all my heart;
She gives me cream, with all her
 might,
 To eat with apple-tart.

She wanders lowing here and there,
 And yet she cannot stray,
All in the pleasant open air,
 The pleasant light of day.

And blown by all the winds that pass
 And wet with all the showers,
She walks among the meadow grass
 And eats the meadow flowers.

Robert Louis Stevenson

Chanticleer

High and proud on the barnyard
 fence
Walks rooster in the morning.
He shakes his comb, he shakes his
 tail
And gives his daily warning.

"Get up, you lazy boys and girls,
It's time you should be dressing!"
I wonder if he keeps a clock,
Or if he's only guessing.

John Farrar

My Hairy Dog

My dog's so furry I've not seen
His face for years and years:
His eyes are buried out of sight,
I only guess his ears.

When people ask me for his breed,
I do not know or care:
He has the beauty of them all
Hidden beneath his hair.

Herbert Asquith

The Hippopotamus

In the squdgy river,
　　Down the oozely bank,
Where the ripples shiver,
　　And the reeds are rank.

Where the purple Kippo
　　Makes an awful fuss,
Lives the Hip-hip-hippo
　　Hippo-pot-a-mus!

Broad his back and steady;
　　Broad and flat his nose;
Sharp and keen and ready
　　Little eyes are those.

You would think him dreaming
　　Where the mud is deep.
It is only seeming —
　　He is not asleep.

Better not disturb him,
　　There'd be an awful fuss
If you touched the Hippo,
　　Hippo-pot-a-mus.

Georgia Roberts Durston

The Snail's Dream

A snail who had a way, it seems,
Of dreaming very curious dreams,
Once dreamt he was — you'll never
　　guess! —
The Lightning Limited Express.

Oliver Herford

Eletelephony

Once there was an elephant,
Who tried to use the telephant —
No! No! I mean an elephone
Who tried to use the telephone —
(Dear me! I am not certain quite
That even now I've got it right.)

Howe'er it was, he got his trunk
Entangled in the telephunk;
The more he tried to get it free,
The louder buzzed the telephee —
(I fear I'd better drop the song
Of elephop and telephong!)

Laura E. Richards

Trot Along, Pony

Trot along, pony.
　　Late in the day,
Down by the meadow
　　Is the loveliest way.

The apples are rosy
　　And ready to fall.
The branches hang over
　　By Grandfather's wall.

But the red sun is sinking
　　Away out of sight.
The chickens are settling
　　Themselves for the night.

Your stable is waiting
　　And supper will come.
So turn again, pony,
　　Turn again home.

Marion Edey and Dorothy Grider

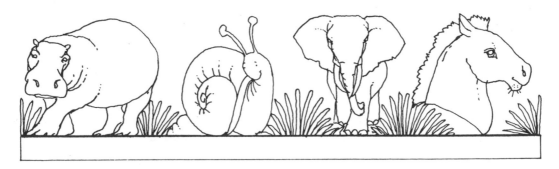

Lion Thoughts

I wouldn't like at all to be
A lion in a zoo,
With people standing there to see
The lion things I do.

I'd rather be in jungle land,
Beneath a jungle tree,
With only jungle animals
To stand and look at me.

Iowna Elizabeth Banker

The Seals

The seals all flap
Their shining flips
And bounce balls on
Their nosey tips,
And beat a drum,
And catch a bar,
And wriggle with
How pleased they are.

Dorothy Aldis

Once I Saw a Little Bird

Once I saw a little bird
  Come hop, hop, hop;
So I cried, "Little bird,
  Will you stop, stop, stop?"

And was going to the window
  To say, "How do you do?"
But he shook his little tail,
  And far away he flew.

The Squirrel

Whisky, frisky,
Hippity hop,
Up he goes
To the tree top!

Whirly, twirly,
Round and round,
Down he scampers
To the ground.

Furly, curly,
What a tail!
Tall as a feather,
Broad as a sail!

Where's his supper?
In the shell,
Snappity, crackity,
Out it fell!

Catkin

I have a little pussy,
  And her coat is silver gray;
She lives in a great wide meadow
  And she never runs away.
She always is a pussy,
  She'll never be a cat
Because — she's a pussy willow!
  Now what do you think of that!

Pussy has a whiskered face,
Kitty has such pretty ways;
Doggie scampers when I call,
And has a heart to love us all.

Christina Rossetti

The Happy Sheep

All through the night the happy
　　sheep
Lie in the meadow grass asleep.

Their wool keeps out the frost and
　　rain
Until the sun comes round again.

They have no buttons to undo,
Nor hair to brush, like me and you.

And with the light they lift their
　　heads
To find their breakfast on their beds,

Or rise and walk about and eat
The carpet underneath their feet.

Wilfred Thorley

Did you ever have a chipmunk for a
　　friend?
　I have one that I call "Chippy."
Sometimes he comes right on my
　　lap,
　If I put bread there,
　And stay very still.
　Then he sits up,
And holds the bread in his thin
　　brown fingers,
Turning it over and over as he eats,
And watching me with his round,
　　bright eye,
And listening with his tiny ears.
　If I even so much as breathe,
He stuffs the bread in his cheek and
　　scampers off.

Jessie Orton Jones
(XII from Secrets)

The Eagle

He clasps the crag with crooked
　　hands;
Close to the sun in lonely lands,
Ringed with the azure world, he
　　stands.

The wrinkled sea beneath him
　　crawls;
He watches from his mountain
　　walls,
And like a thunderbolt he falls.

Alfred Tennyson

What Is It?

Tall ears,
Twinkly nose,
Tiny tail,
And — hop, he goes!

What *is* he —
Can you guess?
I feed him carrots
And watercress.

His ears are long,
His tail is small —
And he doesn't make any
Noise at all!

Tall ears,
Twinkly nose,
Tiny tail,
And — hop, he goes!

Marie Louise Allen

The Caterpillar

Brown and furry
Caterpillar, in a hurry
Take your walk
To the shady leaf or stalk
Or what not,
Which may be the chosen spot.
No toad spy you,
Hovering bird of prey pass by you;
Spin and die,
To live again a butterfly.

Christina Rossetti

I Love Little Pussy

I love little Pussy,
   Her coat is so warm,
And if I don't hurt her,
   She'll do me no harm;
So I'll not pull her tail,
   Nor drive her away,
But Pussy and I
   Very gently will play.

Jane Taylor

The Hummingbird

The hummingbird, the
   hummingbird,
   So fairy-like and bright;
It lives among the sunny flowers,
   A creature of delight.

Mary Howitt

Little Robin Red-Breast

Little Robin Red-breast sat upon a
   tree,
Up went Pussy-cat, and down went
   he;
Down came Pussy-cat, and away
   Robin ran;
Says little Robin Red-breast,
"Catch me if you can."

Little Robin Red-breast jumped
   upon a wall,
Pussy-cat jumped after him, and
   almost got a fall;
Little Robin chirped and sang,
And what did Pussy say?
Pussy-cat said "Mew," and Robin
   flew away.

Choosing a Kitten

A black-nosed kitten will slumber all
   the day;
A white-nosed kitten is ever glad to
   play;
A yellow-nosed kitten will answer to
   your call;
And a gray-nosed kitten I like best of
   all.

Angleworms

I like to watch an angleworm.
He moves with such a funny squirm.
He stretches thin and long, and then
Gets quite short and fat again.

A robin likes him for a meal —
Though he's wiggle-y to feel!
On my hand, he twists and squirms,
But I do like angleworms!

Marie Louise Allen

The Humble Bee

Wiser far than human seer,
  Yellow-breeched philosopher!
Seeing only what is fair,
  Sipping only what is sweet,
Thou dost mock at fate and care.
  Leave the chaff, and take the
    wheat.

Ralph Waldo Emerson

Fuzzy wuzzy, creepy crawly
  Caterpillar funny,
You will be a butterfly
  When the days are sunny.

Lillian Schulz Vanada

The Grasshopper and the Elephant

Way down south where bananas
  grow,
A grasshopper stepped on an
  elephant's toe.
The elephant said, with tears in his
  eyes,
"Pick on somebody your own size."

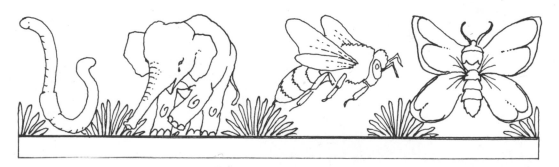

Curiosity

Does the Elephant remember,
In the gray light before dawn,
Old noises of the jungle
In mornings long gone?

Does the Elephant remember
The cry of hungry beasts;
The Tiger and the Leopard,
The Lion at his feasts?

Do his mighty eardrums listen
For the thunder of the feet
Of the Buffalo and Zebra
In the dark and dreadful heat?

Does His Majesty remember,
Does he stir himself and dream
Of the long-forgotten music
Of a long-forgotten stream?

(Circus Elephant)
Kathryn Worth

Why English Is So Hard!

We'll begin with a box, and the
  plural is boxes;
  But the plural of ox should be
  oxen, not oxes.
Then one fowl is goose, but two are
  called geese.
  Yet the plural of moose should
  never be meese.

You may find a lone mouse or a
  whole lot of mice,
  But the plural of house is houses,
  not hice.
If the plural of man is always called
  men,
  Why shouldn't the plural of pan be
  called pen?

The cow in the plural may be cows or
  kine,
  But the plural of vow is vows, not
  vine.
And I speak of a foot, and you show
  me your feet,
  But I give you a boot; would a pair
  be called beet?

If one is a tooth and a whole set are
  teeth,
  Why shouldn't the plural of booth
  be called beeth?
If the singular is this, and the plural
  is these,
  Should the plural of kiss be
  nicknamed kese?

That one may be that, and three may
  be those,
  Yet the plural of hat would never
  be hose;
We speak of a brother, and also of
  brethren,
  But though we say mother, we
  never say methren.

The masculine pronouns are he, his
  and him,
  But imagine the feminine she,
  shis and shim!
So our English, I think you will all
  agree,
  Is the trickiest language you ever
  did see.

The Fishing Pole

A fishing pole's a curious thing;
It's made of just a stick and string;
  A boy at one end and a wish;
  And on the other end a fish.

Mary Carolyn Davies

The Octopus

Tell me, O Octopus, I begs,
Is those things arms, or is they legs?
I marvel at thee, Octopus;
If I were thou, I'd call me Us.

Ogden Nash

If All the Seas Were One Sea

If all the seas were one sea,
What a *great* sea that would be!
And if all the trees were one tree,
What a *great* tree that would be!
And if all the axes were one axe,
What a *great* axe that would be!
And if all the men were one man,
What a *great* man he would be!
And if the *great* man took the *great*
  axe,
And cut down the *great* tree,
And let it fall into the *great* sea,
What a splish splash *that* would be!

A Pin Has a Head

A pin has a head, but has no hair;
A clock has a face, but no mouth
   there;
Needles have eyes, but they cannot
   see;
A fly has a trunk without lock or key;
A timepiece may lose, but cannot
   win;
A corn-field dimples without a chin;
A hill has no leg, but has a foot;
A wine-glass a stem, but not a root;
A watch has hands, but no thumb or
   finger;
A boot has a tongue, but is no
   singer;
Rivers run, though they have no
   feet;
A saw has teeth, but it does not eat;
Ash-trees have keys, yet never a
   lock;
And baby crows, without being a
   cock.

Christina Rossetti

Where Go the Boats?

Dark brown is the river,
   Golden is the sand.
It flows along forever,
   With trees on either hand.

Green leaves a-floating,
   Castles of the foam,
Boats of mine a-boating —
   Where will all come home?

On goes the river
   And out past the mill,
Away down the valley,
   Away down the hill.

Away down the river,
   A hundred miles or more,
Other little children
   Shall bring my boats ashore.

Robert Louis Stevenson

How Doth the Little Crocodile

How doth the little crocodile
   Improve his shining tail,
And pour the waters of the Nile
   On every golden scale!

How cheerfully he seems to grin,
   How neatly spreads his claws,
And welcomes little fishes in
   With gently smiling jaws!

Lewis Carroll

Sandpile Town

It took at least a morning
of working in the sun
and even then our village
was just a sandpile one —
the roads beyond the suburbs
were only just begun,
the little lakes we put in
were only just-for-fun —
how long it must have taken,
how long it must have taken,
how long it must have **taken**
before the World got done!

Aileen Fisher

71

Who Taught Them?

Who taught the bird to build her
          nest
    Of softest wool and hay and moss,
Who taught her how to weave it
          best,
    And lay the tiny twigs across?

Who taught the busy bee to fly
    Among the sweetest herbs and
          flowers;
And lay her store of honey by,
    Providing food for winter hours?

Who taught the little ant the way
    Her narrow hole so well to bore?
And through the pleasant summer
          day,
    To gather up her winter's store?

'Twas God that taught them all the
          way,
    And gave these little creatures
          skill;
And teaches children if they pray,
    To know and do His holy will.

I Often Pause and Wonder

I often pause and wonder
At fate's peculiar ways;
For nearly all our famous men
          were born on holidays.

Moles

Don't you feel sorry
for grubby old moles,
always in tunnels,
always in holes,
never out watching
the sun climb high
or the grass bend low
or the wind race by
or stars make twinkles
all over the sky?

                    Aileen Fisher

How They Sleep

Some things go to sleep in such a
          funny way:
Little birds stand on one leg and tuck
          their heads away;

Chickens do the same, standing on
          their perch;
Little mice lie soft and still, as if they
          were in church;

Kittens curl up close in such a funny
          ball;
Horses hang their sleepy heads and
          stand still in a stall;

Sometimes dogs stretch out, or curl
          up in a heap;
Cows lie down upon their sides
          when they would go to sleep.

But little babies dear are snugly
          tucked in beds,
Warm with blankets, all so soft, and
          pillows for their heads.

Bird and beast and babe — I wonder
          which of all
Dream the dearest dreams that down
          from dreamland fall!

What Robin Told

How do robins build their nests?
    Robin Redbreast told me —
First a wisp of yellow hay
In a pretty round they lay;

Then some shreds of downy floss,
Feathers, too, and bits of moss,
Woven with a sweet, sweet song,
This way, that way, and across;
    THAT'S what Robin told me.

Where do robins hide their nests?
    Robin Redbreast told me —
Up among the leaves so deep,
Where the sunbeams rarely creep,
Long before the leaves are gold,
Bright-eyed stars will peep and see
Baby robins — one, two, three;
    THAT'S what Robin told me.

                    George Cooper

72

The Naughty Boy

There was a naughty boy,
  And a naughty boy was he,
He ran away to Scotland
  The people for to see —
    Then he found
    That the ground
    Was as hard,
    That a yard
    Was as long,
    That a song
    Was as merry,
    That a cherry
    Was as red,
    That lead
    Was as weighty,
    That fourscore
    Was as eighty,
    That a door
    Was as wooden
    As in England —
So he stood in his shoes
  And he wondered,
  He wondered.
He stood in his shoes
  And he wondered.

                    John Keats

A Centipede

A centipede was happy quite
Until a frog in fun
Said, "Pray, which leg comes after
    which?"
This raised her mind to such a pitch,
She lay distracted in a ditch,
Considering how to run.

Flower in the Crannied Wall

Flower in the crannied wall,
I pluck you out of the crannies,
I hold you here, root and all, in my
    hand,
Little flower — but if I could
    understand
What you are, root and all, and all in
    all,
I should know what God and man is.

Alfred Tennyson

Whistles

I want to learn to whistle.
I've always wanted to.
I fix my mouth to do it but
The whistle won't come through.

I think perhaps it's stuck, and so
I try it once again.
Can people swallow whistles?
Where is my whistle then?

Dorothy Aldis

How Doth the Little Busy Bee

How doth the little busy bee
  Improve each shining hour,
And gather honey all the day
  From every passing flower!

How skillfully she builds her cell;
  How neat she spreads the wax!
And labors hard to store it well
  With the sweet food she makes.

Isaac Watts

Favorites

By the shores of Gitche Gumee,
By the shining Big-Sea-Water,
Stood the wigwam of Nokomis,
Daughter of the Moon, Nokomis.
Dark behind it rose the forest,
Rose the black and gloomy pine-
trees,
Rose the firs with cones upon them;
Bright before it beat the water,
Beat the clear and sunny water,
Beat the shining Big-Sea-Water.
There the wrinkled, old Nokomis
Nursed the little Hiawatha,
Rocked him in his linden cradle,
Bedded soft in moss and rushes,
Safely bound with reindeer sinews;
Stilled his fretful wail by saying,
"Hush! the Naked Bear will hear
thee!"
Lulled him into slumber, singing,
"Ewa-yea! my little owlet!
Who is this, that lights the wigwam?
With his great eyes lights the
wigwam?
Ewa-yea! my little owlet!"

Many things Nokomis taught him
Of the stars that shine in heaven;
Showed him Ishkoodah, the comet,
Ishkoodah, with fiery tresses;
Showed the Death-Dance of the
spirits,
Warriors with their plumes and
war-clubs,
Flaring far away to northward
In the frosty nights of Winter;
Showed the broad, white road in
heaven,
Pathway of the ghosts, the shadows,
Running straight across the
heavens,
Crowded with the ghosts, the
shadows.

At the door on summer evenings
Sat the little Hiawatha;
Heard the whispering of the pine-
trees,
Heard the lapping of the water,
Sounds of music, words of wonder;
"Minne-wawa!" said the pine-trees,
"Mudway-aushka!" said the water.

Saw the fire-fly, Wah-wah-taysee,
Flitting through the dusk of
evening,
With the twinkle of its candle
Lighting up the brakes and bushes,
And he sang the song of children,
Sang the song Nokomis taught him:
"Wah-wah-taysee, little fire-fly,
Little, flitting, white-fire insect,
Little, dancing, white-fire creature,
Light me with your little candle,
Ere upon my bed I lay me,
Ere in sleep I close my eyelids!"

Saw the moon rise from the water,
Rippling, rounding from the water,
Saw the flecks and shadows on it,
Whispered, "What is that,
Nokomis?"
And the good Nokomis answered:
"Once a warrior, very angry,
Seized his grandmother, and threw
her
Up into the sky at midnight;
Right against the moon he threw
her;
'Tis her body that you see there."

Saw the rainbow in the heavens,
In the eastern sky, the rainbow,
Whispered, "What is that,
Nokomis?"
And the good Nokomis answered:
" 'Tis the heaven of flowers you see
there;
All the wild-flowers of the forest,
All the lilies of the prairie,
When on earth they fade and perish,
Blossom in that heaven above us."

When he heard the owls at
midnight,
Hooting, laughing in the forest,
"What is that?" he cried in terror;
"What is that?" he said,
"Nokomis?"
And the good Nokomis answered:
"That is but the owl and owlet,
Talking in their native language,
Talking, scolding at each other."

Then the little Hiawatha
Learned of every bird its language,
Learned their names and all their
secrets,
How they built their nests in
Summer,
Where they hid themselves in
Winter,
Talked with them whene'er he met
them,
Called them "Hiawatha's
Chickens."

Of all beasts he learned the
language,
Learned their names and all their
secrets,
How the beavers built their lodges,
Where the squirrels hid their acorns,
How the reindeer ran so swiftly,
Why the rabbit was so timid,
Talked with them whene'er he met
them,
Called them "Hiawatha's Brothers."

(Hiawatha's Childhood)
Henry Wadsworth Longfellow

76

The Village Blacksmith

Under a spreading chestnut tree
  The village smithy stands;
The smith, a mighty man is he,
  With large and sinewy hands;
And the muscles of his brawny arms
  Are strong as iron bands.

His hair is crisp, and black, and
    long,
  His face is like the tan;
His brow is wet with honest sweat,
  He earns whate'er he can,
And looks the whole world in the
    face,
  For he owes not any man.

Week in, week out, from morn till
    night,
  You can hear his bellows blow;
You can hear him swing his heavy
    sledge,
  With measured beat and slow,
Like a sexton ringing the village bell,
  When the evening sun is low.

And children coming home from
    school
  Look in at the open door;
They love to see the flaming forge,
  And hear the bellows roar,
And catch the burning sparks that
    fly
  Like chaff from a threshing floor.

He goes on Sunday to the church,
  And sits among his boys;
He hears the parson pray and
    preach,
  He hears his daughter's voice,
Singing in the village choir,
  And it makes his heart rejoice.

It sounds to him like her mother's
    voice,
  Singing in Paradise!
He needs must think of her once
    more,
  How in the grave she lies;
And with his hard, rough hand he
    wipes
  A tear out of his eyes.

Toiling — rejoicing — sorrowing,
  Onward through life he goes;
Each morning sees some task begin,
  Each evening sees it close;
Something attempted, something
    done,
  Has earned a night's repose.

Thanks, thanks to thee, my worthy
    friend,
  For the lesson thou has taught!
Thus at the flaming forge of life
  Our fortunes must be wrought;
Thus on its sounding anvil shaped
  Each burning deed and thought!

Henry Wadsworth Longfellow

The Bugle Song

The splendor falls on castle walls
And snowy summits old in story:
The long light shakes across the
    lakes,
And the wild cataract leaps in glory.

Blow, bugle, blow,
Set the wild echoes flying,
Blow, bugle; answer, echoes,
Dying, dying, dying.

O hark, O hear! how thin and clear,
And thinner, clearer, farther going!
O sweet and far from cliff and scar
The horns of Elfland faintly blowing!

Blow, let us hear,
The purple glens replying:
Blow, bugle; answer, echoes,
Dying, dying, dying.

O love, they die in yon rich sky,
They faint on hill or field or river:
Our echoes roll from soul to soul,
And grow for ever and for ever.

Blow, bugle, blow,
Set the wild echoes flying,
And answer, echoes, answer,
Dying, dying, dying.

Alfred Tennyson
(from The Princess)

The Apostles' Creed

I believe in God the Father
    Almighty,
  Maker of heaven and earth.
And in Jesus Christ, His Son, our
    Lord;
Who was conceived by the Holy
    Ghost,
Born of the Virgin Mary,
Suffered under Pontius Pilate,
Was crucified, dead, and buried;
He descended into hell;
The third day He arose from the
    dead;
He ascended into heaven,
And sitteth on the right hand of God
    the Father Almighty;
From thence He shall come to judge
    the quick and the dead.
I believe in the Holy Ghost;
The holy Christian Church; the
    communion of saints;
The forgiveness of sins;
The resurrection of the body;
And the life everlasting.
Amen.

Time to Rise

A birdie with a yellow bill
Hopped upon the window sill,
Cocked his shining eye and said:
"Ain't you 'shamed, you sleepy-
    head!"

          Robert Louis Stevenson

I Can

So nigh is grandeur to our dust,
So near is God to man,
When Duty whispers low, *Thou
    must,*
The youth replies, *I can.*

          Ralph Waldo Emerson
          (from Voluntaries, III)

Old Ships

There is a memory stays upon old
    ships,
  A weightless cargo in the musty
      hold —
Of bright lagoons and prow-
    caressing lips,
  Of stormy midnights — and a tale
      untold.
They have remembered islands in
    the dawn,
  And windy capes that tried their
      slender spars,
And tortuous channels where their
    keels have gone,
  And calm blue nights of stillness
      and the stars.

Ah, never think that ships forget a
    shore,
  Or bitter seas, or winds that made
      them wise;
There is a dream upon them,
    evermore —
  And there be some who say that
      sunk ships rise
To seek familiar harbors in the
    night,
  Blowing in mists, their spectral
      sails like light.

David Morton

The Lord is my shepherd; I shall not
want.
He maketh me to lie down in green
pastures:
He leadeth me beside the still
waters.
He restoreth my soul:
He leadeth me in the paths of
righteousness for his name's
sake.
Yea, though I walk through the
valley of the shadow of death,
I will fear no evil: for thou art with
me;
Thy rod and thy staff they comfort
me.
Thou preparest a table before me in
the presence of mine enemies:
Thou anointest my head with oil; my
cup runneth over.
Surely goodness and mercy shall
follow me all the days of my
life:
And I will dwell in the house of the
Lord for ever.

The Bible, Psalm 23

The Destruction of Sennacherib

The Assyrian came down like the
wolf on the fold,
And his cohorts were gleaming in
purple and gold;
And the sheen of their spears was
like stars on the sea,
When the blue wave rolls nightly on
deep Galilee.

Like the leaves of the forest when
Summer is green,
That host with their banners at
sunset were seen;
Like the leaves of the forest when
Autumn hath blown,
That host on the morrow lay
wither'd and strown.

For the Angel of Death spread his
wings on the blast,
And breathed in the face of the foe as
he passed;
And the eyes of the sleepers waxed
deadly and chill,
And their hearts but once heaved,
and for ever grew still!

And there lay the steed with his
nostril all wide,
But through it there rolled not the
breath of his pride;
And the foam of his gasping lay
white on the turf,
And cold as the spray of the rock-
beating surf.

And there lay the rider distorted and
pale,
With the dew on his brow, and the
rust on his mail;
And the tents were all silent, the
banners alone,
The lances uplifted, the trumpet
unblown.

And the widows of Ashur are loud in
their wail,
And the idols are broken in the
temple of Baal;
And the might of the Gentile,
unsmote by the sword,
Hath melted like snow in the glance
of the Lord!

Lord Byron

Monday's child is fair of face,
Tuesday's child is full of grace,
Wednesday's child is full of woe,
Thursday's child has far to go,
Friday's child is loving and giving,
Saturday's child works hard for a
living,
But the child that is born on the
Sabbath day
Is blithe and bonny and good and
gay.

Pop Goes the Weasel

A penny for a ball of thread,
Another for a needle.
That's the way the money goes;
  Pop goes the Weasel!

All around the cobbler's bench
The monkey chased the people;
The donkey thought 'twas all in fun.
  Pop goes the Weasel!

Queen Victoria's very sick;
Napoleon's got the measles;
Sally's got the whooping cough;
  Pop goes the Weasel!

Of all the dances ever planned,
To fling the heel and fly the hand,
There's none that moves so gay and
    grand
  As Pop goes the Weasel!

A penny for a ball of thread,
Another for a needle.
That's the way the money goes;
  Pop goes the Weasel!

Taking Off

The airplane taxis down the field
And heads into the breeze,
It lifts its wheels above the ground,
It skims above the trees,
It rises high and higher
Away up toward the sun,
It's just a speck against the sky
— And now it's gone!

Daffadowndilly

Daffadowndilly
  Has come up to town,
In a yellow petticoat
  And a green gown.

Mother Goose

Little Boy Blue

The little toy dog is covered with
    dust,
But sturdy and staunch he stands;
And the little toy soldier is red with
    rust,
And his musket moulds in his
    hands.
Time was when the little toy dog was
    new,
And the soldier was passing fair;
And that was the time when our
    Little Boy Blue
Kissed them and put them there.

"Now, don't you go till I come," he
    said,
"And don't you make any noise!"
So, toddling off to his trundle-bed,
He dreamt of the pretty toys;
And, as he was dreaming, an angel
    song
Awakened our Little Boy Blue —
Oh! the years are many, the years are
    long,
But the little toy friends are true.

Ay, faithful to Little Boy Blue they
    stand,
Each in the same old place.
Awaiting the touch of a little hand,
The smile of a little face;
And they wonder, as waiting the
    long years through
In the dust of that little chair,
What has become of our Little Boy
    Blue,
Since he kissed them and put them
    there.

Eugene Field

Of Giving

Not what you Get, but what you
    Give
Is that which proves your Right to
    Live.

Arthur Guiterman

The Monkeys and the Crocodile

Five little monkeys
Swinging from a tree;
Leaving Uncle Crocodile,
Merry as can be.
Swinging high, swinging low,
Swinging left and right:
"Dear Uncle Crocodile,
Come and take a bite!"

Five little monkeys
Swinging in the air;
Heads up, tails up,
Little do they care.
Swinging up, swinging down,
Swinging far and near:
"Poor Uncle Crocodile,
Aren't you hungry, dear?"

Four little monkeys
Sitting in a tree;
Heads down, tails down,
Dreary as can be.
Weeping loud, weeping low,
Crying to each other:
"Wicked Uncle Crocodile,
To gobble up our brother!"

Laura E. Richards

Day-Dreamer

Too much thought:
Too little wrought.

Adapted from the German by
Louis Untermeyer

Clementine

In a cavern, in a canyon,
Excavating for a mine,
Dwelt a miner, forty-niner,
And his daughter Clementine.

Light she was and like a fairy,
And her shoes were number nine,
Herring boxes, without topses
Sandals were for Clementine.

Drove she ducklings to the water,
Every morning, just at nine,
Hit her foot against a splinter,
Fell into the foaming brine.

Ruby lips above the water,
Blowing bubbles soft and fine,
Alas for me! I was no swimmer
So I lost my Clementine.

Oh, my darling, oh, my darling,
Oh, my darling Clementine,
You are lost and gone forever,
Dreadful sorry, Clementine.

Under the greenwood tree
Who loves to lie with me,
And turn his merry note
Unto the sweet bird's throat,
Come hither, come hither, come
   hither:
Here shall he see
No enemy
But winter and rough weather.

William Shakespeare

Little Lost Pup

He was lost! — not a shade of doubt
    of that;
For he never barked at a slinking cat,
But stood in the square where the
    wind blew raw
With a drooping ear and a trembling
    paw
And a mournful look in his pleading
    eye
And a plaintive sniff at the passer-by
That begged as plain as a tongue
    could sue,
"O Mister! please may I follow you?"
A lorn wee waif of a tawny brown
Adrift in the roar of a heedless town.
Oh, the saddest of sights in a world
    of sin
Is a little lost pup with his tail tucked
    in!

Now he shares my board and he
    owns my bed,
And he fairly shouts when he hears
    my tread;
Then, if things go wrong, as they
    sometimes do,
He asserts his right to assuage my
    woes
With a warm, red tongue and a nice,
    cold nose
And a silky head on my arm or knee
And a paw as soft as a paw can be.

When we rove the woods for a
    league about
He's as full of pranks as a school let
    out;
For he romps and frisks like a three
    month's colt,
And he runs me down like a
    thunderbolt.
Oh, the blithest of sights in the
    world so fair
Is a gay little pup with his tail in the
    air!

Arthur Guiterman

Fairest Lord Jesus

Fairest Lord Jesus,
    Ruler of all nature,
Son of God and Son of Man!
    Thee will I cherish, thee will I
      honor,
Thou, my soul's glory, joy, and
    crown.

Fair are the meadows,
    Fair are the woodlands,
Robed in the blooming garb of
    spring:
    Jesus is fairer, Jesus is purer,
Who makes the woeful heart to sing.

Fair is the sunshine,
    Fair is the moonlight,
And all the twinkling, starry host:
    Jesus shines brighter, Jesus shines
      purer,
Than all the angels heaven can boast.

The Charge of the Light Brigade

Half a league, half a league,
    Half a league onward,
All in the valley of Death
    Rode the six hundred.
'Forward, the Light Brigade!
Charge for the guns!' he said:
Into the valley of Death
    Rode the six hundred.

'Forward, the Light Brigade!'
Was there a man dismayed?
Not though the soldier knew
    Some one had blundered:
Theirs not to make reply,
Theirs not to reason why,
Theirs but to do and die:
Into the valley of Death
    Rode the six hundred.

Cannon to right of them,
Cannon to left of them,
Cannon in front of them
  Volleyed and thundered;
Stormed at with shot and shell,
Boldly they rode and well,
Into the jaws of Death,
Into the mouth of Hell
  Rode the six hundred.

Flashed all their sabres bare,
Flashed as they turned in air
Sabring the gunners there,
Charging an army, while
  All the world wondered:
Plunged in the battery-smoke
Right through the line they broke;
Cossack and Russian
Reeled from the sabre-stroke
  Shattered and sundered.
Then they rode back, but not —
  Not the six hundred.

Cannon to right of them,
Cannon to left of them,
Cannon behind them
  Volleyed and thundered;
Stormed at with shot and shell,
While horse and hero fell,
They that had fought so well
Came through the jaws of Death,
Back from the mouth of Hell,
All that was left of them,
  Left of six hundred.

When can their glory fade?
O the wild charge they made!
  All the world wondered.
Honour the charge they made!
Honour the Light Brigade,
  Noble six hundred!

          Alfred Tennyson

Oh, what a tangled web we weave,
When first we practice to deceive!
          Walter Scott.
          (from Marmion)

A stitch in time saves nine.

Energy will do anything that can be done in this world.

Johann Wolfgang von Goethe

Wealth is not his that has it, but his that enjoys it.

Benjamin Franklin

Originality is simply a pair of fresh eyes.

T. W. Higginson

Temperance and labor are the two best physicians.

Rousseau

Genius is 90 percent perspiration, 10 percent inspiration.

Nothing dries sooner than a tear.

Truth never hurts the teller.

Elizabeth Barrett Browning

An apple a day
Will keep the doctor away.

When pleasant work is mixed with
    play,
It makes a very happy day.

I mean to make myself a man,
and if I succeed in that,
I shall succeed in everything else.

James A. Garfield

Friends

I like to play with many boys,
   But there's a special one,
For Andy is my truest friend:
We plan together days on end,
   And have a lot of fun.

We have our ups and downs, of
      course,
   And often disagree;
Sometimes I let him have his way,
And sometimes in our work and
      play,
   He does the same for me.

For friends must give and friends
      must take,
And each must do his part to make
   A friendship tried and true.

                              (Friends)

The Sandpiper

Across the narrow beach we flit,
One little sandpiper and I,
And fast I gather, bit by bit,
The scattered driftwood bleached
    and dry.
The wild waves reach their hands for
    it,
The wild wind raves, the tide runs
    high,
As up and down the beach we flit —
One little sandpiper and I.

Above our heads the sullen clouds
Scud black and swift across the sky;
Like silent ghosts in misty shrouds
Stand out the white lighthouses
    high.
Almost as far as eye can reach
I see the close-reefed vessels fly,
As fast we flit along the beach —
One little sandpiper and I.

I watch him as he skims along,
Uttering his sweet and mournful
    cry.
He starts not at my fitful song,
Or flash of fluttering drapery.
He has no thought of any wrong;
He scans me with a fearless eye:
Staunch friends are we, well tried
    and strong,
The little sandpiper and I.

Comrade, where wilt thou be
    tonight
When the loosed storm breaks
    furiously?
My driftwood fire will burn so
    bright!
To what warm shelter canst thou fly?
I do not fear for thee, though wroth
The tempest rushes through the sky:
For are we not God's children both,
Thou, little sandpiper, and I?

Celia Thaxter

Growing Friendship

Friendship is like a garden of
    flowers, fine and rare;
It cannot reach perfection except
    through loving care;
Then, new and lovely blossoms with
    each new day appear —
For Friendship, like a garden, grows
    in beauty year by year.

There's happiness in little things,
There's joy in passing pleasure;
But friendships are, from year to
    year,
The best of all life's treasure.

It's a Funny Thing but True

It's a funny thing, but true,
The folks you don't like, don't like
    you.
I don't know why this should be so,
But just the same I always know
That when I'm sour, friends are few;
When I'm friendly, folks are, too.
I sometimes get up in the morn,
Awishin' I was never born,
And then I make cross remarks, a
    few,
And then my family wishes, too,
That I had gone some other place,
But then I change my little tune,
And sing and smile,
And then the folks around me sing
    and smile.
I guess 'twas catching all the while.
It's a funny thing, but true,
The folks you like, they sure like
    you.

86

Jenny White and Johnny Black

Jenny White and Johnny Black
　　Went out for a walk.
Jenny found wild strawberries,
　　And John a lump of chalk.

Jenny White and Johnny Black
　　Clambered up a hill.
Jenny heard a willow-wren,
　　And John a workman's drill.

Jenny White and Johnny Black
　　Wandered by the dike.
Jenny smelt the meadow sweet,
　　And John a motor-bike.

Jenny White and Johnny Black
　　Turned into a lane.
Jenny saw the moon by day,
　　And Johnny saw a train.

Jenny White and Johnny Black
　　Walked into a storm.
Each felt for the other's hand
　　And found it nice and warm.

Eleanor Farjeon

Friends

How good to lie a little while
　　And look up through the tree —
The Sky is like a kind big smile
　　Bent sweetly over me.

The Sunshine flickers through the
　　　lace
　　Of leaves above my head,
And kisses me upon the face
　　Like Mother, before bed.

The Wind comes stealing o'er the
　　　grass
　　To whisper pretty things;
And though I cannot see him pass,
　　I feel his careful wings.

So many gentle Friends are near
　　Whom one can scarcely see,
A child should never feel a fear,
　　Wherever he may be.

Abbie Farwell Brown

Jesus, Friend of Little Children

Jesus, friend of little children,
Be a friend to me;
Take my hand and ever keep me
Close to Thee.

Teach me how to grow in goodness
Daily as I grow;
Thou has been a child and surely
Thou dost know.

Fill me with Thy gentle meekness,
Make my heart like Thine;
Like an altar lamp then let me
Burn and shine.

Step by step, O lead me onward,
Upward into youth;
Wiser, stronger still, becoming,
In Thy truth.

Walter J. Mathams

A Little Word

A little word in kindness spoken,
   A motion or a tear,
Has often healed the heart that's
      broken,
And made a friend sincere.

Daniel Clement Colesworthy

No one is too small to be able to help
a friend.

A true friend is the best possession.

Talk not of wasted affection,
   affection never was wasted;
If it enrich not the heart of another,
   its waters, returning
Back to their springs, like the rain,
   shall fill them full of refreshment;
That which the fountain sends forth
      returns
   again to the fountain.

                Henry Wadsworth Longfellow
                      (from Evangeline)

The only safe
And sure way
To destroy an enemy:
Make him your friend.

A friend is a person
   who likes you
   for what you are
   in spite of your faults.

In Gratitude for Friends

I thank You, God in Heaven, for
      friends.
When morning wakes, when
      daytime ends.
   I have the consciousness
Of loving hands that touch my own,
Of tender glance and gentle tone,
   Of thoughts that cheer and bless!
If sorrow comes to me I know
That friends will walk the way I go,
   And, as the shadows fall,
I know that I will raise my eyes
And see — ah, hope that never
      dies! —
   The dearest Friend of All.

                Margaret E. Sangster

Make Me Worthy of My Friends

It is my joy in life to find
   At every turning of the road
The strong arms of a comrade kind
   To help me onward with my load.
And since I have no gold to give
   And love alone can make amends,
My only prayer is, "While I live,
   God, make me worthy of my
      friends!"

The Arrow and the Song

I shot an arrow into the air,
It fell to earth, I knew not where;
For, so swiftly it flew, the sight
Could not follow it in its flight.

I breathed a song into the air,
It fell to earth, I knew not where;
For who has sight so keen and
    strong,
That it can follow the flight of song?

Long, long afterward, in an oak
I found the arrow, still unbroke;
And the song, from beginning to
    end,
I found again in the heart of a friend.

Henry Wadsworth Longfellow

Fun and Nonsense

Bibbily Boo, the king so free,
He used to drink the Mango tea.
Mango tea and coffee, too,
He drank them both till his nose
turned blue.

Wollypotump, the queen so high,
She used to eat the Gumbo pie.
Gumbo pie and Gumbo cake,
She ate them both till her teeth did
break.

Bibbily Boo and Wollypotump,
Each called the other a greedy
frump.
And when these terrible words were
said,
They sat and cried till they both were
dead.

(Bibbily Boo and Wollypotump)
Laura E. Richards

There Was an Old Man With a Beard

There was an Old Man with a beard,
Who said, "It is just as I feared! —
    Two Owls and a Hen,
    Four Larks and a Wren,
Have all built their nests in my
    beard."

Edward Lear

Antonio

Antonio, Antonio,
Was tired of living alonio.
    He thought he would woo
    Miss Lissamy Lu,
Miss Lissamy Lucy Molino.

Antonio, Antonio,
Rode off on his polo-ponio.
    He found the fair maid
    In a bowery shade,
A-sitting and knitting alonio.

Antonio, Antonio,
Said, "If you will be my ownio,
    I'll love you true,
    And I'll buy for you,
An icery creamery conio!"

"Oh, nonio, Antonio!
You're far too bleak and bonio!
    And all that I wish,
    You singular fish,
Is that you will quickly begonio."

Antonio, Antonio,
He uttered a dismal moanio;
    Then ran off and hid
    (Or I'm told that he did)
In the Antarctical Zonio.

Laura E. Richards

Roses are red,
Violets are blue,
I copied your paper,
And I flunked too.

Foolish Flowers

We've Foxgloves in our garden;
    How careless they must be
To leave their gloves out hanging
    Where every one can see!

And Bachelors leave their Buttons
    In the same careless way;
If I should do the same with mine,
    What would Mother say?

We've lots of Larkspurs in the
        yard —
    Larks only fly and sing —
Birds surely don't need spurs
        because
    They don't ride anything!

And as for Johnny-Jump-Ups —
    I saw a hornet light
On one of them the other day;
    He didn't jump a mite!

Rupert Sargent Holland

There Were Three Ghostesses

There were three ghostesses
Sitting on postesses
Eating buttered toastesses
And greasing their fistesses
Right up to their wristesses.
Weren't they beastesses
To make such feastesses?

Oh, the Funniest Thing

Oh, the funniest thing
    I've ever seen
Was a tomcat sewing
    On a sewing machine.
Oh, the sewing machine
    Got running too slow,
And it took seven stitches
    In the tomcat's toe.

Five Little Squirrels

Five little squirrels sat up in a tree.
The first one said, "What do I see?"
The second one said, "A man with a
    gun."
The third one said, "Then we'd
    better run."
The fourth one said, "Let's hide in
    the shade."
The fifth one said, "I'm not afraid."
Then BANG went the gun,
And how they did run.

A Tutor Who Tooted the Flute

A Tutor who tooted the flute
Tried to teach two young tooters to
    toot;
    Said the two to the Tutor,
    "Is it harder to toot, or
To tutor two tooters to toot?"

"The time has come," the Walrus
    said,
    "To talk of many things:
Of shoes — and ships — and
    sealing-wax —
    Of cabbages — and kings —
And why the sea is boiling hot —
    And whether pigs have wings."

Lewis Carroll

The Twins

In form and feature, face and limb,
    I grew so like my brother,
That folks got taking me for him,
    And each for one another.
It puzzled all our kith and kin,
    It reached an awful pitch;
For one of us was born a twin,
    Yet not a soul knew which.

One day (to make the matter worse),
    Before our names were fixed,
As we were being washed by nurse
    We got completely mixed;
And thus, you see, by Fate's decree,
    (Or rather nurse's whim),
My brother John got christened *me*,
    And I got christened *him*.

This fatal likeness even dogg'd
    My footsteps when at school,
And I was always getting flogg'd,
    For John turned out a fool.
I put this question hopelessly
    To everyone I knew —
What *would* you do, if you were me,
    To prove that you were *you*?

Our close resemblance turned the
    tide
    Of my domestic life;
For somehow my intended bride
    Became my brother's wife.
In short, year after year the same
    Absurd mistake went on;
And when I died — the neighbors
    came
    And buried brother John!

Henry S. Leigh

93

Inky, dinky spider
Climbed up the waterspout;
Down came the rain
And washed the spider out;
Up came the sun
And drove away the rain;
Inky, dinky spider climbed up the
    spout again.

Poor Old Lady

Poor old lady, she swallowed a fly.
I don't know why she swallowed a
    fly.
Poor old lady, I think she'll die.

Poor old lady, she swallowed a
    spider,
It squirmed and wriggled and
    turned inside her.
She swallowed the spider to catch
    the fly.
I don't know why she swallowed a
    fly.
Poor old lady, I think she'll die.

Poor old lady, she swallowed a bird.
How absurd! She swallowed a bird.
She swallowed the bird to catch the
    spider,
She swallowed the spider to catch
    the fly.
I don't know why she swallowed a
    fly.
Poor old lady, I think she'll die.

Poor old lady, she swallowed a cat.
Think of that! She swallowed a cat.
She swallowed the cat to catch the
    bird,
She swallowed the bird to catch the
    spider,
She swallowed the spider to catch
    the fly.
I don't know why she swallowed a
    fly.
Poor old lady, I think she'll die.

Poor old lady, she swallowed a dog.
She went the whole hog when she
    swallowed the dog.
She swallowed the dog to catch the
    cat,
She swallowed the cat to catch the
    bird,
She swallowed the bird to catch the
    spider,
She swallowed the spider to catch
    the fly.
I don't know why she swallowed a
    fly.
Poor old lady, I think she'll die.

Poor old lady, she swallowed a cow.
I don't know how she swallowed a
    cow.
She swallowed a cow to catch the
    dog,
She swallowed the dog to catch the
    cat,
She swallowed the cat to catch the
    bird,
She swallowed the bird to catch the
    spider,
She swallowed the spider to catch
    the fly.
I don't know why she swallowed a
    fly.
Poor old lady, I think she'll die.

Poor old lady, she swallowed a
    horse.
She died, of course.

(attributed to Pamela Smith)

The Poor Unfortunate Hottentot

A poor unfortunate Hottentot
He was not content with his
    lottentot;
    Quoth he, "For my dinner,
    As I am a sinner,
There's nothing to put in the
    pottentot!"

This poor unfortunate Hottentot
Said, "Yield to starvation I'll
    nottentot;
  I'll see if I can't elope
  With a young antelope —
One who'll enjoy being shottentot."

This poor unfortunate Hottentot
His bow and his arrows he
    gottentot;
  And being stout-hearted,
  At once he departed,
And struck through the Bush at a
    trottentot.

This poor unfortunate Hottentot,
Was not many miles from his
    cottentot,
  When he chanced to set eyes on
  A snake that was pison,
A-tying itself in a knottentot.

This poor unfortunate Hottentot
Remarked, "This for me is not
    spottentot!
  I'd better be going;
  There's really no knowing;
I might on his view be a blottentot."

This poor unfortunate Hottentot,
Was turning to fly to his grottentot,
  When a lioness met him,
  And suddenly ate him,
As penny's engulfed by the
    slottentot.

Moral

This poor unfortunate Hottentot,
Had better have borne with his
    lottentot.
  A simple banana
  Had staved off Nirvana;
But what had become of my
    plottentot?

Laura E. Richards

Some Fishy Nonsense

Timothy Tiggs and Tomothy Toggs,
They both went a-fishing for
    pollothywogs;
  They both went a-fishing
  Because they were wishing
To see how the creatures would turn
    into frogs.

Timothy Tiggs and Tomothy Toggs,
They both got stuck in the
    bogothybogs;
  They caught a small minnow
  And said 'twas a sin oh!
That things with no legs should
    pretend to be frogs.

Laura E. Richards

Fifty Cents

I asked my mother for fifty cents
To see the elephant jump the fence.

He jumped so high,
He reached the sky.

He never came back
'Til the Fourth of July.

Fun

I love to see a lobster laugh
Or see a turtle wiggle
Or poke a hippopotamus
And see the monster giggle,
Or even stand around at night
And watch the mountains wriggle.

Leroy F. Jackson

There was a young lady of Riga,
Who rode with a smile on a tiger;
  They returned from the ride
  With the lady inside,
And the smile on the face of the
  tiger.

There was a young lady of Lynn,
Who was so uncommonly thin,
  That when she essayed
  To drink lemonade,
She slipped through the straw and
  fell in.

The Purple Cow

I never saw a purple cow
I never hope to see one,
But I can tell you anyhow,
I'd rather see than be one!

Gelett Burgess

A cheerful old bear at the zoo
Could always find something to do.
  When it bored him, you know,
  To walk to and fro,
He reversed it and walked fro and to.

On Leslie Moore

Here lies what's left
Of Leslie Moore
  No Les
  No More

State Quiz

What did Delaware?
  She wore her New Jersey.
Where has Oregon?
  He's taking Oklahoma.
What does Iowa?
  She hoes the Maryland.
How did Connecticut?
  She used the New Hampshire.
What does Mississippi?
  She sips her Old Virginia.
How does Florida?
  She died of Missouri.
How did Wisconsin?
  He stole the Nebraska.
What did Tennessee?
  He saw what Arkansas.
What did Massachusetts?
  He chewed his Old Kentucky.

The Ostrich Is a Silly Bird

The ostrich is a silly bird,
  With scarcely any mind.
He often runs so very fast,
  He leaves himself behind.

And when he gets there, has to stand
  And hang about till night,
Without a blessed thing to do
  Until he comes in sight.

Mary E. Wilkins Freeman

Theophilus Thistledown

Theophilus Thistledown, the
  successful thistle sifter,
In sifting a sieve of unsifted thistles,
Thrust three thousand thistles
Through the thick of his thumb.
If then, Theophilus Thistledown,
  the successful thistle sifter,
In sifting a sieve of unsifted thistles,
Thrust three thousand thistles
Through the thick of his thumb,
See that thou, in sifting a sieve of
  unsifted thistles,
Do not get the unsifted thistles stuck
  in thy tongue.

Jaybird

Jaybird a-sitting on a hickory limb;
  He winked at me and I winked
  at him.
I picked up a rock and hit him on the
  chin.
Says he, "Young feller, don't you do
  that again!"

Ashes to ashes
Dust to dust,
Oil those brains
Before they rust.

You can lead a horse to water,
But you cannot make him drink.
You can send a fool to college,
But you cannot make him think.

A Tragic Story

There lived a sage in days of yore,
And he a handsome pigtail wore;
But wondered much and sorrowed
    more,
Because it hung behind him.

He mused upon this curious case,
And swore he'd change the pigtail's
    place,
And have it hanging at his face,
Not dangling there behind him.

Says he, "The mystery I've found —
I'll turn me round," — he turned him
    round;
But still it hung behind him.
Then round and round, and out and
    in,
All day the puzzled sage did spin;
In vain — it mattered not a pin —
The pigtail hung behind him.

And right and left, and round about,
And up and down, and in and out,
He turned; but still the pigtail stout
Hung steadily behind him.

And though his efforts never slack,
And though he twist and twirl and
    tack,
Alas! still faithful to his back,
The pigtail hangs behind him.

William Makepeace Thackeray

A Flea and a Fly in a Flue

A flea and a fly in a flue
Were imprisoned, so what could
    they do?
  Said the fly, "Let us flee,"
  Said the flea, "Let us fly,"
So they flew through a flaw in the
    flue.

On a mule you find two feet behind,
Two feet you find before;
You stand behind before you find
What the two behind be for.

Peas

I always eat peas with honey,
I've done it all my life,
They do taste kind of funny,
But it keeps them on my knife.

The noble Duke of York,
He had ten thousand men,
He marched them up to the top of the
    hill,
And he marched them down again.
And when they were up, they were
    up,
And when they were down, they
    were down,
And when they were only half way
    up,
    They were neither up nor down.

A young theologian named Fiddle
Refused to accept his degree.
"For," said he, " 'tis enough to be
    Fiddle,
Without being Fiddle, D.D."

Buttons

The front ones I can button fine
The side ones keep me busy
But buttons all the way behind
I hunt until I'm dizzy!

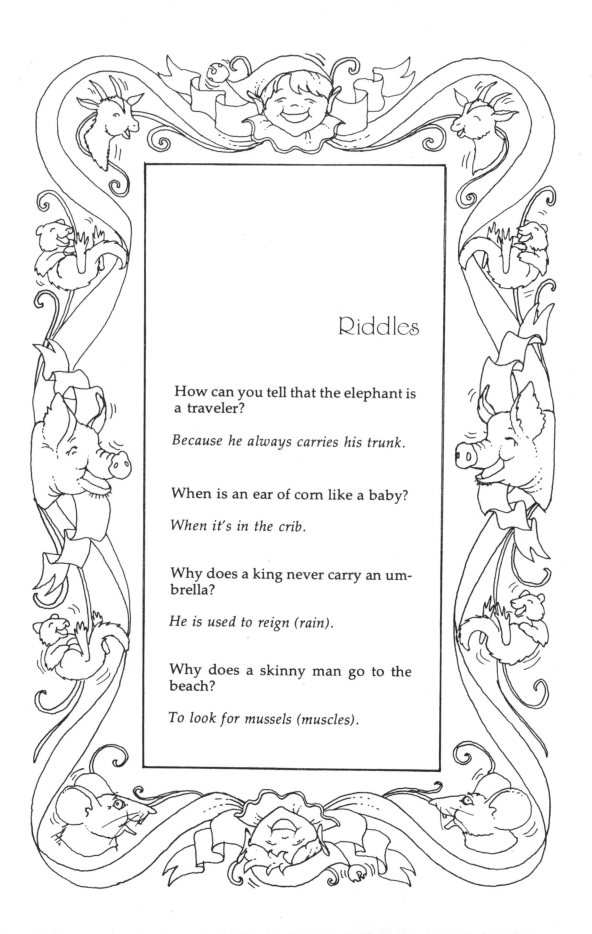

Riddles

How can you tell that the elephant is a traveler?

Because he always carries his trunk.

When is an ear of corn like a baby?

When it's in the crib.

Why does a king never carry an umbrella?

He is used to reign (rain).

Why does a skinny man go to the beach?

To look for mussels (muscles).

What has a tongue and can't talk?

A shoe.

What tool grows sharper with use?

The tongue.

What is it that can be broken without being dropped or hit?

A promise.

What is the best way to keep fish from smelling?

Cut off their noses.

Ten cats were in a boat. One jumped out. How many were left?

None. They were copycats.

Why isn't your nose twelve inches long?

Because it would be a foot.

What do you call a man who is always wiring for money?

An electrician.

Which side of an apple pie is the left side?

The part that isn't eaten.

Which is the strongest day of the week?

Sunday, because all the rest are week (weak) days.

Three men fell into the lake, but only two men got their hair wet. Why?

One was bald.

How can you get into a locked cemetery at night?

Use a skeleton key.

What two animals go with you everywhere?

Your calves.

What is everybody in the world doing at the same time?

Growing older.

What has a foot at each end and one in the middle?

A yardstick.

What is worse than a centipede with sore feet?

A giraffe with a sore throat.

Why is it cheap to feed a giraffe?

He makes a little food go a long way.

What is it you have that everyone else uses more than you do?

Your name.

What is black and white and read all over?

A newspaper.

What is the surest way to double your dollar?

Fold it.

Why is a fraidycat like a leaky faucet?

They both keep running.

When is a man obliged to keep his word?

When no one else will take it.

What can speak every language in the world?

An echo.

What do cats have that children want?

Kittens.

What animal took the most baggage into Noah's ark?

The elephant. He took his trunk.

What animals took the least baggage into Noah's ark?

The fox and the rooster. They only had a brush and a comb between them.

Where was Solomon's temple?

On the side of his head.

What starts with T, ends with T, and is full of T?

A teapot.

Who was the most successful doctor in the Bible?

Job, because he had the most patience (patients).

Who was the straightest man in the Bible?

Joseph, because King Pharaoh made a ruler out of him.

What can't you name without breaking it?

Silence.

Growing Up

Blessings on thee, little man,
Barefoot boy, with cheek of tan!
With thy turned-up pantaloons,
And thy merry whistled tunes;
With thy red lip, redder still
Kissed by strawberries on the hill;
With the sunshine on thy face,
Through thy torn brim's jaunty
    grace;
From my heart I give thee joy, —
I was once a barefoot boy!
Prince thou art, — the grown-up
    man
Only is republican.
Let the million-dollared ride!
Barefoot, trudging at his side,
Thou hast more than he can buy
In the reach of ear and eye, —
Outward sunshine, inward joy:
Blessings on thee, barefoot boy!

Oh, for boyhood's painless play,
Sleep that wakes in laughing day,
Health that mocks the doctor's rules,
Knowledge never learned of schools,
Of the wild bee's morning chase,
Of the wild flower's time and place,
Flight of fowl and habitude
Of the tenants of the wood;
How the tortoise bears his shell,
How the woodchuck digs his cell,
And the ground-mole sinks his well;
How the robin feeds her young,
How the oriole's nest is hung;
Where the whitest lilies blow,
Where the freshest berries grow,
Where the ground-nut trails its vine,
Where the wood-grape's clusters
      shine;
Of the black wasp's cunning way,
Mason of his walls of clay,
And the architectural plans
Of gray hornet artisans!
For, eschewing books and tasks,
Nature answers all he asks;
Hand in hand with her he walks,
Face to face with her he talks,
Part and parcel of her joy, —
Blessings on the barefoot boy!

Oh, for boyhood's time of June,
Crowding years in one brief moon,
When all things I heard or saw,
Me, their master, waited for.
I was rich in flowers and trees,
Humming birds and honey-bees;
For my sport the squirrel played,
Plied the snouted mole his spade;
For my taste the blackberry cone
Purpled over hedge and stone;
Laughed the brook for my delight
Through the day and through the
      night, —
Whispering at the garden wall,
Talked with me from fall to fall;
Mine the sand-rimmed pickerel
      pond,
Mine the walnut slopes beyond,
Mine, on bending orchard trees,
Apples of Hesperides!
Still as my horizon grew,
Larger grew my riches too;
All the world I saw or knew

Seemed a complex Chinese toy,
Fashioned for a barefoot boy!

Oh, for festal dainties spread,
Like my bowl of milk and bread;
Pewter spoon and bowl of wood,
On the door-stone, gray and rude!
O'er me, like a regal tent,
Cloudy-ribbed, the sunset bent,
Purple-curtained, fringed with gold,
Looped in many a wind-swung fold;
While for music came the play
Of the pied frogs' orchestra;
And, to light the noisy choir,
Lit the fly his lamp of fire.
I was monarch: pomp and joy
Waited on the barefoot boy!

Cheerily, then, my little man,
Live and laugh, as boyhood can!
Though the flinty slopes be hard,
Stubble-speared the new-mown
      sward,
Every morn shall lead thee through
Fresh baptisms of the dew;
Every evening from thy feet
Shall the cool wind kiss the heat:
All too soon these feet must hide
In the prison cells of pride,
Lose the freedom of the sod,
Like a colt's for work be shod,
Made to tread the mills of toil,
Up and down in ceaseless moil:
Happy if their track be found
Never on forbidden ground;
Happy if they sink not in
Quick and treacherous sands of sin.
Ah! that thou couldst know thy joy,
Ere it passes, barefoot boy!

(The Barefoot Boy)
John Greenleaf Whittier

Patience is a virtue,
   virtue is a grace;
Both put together
   make a pretty face.

A Boy's Song

Where the pools are bright and
    deep,
Where the gray trout lies asleep,
Up the river, and over the lea,
That's the way for Billy and me.

Where the blackbird sings the latest,
Where the hawthorne blooms the
    sweetest,
Where the nestlings chirp and flee,
That's the way for Billy and me.

Where the mowers mow the
    cleanest,
Where the hay lies thick and
    greenest,
There to trace the homeward bee,
That's the way for Billy and me.

Where the hazel bank is steepest,
Where the shadow falls the deepest,
Where the clustering nuts fall free,
That's the way for Billy and me.

James Hogg

Decision

Golly, it's hard
To decide what to pick . . .
I sure do like lollipops,
They're fun to lick;
But look at those jawbreakers!
They last and last;
Gumdrops are better,
But go down too fast;
Can't get rock candy . . .
Mom says it's too hard;
Bubble gum comes
With a free baseball card;
That pink colored taffy
Is sure nice and chewy;
Might just get caramels,
They're not so gooey!
Golly, it's tough
To pick from so many.
Wish I had a dollar
Instead of a penny!

M. P. Flynn

The Winning of the TV West

When twilight comes to Prairie
    Street
On every TV channel,
The kids watch men with blazing
    guns
In jeans and checkered flannel.
Partner, the West is wild tonight —
There's going to be a battle
Between the sheriff's posse and
The gang that stole the cattle.
On every screen on Prairie Street
The sheriff roars his order:
"We've got to head those hombres
    off
Before they reach the border."
Clippoty-clop and bangity-bang
The lead flies left and right.
Paradise Valley is freed again
Until tomorrow night.
And all the kids on Prairie Street
Over and under ten
Can safely go to dinner now . . .
The West is won again.

John T. Alexander

Aren't You Glad

The world is made of days and
    nights,
    of wind and rain and trees,
Of boys and girls and grownups,
    who grow in families.
I'll tell you about these.

Little girls have soft hair
    and necklaces and lace,
      daintiness and dolls
And sweetness in their face.
    Oh, dance and swirl, dance and
      twirl,
     ballet toes, little girl.

Little boys are rougher,
    with bikes and balls and blocks;
Little boys are tougher
    in corduroys and socks.
Please and tease and lots of noise,
That's the way of little boys.

Little girls who grow up
    are mothers, aunts, and
      grandmas;
Little boys who grow up
    are fathers, friends, and
      grandpas.
    All of these make families.

Little cats are furriness,
Green eyes that glow,
    and purriness.
Slither and prowl, skit and skat
Through the garden, little cat.

Little dogs are woofs and barks,
    pink tongues and wagging tails;
Little dogs are cold, wet noses
    and paws with scratchy nails.
Loppety log, joggety jog,
Your paws go pattery, little dog.

Little girls and little boys,
Little cats and dogs —
    all of these
    make families,
And families live in houses,
    made of windows, doors, and
      stairs,
    of beds and books and bathtubs,
    of tables and of chairs.

Roots and branches and leaves
And the rustling of wind make trees;
    sunny trees rustle and sigh,
    glimmer and shimmer against the
     sky.
The sun outside means time to play
    in its warmth and light-gold light;
But darkness outside and the moon
    up high,
The bed turned down and stars to
    sleep by come at night.

The world is the sun and its light-
    gold light
The bed turned down and the stars
    at night,
The roots and the branches and
    wind in the leaves,
The dogs and the cats and the
    families.
    Oh, aren't you glad
    you're part of these?

Charlotte Zolotow

Mother of the House

Strength and dignity are her
    clothing,
    and she laughs at the time to
      come.
She opens her mouth to wisdom,
    and the teaching of kindness
      is on her tongue.
She looks well to the ways of her
    household,
    and does not eat the bread of
      idleness.
Her children rise up and call her
    blessed;
    her husband also, and he praises
      her:
"Many women have done
    excellently,
    but you surpass them all."

The Bible, Proverbs 31:25-29, RSV

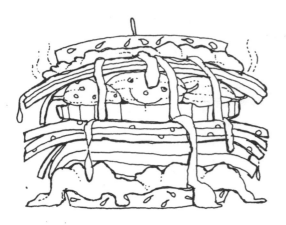

Recipe

I can make a sandwich.
I can really cook.
I made up this recipe
That should be in a book:
Take a jar of peanut butter,
Give it a spread,
Until you have covered
A half a loaf of bread.
Pickles and pineapple,
Strawberry jam,
Salami and bologna
And half a pound of ham —
Pour some catsup on it.
Mix in the mustard well.
It will taste delicious,
If you don't mind the smell.

Bobbi Katz

Down in the Field

Down in the field
  Among tall grass
  and fever weeds that blow —
  I'd go.

Trees about
  And those beyond
  All seemed to know:
I'd put my schoolroom manners
  On the shelf
To play at being no one
  But myself.

M. P. Flynn

A Prayer for the Young and Lovely

Dear God, I keep praying
For the things I desire,
You tell me I am selfish
And "playing with fire" —
It is hard to believe
I am selfish and vain.
My desires seem so real
And my needs seem so sane,
And yet You are wiser
And Your vision is wide
And You look down on me
And You see deep inside,
You know it's so easy
To change and distort,
And things that are evil
Seem so harmless a sport —
Oh, teach me, dear God,
To not rush ahead
But to pray for Your guidance
And to trust You instead,
For You know what I need
And that I'm only a slave
To the things that I want
And desire and crave —
Oh, God, in Your mercy
Look down on me now
And see in my heart
That I love You somehow,
Although in my rashness,
Impatience and greed
I pray for the things
That I want and don't need —
And instead of a crown
Please send me a cross
And teach me to know
That all gain is but loss,
And show me the way
To joy without end,
With You as my Father,
Redeemer and Friend —
And send me the things
That are hardest to bear,
And keep me forever
Safe in Your care.

Helen Steiner Rice

My Shadow

I have a little shadow that goes in
    and out with me,
And what can be the use of him is
    more than I can see.
He is very, very like me from the
    heels up to the head;
And I see him jump before me, when
    I jump into my bed.

The funniest thing about him is the
    way he likes to grow —
Not at all like proper children, which
    is always very slow;
For he sometimes shoots up taller
    like an India-rubber ball,
And he sometimes gets so little that
    there's none of him at all.

He hasn't got a notion of how chil-
    ·dren ought to play,
And can only make a fool of me in
    every sort of way.
He stays so close beside me, he's a
    coward you can see;
I'd think shame to stick to nursie as
    that shadow sticks to me!

One morning, very early, before the
    sun was up,
I rose and found the shining dew on
    every buttercup;
But my lazy little shadow, like an
    arrant sleepy-head,
Had stayed at home behind me and
    was fast asleep in bed.

Robert Louis Stevenson

At the Seaside

When I was down beside the sea
A wooden spade they gave to me
To dig the sandy shore.

My holes were empty like a cup.
In every hole the sea came up,
Till it could come no more.

Robert Louis Stevenson

How Pleasant Is Saturday Night

How pleasant is Saturday night,
When I've tried all the week to be
    good,
Not spoken a word that was bad
And obliged everyone that I could.

School Is Over

School is over,
    Oh, what fun!
Lessons finished,
    Play begun.
Who'll run fastest,
    You or I?
Who'll laugh loudest?
    Let us try.

Kate Greenaway

My Aim

As I grow more and more each day,
I'll try to live the friendly way.
I'll try hard to say and do
Only what is kind and true.

Always it shall be my aim
To play fair in any game,
Keep myself alert but cool,
Try to live the Golden Rule.

Alexander Seymour

If

If you can keep your head when all
  about you
    Are losing theirs and blaming it
    on you;
If you can trust yourself when all
  men doubt you,
    But make allowance for their
    doubting too;
If you can wait and not be tired by
  waiting,
    Or, being lied about, don't deal in
    lies,
Or, being hated, don't give way to
  hating,
    And yet don't look too good, nor
    talk too wise;

If you can dream — and not make
  dreams your master;
    If you can think — and not make
    thoughts your aim;
If you can meet with triumph and
  disaster
    And treat those two impostors just
    the same;
If you can bear to hear the truth
  you've spoken
    Twisted by knaves to make a trap
    for fools,
Or watch the things you gave your
  life to broken,
    And stoop and build 'em up with
    worn-out tools;

If you can make one heap of all your
  winnings
    And risk it on one turn of pitch-
    and-toss,
And lose, and start again at your
  beginnings
    And never breathe a word about
    your loss;
If you can force your heart and nerve
  and sinew
    To serve your turn long after they
    are gone,
And so hold on when there is
  nothing in you
    Except the Will which says to
    them: "Hold on";

If you can talk with crowds and keep
  your virtue,
    Or walk with kings — nor lose the
    common touch;
If neither foes nor loving friends can
  hurt you;
    If all men count with you, but
    none too much;
If you can fill the unforgiving minute
  With six seconds' worth of
    distance run —
Yours is the Earth and everything
  that's in it,
    And — which is more — you'll be
    a Man, my son!

Rudyard Kipling

Mr. Nobody

I know a funny little man,
  As quiet as a mouse,
Who does the mischief that is done
  In everybody's house!
There's no one ever sees his face,
  And yet we all agree
That every plate we break was
  cracked
    By Mr. Nobody.

'Tis he who always tears our books,
  Who leaves the door ajar,
He pulls the buttons from our shirts,
  And scatters pins afar;
That speaking door will always
  speak,
    For, prithee, don't you see,
We leave the oiling to be done
    By Mr. Nobody.

The fingermarks upon the door
  By none of us are made;
We never leave the blinds unclosed,
  To let the curtains fade.
The ink we never spill; the boots
  That lying round you see
Are not our boots — they all belong
  To Mr. Nobody.

There Was a Child Went Forth

There was a child went forth every
    day;
And the first object he looked upon,
    that object he became.
And that object became part of him
    for the day, or a certain part of
    the day, or for many years,
    or stretching cycles of years:
The early lilacs became part of this
    child. . . .
And the apple-trees covered with
    blossoms, and the fruit after-
    ward, and wood-berries, and
    the commonest weeds by the
    road;
And the schoolmistress that passed
    on her way to the school. . . .

The blow, the quick loud word, the
    tight bargain, the crafty lure,
The family usages, the language, the
    company, the furniture — the
    yearning and swelling heart.
The doubts of day-time and the
    doubts of night-time — the
    curious whether and how,
Whether that which appears is so, or
    is it all flashes and specks?
Men and women crowding fast in
    the streets — if they are not
    flashes and specks, what are
    they?

These became part of that child who
    went forth every day,
and who now goes, and will always
    go forth every day.

Walt Whitman

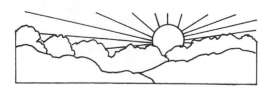

Me

As long as I live
I shall always be
My Self — and no other,
Just me.

Like a tree.

Like a willow or elder,
An aspen, a thorn,
Or a cypress forlorn.

Like a flower,
For its hour,
A primrose, a pink,
Or a violet —
Sunned by the sun
And with dewdrops wet.

Always just me.

Walter de la Mare

He Was One of Us

He was born as little children are
    and lived as children do,
So remember that the Saviour
    was once a child like you,
And remember that He lived on
    earth
    in the midst of sinful men,
And the problems of the present
    existed even then;
He was ridiculed and laughed at
    in the same heartbreaking way
That we who fight for justice
    are ridiculed today;
He was tempted . . . He was
    hungry . . .
    He was lonely . . . He was sad . . .
There's no sorrowful experience
    that the Saviour has not had;
And in the end He was betrayed
    and even crucified,
For He was truly "One of Us" —
    He lived on earth and died;
So do not heed the skeptics
    who are often heard to say:
"What does God up in heaven
    know of things we face today" . . .

For, our Father up in heaven
   is very much aware
Of our failures and shortcomings
   and the burdens that we bear;
So whenever you are troubled
   put your problems in God's hand
For He has faced all problems
   and He will understand.

Helen Steiner Rice

Animal Crackers

Animal crackers, and cocoa to drink,
That is the finest of suppers, I think;
When I'm grown up and can have
   what I please
I think I shall always insist upon
   these.

What do *you* choose when you're
   offered a treat?
When Mother says, "What would
   you like best to eat?"
Is it waffles and syrup, or cinnamon
   toast?
It's cocoa and animals that *I* love
   most!

The kitchen's the cosiest place that I
   know:
The kettle is singing, the stove is
   aglow,
And there in the twilight, how jolly
   to see
The cocoa and animals waiting for
   me.

Daddy and Mother dine later in
   state,
With Mary to cook for them, Susan
   to wait;
But they don't have nearly as much
   fun as I
Who eat in the kitchen with Nurse
   standing by;
And Daddy once said he would like
   to be me
Having cocoa and animals once
   more for tea!

Christopher Morley

Lullaby

Sweet and low, sweet and low,
   Wind of the western sea,
Low, low, breathe and blow,
   Wind of the western sea!
Over the rolling waters go,
Come from the dying moon, and
   blow,
   Blow him again to me;
While my little one, while my pretty
   one, sleeps.

Sleep and rest, sleep and rest,
   Father will come to thee soon;
Rest, rest, on mother's breast,
   Father will come to thee soon;
Father will come to his bird in the
   nest;
Silver sails all out of the west
   Under the silver moon:
Sleep, my little one, sleep, my pretty
   one, sleep.

Alfred Tennyson
(from The Princess)

Little

I am the sister of him
And he is my brother.
He is too little for us
To talk to each other.

So every morning I show him
My doll and my book;
But every morning he still is
Too little to look.

Dorothy Aldis

The Little Elf

I met a little Elf-man, once,
  Down where the lilies blow.
I asked him why he was so small
  And why he didn't grow.

He slightly frowned, and with his
    eye
  He looked me through and
    through.
"I'm quite as big for me," said he,
  "As you are big for you."

              John Kendrick Bangs

Two in Bed

When my brother Tommy
  Sleeps in bed with me,
    He doubles up
    And makes
      himself
      exactly
      like
        a
        V
And 'cause the bed is not so wide,
A part of him is on my side.

              A. B. Ross

I am glad I'm who I am;
I like to be myself.
Even when I do the wrong thing,
I know I am the right person.

              Jessie Orton Jones
              (VIII from Secrets)

Only One Mother

Hundreds of stars in the pretty sky,
  Hundreds of shells on the shore
        together,
Hundreds of birds that go singing
        by,
  Hundreds of lambs in the sunny
        weather.

Hundreds of dewdrops to greet the
        dawn,
  Hundreds of bees in the purple
        clover,
Hundreds of butterflies on the lawn,
  But only one mother the wide
        world over.

              George Cooper

Tea Party

My, it's nice
To visit with you!
So glad you could bring
Your little boy, too.

We haven't had
A tea party this way
For ages and ages —
Why, since yesterday!

              Mary R. Hurley

Growing Up

My birthday is coming tomorrow,
And then I'm going to be four;
And I'm getting so big that already,
I can open the kitchen door;
I'm very much taller than Baby,
Though today I am only three;
And I'm bigger than Bob-tail the
        puppy,
Who used to be bigger than me.

A boy has two jobs.
One is just being a boy.
The other is growing up to be a man.

              Herbert Hoover

Gentle Jesus meek and mild
Look upon a little child
Make me loving, as Thou art
Come and dwell within my heart.
                              Amen.

Mrs. William H. Dietz

Help us to do the things we should
To be to others kind and good
In all our work in all our play
To grow more loving every day.
                              Amen.

Mrs. William H. Dietz

Don't Give Up

If you've tried and have not won,
  Never stop for crying;
All that's great and good is done
  Just by patient trying.

If by easy work you beat,
  Who the more will prize you?
Gaining victory from defeat,
  That's the test that tries you.

Phoebe Cary

The Children's Hour

Between the dark and the daylight,
  When the night is beginning to
    lower,
Comes a pause in the day's
  occupations,
  That is known as the Children's
    Hour.

I hear in the chamber above me
  The patter of little feet,
The sound of a door that is opened,
  And voices soft and sweet.

From my study I see in the
  lamplight,
  Descending the broad hall stair,
Grave Alice, and laughing Allegra,
  And Edith with golden hair.

A whisper, and then a silence:
  Yet I know by their merry eyes
They are plotting and planning
    together
  To take me by surprise.

A sudden rush from the stairway,
  A sudden raid from the hall!
By three doors left unguarded,
  They enter my castle wall!

They climb up into my turret
  O'er the arms and back of my
    chair;
If I try to escape, they surround me;
  They seem to be everywhere.

They almost devour me with kisses,
  Their arms about me entwine,
Till I think of the Bishop of Bingen
  In his Mouse-Tower on the Rhine!

Do you think, O blue-eyed banditti,
  Because you have scaled the wall,
Such an old moustache as I am
  Is not a match for you all?

I have you fast in my fortress,
  And will not let you depart,
But put you down into the dungeon
  In the round-tower of my heart.

And there will I keep you forever,
  Yes, forever and a day,
Till the walls shall crumble to ruin,
  And moulder in dust away!

Henry Wadsworth Longfellow

Even a child is known by his doings,
whether his work be pure, and
whether it be right.

The Bible, Proverbs 20:11

Honour thy father and thy mother:
that thy days may be long upon the
land which the Lord thy God giveth
thee.

The Bible, Exodus 20:12

Happy Memories

On the merry, merry, merry-go-
    round,
The horses go up and the horses go
    down.
Faster and faster they paw and
    prance
In a happy-go-lucky, jerky dance.

On the merry, merry, merry-go-
    round
There's never time for a sigh or
    frown.
In all the world there's no more fun.
I ought to know, I rode on one!

(On the Merry, Merry-Go-Round)
Dorothy McGrath Martin

Merry-Go-Round

Purple horses with orange manes,
    Elephants pink and blue,
Tigers and lions that never were
        seen
    In circus parade or zoo!
Bring out your money and choose
        your steed,
    And prance to delightsome
        sound.
What fun if the world would turn
        some day
    Into a Merry-Go-Round.

Rachel Field

Song for a Little House

I'm glad our house is a little house,
    Not too tall nor too wide;
I'm glad the hovering butterflies
    Feel free to come inside.

Our little house is a friendly house,
    It is not shy or vain;
It gossips with the talking trees,
    And makes friends with the rain.

And quick leaves cast a shimmer of
        green
    Against our whited walls,
And in the phlox the courteous bees
    Are paying duty calls.

Christopher Morley

Slumber Party

My sister had a slumber party.
Girls giggled and ate till almost
        dawn.
They did not sleep nor did they
        slumber.
So why call it a slumber party?
When they just giggled and ate the
        whole night long.

Carson McCullers

The Hut

We built a hut, my brother and I,
Over a sandy pit,
With twigs that bowed and met
        above
And leaves to cover it.

And there we sat when all around
The rain came pouring down.
We knew if we were out in it
We'd both be sure to drown.

And though in puddles at our feet
Drops gathered from the sky,
We smiled through strands of
        dripping hair,
Because we felt so dry.

Hilda Van Stockum

The Swing

How do you like to go up in a swing,
    Up in the air so blue?
Oh, I do think it the pleasantest
        thing
    Ever a child can do!

Up in the air and over the wall,
    Till I can see so wide,
Rivers and trees and cattle and all
    Over the countryside —

Till I look down on the garden green
    Down on the roof so brown —
Up in the air I go flying again,
    Up in the air and down!

Robert Louis Stevenson

The Postman

Eight o'clock,
The postman's knock!
Five letters for Papa;
  One for Lou,
  And none for you,
And three for dear Mamma.

Christina Rossetti

Daffodils

I wandered lonely as a cloud
  That floats on high o'er vales and
    hills,
When all at once I saw a crowd,
  A host, of golden daffodils;
Beside the lake, beneath the trees,
Fluttering and dancing in the
    breeze.

Continuous as the stars that shine
  And twinkle on the Milky Way,
They stretched in never-ending line
  Along the margin of a bay:
Ten thousand saw I at a glance,
Tossing their heads in sprightly
    dance.

The waves beside them danced, but
    they
  Out-did the sparkling waves in
    glee:
A poet could not but be gay,
  In such a jocund company:
I gazed — and gazed — but little
    thought
What wealth the show to me had
    brought:

For oft, when on my couch I lie
  In vacant or in pensive mood,
They flash upon that inward eye
  Which is the bliss of solitude;
And then my heart with pleasure
    fills,
And dances with the daffodils.

William Wordsworth

Break, Break, Break

Break, break, break,
  On thy cold gray stones, O Sea!
And I would that my tongue could
    utter
  The thoughts that arise in me.

O well for the fisherman's boy,
  That he shouts with his sister at
    play!
O well for the sailor lad,
  That he sings in his boat on the
    bay!

And the stately ships go on
  To their haven under the hill;
But O for the touch of a vanish'd
    hand,
  And the sound of a voice that is
    still.

Break, break, break,
  At the foot of thy crags, O Sea!
But the tender grace of a day that is
    dead
  Will never come back to me.

Alfred Tennyson

I Love to Tell the Story

I love to tell the story
Of unseen things above,
Of Jesus and His glory,
Of Jesus and His love.
I love to tell the story,
Because I know 'tis true;
It satisfies my longings
As nothing else could do.

I love to tell the story;
More wonderful it seems
Than all the golden fancies
Of all our golden dreams.
I love to tell the story,
It did so much for me;
And that is just the reason
I tell it now to thee.

I love to tell the story;
'Tis pleasant to repeat
What seems, each time I tell it,
More wonderfully sweet.
I love to tell the story,
For some have never heard
The message of salvation
From God's own holy Word.

I love to tell the story;
For those who know it best
Seem hungering and thirsting
To hear it, like the rest.
And when, in scenes of glory,
I sing the new, new song,
'Twill be the old, old story,
That I have loved so long.

I love to tell the story,
'Twill be my theme in glory
To tell the old, old story
Of Jesus and His love.

Katherine Hankey

Little Girl's Heart

A little girl's heart must be wide and
    deep,
To hold all the things that she likes to
    keep;
A curly-haired doll that holds out its
    hands
And walks and talks when occasion
    demands.

A bright colored bow, her favorite
    book,
A little toy stove that really will cook;
A gay, cheery song, to sing when
    she's glad,
A corner to hide in (when she is
    bad).

There is plenty of room for the girl
    next door
And the blue silk dress in the
    downtown store;
A soft fluffy kitten with playful
    charms
And a welcome spot in her mother's
    arms.

Reginald Holmes

118

When I Was One-and-Twenty

When I was one-and-twenty
   I heard a wise man say,
"Give crowns and pounds and
     guineas
But not your heart away;
Give pearls away and rubies
   But keep your fancy free."
But I was one-and-twenty,
   No use to talk to me.

When I was one-and-twenty
   I heard him say again,
"The heart out of the bosom
   Was never given in vain;
'Tis paid with sighs a-plenty
   And sold for endless rue."
And I am two-and-twenty,
   And oh, 'tis true, 'tis true.

A. E. Housman

The Secret

We have a secret, just we three,
The robin, and I, and the sweet
   cherry-tree;
The bird told the tree, and the tree
   told me,
And nobody knows it but just us
   three.

But of course the robin knows it
   best,
Because he built the — I shan't tell
   the rest;
And laid the four little — something
   in it —
I'm afraid I shall tell it every minute.

But if the tree and the robin don't
   peep,
I'll try my best the secret to keep;
Though I know when the little birds
   fly about
Then the whole secret will be out.

The Popcorn-Popper

The popcorn man
At the park
Has a popping machine
Inside his cart.
   He puts in dry, yellow brown,
   Hard bits of corn
   And soon —
   Afaff afaff afaff —
   The corn begins to laugh
   And dance
   And hop
   And pop, and pop, and pop.

And then —
   I stand
   And hold
   The bag in my hand,
   And the man
   Pours it full
   Of puffy, fluffy, flaky,
   Soft white
      Popcorn.

Dorothy Baruch

Sandlot Days

Summer days were sandlot days
   When I was a boy of ten;
High pop flies and R.B.I.'s
   Were all I cared for then.

The field was just a vacant lot
   Just right for playing ball
Where my Louisville Slugger and I
     went down
   On many a strike-three call.

First and second base were seats
   From two old kitchen chairs,
Third and Home — deflated tires
   Too worn to use for spares.

And, oh, how I remember
   That nothing could replace
The thrill of sliding into Home
   Or getting to steal a base.

Strange, but after all these years
   Every now and then
I long for the good old sandlot days
   That came with being ten.

M. P. Flynn

God's Gifts to Me

Birds and bees, flowers and trees,
   sun and moon to see;
Rain and snow, and winds that
   blow, are God's gifts to me.

Night and day, friends for play, all
   my family;
Love and care, and clothes to wear,
   are God's gifts to me.

Thelma Walton

Memory

My mind lets go a thousand things,
Like dates of wars and deaths of
   kings,
And yet recalls the very hour —
'Twas noon by yonder village tower,
And on the last blue noon in May
The wind came briskly up this way,
Crisping the brook beside the road;
Then, pausing here, set down its
   load
Of pine-scents, and shook listlessly
Two petals from that wild-rose tree.

Thomas Aldrich

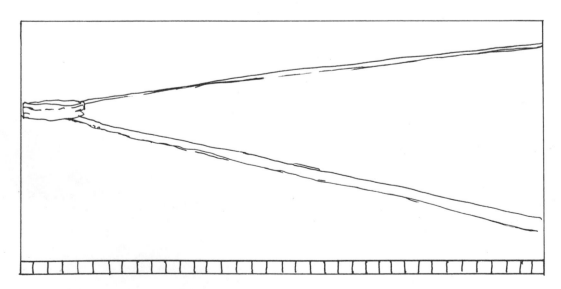

Land of Make Believe

The Owl and the Pussy-Cat went to
          sea
    In a beautiful pea-green boat,
They took some honey, and plenty of
          money
    Wrapped up in a five-pound note.
The Owl looked up to the stars
          above,
    And sang to a small guitar,
"O lovely Pussy, O Pussy, my love,
    What a beautiful Pussy you are,
              You are,
              You are!
    What a beautiful Pussy you are!"

Pussy said to the Owl, "You elegant
          fowl,
    How charmingly sweet you sing!
Oh! let us be married, too long we
          have tarried:
    But what shall we do for a ring?"

They sailed away, for a year and a
     day,
  To the land where the Bong-tree
     grows;
And there in a wood a Piggy-wig
     stood,
  With a ring at the end of his nose,
          His nose,
          His nose,
  With a ring at the end of his nose.

"Dear Pig, are you willing to sell for
     one shilling
  Your ring?" Said the Piggy, "I
     will."
So they took it away, and were
     married next day
  By the Turkey who lives on the
     hill.
They dined on mince and slices of
     quince,
  Which they ate with a runcible
     spoon;
And hand in hand, on the edge of
     the sand,
  They danced by the light of the
     moon,
          The moon,
          The moon,
  They danced by the light of the
     moon.

                (The Owl and the Pussy-Cat)
                    Edward Lear

                The Doze

Through dangly woods the aimless
     Doze
A-dripping and a-dribbling goes.
His company no beast enjoys.
He makes a sort of hopeless noise
Between a snuffle and a snort.
His hair is neither long nor short;
His tail gets caught on briars and
     bushes,
As through the undergrowth he
     pushes.
His ears are big, but not much use.
He lives on blackberries and juice
And anything that he can get.

His feet are clumsy, wide and wet,
Slip-slopping through the bog and
     heather
All in the wild and weepy weather.
His young are many and maltreat
     him;
But only hungry creatures eat him.
He jokes about his mossy holes,
Disturbing sleepless mice and
     moles,
And what he wants he never
     knows —
The damp, despised, and aimless
     Doze.

James Reeves

Twinkle, Twinkle, Little Bat

Twinkle, twinkle, little bat!
How I wonder what you're at?
Up above the world you fly,
Like a tea-tray in the sky.

Lewis Carroll

Jabberwocky

'Twas brillig, and the slithy toves
  Did gyre and gimble in the wabe:
All mimsy were the borogoves,
  And the mome raths outgrabe.

"Beware the Jabberwock, my son!
  The jaws that bite, the claws that
     catch!
Beware the Jubjub bird, and shun
  The frumious Bandersnatch!"

He took his vorpal sword in hand:
  Long time the manxome foe he
     sought —
So rested he by the Tumtum tree,
  And stood awhile in thought.

And, as in uffish thought he stood,
  The Jabberwock, with eyes
    of flame,
Came whiffling through the tulgey
    wood,
  And burbled as it came!

One, two! One, two! And through
    and through
  The vorpal blade went snicker-
    snack!
He left it dead, and with its head
  He went galumphing back.

"And hast thou slain the
    Jabberwock?
  Come to my arms, my beamish
    boy!
O frabjous day! Callooh! Callay!"
  He chortled in his joy.

'Twas brillig, and the slithy toves
  Did gyre and gimble in the wabe:
All mimsy were the borogoves,
  And the mome raths outgrabe.

Lewis Carroll

The Land of Story-Books

At evening when the lamp is lit,
Around the fire my parents sit;
They sit at home and talk and sing,
And do not play at anything.

Now, with my little gun, I crawl
All in the dark along the wall,
And follow round the forest track
Away behind the sofa back.

There, in the night, where none can
    spy,
All in my hunter's camp I lie,
And play at books that I have read
Till it is time to go to bed.

These are the hills, these are the
    woods,
There are my starry solitudes;
And there the river by whose brink
The roaring lions come to drink.

I see the others far away
As if in firelit camp they lay,
And I, like to an Indian scout,
Around their party prowled about.

So, when my nurse comes in for me,
Home I return across the sea,
And go to bed with backward looks
At my dear Land of Story-books.

Robert Louis Stevenson

The Duel

The gingham dog and the calico cat
Side by side on the table sat;
'Twas half-past twelve, and (what do
    you think!)
Nor one nor t'other had slept a wink!
    The old Dutch clock and the
        Chinese plate
    Appeared to know as sure as fate
There was going to be a terrible spat.
    (I wasn't there; I simply state
    What was told to me by the Chinese
        plate!)

The gingham dog went, "bow-
    wow-wow!"
And the calico cat replied, "mee-
    ow!"
The air was littered, an hour or so,
With bits of gingham and calico,
    While the old Dutch clock in the
        chimneyplace
    Up with its hands before its face,
For it always dreaded a family row!
    (Now mind: I'm only telling you
    What the old Dutch clock declares is
        true!)

The Chinese plate looked very blue,
And wailed, "Oh, dear! what shall
    we do!"
But the gingham dog and the calico
    cat
Wallowed this way and tumbled
    that,
    Employing every tooth and claw
    In the awfullest way you ever
        saw —
And, oh! how the gingham and
    calico flew!
    (Don't fancy I exaggerate —
    I got my news from the Chinese
        plate!)

Next morning, where the two had
    sat
They found no trace of dog or cat;
And some folks think unto this day
That burglars stole that pair away!
    But the truth about the cat and pup
    Is this: they ate each other up!
Now what do you really think of
    that!
    (The Old Dutch clock it told me so,
    And that is how I came to know.)

Eugene Field

The Jumblies

They went to sea in a sieve, they did;
    In a sieve they went to sea:
In spite of all their friends could say,
On a winter's morn, on a stormy
    day,
    In a sieve they went to sea.
And when the sieve turned round
    and round,
And everyone cried, "You'll all be
    drowned!"
They called aloud, "Our sieve ain't
    big;
But we don't care a button, we don't
    care a fig:
    In a sieve we'll go to sea!"
        Far and few, far and few,
        Are the lands where the
            Jumblies live:
        Their heads are green, and
            their hands are blue;
        And they went to sea in a
            sieve.

Edward Lear

126

A Swing Song

Swing, swing,
　Sing, sing,
Here! my throne
and I am a king!
　Swing, sing,
　Swing, sing,
Farewell, earth,
for I'm on the wing!
　Low, high,
　Here I fly,
Like a bird
through sunny sky;
　Free, free,
　Over the lea,
Over the mountain,
over the sea!

　Up, down,
　Up, down,
Which is the way
to London Town?
　Where? Where?
　Up in the air,
Close your eyes and
now you are there!
　No, no,
　Low, low,
Sweeping daisies
with my toe.
　Slow, slow,
　To and fro,
Slow — slow — slow — slow.

William Allingham

When Mother Reads Aloud

When Mother reads aloud, the past
　Seems real as every day;
I hear the tramp of armies vast,
I see the spears and lances cast,
　I join the thrilling fray.
Brave knights and ladies fair and
　proud
I meet when Mother reads aloud.

When Mother reads aloud, far lands
　Seem very near and true;
I cross the desert's gleaming sands,
Or hunt the jungle's prowling
　bands,
　Or sail the ocean blue.
Far heights, whose peaks the cold
　mists shroud,
I scale, when Mother reads aloud.

When Mother reads aloud, I long
　For noble deeds to do —
To help the right, redress the wrong;
It seems so easy to be strong,
　So simple to be true.
Oh, thick and fast the visions crowd
My eyes, when Mother reads aloud.

Only My Opinion

Is a caterpillar ticklish?
Well, it's always my belief
That he giggles, as he wiggles
Across a hairy leaf.

Monica Shannon

The Little Man Who Wasn't There

As I was going up the stair
　I met a man who wasn't there!
He wasn't there again today!
　I wish, I *wish* he'd stay away!

Hughes Mearns

The Ichthyosaurus

There once was an Ichthyosaurus
Who lived when the earth was all
　porous,
But he fainted with shame
When he first heard his name,
And departed a long time before us.

There Once Was a Puffin

Oh, there once was a Puffin
Just the shape of a muffin,
And he lived on an island
In the
    bright
        blue
            sea!

He ate little fishes,
That were most delicious,
And he had them for supper
And he
    had
        them
            for tea.

But this poor little Puffin
He couldn't play nothin',
For he hadn't anybody
To
    play
        with
            at all.

So he sat on his island,
And he cried for awhile, and
He felt very lonely
And he
    felt
        very
            small.

Then along came the fishes,
And they said, "If you wishes,
You can have us for playmates,
Instead
        of
            for
                tea!"

So now they play together,
In all sorts of weather,
And the Puffin eats pancakes,
Like you
        and
            like
                me.

Florence Page Jaques

The Invisible Playmate

When the other children go,
    Though there's no one seems to
        see
And there's no one seems to know,
    Fanny comes and plays with me.

She has yellow curly hair
    And her dress is always blue,
And she always plays quite fair
    Everything I tell her to.

People say she isn't there —
    They step over her at play
And they sit down in her chair
    In the very rudest way.

It is queer they cannot know
    When she's there for me to see!
When the other children go
    Fanny comes and plays with me.

Margaret Widdemer

The Land of Counterpane

When I was sick and lay a-bed,
I had two pillows at my head,
And all my toys beside me lay
To keep me happy all the day.

And sometimes for an hour or so
I watched my leaden soldiers go,
With different uniforms and drills,
Among the bed-clothes, through the
    hills;

And sometimes sent my ships in
    fleets
All up and down among the sheets;
Or brought my trees and houses out,
And planted cities all about.

I was the giant great and still
That sits upon the pillow-hill,
And sees before him, dale and plain,
The pleasant land of counterpane.

Robert Louis Stevenson

128

Escape at Bedtime

The lights from the parlour and
  kitchen shone out
   Through the blinds and the
    windows and bars;
And high overhead and all moving
  about,
   There were thousands of millions
    of stars.

There ne'er were such thousands of
  leaves on a tree,
   Nor of people in church or the
    Park,
As the crowds of the stars that
  looked down upon me,
   And that glittered and winked in
    the dark.

The Dog, and the Plough, and the
  Hunter, and all,
   And the Star of the Sailor, and
    Mars,
These shone in the sky, and the pail
  by the wall
   Would be half full of water and
    stars.

They saw me at last, and they chased
  me with cries,
   And they soon had me packed into
    bed;
But the glory kept shining bright in
  my eyes,
   And the stars going round in my
    head.

Robert Louis Stevenson

Wish

If I could wish
I'd be a fish
(For just a day or two)
To flip and flash
And dart and splash
With nothing else to do,
And never anyone to say,
"Are you quite sure you washed
   today?"
I'd like it, wouldn't you?

Dorothy Brown Thompson

My Rocking Chair

I have a little rocking chair
That hides a tiny squeak
  somewhere;
It's quite as if some baby Elf
Were singing to his little self.
I rock and rock, so I can see
Just what he tries to say to me.
My Mother says, "Good gracious,
  child!
That noise will surely drive me
  wild!"
But that's because she doesn't know
An Elf is singing down below!

Doris I. Bateman

Daisies

At evening when I go to bed
I see the stars shine overhead.
They are the little daisies white
That dot the meadow of the night.

And often while I'm dreaming so,
Across the sky the moon will go.
It is a lady, sweet and fair,
Who comes to gather daisies there.

For, when at morning I arise,
There's not a star left in the skies.
She's picked them all
And dropped them down
Into the meadows of the town.

Frank Dempster Sherman

129

Block City

What are you able to build with your
  blocks?
Castles and palaces, temples and
  docks.
Rain may keep raining, and others
  go roam,
But I can be happy and building at
  home.

Let the sofa be mountains, the carpet
  be sea,
There I'll establish a city for me:
A kirk and a mill and a palace beside,
And a harbor as well where my
  vessels may ride.

Great is the palace with pillar and
  wall,
A sort of a tower on the top of it all,
And steps coming down in an
  orderly way
To where my toy vessels lie safe in
  the bay.

This one is sailing and that one is
  moored:
Hark to the song of the sailors on
  board!
And see on the steps of my palace,
  the kings
Coming and going with presents
  and things!

Now I have done with it, down let it
  go!
All in a moment the town is laid low.
Block upon block lying scattered and
  free,
What is there left of my town by the
  sea?

Yet as I saw it, I see it again,
The kirk and the palace, the ships
  and the men,
And as long as I live and where'er I
  may be,
I'll always remember my town by the
  sea.

Robert Louis Stevenson

Mouths

I wish I had two little mouths
Like my two hands and feet —
A little mouth to talk with
And one that just could eat.

Because it seems to me mouths have
So many things to do —
All the time they want to talk
They are supposed to chew!

Dorothy Aldis

The Sugar-Plum Tree

Have you ever heard of the Sugar-
  Plum Tree?
  'Tis a marvel of great renown!
It blooms on the shore of the
  Lollipop Sea
  In the garden of Shut-Eye Town.

Eugene Field

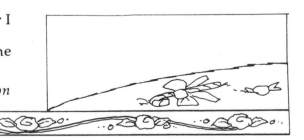

Lessons to Learn

A little kingdom I possess
   Where thoughts and feelings
      dwell;
And very hard the task I find
   Of governing it well.

I do not ask for any crown
   But that which all may win;
Nor try to conquer any world
   Except the one within.

          (My Kingdom)
         Louisa May Alcott

Recessional

God of our fathers, known of old,
  Lord of our far-flung battle-line,
Beneath whose awful Hand we hold
  Dominion over palm and pine—
Lord God of Hosts, be with us yet,
Lest we forget — lest we forget!

The tumult and the shouting dies;
  The Captains and the Kings
          depart:
Still stands thine ancient sacrifice,
  An humble and a contrite heart.
Lord God of Hosts, be with us yet,
Lest we forget — lest we forget!

Far-called, our navies melt away;
  On dune and headland sinks the
          fire:
Lo, all our pomp of yesterday
  Is one with Nineveh and Tyre!
Judge of the Nations, spare us yet,
Lest we forget — lest we forget!

If, drunk with sight of power, we
          loose
  Wild tongues that have not thee in
          awe,
Such boastings as the Gentiles use,
  Or lesser breeds without the
          Law —
Lord God of Hosts, be with us yet,
Lest we forget — lest we forget!

For heathen heart that puts her trust
  In reeking tube and iron shard,
All valiant dust that builds on dust,
  And, guarding, calls not thee to
          guard,
For frantic boast and foolish word—
Thy mercy on thy People, Lord!

                    Rudyard Kipling

Every Day

Love the beautiful,
  Seek out the true,
Wish for the good,
  And the best do!

                    Felix Mendelssohn

Success

Success is speaking words of praise,
In cheering other people's ways,
In doing just the best you can,
With every task and every plan.

It's silence when your speech would
          hurt,
Politeness when your neighbor's
          curt.
It's deafness when the scandal flows,
And sympathy with others' woes.

It's loyalty when duty calls,
It's courage when disaster falls,
It's patience when the hours are
          long,
It's found in laughter and in song.

It's in the silent time of prayer.
In happiness and in despair,
In all of life and nothing less,
We find the thing we call success.

No bees, no honey;
No work, no money.

Be True

Thou must be true thyself
  If thou the truth wouldst teach;
Thy soul must overflow if thou
  Another's soul wouldst reach!
It needs the overflow of heart
  To give the lips full speech.

Think truly, and thy thoughts
  Shall the world's famine feed;
Speak truly, and each word of thine
  Shall be a fruitful seed;
Live truly, and thy life shall be
  A great and noble creed.

Horatius Bonar

Four Things

Four things a man must learn to do
If he would make his record true:
To think without confusion clearly;
To love his fellow-men sincerely;
To act from honest motives purely;
To trust in God and Heaven
    securely.

Henry Van Dyke

Lend a Hand

I am only one,
But still I am one.
I cannot do everything,
But still I can do something;
And because I cannot do everything
I will not refuse to do the something
    that I can do.

Edward Everett Hale

We always have time enough, if we
use it aright.

Johann Wolfgang Von Goethe

The Oak

Live thy life,
  Young and old,
Like yon oak,
Bright in spring
  Living gold;

Summer-rich
  Then; and then
Autumn-changed,
Soberer-hued
  Gold again.

All his leaves
  Fallen at length,
Look, he stands,
Trunk and bough,
  Naked strength.

Alfred Tennyson

When Jesus Walked Upon the Earth

When Jesus walked upon the earth
  He didn't talk with kings,
He talked with simple people
  Of doing friendly things.

He didn't praise the conquerors
  And all their hero host;
He said the very greatest
  Were those who loved the most.

He didn't speak of mighty deeds
  And victories. He spoke
Of feeding hungry people
  And cheering lonely folk.

I'm glad His words were simple
    words
  Just meant for me and you,
The things He asked were simple
    things
  That even I can do.

Marion Brown Shelton

Be Like the Bird

Be like the bird, who
Halting in his flight
On limb too slight
Feels it give way beneath him,
Yet sings
Knowing he hath wings.

Victor Hugo

Footprints made on the sands of
time were never made sitting down.

A winner never quits;
A quitter never wins.

A penny saved is a penny earned.

Practice makes perfect.

Lost

Lost, yesterday, somewhere
between sunrise and sunset,
two golden hours,
each set with sixty
diamond minutes.
No reward is offered
for they are gone forever.

Doubts

Our doubts are traitors,
And make us lose the good we oft
    might win,
By fearing to attempt.

William Shakespeare

To-day

Build a little fence of trust
    Around to-day;
Fill the space with loving deeds
    And therein stay.
Look not through the sheltering bars
    Upon to-morrow;
God will help thee bear what comes
    Of joy or sorrow.

Mary Frances Butts

He that is slow to anger is better than
    the mighty;
And he that ruleth his spirit than he
    that taketh a city.

The Bible, Proverbs 16:32

A soft answer turneth away wrath:
But grievous words stir up anger.

The Bible, Proverbs 15:1

A talebearer revealeth secrets:
But he that is of a faithful spirit con-
    cealeth the matter.

The Bible, Proverbs 11:13

A good name is rather to be chosen
    than great riches,
And loving favour rather than silver
    and gold.

The Bible, Proverbs 22:1

But they that wait upon the Lord
    shall renew their strength;
They shall mount up with wings as
    eagles;
They shall run, and not be weary;
And they shall walk, and not faint.

The Bible, Isaiah 40:31

How happy are those who know
    their need for God,
  for the kingdom of Heaven
    is theirs!
How happy are those who know
    what sorrow means,
  for they will be given courage and
    comfort!
Happy are those who claim nothing,
  for the whole earth will belong to
    them!
Happy are those who are hungry
    and thirsty for true goodness,
  for they will be fully satisfied!
Happy are the merciful,
  for they will have mercy shown to
    them!
Happy are the utterly sincere,
  for they will see God!
Happy are those who make peace,
  for they will be known as sons of
    God!
Happy are those who have suffered
    persecution for the cause of
    goodness,
  for the kingdom of Heaven is
    theirs!
And what happiness will be yours
    when people blame you
  and ill-treat you and say all kinds
    of slanderous things against
    you for my sake!

The Bible, Matthew 5:3-12, Phillips

Blessed is the man
  that walketh not in the
    counsel of the ungodly,
  nor standeth in the way of sinners,
  nor sitteth in the seat of the
    scornful.
But his delight
  is in the law of the Lord;
  and in his law doth he meditate
    day and night.
And he shall be like a tree
  planted by the rivers of water,
  that bringeth forth his fruit in his
    season;
  his leaf also shall not wither;
  and whatsoever he doeth shall
    prosper.

The Bible, Psalm 1:1-3

Go to the Ant

Go to the ant, thou sluggard;
Consider her ways, and be wise:
Which having no guide,
Overseer, or ruler,
Provideth her meat in the summer,
And gathereth her food in the
    harvest.

The Bible, Proverbs 6:6-8

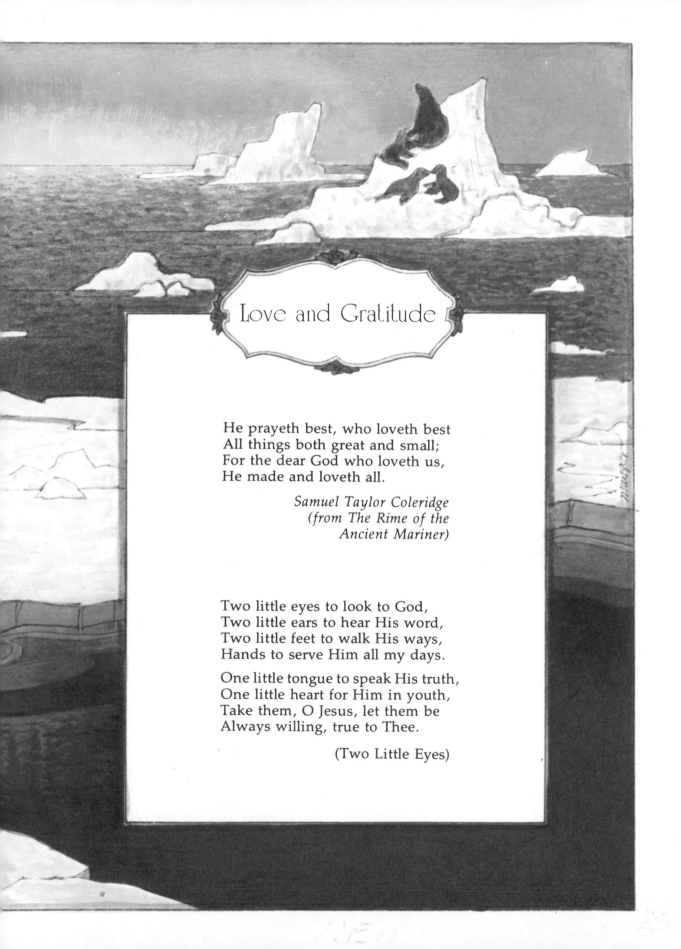

Love and Gratitude

He prayeth best, who loveth best
All things both great and small;
For the dear God who loveth us,
He made and loveth all.

Samuel Taylor Coleridge
(from The Rime of the
Ancient Mariner)

Two little eyes to look to God,
Two little ears to hear His word,
Two little feet to walk His ways,
Hands to serve Him all my days.

One little tongue to speak His truth,
One little heart for Him in youth,
Take them, O Jesus, let them be
Always willing, true to Thee.

(Two Little Eyes)

A Child's Offering

The wise may bring their learning,
  The rich may bring their wealth,
And some may bring their
      greatness,
  And some bring strength and
      health;
We, too, would bring our treasures
  To offer to the King;
We have no wealth or learning:
  What shall we children bring?

We'll bring Him hearts that love
      Him;
  We'll bring Him thankful praise,
And young souls meekly striving
  To walk in holy ways:
And these shall be the treasures
  We offer to the King,
And these are gifts that even
  The poorest child may bring.

We'll bring the little duties
  We have to do each day;
We'll try our best to please Him,
  At home, at school, at play:
And better are these treasures
  To offer to our King,
Than richest gifts without them;
  Yet these a child may bring.

The Book of Praise for Children

They that go down to the sea in
      ships,
  that do business in great waters;
These see the works of the Lord, and
  his wonders in the deep.
For he commandeth, and raiseth the
      stormy wind,
  which lifteth up the waves
      thereof.
They mount up to the heaven, they
  go down again to the depths:
  Their soul is melted because of
      trouble.

They reel to and fro, and stagger
  like a drunken man,
  And are at their wits' end.
Then they cry unto the Lord in their
      trouble,
  and he bringeth them out of
      their distresses.
He maketh the storm a calm, so that
  the waves thereof are still.
Then are they glad because they be
      quiet;
  so he bringeth them unto their
      desired haven.
Oh that men would praise the Lord
  for his goodness,
  and for his wonderful works to the
      children of men!

The Bible, Psalm 107:23-31

Praise ye the Lord.
Praise God in his sanctuary:
Praise him in the firmament of
      his power.
Praise him for his mighty acts:
Praise him according to his
      excellent greatness.
Praise him with the sound of the
      trumpet:
Praise him with the psaltery and
      harp.
Praise him with the timbrel and
      dance:
Praise him with stringed
  instruments and organs.
Praise him upon the loud cymbals:
Praise him upon the high sounding
      cymbals.
Let every thing that hath breath
  praise the Lord.
Praise ye the Lord.

The Bible, Psalm 150

Woodman, Spare That Tree

Woodman, spare that tree!
　Touch not a single bough!
In youth it sheltered me,
　And I'll protect it now.
'Twas my forefather's hand
　That placed it near his cot;
There, woodman, let it stand,
　Thy axe shall harm it not!

That old familiar tree,
　Whose glory and renown
Are spread o'er land and sea,
　And wouldst thou hew it down?
Woodman, forbear thy stroke!
　Cut not its earth-bound ties;
O, spare that aged oak,
　Now towering to the skies!

When but an idle boy
　I sought its grateful shade;
In all their gushing joy
　Here too my sisters played.
My mother kissed me here;
　My father pressed my hand —
Forgive this foolish tear,
　But let that old oak stand!

My heart-strings round thee cling,
　Close as thy bark, old friend!
Here shall the wild-bird sing,
　And still thy branches bend.
Old tree! the storm still brave!
　And, woodman, leave the spot;
While I've a hand to save,
　Thy axe shall harm it not.

George Pope Morris

Deeds of Kindness

Suppose the little Cowslip
   Should hang its golden cup
And say, "I'm such a little flower
   I'd better not grow up!"
How many a weary traveller
   Would miss its fragrant smell,
How many a little child would grieve
   To lose it from the dell!

Suppose the glistening Dewdrop
   Upon the grass should say,
"What can a little dewdrop do?
   I'd better roll away!"
The blade on which it rested,
   Before the day was done,
Without a drop to moisten it,
   Would wither in the sun.

Suppose the little Breezes,
   Upon a summer's day,
Should think themselves too small to
     cool
   The traveller on his way:
Who would not miss the smallest
   And softest ones that blow,
And think they made a great mistake
   If they were acting so?

How many deeds of kindness
   A little child can do,
Although it has but little strength
   And little wisdom too!
It wants a loving spirit
   Much more than strength,
     to prove
How many things a child may do
   For others by its love.

The Night Has a Thousand Eyes

The night has a thousand eyes,
   And the day but one;
Yet the light of the bright world dies
   With the dying sun.

The mind has a thousand eyes,
   And the heart but one;
Yet the light of a whole life dies
   When love is done.

Francis William Bourdillon

Bless the Lord, O my soul:
And all that is within me, bless
   his holy name.
Bless the Lord, O my soul,
And forget not all his benefits:
Who forgiveth all thine iniquities;
Who healeth all thy diseases;
Who redeemeth thy life from
   destruction;
Who crowneth thee with loving-
   kindness and tender mercies;
Who satisfieth thy mouth with good
   things;
So that thy youth is renewed like the
   eagle's.

The Bible, Psalm 103:1-5

What Can I Give Him?

What can I give Him,
   Poor as I am?
If I were a shepherd,
   I would bring a lamb;
If I were a wise man
   I would do my part, —
Yet what can I give Him,
   Give Him my heart.

Christina Rossetti

Thanksgiving Hymn

We gather together to ask the Lord's
    blessing;
    He chastens and hastens his will
        to make known;
The wicked oppressing now cease
    from distressing:
    Sing praises to his Name; he
        forgets not his own.

Beside us to guide us, our God with
    us joining,
    Ordaining, maintaining his
        Kingdom divine;
So from the beginning the fight we
    were winning;
    Thou, Lord, wast at our side: all
        glory be thine.

We all do extol thee, thou Leader
    triumphant,
    And pray that thou still our
        Defender wilt be.
Let thy congregation escape
    tribulation:
    Thy Name be ever prais'd! O
        Lord, make us free!

Words translated by Theodore Baker

Beshrew me but I love her heartily;
For she is wise, if I can judge of her,
And fair she is, if that mine eyes be
    true,
And true she is as she hath proved
    herself,
And therefore, like herself, wise, fair
    and true,
Shall she be placed in my constant
    soul.

William Shakespeare
(from The Merchant of Venice)

Our Wonderful World

How could God think of so many
    kinds of houses?
There are millions of houses that I
    can't even see.
There must be lots of very funny
    ones!
    Mole houses —
        Frog houses —
            Beaver houses —
    Stork nests on chimneys,
    Squirrel nests in trees.
    Houses for everyone!
        And my house
            for me.

Jessie Orton Jones
(XXI from Secrets)

The Wonderful World

Great, wide, beautiful, wonderful
    World,
With the wonderful water round you
    curled,
And the wonderful grass upon your
    breast,
World, you are beautifully dressed.

The wonderful air is over me,
And the wonderful wind is shaking
    the tree —
It walks on the water, and whirls the
    mills,
And talks to itself on the top of the
    hills.

You friendly Earth, how far do you
    go,
With the wheat fields that nod and
    the rivers that flow,
With cities and gardens and cliffs
    and isles,
And the people upon you for
    thousands of miles?

Ah! you are so great, and I am so
    small,
I hardly can think of you, World, at
    all;
And yet, when I said my prayers
    today,
My mother kissed me, and said,
    quite gay,

"If the wonderful World is great to
    you,
And great to Father and Mother, too,
You are more than the Earth, though
    you are such a dot!
You can love and think, and the
    Earth cannot!"

William Brighty Rands

The Wind

I saw you toss the kites on high
And blow the birds about the sky;
And all around I heard you pass,
Like ladies' skirts across the grass —
    O wind, a-blowing all day long,
    O wind, that sings so loud a song!

I saw the different things you did,
But always you yourself you hid.
I felt you push, I heard you call,
I could not see yourself at all —
    O wind, a-blowing all day long,
    O wind, that sings so loud a song!

Robert Louis Stevenson

Little Wind

Little wind, blow on the hilltop,
Little wind, blow on the plain,
Little wind, blow up the sunshine,
Little wind, blow off the rain.

Who Has Seen the Wind?

Who has seen the wind?
    Neither I nor you:
But when the leaves hang trembling
    The wind is passing thro'.

Who has seen the wind?
    Neither you nor I:
But when the trees bow down their
    heads
    The wind is passing by.

Christina Rossetti

The Wind

The wind stood up, and gave a
    shout;
He whistled on his fingers, and

Kicked the withered leaves about,
And thumped the branches with his
    hand,

And said he'd kill, and kill, and kill;
And so he will! And so he will!

James Stephens

O, Look at the Moon

O, look at the moon,
   She is shining up there;
O, mother, she looks
   Like a lamp in the air.

Last week she was smaller,
   And shaped like a bow,
But now she's grown bigger,
   And round like an O.

The Star

Twinkle, twinkle, little star,
How I wonder what you are!
Up above the world so high,
Like a diamond in the sky.

As your bright and tiny spark
Lights the traveler in the dark,
Though I know not what you are,
Twinkle, twinkle, little star.

Jane Taylor

I see the moon,
And the moon sees me;
God bless the moon,
And God bless me.

The Universe

There is the moon, there is the sun
Round which we circle every year,
And there are all the stars we see
On starry nights when skies are
    clear,
And all the countless stars that lie
Beyond the reach of human eye.
If every bud on every tree,
All birds and fireflies and bees,
And all the flowers that bloom and
    die,
Upon the earth were counted up,
The number of the stars would be
Greater, they say, than all of these.

Mary Britton Miller

Things We Can Depend On

The sun is gone down,
   And the moon's in the sky;
But the sun will come up,
   And the moon be laid by.
The flower is asleep,
   But it is not dead;
When the morning shines,
   It will lift up its head.

George MacDonald

The Song of the Brook

I come from haunts of coot and hern,
  I make a sudden sally,
And sparkle out among the fern,
  To bicker down a valley.

By thirty hills I hurry down,
  Or slip between the ridges,
By twenty thorps, a little town,
  And half a hundred bridges.

Till last by Philip's farm I flow
  To join the brimming river;
For men may come, and men may
    go,
  But I go on forever.

I chatter over stony ways,
  In little sharps and trebles;
I bubble into eddying bays,
  I babble on the pebbles.

With many a curve my bank I fret
  By many a field and fallow,
And many a fairy foreland set
  With willow-weed and mallow.

I chatter, chatter, as I flow
  To join the brimming river;
For men may come, and men may
    go,
  But I go on forever.

I wind about, and in and out,
  With here a blossom sailing,
And here and there a lusty trout,
  And here and there a grayling,

And here and there a foamy flake
  Upon me as I travel,
With many a silvery waterbreak
  Above the golden gravel,

And draw them all along and flow
  To join the brimming river;
For men may come, and men may
    go,
  But I go on forever.

I steal by lawns and grassy plots,
  I slide by hazel covers,
I move the sweet forget-me-nots
  That grow for happy lovers.

I slip, I slide, I gloom, I glance,
  Among my skimming swallows;
I make the netted sunbeam dance
  Against my sandy shallows.

I murmur under moon and stars
  In brambly wildernesses;
I linger by my shingly bars,
  I loiter round my cresses;

And out again I curve and flow
  To join the brimming river;
For men may come, and men may
    go,
  But I go on forever.

Alfred Tennyson

The Handiwork of God

I believe in the brook as it wanders
  From hillside into glade;
I believe in the breeze as it whispers
  When evening shadows fade.
I believe in the roar of the river
  As it dashes from high cascade;
I believe in the cry of the tempest
  'Mid the thunder's cannonade.
I believe in the light of the shining
    stars,
  I believe in the sun and the moon;
I believe in the flash of the lightning,
  I believe in the nightbird's croon.
I believe in the faith of the flowers,
  I believe in the rock and the sod,
For in all of these appeareth clear
  The handiwork of God.

Happy Thought

The world is so full of a number of
    things,
I'm sure we should all be as happy as
    kings.

Robert Louis Stevenson

I Saw Some Lovely Things Today

I saw some lovely things today:
I feel, dear God, I'd like to pray.
I saw some tiny, little things —
Some hummingbirds with gauzy
    wings,
A flower with its head held high
As though its blue came from the
    sky.
I saw some lovely things today:
I feel, dear God, I'd like to pray.

I heard some wondrous things
    today:
I feel, dear God, I'd like to pray.
I heard a brook. It seemed to me
To catch the rhythm of the sea.
I heard a bird. It sang to me
A joyous, lilting melody.
I heard some wondrous things
    today:
I feel, dear God, I'd like to pray.

Perhaps, dear Lord, the woodland
    air
Was really breathing out a prayer —
    The prayer I prayed.
The awe and wonder in my heart
Were such a very vital part
    Of what thou callest prayer.

Thanatopsis

To him who in the love of Nature
    holds
Communion with her visible forms,
    she speaks
A various language; for his gayer
    hours
She has a voice of gladness, and a
    smile
And eloquence of beauty, and she
    glides
Into his darker musings, with a mild
And healing sympathy, that steals
    away
Their sharpness, ere he is aware.

William Cullen Bryant

The Creator

The earth *is* the Lord's, and the
    fulness thereof;
    the world, and they that dwell
        therein.
For he hath founded it upon the
    seas,
    and established it upon the floods.
Who shall ascend into the hill of the
    Lord?
    or who shall stand in his holy
        place?
He that hath clean hands, and a pure
    heart;
    who hath not lifted up his soul
        unto vanity,
    nor sworn deceitfully.
He shall receive the blessing from
    the Lord,
    and righteousness from the God of
        his salvation.
This is the generation of them that
    seek him,
    that seek thy face, O Jacob.
Lift up your heads, O ye gates;
And be ye lifted up, ye everlasting
    doors;
    and the King of glory shall come
        in.
Who is this King of glory?
The Lord strong and mighty,
The Lord mighty in battle.
Lift up your heads, O ye gates;
Even lift them up, ye everlasting
    doors;
    and the King of glory shall come
        in.
Who is this King of glory?
The Lord of hosts,
He *is* the King of glory.

The Bible, Psalm 24

Praise to God for things we see —
Growing grass, the waving tree,
Mother's face, the bright, blue sky,
Birds and clouds floating by.
Praise to God for things we see,
Praise to God for seeing.

M. M. Penstone

All Things Bright and Beautiful

All things bright and beautiful,
  All creatures great and small,
All things wise and wonderful,
  The Lord God made them all.

Each little flower that opens,
  Each little bird that sings,
God made their glowing colors,
  He made their tiny wings.

The purple-headed mountain,
  The river running by,
The sunset, and the morning
  That brightens up the sky.

The cold wind in the winter,
  The pleasant summer sun,
The ripe fruits in the garden —
  He made them every one.

The tall trees in the greenwood,
  The meadows where we play,
The rushes by the water,
  We gather every day.

He gave us eyes to see them,
  And lips that we might tell
How great is God Almighty,
  Who doeth all things well.

Cecil Frances Alexander

Rain

The rain is raining all around,
  It falls on field and tree,
It rains on the umbrellas here,
  And on the ships at sea.

Robert Louis Stevenson

This Is My Father's World

This is my Father's world,
  And to my listening ears,
All nature sings, and round me rings
  The music of the spheres.
This is my Father's world
  I rest me in the thought
Of rocks and trees, of skies and seas;
  His hand the wonders wrought.

This is my Father's world,
The birds their carols raise,
The morning light, the lily white,
  Declare their Maker's praise.
This is my Father's world:
  He shines in all that's fair;
In the rustling grass I hear Him pass,
  He speaks to me everywhere.

This is my Father's world,
  O let me ne'er forget
That though the wrong seems oft so
    strong,
  God is the Ruler yet.
This is my Father's world:
  The battle is not done;
Jesus who died shall be satisfied,
  And earth and heaven be one.

Maltbie D. Babcock

Fog

The fog comes
on little cat feet.

It sits looking
over harbor and city
on silent haunches
and then moves on.

Carl Sandburg

Oh, Who Can Make a Flower?

Oh, who can make a flower?
I'm sure I can't. Can you?
Oh, who can make a flower?
No one but God — 'tis true.

Oh, who can make the sunshine?
I'm sure I can't. Can you?
Oh, who can make the raindrops?
No one but God — 'tis true.

Grace W. Owens

Great Is the Lord

Praise ye the Lord:
For it is good to sing praises
   unto our God;
For it is pleasant; and praise
   is comely.
Great is our Lord, and of great
   power:
Who covereth the heaven with
   clouds,
Who prepareth rain for the earth,
Who maketh grass to grow upon the
   mountains.
He giveth to the beast his food,
And to the young ravens which cry.
He giveth snow like wool:
He scattereth the hoarfrost like
   ashes.
He casteth forth his ice like morsels:
Who can stand before his cold?
He sendeth out his word, and
   melteth them:
He causeth his wind to blow, and
   the waters flow.
Sing unto the Lord with
   thanksgiving;
Praise ye the Lord.

The Bible, Psalm 147:1,5,8,9,
16-18,7,20

I'm glad the sky is painted blue;
And the earth is painted green;
And such a lot of nice fresh air
All sandwiched in between.

Baby Seeds

In a milkweed cradle,
Snug and warm,
Baby seeds are hiding,
Safe from harm.
Open wide the cradle,
Hold it high!
Come Mr. Wind,
Help them fly.

The heavens declare the glory of
   God;
   and the firmament sheweth his
     handywork.
Day unto day uttereth speech,
   and night unto night sheweth
     knowledge.
There is no speech nor language,
   where their voice is not heard.
Their line is gone out through all the
   earth,
   and their words to the end of the
     world.
In them hath he set a tabernacle for
   the sun,
Which is as a bridegroom coming
   out of his chamber,
   and rejoiceth as a strong man to
     run a race.
His going forth is from the end of the
   heaven,
   and his circuit unto the ends of it:
And there is nothing hid from the
   heat thereof.

The Bible, Psalm 19:1-6

Silver

Slowly, silently, now the moon
Walks the night in her silver shoon;
This way, and that, she peers, and
   sees
Silver fruit upon silver trees;
One by one the casements catch
Her beams beneath the silvery
   thatch;
Couched in his kennel, like a log,
With paws of silver sleeps the dog;
From their shadowy cote the white
   breasts peep
Of doves in a silver-feathered sleep;
A harvest mouse goes scampering
   by,
With silver claws, and silver eye;
And moveless fish in the water
   gleam,
By silver reeds in a silver stream.

Walter de la Mare

Rules to Live By

Lay not up for yourselves treasures
   upon earth,
Where moth and rust doth corrupt,
And where thieves break through
   and steal:

But lay up for yourselves treasures in
   heaven,
Where neither moth nor rust doth
   corrupt,
And where thieves do not break
   through nor steal:

For where your treasure is, there will
   your heart be also.

The Bible, Matthew 6:19-21

Grizzly Bear

If you ever, ever, ever meet a grizzly
    bear,
You must never, never, never ask
    him *where*
He is going,
Or *what* he is doing;
For if you ever, ever dare
To stop a grizzly bear
You will never meet *another* grizzly
    bear.

Mary Austin

Seldom Can't

Seldom "can't,"
  Seldom "don't";
Never "shan't,"
  Never "won't."

Christina Rossetti

Go to bed late
  Stay very small;
Go to bed early
  Grow very tall.

Today I lost my temper,
  And angry words were said:
Words that did not help at all,
And they are now beyond recall —
  The angry words I said.

Good and Bad

There is so much good in the worst
    of us,
And so much bad in the best of us,
That it hardly becomes any of us
To talk about the rest of us.

Edward Wallis Hoch

Always Finish

If a task is once begun,
Never leave it till it's done.
Be the labor great or small,
Do it well or not at all.

Early to bed, early to rise
Makes a man healthy, wealthy, and
    wise.

An acre of performance is worth a
whole world of promise.

Thomas James Howell

A Bit of the Book

A bit of the Book* in the morning,
  To order my onward way.
A bit of the Book in the evening,
  To hallow the end of the day.

Margaret E. Sangster

* Bible

Fret Not

Fret not thyself because of
    evildoers,
Neither be thou envious against the
    workers of iniquity.
For they shall soon be cut down like
    the grass,
And wither as the green herb.
I have seen the wicked in great
    power,
And spreading himself like a green
    bay tree.
Yet he passed away, and, lo, he was
    not:
Yea, I sought him, but he could not
    be found.
Trust in the Lord, and do good;
So shalt thou dwell in the land,
And verily thou shalt be fed.

The Bible, Psalm 37:1,2,35,36,3

In everything you do
Aim to excel,
For what's worth doing
Is worth doing well.

My son, forget not my law; but let
thine heart keep my commandments;
For length of days, and long life,
and peace, shall they add to thee.
Let not mercy and truth forsake
thee: bind them about thy neck;
write them upon the table of thine
heart:
So shalt thou find favour and good
understanding in the sight of God
and man.

The Bible, Proverbs 3:1–4

Whatsoever things are true,
Whatsoever things are honest,
Whatsoever things are just,
Whatsoever things are pure,
Whatsoever things are lovely,
Whatsoever things are of
    good report;
If there be any virtue,
And if there be any praise,
Think on these things.

The Bible, Philippians 4:8

John Wesley's Rule

Do all the good you can,
In all the ways you can,
In all the places you can,
At all the times you can,
To all the people you can,
As long as ever you can.

Be ye kind one to another.

The Bible, Ephesians 4:32

Be kindly affectioned one to
another with brotherly love; in
honor preferring one another; not
slothful in business; fervent in
spirit; serving the Lord.

The Bible, Romans 12:10,11

Short Sermon

To give — and forgive —
Is a good way to live.

*Adapted from the German by
Louis Untermeyer*

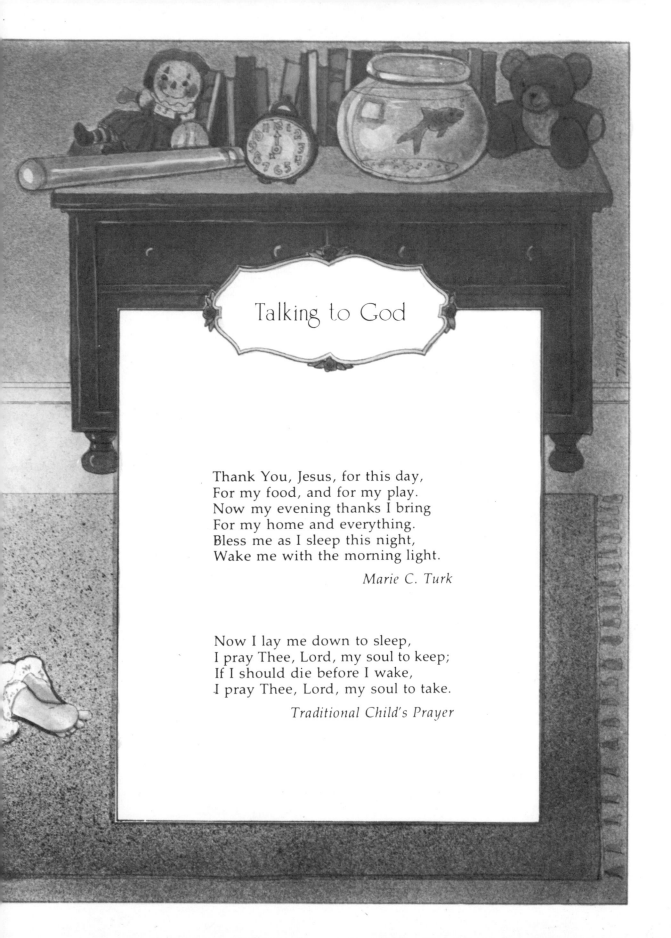

Talking to God

Thank You, Jesus, for this day,
For my food, and for my play.
Now my evening thanks I bring
For my home and everything.
Bless me as I sleep this night,
Wake me with the morning light.

Marie C. Turk

Now I lay me down to sleep,
I pray Thee, Lord, my soul to keep;
If I should die before I wake,
I pray Thee, Lord, my soul to take.

Traditional Child's Prayer

The Lord's Prayer

Our Father which art in heaven,
Hallowed be thy name.
Thy kingdom come.
Thy will be done
   in earth, as it is in heaven.

Give us this day
   our daily bread.
And forgive us our debts,
   as we forgive our debtors.
And lead us not into temptation,
   but deliver us from evil:

For thine is the kingdom,
   and the power,
   and the glory,
   for ever. Amen.

The Bible, Matthew 6:9-13

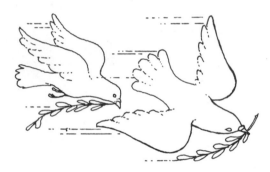

Thanks

Dear Lord, we give Thee thanks for
   the bright silent moon
And thanks for the sun that will
   warm us at noon.
And thanks for the stars and the
   quick running breeze,
And thanks for the shade and
   the straightness of trees.

Give Thanks

Oh, give thanks to Him who made
Morning light and evening shade;
Source and giver of all good,
Nightly sleep, and daily food,
Quickener of our wearied powers;
Guard of our unconscious hours.

It's Me Again, God

I come every day
Just to talk with You, Lord,
And to learn how to pray . . .
You make me feel welcome,
You reach out Your hand,
I need never explain
For YOU understand . . .
I come to You frightened
And burdened with care
So lonely and lost
And so filled with despair,
And suddenly, Lord,
I'm no longer afraid,
My burden is lighter
And the dark shadows fade . . .
Oh, God, what a comfort
To know that You care
And to know when I seek You
YOU WILL ALWAYS BE THERE!

Helen Steiner Rice

Prayer

Prayer is so simple
It is like quietly opening a door
And slipping into the very presence
   of God,
There in the stillness
To listen for his voice.
Perhaps to petition
Or only to listen,
It matters not;
Just to be there,
In his presence,
Is prayer!

A Simple Prayer

Lord, make me an instrument of
    Your peace.
Where there is hatred . . .
    Let me sow love;
Where there is injury . . .
    Pardon;
Where there is doubt . . .
    Faith;
Where there is despair . . .
    Hope;
Where there is darkness . . .
    Light;
Where there is sadness . . .
    Joy.

O Divine Master, grant that I may
    Not so much seek
To be consoled . . .
    As to console;
To be understood . . .
    As to understand,
To be loved . . .
    As to love, for
It is in giving that we receive,
It is in pardoning that we are
    pardoned,
It is in dying that we are born to
    eternal life.

St. Francis of Assisi

The Christian's Prayer

Lord, make me free . . .
    From fear of the future;
    From anxiety of the morrow;
    From bitterness toward anyone;
    From cowardice in face of danger;
    From failure before opportunity;
    From laziness in face of work.

My Savior, Hear My Prayer

My Savior, hear my prayer
Before I go to rest;
It is Your little child
Who comes now to be blest.

Forgive me all my sin,
And let me sleep this night
In safety and in peace
Until the morning light.

Henry L. Jenner

A Thought

It is very nice to think
The world is full of
    meat and drink,
With little children
    saying grace
In every Christian kind of place.

Robert Louis Stevenson

My Choice

Lord, may it be my choice
    This blessed rule to keep —
"Rejoice with them that do rejoice,
    And weep with those that weep."

Each prayer is answered,
That is so;
But for our good
It may be, "No!"

Prayer for a Pilot

Lord of Sea and Earth and Air,
Listen to the Pilot's prayer —
Send him wind that's steady and
    strong,
Grant that his engine sings the song
Of flawless tone, by which he knows
It shall not fail him where he goes;
Landing, gliding, in curve,
    half-roll —
Grant him, O Lord, a full control,
That he may learn in heights of
    Heaven
The rapture altitude has given,
That he shall know the joy they feel
Who ride Thy realms on Birds of
    Steel.

Cecil Roberts

A Prayer for Love

I pray for a child-like heart,
    For gentle, holy love,
For strength to do Thy will below,
    As angels do above.
On friends to me most dear,
    Oh, let Thy blessing fall;
I pray for grace to love them well,
    But Thee beyond them all.

An Evening Prayer

Now I lay me down to sleep,
I pray Thee, Lord, Thy child to keep;
Thy love go with me all the night
And wake me with the morning
    light.

Night Blessing

Good night
Sleep tight
Wake up bright
In the morning light
To do what's right
With all your might.

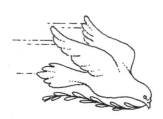

A Prayer

Teach me, Father, how to go
Softly as the grasses grow;
Hush my soul to meet the shock
Of the wild world as a rock;
But my spirit, propt with power,
Make as simple as a flower.
Let the dry heart fill its cup,
Like a poppy looking up;
Let life lightly wear her crown,
Like a poppy looking down,
When its heart is filled with dew,
And its life begins anew.

Teach me, Father, how to be
Kind and patient as a tree.
Joyfully the crickets croon
Under shady oak at noon;
Beetle, on his mission bent,
Tarries in that cooling tent.
Let me, also, cheer a spot,
Hidden field or garden grot —
Placed where passing souls can rest
On the way and be their best.

Edwin Markham

God, Are You There?

I'm way down HERE!
You're way up THERE!
Are You sure You can hear
My faint, faltering prayer?
For I'm so unsure
Of just how to pray —
To tell you the truth, God,
I don't know what to say . . .
I just know I am lonely
And vaguely disturbed,
Bewildered and restless,
Confused and perturbed . . .
And they tell me that prayer
Helps to quiet the mind
And to unburden the heart,
For in stillness we find
A newborn assurance
That SOMEONE DOES CARE
And SOMEONE DOES ANSWER
Each small sincere prayer!

Helen Steiner Rice

Grace for a Child

Here a little child I stand,
Heaving up my either hand;
Cold as paddocks though they be,
Here I lift them up to Thee,
For a benison* to fall
On our meat and on us all,
                              Amen.

Robert Herrick
*blessing

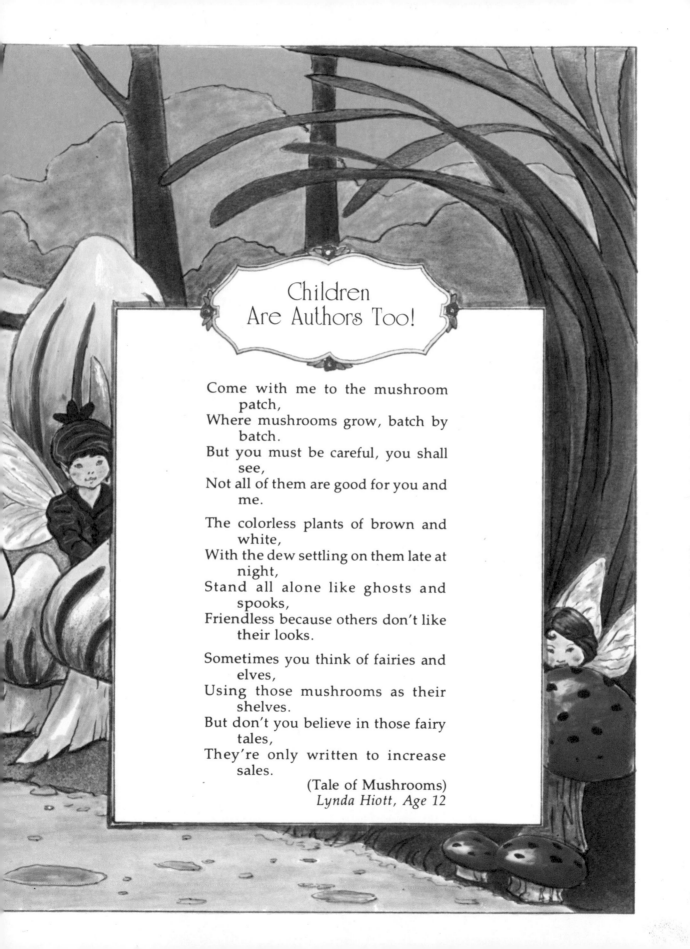

Children Are Authors Too!

Come with me to the mushroom
  patch,
Where mushrooms grow, batch by
  batch.
But you must be careful, you shall
  see,
Not all of them are good for you and
  me.

The colorless plants of brown and
  white,
With the dew settling on them late at
  night,
Stand all alone like ghosts and
  spooks,
Friendless because others don't like
  their looks.

Sometimes you think of fairies and
  elves,
Using those mushrooms as their
  shelves.
But don't you believe in those fairy
  tales,
They're only written to increase
  sales.

(Tale of Mushrooms)
Lynda Hiott, Age 12

Rules to Live By

Never put anybody down.
Remember that everyone else is
    human, too.
Benefit from everything you do.
Last but not least, obey all other
    rules in life for a happy one.

Paula Del Giudice, Age 12

Blind but Happy

O what a happy soul am I!
    Although I cannot see,
I am resolved that in this world
    Contented I will be;
How many blessings I enjoy
    That other people don't!
To weep and sigh because I'm blind,
    I cannot and I won't.

*Fanny Crosby
(written at Age 8)*

Grandma

My grandma likes to play with God,
They have a kind of game.
She plants the garden full of seeds,
He sends the sun and rain.

She likes to sit and talk with God
And knows he is right there.
She prays about the whole wide
    world,
Then leaves us in his care.

Ann Johnson, Age 8

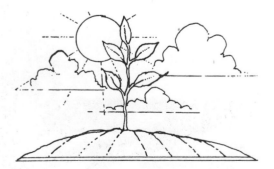

Rhapsodies

There are many things I love to hear
    Of things composed from this past
        year,
The sound of the trumpets, the beat
    of the snare,
    Of music happy and of great
        despair.
But of all the music I have ever
    known
    The rhapsodies that have grown
From the hearts of men so deep and
    still
    Of the power and strength of the
        musician's skill,
Seem to entrance me still
    Into a world of make believe:
Gershwin's Rhapsody in Blue
Chopin's Nocturne, Purple Hue
Beethoven's lovely Moonlight
    Sonata
And Wagner's lively Pitzue Contata
    All these and many more
Have taken the keys and unlocked
    the door
    To many a heart and many a mind
    Of many a person of many a kind.

Judy Turner, Age 13

Dear heavenly Father,
    Thank You for making
        everything,
    Thank You for making me so that
        I could grow up
        and grow old
        and die
        and go to heaven
        and see what You're like.
    I can't see You, God,
        but You can see me! Amen.

*Said at prayer time by Christian Holt,
Age 5, and recorded by his
grandmother, Mrs. Dixie Baer*

Up on the Moon

T'was the night before Christmas,
  and up on the moon
Not a martian was stirring;
  It was a little past noon.
The stockings were hung in the
  crater with care,
In hopes that Santa would come
  right there.
The moon kids were nestled
  all snug in their beds,
And Mama in her craterchief,
  and I in my cap,
Had just settled down
  for a long moon nap,
When out on the moon dust
  arose such a clatter,
I sprang from my bed to see
  what was the matter.
But what to my martian eyes
  should appear,
But a tiny moon buggy and
  eight moondeer,
With a little old martian
  so lively and quick,
I knew in a moment it must be
  St. Nick.
And then in a second, I heard
  on the crater,
The stamping and stomping of hoofs
  grew much greater.
As I was slowly turning and
  glancing around,
Down the crater chimney he came
  with a bound.

He was dressed all in fur,
  from his head to his foot,
And his clothes were all covered
  with ashes and soot;
A bundle of toys he had
  on his back,
And he looked like a peddler
  just opening his pack.
He spoke not a word, but went
  straight to his work;
He filled all the stockings,
  then turned with a jerk,
Putting his head gear over
  his nose,
And with a nod up the crater
  chimney he rose;
He leaped to his moon buggy,
  to his moondeer gave a whistle,
And away they flew just as fast
  as a missile.
But I heard on the intercom as he
  drove out of sight,
"Merry Christmas to all and to all a
  Good Night!"

Nona Maiola, Age 12

I hear but my brain doesn't get the
message.

Andrew Pacheco, Age 12

Definitions by Sixth Graders

A SIXTH GRADER is a person in the middle of growing up.

Sally Evans

ANGER is when someone is tired and emotional.

Mavis Harrison

LOVE is an understanding between two people who have certain feelings for each other and they get along because of it.

Tom Parmityr

PRAYER is talking to God to tell Him you love Him and believe in Him.

Carol Peterson

THE SKY is the seeable space around the earth. During the day it appears to be a blue dome surrounding the earth.

Blair West

A VACATION is a trip to get away from it all.

Terri Hall

WATER is what you drink when there isn't any soda pop.

Kirk Bradley

Do as you're told; don't argue.

Kelly Wignall, Age 12

Don't do unto others what you don't want them to do to you.

Stephanie Johnny, Age 13

The Soap Box Derby

When I was in a soap box derby,
I drove a car by the name of Herby.
  He had red wheels,
  I drove him through fields,
And I won the soap box derby!

Michael L. Kane, Age 10

The Man on the Moon

They say there's a man on the moon,
Who's due for a face-lifting soon.
  "The Russians," they say,
  "Will be there some day,
And wrinkle him up like a prune!"

Judy Turner, Age 10

Tips for Living

Never be rude.
Obey your elders.
Show love to all people
  even if they are not your friends.

Leandra Garcia, Age 11

Homework

Homework, homework,
Most monotonous kind of lone work!
I hate it when wanting to catch fishes,
But I love it when I should be doing dishes!

Gary Hoskins, Age 11

166

Mister Snowman

Look at Mr. Snowman
  Standing in the snow!
But when the sun is shining,
  He surely doesn't grow!
He gets a little shorter,
  With every passing hour,
But where he gently faded,
  Will grow a little flower.

Joleen Urriola, Age 11

Pioneers

These pioneers of olden days,
  With their sure and honest ways,
Helped the people, rich or poor,
  Only to give and help some more.

Clara Barton was one of those;
  She helped all, not a few she
    chose.
She nursed the soldiers, one by one,
  And didn't stop till she was done.

Benjamin Franklin worked and
    wrote,
  Made his stories, note by note.
He worked hard in the printing
    shops,
  Until of writers, he was "tops."

Marie Curie tried and tried,
  She worked on radium until she
    died.
Then she saw that glowing light
  In radium, that made life bright.

Ann Harris, Age 11

Owls

Some owls have big eyes,
And some have small,
But the owls with big eyes
See best of all!

Bob Merkel, Age 13

A Thanksgiving Prayer

On Thanksgiving Day, I'll say a little
    prayer,
To thank our heavenly Father for
    things so rare:
For our parents, kind and dear,
For our friends both far and near,
For the food that helps us grow,
For the rain and for the snow.
All these things I'm thankful for,
Yes, all of these and many more.

Kristy Woodward, Age 11

The Report Card

Violets are blue, roses are red;
Report cards are the one thing I
    dread!
One look at my card and lo and
    behold,
I should have done my work as I was
    told!

Richard Barrows, Age 11

Spring

I saw a bird high in the tree,
He was singing a song to me.
He sang, "Nothing can go wrong,
When I sing my happy song!"
He was as happy as could be,
Away up high in his big tree.

Pat Brennen, Age 7

Definitions by Fourth Graders

TEACHERS are people that help you learn things that you don't know.

COURAGE is when you're going to get spanked and stand up to it.

PATRIOTISM is love and loyal support of your country.

HAPPINESS is when you're going to get spanked and you don't.

A FRIEND is someone that you have fun with and who helps you.

A FATHER is someone you like. He is your mother's husband and loves you and is the boss.

A MOTHER is a person who brought you into the world and loves you and cares for you.

A HOME is a house, but you live in it to make it a home.

Thanks for Hearing

For ears to hear Your outdoor
      music,
   We thank Thee, God.
For birds singing early in the
      morning
And crickets squeaking in our
      gardens at night,
   We thank Thee, God.
For the "drip-drip" of the rain,
The happy chatter of the brook,
The splash and roar of the waves,
   We thank Thee, God.
For the whisper and rustling of the
      leaves,
And sometimes the loud "who-o-o"
      of the wind,
   We thank Thee, God.
For the church bells that sing to us
On a quiet Sunday morning,
   We thank Thee, God.

Written by the children of the Primary Department, First Congregational Church, Bristol, Connecticut

A Mother

I'd like to be a mother,
A mother dear and sweet,
And I want some children,
To keep nice and neat.
I wouldn't want my children
To run and rob a bank.
If they become good grown-ups,
They'll have me to thank.
There are lots of things I want to do,
But more than any other,
When I'm all grown-up,
I want to be a mother.

Victoria C. Armuth, Age 9

Character is something a person has. It is what kind of person he is. Or it will point out some good or some bad thing you did not know about them.

Layne Felsted   Age 12

William Penn

William Penn owned millions of
    acres,
But he gave up a life of ease
To join his friends, the Quakers.

Our hero went to jail,
A dirty place, indeed.
Another man joined him,
His name was William Mead.

Penn went to the king, and said,
"Have mercy on our band,
We want a peaceful settlement in
Your wonderful new land."

William didn't have colorful things,
His clothes were not very showy,
But he always was able and ready,
In weather both clear and snowy.

From the Old Country,
England, they came.
They founded their own city,
Philadelphia was its name.

Carol Harriman, Age 11

Mice Are Pets?

Mice are small,
Mice are fat,
Mice make
    good pets for cats!

Diana Taufer, Age 13

A Kite

If I were a kite, high in the sky,
I might see many types of birds go
    by.
Whenever my master tugged on the
    line,
That would be the signal to climb.

It's good to fly and be a kite;
Maybe some day I'll make a long
    flight.
The trouble begins when I'm caught
    in a storm:
If it's bad, I may come down torn.

I'm glad that I'm a free-flying kite —
The views that I see are a wondrous
    sight.
Some day when you see me pass by,
You'll wish that you were a kite in
    the sky.

Scott Trevor, Age 12

Mice

E-E-K!
Is
The noise
My mother
Makes when
She sees one!

David Marsh, Age 13

Acknowledgments

ABINGDON PRESS for "The Handiwork of God" and "Always Finish" by unknown authors on pages 136 and 145 of *Great Art and Children's Worship* by Jean L. Smith. Copyright 1948 by Stone and Pierce.

ASSOCIATION FOR CHILDHOOD EDUCATION INTERNATIONAL for "Fuzzy, Wuzzy, Creepy, Crawly" by Lillian Schulz Vanda from *Sung Under the Silver Umbrella*. Copyright 1948 by the Association for Childhood Education International.

ATHENEUM PUBLISHERS for "The Travelers" by Patricia Hubbell from *The Apple Vendor's Fair*. Copyright © 1963 by Patricia Hubbell.

MRS. PETRA CABOT for "The Little Man Who Wasn't There" by Hughes Mearns from *Creative Youth Anthology of Lincoln School Verse*.

CENTURY CO. for "The Little Elf" by John Kendrick Bangs from *St. Nicholas Book of Verse*. Copyright 1923 by The Century Company.

WILLIAM COLE for the poem beginning "It's such a shock, I almost screech" from *Rhyme Giggles*. Copyright © 1967 by William Cole.

CONCORDIA PUBLISHING HOUSE for "Thank You, Jesus, for This Day", "My Savior, Hear My Prayer," and "Two Little Eyes" from *Little Children Sing to God!* Compiled and edited by A. H. Jahsmann and A. W. Gross and copyright © 1960 by Concordia Publishing House.

DODD MEAD & COMPANY for "The Owl and the Pussy-Cat", "They Went to Sea in a Sieve, They Did," "There Was an Old Man with a Beard," and "Twinkle, Twinkle Little Bat," by Edward Lear from *The Complete Nonsense Book*.

DOUBLEDAY & CO. for "Circus Elephant" by Kathryn Worth Curry from *Poems For Josephine*. Copyright 1937 by Kathryn Worth Curry. For "Mice" by Rose Fyleman from *51 New Nursery Rhymes*. Copyright 1932 by Doubleday and Company. For "Only My Opinion" by Monica Shannon from *Goose Grass Rhymes*. Copyright 1930 by Doubleday & Co. For "Fourth of July" by Rachel Field from *A Little Book of Days*. Copyright 1927 by Doubleday & Co.

DUCKWORTH & CO. LTD. for "The Frog" by Hilaire Belloc from *Cautionary Verses*.

EYRE METHUEN LTD. and the NATIONAL TRUST for "If" by Rudyard Kipling from *Rewards and Fairies*.

AILEEN FISHER for "Sandpile Town" from *That's Why*. Copyright 1946, renewed 1974, and published by Thomas Nelson & Sons. For "Benjamin Jones Goes Swimming" which first appeared in *Child Life*, published in July 1942 by *The Saturday Evening Post*.

GOSPEL LIGHT PUBLICATIONS for lyrics to "God's Gifts to Me" from *Two-n-Three Time Songs*.

COLLECTED POEMS for "When I Was One-and-Twenty" by A. E. Housman for world rights, excluding the USA.

THE SOCIETY OF AUTHORS as the literary representative of the Estate of John Masefield for "Sea Fever" by John Masefield from *Poems*.

MELVIN STEADMAN JUNIOR for the following poems by Nancy Byrd Turner. "God's Plan for Spring" from *Children's Religion*; "Black and Gold" from *Poetry for Holidays*; and "Clementine" from *Exploring Music*.

TEACHER for "Lion Thoughts" by Iowna Elizabeth Banker and "On the Merry, Merry-Go-Round" by Dorothy McGrath from *Grade Teacher*, June 1958. Copyright © by MacMillan Professional Magazines Inc.

MRS. JOSEPHINE THACKER, Administrator of Dixie Willson Estate for "The Mist and All" by Dixie Willson from *Child Life* Magazine. Copyright 1924, 1952 by Rand McNally & Co.

UNITED CHURCH PRESS for "When Jesus Walked Upon the Earth" by Marion Brown Shelton from *The Pilgrim Elementary Teacher*.

YALE UNIVERSITY PRESS for "Chanticleer" by John Farrer from *Songs For Parents*. Copyright 1921 by Yale University Press.

Grateful thanks is made to the following authors whose addresses, publishers, agents, and/or trustees I was unable to locate:

James Barton Adams for "The Cowboy's Life"; William Henry Davies for "Leisure"; F. E. Elwell for "Courtesy"; Edwina Fallis for "Wise Johnny"; Louis and Linka Friedman for "April Rain" ("The Rain Song" or "Song") by Robert Loveman; Esther Gillespie for "God Is Everywhere" and "Who Taught Them?" by unknown authors; Reginald Holmes for "Little Girl's Heart"; W. D. Howard for "Young Men!"; Ann Johnson for "Grandma"; Richard Le-Gallienne for "I Meant to Do My Work Today"; Mary Wright Saunders for "Remembering Day"; James Stephens for "The Wind"; Dorothy Brown Thompson for "Wish"; and Thomas H. B. Webb for "An Ancient Prayer."

 Index of Titles and First Lines

*The first lines of Scripture are italicized

 Index of Authors and Sources

Contents

Photo Acknowledgements

Action Plus: 175, 268, 327
Alamy: 9b, 13, 22, 26–7, 32, 39, 44–5, 55, 59, 60, 86, 95, 97, 106, 115, 117, 119, 121, 122, 127, 129, 130, 132, 177, 179, 219, 242, 246, 247, 253, 254, 256, 257, 258, 263, 263, 264, 267, 270, 272, 273, 274, 277, 293, 293, 318, 336, 340, 342, 343, 353, 355, 355
Corbis: 47, 57, 148, 156, 166, 253, 295, 302, 310, 311, 341, 356
Cycleandstyle.com: 139
Food Standards Agency (Crown copyright): 234
Getty Images: 20, 21a, 21b, 22, 23, 26–7, 29, 30a, 30b, 32, 33, 35, 37, 39, 41, 44–5, 47, 48, 49a, 49b, 51, 53, 55, 57, 58, 59, 60, 84–85, 86, 88, 89, 112, 114, 115, 116, 117, 119, 121, 122, 125, 126, 127, 129, 130, 132, 136, 139, 140, 141, 143, 144, 146, 148, 148, 148, 148, 150, 151, 153, 155, 156, 157, 158, 159, 166, 168, 169, 170, 172, 174, 175, 176, 177, 179, 180, 181, 182, 183, 186a, 186b, 190, 191, 193, 197, 198, 200, 203, 205, 207, 210, 212, 213, 215, 219, 221, 222, 224, 227, 230, 232, 234, 236, 239a, 239b, 241, 241, 242, 245, 246, 247, 250, 253a, 253b, 254, 255, 256, 257, 258, 259, 261a, 261b, 263a, 263b, 264, 265, 266, 267, 268, 269, 270, 272, 273, 274, 275, 277, 280, 283, 284, 287, 289, 293a, 293b, 295, 299, 301, 302, 303, 306, 308, 309, 310, 311, 312, 313, 315, 316, 318, 320, 321, 322, 323, 324, 325, 326, 327, 328, 329, 332, 335a, 335b, 336, 337, 338, 339, 340, 341, 342, 343, 344, 345, 346, 347, 348, 349, 350, 351, 352, 353, 355a, 355b, 356, 357
iStockphoto: 11, 21a, 21b, 23, 29, 35, 37, 48, 49a, 49b, 53, 58, 93, 94, 100, 102, 103a, 103b, 105, 126, 136, 150, 151, 158, 169, 180, 210, 213, 215, 232, 239a, 239b, 241, 245, 259, 309, 312, 322, 324, 326, 328
Natalie Andrews: 198
NCSA-lift.org: 144
Patrick Eagar: 352
Photo Library: 148
Rex Features: 125, 320, 335, 357
Shutterstock: 2–4, 5, 7, 9, 12, 30a, 30b, 33, 41, 51, 84–85, 90, 96, 99, 112, 114, 146, 148, 153, 155, 159, 168, 174, 176, 183, 200, 203, 205, 212, 227, 230, 236, 241, 261, 266, 280, 283, 287, 289, 299, 301, 303, 306, 308, 315, 316, 325, 329, 335
Science Photo Library: 140, 221, 222, 224
Sport for All: 116

Introduction

Welcome to BTEC Level 3 Sport.

This course book is written for students aiming to achieve one of the following BTEC Level 3 Sport awards:

BTEC Level 3 National Certificate in Health and Social Care	(30 credits)
BTEC Level 3 National Certificate in Sport	(30 credits)
BTEC Level 3 National Subsidiary Diploma in Sport	(60 credits)
BTEC Level 3 National Diploma Sport	(120 credits)
BTEC Level 3 National Extended Diploma Sport	(180 credits)

The material in this book covers fifteen units of the BTEC Level 3 Sport award. All the units you need to complete to obtain a certificate or subsidiary diploma award are contained in this book. Most of the mandatory units required for the diploma awards for the Performance and Excellence or Development, Coaching and Fitness pathways are also covered in this book.

Each chapter of the book covers a specific BTEC Level 3 National Sport unit. You will see that the chapters are divided into topics. Each topic provides you with a focused and manageable chunk of learning and covers all of the content areas that you need to know about in a particular unit. You should also notice that the material in each topic is clearly linked to the unit's pass, merit and distinction grading criteria. This mapping of the content against the grading criteria should help you to prepare for your assignments and practical assessments. The assignments that you are given by your tutor will require you to demonstrate that you have the knowledge and are able to do the things which the pass, merit or distinction criteria refer to. Obviously, many of the assignments will be practical.

The book provides suggestions for methods of achieving particular grades, and scenarios that relate to specific sports. However, alternative approaches of assessment are acceptable, and centres may choose to examine different sports and use examples that occur in those activities. Work will be assessed and checked by your tutor. The checklist at the end of each unit will help you to match the work you produce to the grades you are trying to achieve.

Overall, this course book provides a comprehensive resource for the units of the BTEC Level 3 National Sport programme that it covers. You can be sure that the content is closely matched to the BTEC specification and is designed and presented to help you achieve the grades you are aiming for and which you are capable of. The book provides case studies, activities and realistic examples to develop your interest in, and understanding of, Sport.

Students often begin a BTEC National Sport course with the aim of undertaking further professional training or to get a job in industry. We hope that the material in the book is accessible, interesting and inspires you to pursue and achieve this goal. You will find an extensive further reading list at the back of this book. Good luck with your course!

The authors

1 | Principles of anatomy and physiology in sport

LO1 Know the structure and function of the skeletal system

- There are several major bones in the skeleton and it is important to know their location.

- One of the five functions of the skeleton is to allow movement.

- The skeleton is connected by joints and these allow different types of movements to occur.

LO2 Know the structure and function of the muscular system

- Muscles are located in different parts of the body and each performs a specific function.

- The different types of muscles allow our bodies to function in different ways.

- There are different types of muscle fibre and each one can be associated with specific sports.

LO3 Know the structure and function of the cardiovascular system

- The heart is made up of different parts and it performs the function of the 'pump' for the cardiovascular system.

- A major function of this system is to ensure that oxygen is delivered to all parts of the body.

- Blood transports oxygen and also clots to seal wounds and fight infection.

LO4 Know the structure and function of the respiratory system

- ▶ There are different airways which allow air to enter the body and breathing to occur.

- ▶ The lungs are the organs which allow the exchange of oxygen and carbon dioxide.

- ▶ Various depths of breathing are possible when breathing in and out.

LO5 Know the different types of energy systems

- ▶ Different sports may require different energy systems to be used.

- ▶ Even within one sport different energy systems may be used at different times.

- ▶ Sports performers have to consider the recovery times which are relevant to their sport.

Structure and function of the skeletal system

You must be able to describe the **axial skeleton**, the **appendicular skeleton**, the different types of bone in the skeleton, and be able to locate all of the major bones in the body. You also need to be able to describe the function of the skeletal system.

Your assessment criteria:

P1 Describe the structure and function of the skeletal system

P1 Structure of the skeletal system

The skeleton is made up of a variety of different types of bone, as shown in Figure 1.1.

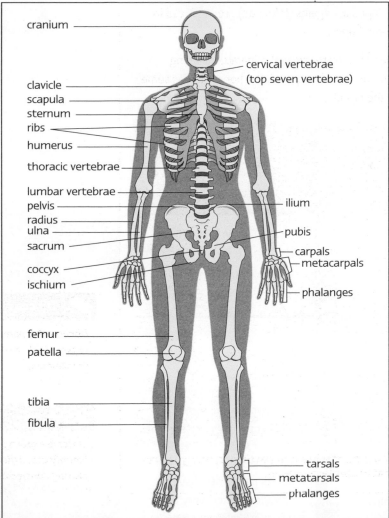

Figure 1.1 The main bones in the human body

Function of the skeletal system

The skeletal system has five functions:

1. *Protection* – all of the vital organs in your body are protected by bones. Your brain is encased within your cranium and your heart and lungs are behind your ribs.

2. *Attachment for skeletal muscles* – the bones do not move on their own as movement only occurs through the combined action of bones and muscles.

3. *Support* – the skeleton keeps everything in place and provides support for muscles and some of the other more delicate vital organs. It is the framework around which our bodies are constructed and without it our bodies would collapse.

4. *Blood cell production* – red blood cells (which carry oxygen) and white blood cells (which protect against infection) are produced in the bone marrow of some bones.

5. *Mineral storage* – bone tissue stores several minerals, including calcium and phosphorus, and when required, the bone releases some of these minerals into the blood.

Although the cranium protects the brain in particular, many sports performers use additional protection as well.

 Discuss

Discuss other parts of the body or vital organs which are clearly protected by the skeleton.

 Practical

Observe a sports performer moving. Identify the particular bones that are moving during that activity.

Joints

A joint is where two or more bones meet. There are over 100 joints in the body. You need to know the different types of joints and the movements they allow.

P2 Types of joint

Joints are classified into three groups:

1. Fixed joints – these are sometimes referred to as immoveable joints. The main examples of these are in the pelvis and cranium.

2. Slightly moveable joints – as the name suggests, some movement occurs at these joints. The main examples of these are the vertebrae in the spine.

3. Synovial or freely moveable joints – these are the most common joints in the body and are sub-divided into the following types of joint:

   • gliding joints, e.g. in the hands and feet (Figure 1.2)

   • hinge joints, e.g. in the elbow and the knee (Figure 1.3)

   • pivot joints, e.g. at the top of the neck and the bottom end of the arm (Figure 1.4)

   • ball and socket joints, e.g. the hip and the shoulder (Figure 1.5)

   • condyloid joints, e.g. the wrist (Figure 1.6).

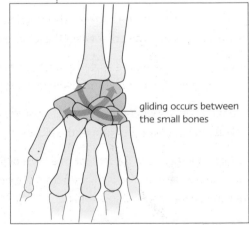

gliding occurs between the small bones

Figure 1.2 Gliding joints in the hand.

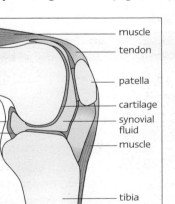

muscle
tendon
patella
cartilage
synovial fluid
muscle
femur
capsule
synovial membrane
tibia

Figure 1.3 The knee is a hinge joint.

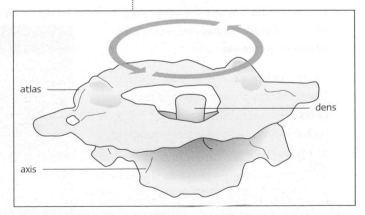

atlas
dens
axis

Figure 1.4 The pivot joint in your neck allows you to turn your head.

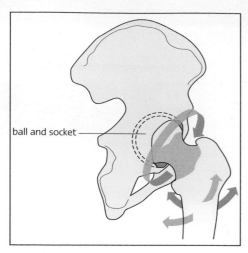

Figure 1.5 The hip is a ball and socket joint.

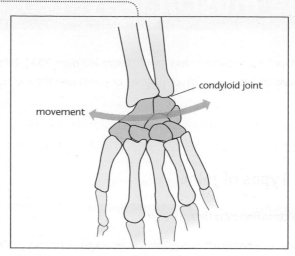

Figure 1.6 The condyloid joint in the wrist allows some sideways movement.

Movement of joints

Every movement which the body is able to perform has a specific technical name and these occur when the joints are used or moved.

- *Flexion* – this is where the angle between the two bones is increased, such as bending your arm at the elbow (a hinge joint).

- *Extension* – this is where the angle between the two bones is decreased, such as straightening your arm at the elbow.

- *Abduction* – this is the movement of a bone or limb away from your body, such as raising your arm away from the side of your body from your shoulder (a ball and socket joint).

- *Adduction* – this is the movement of a bone or limb towards your body, such as bringing your raised arm back into your body.

- *Rotation* – this is where the bone is able to move around in an arc, such as in the shoulder (a ball and socket joint) when you rotate your arm.

- *Circumduction* – this is a combination of flexion, extension, abduction and adduction (a combination of hinge joints and ball and socket joints) in a circular movement, such as a pitcher delivering a ball in softball or baseball.

- *Condyloid* – this allows some sideways movement, such as in the wrist (Figure 1.6).

Practical

Observe a sports performer carrying out some basic movements. Name the movements in the joints using the correct technical terms.

This circular delivery movement is circumduction.

7

Structure and function of the muscular system

P3 ▶ The major muscles

The muscular system has to work together with the skeletal system as movement can only take place when the two body systems work together. There are approximately 639 skeletal muscles in the body, but you only need to know about the location of those shown in Figure 1.7.

You should be able to identify many of the skeletal muscles from this bodybuilder's very well defined physique.

Types of muscle

There are three types of muscle:

- *Skeletal muscles* are attached to the skeleton and they make up the majority of muscles in the body.

- *Cardiac muscles* are a specific type of muscle that is only found in the wall of the heart.

- *Smooth muscles* are ones which contract and relax automatically and are found in the digestive and circulatory systems.

The three types of muscle perform different functions:

- The skeletal muscles are under your conscious control so they allow voluntary movements to occur.

- The cardiac muscles in the heart allow the heart to beat, enabling the cardiovascular system to function.

- The smooth muscles are involuntary muscles which means that they are not under conscious control, but contract and relax automatically.

Your assessment criteria:

P3 Identify the location of the major muscles in the human body

 Discuss

Discuss the reasons why the cardiac and smooth muscles work automatically and are not under conscious control like the skeletal muscles.

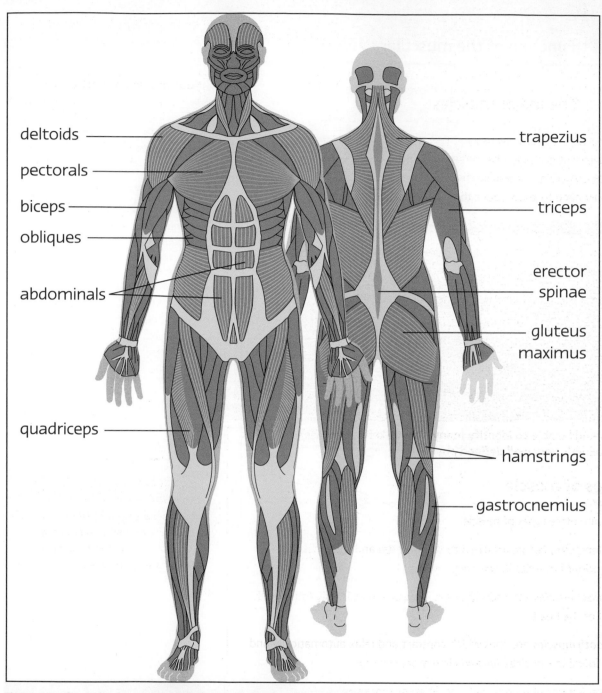

Figure 1.7 The skeletal muscles of the human body

  Practical

Observe a sports performer carrying out some basic movements. Identify and name the particular muscles which are moving.

P4 Function of the muscular system

Your assessment criteria:

P4 Describe the function of the muscular system and the different fibre types

The muscles which perform specific movements have names.

Muscle movement

It is important to be aware that muscles can only pull and that they cannot push. For this reason, they are always arranged in pairs so that one **contracts** (gets smaller) and the other relaxes (becomes longer) to allow a movement. The pair of muscles then reverse their roles to allow the opposite movement to happen as can be seen in the example of the movement in the elbow joint in Figure 1.8. These pairs of muscles are antagonistic pairs.

The following terms refer to specific muscle movements:

Key terms

Contract: to reduce in size by drawing together

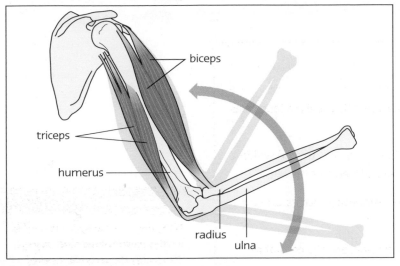

Figure 1.8 Muscle movement in the elbow joint

* antagonist – the muscle which relaxes and lengthens

* agonist – the muscle which contracts and shortens

* synergist – the muscles which help or assist in the movement

* fixator – the muscles which prevent any other unnecessary movement by fixing or stabilising other areas.

Practical

Observe a sports performer carrying out a movement. Identify which are the antagonist and agonist muscles involved in the movement.

This sprinter will rely on the conscious control of their skeletal muscles to get off to a fast start.

P4 ▶ Types of contraction

Muscles must contract in order to allow movement. There are four types of contraction:

- *Isometric* – the muscle stays the same length, there is tension within the muscle, but the distance between the ends remains the same.

- *Concentric* – the muscle shortens when a movement occurs, and the ends of the muscle move closer together.

- *Eccentric* – the muscle lengthens under tension, and the ends of the muscle move further apart.

- *Isokinetic* – the muscle contracts and shortens at constant speed.

Fibre types

Muscle fibres are classified in three groups:

- *Type 1* – these are also known as 'slow twitch' fibres and they contain large amounts of myoglobin with many blood capillaries. These fibres are red and split **ATP** at a slow rate, having a slow contraction velocity which makes them very resistant to fatigue. A high number of these are an advantage to any performer in endurance or aerobic-type events or sports.

 Discuss

Using the movement you observed to identify muscle movements on page 10, identify the particular types of muscle contraction which occurred and which muscle was involved.

P4 ▸ Fibre types *continued*

- *Type 2a* – these are known as 'fast twitch' fibres and they contain very large amounts of myoglobin with very many blood capillaries. These fibres are red with a very high capacity for generating ATP, and have a fast contraction velocity which makes them resistant to fatigue. A high number of these are an advantage to any performer in long-term anaerobic-type events or sports.

- *Type 2b* – these are also known as 'fast twitch' and they contain low levels of myoglobin with relatively few blood capillaries. The fibres are white and have a fast contraction velocity which means that they fatigue easily. A high number of these are an advantage to any performer in short-term anaerobic-type events or sports.

Most skeletal muscles of the body are a mixture of all three types, but their proportions vary between individuals.

A marathon runner has a high proportion of aerobically-trained muscle tissue.

Your assessment criteria:

P4 Describe the function of the muscular system and the different fibre types

M1 Explain the function of the muscular system and the different fibre types

D1 Analyse the function of the muscular system and the different fibre types

M1 ▸ Explain the function of the muscular system

All movements are only possible if the muscular system functions correctly. The best way to explain a movement is to observe it and then describe each phase of the movement in relation to the ways in which the antagonistic pairs work together, and the type (or types) of contraction which occur.

 Practical

Bend and straighten your arm. As you do so, use the fingers of the other hand to press gently on the tricep and bicep muscles. See if you can feel the movement which is taking place, and try to feel the location of the origin and insertion of the muscles at the shoulder and the elbow.

D1 Analyse the function of the muscular system

The best way to analyse the muscular system in operation is to slow down the movement in order to be able to see more clearly what is happening. The practical activity describes various ways in which this can be done.

🏃 Practical

Use a recording device (video camera, flip-cam or digital camera) to record a muscular movement, or a series of movements, and play it back on Real Player where it will be possible to scroll through the movement, freeze-frame it and slow it down. This will give you the opportunity to analyse the muscle movement in detail.

Alternatively, a video or DVD player can be used with a recorded performance where the same functions of freeze-framing and slow motion can be used.

Structure and function of the cardiovascular system

The cardiovascular system is a combination of the circulatory system and the respiratory system working together.

P5 Structure of the cardiovascular system

The heart

The most vital component of the cardiovascular system is the heart (Figure 1.9).

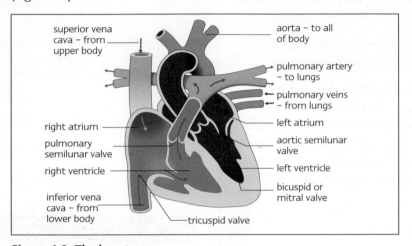

Figure 1.9 The heart

The heart is a pump and it works with the blood and the blood vessels to make up the circulatory system. There are several main blood vessels leading into and out of the heart: the aorta, pulmonary vein, pulmonary artery and vena cava.

Blood vessels

All of your blood flows through blood vessels. There are five types:

- *Arteries* – these have relatively thick walls and carry the oxygenated blood at high pressure away from the heart to the cells, tissues and organs of the body. They have no valves and the walls are more elastic than veins.

- *Arterioles* – these are small blood vessels which branch out from the arteries and transport blood from the heart to the body tissues.

- *Capillaries* – these are microscopic vessels which link the arteries with the veins. They are very narrow and allow carbon dioxide, oxygen, nutrients and waste products to pass through their thin walls.

- *Veins* – these carry deoxygenated blood back to the heart and have thinner walls than arteries. They are also far less elastic and have valves to ensure that the blood does not flow backwards through the vein.

- *Venuoles* – these branch off the veins and link to the capillaries. They drain the deoxygenated blood from the capillaries and take it to the veins to return to the heart.

Function of the cardiovascular system

The cardiovascular system has three main functions:

- *Delivery of oxygen and nutrients* – this is a transport function as the blood, water, oxygen and nutrients are carried throughout the body. The blood transports oxygen from the lungs to the body's tissues, and then carries carbon dioxide back to the lungs to be breathed out.

- *Removal of waste products* – the same system is responsible for removing products such as carbon dioxide and lactic acid.

- *Thermoregulation* – this function relates to temperature control and regulation. The body temperature is controlled as the blood absorbs body heat and carries it to the lungs. From there it is taken to the skin where it is released through the veins and capillaries. The blood vessels widen (vasodilation) to allow this process to take place and then they return to their normal size and become narrow again (vasoconstriction).

Function of the blood

The blood has three functions:

- *Oxygen transport* – this is via the red blood cells.

- *Clotting* – platelets (small fragments or particles of larger cells) help to seal the skin and perform the same function on damaged blood vessels.

- *Fighting infection* – the white blood cells are the body's main defence against infection and disease and some produce antibodies that protect the body from infection.

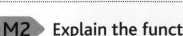 **M2** Explain the function of the cardiovascular system

Each part of the cardiovascular system is designed to fulfil a specific function, so any explanation must consider all of the components and the function they perform to enable the system to work efficiently.

 Design

In the form of a laboratory report, hand-draw the structure of the heart and blood vessels and label each part.

? | Did you know?

Many people's faces appear to go red when they are exercising vigorously because the blood vessels at the surface of the skin open up (dilate) to allow the heat to escape. This causes the 'flushed' or reddening effect as it is most obvious in the face.

Structure and function of the respiratory system

The respiratory system works with the cardiovascular system. It is the respiratory system which allows the body to take in oxygen which is transported through the blood, providing the energy needed for the body to function properly.

Your assessment criteria:

P6 Describe the structure and function of the respiratory system

P6 Structure of the respiratory system

The respiratory system is made up of the following parts:

- *Nasal cavity* – this is the hollow space into which air passes from the nose and mouth.

- *Epiglottis* – this is a flap of tissue at the base of the tongue, which prevents food from going into the trachea.

- *Trachea* (also known as the windpipe) – this is the tube through which air enters the lungs.

- *Bronchus* – the trachea divides into two tubes, each called a bronchus (plural bronchi), and each leading to a lung.

- *Bronchioles* – these are the smaller tubes that branch off the bronchi.

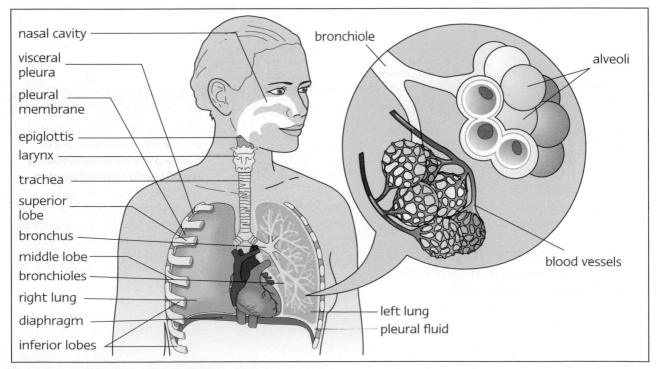

Figure 1.10 The respiratory system

nasal cavity
visceral pleura
pleural membrane
epiglottis
larynx
trachea
superior lobe
bronchus
middle lobe
bronchioles
right lung
diaphragm
inferior lobes

bronchiole
alveoli
blood vessels
left lung
pleural fluid

- *Alveoli* – these are the air sacs at the end of the bronchioles, and it is here that the exchange of oxygen and carbon dioxide takes place.

- *Diaphragm and intercostal muscles* – these are the two muscles which assist in the breathing process. The diaphragm is a large, dome-shaped muscle sheet under the lungs which seals the chest cavity from the abdominal cavity. The intercostal muscles connect the ribs, allowing them to move and the area which consists of the ribcage and intercostal muscles (see Figure 1.11) is known as the thoracic cavity.

Function of the respiratory system

Mechanisms of breathing

The first movement in the action of breathing is *inspiration* or breathing in (Figure 1.11). This happens when the intercostal muscles contract, lifting the ribs upwards and outwards. At the same time, the diaphragm becomes flatter and moves downwards. This makes the chest cavity larger, which reduces the pressure inside the cavity, and causes air to be sucked into the lungs.

? Did you know?

If you cross your arms across your chest and place your palms downwards on your chest you can feel the interaction of the intercostal muscles lifting the ribs outwards and upwards as you breathe in. You will find that your arms are raised upwards and outwards, and they will then drop down as you breathe out.

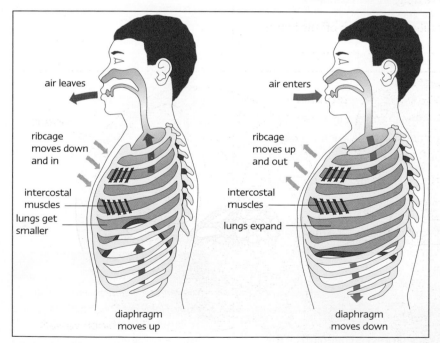

air leaves

ribcage moves down and in

intercostal muscles

lungs get smaller

diaphragm moves up

air enters

ribcage moves up and out

intercostal muscles

lungs expand

diaphragm moves down

Figure 1.11 How we breathe

? Did you know?

With an average breathing rate of 14 to 16 breaths a minute, the neural breathing rate will be approximately 20,000 breaths a day and therefore 141,120 in a week. As this is the resting breathing rate, the weekly rate is likely to be far more as the rate increases when any exercise takes place.

P6 Function of the respiratory system *continued*

The second movement is *expiration* or breathing out, and is the reverse of the inspiration process. The diaphragm relaxes at the same time as the intercostal muscles. The chest cavity returns to its normal size, and the pressure on the lungs is increased, forcing the air out.

Figure 1.12 shows the process of *gaseous exchange* which allows oxygen to be taken from the air and exchanged for carbon dioxide.

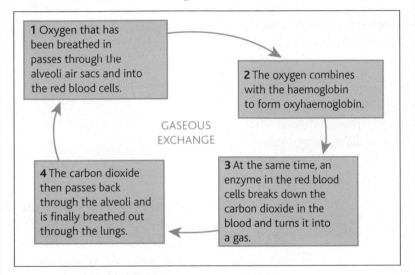

1 Oxygen that has been breathed in passes through the alveoli air sacs and into the red blood cells.

2 The oxygen combines with the haemoglobin to form oxyhaemoglobin.

GASEOUS EXCHANGE

4 The carbon dioxide then passes back through the alveoli and is finally breathed out through the lungs.

3 At the same time, an enzyme in the red blood cells breaks down the carbon dioxide in the blood and turns it into a gas.

Figure 1.12 The process of gaseous exchange

Lung volumes

Tidal volume is the amount of air you breathe in and out in a normal breathing cycle. When this increases, you are able to deliver more oxygen and remove carbon dioxide more quickly.

Vital capacity is the total volume of air that you can move in and out of your lungs in one deep breath.

Residual volume is the amount of air left in the lungs after a maximal exhalation, or the amount of air always left in the lungs which can never be expired.

Control of breathing

Neural breathing occurs when the breathing process is controlled by the central nervous system as an automatic action.

Chemical breathing occurs when receptors in the brain monitor rates of carbon dioxide concentration to increase the rate and depth of breathing.

? Did you know?

You can 'test' neural breathing quite easily. Hold your breath for as long as you possibly can, and you will find that your body will automatically start breathing again as the central nervous system takes over and forces you to breathe.

M3 ▸ Explain the function of the respiratory system

The respiratory system, and especially the mechanics of breathing, plays a vital role in enabling the body to function properly. This is particularly the case when taking part in any form of physical activity as the system must supply all of the working muscles with an adequate oxygen supply.

 Practical

To understand how important the nasal cavity is in the action of breathing, try the following. Pinch your nose very tightly (to stop any air at all from being breathed in) and breathe in as deeply as possible only using your mouth. Note how difficult it is to fully inflate your lungs when you are doing this.

? | **Did you know?**

If you work very hard during a physical activity, you may find that you are out of breath for quite some time after you have finished. This is because your body has needed more oxygen than you were able to supply, and you have experienced oxygen debt. This feeling of being short of breath after exercising is not unusual, but you need to repay the oxygen debt and also disperse the lactic acid that has built up. One of the best ways to do this is to exercise lightly after you have finished – this is called the cool down!

 Practical

Monitor your own breathing rate by checking how high the level goes following strenuous exercise.

Cooling down and stretching after exercise

Types of energy systems

Three different energy systems are used to provide the amount of energy required by the body during exercise. This depends on the intensity and duration of the exercise. Many sports require a combination of these systems at different times or in different phases.

Your assessment criteria:

P7 | Describe the three different energy systems and their use in sport and exercise activities

P7 | Energy systems and their use in sport

Phosphocreatine system

As it does not require oxygen, this is the fastest system to generate ATP (adenosine triphosphate), an energy source used by the body which is produced when the body breaks down food. This is the first energy system the body uses in almost every activity and movement. As soon as the body senses that it is going to require a maximum effort, this energy system starts up, but it can only last for 5 to 8 seconds of sustained maximum effort. As a result, this energy system is the primary energy source for initial short sprints in invasion games, long and high jump, and any other activities that require very quick bursts of energy, such as serving in tennis.

? | Did you know?

Sprinters in the 100-metre race do not breathe throughout the race. They only use the phosphocreatine system. Top sprinters finish the race within 10 seconds so they take a breath right at the start and continue to breathe normally once they have finished the race!

Lactic acid system

This is the second fastest system. Again, it does not require oxygen, but it can last for about 60 to 180 seconds (one to three minutes) of all out effort. As a result, this system is the primary energy source for any short-distance running events such as the 100-200- and 400-metre events.

Aerobic energy system

This is the long-term energy system which is used when a performer continues with an activity for a long period of time. This energy system requires oxygen in order to produce energy, so it is not as dependent on ATP as the previous two systems, and the rate that the ATP is supplied is relatively slow. Any long distance (or endurance) event uses this system. This system produces the largest amounts of energy at the lowest intensity, but at the start of exercise the body cannot deliver oxygen to the muscles fast

This performer needs to replace the oxygen used up after a strenuous burst of exercise.

20

enough so the phosphocreatine system and lactic acid system are required for the first couple of minutes.

Sports that use energy systems

This sprinter who has just left the blocks is only in the first second of her activity. This means that she is using the phosphocreatine system at the start of the race, and is then moving on to the lactic acid one. If she is competing in a sprint event, she is likely to only make use of these two particular systems, requiring ATP to be produced at a fast rate throughout.

This rugby player may have required the phosphocreatine system at the start of this ball carrying run, also moving on to the lactic acid one if his run continues. However, to continue playing at a high intensity for the full 80 minutes of a game, he will make use of the aerobic system as well.

Discuss

Choose three different sports or physical activities and discuss which energy systems are being used in these activities. Also, consider which systems are being used at particular times if more than one energy system is being used.

Did you know?

'Aerobic' and 'aerobics' are terms which are often confused. Aerobic literally means 'with oxygen' and aerobics is a type of physical exercise which combines rhythmic aerobic exercise with stretching and strength training routines. Aerobics sessions are often taken by an instructor or leader and performed to music.

P7 Energy systems and their use in sport
continued

Recovery time

Performers generally recover quicker after using just the phosphocreatine and lactic systems than they do after using the aerobic one. This is why sprinters can generally run races with relatively short rest periods (often two in a day in major competitions), and endurance athletes require several days between races or even longer spells for events such as a marathon.

Your assessment criteria:

P7 Describe the three different energy systems and their use in sport and exercise activities

M4 Explain the three different energy systems and their use in sport and exercise activities

D2 Analyse the three different energy systems and their use in sport and exercise systems

? Did you know?

When Usain Bolt won the 100 metres Olympic title in Beijing in 2008 (setting a world record time of 9.69 seconds), he had to run three races in two days. He ran heats on 15th August, and then ran a semi-final and final on 16th August, and still managed to save his fastest run until the final race!

M4 Explain energy systems

Every sporting situation involves the use of energy systems, and certain sports will make use of one system in particular. You should consider each energy system individually to see which sports and exercise activities it applies to most closely.

D2 Analyse energy systems

To analyse an energy system, you need to consider specific sports or exercise activities and the physical demands of those activities.

Case study

Helen is a sports therapist who regularly applies her anatomical knowledge to sports and exercise activities. She has two new clients who have come to her for advice relating to the demands their activities may be having on them.

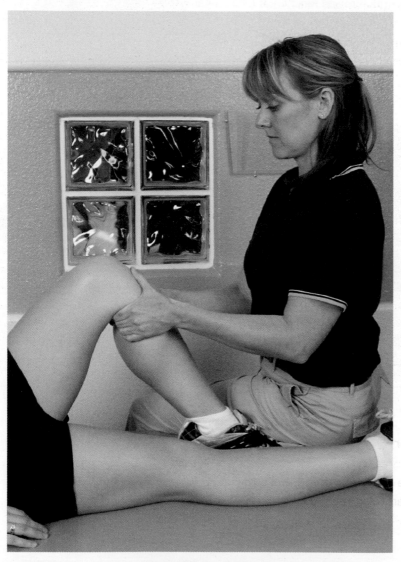

One client is a county standard 400-metre runner who is hoping to do well in the forthcoming national trials, and the other is an up-and-coming rugby player who is currently in the squad for a high standard rugby team.

What advice is Helen likely to be able to give to both of these performers relating to the energy systems they are using and the recovery times they should allow?

Assessment checklist

To achieve a pass grade, my portfolio of evidence must show that I can:

Assessment Criteria	Description	✓
P1	Describe the structure and function of the skeletal system.	☐
P2	Describe the different classification of joints.	☐
P3	Identify the location of the major muscles in the human body.	☐
P4	Describe the function of the muscular system and the different fibre types.	☐
P5	Describe the structure and function of the cardiovascular system.	☐
P6	Describe the structure and function of the respiratory system.	☐
P7	Describe the three different energy systems and their use in sport and exercise activities.	☐

To achieve a merit grade, my portfolio of evidence must show that I can:

Assessment Criteria	Description	✓
M1	Explain the function of the muscular system and the different fibre types.	☐
M2	Explain the function of the cardiovascular system.	☐
M3	Explain the function of the respiratory system.	☐
M4	Explain the three different energy systems and their use in sport and exercise activities.	☐

To achieve a distinction grade, my portfolio of evidence must show that I can:

Assessment Criteria	Description	✓
D1	Analyse the function of the muscular system and the different fibre types.	☐
D2	Analyse the three different energy systems and their use in sport and exercise activities.	☐

2 | The physiology of fitness

LO1 Know the body's response to acute exercise

- ▸ The musculoskeletal system (the combination of your muscles and bones) reacts and responds to exercise.

- ▸ The energy systems in your body adapt and respond when you exercise.

- ▸ The cardiovascular system responds to the demands which are made on it during exercise.

- ▸ The respiratory system (and in particular your breathing) responds to acute exercise.

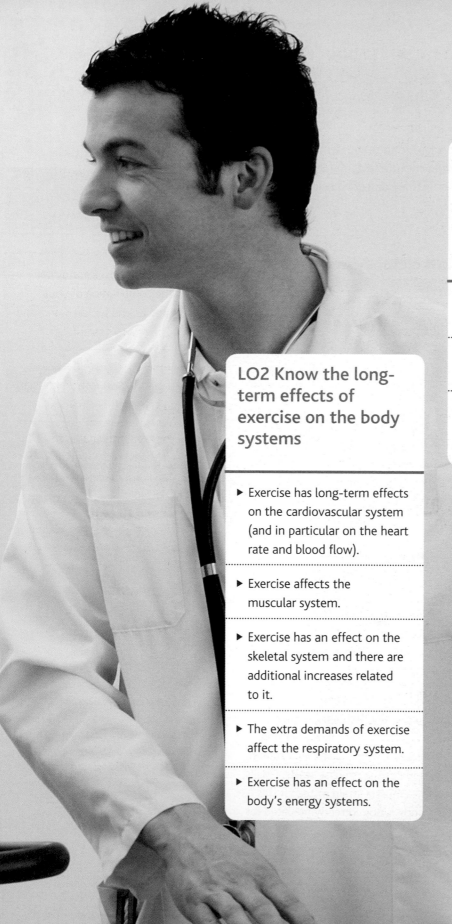

LO3 Be able to investigate the physiological effects of exercise on the body systems

- ▶ There are various different types of exercise.

- ▶ You can make use of a range of methods of investigation.

- ▶ Carrying out a review of your investigation is important and valuable.

LO2 Know the long-term effects of exercise on the body systems

- ▶ Exercise has long-term effects on the cardiovascular system (and in particular on the heart rate and blood flow).

- ▶ Exercise affects the muscular system.

- ▶ Exercise has an effect on the skeletal system and there are additional increases related to it.

- ▶ The extra demands of exercise affect the respiratory system.

- ▶ Exercise has an effect on the body's energy systems.

The body's response to acute exercise

When you exercise, your body has to adapt to the extra demands you are making on it. All sports performers experience these demands. The body systems respond to exercise and the effects are described below.

Your assessment criteria:

P1 Describe the musculoskeletal and energy systems' responses to acute exercise

P1 How the musculoskeletal system responds to exercise

The musculoskeletal system responds in a variety of ways to a single bout of exercise:

- Increased **blood supply** – the muscles require more blood because the demand has increased.

- Increase in **muscle pliability** – the muscles have to move quickly and often.

- Increased range of movement – acute exercise is active and energetic, requiring a much greater range of movement than normal.

- Muscle fibre micro tears – this is a negative effect as it is a form of injury caused by resistance exercise.

A warm-up is necessary because of the ways in which the musculoskeletal system responds. This is the correct way in which to prepare the body for these responses in order to avoid injury due to the change of state which occurs. It is a common misconception that a warm-up gets the blood flowing – it is already flowing! The warm-up increases the blood flow which is important as the muscles respond immediately to the additional demand being put upon them.

Muscles need to be warmed up gradually in order to become pliable as the exercise makes movements both quicker and frequent. A run can triple the amount of movement which is required for merely walking. The range of movement will also be greater (a stride pattern for running is far greater than one for walking) as soon as the exercise starts. Finally, there is a chance of an injury, especially a muscle strain or tear, if this warm-up does not take place and the body is not correctly prepared for the acute exercise which is to occur.

Key terms

Blood supply: the volume of blood supplied to an organ or part of the body at any particular time

Muscle pliability: the way in which muscles are quickly receptive to change

? Did you know?

There is no such thing as being double-jointed. Flexibility is the range of movement at a joint, and everyone has the capacity to increase this range through regular stretching and mobility exercises. As exercise requires a greater range of movement than normal, being very flexible can be a real advantage for a performer.

How the energy systems respond to exercise

The energy systems respond in the following ways to a bout of exercise of approximately 30 minutes:

- The phosphocreatine is the fastest system to generate ATP so this system responds initially when the acute exercise gets underway.

- As the body responds, the lactic acid system is called into action in conjunction with the phosphocreatine system initially and then as the main energy source from 60 to 180 seconds.

- The aerobic system is the third system to respond as this is a more long-term system which takes over as the exercise demands continue for more than about three minutes. Very few activities which are undertaken last for less than three minutes so this system is a very important one for all sports performers. It is for this reason that the majority of performers include some form of aerobic training in their training schedule as they would expect to continue with exercise for quite some time beyond the three-minute barrier.

- The energy continuum is the concept used to describe the type of respiration you use depending on the type of physical activity you are undertaking. The more energetic (or acute) this is, the lower down the continuum it will be and the greater the demand will be.

- The energy requirements of different sport and exercise activities will vary as some are clearly more active than others (this relates to the energy continuum described above), and you should be aware that the body responds differently to a greater demand which a particular activity might make.

Key terms

ATP: adenosine triphosphate, the molecule that cells use to store energy for future use

Lactic acid: a syrupy, water-soluble liquid which is a mild poison and which is produced in muscles as a result of anaerobic exercise

Discuss

Observe someone carrying out energetic (acute) exercise, or you can exercise yourself.

1. *Discuss which of the effects described here occur as the musculoskeletal system responds.*

2. *Discuss which energy systems are being used and at which times.*

Acute exercise movements such as these clearly result in an increase in the range of movement.

29

P2 How the cardiovascular system responds to exercise

Your assessment criteria:

P2 Describe the cardiovascular and respiratory systems' responses to acute exercise

The cardiovascular system responds in a variety of ways to a single bout of exercise of approximately 30 minutes:

- Heart rate anticipatory response – the heart rate starts to increase even before activity gets underway in anticipation of the demands which are to be made. A performer will be well aware of the session they are about to start even if it is simply a training session. For a sprinter lining up at the start of a race, there will be a great deal of tension which will lead to an increase in heart rate.

- Activity response – this is the actual demand which the activity will make. All activities require different levels of response. An outfield player in football has a greater demand upon their cardiovascular system than a goalkeeper despite the fact that they will be playing in the same game and for the same amount of time. Different activities have different demands as can be seen by comparing golf with marathon running. A round of golf is likely to take as long as running a marathon, but the distance covered (just over 26 miles in the case of the marathon) is far greater for the marathon and therefore requires a different activity demand response.

The demands of playing golf and running a marathon may be similar in terms of time taken, but the marathon run will require a greater cardiovascular response.

- Increased **blood pressure** – greater demand means that more blood is required, so the pressure needed to increase this flow also increases. The blood carries the oxygen to the working muscles and as the demand on the muscles increases, so the blood pressure must increase accordingly.

- **Vasoconstriction** – as the blood flow increases, so the blood vessels narrow as contractions occur. This increase will cause contractions to take place far more rapidly and far more often.

- **Vasodilation** – as the blood vessels relax, following initial contractions, they expand as the opposite action. For each vasoconstriction there must be vasodilation, so these will increase accordingly.

How the respiratory system responds to exercise

The respiratory system responds to acute exercise in the following ways:

- Increase in **breathing rate** – this will go up from the normal rate of approximately 12 breaths per minute depending on how active the exercise demand is. If the activity is particularly demanding, then the breathing rate is likely to increase by up to three times the normal resting rate. Even a slight increase in demand will result in the breathing rate increasing. This is related to the neural control (the automatic action your nervous system controls) and the chemical control (where the brain registers the levels of carbon dioxide controls) of breathing rates.

- Increased **tidal volume** – this is the normal amount of air you breathe in and out and the increased demand during exercise will mean that this will increase. The demand will no longer be the normal amount required at rest, so this is bound to increase as well.

Key terms

Blood pressure: the pressure exerted by the blood against the walls of the blood vessels, especially the arteries

Breathing rate: the frequency and speed of breathing in

Tidal volume: the normal amount of air you breathe in and out

Vasoconstriction: the narrowing of a blood vessel (the opposite of vasodilation)

Vasodilation: the expansion of a blood vessel (the opposite of vasoconstriction)

Practical

Monitor increases in your heart rate in relation to activity response by taking your pulse and seeing how much higher it goes when exercising energetically compared to what it is when you are resting.

Did you know?

Stitch is related to the respiratory system as it is caused by a spasm in the diaphragm muscle which causes an intense stabbing pain under the lower edge of the ribcage. It is commonly experienced by performers when the respiratory system is put under stress during intense exercise.

M1 ▶ Musculoskeletal system

Your assessment criteria:

M1 Explain the responses of the musculoskeletal, cardiovascular and respiratory systems to acute exercise

Increased blood supply

During exercise, the blood supply to the major muscles has to increase quite significantly. The amount of blood in your body is constant, but it is the transport system which provides energy in the form of oxygen, so this increased blood supply ensures a greater supply of oxygen.

Increase in muscle pliability

Exercise affects the muscles as they have to relax and contract much faster and more often. Their increased pliability is crucial as it enables them to react quickly and efficiently and reduces the risk of injury.

Increased range of movement

During any acute exercise, the range of movements which muscles, or muscle groups, go through is greatly increased. A gymnast performs a number of complex and difficult movements in a floor routine which are far more demanding than simply walking about.

Muscle fibre micro tears

The greater the demand which a performer makes upon the body, the greater the risk is of injury. Failing to warm up properly before acute exercise can result in muscle tears and micro tears can cause soreness in the muscles. This is not always considered to be a negative effect as this can cause the muscles to react by becoming stronger to combat this effect.

Cardiovascular system

Heart rate anticipatory response

Anticipatory response heart rates can be linked to the types of activities being undertaken. A sprinter who is about to run a race for 10–20 seconds may have a very high anticipatory rate as they know there can only be one winner and poor starts can cost them the race.

In this floor routine, ranges of movement are greatly increased compared to normal.

Activity response

Different types of activity can have very different levels of activity response. A weightlifter carries out a lift which only lasts a matter of a few seconds from start to finish so they have to respond quickly and for a short time, whereas another performer may have longer ongoing demands.

Increased blood pressure

Normal blood pressure is 130 over 85, and in order for the blood to increase its flow to the body parts which require it, the blood pressure rises. (Do not confuse this with resting blood pressure values which are related to being in good health.) The blood vessels react to this higher pressure by expanding (vasodilation) and contracting (vasoconstriction) far more than when you are at rest.

Respiratory system

Increase in breathing rate

As the muscles require more oxygen, breathing rates can increase up to four times. This means that the muscles do not fatigue so quickly and the performer is able to exercise for longer. The chemical control takes over as the carbon dioxide has to be exhaled while the oxygen is inhaled, and it is not possible to hold your breath (which you can do at rest) when you are exercising at a high level – you are more likely to be gasping for breath!

Increased tidal volume

As your breathing rate increases, your tidal volume also increases. The demand you are making is far more than normal so normal amounts of air are not sufficient.

Q | Research

1. *Choose three different sports or exercise activities and find out what the increases in breathing rate are likely to be for each one.*

2. *Research the increased heart rate levels which each of the performers are likely to be experiencing.*

? | Did you know?

The world record for someone holding their breath is an astonishing 19 minutes 21 seconds held by Swiss freediver, Peter Colat. Like any other body system, the respiratory system can be trained to improve. How long can you hold your breath?

Freedivers undertake specific training to be able to hold their breath for a very long time.

The long-term effects of exercise on the body systems

Acute exercise has many immediate effects on the body, whereas regular exercise has many long-term effects on the body. Regular exercise affects five body systems in a variety of ways.

P3 ▶ Adaptations of the musculoskeletal and energy systems

The musculoskeletal system and energy systems are affected in the following ways by long-term exercise such as a six-week training programme:

The muscular system

- **Hypertrophy** (more precisely muscular hypertrophy as the muscles increase in size) – as the demand on the muscles increases, so they will adapt to this demand and increase in size to cope (known as the overload principle in relation to training).

- Increase in tendon strength – as the tendons are the connective fibrous tissue which connects bone to muscle, these increase in the same way as the muscle size increases.

- Increase in **myoglobin** stores – the myoglobin stores become used to the demands of exercise and the work placed upon them, so the stores increase as they are needed.

- Increased number of **mitochondria** – as the muscular system has an increased demand put on it, so the cells which help to produce this power also increase accordingly.

- Increased storage of glycogen and fat – these are used as energy sources with glycogen being a particularly important 'instant' source.

- Increased muscle strength – with the increased muscle size it is inevitable that muscle strength will increase as well.

- Increased tolerance to lactic acid – this is the by-product of exercise which is always produced, but in the long term the body becomes used to tolerating it without adverse effects such as cramp and soreness in the muscles.

The skeletal system

- Increase in bone calcium stores – the bones effectively become stronger, and it is this increase in calcium stores which contributes to this.

- Increased stretch in the ligaments – it is the ligaments which are the strong fibrous bands which stabilise the joints, and as the range of movement is increased, so these need to adapt accordingly.

Your assessment criteria:

P3 Describe the long-term effects of exercise on the musculoskeletal system and energy systems

P4 Describe the long-term effects of exercise on the cardiovascular and respiratory systems

Key terms

Hypertrophy: the growth and increase of the size of muscle cells

Mitochondria: the cell power producers which convert energy into a form which is usable in the cell

Myoglobin: an iron and oxygen binding compound found in muscle tissue

- Increased thickness of hyaline cartilage – this is the cartilage which provides flexible strength and it is also the mechanism by which the bones grow in length.

- Increased production of **synovial fluid** – as the joints are being used more energetically and often, the synovial fluid has to perform the function of lubricating the joints so that the movements are not painful or restricted.

The energy systems

- Increased aerobic and anaerobic enzymes – aerobic enzymes effectively become 'supercharged' and become better at processing the lactic acid.

- Increased use of fats as an energy source – fats provide the highest concentration of energy of all the nutrients and are the main fuel source for long duration.

Key terms

Stroke volume: *the volume of blood pumped from one ventricle of the heart with each beat*

Synovial fluid: *a clear viscous fluid which acts as a lubricant in joints*

Discuss

In a small group discuss the ways in which both your muscular system and energy systems have improved as you have got older. Compare your levels of fitness and performance now to when you first started secondary school and try to consider these in relation to the bullet points.

 P4 Adaptations of the cardiovascular system

The cardiovascular system is affected in the following ways by long-term exercise such as a six-week training programme:

- Cardiac hypertrophy – this is a thickening of the heart muscle which effectively enlarges the heart.

- Increase in **stroke volume** – over a period of time this increases as a greater volume of blood is pumped with each heart beat.

- Increase in cardiac output – this is an increase in the volume of blood which is pumped by the heart per minute.

- Decrease in resting heart rate – a lower resting heart rate is a good thing and is used as a measure of fitness levels.

- Capillarisation – this is the development of a capillary network to a part of the body and the number of these increases.

- Increase in blood volume – the average adult has approximately five litres of blood but it is possible to increase this.

- Reduction in resting blood pressure – high blood pressure can indicate a health risk so a reduction is a positive factor.

- Decreased recovery time – this is the time it takes for your body to return to normal levels, and being able to get back to normal quickly is an indicator of good fitness levels and a positive factor.

- Increased aerobic fitness – this relates to the way in which your body is able to cope with the aerobic demands of ongoing exercise in the presence of oxygen.

Cross-country skiers enjoy the benefits of the long-term effects of exercise as it increases their endurance levels.

? Did you know?

Miguel Indurain, a Spanish Tour de France cyclist, had a recorded resting heart rate of 28 beats per minute which is one of the lowest ever recorded and 44 beats lower than the average of 72!

P4 Adaptations of the respiratory system

The respiratory system is affected in the following ways by long-term exercise such as a six-week training programme:

- Increased **vital capacity** – the volume of air you are able to breathe in and out in one breath is increased.

- Increase in minute ventilation – this is an increase in the volume of air which can be inhaled and exhaled in one minute.

- Increased strength of respiratory muscles – the increased demand put on these results in an overall increase in their strength. These are the intercostal muscles which will be adapting in size and strength due to the increased overload.

- Increase in oxygen diffusion rate – this is related to the lungs' capacity to transfer gases, so the rate at which the oxygen is being transferred increases.

M2 The long-term effects of exercise on the body systems

The musculoskeletal, cardiovascular, respiratory and energy systems are affected in the following ways by long-term exercise such as a six-week training programme:

The musculoskeletal system

The more exercise the body is subjected to, the more it adapts through the principle of overload, enabling the body to increase its capacity to cope with the extra demands being made upon it. Overload can be achieved by increasing the frequency of your training which means training more often, increasing the intensity of your training which means working harder, or increasing the 'load' in each session. The last aspect of overload involves increasing the overall time of each training session and effectively carrying on for longer. The principle of progression should be considered too as any overload must be added gradually and progressively. Taking on too great a load too quickly can cause harm or damage. The process results in hypertrophy as the muscles gradually increase in size, and in an increase in tendon strength as the tendons adapt in a similar manner. These two factors contribute to the overall increase in muscle strength and the body becomes more used to dealing with, and tolerating, the levels of lactic acid which the body produces.

Your assessment criteria:

P4 Describe the long-term effects of exercise on the cardiovascular and respiratory systems

M2 Explain the long-term effects of exercise on the musculoskeletal, cardiovascular, respiratory and energy systems

Key terms

Vital capacity: the total volume of air that you can move in and out of your lungs in one deep breath

Research

Use some testing or monitoring equipment to measure your vital capacity and find out what the levels are within your group. Alternatively, use the internet to research the vital capacity levels of some top level performers.

The myoglobin stores increase due to the additional demands the body is making on the muscles and therefore the myoglobin (the oxygen carrying protein in the muscle tissue) must increase accordingly. The mitochondria (the cell power producers) increase their stores similarly to cope with this additional demand. Glycogen and fats are required in greater numbers as they too provide the 'fuel' for the additional demands, therefore their levels also increase.

The increased stretch in the ligaments (the strong fibrous bands which stabilise the joints and control movement) occurs when the ligaments adapt to the hypertrophy and increase in muscle strength. Similarly, the hyaline cartilage (the smooth shiny cartilage which covers the surfaces of bones and which reduces friction between bones at a joint) increases in thickness as far more movement is occurring. The synovial fluid (the lubricant in these joints) also has increased production for exactly the same reasons.

The cardiovascular system

The general overall effect is that the efficiency of the system will improve considerably as the body adjusts to transport oxygen to the working muscles quickly and effectively. This is the main purpose of the cardiovascular system and the adaptations which are made through taking part in exercise positively aid this process. The overall effect is most apparent for a performer in the areas of decreased recovery time and increased aerobic fitness which will increase general fitness levels.

The respiratory system

The respiratory system is responsible for the intake of oxygen into the body and it is the oxygen which provides the energy for the working muscles which are experiencing the greater demand as exercise increases. Therefore, the increases in vital capacity and minute ventilation are significant factors in ensuring that this system is far more effective and responsive by allowing a greater level of oxygen intake to satisfy this demand.

The energy systems

Increases occur in the energy systems and again this is due to the increased demands and the body adapting to them. The increased levels of exercise boost these enzymes (particularly the anaerobic enzymes) as part of the process of producing more energy. Similarly, fats are used as an energy source and particularly for long duration exercise, so there is an increased use of these.

Bodybuilders rely on hypertrophy to increase their muscle size and strength and they can only achieve this over a long period of high level exercise.

Q   Research

Checking or monitoring the long-term effects of exercise on the body systems is quite difficult as it is a very gradual process. However, you could take part in a six-week exercise training programme where you carry out a series of pre- and post-programme physiological tests and explain the effects which you and other members of your group are able to measure.

The physiological effects of exercise on the body systems

In order to investigate the **physiological** effects of exercise, it is important initially to think about the different forms of exercise which can be used:

Aerobic: this is any form of exercise which involves continuing for fairly long periods of time so that oxygen is being used as the main energy source. This can be simply jogging or distance running, cycling, rowing or using gym machines such as treadmills, cross-trainers or rowing machines.

Resistance: this usually involves using weights which can either be free-standing or an integral part of weight training machines such as those found in gyms.

Circuit: this is a form of exercise training which involves taking part in a variety of different exercises, movements or skills in a continuous loop moving from one to the other.

Interval: this is a form of exercise consisting of periods of work followed by periods of rest. The two forms of this are long interval, where the work periods are long with corresponding long rest periods in between, and short interval, where the exercise period can be as short as 10–15 seconds with relatively short recovery periods as well.

You can use different investigation methods, and it is also possible to combine some of them.

To compare pre-exercise, exercise and post-exercise physiological readings, you can use the following methods:

- resting heart rate – the rate per minute when the body is at rest

- exercise heart rate – the rate which is achieved when exercise is fully underway

- percent heart rate maximum – the maximum heart rate is 220 minus age (so for a 16 year old, this would be 220 – 16 which is 204)

- percent heart rate reserve maximum – this is the difference between the maximum heart rate and the resting heart rate

- rating of perceived exertion – this makes use of the Borg scale which assigns numbers according to how you feel about the amount of exertion from a level 6 (no exertion at all) to level 20 (maximal exertion) with descriptive criteria assigned to each of the levels/numbers

- flexibility tests – the most common is the sit and reach test which measures the level of flexibility in the hamstrings and lower back

- blood pressure which is easily measured and monitored by using a blood pressure monitor

- **spirometry** which is measured by using a spirometer.

Key terms

Aerobic: *activity or exercise performed over a long period of time requiring oxygen as the energy source*

Physiological: *relating to the study of the function and processes of the human body*

Resistance: *usually referring to weights or any form of load which the muscles have to deal with*

Spirometry: *the measuring of breath*

P5 ▶ Collect physiological data with tutor support

You should carry out the investigation *with tutor support*. You should select at least two different types of exercise in order to determine how the different types of exercise result in different adaptations. You must examine the acute response to the selected exercise as well as the long-term effects, and you should record the physiological data before, during and after exercise.

M3 ▶ Collect physiological data with limited tutor support

You should carry out the investigation *with limited tutor support*. You should select at least two different types of exercise in order to determine how the different types of exercise result in different adaptations. You must examine the acute response to the selected exercise as well as the long-term effects.

 Practical

Being able to both take and monitor your heart rate is crucial for many of the tests you will be involved in. Make sure that you are able to locate and check your own heart rate and practise using a heart rate monitor so that you are able to operate it correctly and accurately.

D1 ▶ Collect physiological data independently

You should carry out the investigation *independently*. You should select at least two different types of exercise in order to determine how the different types of exercise result in different adaptations. You must examine the acute response to the selected exercise as well as the long-term effects.

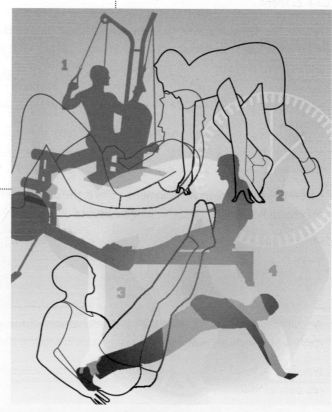

Circuit training is an appropriate type of exercise to select for your investigation.

It is important to review the physiological data which you have collected relating to the effects on the musculoskeletal, cardiovascular, respiratory and energy systems. You need to consider the following factors in your review:

- both the acute and long-term effects of exercise on the body systems

- pre-exercise, exercise and post-exercise physiological data

- practicality of exercise activities selected

- advantages and disadvantages

- strengths and areas for improvement.

There are different requirements for each of the three awards:

P6 ▶ Review physiological data by describing the effects of exercise on the body systems

You must examine the data collected and review the results by *describing* (this means giving a general account of the results) how the body responds to each type of exercise during the acute phases and also the long-term effects of the selected exercises on the body systems. It is important to review physiological data collected before, during and after exercise. You should consider the practicality of the exercise activities selected and any advantages or disadvantages encountered during data collection. You should also describe the strengths and areas for improvement of the investigation in the review.

M4 ▶ Review physiological data by explaining the effects of exercise on the body systems

You must examine the data collected and review the results by *explaining* (this means making the information plain and understandable) how the body responds to each type of exercise during the acute phases and also the long-term effects of the selected exercises on the body systems. It is important to review physiological data collected before, during and after exercise. You should consider the practicality of the exercise activities selected and any advantages or disadvantages encountered during data collection. You should also describe the strengths and areas for improvement of the investigation in the review.

Your assessment criteria:

P6 Review physiological data collected, describing the effects of exercise on the musculoskeletal, cardiovascular, respiratory and energy systems

M4 Review physiological data collected, explaining the effects of exercise on the musculoskeletal, cardiovascular, respiratory and energy systems

D2 Review physiological data collected, analysing the effects of exercise on the musculoskeletal, cardiovascular, respiratory and energy systems

? Did you know?

Elite performers in all forms of sport are constantly reviewing and analysing the effects of exercise on their body systems. This is how they keep check of their current levels of fitness, and they pay particular attention to strengths and areas for improvement as this is where they will make changes. For a professional sportsperson, reviewing physiological data will be an ongoing process.

D2 Review physiological data by analysing the effects of exercise on the body systems

You must examine the data collected and review the results by *analysing* (this means examining in detail and explaining the meaning of the results) how the body responds to each type of exercise during the acute phases and also the long-term effects of the selected exercises on the body systems.

You should analyse the practicality of the exercise activities selected and the advantages or disadvantages encountered during data collection. You should include an analysis of the strengths and areas for improvement of the investigation in the review.

Research

Consider all of the factors listed on page 40 as part of your review and make sure that you have ways to record all of the data you collect. Use SMART target setting to help you with the areas for improvement which you should cover.

Using resistance machines is another type of exercise you can use to collect the data for your review.

 ## Case study

Adnan has chosen aerobic and resistance as his two forms of exercise. He intends to go jogging and go to the gym to use the weight training machines. Adnan has been allocated a six-week period during his course for this component of his coursework, but he is aiming to achieve D1 and D2 so he is not allowed any tutor help in collecting his data.

1. What are the main differences between the forms of exercise Adnan has chosen?

2. Will Adnan be able to use all of the methods of investigation for both of his forms of exercise? Which will be most relevant to each form?

3. How would you recommend that Adnan organises his exercise sessions throughout his six-week period?

4. What are likely to be the main advantages and disadvantages of each of the forms of exercise which Adnan has chosen?

Assessment checklist

To achieve a pass grade, my portfolio of evidence must show that I can:

Assessment Criteria	Description	✓
P1	Describe the musculoskeletal and energy systems' responses to acute exercise.	☐
P2	Describe the cardiovascular and respiratory systems' responses to acute exercise.	☐
P3	Describe the long-term effects of exercise on the musculoskeletal system and energy systems.	☐
P4	Describe the long-term effects of exercise on the cardiovascular and respiratory systems.	☐
P5	Collect physiological data to investigate the effects of exercise on the musculoskeletal, cardiovascular, respiratory and energy systems, with tutor support.	☐
P6	Review physiological data collected, describing the effects of exercise on the musculoskeletal, cardiovascular, respiratory and energy systems.	☐

To achieve a merit grade, my portfolio of evidence must show that I can:

Assessment Criteria	Description	✓
M1	Explain the responses of the musculoskeletal, cardiovascular and respiratory systems to acute exercise.	☐
M2	Explain the long-term effects of exercise on the musculoskeletal, cardiovascular, respiratory and energy systems.	☐
M3	Collect physiological data to investigate the effects of exercise on the musculoskeletal, cardiovascular, respiratory and energy systems, with limited tutor support.	☐
M4	Review physiological data collected, explaining the effects of exercise on the musculoskeletal, cardiovascular, respiratory and energy systems.	☐

To achieve a distinction grade, my portfolio of evidence must show that I can:

Assessment Criteria	Description	✓
D1	Independently investigate the physiological effects of exercise on the musculoskeletal, cardiovascular, respiratory and energy systems.	☐
D2	Review physiological data collected, analysing the effects of exercise on the musculoskeletal, cardiovascular, respiratory and energy systems.	☐

3 | Assessing risk in sport

LO1 Know the key factors that influence health and safety in sport

▶ There are different forms of legislation and laws which are currently in place.

▶ There are different types of law and legal factors which apply.

▶ Organisations, known as regulatory bodies, are also influential.

LO2 Be able to carry out risk assessments

▶ Risk assessment has some very specific aims.

▶ There are some very specific objectives linked to these aims.

▶ It is very important to ensure that risk controls are put in place.

▶ Various types of training are available to help carry out risk assessment.

LO3 Know how to maintain the safety of participants and colleagues in a sports environment

▶ There are a variety of different procedures which need to be put in place.

▶ It is very important to follow specific protocols.

▶ The various governing bodies provide very clear and precise guidelines which should be followed.

▶ It is important to be aware of others who you should consult with.

LO4 Be able to plan a safe sporting activity

▶ Different roles and responsibilities should be established as part of the planning process.

▶ There are many factors relating to the site to be used which will need consideration.

▶ It is essential to undertake a comprehensive review.

Key factors that influence health and safety in sport

One of the main attractions of taking part in sport is the challenge it offers, but this has to be balanced against ensuring that taking part is safe. Rules and guidelines are always in place for all sporting activities, so it is important that participants are aware of them and know why they are there.

P1 Legislative factors

There is a variety of legislation relating to health and safety in sport:

- Health and Safety at Work Act (1974)
- additions to the (1974) Health and Safety at Work Act (Reporting of Injuries, Diseases and Dangerous Occurrences Regulations (RIDDOR))
- Management of Health and Safety at Work Act (Amendment) Regulations (1994)
- Personal Protective Equipment (PPE, 2002)
- Control of Substances Hazardous to Health (COSHH, 2002)
- Health and Safety (First Aid) Regulations (1981)
- Manual Handling Operations Regulations (1992)
- Management of Health and Safety Regulations (1999)
- Fire Safety and Safety of Places of Sport Act (1987)
- Adventurous Activities Licensing Authority Regulations (2004).

P2 Legal factors

There are various health and safety regulations in place, and organisations known as regulatory bodies have the **legal** responsibility of making sure that these regulations are complied with. This is particularly important in a sporting situation, where the health and safety of all those involved is paramount.

The following legal factors influence health and safety in sport:

Your assessment criteria:

P1 Describe four legislative factors that influence health and safety in sport

P2 Describe the legal factors and regulatory bodies that influence health and safety in sport

 Key terms

Legal: *relating to the law or official accepted rules*

The House of Commons is where legislation is passed after parliamentary debate.

The law

The law consists of three categories:

- *Statutory* law is written down, for example the law relating to the wearing of jewellery.

- **Civil law** is closely linked to individuals' rights, for example someone being sued for negligence.

- **Case law** is based on laws which have been shown to be enforced legally by the courts, or where judges make a judgement taking into account previous judgements (or 'cases') which have already been decided upon.

In loco parentis

If someone is **in loco parentis**, they are required to behave in a way in which parents would be expected to behave as they are taking their place. For example, a PE teacher taking a group away for a sporting fixture would be expected to care for the group just as a parent would in terms of getting the individuals to the match, supervising the game and then ensuring that they get home safely.

Duty of care

If an individual has a duty of care, it means that a legal obligation is imposed on them to make sure that no harm comes to them. 'Reasonable care' must be employed, which means that individuals should not be asked to perform an unreasonable movement or activity. An example of this would be performing a gymnastic movement in its entirety without having performed the preparatory progressions first.

P2 Legal factors *continued*

Higher duty of care

A higher duty of care has to be in place in circumstances where the likelihood of harm occurring is increased, such as in very challenging sporting environments and particularly when someone is taking on the role of leading. For example, a cross-country run which involves going off the school site, running through woods and beside a river is a potentially more dangerous environment than running around the school fields within a perimeter fence.

Negligence

Negligence is when someone is seen to act unreasonably or without due care and this contributes to a possible hazardous situation or danger. For example, it is negligent if the runners in a cross-country run have to cross a deep stream or river as part of their run, because the course has not been checked carefully beforehand, the hazard identified and the route changed.

Regulatory bodies

There are a number of regulatory bodies that influence health and safety in sport.

The Health and Safety Executive (HSE) sets out the guidelines which are appropriate to all activities.

Other regulatory bodies include local authorities (local and district councils), local educational authorities and the police. Some regulatory bodies are responsible for specific activities or specific types of activities, such as the Adventurous Activities Licensing Authority (AALA) and the national governing bodies of different sports (NGBs).

M1 Compare and contrast the influences of legislation, legal and regulatory bodies

There is a difference between **statute** and case law, and a responsible sports leader must be aware of how important these are in any sporting situation. Some background research and knowledge is crucial if a leader is to have sufficient knowledge to be safely involved in an activity.

Your assessment criteria:

P2 Describe the legal factors and regulatory bodies that influence health and safety in sport

M1 Compare and contrast the influences of legislation, legal factors and regulatory bodies on health and safety in sport

A higher duty of care would be necessary when taking part in an activity as potentially dangerous as climbing.

? | **Did you know?**

The RFU (Rugby Football Union), as the governing body for rugby, recommends that all teachers have at least some basic training before teaching rugby, and recommends that a teacher has at least a Level 1 coaching qualification before they teach any school sessions. Some schools insist that their PE staff have this qualification before they teach any rugby groups.

Key terms

Statute: *a written piece of legislation which becomes a law*

You need to consider the content in P1 and P2 in order to be able to make the links between the legal definitions, and to demonstrate good knowledge of legal factors and regulatory bodies. This information is vital to be able to compare and contrast.

These are two contrasting activities in terms of the types of rules and regulations their NGBs have in place regarding health and safety.

 ## Case study

Steve decides to compare and contrast trampolining and football as two activities and he looks into the regulations of each activity. He goes to the local trampoline club to talk to the club coach about the rules and regulations they have to comply with, and as he is already a Level 1 football coach, he feels he has enough knowledge about football.

Steve is surprised to find that the national governing body for trampoline is British Gymnastics and finds out that only registered and qualified coaches can take any trampoline sessions. He has quite a long conversation with the centre manager where the trampoline club is based, talking about the regulations in place relating to the storage and locking up of the trampolines and the rules for setting them up and putting them away.

Steve finds that the rules and regulations from the FA (as the national governing body for football) are far less detailed, and that he can book the football pitch to play on quite easily.

1. What are the main contrasts between the two sports which Steve decides to consider?

2. Can you make any direct comparisons between the two sports in terms of factors they have in common?

3. Which activity seems to have a higher duty of care, and why?

The main reason for going through the risk assessment process is to develop awareness of the importance of the health and safety legislation, regulations and legal responsibilities of all those working in sporting situations. The factors identified in the previous pages are crucial for a comprehensive risk assessment to be carried out effectively.

Your assessment criteria:

P3 Carry out risk assessments for two different sports activities, with tutor support

P3 Risk assessments

Risk assessments must be completed for two different sporting activities, with tutor support. A risk assessment reporting sheet (similar to the one in Figure 3.1) should be available in individual centres or can be obtained from the Health and Safety Executive website, so there is no need for an individual to provide their own.

Figure 3.1 An example of part of a risk assessment sheet

Activity: Introduction to surf kayaking for intermediate paddlers						
Venue: Sunny Sands Beach						
Risk assessment carried out by: _____						
Date of risk assessment: _____ Date for reiew: _____						
Hazard	Who is affected?	Potential outcome/Injury	Control measures	Severity of hazard	Likehood of occurrence	Risk rating
Surf/water (beach wave)	Kayakers, other surfers	Loss of control over kayak Loss of consciousness Drowning	Check forecast and conditions. Surf in appropriate and relevantconditions/location. Set boundaries/identify a surf zone. Ensure safety cover is in place, e.g. surf as a group and look out for each other or use a buddy system. Wear wetsuit and buoyancy aid. Avoid other surfers.	1	C	Medium
Reef/rocks	Kayakers	Head injury Cuts and bruises Drowning Damage to equipment	As above, plus: Avoid reef and rocks through use of a surf zone. Wear helmets.	1	C	Medium
Jellyfish	Kayakers	Sting	Avoid if possible. Cover up if jellyfish seen, e.g. wear gloves. Carry vinegar as part of first aid kit.	3	C	Low
Poor technique	Kayakers	Damage to muscles Dislocated shoulder	Ensure surfers have been coached on correct technique. Don't push off bottom with paddle. Provide feedback.	2	B	Medium

An activity such as surf kayaking requires a comprehensive risk assessment to be carried out.

Aims

A risk assessment must have the following aims:

- to eliminate any **hazards** (e.g. picking up broken glass from a playing area)

- to minimise any hazards (e.g. making sure that all participants are wearing the correct protective clothing)

- to protect participants from harm (e.g. providing basic safety equipment and making sure it is used, such as cricket batting gloves and pads).

Objectives

A risk assessment must have the following objectives:

- to identify any hazards

- to identify those who might be at risk

- to assess the chance of a hazard causing harm

- to grade the risks (across three levels of severity).

Key terms

Hazard: something which could cause injury or harm

Did you know?

Outdoor activity centres complete full, comprehensive risk assessments for all the activities they offer. These are inspected when the centres are checked, as all centres must have a licence to provide these challenging activities. If risk assessments are not in place, the centre may be closed down.

Figure 3.2 An example of a risk rating table

Severity			
3	Medium	Medium	Low
2	High	Medium	Medium
1	High	High	High
	A	B	C
Likelihood			

Key
Severity: 1 = death or major injury; 2 = injury lasting more than 3 days; 3 = minor injury, damage to equipment, etc.
Likelihood: A = extremely likely; B = may happen occasionally; C = extremely unlikely

P3 ▶ Risk assessments *continued*

Risk controls

In any risk assessment, it is important to consider risk controls, including:

- Not doing the activity – in extreme cases this would mean changing plans and not doing it all. For example, it may be too dangerous to continue playing golf in a thunder storm as lightning may strike.

- Modifying the activity – for example, moving to an indoor environment rather that an outdoor one, or even shortening a cross-country course to avoid a swollen stream.

- Protecting participants from a hazard – once a hazard has been identified, the participants must be protected from it. For example, an unstable rock face could not be used for climbing once the hazard had been identified.

- Providing appropriate safety equipment – when safety equipment is available, it should always be used, for example safety helmets in any climbing areas.

- Providing appropriate training – ideally all leaders and staff will be fully qualified, they must be trained in the use of equipment and facilities, and their training must be updated regularly.

- Providing appropriate supervision for participants – often participants are either unaware of hazards or may choose to ignore them, so they must be supervised at all times.

Your assessment criteria:

P3 Carry out risk assessments for two different sports activities, with tutor support

M2 Independently carry out risk assessments for two different sports activities

D1 Review the risk assessment controls and evaluate their effectiveness

Case study

Andy decides to carry out one of his risk assessments at the indoor climbing centre which has just opened in his area. He does not take part in this activity himself, so has no prior knowledge about climbing. He is planning a visit to the centre and has arranged to meet the manager of the centre and the lead climbing instructor.

1. What is the national governing body for this particular activity?

2. Does it matter that Andy has no experience of climbing?

3. Who would be the best person for Andy to talk to about training provisions?

4. Who would be the best person for Andy to talk to about appropriate risk controls?

M2 ▶ Carry out risk assessments independently

You should carry out two risk assessments autonomously (on your own), and then consider any appropriate risk controls.

D1 ▶ Review and evaluate the risk assessment controls

Risk assessment controls are put in place for a purpose, and it is essential that they fulfil their function of ensuring that activities are carried out correctly and safely. Evaluating their effectiveness is an important part of the risk assessment process as the main purpose is to eliminate risk altogether, or at the very least to minimise it.

📋 Case study

Chloe is carrying out a risk assessment of the throwing events at the school sports day. She liaises with the teacher in charge of the whole event, and helps to put the risk controls in place for the discus, javelin and shot put events. Chloe makes sure that the throwing areas are roped off and out of bounds to all spectators, and that competitors are kept in a 'holding area' away from the throwing area before they come up for their throws. Chloe also meets with the officials who measure the distances of the throws, and she appoints another person to brief the competitors on when to throw and when to collect.

A school sports day requires a detailed risk assessment, providing an opportunity for a school to review their controls and their effectiveness.

Throughout the competition there are no major problems, and the only incident is when one boy gets a splinter in his hand from a wooden discus.

1. Consider what safeguards Chloe puts in place, and explain why she plans them and who she is protecting.

2. Are there any controls in place which Chloe might need to review?

3. How effective overall do Chloe's controls appear to be?

4. Consider the planning which would go into a specific sports event in terms of risk assessment, and think about how your review could apply to this. Remember that the review must be specifically related to completed risk assessments.

 Discuss

In a group, discuss what the main risk assessment controls are which would need to be put in place for the school sports day track events (including the hurdles) and the two field jumping events of high jump and long jump. In particular, focus on any equipment which it might be necessary to use.

It is important to make sure that the safety levels in a sporting environment remain in place for the duration of the event or activity.

Your assessment criteria:

P4 Describe three procedures used to promote and maintain a healthy and safe sporting environment

P4 Health and safety procedures

Operating procedures and good practice

The following procedures and practices are essential for maintaining a healthy and safe sporting environment. The sport of rugby is used here as an example:

- *Staff training* – this includes all of the staff involved. If this is a top level game of rugby, it will include the match stewards who are responsible for spectators, the administrators who are responsible for support staff such as first aid, and all team officials including managers, coaches and physiotherapists.

- *Staff development* – this includes all the staff who are involved on a day-to-day basis with the rugby club and team. Their own particular roles must be developed, and they must be updated on any changes to procedures or regulations, such as changes to the emergency evacuation procedure.

- *Risk assessments* – all staff must be made aware of the risk assessment procedure and its importance, especially where any risk assessment particularly applies to them. For example, ground staff are responsible for keeping the pitch in good order by inspecting it and removing dangerous or sharp objects, and maintaining the safety pads on the posts.

- *Emergency procedure* **protocols** – in the case of a large rugby club, this may include evacuating the ground in the event of a fire or serious incident, or dealing with a particularly serious injury which requires an ambulance to enter and leave the ground.

- *First aid* – this may involve players, staff, officials or spectators as any of them could require first aid. It must be accessible and available to all of these groups of people.

- *Communications* **cascade** *system for notification of incidents* – each person involved in an incident must know who to give directions to and who to receive them from. Most senior stewards in grounds use communication devices to keep in touch with the various members of their team, and grounds have a public address system where announcements can be made to everyone in attendance.

Key terms

Cascade: a continuing series that is passed on

Protocols: a formal set of rules or regulations

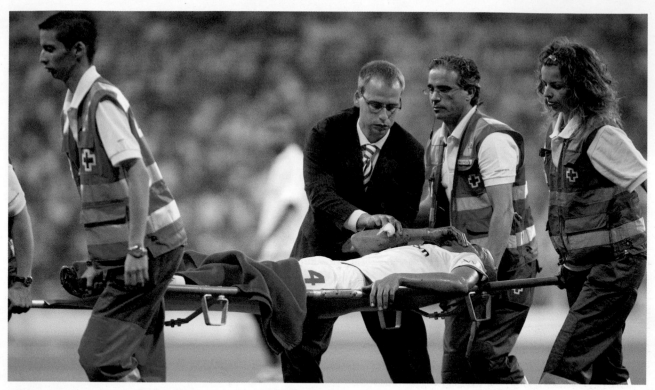

First aid facilities must be available for the duration of events.

 ## Case study

Sandeep decides to organise a five-a-side football tournament for year 6 pupils and 20 teams enter the tournament. She plans to use five pitches and have four teams in each group who will each be allocated to one of the pitches. Four of the pitches are right next door to each other and in front of the area Sandeep intends to use as her 'base', but unfortunately the fifth one is a six-minute walk away on an adjoining field surrounded by high hedges so it is not in sight of the base. Sandeep, therefore, realises that she will have to use a split-site venue and is planning accordingly.

1. Which NGB should Sandeep turn to for possible advice and guidance on running her tournament?

2. What are the implications for the first aid provision on this split-site?

3. How might this site cause problems for the communications cascade system?

4. Are there any simple organisational changes that Sandeep could make which would make the organisation easier?

Q | Research

In May 1985, a wall collapsed in the Heysel Stadium in Brussels during the European Cup Final between Liverpool and Juventus, and 39 football fans were killed. In 1989 an even worse disaster occurred at Hillsborough which also involved Liverpool fans.

Research another serious incident which occurred in a sporting situation in the past. Investigate the particular health and safety issues relating to this incident.

P4 Health and safety procedures *continued*

Safety procedures and protocols

There are also safety procedures and protocols which are important for maintaining a healthy and safe sporting environment:

- Established to maintain a safe environment – in stadiums there are rules for spectators to be seated as this avoids problems in standing room only spaces when crowds are not segregated.

- Governing body guidelines – the RFU (Rugby Football Union) as the national governing body will have many procedures in place ranging from regulations about safety equipment, the level and qualification of officials and first aid provision which must be available to recommendations on playing conditions and when games should be played.

- Equipment manufacturers' guidelines – all specialist equipment which is used (including the touchline and sideline flags which have special designs to prevent impact injuries) comes with installation and maintenance instructions which must be followed.

- When to consult with others – one person may not be qualified to make all decisions, for example a referee will ask one of the medical staff for guidance if a player is injured, and may demand they are replaced in some circumstances. Referees will often consult with the ground staff to decide if a pitch is fit for play.

- Who to consult with – a written set of procedures and responsibilities should be available so that everyone knows everybody else's responsibilities. For example, if a faulty piece of equipment needs attention, the team then know who is responsible for it.

- Local and national requirements – in a sport such as rugby these are likely to be the same, but in some other activities procedures may vary. For instance, most stadiums require a local health and safety licence to be able to host competitive matches with crowds attending.

M3 Explain health and safety procedures

If you were involved in a rugby event, you would need to consider the following procedures:

- Emergency procedure protocols would have to take into account the fact that rugby is a contact sport, so there are likely to be quite frequent impact injuries. Procedures to deal with these would need to be established.

Your assessment criteria:

P4 Describe three procedures used to promote and maintain a healthy and safe sporting environment

M3 Explain three procedures used to promote and maintain a healthy and safe sporting environment

D2 Analyse three procedures used to promote and maintain a healthy and safe sporting environment

? Did you know?

Following on from the Heysel and Hillsborough disasters, a major report known as the Taylor Report (1989) reviewed and changed arrangements for stadiums and spectators. As a result, all of the major stadiums were converted so that all spectators had tickets and were seated. Other rules were also introduced concerning alcohol, crash barriers, fences, turnstiles and ticket prices. Many of the rules and regulations which are now taken for granted were not in place prior to 1989.

- The RFU has very specific guidelines on age groups and officials for safety reasons. All competitive rugby is played strictly in age groups at junior level to ensure that size and strength is roughly equal, as well as to make contests more even.

- Maintaining a safe environment requires the environment to be safe in the first place for both players and spectators, and there is then a responsibility to make sure these safety precautions are kept in place throughout play. Pre-match checks are always carried out, the officials are responsible for checking the playing area and the home team is responsible for making sure that the spectator environment is safe. If, for any reason, the situation changes and the environment becomes unsafe, then play should be stopped, or at least suspended.

> **? Did you know?**
>
> *The cricket test match between England and the West Indies in Antigua in 2009 was the shortest test match in history as it only lasted for ten balls! The umpires made the decision that the bowler's run-ups were so poor on the pitch that it became unfit for play. The entire match therefore lasted only 16 minutes before being abandoned.*

D2 Analyse health and safety procedures

Once procedures are put in place, it is important to analyse how successful they are in achieving the intended aims. It is often not until incidents take place that the procedures are fully tested, so it is then that any problems come to light.

Case study

Robert makes sure that he has a registered first aider in attendance at his rugby tournament as he is aware that that this is one of the procedures he must have in place. Unfortunately, there are two separate incidents on two pitches which are being played on. There is only one first aider, and it looks as if one of the incidents has resulted in a dislocated shoulder.

Discuss how successful Robert's procedures are in terms of:

- emergency procedure protocols

- first aid arrangements

- maintaining the safe environment.

> **Q Research**
>
> *Identify the NGB for one particular major sport and find out what guidelines they have in place for age groups and officials who are participating in that particular sport. Find out if they have a particular safety policy or policies which identify the main concerns which that sport has in relation to the safety of its participants.*

P5 ▶ Produce and review a sports activity plan

Planning an activity is a complex task, and taking all the safety aspects into account is challenging. As well as planning the activity, it is important to review the plan in order to assess what is going well and any aspects which might need to be improved.

You must plan for leaders to take sessions safely.

Plan

The following factors are very important in the planning of a sports activity:

- *Roles and responsibilities* of all the people who are involved, e.g. leaders, coaches and first aid. All of these people have specific roles, and they must know what is required of them, especially in terms of where they should be and when they must be available. For example, the coaches are directly involved with the players at all times, whereas the first aiders have to be available to anyone who needs them which may include the players, other staff and spectators.

- *Equipment* – all the correct equipment must be provided, and there must be enough to go round. For example, being short of a set of portable goals when organising a five-a-side football tournament would be disastrous, and not having enough bibs for all players to wear or being short of cones for marking out playing areas would also cause problems.

Your assessment criteria:

P5 Produce a plan for the safe delivery of a selected sports activity and review the plan

---

? Did you know?

Anyone who is involved in any activities involving young people must have a CRB check. The CRB or Criminal Records Bureau is an agency which carries out checks on individuals to ensure protection for young children and vulnerable adults. They make sure that individuals are suitable for certain work and roles they may be given.

- *Suitability of the site* which is to be used. This may include making sure it is big enough to cope with the demand, it is accessible to everyone, there are enough parking spaces available, the gates are wide enough to allow vehicles through or the surface is suitable for vehicles to drive on. Grass areas surrounding pitches can get very churned up in poor weather and vehicles can get stuck in deep mud. A site which is too remote can be viewed by some people as inaccessible due to the distance they would have to travel, especially if there is a lack of public transport.

- *Suitability of the participants to the activity*. This may mean making sure that the age of the participants matches the type of activity offered. In most game activities (such as football, netball, hockey, basketball and rugby) and athletics, events are arranged very strictly in age groups, and often related to year groups in schools, such as year 6 or 7. Some other activities, such as martial arts, expect people to have some level of grading or experience in that sport before taking part.

- *Guidelines* are given to both the participants and the leaders, and cover all of the planning which has been put into place. The leaders need to know where and when their teams have to be at a given point, what time to arrive and what the estimated finish time is. They might even need to know if refreshments will be available and if water will be supplied – this could be very important in an outdoor event on a hot day in summer. This information is often provided in writing prior to the event and displayed somewhere prominent. Information about the draw, rules and order of play, for instance, is important for all of those taking part.

- *Insurance* factors must be considered as there is always the possibility of an accident or injury at a sporting event. Most events must have their own insurance in place, and if the event is sanctioned by a governing body, the insurance might be covered by them.

Discuss

1. *In a group, choose three different activities and discuss what factors must be taken into account to ensure that the participants are suited to the activity.*

2. *Discuss the factors which would definitely result in the participants not being suited to the activity.*

P5 **Produce and review a sports activity plan** *continued*

Review

The factors of the review process which need to be considered include the effectiveness of risk management, injuries, near misses and dangerous occurrences, the suitability of the group for the activity, the effectiveness of briefings and the suitability of equipment. The support of other agencies such as governing bodies, local authorities and the police also needs to be considered.

The strengths and areas for improvement have to be considered as part of the review process.

Your assessment criteria:

P5 Produce a plan for the safe delivery of a selected sports activity and review the plan

M4 Explain the plan for the safe delivery of a selected sports activity and review the plan

The police are one of the most commonly used outside agencies involved in sporting events with the main function of assisting with crowd control.

 Discuss

1. Choose a sporting event which you attended, and discuss which planning factors you were aware of being in place.

2. Think about the review factors, and discuss how successful they were.

M4 Explain and review a sports activity plan

Once the strengths and areas for improvement have been identified (as part of the review process in your P5 criteria), it is important to explain some aspects of the plan, such as why certain planning factors were put in place and the likely outcomes. For example, the coaches would need to be assigned to particular individuals and teams, and their duties would need to be clear to them. They would need to know if they are responsible for team selection and tactics before the event, as well as warming up the team and making changes once play is underway.

 Practical

Deliver at least part of your plan so that you are able to see how successful the different parts of your plan are. This will enable you to carry out your review with full explanations as you will have actual examples to consider.

 Case study

John decides to take on the responsibility for planning an inter-school rugby sevens tournament. This is an event which regularly takes place in his area, but the organisers have agreed to let him work with them to assist in the delivery. John has already carried out a risk assessment on rugby as one of his two sports activities.

1. How much will John benefit from already having carried out his risk assessment on rugby, and why?

2. How much help will John get in assisting with an event which is already regularly running, and what will be the advantages to him?

3. As rugby is a contact sport, which particular procedures will John have to consider for the participants and make a priority for this activity?

4. Which other agencies will John have to consider being involved in this event?

Assessment checklist

To achieve a pass grade, my portfolio of evidence must show that I can:

Assessment Criteria	Description	✓
P1	Describe four legislative factors that influence health and safety in sport.	☐
P2	Describe the legal factors and regulatory bodies that influence health and safety in sport.	☐
P3	Carry out risk assessments for two different sports activities, with tutor support.	☐
P4	Describe three procedures used to promote and maintain a healthy and safe sporting environment.	☐
P5	Produce a plan for the safe delivery of a selected sports activity and review the plan.	☐

To achieve a merit grade, my portfolio of evidence must show that I can:

Assessment Criteria	Description	✓
M1	Compare and contrast the influences of legislation, legal factors and regulatory bodies on health and safety in sport.	☐
M2	Independently carry out risk assessments for two different sports activities.	☐
M3	Explain three procedures used to promote and maintain a healthy and safe sporting environment.	☐
M4	Explain the plan for the safe delivery of a selected sports activity and review the plan.	☐

To achieve a distinction grade, my portfolio of evidence must show that I can:

Assessment Criteria	Description	✓
D1	Review the risk assessment controls and evaluate their effectiveness.	☐
D2	Analyse three procedures used to promote and maintain a healthy and safe sporting environment.	☐

4 | Fitness training and programming

LO1 Know different methods of fitness training

▶ Physical fitness can be divided into six main components.

▶ Each component has a specific training method that an athlete can use to develop his or her fitness.

LO2 Be able to plan a fitness training session

▶ Training sessions need to be planned so that specific training can be completed at the appropriate intensity and time.

▶ Training needs to take into account the fitness level and experience of a sports person.

▶ Cardiovascular training needs to be specific. If the intensity is not high enough the body will burn calories and not develop aerobic fitness.

▶ Resistance training includes the use of free and fixed weight machines. Training for strength, power or muscular endurance can take place using a variety of methods. Recommendations for training have been established by the ACSM (American College of Sports Medicine).

▶ Flexibility training should be completed towards the end of a training session. PNF stretches are the most effective type of flexibility training. Static stretches are the safest but the least effective.

▶ Speed training is essential in most sports but is often neglected as athletes struggle for facilities. Training requires significant amounts of motivation and commitment.

LO3 Be able to plan a fitness training programme

▸ Collecting information on training methods and intensities is difficult as there is a huge amount of unscientific evidence published in magazines. Training methods are often guessed rather than tested. However, there is a wide body of scientifically proven evidence available (YMCA, ACSM).

▸ Training needs to follow a number of principles to make sure that it is specific enough to achieve the desired effect.

▸ An elite athlete will have to divide their training into periods during which they can focus on specific training needs such as speed. Training and fitness need to peak for big competitions.

▸ Maintaining an accurate training diary is the key to monitoring and building successful performances.

LO4 Be able to review a fitness training programme

▸ Coaches and fitness trainers need to monitor an athlete at regular intervals. Sports people need motivation and advice throughout their careers.

▸ Coaches, fitness trainers and athletes need to use a reflective approach to identify training that has been successful and areas that need improvement. Regular organised meetings and reviews assist sportspeople in reaching elite standards.

Fitness training methods

Fitness is extremely important in all sports and will determine the success or failure of a performance. Fitness components may vary significantly between sports. For example, a sprinter may require great speed and acceleration, but a marathon runner will need to focus on aerobic endurance. The components of fitness may also vary in a team. For example, a winger may require more speed than a prop in rugby. An athlete needs to understand the important components of their sport to train and be successful in it. They also need to understand how to train each component, and which methods of training are most appropriate for their requirements.

Your assessment criteria:

P1 Describe one method of fitness training for six different components of physical fitness

P1 Fitness components and methods of training

There are six main components of fitness that affect most sports: flexibility, strength, muscular endurance, power, aerobic endurance and speed. Each component needs to be trained separately and specifically in order for the body to adapt and improve. However, there is often a variety of possible training methods for each component. Your ability, level and personal circumstances may determine the methods you choose.

Flexibility

Flexibility training is often done at the start of training after a warm-up. This is thought to reduce the risk of injury. Many sports now also include it at the end of the training programme. Flexibility should be included in a training programme to develop range of motion. The main muscle groups should be stretched 2–3 days per week for a period of 10–30 seconds. This should be repeated at least four times.

There are three main methods of flexibility training:

- *Static flexibility* involves holding a stretch at the limit of its length. The relaxation of the muscle at its maximum length should encourage the muscle to lengthen.

- *Ballistic stretching* is more dangerous but is very effective at increasing flexibility. It involves kicking and bouncing actions, for example placing your hand on a wall while standing parallel to the wall and swinging your leg backwards and forwards as high as possible 10–20 times.

Research

1. Research the typical range of movement for the main joints associated with exercise in your activity.

2. Using a goniometer, calculate and compare your range of movement and identify your strengths and weaknesses. This will enable you to identify areas that require specific training.

Key terms

Flexibility: the range of movement that can occur around a joint

Measurement of joint angle using a goniometer

Ballistic stretching can produce minor tears in the muscle, so it needs to be undertaken carefully after a thorough warm-up.

• *Progressive neuromuscular facilitation (PNF)* is a method of flexibility training performed with the help of a partner, although gravity and body weight can also be used. PNF stretches should include a 6-second contraction followed by 10- to 30-second assisted stretch. Working with a partner, the athlete moves into a static passive stretch (6-second contraction). After the hold the muscle will release. The athlete's partner then stretches the muscle slightly further (10- to 30-second assisted stretch).

 Did you know?

Flexibility exercises can help to improve joint function. The goal of these exercises is to gently increase range of motion while decreasing pain, swelling and stiffness.

Describe

Identify an activity/sport which you currently take part in.

1. *List the main muscle groups that are important to the activity.*

2. *Describe the stretches that could be used to improve flexibility in your activity.*

A static stretch

A PNF stretch

A ballistic stretch

P1 Fitness components and methods of training *continued*

Strength training

Strength is the maximum force in a muscle or group of muscles during a single maximal contraction. It is an important component of fitness in a number of sports, for example the maximum force in a punch (boxing), deadlift (weightlifting) and drive out of the blocks (sprinting).

It can be trained with two methods: fixed weight resistance machines and free weights. Fixed weight resistance machines are designed for building strength, muscle tone and to work targeted muscles in isolation. Free weights (barbells, dumbbells and machines that provide the same equal resistance to a muscle) target a particular muscle group and engage other muscles that assist in the work. The assisting muscles may help you to increase the weight you use in training to stimulate the most growth in muscle fibres. They can also help support limbs and maintain posture during a lift.

The amount of weight you need to lift to develop strength is based on a percentage of your 1 rep max (1RM), or the maximum amount of weight that you can lift once. It is also based on your level of experience. See Figure 4.1.

Figure 4.1 The amount of weight you need to lift to develop strength

Level	% of 1rm	No. of sets	No. of reps	Minutes rest	Times per week
Novice	60–70	1–3	8–12	2–3	2–3
Intermediate	70–80	1–3	6–12	2–3	2–4
Advanced	100	1–3	1–12	2–3	4–6

A novice athlete starting strength training will need to perform lifts at 60% of their maximum. They will need to perform at least 8 repetitions in 1 set. If they choose to perform 2 sets, they need to rest for at least 2 minutes between sets. Training will need to be completed at least twice a week. An advanced performer may need to lift their maximum lift up to 12 times per set, with 2 minutes' rest, between sets. This will need to be repeated up to 6 times per week. It is essential that at least one day during the week is used for recovery.

Power training

Power is the ability to perform a strength exercise with speed. It can be trained in a number of different ways: resistance training (similar to strength training), and plyometrics. Power is trained on the principle of: power = force × velocity. Improving strength or shortening the time of a muscle contraction will improve performance.

For resistance training the 1 rep max loadings are similar to strength, as shown in Figure 4.2.

Figure 4.2 The amount of weight you need to lift to develop power

Level	% of 1rm	No. of sets	No. of reps	Minutes rest	Times per week
Novice	60–70	1–3	8–12	1–2	2–3
Intermediate	70–80	multiple	6–12	1–2	2–4
Advanced	70-100	multiple	1–12	2–3	4–6

Plyometric training focuses on improving the speed at which the muscle shortens. In plyometric training the muscle is lengthened (eccentric contraction) before a powerful shortening of the muscle (concentric contraction) occurs. Exercises that can be used in plyometrics include bounding, hopping, depth jumps, medicine ball throwing.

Practical

Organise into a routine the exercises for which you have calculated a training load. This should be structured so that multiple-muscle exercises are first, single-muscle exercises second.

Describe

Describe the reason for placing multiple exercises before single exercises in the routine you have organised.

Did you know?

The world record for the vertical jump is 1.5 m (60 inches), by Kadour Ziani, a basketball player who is only 1.78m (5'10). This is more than twice the average NBA vertical leap of 0.71m (28 inches).

Plyometric jumping

P1 Fitness components and methods of training *continued*

Muscular endurance

This form of training is required in most sports because movements are repeated. In football it is important for the leg muscles to last a full match without cramping. Tennis players should be able to play for up to five sets without suffering from fatigue. Athletes can train for muscular endurance in a variety of ways, including resistance training and circuit training.

To train for muscular endurance using resistance machines or free weights, the system shown in Figure 4.3 can be used.

Figure 4.3 Developing muscular endurance using resistance machines or free weights

Level	% of 1rm	No. of sets	No. of reps	Minutes rest	Times per week
Novice	50–70	1–3	10–15	1	2–4
Intermediate	50–80	multiple	10–15	1	2–4
Advanced	50–80	multiple	10–25	2	4–6

Circuit training involves performing a number of exercises in succession, such as abdominal curls, step ups, calf raises and press ups. Circuit training is adaptable to strength, power, endurance or cardiovascular fitness. A minimum of 8–10 exercises involving the major muscle groups (chest, shoulders, arms, abdomen, back, hips and legs) should be performed 2–3 days per week. The exercises should be performed a minimum of 8–12 times or to near fatigue. The circuit can be repeated so that several sets have been performed by the athlete.

Your assessment criteria:

 P1 Describe one method of fitness training for six different components of physical fitness

Key terms

Aerobic endurance: the ability of the cardiovascular system to transport and use oxygen during sustained exercise, ensuring that an athlete does not tire

Muscular endurance: the ability of a muscle to sustain repeated contractions over an extended period of time

Speed: the maximum rate that a person can move over a specific distance; or the ability to get body parts moving quickly

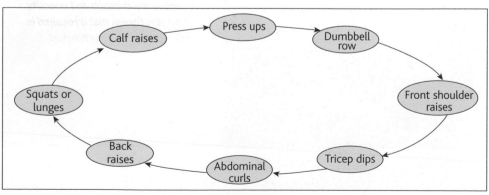

Figure 4.4 An example of a muscular endurance circuit

Speed

Speed training is an important part of most sports. In netball speed is required for breaking away from a player or closing down the opposition. In badminton speed is required to smash the shuttle and accelerate across the court. It is typically trained through interval training. The intervals should be similar to the intervals that are used in the athlete's sport. For example, in the 100m event athletes can train by completing a variety of sprint distances: 8 × 30m at maximum pace with a full recovery between each sprint (to practise the acceleration phase) and 3 × 80m at maximum pace with a full recovery between each sprint (to practise the full event).

Aerobic training

Aerobic endurance training is important in a wide range of individual (e.g. marathon) and team (e.g. hockey) sports. Two main training methods can be used.

Continuous training involves completing 20–60 minutes of continuous or intermittent (minimum 10-minute bouts accumulated throughout the day) aerobic activity, to be completed at 55/65%–90% of maximum heart rate. Training should be completed 3–5 days per week. It should be an activity that is used in the sport (e.g. runners should run, swimmers should swim), but it can be any continuous, rhythmic, aerobic activity that uses large muscle groups, such as jogging, cycling, cross-country skiing, aerobic dance.

You can calculate your training zone using the Karvonen Formula. You need to record your resting heart rate (hr rest) and to work out your maximum heart rate (hr max).

Maximal heart rate = 220 – age

Training heart rate = 65% or 0.65 (hr max – hr rest) + hr rest

In *fartlek training* the intensity varies so that the aerobic system and anaerobic system are both stressed. For example, an athlete could jog 100m in their aerobic zone, then run 20m anaerobically, repeating the pattern three more times before walking for 60 seconds to recover. They would then repeat everything until 40 minutes of exercise had been completed.

Aerobic training

Research

Using the activity selected previously:

- Identify the muscle groups that need to be trained (power/muscular endurance).
- Using the equipment in your gym, calculate your training load for each muscle group.
- Research plyometric exercises that could be used to train the muscle groups that are important to your sport.
- List the aspects of speed that are important in your activity (whole body/body part).
- Research and describe speed training drills/exercises that could be important to your sport.

Example calculation:

220 – 20 yrs = 200 hr max

Resting pulse recorded = 65bpm

Training heart rate at
65 % of hr max = 0.65 (200–65) + 65
= 0.65 × 135 + 65
= 153 bpm

Describe

Describe the duration and intensity of aerobic fitness that is required in training for your activity/sport.

M1 Flexibility

Static flexibility training is often encouraged in health and fitness because it is safer. The exercises used do not create long-term joint problems. However, static flexibility is often not sports related and not specific enough to most sports activities to develop appropriate flexibility in the muscles and tendons. Ballistic and PNF stretches produce greater flexibility improvements. An athlete needs to choose and often mix a range of flexibility exercises to suit their performance.

Strength

An athlete needs to choose a specific load based on their 1 rep max. As they progress, they become more used to the intensities and movements involved, and more tolerant of the discomfort they go through, so they can start to train at higher levels. The body becomes stronger and more tolerant of the extra intensity. The body's tolerance to lactic acid improves and muscle soreness decreases.

An advanced athlete can do fewer repetitions, as they may only be able to lift their maximum lift a few times. This will still be sufficient to provide enough stress for the body to adapt. Training can be completed up to six days per week.

Novice to intermediate athletes should use free-weight and machine exercises. However, for advanced resistance training the emphasis should be on free-weight exercises, with only occasional use of machines.

The speed at which the exercises are completed depends on the athlete's experience. Slow to moderate speeds should be used by novice and intermediate individuals, moderate and fast repetition speeds by advanced athletes.

Free-weight bicep curl

Power

The recommended training frequency for novice athletes is the same as for strength training. Intermediate athletes should either train their total body or divide the workout into a routine split between the upper and lower sections. Advanced athletes should focus on trying to split their routine between upper and lower body sections. This enables them to focus on specific body parts and increase their training to multiple sets.

The rest periods for power training gradually increase as the load increases. This allows the body to recover between sets. The exercises should be performed with an explosive velocity (power = strength × speed).

Muscular endurance

The intensity level for muscular endurance training is lower than for strength and power. The repetition level is higher so that repeated contractions can take place. The rest periods for muscular endurance training are shorter because the energy supplies in the muscle are replaced relatively quickly. The speed at which the exercises should be completed is slow for a novice and intermediate (10–15 reps). However, for large numbers of reps (1–25 or more) the speed can be moderate to fast. Increasing the time that a muscle is under tension increases muscle fatigue. The muscle fatigue level is important in developing muscular endurance.

Squat with weight

Speed

This training method may involve a range of movements that include acceleration and reaction drills, power training for specific muscle groups using explosive movements, sprinting drills at an intensity of between 85% and 100% maximum speed and overspeed training. Overspeed training involves working at a level that is 5%–10% faster than the body is normally used to. This can be achieved by sprint tows using a faster athlete, using bungy cords, sprinting down hill and working on cadence or leg speed.

Aerobic training

How much training is enough? Many athletes try and guess their training level and sometimes do too much. Aerobic training needs to be specific. Unfit athletes can work at 55%–65% maximum heart rate (hr max) to achieve some improvement, but fitter athletes need to work at higher intensity levels of 65%–90% hr max, though this can produce a greater cardiovascular risk. At 60%–70% hr max the exercise is easy to complete and enables fat burning and recovery; 70%–80% enables an athlete to develop good cardiovascular fitness; 80%–90% starts to work close to or on an athlete's anaerobic threshold. This means the body will be working anaerobically, developing lactic acid. For continuous training an athlete needs to target the aerobic zone. For fartlek training an athlete could move between 60% and 90% hr max throughout their run (this would include small anaerobic and recovery sections).

 Research

1. Research different types of training circuits that could be used to train strength.

2. Identify the speed which you need to train at to reach the lower end of your training zone.

Discuss

Discuss the differing training needs of a novice triple jumper and an elite shot putter. You will need to think about intensity, type of exercise, progressions and safety factors.

Planning a training session

Training plans need to be specific. They should indicate the intensity, time and type of exercise, so the athlete is able to track improvements. The intensity can be the speed or level on a treadmill, the heart rate at which the athlete is exercising, or the level indicated. However, in some instances several things will need to be recorded, for example if you are rowing you can record the level, pull rate and stroke rate. You will need to check your pulse on the equipment so that you can make sure the level set is specific to your target training zone.

The levels at which an athlete trains need to be specific to their level of fitness (elite, trained, untrained).

Your assessment criteria:

P2 Produce training session plans covering cardiovascular training, resistance training, flexibility training and speed training

P2 Cardiovascular training

Exercise intensities can be monitored in a variety of ways: heart rate monitoring, rate of perceived exertion and general observation. Rate of perceived exertion is a subjective scale that relates directly to heart rate:

- 60%–70% hr max should feel moderate to hard, you should be able to talk and feel that you could hold this pace for a long time

- 70%–80% hr max is described as hard and leaves you feeling that you have worked hard and completed a challenging workout.

Resistance training

The number and choice of exercises must be carefully thought through. To design an effective resistance programme you will need to follow several stages.

1. Identify the muscles to be trained.

2. Consider the equipment to be used (fixed/free weights).

3. Organise the exercises into a routine (multiple-muscle exercises first, single-muscle exercises second) and decide whether you want to split your routine (e.g. chest + biceps, back + triceps, legs + shoulders).

4. Decide on the order: large before small muscle group exercises; multiple-joint exercises before single-joint exercises; higher intensity before lower intensity exercises.

Q Research

1. Identify a sportsperson whom you will design a six-week training programme for.

2. Organise a meeting with your client to identify their fitness goals and level of experience.

3. Identify the training venues your client can use.

4. Identify the main exercises your client needs to perform, e.g. bicep curls.

Q Research

Research training plans for two different sports. Any information found will help you to identify activities that you could use for your client.

5. Decide which component of fitness to train on each exercise (strength/power/muscular endurance).

6. Identify the load, reps, sets and rest periods needed and the speed required.

Flexibility training

Flexibility training also needs to be thought through and planned carefully. It is an area of training that is often neglected by athletes.

Identify the muscles to be trained and the exercises required. Decide on static, ballistic, PNF stretches or a mixture of any combination. Identify the time that is required and the number of repetitions.

Speed training

Ensure that the training distance is appropriate to your sport or activity. Identify the number of repetitions, rest/work ratios and sets.

Q | Research

1. *Identify the intensity level of each activity you have chosen for your client.*

2. *Identify the duration of each activity you have chosen.*

Athletes sprinting out of blocks

M2 Detailed training session plans

A specific warm-up is required for each training method.

- *Cardiovascular training* warm-ups can include brisk walking, cycling or rowing at 50% of the training intensity for between 5 and 15 minutes, depending on a person's age and fitness level.

- *Resistance training* warm-ups can include a light set of 8–10 reps prior to training the muscle.

- *Flexibility and speed* warm-ups can include shuttle running, with a gradual increase in intensity for speed work.

Your assessment criteria:

M2 Produce detailed training session plans covering cardiovascular training, resistance training, flexibility training and speed training

D1 Justify the training session plans covering cardiovascular training, resistance training, flexibility training and speed training

🔍 **Research**

1. *Identify the cardiovascular exercises that you will include as a warm-up for your client.*

2. *Calculate the intensity level and duration of each exercise.*

D1 Justify training session plans

An athlete needs to be treated as an individual and trained at the level of fitness and experience appropriate to them. Training sessions need to be carefully planned around several factors. They should provide activities that are suitable to the athlete's sport and position. Plans should address each of the specific components of fitness and take into account the strength, age and ability of the person to be trained. Previous injuries may also determine the exercises that could be used. For example, an athlete recovering from a hamstring injury may be better completing static stretches than ballistic or PNF. The type of exercise needs to be carefully planned to mimic the actual sport as closely as possible so that any developments in fitness translate into real-life performance differences and are not only improvements seen in the gym.

Design a fitness training programme

Athletes have to be dedicated and organised. Most sports people have to plan their training to reach their peak potential at the right time. The timing could be every four years (Olympics), yearly (World Championships), for a tour (Lions) or simply for a very big game (derby). Athletes cannot maintain peak fitness as this might damage their health. They need to plan how and when they will achieve the targets they set themselves.

Practical

1. Carry out an induction of your client. This will enable you to check that the intensity levels and duration that you have chosen are appropriate.

2. During the induction, identify the level that the prescribed intensity level dictates on each piece of equipment.

? Did you know?

Andy Murray has risen to 4th in the ATP World Rankings partly because of his training. Murray divides his training into two periods: tournament and out of tournament.

Out of tournament he trains for a month, exercising in hot temperatures for six hours a day. This includes one hour of aerobic sprint training, running 400-metre laps at intervals of five minutes, and sideways jump hurdles, to improve balance.

This is followed by a one-hour upper body weight training session in the gym.

He then uses 90-minute yoga sessions to help develop dynamic flexibility. This is done in a room heated to 40°C, in which he burns 1600 calories.

His workout is completed with a two-hour tennis practice session with his coach.

In season, his gym sessions are reduced, as he uses the practice court for two hours before a match.

Training and monitoring performance

Designing a programme for an athlete is a rewarding and challenging experience. It involves the collection of a range of information from the athlete to make sure that the programme is suitable.

Monitoring the performance of an athlete is the key to ensuring success. Detailed record keeping is important to check the level of progress being made.

P3 Design a programme

Fitness professionals working with elite performers and fitness instructors are often asked to develop new motivational plans, but it is really important to remember that the programme must follow clear objectives and take account of the principles of training.

Planning

Identify target dates and set goals. At least three goals should be included: short term (week), medium term (month) and long term (the event itself).

Clear targets should be set against each goal. Each target must be specific, measurable, achievable, realistic and time managed (SMART). Targets can cover lifestyle factors such as smoking and drinking, and dietary changes as nutrition is also important to any fitness development. Medical history, including previous injuries, can also be used to set objectives. For example, a person may have injured their calf and as a result lost muscle mass. A target could be set to regain strength in the injured calf until it reaches the strength of the uninjured limb. Physical activity history is also useful so that targets can be set to gradually increase the frequency and intensity at which a person trains.

Principles of training

Each exercise must be specific and clearly designed for the individual athlete.

The training programme should demonstrate how the body is placed under increasing stress (overload), enabling it to adapt and improve. For each exercise, frequency, intensity, timing and type must be included. Frequency is very important if an athlete is to reach their target.

Your assessment criteria:

P3 Produce a six-week fitness training programme for a selected individual that incorporates the principles of training and periodisation

P4 Monitor performance against goals during the six-week training programme

Key terms

Periodisation: this a method of dividing the training needs of an athlete into specific sections or periods so that training can be planned and can have specific goals

Training diary: a detailed log that records each training session's performance

 Discuss

Discuss your client's access to facilities and equipment, the costs involved and any problems with training.

Periodisation

Athletes need to develop a base, building on the basics and peaking at the right time.

Periodisation is an important aspect of a fitness training programme. Training can be broken down to individual sessions (microcycle), blocks of sessions focusing on a goal (mesocycle), and a number of mesocycles, often six months to a whole year (macrocycle). For example, a football player may keep a base level of aerobic fitness during pre-season. Moving into the season they will try to improve their aerobic fitness and start to focus on speed and power. Leading into important matches, they may focus on speed and power to improve performances.

Research

Using the individual that you selected previously:

1. *Describe the microcycles, mesocycles and macrocycles of their training calendar.*

2. *Identify clear SMART targets for each cycle.*

Design

Design a training diary that could be used by your client. It should include details of equipment, reps, sets, loads, rest, warm-ups and targets.

Monitor a programme

Regular record keeping makes it easy to see the strengths and weaknesses of training and identify problems as they arise. It also allows you to track your performance against your goals. Good record keeping also helps motivate an athlete, as they can see their progress session by session.

It is important to maintain a **training diary**. All training should be logged, including reps, sets, loads, levels and time. A training diary will enable you to track an athlete's progress and help you to motivate them. It will also give you a clear indication of how close they are to their goals and objectives.

Being able to maintain a diary will give a clear indication of how professional an athlete's attitude is to training. The diary will enable you to review their performance against the goals you have set in your programme. The athlete should also try to get comments/reviews from coaches as additional evidence. These comments can be a valuable tool in identifying progress towards agreed goals.

Name: Paul Connery			Sport: Football		
Date of birth:					
Goals	1		2		
Targets	1		2		
	3		4		
Cardiovascular exercise intensity = 65%		Max hr = 153 bpm		RPE = moderate/hard	
Date			7/12/10	9/12/10	11/12/10
Warm-up	Intensity		Level/Time	Level/Time	Level/Time
Pulse raiser (treadmill)	50%		6.5 mph/5 min		
Stretches			Q/H/B/C		
Cardiovascular training	Intensity		Level/Time	Level/Time	Level/Time
Treadmill	155 bpm		8.5 mph/10 min		
Cross trainer	155 bpm		Level 7/10 min		
Resistance training	S/P/E	% 1rm	Reps/Sets	Reps/Sets	Reps/Sets
Chest press	Strength	70–80%	6–12/2		
Leg extension	Power	80%	6–12/3		
Speed work	Distance	Shuttles			
Sprinting	30	8	✓		
Flexibility	Duration				
Hamstring pnf	30s × 5		✓		

Figure 4.5 An example of a workout and exercise log

Reviewing training and providing feedback

Feedback is provided to sports people by coaches and fitness professionals on a regular basis. Athletes spend a lot of time trying to obtain good advice and help with their training. Professionals that can analyse training and correct problem areas are sought after.

P5 Review training

Feedback after a training programme needs to be professional and sensitive. Feedback to an athlete or individual can take into account a range of factors from amount of progression to attitude and motivation. It should link these factors to goals. For example, if motivation has been high throughout the programme, there should be clear evidence of progress and excellent record keeping.

Feedback needs to be clearly divided into three sections: general feedback, strengths and weaknesses.

Key terms

Feedback: a reflective assessment of progress made during training; the identification of strengths and weaknesses; an evaluation of training

Discuss

Conduct a review with your client and discuss the strengths and weaknesses of their six-week programme.

Client appraisal meeting

M3 Explain areas for improvement

Providing detailed explanations for strengths and weaknesses in training is essential to an athlete's development. Weaknesses can clearly identify problem areas and probable causes. For example, problems with strength development goals could be down to a variety of factors, such as not adhering to the loadings/reps and sets, insufficient frequency, injury, motivation and nutrition. Explaining strengths and weaknesses enables a detailed review and a reflective approach to take place, allowing the athlete to learn from their mistakes.

Discuss

Discuss your client's strengths and weaknesses and possible areas for improvement.

D2 Evaluate progress and provide recommendations

A comprehensive evaluation of training can enable an athlete to develop quickly. The evaluation can take into account the quality of evidence available. It is important that the evaluation is undertaken with the athlete so that recommendations can be agreed and acted upon. Any modifications will then allow the athlete to reach and achieve their planned goals. These might be, for example:

- changing the identified level for load (strength/power/muscular endurance) from novice to intermediate or advanced

- changing target heart rates/RPE scale

- changing the type of training from continuous to fartlek.

Discuss

Evaluate the progress made by your client.

Discuss recommendations for future training with either the client or another member of your class.

 Case study

Paul has booked a six-week review of his training. You have already been given a copy of his training log so that you can evaluate his performance. During the consultation you identify that although his cardiovascular fitness has improved, he is disappointed with his level of progress. He has trained three times per week, but does not like running on a treadmill and has struggled to work at the appropriate level because he is losing motivation. His strength and power have improved. He is using fixed-weight resistance machines and has increased the number of sets for each exercise. However, his training is starting to take too long to complete.

1. Discuss your recommendations for amendments to Paul's cardiovascular training.

2. Discuss your recommendations for strength and power training.

3. Suggest strategies that could be used to help with Paul's motivation.

Assessment checklist

To achieve a pass grade, my portfolio of evidence must show that I can:

Assessment Criteria	Description	✓
P1	Describe one method of fitness training for six different components of physical fitness.	☐
P2	Produce training session plans covering cardiovascular training, resistance training, flexibility training and speed training.	☐
P3	Produce a six-week fitness training programme for a selected individual that incorporates the principles of training and periodisation.	☐
P4	Monitor performance against goals during the six-week training programme.	☐
P5	Give feedback to an individual following completion of a six-week fitness training programme, describing strengths and areas for improvement.	☐

To achieve a merit grade, my portfolio of evidence must show that I can:

Assessment Criteria	Description	✓
M1	Explain one method of fitness training for six different components of physical fitness.	☐
M2	Produce detailed training session plans covering cardiovascular training, resistance training, flexibility training and speed training.	☐
M3	Give feedback to an individual following completion of a six-week fitness training programme, explaining strengths and areas for improvement.	☐

To achieve a distinction grade, my portfolio of evidence must show that I can:

Assessment Criteria	Description	✓
D1	Justify the training session plans covering cardiovascular training, resistance training, flexibility training and speed training.	☐
D2	Give feedback to an individual following completion of a six-week fitness training programme, evaluating progress and providing recommendations for future activities.	☐

5 | Sports coaching

LO1 Know the roles, responsibilities and skills of sports coaches

- ▶ A coach may be asked to perform a variety of roles including manager, educator and trainer.

- ▶ A coach must make sure that they meet the requirements of child protection, health and safety and equal opportunities.

- ▶ An effective coach should have a range of personal skills. They must be an excellent communicator and be responsible, organised and prompt.

LO2 Know the techniques used by coaches to improve the performance of athletes

- ▶ A coach uses a wide range of tools to assess athletes and evaluate performance. This can vary from simple observation to detailed video analysis.

LO4 Be able to deliver and review a sports coaching session

▶ A coach must be able to deliver the plan that they have produced. This can include organising warm-ups, demonstrating techniques, extending performance and reviewing progress.

LO3 Be able to plan a sports coaching session

▶ Each sports session must be planned effectively. The venue, equipment, group and activity to be undertaken need to be planned in advance, so that the session is suitable and safe.

▶ Reviewing each session is an important skill. Taking a reflective approach will assist in planning additional activities. A coach needs to reflect on the athletes and their own performance.

Coaching roles and responsibilities

Sports coaching is a challenging and rewarding career for a large number of people. There are a wide range of opportunities working with voluntary groups, children, sports clubs and athletes. There are also opportunities to work and assist in large sporting events. Coaching will play a significant part in the success of Britain's performance at the 2012 Olympics. It is important to develop coaches who have the skill and ability to gain the best out of an athlete. Successful coaches are highly sought-after by schools, clubs and professional athletes. A coach's reputation and employment is often based on their knowledge, experience and their ability to improve performance at the level they are working at.

There are a range of **roles**, **responsibilities** and skills that a coach must develop to be successful. Coaching must be carefully planned, carried out and evaluated. Coaching can be a fantastic career in a practical and fun environment. However, a new coach has to walk through a minefield of problems. Poor planning can result in serious injury and the danger of legal action. A coach must have a range of skills to deal with a variety of situations and people. They must also be a good communicator.

Your assessment criteria:

P1 Describe four roles and four responsibilities of sports coaches, using examples of coaches from different sports

Key terms

Innovator: a person that designs and introduces new practices

Manage: to supervise and control individuals and groups

Responsibilities: the different aspects of coaching that you are directly responsible for

Roles: the functions that you will perform or the jobs that you will undertake

P1 Roles

There are a number of roles that a sports coach has to perform.

Innovator

Coaching involves planning, designing new practices, and thinking on your feet when things do not go to plan. A coach needs to have a fall-back plan, or should be able to adapt a session so that it is appropriate for the group that they are working with. Alex Ferguson is an excellent **innovator** who can change the tactics that a team uses.

Managing people in sport

Manager

A coach **manages** sports people that they work with. Monitoring attendance is important to determine if there are any problems in a

86

group. It also ensures that a coach can track the number of students at each session, and check that they are fulfilling their child protection responsibilities. A coach acts *in loco parentis*. They are responsible for a child in their care until the child's parents collect them. Setting clear targets and maintaining enthusiasm for the sport is a management role. Managing behaviour, keeping students on task and maintaining control and discipline are also important. Athletes must remain focused to be able to develop and learn. Martin Johnson is a good example of a manager. He developed a new code of behaviour for players after the Rugby Football Union charged four unnamed players in his team with misconduct.

Trainer

A coach may have to organise fitness sessions and provide advice and training guidance. This can include designing resistance training sessions to help with strength, organising skill and speed sessions or providing nutritional advice. Marg Caldow, England Netball's open squad coach is a good example of a trainer, as she instilled new confidence and training commitment in the England squad.

Educator

It is important that each session has a clear learning objective so that an athlete or student can review what they have achieved and see clear progress. Each session should be progressive, building on previous knowledge.

Friend

There are times when a coach may have to act as a **friend** and show sympathy and understanding. This may be when an athlete suffers an injury, or is struggling to achieve a difficult target and therefore needs support and encouragement.

Role model

A coach acts as a role model to the athletes and students that they work with. Presentation, appropriate behaviour and professionalism are important. A coach should set high expectations for the people that they are working with. Bobby Robson, England and Newcastle Manager, was an excellent role model to many players and fans.

Discuss

1. *Discuss the roles that a coach may be required to perform. The roles will vary according to a person's level of involvement, experience and the sport or activity that they are involved in.*

2. *Prioritise the roles you have identified from most to least important.*

? Did you know?

Lee Westwood's coach, Peter Cowen, was named UK Coach of the Year at the 2010 UK Coaching Awards. He has helped Westwood overtake Tiger Woods to become the highest rated golfer in the world.

Key terms

Friend: a person who provides support, help and advice to someone and acts in their best interest

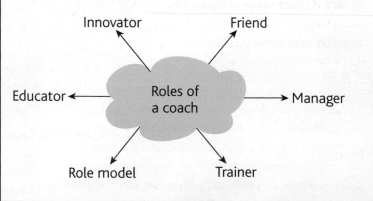

Figure 5.1 The roles of a coach

P1 Responsibilities

A coach has a variety of responsibilities that they must adhere to. These include legal obligations, professional conduct, health and safety, equal opportunities and knowledge of the coaching environment.

Legal obligations

A coach must ensure that children are always protected from physical, sexual and emotional abuse or neglect. Physical abuse can include threatening behaviour from other children. Sexual abuse can be associated with inappropriate contact and touching. Emotional abuse can be caused through bullying, either by a coach or other children. Neglect can include not supervising a session sufficiently and leaving children on their own if a parent is late.

Insurance

A coach must make sure that both they and the centre that they work in are appropriately insured. This should include insurance for legal aid, personal injury and public liability. Public liability insurance is important because it covers the cost of compensation and damages that are the result of an injury or damage to property because of the coach's business.

Professional conduct

A coach must behave professionally at all times. This includes the language that they use, the relationships and respect that they build with the people they are working with, and the behaviour that they encourage. Positive encouragement should focus on hard work, team building, working together, fair play and honesty.

Health and safety

A coach needs to follow strict health and safety procedures for the sport that they are working in. This can include risk-assessing a venue or activity, preparing in advance the people who are involved, checking that participants are wearing appropriate clothing, setting up equipment, completing a warm-up, directing an activity and supervising the participants' departure from the venue.

Checking climbing equipment

Equal opportunities

A coach must ensure that different genders and races have equal opportunities to participate. This may mean adapting an activity so that everyone can take part. For example, a coach may have to decide on appropriate clothing for an activity, modify rules to reduce the danger of physical contact or even create an atmosphere of acceptance and inclusion. In taekwondo Muslim women are now allowed to wear a headscarf in competition.

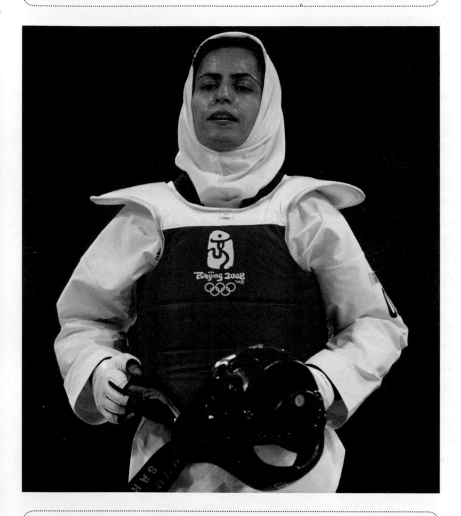

Knowledge of the coaching environment

A coach must make sure that they have the appropriate qualification to be able to deliver the sport and the level of activity. For example, a coach should have at least a Level 2 coaching qualification in the relevant sport to lead a session. A Level 2 course will only enable teaching up to a certain standard, for example front somersaults, but not double somersaults in trampolining. It is advisable for a coach to regularly update the qualification for more dangerous activities.

 Describe

1. Describe rules and regulations that can be adapted in a variety of sports for different genders and races.

2. Describe the health and safety regulations that relate to a sport of your choice.

 Design

Design a leaflet that clearly states the coaching policy for child protection at your venue.

M1 Explain roles

Innovator

A good innovator is able to design practices and maintain enthusiasm by providing variety. Athletes often become bored with routines. An athlete may find that training reaches a certain level and then little progress is made. A coach has to find a solution, often coming up with an original idea or new way of working. Innovations are often seen in ice skating, diving and gymnastics where new techniques are developed to try to beat the opposition. An example of this is the Yurchenko vault, named after Natalia Yurchenko.

Manager

A coach manages a session and the people involved. Managing attendance includes keeping accurate records of who is present and the reasons for any absences.

Managing behaviour involves establishing expected behaviours in a team and also disciplining people who do not follow them. This can include a quiet talk, excluding someone from an activity or session, sending someone off in a game, fining a player or even excluding them from a team. As a manager, a coach may speak to the press on behalf of a player and represent the player's views.

Trainer

A coach may be responsible for training athletes. This includes setting targets for the season, agreeing training priorities and methods, and providing advice and guidance on nutrition. A coach must ensure that the person in their care is trained to meet the requirements of

Your assessment criteria:

M1 Explain four roles and four responsibilities of sports coaches, using examples of coaches from different sports

The Yurchenko vault

the sport they are involved in. They may organise fitness assessments and tests to reveal problem areas in strength, stamina and flexibility. This will enable them to design a training programme that develops the problem area.

Educator

One of the main roles of a coach is to educate the people they work with. This may simply be introducing people to a sport through a taster session, or may be developing performance at elite level. Education is about the skills, tactics, rules and regulations in sport, for example helping someone to volley, understand their position and role in a 4-4-2 formation in football, or learn about the offside rule.

Friend

A coach often acts as a friend when the person they are working with needs advice and guidance. People's personal lives affect their ability to train and perform. Tiger Woods is an example of this. A coach must be approachable so that they can help resolve conflict and limit the effect that this may have on training. A coach may have to resolve personal problems between two people in the same group.

Captain settling new player

Role model

A coach should be a good role model for their sport. They should dress smartly and appropriately for the activity, demonstrate good behaviour and foster an attitude of openness and equal respect. They should be inspirational, creating drive and commitment from players. Bobby Robson was an excellent role model. He discussed situations with his players and respected their points of view. He maintained control because people wanted to play for him and did not want to let him down. He did not need to swear or scream at a player to get the best out of him. *Compare to role model* *in sji predicto*

M1 ▸ Explain responsibilities

Your assessment criteria:

M1 Explain four roles and four responsibilities of sports coaches, using examples of coaches from different sports

Legal obligations

A coach is responsible for the welfare of the people they are teaching. A coach should monitor behaviour and intervene if a difficult situation starts to develop. Separating people and placing them on different teams or in different groups is an effective way of resolving some problems. The danger of sexual abuse can be limited by ensuring that any assistant coaches are CRB checked (Criminal Records Bureau). A coach should also make sure that students are supervised at all times. Bullying must not be tolerated. This includes stopping students from ridiculing those who have less ability than themselves.

Insurance

Governing bodies of sports often offer specific insurance for coaches in their sport. It is essential that a coach checks the activities that the insurance covers, the length of time the insurance runs for, and whether the insurance allows for transportation to and from events.

For example, British Gymnastics offers Legal Liability Cover. This provides protection for all activities including training, competitions and displays as well as any social, fund-raising and administrative activities, recognised or approved by British Gymnastics.

Professional conduct

A coach should demonstrate clear professional conduct at all times. The relationships that they develop should be focused on work and student development. A coach must be firm but fair. They must be able to handle behavioural problems without losing control and resorting to bad language. They should deal with any requests from outside agencies promptly. A coach should treat all students in the same way, showing no favouritism.

Health and safety

Health and safety is often activity-specific. A coach must be aware of all of the risks involved in planning and running an activity. A sports governing body will dictate how equipment should be set up. It will also determine the appropriate clothing and safety equipment for the activity. For example, the FA clearly states that players should wear shin pads at all times. The governing body may also determine the season that players can compete in. For example, rugby can only be played at certain times in the year as the ground becomes too hard and may cause injury. It is the responsibility of the coach to make sure that their players adhere to the policy set.

 Design

Design a code of conduct that could be used by coaches in your sport.

Football player wearing shin pads

Equal opportunities

Everyone should have an equal opportunity to participate. A coach needs to examine rules to see what amendments can be made to include groups. They need to take into account differences in strength and fitness. Practices may, however, focus on skill rather than these two elements, to encourage groups to train together. Sports such as golf have different lengths of course to emphasise the skill, rather than focus on strength and drive length.

Knowledge of the coaching environment

A coach must understand the level that they can work at and what they are allowed to do. The FA, for example, has a clear progression for coaches:

Coaching Level 1: assists other qualified coaches in delivering football coaching sessions.

Coaching Level 2: leads football coaching sessions and works as a football coach in local amateur junior/senior clubs, FA Charter Standard clubs and schools, local authority community football schemes and Football in the Community schemes.

Coaching Level 3 (UEFA 'B'): works as a football coach in a club, academy or centre of excellence.

UEFA 'A': develops knowledge in advanced skills, tactics, strategies and systems of play.

UEFA Pro Licence: compulsory for all Premier League managers, it focuses on employment law, finance, the media, technology, business management and club structure.

🔍 Research

1. *Research the responsibilities of either a professional coach or a local club coach.*

2. *Research the levels of award in a sport of your choice. Find out what each level allows you to teach.*

3. *Research codes of conduct that are used in different sports.*

Comparing roles, responsibilities and skills of successful coaches

D1 ▶ Compare and contrast coaches from different sports

A coach who is good at everything is quite rare. Coaches have strengths and weaknesses.

In **comparing** and **contrasting** the roles, responsibilities and **skills** of successful coaches, you will need to examine two coaches from different sports. It is advisable to choose sports that are very different from each other. You could choose coaches who work at different levels, and compare and contrast their work. For example, a Level 2 rugby coach and a tennis coach may perform similar roles. Each coach will probably need to develop new practices, manage players, act as role models and educate their players in tactics. Each coach may also have similar responsibilities for insurance and professional conduct. However, the rugby coach will need to spend more time and effort planning health and safety for practices, as the sport is more dangerous. Child protection issues may also be more of a challenge in rugby. A coach will need to group players of similar sizes and ages in practices to prevent injury. There is also more chance of conflict and aggression in a rugby match when tempers flare up.

Your assessment criteria:

D1 Compare and contrast the roles, responsibilities and skills of successful coaches from different sports

Key terms

Analyse: *to assess skill, ability or team performance*

Compare: *to make an analysis that looks at similarities*

Contrast: *to make an analysis that looks at differences*

Skills: *personal factors that contribute to successful coaching*

Discuss

Discuss two coaches from different sports, comparing and contrasting their roles, responsibilities and skills.

Research

Research successful coaches from two different sports.

Individual tennis coaching

The skills required of a rugby coach may be different from a tennis coach. Communication on a rugby field will be more difficult than on a tennis court because of the distance and the number of players involved. Rugby will require different organisational skills because it is a team sport. A coach needs to be able to select players for a variety of positions. A small quick player may be better on the wing, whereas a tall strong player may be better playing as a lock or number 8.

Analysing the sport may require a combination of individual analysis, examining skill (can a player pass off both hands with equal effect?) and group tactical analysis (can they play as a unit with the forwards rucking and mauling effectively?). In tennis the analysis may focus more on individual skill/tactics and fault correction (can the player serve accurately with top spin, can they serve and volley?).

 Did you know?

Rinus Michels was named Coach of the Century by FIFA in 1999. He was the originator of Total Football, and won the European Cup with Ajax, the Spanish league with Barcelona and Euro, 88 with Holland. He should also have won the 1974 World Cup.

Key terms

Analyse: *to assess skill, ability or team performance*

Rugby coach organising training

95

Skills common to successful sports coaches

P2 Skills of a sports coach

A coach needs a variety of skills to successfully deliver and **evaluate** a sports session.

Communication skills

A coach must be able to explain and demonstrate sports skills and practices. They should be clear and precise in their instructions, projecting their voice and appearing confident and in charge. A coach's body language is also important as it should send out a message of authority, interest and enthusiasm.

Organisation

Good organisation is essential if a session is to run smoothly. There are various stages in every coaching session that need to be planned. Thorough planning of the following stages means that the session should flow with good pace and few interruptions:

- set up equipment

- introduction and warm-ups that are linked to the activity to be undertaken

- practices that are simple, but eventually progress into a more realistic game-like situation under pressure.

- competition or a small-sided game

Your assessment criteria:

 P2 Describe three skills common to successful sports coaches, using examples of coaches from different sports

 Key terms

Evaluate: to assess the performance of a coaching session against its objectives

? Did you know?

Speaking well is a learned skill.

Keep your voice relaxed, clear, and control the speed you speak at. If you mumble, it will be hard for people to understand what you are trying to explain.

Vary your voice tone. A monotone voice can be boring. Varying the tone of your voice can make you sound more dynamic and will help maintain attention. It can also help to emphasise important points that people have to remember.

- cool down
- review
- check equipment and put away.

Analysing

A coach should be able to observe practices and identify an athlete's strengths and weaknesses. In individual performance this may involve comparing the sportsperson to a coaching model. In a team performance this may involve checking the team against the tactics that the team are using.

Problem-solving

A coach needs to be able to think on their feet. Activities sometimes do not run to plan and need changing. For example, decreasing or increasing the playing space because of fitness levels, and simplifying the skill if a sportsperson is struggling to learn it.

Evaluating

It is important to evaluate the learning that has taken place. At the end of a coaching session a coach should review the performance of the people that they are working with. Feedback should focus on learning, motivation, enthusiasm and success. A coach should also review their own successes and failures within the session as this will aid future planning and performance.

Time management

A coach should arrive 10 to 15 minutes before the session is due to start to make sure that everything is ready and that they are fully prepared. A coach must have good time management skills to progress through the stages of the session and finish on time.

 Describe

1. Describe different ways that you can communicate with a group.

2. Rate your personal skills on a scale of 1 to 5 using the headings in this section.

 Discuss

1. You have planned a football coaching session that focuses on dribbling skills. You had planned to teach outside on the field but the pitch is waterlogged. There is the possibility of moving the practice indoors but this will mean amending your session. Discuss the implications of moving your session from outdoors to indoors and the possible changes that you will need to make.

2. You have planned a badminton coaching session that focuses on the smash. You had planned for people to work in pairs but one person is off sick. Discuss ways of amending your practices that will ensure that everyone is involved in the session.

M2 ► Explain the skills of a sports coach

Communication skills

A coach must have effective communication skills. They need to organise a group by giving instructions that each person in the group can hear clearly. A coach's instructions must be clear and precise, and they should check people's understanding before starting an activity. All practices should be explained, demonstrated, observed and checked. A coach should be able to adapt their practices to include athletes with hearing or visual problems, making sure that they talk to a group face to face or identifying the distance that athletes can hear. A coach should be able to break down practices into simple parts to assist learning.

Organisation

Good organisation requires planning and thought. Lining a group up at the start of a demonstration needs to be planned so that everyone can hear and see. A coach also needs to consider how a group should be divided up for a practice. Groups can be divided according to ability, height, age and experience. Groups should be carefully organised throughout a session to avoid confusion. An easy way to organise this is by forming a group into pairs, pairs can then join to form fours, then eights, and so on. It is much more difficult and time-consuming forming groups of two and then changing them into groups of three. The use of grids and channels are useful in organising practices. They can be set up in advance of a session, enabling a lesson to move from the warm-up, to skills practices and a game without having to stop a group and reorganise the equipment.

Analysing

Analysis can involve individual observational assessments, video analysis and biomechanical analysis. A detailed coaching model is needed for a comparison so that specific coaching points can be examined. For simple fault corrections, observational analysis is often sufficient to be able to identify problems. However, when an athlete starts to perform more complicated moves or if the activity happens quickly, video analysis may be more appropriate, as it gives the coach and athlete more time to review the performance. For team and tactical analysis, and match analysis, real-time data can be used. However, it is useful to have a team discussion that reviews tactics during a video replay of the performance.

Problem-solving

A coach may need to adapt practices if people are missing from the session. In badminton, for example, the ideal situation is to have people

working in pairs. If someone is missing, the groupings may have to be changed to groups of three; two people play and the third person either umpires or checks the performance of the players practising, then the group rotates.

Another common situation is when a student turns up with a slight injury. A coach has to think carefully about how they can include the player in the session and what role they may take.

Evaluating

A coach should review a lesson to find out if the objectives have been met. For example, if the aim was to teach students to play a forward defensive stroke in cricket, the coach must assess whether all students can complete the stroke successfully. A coach can review each stage of the coaching session by completing an evaluation. There are a number of questions that an evaluation can ask: were the activities suitable for the group? Did each person show clear progress? Was the session well organised? Did the session start and finish on time?

Time management

A coach must be able to manage time within their coaching session. If a practice goes on for too long, participants can become bored. A coach must plan how long each activity should take. They should monitor participants and look for signs that it is time to move on or shorten the activity. It is important that a session finishes on time as often another group will be using the facility afterwards.

 Describe

1. Carry out an analysis of a performer completing a simple task.

2. Describe and rate your communication skills, and identify your strengths and weaknesses.

 Discuss

1. Discuss details that you need to plan for prior to your coaching session.

2. Discuss time management issues that you need to prepare and plan for during your coaching session.

Techniques that coaches can use to improve performance

Coaches use a wide variety of techniques to improve the performance of athletes. The method that they choose may be determined by the athlete's ability, age, experience and level of competition. Most techniques require good attention to detail and excellent observational skills.

P3 Techniques

Techniques can be divided into those that a coach is directly responsible for, i.e. effective demonstration and technical instruction, and those that the coach can carry out to assist with learning, i.e. observation analysis.

Effective demonstration

A demonstration of a practice gives an athlete a good understanding of what a skill should look like or how a practice should be run. The demonstration should include key points for an athlete to remember. It may either be the whole skill or part of a skill. If a coach cannot demonstrate the technique, they may be able to use a member of the group to demonstrate instead. It is important that the demonstration is technically correct as athletes will attempt to copy the demonstration that they have seen.

Technical instruction

An athlete needs to learn the coaching points for a technique. The coaching points must be specific and accurate. There are two different ways that coaches can approach this. A coach can teach the whole

Your assessment criteria:

P3 Describe three different techniques that are used by coaches, to improve the performance of athletes

M3 Explain three different techniques that are used by coaches, to improve the performance of athletes

Key terms

Observation analysis: monitoring performance through watching and checking skills

Technical instruction: teaching of specific skill work

Describe

Describe the technical components of a skill of your choice.

Practical

Teach the skill to a partner. Make sure that you have an observer who can review and feed back on your performance.

technique and then shape the athlete gradually until they have mastered it. The second method is for the coach to break the technique down into small parts and teach each part separately.

Observation analysis

A coach needs to watch an athlete to determine the parts of a technique or practice that they can perform successfully. The coach needs to know the coaching points of the technique so that they can easily work out the problems that the performer has from an observation. They can then explain and demonstrate any fault corrections. A coach can also record the performance using a camera and analyse the information in slow motion.

M3 Explain techniques

Effective demonstration

A coach must be familiar with the coaching points linked to the demonstration and should either be able to perform the whole demonstration, or should be able to talk someone through the parts of the demonstration. An effective demonstration allows athletes to copy the performance. Athletes need a clear picture; if the demonstration is not effective or accurate, athletes will learn to complete the technique incorrectly. A coach must always encourage good technique, focusing on developing simple skills first. Most techniques have clear progression stages. These are stages of learning that must be completed before a performer can progress to harder skills.

Technical instruction

In developing good technique a coach must ensure that they do not provide too much information at once. For example, a coach may demonstrate the whole skill of a seat drop in trampolining to give performers a clear picture, but they would not go on to describe all of the technical points. The coach should break down the technique into parts, explaining, demonstrating and practising each part. The first practice in the seat drop involves identifying the seat drop position on the trampoline (with no movement). The coach makes sure that a performer can identify the main points linked to the technique on landing. The second practice focuses on the coaching points needed to move from sitting on the trampoline to bouncing and standing up.

 Research

Research the progressive stages of a skill that you would like to teach.

 Discuss

1. *Discuss how you could demonstrate and explain the skill to a group.*

2. *Discuss how the skill can be extended for performers.*

M3 ▸ Explain techniques *continued*

Observation analysis

Observation analysis can be completed in several ways. A coach can watch a performer and feed back information. They can also record and review evidence using a camera. Observation analysis is often used for beginners or when performances have been poor. It is easy to identify individual faults from just watching. Video evidence is easier to review, because practices can be paused or played in slow motion. It enables a team to review their performance after a match, allowing players to discuss problems and make suggestions for improvement.

To complete observation analysis a coach must choose a position where they are able to observe accurately. If a camera is to be used, it needs to be carefully placed so that the information to be reviewed is recorded.

The final method is notational analysis. A coach records information about a performance from observation. This record can include strengths (e.g. the number of successful smashes, drop shots and net shots in badminton) and weaknesses (e.g. errors from poor shots and unsuccessful serves).

Your assessment criteria:

M3 Explain three different techniques that are used by coaches, to improve the performance of athletes

D2 Evaluate three different techniques that are used by coaches, to improve the performance of athletes

Notational analysis of basketball shooting

D2 Evaluate techniques

Effective demonstration

A demonstration of a technique can give an athlete an idea of what the performance should look like. It provides a target and enables an athlete to make a comparison so that they can determine when the technique has been mastered. However, it only provides a starting point. An athlete still has to learn each of the movements. An athlete has to go through several stages of fault correction to complete their learning. They may also struggle to grasp an important aspect that repeated demonstrations will not correct.

It may be necessary to record, analyse and play back a performance to identify problems. It may require a combined effort from the athlete and the coach to work out what is going wrong.

An effective demonstration

Technical instruction

Providing instruction on technique will improve skill level. An athlete may perform the best technical serve in tennis, but does this make them an effective performer? There are a number of skills in each sport, but a competitor must be able to make the right choice of which one to use and when. A competitor must know, for example, when to play a lob, forehand or volley in a game of tennis. Technical instruction can also produce a production line of athletes that all play the same way. This does not mean that the current technique is correct. It simply means that it is the best one known to date.

Observation analysis

Observation analysis is an excellent tool for identifying strengths and weaknesses. It is also effective in helping to set targets for athletes, but it still falls on the coach to provide solutions. If someone has a problem with their golf swing, errors can be identified. A coach needs to provide solutions for each error and then correct the technique of a performer by repeated practice, using demonstrations and technical instruction to help.

🔍 Research

Research a range of techniques that could be used to improve performance.

 Discuss

Which of the techniques do you feel has the biggest impact on performance?

Planning a coaching session

Coaches need to spend time researching and planning sessions. A coaching session will only be as good as the plan that is produced for it. A detailed session plan will provide you with a reminder of the stages of your session and the key coaching points for each of the practices that you have developed. It will also enable you to think carefully about the aims and objectives of the session, the timings of practices, and the order of the practices.

Your assessment criteria:

P4 Plan a sports coaching session

P4 Aims and objectives

Each coaching session should have a clear aim. For example, the aim of a session could be to enable players to shoot a successful lay-up in a basketball game. Several objectives can also be set so that the aim is achieved. For example, players should be able to perform an effective dribble and pick up, players must also be able to lay up without travelling and finally players should be able to lay up successfully in a game against opposition.

Smart targets

Targets need to be set for each practice so that athletes have something to aim for. For example, in the lay-up activity, targets could be set at the start of the practice. (Every player should be able to score two out of every three lay-ups by the end of the practice and good players should be able to score three out of three.)

Each target needs to be smart. **Smart targets** should be specific to a practice, measurable (easy to track and check), achievable (they should not be too hard), realistic (appropriate) and time-bound (have a specific timescale).

Roles and responsibilities

There are occasions when coaches work together. They often team teach. It is important that each coach clearly understands the parts of the coaching session that they are responsible for. One coach often takes overall control of the session and the other coach assists. The group may sometimes be split into two parts, and each coach either delivers the same practice with a small group to make it easier, or each delivers different practices (for example, one group works on attack and the other on defence).

 Key terms

Smart targets: targets which are specific, measurable, achievable, realistic and time-bound

 Describe

1. Describe the aims and objectives of your sports coaching session.

2. Describe the participants that you will be working with and the resources that you need to conduct the session.

Participants

A coach should identify the people that will be involved in the session. They must know their age and gender so that practices are appropriate. They also need to know how many people will be involved so that they have enough equipment. The ability of the **participants** also needs to be considered. Beginners may need different types of practices than advanced players.

Resources

All of the **resources** or equipment that is needed for the session should be highlighted on the lesson plan, and any costs involved should be indicated. Human resources such as assistant coaches or helpers must also be recorded.

Health and safety

Sports coaches must ensure that activities are safe. A coach needs to assess the risk involved in any activity and plan to reduce the risk where possible to minimise any safety problems. This may include getting a group to walk the pitch to check for any sharp objects, checking that a floor is clean and dry and checking equipment is set up properly. Risk must be assessed in the activity itself. For example, in rugby tackling practices can be dangerous. A method of reducing risk is to pair players of equal size and ability. Practices need to be progressive, starting with easy, slow practices then developing into faster and more difficult ones.

Key terms

Participants: *the people taking part in the session*

Resources: *equipment that is needed to run the coaching session*

Discuss

Discuss the safety risks of your activity with a qualified coach to make sure that your plan is safe.

Footballers checking the pitch before a practice

P4 ▸ Emergency procedures

Your assessment criteria:

P4 Plan a sports coaching session

Before a coach starts a session, they must make sure that all participants are aware of emergency procedures, including fire drills and the evacuation of the building. Participants need to know where to get help, where to locate the nearest telephone and first aid procedures.

Contingencies

A coach must always have a back-up plan. Illness may mean that they do not have enough participants to run a planned activity. Coaches need to be able to think on their feet and adapt practices to accommodate different group sizes. This can be achieved in a variety of ways. Ball handling practices can be organised into continuous relays. Skills practices can be organised into performers and reviewers so that even numbers are not required. The weather can also mean that plans have to change. It is important that a wet weather alternative is planned so that an activity can be run indoors if necessary. This may require modification of the original activity. For example, rugby practices would require significant changes to move the activity indoors. Physical contact may have to be prevented to avoid injury from hard floor surfaces. The game could be changed to tag rugby instead.

Small-sided tag rugby game

Components of a session

There are several parts to a successful session. A coach should introduce the aim of the session and then warm up participants with an appropriate activity. They should then move on to introducing the main part of the lesson. This may include unopposed skills or practices giving participants time to develop without pressure (e.g. individual dribbling). Practices can then be performed against a static or active defence (e.g. dribbling against a defender), or, in the case of individual sports such as trampolining, can be extended (e.g. front drop progresses to front drop with a half twist).

 Describe

Describe contingency plans that you need to make for your session. This could include planning for wet weather, reduced numbers or reduced equipment.

The session should then contain some form of game or fun activity that uses the skill. This can be a small-sided game, or a game with adapted rules. Finally, the session should conclude with a cool-down activity, before the aims and objectives are reviewed. Equipment can then be put away.

Sequencing

When coaching a technique, a coach needs to think about the sequence that the technique should be taught in. For example, when teaching the seat drop in trampolining, a coach should complete the following sequence: static position on the trampoline, seat bouncing without return to feet, three seat bounces with supported return to feet, push and go feet to seat to feet. This sequence is necessary for safety.

In other activities a coach may choose to demonstrate the whole skill and break it down into small parts (similar to the previous example), getting the athlete to practise each section before practising the whole skill again.

An alternative method is to try to shape the athlete by getting them to practise the whole skill all of the time, concentrating on specific aspects of the skill. The athlete can gradually shape the skill until it looks right.

Feedback

Coaches should give feedback to the group about their performance. This should focus on the learning that has taken place, and can include which participants have performed well, comments on fair play and teamwork, and areas that still need further development.

Feedback should occur throughout the coaching session. Each performer should feel that they have received some comments about their performance and have had opportunities to improve.

Feedback is often verbal, but can also include additional demonstrations that reinforce points about techniques and skills. It is important that a coach reviews performances at the end of a session so that athletes know how well they have done.

Q | Research

1. Research coaching plans for different sports and examine the content and layout.

2. Research activities in a sport of your choice that you could include in a coaching session.

Design

Design the components of your coaching session. The sequence should be logical and ensure that the session flows.

Delivering and reviewing a coaching session

An effective coach must be able to deliver a successful coaching session. They need to use all of their skills to make sure that the session is educational, fun and enjoyable. A good coaching session will motivate participants and encourage them to continue or take up the sport.

P5 M4 Deliver a coaching session

The final part of the unit will require you to **deliver** a coaching session that you have planned. Your tutor will provide you with a date and time for your assessment and will complete an observational checklist to assess your ability. If the session is delivered independently, you will meet the requirements of M4. If your tutor provides advice and support so that the session is successful, you will achieve P5.

P6 Review a coaching session

Good coaches constantly **review** their performance to develop and improve. A coach should examine their strengths and weaknesses in all aspects of the session (including planning, delivery and feedback):

• Were the session's aims and objectives appropriate?

• Were the activities appropriate for the group?

• Were the targets for participants met?

• Which aspects of the lesson went well?

• Which aspects would you improve?

• What problems did you have?

M5 Evaluate a coaching session

A simple method of evaluating planning and delivery is to use a checklist and comment box. Each statement can be graded and an explanation provided. Areas for improvement can be easily seen and suggestions for improvement made.

Your assessment criteria:

P5 Deliver a sports coaching session, with tutor support

M4 Independently deliver a sports coaching session

P6 Carry out a review of the planning and delivery of a sports coaching session, identifying strengths and areas for improvement

M5 Evaluate the planning and delivery of a sports coaching session, suggesting how improvements could be reached in the identified areas

D3 Justify suggestions made in relation to the development plan

Key terms

Deliver: *carry out your planned coaching session*

Review: *an evaluation of the coaching session that you delivered*

Practical

Deliver a coaching session.

Figure 5.2 Example evaluation checklist

Planning and evaluation checklist		
Planning	**Scale**	**Explanation of evaluation**
Information was up-to-date and comprehensive.	1 2 3 4 5	
Participants' needs were effectively identified and summarised on the produced plans.	1 2 3 4 5	
Medical conditions likely to endanger self and/or others were identified.	1 2 3 4 5	
Session plans included suitable, technically appropriate and progressive activities for participants.	1 2 3 4 5	
Plans had appropriate timings.	1 2 3 4 5	
Plans followed expectations of the health and safety of the chosen sport.	1 2 3 4 5	
Plans took into account sufficient space and met health and safety requirements of the sport.	1 2 3 4 5	
Suggestions for improvements		
1.		
2.		
3.		
Coaching self-evaluation		
Was the aim of the session appropriate to the participants' needs?	1 2 3 4 5	
Was the organisation of the session adequate and appropriate?	1 2 3 4 5	
Was the content appropriate to the group's needs and expectations?	1 2 3 4 5	
Were your coaching techniques and communication appropriate to the content and participants?	1 2 3 4 5	
Were any changes made during the session?	1 2 3 4 5	
Did the participants' performance improve as expected?	1 2 3 4 5	
Suggestions for improvements		
1.		
2.		
3.		

D3 Justify suggestions

You will need to provide reasons for the improvements you suggest in both your planning and coaching evaluation. For example, if you only score three on planning because your lesson practices are out of date, this gives you an area for future development. One of your evaluative statements could be that you need to review your coaching knowledge, and to do this you intend to take an updated course in the sport that you are analysing.

Reflect

1. Complete a review of your coaching session.

2. Copy and complete the checklist shown in Figure 5.2 and evaluate your coaching session.

Assessment checklist

To achieve a pass grade, my portfolio of evidence must show that I can:

Assessment Criteria	Description	✓
P1	Describe four roles and four responsibilities of sports coaches, using examples of coaches from different sports.	☑
P2	Describe three skills common to successful sports coaches, using examples of coaches from different sports.	☑
P3	Describe three different techniques that are used by coaches, to improve the performance of athletes.	☑
P4	Plan a sports coaching session.	☑
P5	Deliver a sports coaching session, with tutor support.	☑
P6	Carry out a review of the planning and delivery of a sports coaching session, identifying strengths and areas for improvement.	☑

To achieve a merit grade, my portfolio of evidence must show that I can:

Assessment Criteria	Description	✓
M1	Explain four roles and four responsibilities of sports coaches, using examples of coaches from different sports.	☑
M2	Explain three skills common to successful sports coaches, using examples of coaches from different sports.	☑
M3	Explain three different techniques that are used by coaches, to improve the performance of athletes.	☑
M4	Independently deliver a sports coaching session.	☑
M5	Evaluate the planning and delivery of a sports coaching session, suggesting how improvements could be reached in the identified areas.	☑

2

To achieve a distinction grade, my portfolio of evidence must show that I can:

Assessment Criteria	Description	✓
D1	Compare and contrast the roles, responsibilities and skills of successful coaches from different sports.	☐
D2	Evaluate three different techniques that are used by coaches, to improve the performance of athletes.	☐
D3	Justify suggestions made in relation to the development plan.	☐

6 | Sports development

LO1 Know key concepts in sports development

▶ The sports continuum exists at different levels and is the basis of organised sport.

▶ Barriers exist which can reduce levels of participation.

▶ Sport is particularly aimed at specific target groups to increase their participation.

LO2 Know the key providers of sports development

▶ There are a variety of different categories of sports providers.

▶ The various providers offer significantly different benefits for participants.

▶ All providers must have high levels of structural organisation for their provision.

▶ The various providers have different roles.

LO3 Understand how quality is measured in sports development

▸ Quality can be measured using a variety of methods.

▸ Quality is measured for a variety of purposes.

▸ Measuring the quality of the provision has a number of distinct advantages.

▸ There are some disadvantages associated with measuring quality.

LO4 Know about sports development in practice

▸ There are currently a number of major initiatives in place which enhance sports development.

▸ Sports development also exists at a local level where many programmes are available.

▸ National governing bodies have an important role in contributing to the overall development.

Key concepts in sports development

There has been a specific emphasis on developing sport in the last 20 years, whereas sport had previously carried on in its various forms with individuals choosing whether or not to take part. A more formal and organised approach is now in place to make sure that sport does not just happen, but that it is developed as well. This unit considers the sports development **continuum** at its various levels and gives examples of the ways in which initiatives have been used in the past to try to raise public awareness.

Your assessment criteria:

P1 Describe three examples of the sports development continuum, from three different sports

P1 ▶ The sports development continuum

This is now well established and an industry in its own right with the main aim of enabling people to have a healthy, active lifestyle. The following aspects of this development are important.

Key terms

Continuum: a continuous extent or series

Foundation: a first level or lowest division

Levels

Like any other industry, sports development exists at various levels and four specific ones can be identified. The sport of gymnastics is used here as an example of the way these four levels can be applied to a particular sport.

? Did you know?

The sport of gymnastics has a significant increase in participation levels every four years! This is because the media coverage of the Olympic Games raises the profile of the sport by showing it on television far more than it is normally.

- *Foundation* is the basic and first level. This is where the sport is organised and much of the administration is carried out, clubs are formed to make sure there is a provision for the activity to take place and the first levels of involvement occur. Some basic facilities, such as school gyms, sports halls or leisure centres are the most common ones which are used. Gymnastics requires specialist equipment from basic mats to beams and vaulting apparatus, and qualified people to organise and run sessions. The foundation stage makes sure that these requirements are met so that everything is in place for the activity to be provided.

At the lower levels of gymnastics, the foundation clubs offer basic participation.

114

- *Participation* is the second level. As its name suggests, this is where there is actual participation in the sport or activity, so this is where gymnasts go along to clubs to take part in their sport.

- *Performance* is the third level. This is where some form of competition is introduced, so a gymnast moves from learning and practising gymnastic skills to actually taking part in a competition where their skills are matched against others. There are many different gymnastic events and the sport also tends to be organised in age groups, so there are a great number of organised performances which can range from displays to quite high level competitions.

- *Excellence* is the fourth and highest level. This is where elite performers at the top level of the sport have the opportunity to receive specialist training from top coaches using the very best purpose-built facilities.

 Discuss

1. *Discuss how many of the group have been involved at performance level in one or more different sports, and find out which sport was the most popular.*

2. *Discuss how many people are still actively involved in that sport.*

Beth Tweddle is the most successful British gymnast and the first to win a major world title.

P1 ▸ The sports development continuum
continued

Purpose

The main purpose of the continuum is to show and allow progression. The gymnastics example shows how a very young participant can join an organised club and continue in the sport throughout their lifetime. Many gymnasts go on to practise, then compete and possibly even reach the excellence level, but they then go on to organise and coach others as their performing career draws to an end.

Appropriateness

It is important that sports are appropriate, and this is one of the ways in which they become successful. They must appeal to certain people for them to want to take part. For example, a rugby club would be more likely to launch an initiative to recruit young players rather than the 50+ age group, but a golf club would be very likely to target 50+ for their seniors section. Golf is played by many people well into their 50s, 60s and even 70s, but it is most unusual to find a rugby player participating beyond their 40s.

Specific **target groups** are often identified and whole, or parts, of communities are also considered to ensure that they are being included.

Cross-cutting agendas

These would be any initiatives which aim to cover some specific, identified areas of concern or priority. Examples of these would include pro-health, pro-education, anti-drug, anti-crime and **regeneration**. These are examples of cross-cutting agendas which have been introduced by the Sports Council in the past:

- *Sport for All* was the first in 1972 and was intended to encourage all members of the community to participate in sport.

- *Fifty Plus – All to Play For* targeted the specific age range of 50–60 in 1983.

- *Ever Thought of Sport?* was a campaign launched in 1985 aimed at the 13–24 age group to try to raise their levels of involvement in sport and this coincided with the International Year of the Youth.

Your assessment criteria:

P1 ▸ Describe three examples of the sports development continuum, from three different sports

M1 Compare and contrast three examples of the sports development continuum, from three different sports, identifying strengths and areas for improvement

🔑 **Key terms**

Regeneration: *to revive or produce something anew*

Target groups: *specific sections of the community which are identified as priorities*

Figure 6.1 'Sport for All' logo

M1 Compare and contrast examples of the continuum

Not all sports are dealt with equally in terms of sports development. This often depends on the profile which the sport has. A very popular sport such as football has a large amount of provision which will reflect the large numbers involved at the foundation, participation and performance levels. This is in contrast to a so-called 'minority sport' such as table tennis which involves far lower numbers. Recent figures indicate that football has 7 million participants, plus 5 million in schools compared with 120,000 for table tennis!

 Discuss

1. *What is likely to be the highest level participation sport in your particular area and what would be the main target group for it?*

2. *What provision is there in that sport for progressing to a level of excellence?*

? Did you know?

The fastest growing sport in the UK is women's football. Until comparatively recently, it was seen as a male only sport and was not often taught to girls in school. Participation levels of more traditional female sports such as netball are decreasing as a result of this.

Football is already a highly developed sport with large numbers of participants at the lower levels.

Describe barriers to participation

These come under several headings, but it must be remembered that they are possible **barriers** and are not to be considered as factors which will always have a negative effect.

Cultural

The particular culture an individual belongs to may have certain rules and traditions which can make taking part in sport more difficult. For example, in the Muslim community it may be inappropriate for young women to wear sports clothing as their culture dictates that their bodies should be covered up, or at least when in the presence of men. Religion may link to the **cultural** barrier as some cultures do not expect sport to take place at the same time as religious festivals or even on Sundays.

Social

The social barrier is increasingly being broken down and there is less distinction between social classes. However, some activities are still seen to be more suited to the upper social classes (for example, polo) and other activities more suited to the working social class (for example, football).

Some activities are considered to be more social in a different sense of the word as they involve more personal interaction and 'socialising'. Major team games such as football, hockey, netball and rugby fall into this category, whereas individual sports, such as gymnastics, are considered to be less appealing socially.

Economic

This is one of the major barriers as the cost of participating in some sports is much higher than others. This can include paying for the specialist equipment that is required, membership of a club (if necessary), transport costs, match fees and coaching/tuition. Joining a golf club and buying a full set of golf clubs is far more expensive than buying a pair of boots and shin pads for football.

Historical

In the past, certain sports were considered to be suited to either males or females. Until relatively recently, football was seen as a man's sport and netball as a women's sport, and participation reflected this.

History may be linked to culture. A particular community, or culture, may have a historic connection with a specific sport, for example, the West Indies or India with their links to cricket. Many of the old British

Your assessment criteria:

 Describe barriers to participation for individuals from three different target groups at different levels of the sports development continuum

🔑 Key terms

Barriers: *factors which prevent or make participation more difficult*

Cultural: *relating to a culture which is the shared beliefs, attitudes and behaviour of a particular community*

❓ Did you know?

Physical education is one of the few subjects which must be taught in school by law. It is a provision which every school must make because of the benefits it can bring for health and fitness.

Discuss

Discuss the different economic factors applicable to football and golf which could become barriers to participation.

Commonwealth countries historically played traditional British games such as cricket and rugby because these were the games their rulers brought with them.

Educational

Not all people receive the same level of education and the opportunities that this can bring in terms of sporting experiences. This may be due to a lack of facilities (a school without a swimming pool cannot offer swimming) or staffing (PE staff tend to concentrate on activities they favour and are experienced in).

Target groups

It is important for sports providers to target the following groups in society so that they can have greater access to sport and exercise.

Women

Many providers identify mothers with toddlers in this group because women who are mothers often find it difficult to participate in sport. One of the campaigns in the 1980s was *Milk in Action for Women* (1989) which encouraged women to take part in 'taster sessions' which were set up all over the country. The *Everyday Sport* campaign (2005) stated that 76 per cent of women were not carrying out the recommended level of physical activity, and as a result they have been targeting women to increase their participation in the run up to the 2012 Olympics.

Young people

Although young people have to take part in sport through physical education lessons in school, they do not always take part out of school, or continue once they have left. For this reason, they are targeted to keep up levels of exercise and activity.

BMEs

This stands for black and ethnic minority groups. The Race Discrimination Act (1975) put an end to racial prejudice, but BMEs have not always been totally integrated into all sports.

 Did you know?

Viv Anderson was the first black footballer to play for England in 1978, but in the 2010 England World Cup squad, over half of the team members were black.

Discuss

Why do you think young people are a target group? Why does there appear to be little involvement in sport outside school, and a drop off in involvement when young people leave school? Come up with some ideas which might help to change this.

Viv Anderson became the first black footballer to play for England in 1978.

P2 ▸ Target groups *continued*

50+

This is the upper age of the middle-age bracket, and it is seen as a time when many adults give up some of the more active sporting activities they have been involved in. They are targeted to encourage them to take up other activities which might not be quite so demanding, but which still have health benefits.

Disabled people

The many changes in the law have ensured that the disabled can access sporting facilities much more easily, and governing bodies do all they can to adapt their particular sport to the needs of the disabled. The Paralympic Games has also raised the profile of disabled people participating in sport, and in some cases, they compete on equal terms with the able-bodied.

M2 ▸ Explain barriers to participation

In order to effectively explain the barriers which exist, it is useful to look at some local and national examples. A local disabled group would be an interesting starting point as they would be able to provide details specifically relating to the social and economic barriers which are present at a local foundation level.

Case study

Gavin was involved in a serious car accident and as a result is now paralysed from the waist down and confined to a wheelchair. He was a keen and able basketball player prior to his accident, and wants to continue playing competitive sport. Gavin lives in a rural area, his nearest leisure centre is three miles away, but the nearest organised wheelchair club is 25 miles away in the nearest large town. As far as Gavin knows, there are only two other wheelchair athletes in his immediate area. Gavin has a standard wheelchair which he uses to get about, but he relies on his parents for transport as he does not yet have a disabled adapted vehicle to drive.

1. What are the main social barriers which Gavin is likely to come across?

2. What are the main economic barriers which Gavin might have to face?

3. What transport problems will Gavin have to overcome to fulfil his wish to play competitive basketball?

Your assessment criteria:

P2 Describe barriers to participation for individuals from three different target groups at different levels of the sports development continuum

M2 Explain barriers to participation for individuals from three different target groups at different levels of the sports development continuum

D1 Analyse the barriers to participation for individuals from three different target groups at different levels of the sports development continuum, providing effective and realistic solutions

Key terms

Paralympic Games: an international competition for athletes with disabilities

Wheelchair basketball is one of the most popular sports for athletes with disabilities.

D1 Analyse barriers to participation

One of the main aims of sports development is to overcome the barriers to participation by encouraging participation at all levels. A full analysis of the existing provision needs to be carried out before solutions can be identified. In the case of Gavin on page 120, there are several issues which would need to be considered. As the nearest organised disabled club is so far away, it would be worth finding out if the nearby leisure centre could help with some provision, such as a practice facility. Disabled access, parking and changing/toilet facilities would all have to be considered.

It may well be the case that raising awareness among sections of society could be a factor in relation to the target groups of disabled people and BMEs, and this could be tested out through debates and discussions.

 Discuss

In your group, discuss and identify a particular scenario relating to a local disabled sports performer. Find out what barriers they might be facing in order to come up with some possible realistic and effective solutions.

Research

Find out what provision exists in your local area for disabled sports performers. This may be general sport provision, or provision offered in a specific sport.

Key providers of sports development

The key providers are the organisations that have the main responsibility for sports development, those that have more general responsibilities, such as local authorities, and others that have very specific ones, such as national governing bodies. Knowing who these organisations are, and what contribution they make, is very important as is an awareness of the existing links between them.

P3 Providers

All key providers fall into one of the following categories.

National organisations

These include:

- Sport England (www.sportengland.org), formerly known as the Sports Council, is the body mainly responsible for the distribution of lottery funding whose main focus is 'the creation of a world-leading community sport system'.

- sports coach UK (www.sportscoachuk.org) supports the 46 national governing bodies of sport and the 49 county sports partnerships to recruit, develop and retain coaches to help achieve sports participation and performance goals.

- Youth Sport Trust (www.youthsporttrust.org) is an independent charity which was first established in 1994 to 'build a brighter future for young people through PE and sport'.

Local authorities

These are often referred to as local councils or local government. England is divided into nine regions which are then further divided into county, district and parish levels. They are all involved in sports development at some level. For example, a village cricket team (in a parish) might play in a district league which gives players of all standards the opportunity to play cricket. Through various youth teams, and links with local schools, younger players may progress to county trials. If a player lives in a local authority such as Hampshire, they may even play in the county team which would give them the opportunity to play first-class cricket at a venue such as The Rose Bowl in Hampshire.

The Rose Bowl in Hampshire is the home of the county cricket team and a test match venue.

Governing bodies

These bodies are responsible for individual sports and they exist at four levels:

- local

- regional

- national

- international.

The international governing body for rugby union is the IRB (International Rugby Board) and the national governing body is the RFU (Rugby Football Union). At regional level, there are 35 CBs (constituent bodies) and 1,900 rugby clubs at local level.

Voluntary organisations

There are many of these whose main aim is to offer sport, for example martial arts clubs and cheerleading groups. Others, such as the Scouts, Cub Scouts, Guides and youth clubs offer sporting experiences as part of their provision.

Private sector providers

These are clubs and organisations which are privately owned, but which make a provision for their members, for example golf clubs and gyms. A golf club is very keen to develop the standard of the golf played by their members so they have a 'club professional' to run coaching sessions. Gyms often link very closely to national initiatives, for example the 'GP referral scheme' where doctors 'prescribe' exercise for patients to help with weight loss and to increase exercise levels.

Professional providers

These are professional sports clubs which provide facilities and training, especially for youngsters.

Associated benefits

All of the above providers contribute to the associated benefits gained through this provision which include:

- improving performance

- providing opportunities

- encouraging healthy lifestyles

- contributing to the various cross-cutting agendas such as UK Sports Mission 2012, linked to the 2012 Olympics and other initiatives which may be launched.

? Did you know?

There are 150 separate sports registered and recognised in the UK and some of these sports have more than one national governing body regulating them. For example, the sport of bowls has nine NGBs, each one representing a different section of the sport.

? Did you know?

There are over 2,500 golf clubs in the UK, and approximately 1,900 of these are private members clubs. The most expensive ones charge visitors up to £150 for a round of golf!

P3 ▸ Structure

All providers have a basic **structure** for their organisation which enables them to deliver their provision, and which makes it clear to potential participants how the organisation works.

Committees

These are groups of people who are delegated certain jobs and functions in any organisation. They are usually led by a chairperson who has a secretary and treasurer to help them. There are often several sub-committees which have specific responsibilities for certain areas. One of the main committees in a sports club is the selection committee which chooses the teams and players for particular matches and fixtures. Sports clubs also have a disciplinary committee which deals with any inappropriate actions or behaviour.

Working groups

These are groups of people who work together until a specific goal is achieved, so they are not necessarily groups which stay together for a long period of time or permanently.

Forums

This is a form of open debate or discussion. There are many internet devices available which make setting up a forum very straightforward, so this is a rapidly developing area. An example is www.thefootballforum.net which was established in 2002 and has more than 25,000 members sharing opinions on matters such as 'referees and the law' and world football links.

Consultation groups

This is where a specific group is called together or consulted because they have a particular interest or contribution to make. For example, if a sports development was planned in a certain area, the residents would meet as a consultation group to provide their comments.

Roles

Within the wide area of sports development, there are many different **roles** available for both individuals and groups of people, including the following:

 Key terms

Role: something that is expected of a group or an individual

Structure: the way something is arranged or put together

? Did you know?

The organisers of the 2012 Olympic Games are recruiting just over 70,000 volunteers to help with the organisation of the event.

- Enabling and facilitating – this involves making sure that decisions which have been made are actually put into place (e.g. ensuring that planned facilities have opened).

- Direct delivery – this is carrying out the service that is being provided (e.g. a coach delivering coaching sessions).

- Strategic – this is involvement in the policies which are being formed and decided upon (e.g. a strategy would be chosen for a sporting contest situation).

- Operational – this is being part of the delivery team rather than part of the office-based administration of an organisation (e.g. a sports development officer running coaching or training courses for new or established players).

- Advisory – this involves people with specific skills or areas of knowledge who can give help and advice to other members of the team.

- Participation – this includes the people who were targeted and who are actually taking part.

- Volunteers – these are the people who work for no pay and they often make up the largest group within most organisations.

- Performance personnel – these are the people who are directly involved with the participants and they are usually known as sports development officers. There are three main categories of these: sports-specific, non-sports-specific and community officers.

? Did you know?

A sports development officer has many roles and responsibilities. This is the job description for a sports development officer:

- *to work with local communities to identify the need and demand for new activities*

- *to improve access to sport for young people, people with disabilities and people from disadvantaged communities*

- *to support the work of school sport partnerships*

- *to support community amateur sports clubs (CASCs)*

- *to organise national governing body (NGB) qualification courses*

- *to organise sport and physical activity events*

- *to support initiatives to reduce crime and rehabilitate offenders.*

The Beijing Olympics set the record for the number of volunteers at a games. There were 100,000 involved with direct services and 400,000 provided for information consultation.

Measuring quality in sports development

All organisations are regularly checked to make sure they are fulfilling their roles and providing what they claim. This is done through quality assurance which not only provides feedback on how well they are doing, but it also helps them to plan for improvement in the future.

Your assessment criteria:

P4 Explain two methods of measuring quality in sports development

P4 Explain methods of measuring quality

Methods

There are various methods which can be used to measure or gauge quality, such as benchmarks and quality schemes. Some companies offer quality schemes, for example:

- *Quest* – a UK quality scheme for sport and leisure which measures performance against 188 best practice principles and carries out a two-day external audit

- *Investors in People (IiP)* – a national standard developed by the Government in 1991 which provides a framework for improvement using four key principles of commitment, planning, action and evaluating outcomes

- *Customer Service Excellence* – the Government's national standard for excellence in customer service

- *Clubmark* – the national cross sports quality accreditation scheme for clubs with junior sections which has core criteria to ensure that clubs operate a set of consistent, accepted and adopted minimum operating standards (www.clubmark.org.uk).

If a provider does not choose to use agencies and schemes to measure quality, they can opt to carry out internal or self-assessment. This is where they come up with their own criteria to judge how well they are doing in achieving the quality of service they want to offer. If a provider chooses this method, they are likely to use some sort of external audit when an independent body is invited to check the findings they have made.

Some national governing bodies assist in this process with their own schemes. The Amateur Swimming Association (ASA) introduced a scheme called swim21 in 2002. This is an accredited scheme which is the ASA's 'quality mark', recognising clubs that are committed to providing

Key terms

Accreditation: a system of granting credit or recognition, often resulting in the attainment of an award

Audit: a thorough check or examination

Benchmark: a standard by which something can be measured or judged

safe, effective and quality services for the benefit of their members and which can receive Clubmark status.

Purpose of measuring

Measuring quality must be carried out for the following reasons:

- To measure improvement – every organisation has improvement as one of its main aims. Their goal should be to achieve continuous improvement over a period of time, such as improving levels of customer care and satisfaction.

- To achieve standardisation – when a standard has been successfully established, it must be regularly checked for it to be maintained.

Advantages of measuring quality

There are a number of advantages of measuring quality:

- To benchmark the quality which is being achieved – this is very closely linked to targets, and benchmarking is a good way of checking whether these targets have been met. For example, a sports developer may be aiming at a specific level of female participation which it can set as a benchmark level. This would be very easy to check and policies could be put in place to make sure that it is maintained.

- Accessing funds – many organisations receive funding depending on the results they achieve, so being able to prove that they are successful can affect the amount of funding they receive. This is particularly true of National Lottery funding as sports receive quantities of money related to how successful they are in international performance. Sport England has a small grants programme which can support community sports projects for any sum from £300 to £10,000, but the total project cost cannot exceed £50,000. In contrast, the sport of hockey has been granted an additional £1 million to enable both the men's and women's teams to prepare for the 2012 Olympic Games.

- Quality delivery – measuring is designed to ensure that quality delivery is maintained, so it effectively acts as a measuring device in the area of performance as this is the actual point of delivery for all sports.

- Recognition – all sports developers seek recognition that they are doing a good job and achieving their aims, so through measuring their success they are able to gain this recognition. The highest level of recognition is achievement at the highest level, especially if the sport is a competitive one. For sports where competition has a lower profile, it may be increased levels of participation which indicate success.

> **? Did you know?**
>
> *In December 2010, the funding for boxing, canoeing, gymnastics, hockey, rowing and taekwondo was increased, whereas the funding for badminton was decreased. The six sports were rewarded for strong performances in major international competitions, but badminton had a disappointing year.*

> **? Did you know?**
>
> *All major companies and organisations have Q & A departments (Quality Assurance) whose job it is to ensure that two priority principles are upheld. These are that products are 'fit for purpose' and that they are 'right first time' in terms of satisfying the needs of both customers and employees alike.*

P4 Explain methods of measuring quality
continued

Disadvantages of measuring quality

It is important to remember that the following are possible disadvantages and they might not all apply all of the time:

- Cost – measuring quality can be an expensive process, especially if an external body is brought in to carry out all or part of the process. These external companies are businesses in their own right who specialise in carrying out quality measurement, so even for a relatively small organisation the costs for this could run into thousands of pounds.

- Time – measuring quality is not a quick process and it is often something which is ongoing and takes up a lot of time.

- Expertise – a specialist skill or team is required to carry out the process and this expertise may not exist within the organisation. If this is the case, then there is an additional cost involved in paying for this service.

 M3 Evaluate methods of measuring quality

In order to evaluate the methods, you must consider the methods in detail and fully evaluate the purpose of the quality measurement. Once you have identified the advantages and disadvantages, you could recommend some action based on the detailed information from the evaluation.

Using one of the external quality schemes, such as Clubmark, will ensure that there is some actual data which can be used relating to a particular sports development (swim21, for example, which is accredited by Clubmark), and this should provide evidence relating to the purpose and whether or not it was achieved and met.

Your assessment criteria:

 P4 Explain two methods of measuring quality in sports development

M3 Evaluate two methods of measuring quality in sports development

Key terms

Expertise: special skill, knowledge or judgement

Research

The majority of schools have an Investors in People award displayed in their schools. Find out if your school has this award, and talk to the member of staff responsible for achieving it to find out more about its guidelines and requirements.

Did you know?

Swim21 states that the award is not just 'a badge of honour', but it is a planning tool based on long-term athlete development, enabling clubs to help athletes, teachers, coaches and administrators to achieve their full potential.

Case study

John has arranged a meeting with Rachel who is the local sports development officer. John has already found out that the local swimming club has swim21 accreditation and that the main leisure centre in the town, where Rachel is based, has an Investors in People award.

1. Which other methods of measuring quality is John likely to be able to find out about in his local area, and where should he go to find out about them?

2. Who is likely to be the best person to contact about the local swimming club's award?

3. What information does John need to get from Rachel in order to help him to carry out an evaluation?

? Did you know?

Clubmark specifically identifies 11 separate benefits that are gained through the award. These include:

• increased membership because parents are more confident due to the fact that child protection and equity are checked

• retaining membership due to the emphasis on boosting morale and giving full recognition for volunteers

• continuous improvement as it encourages more organised structures and systems to be in place

• funding as some agencies state that organisations must be Clubmark credited before they can be considered to receive funding.

These services and awards have a high profile and are therefore important to organisations.

Sports development in practice

It is through **initiatives** that sports development can happen. One of the biggest sporting initiatives in UK history is the 2012 Olympic Games, but there are a great many other initiatives currently underway and many more to come.

Your assessment criteria:

P5 Describe two different sports development initiatives

P5 Sports development initiatives

Some of these are related to a specific sport or activity, and others are linked to a specific event or organisation. Here are some important examples:

🔑 **Key terms**

Initiative: a beginning, first step or action

London 2012 Olympic Games and Paralympic Games

In July 2005, the 2012 Olympic Games were awarded to London and it is the single biggest sports development initiative. Whenever an Olympic Games is awarded, the Paralympic Games are included and these start soon after the main games have finished.

The costs involved in this project are staggering. The initial estimate for the stadium alone was originally £525 million and it increased by £22 million to £547 million. The aquatic centre where swimming events will take place, is estimated to cost £251 million and the velodrome where cycling events will be based, is estimated to be £105 million. The original overall budget for the games was set at £9.3 billion!

Awards for All

This is a National Lottery funded grants scheme which funds small local community-based projects in the UK. Awards can vary from £300 to £10,000 for many different aspects of acceptable projects, and further details can be checked on the official website (www.awardsforall.org.uk). Over £2.8 billion of funding has already been awarded, and the organisation has a helpline where advisors give help and guidance to potential bidders.

Big Lottery

This is the body which is responsible for awarding the funds raised by the National Lottery. The money is targeted to community groups and projects that improve health, education and the environment. Some

sports developments are eligible to receive money from this organisation as well as from Awards for All as they are two separate organisations.

Private sector programmes

These programmes involve any development which does not depend on public funds (such as those raised by taxation or the National Lottery), for example national companies or even individuals may be prepared to fund specific programmes.

Local programmes

These programmes involve fairly small local businesses or organisations that are prepared to put funds into local initiatives to benefit their local community. Sponsorship is one of the most common forms, where a local firm may supply kit for a local team in return for having advertising on it.

Providers

- Local authority sports development – local authorities have a responsibility for sports development, and sports development officers are usually responsible for this. Providing facilities is one of the major responsibilities for local authorities.

- Governing body sports development – each of the individual governing bodies has their own developments in place at all levels of the sport. These are specific to each individual sport, and often take the form of help with equipment, such as outdoor basketball boards and hoops.

- Voluntary clubs – there are literally thousands of these within the UK and all of them have a target of developing their sport. This is especially true of the junior sections as they guarantee the future members of the clubs. The clubs have to fund themselves, so the more people who get involved, the more revenue they can raise to develop their sport for the good of all their members.

- Partnerships – very few providers work solely on their own as they form partnerships with other interested groups. For example, small local voluntary clubs are usually members of the national governing body, and liaise with their local sports development officer as well.

Areas of work

Sports development targets particular areas. One of the most important is target groups (see page 119), and the other is sport-specific. Targeting groups may not be about one specific sport, but about developing an involvement with sport in general.

(see page 119)

? Did you know?

Since it was first launched in 1994, the National Lottery has raised over £25 billion for 'good causes' and it is contributing a total of £2.175 billion towards the 2012 Olympic Games and Paralympic Games. Over £7450 million of this was from sales at 'designated games' which were targeted to raise money for the Olympics in particular.

Discuss

In your group, discuss how many voluntary clubs exist in your local area.

Q Research

Research how many members there are in these voluntary clubs.

P5 ▶ Sports development initiatives *continued*

Location

Location is one of the most important factors in sports development, and it has various related factors:

- Population – this is the number of people close enough to be involved. **Urban** areas may have greater numbers, but **rural** areas may be more difficult to cater for.

- Access – this may simply be access to facilities (such as disabled access), or may relate to transport issues such as how easy it is to get to a development.

- Cost – locating a development can be very expensive in some central urban areas.

Effectiveness

This factor is linked to measuring quality, as any sports development must prove itself to be effective if it is to continue to exist and be further developed.

🔑 Key terms

Rural: *related to or located in the country*

Urban: *related to or located in a town or city*

M4 ▶ Identify strengths and areas for improvement

In order to compare and contrast, and identify particular strengths and areas for improvement, it is important to choose two very different types of sports development.

For example, the 2012 Olympic Games are a major sports development initiative and the largest one the UK has ever been involved in. This could be compared and contrasted with a much smaller scale local initiative which has far lower levels of funding, fewer provider partnerships and a very specific target group.

The main site for the 2012 Olympic stadium was chosen as an area which could be developed relatively cheaply.

🔍 Research

Choose a particular sports development which is a recent initiative. Research and describe the following:

- *the providers associated with it*

- *the particular areas of work it is associated with*

- *the exact location (or locations if there are more than one)*

- *the overall effectiveness of the initiative.*

Case study

Amy lives in Weymouth in Dorset which will be the venue for the 2012 Olympic and Paralympic sailing competitions. She also knows about a local bowls club which received lottery funding to improve their changing rooms. Amy has chosen to use these for her comparison as they are both local developments.

1. Do you think Amy has made a wise choice? Why?

2. Where is the funding for the Olympic sailing competition likely to have come from?

3. Which funding agency is the local bowls club likely to have used?

4. Which do you think is the most significant development for Amy's area? Why?

Discuss

1. *In your group, discuss where the major sports facilities are located in your own particular area. This should include both indoor and outdoor facilities, and all the categories of providers listed.*

2. *Choose one of the facilities you identified and consider how accessible it is, both in terms of the transport links which enable access, and the access to the facilities themselves, particularly from a disabled athlete's perspective.*

D2 ▶ Make recommendations for improvement

In order to offer recommendations for improvement, you must first analyse two different initiatives. Choosing two quite different ones will make this task easier. You must consider the ways in which the quality is measured in these two initiatives as this should highlight particular areas where improvements and strengths are identified through the checking process.

Case study

Andrei decides to carry out a SWOT analysis of the 2012 Olympics and the local cricket club. Andrei lives in East London, not far from the Olympic stadium site. The cricket club has obtained some funds from both Awards for All and Big Lottery, and has an identified target group for development of junior players.

1. Which of the two groups is Andrei likely to be able to find out the most background information on?

2. Which of the two groups is likely to have the greatest amount of information on the measurement of quality?

3. Why do you think the cricket club has identified juniors as the particular target group they are aiming their initiative at?

4. Is the fact that Andrei lives near the Olympic stadium site likely to be of any advantage to him when he is gathering information?

? Did you know?

The most expensive facility to provide is a swimming pool. This is not just due to the cost of the building, but to the high maintenance and running costs. There is no pool in the UK which makes money, and the cost of keeping one pool open for a year is the same as the cost of building a sports hall!

Assessment checklist

To achieve a pass grade, my portfolio of evidence must show that I can:

Assessment Criteria	Description	✓
P1	Describe three examples of the sports development continuum, from three different sports.	☐
P2	Describe barriers to participation for individuals from three different target groups at different levels of the sports development continuum.	☐
P3	Describe the structures and roles of three sports development providers in the UK.	☐
P4	Explain two methods of measuring quality in sports development.	☐
P5	Describe two different sports development initiatives.	☐

To achieve a merit grade, my portfolio of evidence must show that I can:

Assessment Criteria	Description	✓
M1	Compare and contrast three examples of the sports development continuum from three different sports, identifying strengths and areas for improvement.	☐
M2	Explain barriers to participation for individuals from three different target groups at different levels of the sports development continuum.	☐
M3	Evaluate two methods of measuring quality in sports development.	☐
M4	Compare and contrast two different sports development initiatives, identifying strengths and areas for improvement.	☐

To achieve a distinction grade, my portfolio of evidence must show that I can:

Assessment Criteria	Description	✓
D1	Analyse the barriers to participation for individuals from three different target groups at different levels of the sports development continuum, providing effective and realistic solutions.	☐
D2	Analyse two different sports development initiatives, offering realistic recommendations for improvement.	☐

7 | Fitness testing for sport and exercise

LO1 Know a range of laboratory-based and field-based fitness tests

▶ Sports people can select from a wide variety of fitness tests to check a person's fitness level. Each test can be used to test a specific component of fitness.

▶ Every fitness test has advantages and disadvantages. You need to look at the results that you get and interpret what they mean. Some tests have accuracy problems or may just test motivation rather than fitness, unless both the athlete and tester follow procedures carefully.

LO3 Be able to administer appropriate fitness tests

▶ Fitness tests must be carefully thought through. The tests that are appropriate for a sport will be determined by the important components of fitness in that sport. The preparation for a bank of tests, and the order that the tests are conducted in could influence the results. In choosing which tests to use, reliability, validity and practicality should be considered.

▶ Fitness testing can have problems. Tests should be explained so that the person being tested knows what the test involves. The subject in each test needs to be monitored to ensure their safety. They may need to withdraw or be withdrawn for safety reasons. At the end of a test the results should be recorded and checked.

LO2 Be able to use health screening techniques

▶ Health screening is important in a range of occupations. Health promotion officers, fitness trainers, and occupational health workers often use health screening to determine a person's risk level before they exercise or start a new job. Screening procedures require the use of a range of interpersonal skills and a number of checks.

▶ There are five main health monitoring tests that are often used for screening purposes: heart rate, blood pressure, lung function, waist-to-hip ratio and body mass index.

LO4 Be able to interpret the results of fitness tests and provide feedback

▶ Every test has been designed for a specific group, for example elite athletes or 16 to 19-year-old sports students. There are a range of published tables that show clearly how your results can compare to these groups.

▶ At the end of an organised fitness test, it is important to give feedback to the person who has been tested, identifying their strengths and weaknesses. You should also provide recommendations for future training.

Fitness testing methods

Fitness testing is used in a variety of professions. Fitness professionals often use tests to assess the effectiveness of a personal training programme and to assist in the setting of targets. Sports professionals also use testing for a variety of different reasons. A football team may test a player to analyse their risk of injury and to determine if they are fit enough to play for the first team. Athletes use testing to check that their training is effective (for example, sprint times can be monitored to see if a power training programme has had any effect on performance).

There are a number of fitness tests that can be used. Each test examines a specific component of fitness. For example, the sit and reach test tests hamstring flexibility. Fitness testing must be planned carefully. Some tests have potential dangers as they push a person to their maximum level of performance. It is very easy to influence the results of a test by changing the method, timing and order of a test. Fitness testing is only reliable if the exact testing procedure is carried out. The results also need to be interpreted carefully because a person's motivation level can often affect the score.

P1 ▶ Fitness tests and their advantages and disadvantages

There are a number of tests that can be used to assess a person's performance and ability. Each test has a variety of advantages and disadvantages which must be taken into account when deciding which tests to use.

Flexibility

The sit and reach test is often used in sport. This test is designed to test lower back and hamstring flexibility. To carry out the test, a person removes their shoes and places their feet flat against a sit and reach board with their legs straight. They reach forward and push their fingers slowly along the board as far as possible, holding the position for one to two seconds (without bouncing). The distance from finger tips to feet (usually point 0 on the sit and reach board) is then measured. Three trials should be attempted with the best score recorded.

If a sit and reach board is not available, a table and ruler can be used.

Advantages: the sit and reach test is easy and quick to perform. It requires very little equipment and is therefore simple and portable. Most people can perform a sit and reach test.

Disadvantages: differences in arm, leg and trunk length can make comparisons difficult. The test measures the flexibility of the lower back and hamstrings, but there is no way to determine which muscle group's flexibility has changed. No warm-up should be done before the test. Any amount of activity before the test can influence the result.

 Did you know?

You can be born with short hamstrings.

 Did you know?

Women tend to be more flexible than men.

Practical

Complete the sit and reach test and identify your level of flexibility against normative data.

Figure 7.1 Normative data for the sit and reach test: national norms for 16–19-year-olds. (Source: Davis, B. et al, *Physical Education and the Study of Sport*, 2000)

Gender	Excellent	Above average	Average	Below average	Poor
Male	>14	11–14	7–10	4–6	<4
Female	>15	12–15	7–11	4–6	<4

Hamstring flexibility is important in a range of sports. Footballers must undergo a sit and reach assessment and medical before they change clubs and sign a new contract. This helps determine whether a player is fit to play and helps to identify future training needs. Tight hamstrings can cause postural problems as they will pull the pelvis out of its normal position. Pressure in your lower back can cause pressure on your sciatic nerve, causing the hamstrings to tighten. This can increase the chance of a muscle rupturing during an activity.

 Discuss

1. *Discuss and compare your level of flexibility with other people in your class.*

2. *Work out who has the best flexibility in your class, and try to determine whether this is due to natural ability or the effects of training and/or lifestyle.*

P1 Fitness tests and their advantages and disadvantages *continued*

Strength

There are a number of methods for testing strength. These include the use of a variety of 1 RM (rep max) lifts (the maximum amount of weight that can be lifted once) and grip **dynamometer** tests. Each test assesses specific muscle groups.

The grip dynamometer test assesses an athlete's grip strength. To carry out the test, the athlete holds the dynamometer with a straight arm over their head. They squeeze the dynamometer and gradually bring it down to waist level. The test should be repeated three times and the highest score recorded.

Advantages: the test is portable and simple to use. The results are reliable assuming technique and rest is taken into account.

Disadvantages: the test is a poor measure of general strength as it only measures forearm strength. The

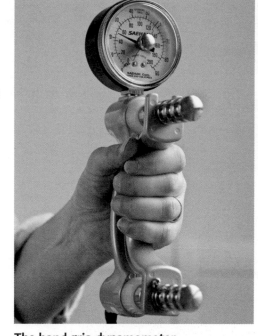

The hand grip dynamometer

dynamometer needs to be adjusted to hand size and the adjustment can affect the accuracy of the scores produced.

Key terms

Dynamometer: a device to measure force

Did you know?

The current world record for the deadlift was set in 2010 by Andy Bolton at 457.5kg.

Practical

Examine the grip strength test. Calculate your grip strength.

Figure 7.2 Normative data for the grip strength test: national norms for 16–19-year-olds. (Source: Davis, B. et al, *Physical Education and the Study of Sport*, 2000)

Gender	Excellent	Good	Average	Fair	Poor
Male	>56	51–56	45–50	39–44	<39
Female	>36	31–36	25–30	19–24	<19

Research

Compare your scores to relevant tables for your age or level of experience.

MSF test

The **MSF test** (multi-stage fitness test) monitors an athlete's maximum oxygen uptake. A distance of 20 metres is measured on an athletics track and marked with cones. The athlete can warm up and stretch prior to the test starting. Athletes line up at the start of the test and then run for as long as possible in time with the beeps. If the athlete arrives at the end of a shuttle before the beep, they must wait for the beep before continuing to run. The athlete runs until they cannot keep up with the prescribed speed. They then either drop out voluntarily, or the tester withdraws them from the test after three shuttles. The level and shuttle that the athlete reaches is recorded.

A person completing the multi-stage fitness test is given a level and VO2 max score. VO2 max is the maximum amount of oxygen in millilitres that can be used by working muscles in one minute per kilogram of body weight. People who have a high level of aerobic fitness have high VO2 max scores.

The multi-stage fitness test

Advantages: the test is portable and can be conducted both indoors and outdoors. It is suitable for testing team sports such as football and basketball. The test is reliable if people are motivated to work to their maximum ability.

Disadvantages: the test is carried out to exhaustion and can cause problems for some people. It gives a prediction, not absolute scores. The test is not as accurate for sports that do not involve running with a change of direction.

Key terms

MSF test: multi-stage fitness test (also known as the bleep test)

? Did you know?

The highest ever recorded VO2 max was by two cross-country skiers at 94ml/kg/min for men and 77ml/kg/min for women.

Practical

Complete the multi-stage fitness test.

Research

Research the recommended levels that athletes should achieve in two different sports, and compare your scores with these levels.

Figure 7.3 Normative data for the VO2 max test. (Source: *The Physical Fitness Specialist Certification Manual,* **The Cooper Institute for Aerobics Research, Dallas TX, revised 1997, printed in** *Advance Fitness Assessment & Exercise Prescription,* **3rd Edition, Vivian H. Heyward, 1998, page 48)**

Female (values in ml/kg/min)						
Age	Very poor	Poor	Fair	Good	Excellent	Superior
13–19	<25.0	25.0–30.9	31.0–34.9	35.0–38.9	39.0–41.9	>41.9
20–29	<23.6	23.6–28.9	29.0–32.9	33.0–36.9	37.0–41.0	>41.0
30–39	<22.8	22.8–26.9	27.0–31.4	31.5–35.6	35.7–40.0	>40.0
40–49	<21.0	21.0–24.4	24.5–28.9	29.0–32.8	32.9–36.9	>36.9
50–59	<20.2	20.2–22.7	22.8–26.9	27.0–31.4	31.5–35.7	>35.7
60+	<17.5	17.5–20.1	20.2–24.4	24.5–30.2	30.3–31.4	>31.4
Male (values in ml/kg/min)						
Age	Very poor	Poor	Fair	Good	Excellent	Superior
13–19	<35.0	35.0–38.3	38.4–45.1	45.2–50.9	51.0–55.9	>55.9
20–29	<33.0	33.0–36.4	36.5–42.4	42.5–46.4	46.5–52.4	>52.4
30–39	<31.5	31.5–35.4	35.5–40.9	41.0–44.9	45.0–49.4	>49.4
40–49	<30.2	30.2–33.5	33.6–38.9	39.0–43.7	43.8–48.0	>48.0
50–59	<26.1	26.1–30.9	31.0–35.7	35.8–40.9	41.0–45.3	>45.3
60+	<20.5	20.5–26.0	26.1–32.2	32.3–36.4	36.5–44.2	>44.2

Figure 7.4 Normative data for the VO2 max test (Source: Leger, L. A. & Lambert, J., 'A maximal multistage 20m shuttle run test to predict VO2 max', *European Journal of Applied Physiology,* Vol. 49, pages 1–5)

Multi-stage fitness test levels								
Level	Shuttle	VO2 max	Level	Shuttle	VO2 max	Level	Shuttle	VO2 max
4	2	26.8	5	2	30.2	6	2	33.6
4	4	27.6	5	4	31.0	6	4	34.3
4	6	28.3	5	6	31.8	6	6	35.0
4	9	29.5	5	9	32.9	6	8	35.7
						6	10	36.4
Level	Shuttle	VO2 max	Level	Shuttle	VO2 max	Level	Shuttle	VO2 max
7	2	37.1	8	2	40.5	9	2	43.9
7	4	37.8	8	4	41.1	9	4	44.5
7	6	38.5	8	6	41.8	9	6	45.2
7	8	39.2	8	8	42.4	9	8	45.8
7	10	39.9	8	11	43.3	9	11	46.8
Level	Shuttle	VO2 max	Level	Shuttle	VO2 max	Level	Shuttle	VO2 max
10	2	47.4	11	2	50.8	12	2	54.3
10	4	48.0	11	4	51.4	12	4	54.8
10	6	48.7	11	6	51.9	12	6	55.4

Level	Shuttle	VO2 max	Level	Shuttle	VO2 max	Level	Shuttle	VO2 max
10	8	49.3	11	8	52.5	12	8	56.0
10	11	50.2	11	10	53.1	12	10	56.5
			11	12	53.7	12	12	57.1

Level	Shuttle	VO2 max	Level	Shuttle	VO2 max	Level	Shuttle	VO2 max
13	2	57.6	14	2	61.1	**15**	**2**	**64.6**
13	4	58.2	14	4	61.7	15	4	65.1
13	6	58.7	14	6	62.2	15	6	65.6
13	8	59.3	14	8	62.7	15	8	66.2
13	10	59.8	14	10	63.2	15	10	66.7
13	13	60.6	14	13	64.0	15	13	67.5

Level	Shuttle	VO2 max	Level	Shuttle	VO2 max	Level	Shuttle	VO2 max
16	2	68.0	17	2	71.4	18	2	74.8
16	4	68.5	17	4	71.9	18	4	75.3
16	6	69.0	17	6	72.4	18	6	75.8
16	8	69.5	17	8	72.9	18	8	76.2
16	10	69.9	17	10	73.4	18	10	76.7
16	12	70.5	17	12	73.9	18	12	77.2
16	14	70.9	17	14	74.4	18	15	77.9

Level	Shuttle	VO2 max	Level	Shuttle	VO2 max	Level	Shuttle	VO2 max
19	2	78.3	20	2	81.8	21	2	85.2
19	4	78.8	20	4	82.2	21	4	85.6
19	6	79.2	20	6	82.6	21	6	86.1
19	8	79.7	20	8	83.0	21	8	86.5
19	10	80.2	20	10	83.5	21	10	86.9
19	12	80.6	20	12	83.9	21	12	87.4
19	15	81.3	20	14	84.3	21	14	87.8
			20	16	84.8	21	16	88.2

P1 Fitness tests and their advantages and disadvantages *continued*

Your assessment criteria:

P1 Describe one test for each component of physical fitness, including advantages and disadvantages

Speed

There are a various tests of speed and sprinting ability. One of the easiest to conduct is the 30-metre acceleration test. A distance of 30 metres is measured on an athletics track. The test is conducted from a standing start or from starting blocks. The athlete has three attempts to sprint with a full recovery between each attempt. Their best score is used to determine their ability.

? Did you know?

Usain Bolt can run 30 metres in 3.76 seconds.

Figure 7.5 Normative data for the 30 metre test: national norms for 16–19-year-olds. (Source: Davis, B. et al, *Physical Education and the Study of Sport*, 2000)

Gender	Excellent	Above average	Average	Below average	Poor
Male	<4.0	4.2–4.0	4.4–4.3	4.6–4.5	>4.6
Female	<4.5	4.6–4.5	4.8–4.7	5.0–4.9	>5.0

Advantages: the test is designed to measure sprinting ability and can be used for any sport that contains aspects of sprinting. It can be conducted both inside and outside and requires very little equipment.

Disadvantages: the results are dependent on the accuracy of the timing. Hand timing can produce errors. The results can also be influenced by wind speed and direction and other weather conditions.

Figure 7.6 Normative data for the Sargent jump test. (Source: Davis, B. et al, *Physical Education and the Study of Sport*, 2000)

National norms for 16–19-year-olds					
Gender	Excellent	Above average	Average	Below average	Poor
Male	>65cm	50–65cm	40–49cm	30–39cm	<30cm
Female	>58cm	47–58cm	36–46cm	26–35cm	<26cm
National norms for adults					
Gender	Excellent	Above average	Average	Below average	Poor
Male	>65cm	60m	55cm	50cm	<46cm
Female	>55cm	50cm	45cm	40cm	<36cm

Power

A good test of **power** is the Sargent jump. It tests an athlete's elastic leg strength. The athlete stands sideways onto a wall and then marks the point that their finger tips can reach on the wall, keeping both feet on the ground. They then squat and jump as high as possible and mark the wall. Marking can be done with chalk or from visual observation using a Sargent jump board. The athlete's initial reach height is then deducted from their jump height.

Advantages: the test is easy to conduct and accurate as long as the tester monitors jump and reach heights. The test can be used for sports that contain aspects of a vertical jump such as basketball.

Disadvantages: the test can be influenced through jumping technique. Athletes who are not involved in jumping may improve through practice. The results can be affected by the amount of warm-up or activity prior to the test being conducted.

Key terms

Power: a combination of speed and strength

? Did you know?

The world record vertical jump is 61 inches (155cm) by Kadour Ziani.

Practical

1. *Calculate the power that you can produce using the following equation:*

   peak power (W) = 61.9 x VJ (cm) + 36.0 x mass (kg) + 1822

2. *Compare your scores with other people in your class, and determine who can produce the highest peak power.*

Case study

Paul is a 20-year-old basketball player who plays for a local team. He has recently approached you with a request to test his power and jump height. Paul would like to improve his ability to slam dunk the basketball and reach extra height on his lay-ups.

You have managed successfully to test Paul and he has produced a score of 40cm. You have arranged to retest Paul on a regular basis, and provide him with training recommendations to help him achieve his goal.

1. How does 40cm compare with normative data?

2. Are there any factors that may affect the results when regularly testing Paul to see if there has been any improvement?

3. What training recommendations would you make to ensure that Paul can reach his target?

4. Are there any factors in a lay-up or slam dunk that Paul could benefit from practising?

P1 Fitness tests and their advantages and disadvantages *continued*

Muscular endurance

Muscular endurance can be tested on a range of muscle groups. Two tests that are often used are the *press up test* and *sit up test*.

The muscle groups used in a press up are the triceps and pectorals. The deltoids may also contribute to the exercise.

The press up test can be conducted in two ways, using either full or modified press ups. The athlete performs the test to exhaustion. The athlete lies on a mat with hands shoulder width apart and their arms fully extended. They lower their body until their elbows reach 90 degrees and then fully extend their arms. The press ups must be continuous with no rest. If an athlete pauses, the test is concluded.

? Did you know?

The world record for non-stop press ups stands at 10,507 by Minoru Yoshida from Japan (October 1980).

? Did you know?

The main muscles used in a press up are the pectoralis major, the anterior deltoid and the tricpes brachii.

Full body press ups

? Did you know?

You can train to improve your press up scores either by performing push ups with knees bent on the floor, completing full body press ups or by elevating your feet while having a partner hold a weight on your back.

? Did you know?

Press ups can be performed in a number of ways: slow press ups, pulses, clap press ups and single-arm press ups.

Advantages: the test is accurate and easy to complete anywhere.

Disadvantages: some athletes with weak upper body strength may struggle to complete the test. The test is also influenced by a person's motivation.

Figure 7.7 Normative data for the full body press up test. (Source: McArdle, B. D. et al, *Essentials of Exercise Physiology***, 2000)**

Age	Excellent	Good	Average	Fair	Poor
20–29	>54	45–54	35–44	20–34	<20
30–39	>44	35–44	25–34	15–24	<15
40–49	>39	30–39	20–29	12–19	<12
50–59	>34	25–34	15–24	8–14	<8
60+	>29	20–29	10–19	5–9	<5

Figure 7.8 Normative data for the modified press up test for females. (Source: McArdle, B. D. et al, *Essentials of Exercise Physiology***, 2000)**

Age	Excellent	Good	Average	Fair	Poor
20–29	>48	34–38	17–33	6–16	<6
30–39	>39	25–39	12–24	4–11	<4
40–49	>34	20–34	8–19	3–7	<3
50–59	>29	15–29	6–14	2–5	<2
60+	>19	5–19	3–4	1–2	<1

The muscle groups used in a sit up are the abdominals and hip flexors.

The sit up test monitors an athlete's abdominal endurance. The athlete lies flat on a mat with their knees bent and their feet flat on the floor. They must fold their arms across their chest during the test. Upon a signal from the tester, the athlete has 30 seconds to perform as many sit ups as possible, lifting up to 90 degrees and then lowering down until their back touches the floor.

Advantages: the test is simple to conduct and only requires a mat and stop watch.

Disadvantages: the test is dependent on the motivation of the athlete.

Figure 7.9 Normative data for the sit up test: national norms for 16–19-year-olds. (Source: Davis, B. et al, *Physical Education and the Study of Sport***, 2000)**

Gender	Excellent	Above average	Average	Below average	Poor
Male	>30	26–30	20–25	17–19	<17
Female	>25	21–25	15–20	9–14	<9

P1 Fitness tests and their advantages and disadvantages *continued*

Body composition

This can be measured in a variety of ways including the use of skinfold callipers, bioelectrical impedance and hydrodensitometry. Skinfold callipers determine the amount of fat that a person has. There are various different calliper tests. The simplest is often taken from four skinfold sites. The test is conducted using a set of plastic or metal skinfold callipers. Skinfolds on the right side of the body are measured to the nearest millimetre. To measure the skinfold, the index finger and thumb are used to pick the fold and the callipers are applied 1cm from the fingers.

There are four skinfold measurement sites:

- triceps (taken with a relaxed arm by the side of the body, the skinfold should be a vertical fold midway between the shoulder and the elbow)

- biceps (taken with a relaxed arm, the skinfold should be between the elbow and the top of the shoulder)

- subscapular (a diagonal fold below the shoulder blade and across the back)

- sacroiliac (a diagonal fold just above the hip bone).

The four measurements are added together and compared with an appropriate chart. The average body fat percentage for men is between 15 per cent and 17 per cent and for women between 18 per cent and 22 per cent. Elite athletes have lower levels of body fat with scores of 6 per cent to 12 per cent for men and 12 per cent to 20 per cent for women.

Advantages: this is an accurate measurement of body fat that is quick to complete.

Disadvantages: the test is uncomfortable and some people find it distressing. There are problems testing between genders. The results are dependent on the skill of the tester and the accuracy of the skinfold measurements.

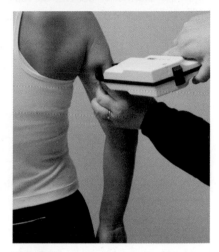

Triceps

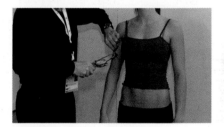

Biceps

Subscapular

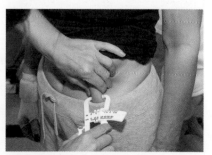

Sacroiliac

 Research

Research recommended body fat percentage in a variety of sports. Use the information you have found to identify the sport in which athletes tend to have the lowest body fat percentage.

Discuss

Athletes often have very low body fat levels. Are athletes that have a low body fat percentage healthy?

Figure 7.10 Body fat percentage versus skin fold thickness data. (Source: adapted from www.harpendencalipers.co.uk/lookup-tables-for-the-4-site-system.html)

Skinfold thickness	Male Age					Female Age				
	17–19	20–29	30–39	40–49	50+	17–19	20–29	30–39	40–49	50+
10mm	0.41	0.04	5.05	3.30	2.63	5.34	4.88	8.72	11.71	12.88
12mm	2.46	2.1	6.86	5.61	5.20	7.60	7.27	10.85	13.81	15.10
14mm	4.21	3.85	8.40	7.58	7.39	9.53	9.30	12.68	15.59	16.99
16mm	5.74	5.38	9.74	9.31	9.31	11.21	11.08	14.27	17.15	18.65
18mm	7.10	6.74	10.93	10.84	11.02	12.71	12.66	15.68	18.54	20.11
20mm	8.32	7.96	12.00	12.22	12.55	14.05	14.08	16.95	19.78	21.44
22mm	9.43	9.07	12.98	13.47	13.95	15.28	15.36	18.10	20.92	22.64
24mm	10.45	10.09	13.87	14.62	15.23	16.40	16.57	19.16	21.95	23.74
26mm	11.39	11.03	14.69	15.68	16.42	17.44	17.67	20.14	22.91	24.76
28mm	12.26	11.91	15.46	16.67	17.53	18.40	18.69	21.05	23.80	25.71
30mm	13.07	12.73	16.17	17.60	18.56	19.30	19.64	21.90	24.64	26.59
32mm	13.84	13.49	16.84	18.47	19.53	20.15	20.54	22.70	25.42	27.42
34mm	14.56	14.22	17.47	19.28	20.44	20.95	21.39	23.45	26.16	28.21
36mm	15.25	14.90	18.07	20.06	21.31	21.71	22.19	24.16	26.85	28.95
38mm	15.89	15.55	18.63	20.79	22.13	22.42	22.95	24.84	27.51	29.65
40mm	16.51	16.17	19.17	21.49	22.92	23.10	23.67	25.48	28.14	30.32
42mm	17.10	16.76	19.69	22.16	23.66	23.76	24.36	26.09	28.74	30.96
44mm	17.66	17.32	20.18	22.80	24.38	24.38	25.02	26.68	29.32	31.57
46mm	18.20	17.86	20.65	23.41	25.06	24.97	25.65	27.24	29.87	32.15
48mm	18.71	18.37	21.10	24.00	25.72	25.54	26.26	27.78	30.39	32.71
50mm	19.21	18.87	21.53	24.56	26.35	26.09	26.84	28.30	30.90	33.25
52mm	19.69	19.35	21.95	25.10	26.96	26.62	27.40	28.79	31.39	33.77
54mm	20.15	19.81	22.35	25.63	27.55	27.13	27.94	29.27	31.86	34.27
56mm	20.59	20.26	20.73	26.13	28.11	27.63	28. 7	29.74	32.31	34.75
58mm	21.02	20.69	23.11	26.62	28.66	28.10	28.97	30.19	32.75	35.22
60mm	21.44	21.11	23.47	27.09	29.20	28.57	29.46	30.62	33.17	35.67
62mm	21.84	21.51	23.82	27.55	29.71	29.01	29.94	31.04	33.58	36.11
64mm	22.23	21.90	24.16	28.00	30.21	29.45	30.40	31.45	33.98	36.53
66mm	22.61	22.28	24.49	28.43	30.70	29.87	30.84	31.84	34.37	36.95
68mm	22.98	22.65	24.81	28.85	31.17	30.28	31.28	32.23	34.75	37.35
70mm	23.34	23.01	25.13	29.26	31.63	30.67	31.70	32.60	35.11	37.74
72mm	23.69	23.36	25.43	29.66	32.07	31.06	32.11	32.97	35.47	38.12
74mm	24.03	23.70	25.73	30.04	32.51	31.44	32.51	33.32	35.82	38.49
76mm	24.36	24.03	26.01	30.42	32.93	31.81	32.91	33.67	36.15	38.85
78mm	24.68	24.36	26.30	30.79	33.35	32.17	33.29	34.00	36.48	39.20
80mm	25.00	24.67	26.57	31.15	33.75	32.52	33.66	34.33	36.81	39.54

M1 Explain advantages and disadvantages

Sit and reach test (flexibility)

Advantages: the test is easy to complete and can be undertaken using a variety of methods. A sit and reach box can be used, or simply a bench and ruler if a box is not available. The test is simple to conduct.

Disadvantages: the sit and reach test is affected by temperature. Any warm-up can alter the scores achieved. Performance can also be influenced by the length of limbs.

Grip dynamometer test (strength)

Advantages: the equipment is small and portable, suitable for testing anywhere and requires very little space. The test only takes a small amount of time. Although the test is a measure of strength, it is not difficult to perform.

Disadvantages: the **validity** of the test has been questioned as a measure of strength. The test only measures forearm strength and does not measure strength in other areas. The dynamometer must be adjusted to hand size and this is difficult to achieve accurately for people who are new to testing. The adjustment may affect the results achieved. There is also a difference in scores between dominant and non-dominant hands.

Key terms

Validity: being an accurate test for the purpose it was designed for

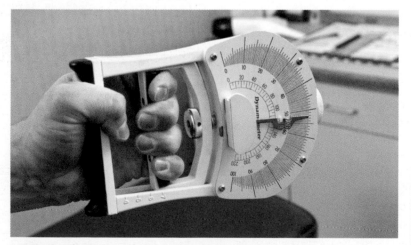

A grip dynamometer with adjustment

Multi-stage fitness test (maximum oxygen uptake)

Advantages: the correlation to VO2 max scores is high. If the test is conducted with motivated subjects, the results are accurate.

? Did you know?

The dominant hand is usually 10 per cent stronger than the non-dominant hand.

? Did you know?

Handgrip dynamometer scores can vary by 0.1kg due to the reliability of the meter itself.

Disadvantages: the test is suitable for sports teams, but may be a problem for people with cardiovascular problems. The results can be influenced by a number of factors. An athlete's running and turning technique can improve with practice. The motivation of people conducting the test may be influenced by either an audience or the number of people performing the test at a relevant level. Scores can be affected by temperature, the testing surface and the clothing that an athlete wears during testing. The environment and weather can influence scores if the test is conducted outside.

Press up and sit up tests (muscular endurance)

Advantages: both tests are easy to carry out, can be completed anywhere and require very little space. The equipment is portable and can be transported easily. Each test can be an accurate indicator of muscular endurance performance if the procedures are followed accurately and the subject is motivated.

Disadvantages: upper body strength may be a problem in completing the press up test. For full press ups, an athlete needs to be able to lift almost 75 per cent of their body weight for each push up. A person's motivation and tolerance to lactic acid can influence how far they can push themselves in both tests. Scores can improve because of improvements in technique rather than fitness levels.

Sargent jump (power)

Advantages: the test is simple to perform and can be completed anywhere. Specialist equipment is not required. The results are easy to calculate.

Disadvantages: technique can play a significant part in the score an athlete achieves. During repeated testing, technique will improve. Factors such as explosive use of the legs from a squatting position, movement of the shoulders in the jump and the position of the arms can alter the score. Temperature also affects score levels as muscles work and contract better when they are warm.

? | Did you know?

Power can be estimated in the Sargent jump by using the following formula:

Peak power (W) = 61.9 x VJ (cm) + 36.0 x mass (kg) = 1822

? | Did you know?

A heavy person has to do more work than a light person when jumping the same height as they have a larger mass to move.

🏃 | Practical

1. *Complete the Sargent jump and calculate your power level.*

2. *Compare your results with other people in your class.*

Describe

1. *Describe the advantages and disadvantages of fitness tests.*

2. *Order the fitness tests described above from the easiest to administer to the most difficult. Explain your order.*

Health screening techniques

Health screening ensures that a check has been completed to identify any risk factors that a person may have before they exercise. There has been a gradual increase in the membership of sports clubs and gyms. People of all ages train, however risk increases with age. It is important to identify risk to ensure that people can exercise safely. Training programmes may need to be amended to take into account a person's specific health problems.

Your assessment criteria:

P2 Prepare an appropriate health screening questionnaire

P3 Devise and use appropriate health screening procedures for two contrasting individuals

P2 Health screening procedures

Health screening questionnaire

Fitness professionals providing exercise equipment and testing should conduct pre-participation health screening of everyone regardless of age. A detailed health questionnaire is useful to assess a person's risk of disease. This should include a history of symptoms, recent illness, lifestyle habits, exercise history and family history of heart disease. A useful questionnaire to use is the Par-Q1. This was revised in 1998 and is a safe pre-exercise screening measure for people who take part in low to moderate exercise.

People should also be evaluated for coronary heart disease risk including family history of a heart attack; sudden death before 55 years of age (father) or 65 years (mother); cigarette smoking (current or stopped in the last six months); hypertension (BP >140 systolic pressure/>90mm hg diastolic pressure); obesity (body mass index >30kg/m²); waist girth >100cm; sedentary lifestyle, i.e. not participating in regular exercise programmes or meeting minimal activity recommended levels.

Medical referral

Once screening has been completed, risk levels are assessed and the number of risks identified. The American College of Sports Medicine recommends that risk should fall into three categories:

- *low risk:* men of less than 45 years and women of more than 55 years of age who meet no more than one risk factor
- *moderate risk:* men of less than 45 years and women of more than 55 years of age or those who meet two or more risk factors
- *high risk:* individuals with one or more signs or symptoms of known cardiovascular, pulmonary or metabolic disease including diabetes mellitus.

Key terms

Diastolic pressure: the lowest arterial pressure as the ventricles of the heart relax and fill with blood

Systolic pressure: the highest arterial pressure as the left ventricle of the heart contracts

A medical examination is not needed for low risk categories or those at moderate risk, training at a moderate intensity of 40 per cent to 60 per cent VO2 max.

A medical examination is recommended for high risk individuals and those at moderate risk, exercising at 60 per cent or higher VO2 max.

P3 Health screening issues

Client consultation

During any consultation, it is important to develop a good relationship and show discretion. You should ask questions and listen to the responses that are given. You may be able to explore and pose additional questions from the answers that you receive. The consultation should be a relaxed and professional discussion. A person's body language and tone of voice will provide indications of how you are making them feel.

Client confidentiality

The information you obtain from your client is very personal and should be treated sensitively. It is your responsibility to ensure that records are only viewed by yourself, the client and your assessor. The information should be kept securely and should not be discussed outside the consultation process.

Informed consent

Each person to be tested must provide informed consent before they take part. This consent means that they have been notified of the tests and risks involved and have declared any medical information that may be a problem. The client must sign a declaration that states they understand the testing method, know what is required and provide their consent to take part. A client must know that they can ask questions about a test and withdraw their consent from the test at any time. The form should be signed by the individual to be tested (and their parent or guardian if under 18), the person conducting the testing and a witness.

 Design

Prepare a health screening questionnaire that you could use.

 Reflect

Use your health screening questionnaire to evaluate the health of two contrasting individuals. The contrast can be male and female, or from distinctly different groups such as 16 to 19-year-olds and adults.

Administering fitness tests

Health monitoring tests

There are a range of tests that are used to monitor health, including heart rate, blood pressure, lung function, waist-to-hip ratio and BMI. They are usually quick tests that can be used to identify potential health problems that a person may have.

Heart rate

A person's resting heart rate is an indicator of their fitness level. The test is conducted by placing two fingers either on the radial or carotid arteries and feeling the pulse of the heart beating. The pulse is recorded for 15 seconds and multiplied by four.

Key terms

BMI *(body mass index):* a measure of body composition to determine if a person is overweight

Lung function: the efficiency of your lungs in delivering gas through inspiration and expiration

Figure 7.11 Resting heart rate scores

Resting heart rate			
Male			
Age	Poor	Reasonable	Excellent
20–29	85+	84–61	<60
30–39	85+	84–63	<62
40–49	89+	87–65	<64
50+	89+	87–67	<67
Female			
Age	Poor	Reasonable	Excellent
20–29	95+	94–72	<72
30–39	97+	96–72	<72
40–49	99+	98–74	<74
50+	103+	102–76	<76

Blood pressure

Blood pressure is measured using a digital monitor on the arm or wrist (arm monitors are more accurate). When blood pressure is measured, the client must be relaxed. Factors such as stress, anxiety, exercise, alcohol, smoking and a full bladder can affect the scores. Blood pressure should not be measured just after eating and caffeine should be avoided for at least 30 minutes before the test is due to take place. The test should be

Did you know?

In checking blood pressure it is useful to take readings at the same time of day. Results will then be consistent.

conducted in a quiet place with the subject seated (feet flat on the floor) for five minutes prior to the test.

The cuff should be placed on the upper arm, 2cm above the crease in the elbow. The cuff should be tight, but not too tight, so that you can push a finger inside. The arm should be rested at the height of the heart. The monitor is turned on to inflate the cuff and the cuff tightens. The display gives both the systolic and diastolic scores. Readings can vary, so the test should be repeated three times and the results averaged.

- *Normal blood pressure is (120 systolic/80 diastolic):* this is the ideal blood pressure for people wishing to have good health and they will have a lower risk of heart disease or stroke. If the score is above 120/80mmHg, it should be lowered.

- *Blood pressure level of 135/85mmHg:* a person is twice as likely to have a heart attack or stroke as someone with a reading of (115/75). The lower level can be achieved through weight loss and aerobic exercise.

- *Blood pressure level of 140/90mmHg or above, but below 160/100mmHg:* the risk from mild high blood pressure is small, but some people with blood pressure in this range are advised to take medication to lower it. This can include people with diabetes, coronary heart disease and heart or kidney damage.

- *Blood pressure of 160/100mmHg or above:* all people with a blood pressure that is sustained at this level are usually given medication to lower it.

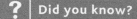

? Did you know?

There are a variety of blood pressure machines available that can check different areas. However, finger monitors do not give accurate readings, and wrist monitors are less reliable than upper arm monitors.

? Did you know?

There can be a difference between the readings on each arm. Use the monitor to check both left and right arms to start with, then recheck whichever arm gives the higher reading.

🏃 Practical

1. Measure the blood pressure of a member of your class.

2. Compare the scores with normative data.

3. Provide advice or recommendations that may help improve a person's blood pressure scores.

🏃 Practical

1. Measure the resting pulse of a member of your class.

2. Compare the scores with normative data.

3. Provide recommendations to your client to help them improve their scores in the future.

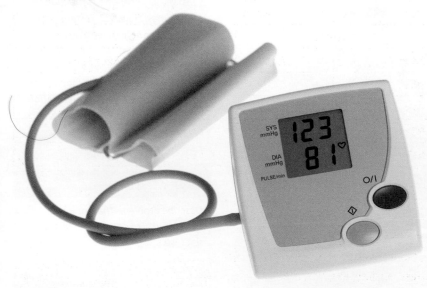

A blood pressure monitor

P4 Health monitoring tests *continued*

Lung function

A lung function test can assist in the diagnosis of asthma and monitors the efficiency of the lungs. The client starts with a full inspiration and is then requested to blow as hard and fast as they can until their lungs are empty. Three trials should be performed. The spirometer records forced vital capacity (the total volume of air that is expired) and **FEV1** or forced expiratory volume in 1 second (the total volume of air expired in 1 second).

Normal spirometry results are 75% of vital capacity after 1 second, 94% after 2 seconds and 97% after 3 seconds. FEV1 scores can be used to check if there is an obstruction from asthma or other lung diseases.

Figure 7.12 FEV1 scores

<40% – severe obstruction
40%–59% – moderate obstruction
65% –79% – mild obstruction

There are a number of irritants that can cause problems to a person's lung function. These include tobacco smoke, strong odours, air pollutants, chemicals, dust, gases or aerosols. Allergens can also cause a problem with breathing, for example mould, animal hair, house dust mites and pollen.

A spirometer

Key terms

FEV1: *total lung volume expired in 1 second*

? Did you know?

Many doctors and nurses use peak flow measurements as part of asthma care.

? Did you know?

Asthma results in approximately 127,000 hospital admissions every year.

? Did you know?

Regular exercise does not substantially change the function of the lungs. However, testing lung function can help determine if an athlete has an undiagnosed asthma problem. This can then be treated by a doctor who can prescribe medication to dilate the bronchi. The medication can improve performance in the person being treated.

Describe

Describe problems that may be associated with conducting health risk tests.

Waist-to-hip ratio

This is a simple test to predict health risks linked to excessive abdominal fat. It is often used to help predict strokes, diabetes and CHD. It is measured by recording hip circumference at its widest point and waist circumference at its narrowest point (the belly button or just above). The ratio is calculated using the following equation:

$$WHR = \frac{\text{waist cm}}{\text{hip cm}}$$

Men are at risk if their ratio is above 0.95 and women are at risk with a ratio over 0.8.

Body mass index (BMI)

This test is used to determine whether a person is overweight. It is an estimate and does not take into account body composition (such as muscle). The test is easy to conduct. A person's height is compared with their weight using a BMI chart. Examples of BMI charts can be found online, for example, at www.lowfatdietplan.org

 Discuss

1. *Discuss which health screening test provides the best indicator of health risk.*

2. *Discuss why body fat percentage may be a better indicator of health risk than BMI.*

Key terms

CHD: coronary heart disease

 Practical

1. *Complete each health screening test and evaluate your own health risks. This will enable you to practise each of the tests and become familiar with the information you need to use.*

2. *Conduct health screening tests on two contrasting individuals. You should use the same individuals that were assessed using your health screening questionnaires.*

Providing feedback

You need to divide your client's results into two sections, strengths and areas for improvement, as shown in the example below. Strengths are scores that indicate there is no risk, and areas for improvement are scores in which the client demonstrates a risk factor. The feedback you provide should be drawn from both the test results and your questionnaire.

Figure 7.14 Example of client feedback

Strengths	Areas for improvement
Blood pressure 122 systolic/83 diastolic Result – normal, no risk	BMI – weight = 95.5kg, height = 172cm Result – BMI = 32, obese Increased risk of CHD/stroke/diabetes
Lung function FEV1 = 80% vital capacity after 1 second Result – normal, no risk	Waist-to-hip ratio Waist = 90cm, hip = 75cm Result – WHR = 1.2 Risk of CHD/diabetes/stroke
	Resting heart rate 20-year-old male Pulse = 87 Result – poor
	Sedentary lifestyle
	Smokes currently 15 per day
	Previous calf injury which still causes some discomfort

Your assessment criteria:

M2 Describe the strengths and areas for improvement for two contrasting individuals using information from health screening questionnaires and health monitoring tests

D1 Evaluate the health screening questionnaires and health monitoring test results and provide recommendations for lifestyle improvement

Reflect

1. Reflect on the comments provided in your health screening questionnaire.

2. Reflect on your client's fitness test scores. Identify which tests they have scored well in and which tests are regarded as a weakness.

Discuss

Discuss your client's category or level of risk and any potential problems that need to be taken into account if they undertake fitness testing or training. Are there any recommendations that you can make that could improve their health?

D1 Evaluation and recommendations

You must be able to evaluate the responses provided in the health screening questionnaires and the results of health screening tests. A lifestyle improvement should be recommended for each weakness. Some of the information provided in Unit 4 Fitness training and programming will help you to provide many of the recommendations required.

In the example in M2, the client needs to improve their BMI and waist-to-hip ratio scores. They must undertake cardiovascular exercise to burn up additional calories. This will enable general weight loss, resulting in an improvement in both scores and a gradual reduction of risk. Cardiovascular training will also result in a gradual reduction of the client's resting heart rate. The client may still have a problem with their previous calf injury. The cardiovascular training could focus on cycling or rowing rather than running, to reduce the force that is exerted on the calf so that it is not placed under excessive strain. Recommendations for a gradual reduction in smoking could also be provided.

 ## Case study

Mandeep is a 35-year-old hockey player who has played socially for a number of years. She used to play for fun and to improve her performance, but recently her emphasis on training has changed. Mandeep has become increasingly concerned about her lifestyle and long-term health and now wants to use hockey to improve her health.

Mandeep has asked you to assess her health and to identify any areas that require improvement. She has produced the following results from tests:

- blood pressure – 140/80
- BMI – 29
- waist-to-hip ratio – 1.3
- resting pulse – 95.

1. Identify Mandeep's risk for each of the tests.

2. Provide recommendations for future training.

3. As this is the first time you have met Mandeep, do you think her blood pressure score can be accurate?

4. Is hockey a good sport to play to improve your health?

 Discuss

Discuss the results of the fitness tests with your client. Do they have any lifestyle factors that can explain the strengths they have? Can they explain why they have underperformed in some tests?

Research

Research recommendations that could be used to improve each specific component of fitness. A useful organisation to check for current guidelines is ACSM. (See also Unit 4 Fitness training and programming for recommendations for each component of fitness.)

P5 Administration of fitness tests

Your assessment criteria:

P5 Select and safely administer six different fitness tests for a selected individual, recording the findings

M3 Justify the selection of fitness tests commenting on suitability, reliability, validity and practicality

You should be able to select and prepare six different fitness tests. The selection of tests must be related to the components of fitness of the sport that your client is involved in. For example, in testing a rugby player, you may decide to test the following six components of fitness:

- cardiovascular fitness – to measure your client's ability to run over 80 minutes

- power – to monitor jumping ability in the lineout

- flexibility – to determine the risk of injury to the hamstrings

- speed – to measure ability to sprint to get the ball

- body fat percentage – to monitor excess weight as this may hamper performance

- strength – to monitor the ability of grip enabling your client to rip the ball off someone or pull them back in a tackle.

You also need to think about the purpose of testing. Are you testing so that you can set a specific programme for your client? Are you providing a benchmark to measure improvements? Is the purpose to educate your client about fitness in their sport?

Once you have selected the tests that you intend to carry out, you must plan the sequence that they will be conducted in. The order that the tests are carried out in can affect the results of some tests. Some tests are affected by a warm-up (such as flexibility, blood pressure and resting heart rate). Strength and muscular endurance tests must have sufficient rest periods to enable recovery between tests. Exhaustive tests such as the multi-stage fitness test should be either completed at the end of a session or on another day.

In administering the tests, there are several steps that you must follow:

- Your client must complete an informed consent form.

- You must set up and carefully check the equipment you are going to use.

- You must fully explain and demonstrate each test before your client is tested.

- You must monitor your client's health and safety during each test and if there are any signs of risk to their health, the test should be terminated.

- You should record results upon completion of the test.

Describe

Describe six components of fitness, and why they are important to your sport.

Reflect

Identify the six tests that you could use to assess the components of fitness.

When you select fitness tests, consider all of the components of fitness in the sport of your choice. Rate the components of fitness to determine the ones that are of greater importance. The top six will be the ones that you should then test. You may need to think about a certain position in the sport, for example in football each player may have a slightly different profile (wingers are different from goalkeepers).

It is beneficial if you can set up all of the fitness tests in advance. This will save your client time, and will also make it easier for you to plan and progress through the bank of tests that you have chosen.

Discuss

Discuss problems of validity with tests that you have chosen. For example, the multi-stage fitness test may not be as relevant to swimmers as it is to team sport players.

Practical

Plan the layout of your tests. Where will each one be placed to ensure a smooth transition between tests?

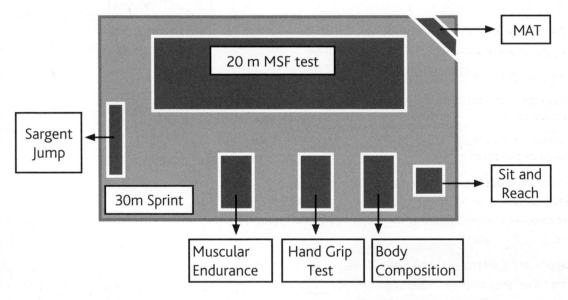

Figure 7.15 This layout enables you to set up and then concentrate on explaining, demonstrating and conducting the tests. However, the 30m sprint test crosses the shuttle run test, so these two tests obviously cannot be conducted at the same time.

M3 Selection of appropriate fitness tests

You must think about the suitability, reliability, validity and practicality of the tests that you have selected. A fitness test is suitable if it monitors the component of fitness that you have chosen to analyse. A test is valid if it assesses the fitness component in a suitable environment. It is best to assess rugby players' aerobic fitness on the pitch they play on rather than in a sports hall. Swimmers' aerobic fitness should ideally be assessed in a pool. This may not make the test very practical though, so there are compromises that you may have to make. The compromises, however, may affect the reliability of the test.

Key terms

Practicality: being easy to follow with the available facilities

Reliability: producing results that are repeatable

Suitability: relating to the component of fitness in the relevant sport

P6 Comparison with normative data

Once the tests are completed, each of the scores needs to be compared to normative data. These are published tables that determine how a person has performed in the relevant test. Some tables are designed for a particular age group or sports performance level. It is important that you compare your client to data that is relevant to them.

You should be able to provide your client with a description of how they have performed in each test (for example, good, below average, etc.). The feedback that you give to your client can be verbal or written and should include an explanation of why the tests were chosen and what the results mean.

M4 Identify strengths and areas for improvement

Feedback should ideally be divided into two areas: strengths and weaknesses. You should focus on the strengths first so that the client receives some positive feedback. You should consider the weaknesses towards the end of the meeting so that areas for improvement can be identified and discussed.

Your assessment criteria:

P6 Give feedback to a selected individual, following fitness testing, describing the test results and interpreting their levels of fitness against normative data

M4 Compare the fitness test results to normative data and identify strengths and areas for improvement

D2 Analyse the fitness test results and provide recommendations for appropriate future activities or training

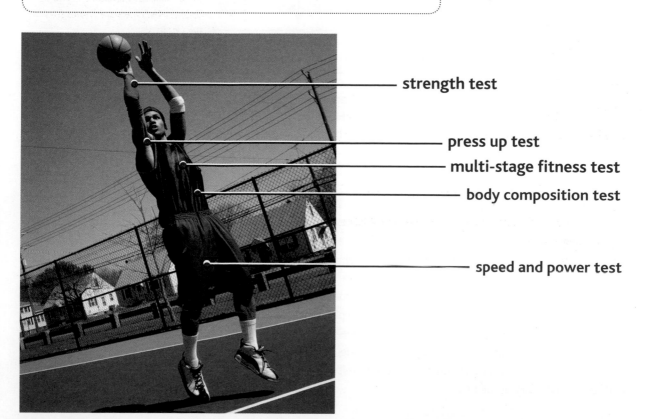

strength test

press up test

multi-stage fitness test

body composition test

speed and power test

D2 Provide recommendations

Recommendations should be provided at the end of a feedback and review meeting. If your client has performed exceptionally well in a test, the recommendation may be to maintain their current training. However, in tests where your client has performed below an excellent level, you should make a recommendation for additional training. The recommendations must focus on training in the appropriate fitness component. See Unit 4 Fitness training and programming for information on recommendations.

 ## Case study

John is 17 years old and regularly plays for a local football team as a goalkeeper. He has been trying to improve his fitness recently as he knows there is a scout due to watch a game in the near future.

John has asked you to check his level of fitness and provide him with recommendations that he can use to enhance his training.

John's weight is 80 kg and his height 175cm.

John has completed a range of tests and produced the following results:

Sargent jump = 40cm

30m sprint = 4.3 seconds

MSF test = 9.2

body fat percentage = 19%

muscular endurance press up test = 45

hand grip test = 42kg/f.

1. Assess each score and determine John's fitness rating.

2. Provide recommendations for each test (see Unit 4 Fitness training and programming, page 64).

 ### Practical

1. Select six appropriate fitness tests for a client of your choice.

2. Identify the purpose of the assessment.

3. Identify the fitness test sequence.

4. Explain the validity, suitability, reliability and practicality of the tests you have chosen.

5. Arrange a suitable time with your client and conduct the fitness tests.

6. Record the results.

7. Provide feedback and future recommendations.

Research

1. Research the American College of Sports Medicine's guidelines for weight loss.

2. Research strength development.

3. Identify how long it will take to increase the size of a muscle through strength and power training.

 ### Discuss

Discuss how long it may take for John to reduce his body fat percentage.

Assessment checklist

To achieve a pass grade, my portfolio of evidence must show that I can:

Assessment Criteria	Description	✓
P1	Describe one test for each component of physical fitness, including advantages and disadvantages.	☐
P2	Prepare an appropriate health screening questionnaire.	☐
P3	Devise and use appropriate health screening procedures for two contrasting individuals.	☐
P4	Safely administer and interpret the results of four different health monitoring tests for two contrasting individuals.	☐
P5	Select and safely administer six different fitness tests for a selected individual, recording the findings.	☐
P6	Give feedback to a selected individual, following fitness testing, describing the test results and interpreting their levels of fitness against normative data.	☐

To achieve a merit grade, my portfolio of evidence must show that I can:

Assessment Criteria	Description	✓
M1	Explain the advantages and disadvantages of one fitness test for each component of physical fitness.	☐
M2	Describe the strengths and areas for improvement for two contrasting individuals using information from health screening questionnaires and health monitoring tests.	☐
M3	Justify the selection of fitness tests commenting on suitability, reliability, validity and practicality.	☐
M4	Compare the fitness test results to normative data and identify strengths and areas for improvement.	☐

To achieve a distinction grade, my portfolio of evidence must show that I can:

Assessment Criteria	Description	✓
D1	Evaluate the health screening questionnaires and health monitoring test results and provide recommendations for lifestyle improvement.	☐
D2	Analyse the fitness test results and provide recommendations for appropriate future activities or training.	☐

8 | Practical team sports

LO1 Know the skills, techniques and tactics required in selected team sports

- There are a variety of team sports that can be selected.
- Some sports have specific skills which are only used in that sport.
- The techniques required for each sport vary, and many are particularly suited to that sport.

LO2 Know the rules and regulations of selected team sports

- There are rules, or laws, in place for all sports.
- Specific regulations provide an additional level of organisation for sports.
- There are rules and regulations which relate to specific situations.

LO3 Be able to assess own performance in selected team sports

▶ A starting point for assessment is carrying out a self-analysis.

▶ There are various assessment methods which can be used to assess performance.

▶ The overall aim should be to achieve significant personal development.

LO4 Be able to assess the performance of teams in selected team sports

▶ A performance analysis of a selected team has to be initially carried out.

▶ There are different assessment methods which can be used to assess performance.

▶ Finally, the various options should be considered, and suggestions made for future development.

Skills, techniques and tactics of selected team sports

To be successful in a team sport, a performer must be familiar with all the basic essentials to play effectively. Developing the necessary knowledge and understanding makes for a more effective performer.

P1 Skills, techniques and tactics of two team sports

Team sports

There is a great deal of common ground in many team sports. Transferable **skills** are skills which are learnt or developed in one team sport, and which are valuable and used in another.

The team sports to choose from are: association football; basketball; cricket; hockey; netball; rugby union; rugby league; rounders; volleyball; lacrosse; adapted team sports such as wheelchair rugby, wheelchair basketball and goalball.

Skills and techniques

Once the two sports have been chosen, it is important to specifically identify the skills and **techniques** associated with them. The following skills and techniques are required to perform effectively in various team sports: passing; throwing; receiving; catching; shooting; movement; turning; intercepting; tackling; footwork; marking; dodging and creating space.

Tackling, including physical contact, is allowed in hockey.

168

Figure 8.1 Examples of skills and techniques for two different team sports

Team sport	Passing	Receiving	Shooting	Tackling	Marking
Basketball	Basic passes include chest pass, bounce pass and overhead pass. All require the ball to be passed by the hands.	The hands have to be used to receive (catch) the ball and the body must be in the correct position to receive it.	Different techniques are used for different distances from the basket. This can include skills such as the lay-up or set shot.	This must be discouraged as no physical contact is allowed.	As there are only five players in each team, this is usually 'man-to-man' or zonal marking.
Hockey	All passes have to be made using a hockey stick. Different techniques of striking the ball can be used (such as a hit, push, etc.) and they can be over short or long distances.	The ball can only be received using the stick, and only one side of the stick can be used. It is important that the body is in the correct position to receive the ball.	There are specific rules about where shots can be taken from. Any type of hit with the stick is allowed, distance from the goal is a factor. This is a sport which has a goalkeeper.	Tackling another player with the ball is allowed, but there are specific rules that govern which techniques can be used.	There are eleven players in each team so there may be man-to-man or zonal marking.

Tactics

The following **tactics** are relevant to selected sports: **offence**/attacking; defence; setplays; team formations; movement; communication and phases of play. In the examples of basketball and hockey, all of these tactics apply, but in cricket setplays do not apply.

Key terms

Offence: where a team, or player, is attacking

Tactics: the choices made in the selection of a skill or method of play

Discuss

Discuss the skills and techniques listed on page 168. which do not appear in Figure 8.1, and compare them in the sports of basketball and hockey.

No physical contact is allowed in basketball.

P3 Demonstrate skills, techniques and tactics in two team sports

To perform effectively in different sports, a performer must be able to use skills, techniques and tactics, and select the appropriate ones at the right time. They must also be appropriate to the sport. For example, tackling techniques are completely different in rugby and football, and if you perform a slide tackle in rugby, you are likely to be sent off!

Making use of a range of skills (especially the core skills) and tactics is important as these have to be adapted to particular game situations. In football, only the goalkeeper is allowed to handle the ball, so they must focus on handling skills. However, in rugby the ball has to be passed using the hands, so all team members must learn and master ball handling skills. Kicking the ball is allowed in both games, but it is a more complex skill in rugby due to the oval shape of the ball which makes accurate kicking far more difficult. This is why penalty kicking and place kicking is left to a selected specialist player in a rugby team.

Team skills in the sports of rugby and football are also significantly different. In football the teams are divided up into defence, midfield and attack, and various formations can be used for the 11 players in the team, taking into account that the goalkeeper is a specialist position. Even though there are more players (15) in rugby union, the team is considered to be composed of two units, forwards and backs, and there are certain situations within games when they must line up as such. This includes all scrums and lineouts, and the laws of the game dictate that the forwards must be in the scrum with the backs in position behind them.

In these two sports, tactics are quite different as the majority of football tactics are based on the formation the team adopts on the pitch. The formation is not an option in rugby.

M1 Explain skills, techniques and tactics in two team sports

In order to explain the skills, techniques and tactics, it is important to refer carefully to the different sports as there is a lot of variation between them. For example, a lay-up shot in basketball can only be performed in a particular area of the court, and there are restrictions imposed by the rules on dribbling to consider here. The skills required are a combination of dribbling and jumping just before the shot is released. This involves starting the move at an appropriate distance from the basket in order to be close enough to release the ball when the final phase of the shot is made.

Similarly, zone defence is a form of defensive formation which can be described in detail, and a diagram can be used to show where the five players are positioned on the court. The roles of each of these players can then be described.

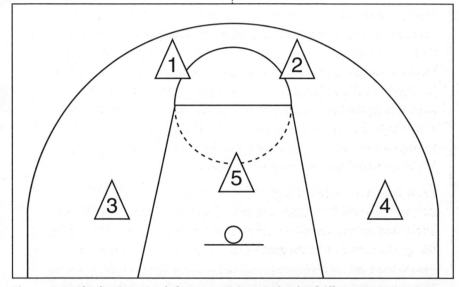

Figure 8.2 The basic zone defence positions in basketball

 Case study

Alex has chosen football and rugby as the two team sports to demonstrate his skills, techniques and tactics. He plays in goal at football and considers that this concentration on ball handling skills, and the fact that he has to kick the ball often means that he can use some common skills and techniques in the two sports.

1. Do you think it is sensible to choose two team games which are likely to have common skills and techniques?

2. Would you agree with Alex that these are common skills which he identified?

3. What would be the main differences between the two sports which Alex might not have considered?

4. Are there likely to be any tactics which could be used in both of these sports?

Describe

Explain how the players in the diagram would be placed for a particular attacking or defensive situation or setplay.

Design

Choose a team sport and draw a diagram of the pitch or court with all of the identified players on it.

Rules and regulations of selected team sports

It is not possible, or sensible, to take part in any team sport without knowing the **rules** and **regulations**. Being aware of them will make you a better and more effective player.

Rules and regulations exist in all team sports.

P2 Rules and regulations of two team sports

Rules (also known as laws in some sports) are produced by the governing body of the sport, and they must be enforced. There are also unwritten rules (known as **etiquette**) which must be followed. For example, it is a rule of football that all players must wear shin pads, but it is good etiquette to kick the ball out of play when an opponent is injured to allow them to be treated. Not wearing shin pads would mean that the referee would not allow you to play, but not kicking the ball out would not get you into trouble with the officials, but it might upset the opposition!

Football officials enforce the rule regarding studs on boots being safe for play.

There are regulations in sport which refer to the following:

The players

Each sport has a set number of players, and there are additional rules for replacements and substitutions.

Your assessment criteria:

P2 Describe the rules and regulations of two different team sports and apply them to three different situations for each sport

Key terms

Etiquette: the unwritten rules or conventions of any activity

Regulations: regulations relate to the greater detail about the field of play, size, game times, and equipment used, for example the size of the trampoline or how long a sequence should be

Rules: rules relate to general playing or performing of a sport, for example a routine should stop immediately if there is contact with the matting around a trampoline or the main structure

Officials

The number of officials varies with different sports and at different levels. For example, most tennis matches would just have an umpire, but at the top level there are line judges and a net cord judge which could mean an additional seven officials being on court.

Spectators

Most regulations relate to safety of the spectators, but there are also regulations which concern their behaviour. At junior level football, teams are responsible for the spectators' behaviour towards the officials, especially in terms of unacceptable comments which might be made.

Facilities

The facility provision for each sport is regulated very strictly in terms of what must be provided, for example acceptable lighting levels, changing facilities, disabled access and car parking.

Equipment

Each sport sets out the equipment which must or may be used. For example, in cricket any protective equipment is optional at senior level, but there are guidelines on the size and materials used for cricket bats.

Playing surface

For indoor sports there may be options in terms of the materials used for the surface, but for outdoor sports the condition of the surface is regulated. The marking out of the surface has regulations as well.

Health and safety

Health and safety regulations apply in many areas of life, but they must be very strictly applied to sporting situations. Each facility has to be licensed under health and safety regulations.

Child protection

This can apply to young people actively involved in the sport itself or as spectators.

? Did you know?

In 1979, Australian fast bowler Dennis Lillee went out to bat against England with an aluminium bat! There were no rules against this at the time. The first ball Lillee hit went for three runs, but his captain thought it should have gone for four, so instructed Lillee to replace it with a wooden one. In the meantime, the England captain had complained to the umpires that the bat was damaging the ball. There was a ten-minute delay, Lillee threw the bat away in a fit of temper, and within months the rules of the game had been changed to only allow wooden bats.

P2 ▶ Rules and regulations of two team sports *continued*

Insurance

All sporting situations must be fully covered by insurance as there is always the likelihood of accidents or injuries occurring.

Administration

Regulations are in place to make sure that all sports, and clubs in particular, are administered correctly and that no illegal activities take place.

Scoring systems

These vary greatly. Tennis has a scoring system of love, 15, 30, 40 and game, and rugby union has five points for a try, two for a conversion and three for a penalty or drop goal. Football and netball have goals with a value of one, but in basketball you can score two points or three depending on how far out you are when you shoot. Each sport has its own unique system.

Situations

In any team sport there are situations which players must be aware of, for example a player in an illegal position (the offside rule occurs in many games); player injuries (play continues while a player is treated on the pitch in rugby, but play is stopped in football); the ball being out of play (the line is out of play in rugby, but the ball must cross the line in football) and illegal challenges (contact is allowed in rugby and football, but not in basketball and netball). Each sport has its own particular interpretation of these.

Your assessment criteria:

P2 Describe the rules and regulations of two different team sports, and apply them to three different situations for each sport

M2 Explain the application of the rules and regulations, of two different team sports, in three different situations for each sport

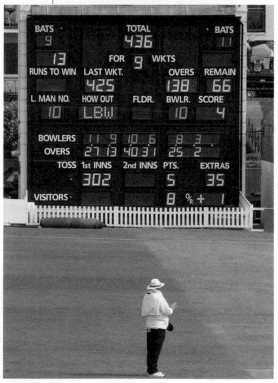

The scoring system for cricket is quite complex as shown on this scoreboard.

? | Did you know?

The ball out of play rules and regulations varies with different sports. If the ball touches the try line in rugby, it is deemed to be in, so a ball touched down on that line is a try. However, in football the ball has to cross the line to be in another area, so the ball has to cross the goal line for a goal to be awarded. If the ball touches the boundary in cricket, then it is deemed to have crossed it for either a four or six, so this is similar to the rugby rules.

M2 ► Explain the application of rules and regulations

All sports performers must be aware of the rules and regulations before they take part in a team sport. However, it is the officials in charge who are responsible for ensuring that performers adhere to these once a game is underway. For example, a hockey player, rugby player or footballer will be aware of the offside rule in their sport and try to stay onside, but it is the official who will apply the rule and make the decision.

Practical

1. *Observe an official taking charge of a game situation and consider the ways in which they apply the rules to particular situations.*

2. *Write a brief report as if you were the official's assessor, and comment on how well they apply the rules and regulations in your opinion.*

Did you know?

Premier League football referees are formally assessed and marked on their performance in every match they take charge of. They are only selected to take charge of Premier League games after several years of officiating in lower leagues, and they have to maintain high ratings and standards to be allowed to take charge at the highest level.

Assessing own performance in selected team sports

To improve performance in a team sport, a performer should assess their levels at any particular time and then set themselves targets for improvement. Self-assessment can be difficult, so it is important to be aware of the various assessment methods that can be used.

Your assessment criteria:

P4 Carry out a self-analysis using two different methods of assessment, identifying strengths and areas for improvement in two different team sports

P4 Self-analysis

The starting point for this assessment is to carry out a self-analysis which involves looking in detail at individual performance levels. This needs to be carried out under the following headings:

Specific to sport

There may be sport-specific criteria to consider. In many sports there are specialist positions, such as goalkeepers in football and hockey, and these have specific responsibilities, skills and techniques which apply only to them.

Application of skills

Skills must be applied in a game situation to be effective. Cricketers can practise batting in the nets, but they must be able to play different shots to different bowlers in a match situation where the pace of delivery may be varied and where they may be facing slow, spin bowling for one over, and then quick, pace bowling in the next.

A goalkeeper in hockey is considered to be a specialist position.

Techniques and tactics

Techniques and tactics must be assessed in terms of how successfully they were selected, and how effective they were.

Strengths and areas for improvement

All aspects of the performance should be considered, and both the strengths and areas for improvement must be prioritised in terms of which are the most important and significant.

Assessment methods

Different methods may be more relevant to particular sports, but the following can be used.

? | **Did you know?**

In cricket games many captains will use the different skills of their bowlers as a tactic. They will select a slow bowler to bowl an over from one end, and a fast bowler to bowl from the other end so that the batters cannot settle into a rhythm by facing one particular type of bowling.

Objective performance data

Objective performance data can be used to record how successful a performance was. This involves making a note of the specific skills and techniques for a particular sport and recording how successfully each one was achieved. For example, in netball, hockey, football and basketball you could record the number of passes made and whether they were accurate and successful.

Subjective observations

Subjective observations require an opinion to be given on how successful an aspect of performance was, or how successful the performance was overall.

Technology

Technology can be used as an aid to the self-assessment process and often involves the use of some sort of visual analysis software such as the Dartfish system which is available in some clubs and schools. Any form of recording device such as DVD, video cameras or flip cams which play back on a computer, or video/DVD players can be used for this. This enables a performance to be recorded, played back and considered in greater detail.

SWOT analysis

A SWOT analysis divides statements into strengths, weaknesses, opportunities (to develop and improve) and threats (to improvement and long-term improvement).

Testing

Testing can be carried out, but this must be against a factor which can be clearly identified and accurately tested.

Interviews

Interviews with other people who have observed a performance can be useful. This is another form of subjective assessment. Asking the rest of the team (or even opponents) for their views is a good method of assessment.

Performance profiling

This involves identifying the particular aspects of a sport which need the most consideration, and assessing the level of each skill necessary to complete a competent performance.

Key terms

Objective: *clearly defined and measurable*

Subjective observations: *observations based on the opinions of the observer*

Practising and recording the skill of batting in the nets helps to assess technique for identified improvement.

Key terms

SWOT analysis: *analysis that divides statements into strengths, weaknesses, opportunities and threats*

Did you know?

Many professional performers negotiate with television companies to get video recordings of their performances so that they are able to carry out their own self-analysis straight after a performance.

P4 Development

Initially the aims and objectives must be identified to establish what the focus of development is to be. This will be linked very closely to the goals which should be matched to SMART targets:

- **S**pecific – particular targets are identified

- **M**easurable – targets are measured against how successfully they are achieved

- **A**chievable – targets are possible in the time available

- **R**ealistic – targets are possible in terms of levels of ability and time available

- **T**ime-bound – targets are achieved in a specific amount of time.

There may be opportunities for development, such as specific training, attending courses and gaining qualifications. However, there are also possible barriers to development.

Your assessment criteria:

P4 Carry out a self-analysis using two different methods of assessment, identifying strengths and areas for improvement in two different team sports

M3 Explain identified strengths and areas for improvement in two different team sports, and make suggestions relating to personal development

D1 Analyse identified strengths and areas for improvement in two different team sports, and justify suggestions made

M3 Explain strengths and areas for development

A self-analysis should be carried out, using the various assessment methods to identify the main strengths and areas for development. These should then be prioritised as specific suggestions for personal development.

In carrying out a self-analysis, it is important to focus on some specific aspects rather than attempt to analyse the whole of a performance. A team game may last 90 minutes (football) or 80 minutes (rugby) and this would provide a very large amount of data or information to analyse. For this reason, some aspects of the performance can be focused on and analysed in detail (such as passing and receiving success rates), rather than a general overview. Also, it is sometimes difficult for an individual to be totally engaged in any team game for its entire duration, so there will be times when they will be more actively involved than others. Therefore, these should be focused on.

 Practical

1. *Use a simple recording device, such as the video function on digital camera or a mobile phone, to record a short sequence of personal sporting activity.*

2. *Complete a very basic self-analysis of at least part of a performance.*

 Case study

Dan has carried out a self-analysis of two performances in his chosen sports of rugby and cricket. In both sports, he felt he was able to apply skills successfully as the objective performance data he collected showed that

he passed and received the ball very well during his rugby performance, and he scored runs quickly and consistently when batting in cricket.

However, Dan found that he struggled to complete the whole game in the rugby match, and he was also tiring quite quickly towards the end of his innings in the cricket game. He did not bowl in the cricket game, as he considers himself to be a specialist batter.

Dan needs to think about an action plan for his development.

1. What would Dan consider to be his main strengths across the two sports?

2. In which sport would he consider himself to have made the most effective performance, and why?

3. What might he consider to be the main area for improvement which would apply to both sports?

D1 Analyse strengths and areas for improvement

Any targets which are set for future development should be justified in line with the identified strengths and areas for improvement.

Being able to analyse (examine in detail) helps in the process of justifying suggestions. For example, if a particular skill or technique is not proving successful, it is helpful to look closely at how it is being performed. Using video or visual analysis software can assist in this process as it allows detailed analysis to take place, usually through slowing down the movement to allow each phase to be examined. This can then be compared with another performer successfully performing the skill or technique, and the differences can be noted.

Using slow motion and even one-by-one frame advancement allows the performance to be analysed in minute detail, and aspects such as balance, control, core stability, starting positions and finishing positions can be considered. All phases of the movement must be covered, rather than one particular phase within it. Using an 'exemplar' demonstration from another performer (an elite performer would be ideal) allows the analysis to be considered against a high level example. This is likely to provide contrasts between the two examples which will help in the process of making suggestions for improvement.

 Practical

Arrange for a practical team sport session to be videoed so that it is possible to carry out a detailed analysis of any strengths or areas for improvement which have been identified.

Assessing team performance in selected team sports

One of the best ways an individual can gain the necessary knowledge to improve is to watch others performing in particular sports and reflect on those performances.

P5 Performance analysis

A **performance analysis** covers the overall performance, and the following aspects of the performance have to be considered.

Specific to sport

There may be sport-specific aspects which are relevant to that particular sport. For example, both volleyball and basketball are played in an indoor setting, so environmental factors such as the weather and climate do not need to be considered. Also, in a sport such as cricket a scorebook records the contribution made by players in terms of runs scored and bowling figures, so this makes gathering analysis data far easier. Basketball scorebooks also record similar individual information, especially in relation to successful shooting and the number of fouls committed.

Application of skills

It may be useful to identify particular skills prior to the performance. As there are a variety of skills available in most team sports, it is very difficult to analyse every one of them. For example, a scrum half in rugby is responsible for distribution of the ball from line-out, scrums, rucks and mauls, so it would be sensible to concentrate on the number of successful passes which are made. An additional factor could be whether these are passes made to the right or the left, and the number of successful team passes could be considered as opposed to just one individual's passes.

Techniques and tactics

Specific techniques might need to be identified prior to the performance, but tactics can be noted as they occur. However, it may be useful to

have a discussion with the team prior to the performance to find out what tactics they intend to use so that these can be noted. In most team games the most threatening opposition player will have been identified and plans made for them, such as man-for-man marking. For corners in football, certain players will be designated to mark others defensively (usually a choice made on height), and in cricket, plans will be made to exploit perceived weaknesses in certain batters such as poor hook shots to short-pitched bowling.

Achievements

These may be achievements by the team in general (such as scoring, or even preventing the opposition scoring), or by particular individuals within the team who make a significant contribution.

Strengths and areas for improvement

These do need to be identified, but the strength of the opposition is a factor which has to be considered. A match resulting in a loss against a strong team could still display many strengths, but the fact that it is a loss may indicate that areas for improvement are the major factor.

Assessment methods

These are the same assessment methods which were available for the self-analysis, but the important difference is that any personal involvement cannot be commented on and considered. Where methods prove successful and easy to administer, it is advisable to use these again. Two methods have to be used, so the two most successful should be chosen. The choices include:

• objective performance data

• subjective observations

• technology

• SWOT analysis

• testing – might be problematic with large teams

• interviews – with individual team members, the team as a whole, managers/coaches or even the opposition team

• performance profiling.

> **? Did you know?**
>
> *In some sports there are even rules relating to techniques. For example, there are specific rules in football for the throw in which, if broken, result in a foul throw, and in cricket the umpire has to check that the bowler's technique is correct or they will signal a no ball.*

P5 Development

Once the analysis has been carried out, the team's development is important, and the following aspects of their development should be considered:

- identified aims and objectives

- identified specific goals which are related to the aims and objectives

- SMART target setting

- opportunities which might be available to the team, or to identified individuals within it, e.g. specific training, courses and qualifications

- any identified barriers.

M4 Explain strengths and areas for improvement

A full performance analysis must be carried out before the strengths and areas for improvement can be explained to the team. The use of video evidence and video analysis technology may help with the explanation.

Explaining the strengths to an entire team can be a challenging exercise, so it is useful to identify the particular units of a team in order to do this. This may include the defensive or offensive unit (for example, in football, hockey and netball), or even individual specialist positions which exist in some team sports (for example, the seven clearly identified positions within netball, or goalkeepers in hockey and football). It is important that the team identity is identified and considered, and that individuals within the team are not singled out and criticised, particularly those identified as areas for improvement.

The use of video evidence and/ or video analysis technology helps to make a clear and detailed explanation. The strengths and areas for improvement must be considered in equal proportion without giving a particular emphasis to one. This may help to avoid the issue of one individual making a poor contribution which may have led to a lack of success in the game situation.

Your assessment criteria:

P5 Carry out a performance analysis using two different methods of assessment, identifying strengths and areas for improvement in the development of a team in a team sport

M4 Explain identified strengths and areas for improvement in the development of a team in a team sport, and make suggestions relating to development of a team

D2 Analyse identified strengths and areas for improvement in the development of a team in a team sport, and justify suggestions made

 Discuss

Prior to your team's performance, discuss any particular tactics they are considering using, and what they consider to be their main strengths and areas for improvement.

One individual mistake should not be allowed to dominate a team performance when it is analysed.

D2 Justify suggestions made

After a full analysis has been carried out, any suggestions for improvement must be justified. Therefore, these suggestions need to be backed up by reliable evidence which has been clearly and correctly gathered in the assessment process, and through sharing the information obtained by the chosen assessment methods. Using objective evidence is advisable as it is far easier to justify than large amounts of subjective evidence.

Once again, the emphasis must be on improvements to the team as a whole rather than individuals, or particular units, within the team.

Practical

You are the consultant for a team in a team sport with the role of identifying their strengths and areas for improvement, and using these to make suggestions for their future development. Gather all your assessment evidence, and write a detailed report for the team.

Case study

Lara chooses to carry out her team sport assessment on the school netball team. She carries out a full performance analysis, and chooses to use objective performance data and subjective observations as her two assessment methods. For her objective performance data, she gathers evidence on how many successful passes are completed by the team in a whole match, and how many centre pass restarts result in the ball being successfully passed on for a shot on goal to be taken. For her subjective assessment, she gives the team a rating out of ten for their overall performance, using her own rating scales from poor to excellent. She completes a written report which she is preparing to present to the team in a feedback session.

1. Which of the two assessment methods Lara chooses is the most difficult to complete, and why?

2. Do you think that the methods she chooses are appropriate?

3. Would you recommend that Lara uses another assessment method? If so, why?

4. When Lara gives her feedback to the team, which method of assessment might make it more difficult for her to justify her suggestions?

A game such as netball is more easily observed due to the number of players and the relatively small playing area.

Assessment checklist

To achieve a pass grade, my portfolio of evidence must show that I can:

Assessment Criteria	Description	✓
P1	Describe skills, techniques and tactics required in two different team sports.	☐
P2	Describe the rules and regulations of two different team sports and apply them to three different situations for each sport.	☐
P3	Demonstrate appropriate skills, techniques and tactics in two different team sports.	☐
P4	Carry out a self-analysis using two different methods of assessment, identifying strengths and areas for improvement in two different team sports.	☐
P5	Carry out a performance analysis using two different methods of assessment, identifying strengths and areas for improvement in the development of a team in a team sport.	☐

To achieve a merit grade, my portfolio of evidence must show that I can:

Assessment Criteria	Description	✓
M1	Explain skills, techniques and tactics required in two different team sports.	☐
M2	Explain the application of the rules and regulations, of two different team sports, in three different situations for each sport.	☐
M3	Explain identified strengths and areas for improvement in two different team sports, and make suggestions relating to personal development.	☐
M4	Explain identified strengths and areas for improvement in the development of a team in a team sport, and make suggestions relating to development of a team.	☐

To achieve a distinction grade, my portfolio of evidence must show that I can:

Assessment Criteria	Description	✓
D1	Analyse identified strengths and areas for improvement in two different team sports, and justify suggestions made.	☐
D2	Analyse identified strengths and areas for improvement in the development of a team in a team sport, and justify suggestions made.	☐

9 | Practical individual sports

LO1 Know the skills, techniques and tactics required in selected individual sports

▶ Each sport has its own set of skills and techniques. Some skills and techniques are common to several sports, but many are only relevant to a particular sport.

▶ Each sport has its own set of tactics including offence/defence, and/or movement.

LO2 Know the rules and regulations of selected individual sports

▶ Sports' rules and laws are determined by the governing body of that sport. For example, Badminton England and British Gymnastics determine the rules and laws of badminton and trampolining.

▶ The regulations for each sport differ because of the nature of the activity. The officials, equipment and scoring will be relevant to only one sport.

LO3 Be able to assess own performance in selected individual sports

▶ Analysis can be carried out in a variety of ways. Self-analysis enables you to reflect on your application of the skills that you have learnt. You can also comment on tactics, strengths and improvements.

▶ Analysis can also be objective, carried out through observation by another performer, judge or umpire.

▶ Your analysis will help you to set goals for your development in the sports that have been selected. It will also help you to identify opportunities for your future development as a sportsperson.

LO4 Be able to assess the performance of other individuals in selected individual sports

▶ Having the skill to assess another performer will enable you to enhance your coaching skills and confirm your understanding of skills, techniques and tactics.

Skills, techniques and tactics of trampolining

Sport has seen substantial growth in participation rates. There is a wide range of opportunities for people to become actively involved in sport and there is increasing recognition that sport is important in establishing a healthy lifestyle.

Sports can be categorised into two distinct areas: individual and team. Both areas will help you to develop your knowledge in the sports selected and in your ability to play or compete. The knowledge that you gain in these areas will also help you to develop subject knowledge for coaching, sports development and PE teaching.

There are a wide range of individual sports that can be selected. Each sport's **skills** and **techniques** tend to be different. This unit focuses on two very different sports, badminton and trampolining. Each sport is covered from initial technique to competition and assessment.

Key terms

Skills: techniques that are automatic, learnt, fluid and that can be applied in game situations under pressure

Techniques: individual movements allowing the performance of a physical task

P1 ▶ Describe skills and techniques of trampolining

There are a range of techniques that should be practised to develop a basic trampoline routine. Techniques in trampolining are progressively graded in difficulty level through a tariff system. To complete an assessment in trampolining, you must learn the techniques that are involved in completing a set compulsory routine. You will also have the opportunity to learn additional techniques that could be selected to complete a voluntary routine. The order and completion of your routine will demonstrate a tactical choice of how difficult you want to make your voluntary routine. It will also clearly demonstrate your level of skill.

There are a range of techniques in trampolining. This unit focuses on the techniques up to and including front and back somersaults. Each technique has progressive stages that should be worked through to ensure that the technique is safe and that each part of the technique has been learnt properly. Techniques develop into skills when they can be performed naturally, with good movement, and become automatic.

Straight jump

Your feet are no more than hip width apart. Your back is straight, head in natural alignment and eyes looking forward and slightly down. The ankles are flexed on leaving the trampoline, then fully extended. Circle your arms backwards, just high enough to match your jump height. Your arms go up as you go up, and down as you go down.

Reflect

Reflect on your practice performances. Identify aspects that you have completed well and aspects where you have struggled.

Discuss

1. Discuss technique problems that you have with a coach and record any advice that you receive.

2. Discuss elements of physical training that would improve your performance.

Practical

Try to perform each of the techniques in the following order: straight jump, tuck, pike, half twist, full twist, 1½ twist.

Tuck jump

At the top of a straight jump, bring your knees close to your chest, with one hand grasping each leg on the shin. The knees are brought close together and the toes are pointed. Regain the straight jump shape prior to landing.

Pike jump

At the top of a straight jump, bring your legs up to an angle of 90 degrees, with toes pointed. Bring your arms down towards your legs at the same time. Regain the straight jump shape prior to landing.

Straddle jump

At the top of a straight jump, bring both legs up to an angle of 90 degrees, with toes pointed. Your legs should also be at least 90 degrees apart. Bring your arms down towards your legs at the same time.

Half twist

At the start of the straight jump, twist your arms and shoulders. Maintain an upright position and keep your arms straight. Your arms need to be turned wider than shoulder width. The action should be gentle.

The straight jump

Full twist

The full twist uses the same technique as the half twist. You can accelerate the twist by bringing your arms closer to your body by either wrapping your arms across your chest, keeping them by your sides or above your head. You can slow down the twist for landing by bringing your arms wider than your body.

1½ twist

Follow the stages of the full twist, but start the twist with the arms wider and look down throughout.

 Practical

Perform a straight jump, tuck jump, pike jump and straddle jump in sequence.

 Describe

Record your performance and describe your strengths and weaknesses.

Seat drop

Initiate the seat drop with a straight jump. At the top of the jump, pike your legs and bring your arms down towards your legs at the same time. The landing should be flat with contact between your heels and your hips. Your hands are just behind your hips, with your fingers pointing forwards. After contact push with your hands, press down with your legs and push your hips forwards. Raise your arms above your head on takeoff.

The seat drop

Seat drop half twist to feet

Follow the stages of the seat drop, but include a half twist after contact with the trampoline. Stretch up after contact.

Half twist to seat drop

Reach up with straight arms. Your hips and legs should move slightly backwards at takeoff. Aim to land on the same point as the takeoff. Place your hands flat on your hips, with the fingers pointing forwards.

Front drop

Displace your hips backwards to begin the rotation. Use the natural rebound of the trampoline to achieve the front drop position. Aim to land with your navel exactly at the point that you took off. The landing should be flat with contact between the knees and chest. Your elbows are wide with finger tips nearly touching flat and in front of the face, so that the arms take no force on landing. Kick your legs down to aid rotation back to feet and the arms push.

Your assessment criteria:

P1 Describe skills, techniques and tactics required in two different individual sports

? | Did you know?

Power is required to achieve height. This gives you time to execute each of your skills.

? | Did you know?

International trampolinists can spend 2 seconds in the air and jump 9.14m. However, 5m is typical for beginners.

Q | Research

Research how often elite trampolinists train each week.

Back drop

Start the back drop with a lift of the hips into a jump. Rotate your body until there is contact with the trampoline. Your neck must remain firm throughout the move, with your head looking down towards the chest. Contact with the trampoline is with a flat back.

When contact occurs, beat your legs down towards the trampoline. Push your hips forward and up at takeoff, returning to your feet.

Seat drop to front drop

Follow the stages of the seat drop. Push the hips back at takeoff from the seat drop. Look down to spot your landing and stretch to front drop.

Front drop to seat drop

Follow the stages of the front drop. Kick down on contact with the trampoline and push your hips forward as you leave the trampoline. Resist piking too early.

Half twist to back drop

Perform a half twist. Move your hips up as you twist. Start the twist with your arms and shoulders. Displace your hips backwards on takeoff. Spread your arms wide to control the twist on landing.

Half twist to front drop

Perform a half twist and displace hips forward at takeoff.

Front drop half twist to feet

Perform a front drop, then use your hands and arms to direct the twist whilst in contact with the trampoline.

Front somersault

Initiate an off-centre force forwards during the jump to start rotation. Displace your hips backwards at takeoff, then tuck in your body to accelerate the rotation. Open out to reduce rotation speed before landing.

Backward somersault

Jump and push your hips forward to create rotation. Tuck in to increase the speed of rotation. Keep your eyes open to identify a point that you need to open out on. Kick your feet out when your head is parallel to the floor. Open out to reduce your rotation and land on your feet.

The backward somersault

 Practical

1. *Perform a seat drop, half twist to seat drop, half twist to feet drop, front drop and back drop in sequence.*

2. *Perform a tuck jump, front somersault and tuck jump in sequence.*

3. *Perform a tuck jump, back somersault and straight jump in sequence.*

4. *Record your performance.*

P1 Describe tactics of trampolining

Trampolining **tactics** involve the selection of a tariff score for a routine. The tariff for the compulsory routine is set at a point score of 10. The tariff for a voluntary routine can change. The routine is given a start tariff of 10, but then has a difficulty tariff added to it.

Figure 9.1 The tariff score for a routine

Name	Compulsory	Deductions	Voluntary	Deductions
	1 Half twist		1	
	2 Straddle jump		2	
	3 Seat drop		3	
	4 Half twist to seat		4	
	5 Half twist to feet		5	
	6 Pike jump		6	
	7 Front drop		7	
	8 Straight jump		8	
	9 Tuck jump		9	
	10 Full twist		10	
Totals	10	10 − D =	10 + tariff =	Total − D =

The tariffs shown in Figure 9.2 can be used to calculate your difficulty level.

Tactics in trampolining are about how difficult to make a routine. There is a choice between performing an easy routine with the probability of few mistakes and deductions, and performing a difficult routine but the chance of more mistakes and deductions. Deductions are made for neatness of a skill or form, control and height consistency. Both routines must be memorised and performed in sequence.

Figure 9.2 The tariff score for difficulty level

Straight jump	0
Tuck/pike/straddle	0
Seat drop	0
Half twist	0.1
Full twist	0.2
1½ twist	0.3
Front drop	0.2
Back drop	0.2
Front drop half twist	0.3
Back drop half twist	0.3
Front somersault	0..5
Back somersault	0.5

M1 Explain skills and techniques of trampolining

An understanding of movement and biomechanics is necessary to be able to explain how techniques and skills are performed. Each skill has a specific coaching point that must be focused on to perform the skill effectively.

- Straight jump – the centre of mass should be maintained over the base of support for balance.

- Tuck/pike and straddle – the legs and arms must move at the same time to ensure stability.

- Half twist – the twist is produced by a transfer of momentum from the arms and shoulder action by the reaction of the trampoline against the twisting action.

- Full twist – reducing and increasing the moment of inertia causes acceleration and deceleration of the speed of twist.

- Seat drop – the centre of mass must be above the base of support on landing.

- Front drop – an off-centre force is produced on takeoff and is directed backwards through displaced hips.

- Back drop – an off-centre force from the hip lift produces backward rotation. On contact with the trampoline, a leg beat transfers momentum producing forward rotation back to the feet.

- Front somersault – tucking reduces the radius of gyration, increasing angular velocity.

Explain tactics of trampolining

In a performance of a ten bounce routine, it is important to carefully select the order and tariff difficulty of techniques that you want to use. Tucks, pikes, straddles and straight jumps are used to provide height in a routine. If you have chosen a difficult technique, you may want to include one of these as the next move to provide height and stability. The most difficult technique or tariff is often left until the end. There can be no interruption during your routine. If you make an error and cannot complete the routine without taking additional bounces, the routine has not been successful. However, if you make a mistake on the last skill or technique, you will only have a large deduction for the error.

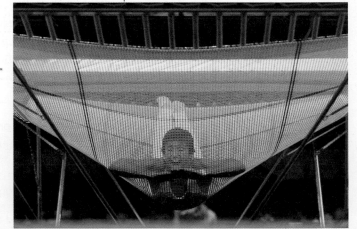

A performer maintaining position in the centre of the trampoline.

Describe

1. Describe the tactical choices that you have made.

2. Calculate the tariff difficulty score for your voluntary routine.

Rules and regulations of trampolining

A trampoline competition comprises of three rounds: compulsory and voluntary, plus a final round for the top ten performers after the first two rounds. Athletes can perform their routines wearing socks or special shoes, but cannot be barefoot. Athletes who do not obey these regulations, or who wear jewellery during the competition, may face the penalty of expulsion.

Round 1 – each participant performs the same compulsory routine. This round is judged for form. Five judges assess each skill and deduct marks for errors in performance. Each skill starts with a mark of 1. Judges may deduct up to a maximum mark of 5 for the entire routine. A very good routine will probably score over 8.8. Average routines score between 7.5 and 8. Judges should display their scores at the same time. All scores are recorded, but the highest and lowest are discounted. The total score is the average of the remaining scores.

Round 2 – each participant performs their own voluntary routine that has been memorised. Judges also assess the difficulty tariff.

Judges' deductions

Deductions may be made for a variety of reasons:

- Form – this is the quality of each movement. In all positions, the feet and legs should be together and the feet pointed. In a pike jump, the feet must be at least shoulder width apart. In the tuck jump, the hands should be below the knees. During all moves the head should be in natural alignment, and the arms should be straight or close to the body whenever possible.

- Control – judges can make deductions for any movement or travel on the trampoline. All skills should be performed close to the centre of the bed.

- Height – all skills in a routine should be performed at the same height.

- Stability – at the end of a routine, the performer must land on both feet with no additional movement. One step forward deducts 0.1, two steps 0.2 and a double bounce 0.3.

The routine is stopped if the performer does not maintain rhythm (stops jumping), lands on one foot, touches the frame, fails to perform the routine in its correct sequence, or leaves the trampoline. as these are against the rules.

Your assessment criteria:

P2 Describe the rules and regulations of two different individual sports, and apply them to three different situations for each sport

M2 Explain the application of the rules and regulations, of two different individual sports, in three different situations for each sport

P3 Demonstrate appropriate skills, techniques and tactics in two different individual sports

Key terms

Regulations: regulations relate to the greater detail about the field of play, size, game times and equipment used, for example the size of the trampoline or how long a sequence should be

Rules: rules relate to general playing or performing of a sport, for example a routine should stop immediately if there is contact with the matting around a trampoline or the main structure

M2 ▸ Explain rules and regulations of trampolining

Deductions for form depend on how large an error is. This will depend on the skill involved. For some skills or techniques the deduction may be small such as bending the legs. For others there may be a higher deduction such as in the tuck jump example below.

Loss of height deductions will depend on the amount of height lost in the routine. For example, if one skill has lost three-quarters of the routine's normal height, there will be a deduction of 0.3.

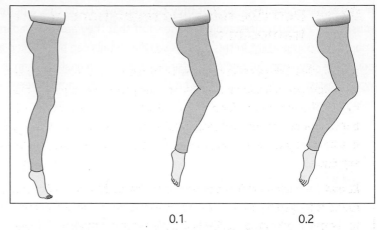

0.1   0.2

Figure 9.3 Bending the legs deductions

P3 ▸ Demonstrate the skills, techniques and tactics of trampolining

You will need to demonstrate your ability in trampolining. This can be achieved in several ways. During your practical work when you are learning techniques and developing skills, you should record your performance and comment on your strengths and weaknesses. This can be supported by a witness statement from your coach or tutor. You may also receive observational feedback from your coach on your performance during the end of unit competition.

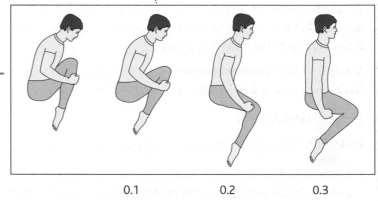

0.1   0.2   0.3

Figure 9.4 Tuck jump deductions

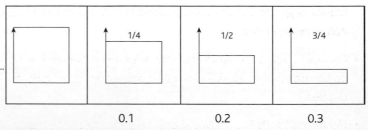

0.1   0.2   0.3

Figure 9.5 Loss of height deductions

🏃 Practical

1. Observe and score another performer's routine.

2. Calculate the deductions that you will take away from their initial score.

3. Present the final score to the performer with an explanation for the deductions.

Performance analysis of trampolining

Performers must be able to reflect on each performance and learn from the mistakes they have made so that they can improve. To do this, a performer must have a good understanding of the sport that they are involved in. The coach is also important in this process so that details can be checked and advice for development and progressions given. Video analysis is an excellent way to assist in assessment. It can be played frame by frame if necessary, so that movement can be compared with relevant coaching points.

P4 Performance self-analysis

Self-analysis can be carried out in trampolining during the final competition. The voluntary routine of the competition will demonstrate how much progress a performer has made as it gives them a chance to select their difficulty level.

During the competition, each athlete's routine should be recorded using a video camera so that the athlete can review their own performance. Scores and comments can also be collected from the five judges. The final score will be based on **subjective observations** and will provide information that can be analysed. Notes can also be made on reasons for any deductions.

During the review of a performance, an athlete should reflect on each of the skills that they have learnt and describe the reasons for their routine selection. This can take the form of a simple checklist. An athlete can carry out a **SWOT** analysis in which they describe their strengths and weaknesses in trampolining. They then describe the threats or problems that they have had. Threats could include barriers to learning, problems with particular skills, illnesses or injuries. Finally, they describe opportunities for improvement. These can include access to a local trampolining club, progression to regional or national events or the development of a new club if suitable coaching can be found.

⚲ | Key terms

Subjective observations: observations based on the opinions of the observer

SWOT: analysis that divides statements into strengths, weaknesses, opportunities and threats

Your assessment criteria:

P4 Carry out a self-analysis using two different methods of assessment, identifying strengths and areas for improvement in two different individual sports

M3 Explain identified strengths and areas for improvement in two different individual sports, and make suggestions relating to personal development

D1 Analyse identified strengths and areas for improvement in two different individual sports, and justify suggestions made

P5 Carry out a performance analysis using two different methods of assessment, identifying strengths and areas for improvement in the development of an individual in an individual sport

M4 Explain identified strengths and areas for improvement in the development of an individual in an individual sport, and make suggestions relating to development of an individual

D2 Analyse identified strengths and areas for improvement in the development of an individual in an individual sport, and justify suggestions made

M3 Explain strengths and areas for improvement

Strengths and weaknesses can clearly address specific problems. For example, a performer may be able to complete all techniques individually, but may not be able to perform several of them fluidly in a routine. Moving from a back drop into a half twist front drop and then progressing to a somersault, is more difficult than moving from a straight jump into a somersault and then into a tuck. You need to come up with suggestions for improvement for each of the weaknesses described in P4. For example, if a performer is over-rotating on their somersault, they may need to start to open out earlier so that they can slow the speed that they rotate, enabling them to land with stability.

Analysis of performance

D1 Analyse strengths and areas for improvement

You must justify each of the weaknesses in M3. In the example above, the performer has a problem with over-rotation. This is often caused by throwing the shoulders and head down and forward at the start of the somersault. The athlete needs to concentrate on lifting their hips up and back and slowing down a little. As they turn, they also need to open out of the tuck a little earlier, pushing their chest up and hips back.

 Practical

1. *Review and analyse a video of your compulsory routine.*

2. *Video the performance of a performer in the final round of the competition and analyse their performance.*

P5 M4 D2 Performance analysis of an individual

P5, M4 and D2 can all be achieved by completing an analysis of one of the performers in the final round of the competition. The final round is another voluntary routine that the performer must memorise. The analysis can be carried out in the same way as the self-analysis.

Skills, techniques and tactics of badminton

P1 Describe skills and techniques of badminton

Your assessment criteria:

P1 Describe skills, techniques and tactics required in two different individual sports

There are a range of techniques that must be practised to enable the development of badminton. Techniques in badminton can be progressed from simple skills such as a serve to more advanced techniques such as a smash. To complete an assessment in badminton, you need to learn the techniques that are involved in singles play, and compete in an end of unit competition. You can demonstrate tactical choices in singles in the shots you select and in your movement.

There are a range of techniques that are played in singles badminton. Each technique takes time to practise and develop through co-operative work. The techniques only progress into skills when they are automatic, and can be played in a game under pressure.

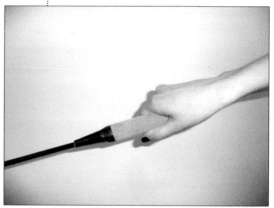

The forehand grip

Grip

Forehand grip – this is used to play forehand shots or shots around the head. The racket is held as if shaking hands with it, with a V between the thumb and index finger. It should rest loosely in the hand.

Backhand grip – this grip is used to perform backhand shots. Hold the racket in a forehand grip, but turn the racket anticlockwise. Place your thumb on the handle for better grip, movement and power.

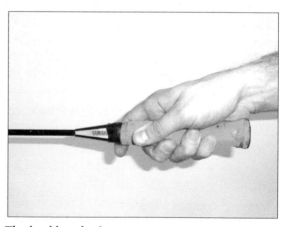

The backhand grip

Serving

There are a range of serving techniques: high, low, forehand, backhand, flick and drive.

High serve – this tactic is used to push your opponent to the back of the court, thus opening space at the front of the court. Play the serve with a forehand underarm action from two feet behind the service line. The non-racket leg leads. Bring back the racket to shoulder level and then swing forward smoothly. Hold the shuttle by the feathers and drop it in front of

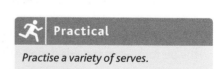

Practical

Practise a variety of serves.

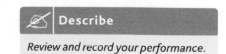

Describe

Review and record your performance.

you. Hit the shuttle with the flat face of the racket and allow the racket to follow through.

Low serve forehand – this tactic is used to make your opponent lift the shuttle. Stand two feet behind the service line, leading with the non-racket leg. Bring the racket back to waist level before the swing. Hold the shuttle by the feathers, but bring it towards the racket rather than dropping it as in the high serve. Hit the shuttle at a higher point but below waist line. Push it with the racket face, skimming the net if possible.

Low serve backhand – the racket hand starts in front, leading with the racket leg. Start the serve with a short back swing. Hold the shuttle by the tips of the feathers in front at waist level. It should be pushed with the racket face, skimming the net if possible.

Flick serve – this tactic is used when an opponent is likely to rush forward and attack the serve. You should disguise the shuttle so that it looks like a low serve is about to be performed. Use your wrist at the last minute to flick the shuttle to the back of the court.

Drive serve – this tactic is used as an attacking serve. The shuttle travels at a flat trajectory and with speed, giving the opponent little time to react. Play this serve with a forehand underarm action, leading with the non-racket leg. Hold the racket below waist level, swing forward and follow through. The shuttle should still pass close to the net, but travels to the back of the court.

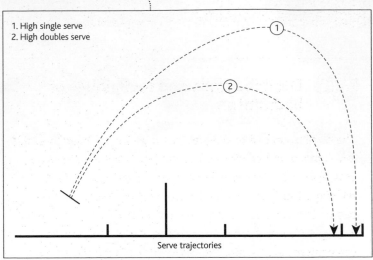

1. High single serve
2. High doubles serve

Serve trajectories

Figure 9.6 The shot trajectory and end position of the high serve

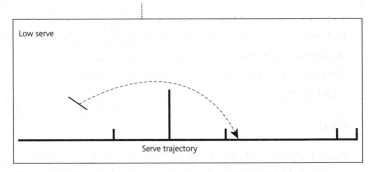

Low serve

Serve trajectory

Figure 9.7 The shot trajectory and end position of the low serve

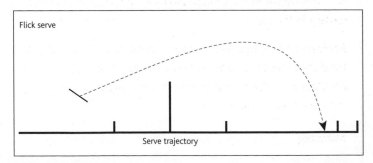

Flick serve

Serve trajectory

Figure 9.8 The shot trajectory and end position of the flick serve

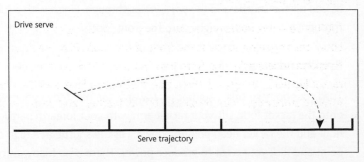

Drive serve

Serve trajectory

Figure 9.9 The shot trajectory and end position of the drive serve

P1 Describe skills and techniques of badminton *continued*

Overhead clear

This shot is used to move your opponent to the back of the court creating space at the front. It can also allow you time to get back into position depending on the type of clear that you play.

Clears can be attacking or defensive. The attacking clear is played flat and fast to the back of the court giving little time for your opponent to react and move. The defensive clear is hit high and long. This gives you time to recover and return to the centre of the court.

The action for both clears is the same. Turn your body sideways to the net with your weight on the back foot. The non-racket hand should point to the direction of the shuttle. Hit the shuttle with the contact as high as possible and in front of the body using a throwing action. The elbow straightens as you hit the shuttle and the wrist whips through. Finish with a follow through, moving your weight onto the front foot.

Backhand clear

Turn your body so that your back is towards the net. Move your weight onto the racket foot. Lift your racket arm with your forearm parallel to the floor and the racket head pointing down. Hit the shuttle at a high contact point and flick your wrist to produce power. There is no follow through.

Practical

Practise clears, drop shots and smashes.

Describe

Review and record your performance in each of the practices, commenting on strengths and weaknesses.

Underarm clear

The underarm clear is used to push your opponent to the back of the court, creating space at the front. Extend the racket upwards with the point of contact in front and as high as possible, using your wrist to flick and add power. Add a follow through.

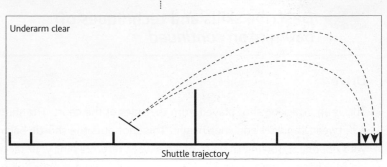

Figure 9.10 The shot trajectory and end position of the underarm clear

Drop shot

This shot can be used to move your opponent to the front of the court, creating space behind them. Drop shots can be slow or fast. A slow drop shot lands in the forecourt area, close to the net. You should hit the shuttle above the racket shoulder in a similar position to the clear, but with the wrist disguising the shot by slowing the movement down. Slicing or tapping the shuttle reduces the shuttle speed.

A fast drop shot lands in the middle of the court, close to one of the side lines. You should hit the shuttle slightly more in front of your body.

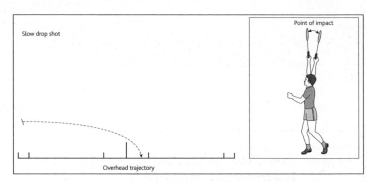

Figure 9.11 The shot trajectory and end position of the slow drop shot

Backhand drop shot

This shot is performed in a similar way to the backhand clear. You slice or tap the shuttle as you hit it. The angle of the racket face determines the direction of the shot.

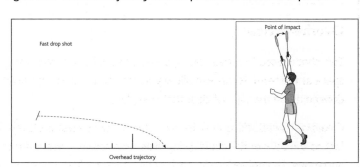

Figure 9.12 The shot trajectory and end position of the fast drop shot

Smash

This shot is used as an attacking shot with power and speed. It is important to make sure that the shuttle is targeted downwards. You hit the shuttle more in front of your body than the clear or drop shot.

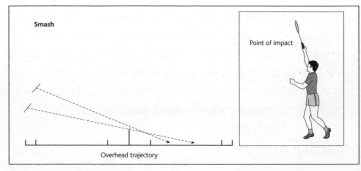

Figure 9.13 The shot trajectoryw and end position of the smash

P1 Describe skills and techniques of badminton *continued*

Drive

This is an attacking shot played from the sides of the court. The shuttle is between shoulder and knee height. This shot puts the shuttle behind your opponent, forcing them to make a weak return. Point your racket leg towards the sideline. Start with a back swing, and put your body weight on the racket leg as you swing forward. Extend your racket arm, turn the forearm and flick your wrist on contact. Hit the shuttle at the highest point possible. Direct the racket head to place the shot, inwards (for cross court), or square (to hit down the line).

Cross over the racket leg to the backhand side. Draw the racket arm back, keeping the racket parallel to the floor. Your body weight is transferred to the front leg as you swing the racket, and you hit the shuttle in front of the leading leg at the highest point possible.

Describe tactics of badminton

There are a variety of tactics that can be used in badminton. Here are some examples:

- Play flat and attack. This encourages your opponent to lift the shuttle making it easier to attack.

- Vary play and use space. This can be achieved by playing alternative clears and drop shots, playing to the back and front of the court.

- For weaker opponents, dominate the court by overpowering the player.

- Play against your opponent's weaknesses. This is typically their backhand shot, but could be another area.

M1 Explain skills and techniques of badminton

When a technique becomes automatic, it develops into a skill. A good player does not have to think about the technique, they think about where the shuttle should go. A technique becomes a skill when a player achieves a degree of accuracy and they can move and place the shuttle in the direction and area that it was intended. Good players can hit regularly within a foot of each sideline.

Your assessment criteria:

P1 Describe skills, techniques and tactics required in two different individual sports

M1 Explain skills, techniques and tactics required in two different individual sports

Did you know?

Badminton is the fastest racket sport with shuttles travelling at speeds of over 200mph.

Reflect

Reflect on the tactics that you can currently use. Identify tactical areas of your game that need to improve.

Badminton is also about movement, speed, power and flexibility. Court dominance, recovering to the centre and maintaining balance are essential to good game play. Footwork is often a neglected area. Players can play the correct shots, but struggle to cover the court with quick feet. They must be able to perform lunges to reach and recover from a shot. Defence is equally important, as a game often ebbs and flows. A player must show good reactions to block a smash and must choose appropriate shots that allow them to recover and turn defence into attack.

Explain tactics of badminton

- Play flat and attack. Hitting down will encourage your opponent to lift or block the shuttle. This will create more attacking opportunities and enable you to smash more.

- Vary play and use space. Moving a player around the court will force them to play off balance at times. They are more likely to play poor shots. Moving a player will also give them less time to think about where to place the shuttle and how to attack.

- For weaker opponents, dominate the court by overpowering the player. Attacking clears need to be used so that your opponent has less time to react. These should be flat and driven to the back of the court. A weak opponent will probably produce a poor clear or allow you to move into a dominant position in the centre of the court.

- Play against your opponent's weaknesses. Playing to a player's weak backhand will probably produce a weak or short shot allowing you to attack with a smash or to move forward to dominate the court.

 Describe

1. *Describe the tactics that you can use effectively in a game.*

2. *Describe tactics that you find difficult and provide suggestions on how you can improve.*

Rules and regulations of badminton

P2 ▷ Describe rules and regulations of badminton

Badminton has a variety of rules and regulations. A match consists of the best of three games. Each game is won by the side that scores 21 points or that wins by two clear points over 20 points. A point is scored by the player that wins a rally. A rally is won if the opposing side commits a fault or the shuttle touches the surface of the court inside the opponent's court. The side winning a game serves first in the next game. Players should change ends after each game, and change ends in the final game when a player reaches 11 points. The server and receiver stand diagonally in opposite service courts. The serve must start with the shuttle below the server's waist when it is hit. A player serves from the right side of the court when their score is even and from the left side of the court when their score is odd. In singles play, the service lines are short and long. Side lines are out throughout the game. The back lines are counted in for the serve and throughout the game. A fault is a shot into the net or outside the boundaries of the court. A fault is also counted if the shuttle hits a player, or is hit twice by a player without going over the net. Finally, a fault is called if a player touches the net with their racket.

Your assessment criteria:

P2 Describe the rules and regulations of two different individual sports, and apply them to three different situations for each sport

M2 Explain the application of the rules and regulations, of two different individual sports, in three different situations for each sport

P3 Demonstrate appropriate skills, techniques and tactics in two different individual sports

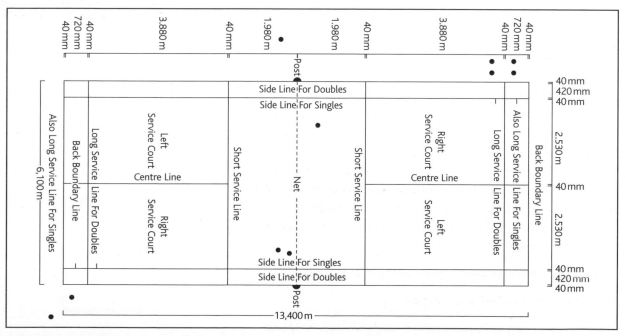

Figure 9.14 The markings of a badminton court

M2 Explain rules and regulations of badminton

Before play starts, a toss should be conducted and the side winning the toss has a choice of receiving the serve or playing at one end of the court. The side losing the toss will have the alternative choice. If players have not changed ends as previously mentioned, they should do so as soon as the mistake is discovered. The serve should not be unduly delayed. Once the serve has started and the racket moves forward, it cannot be stopped and restarted. During play a player cannot deliberately distract an opponent by shouting or making gestures. If the score reaches 29 all, the side scoring 30 points wins the game.

 Describe

1. Describe the rules and regulations of badminton to a partner.

2. Ask your partner to check your knowledge and identify areas that you misunderstand.

 P3 Demonstrate the skills, techniques and tactics of badminton

You will need to demonstrate your ability in badminton. This can be achieved in several ways. During your practical work when you are learning techniques and developing skills, you should record your performance and comment on your strengths and weaknesses. This can be supported by a witness statement from your coach or tutor. You may also receive observational feedback from your coach on your performance during the end of unit competition.

 Case study

Anna has just finished a singles competition and is reviewing her performance before she leaves the venue so that she can learn from the experience. She has played several very close games, but is frustrated because she has lost several points because of rule infringements. In the first game she lost points on her serve because her hand position was incorrect. In the second game Anna tried to move her opponent around the court but lost points for serving too wide. In the third game she started to tire and her decision making suffered. She lost two points for serving to the wrong side of the court.

1. Explain the rules for the hand position during a serve.

2. Explain the line rules during singles play.

3. Describe the scoring system and explain which side a player should serve from for a particular score.

Performance analysis of badminton

P4 ▶ Performance self-analysis

Self-analysis can be carried out in badminton during the final competition. Each performer can review one match. During the competition, a player's game should be recorded using a video camera so that the player can review their own performance. Scores and comments can be collected from the umpire. The final score will be based on subjective observations and will provide objective information.

During the review of a performance, a player should reflect on each of the skills that they have learnt and describe the reasons for their choice of tactical play. This can take the form of a simple checklist. A player can carry out a SWOT analysis in which they describe their strengths and weaknesses in badminton. They then describe the threats or problems that they have had. Threats could include barriers to learning, problems with particular skills, illnesses or injuries. Finally, they describe opportunities for improvement. These can include access to a local badminton club, progression to regional or national events or the development of a new club if suitable coaching can be found.

The following aspects may assist when carrying out your review:

Figure 9.15 Aspects to consider when carrying out your badminton review

1. High serve – ability to serve with control and variation in height and direction
2. Short serve – ability to hit low over the net with controlled variation in direction
3. Overhead clear (forehand and around the head) – ability to hit deep to move an opponent backwards to the rear of the court
4. Overhead drop shot (forehand and backhand) – ability to use disguise (preparation identical to overhead clear) and place shuttle away from the opponent
5. Smash – ability to hit down sharply as fast as possible to open space, or at an opponent's body
6. Net shots – ability to hit an appropriate net shot
7. Skills improvement – action to improve skill proficiency
8. Initiation of tactics – ability to move an opponent around the court and open space to dominate play

? Did you know?

Badminton originated at the home of the Duke of Beaufort in Gloucestershire.

? Did you know?

Badminton competitions in Malaysia and Indonesia have crowds of 15,000 people in stadiums regularly watching the game.

M3 ▶ Explain strengths and areas for improvement

Strengths and weaknesses can clearly address specific problems in movement, fluidity of play and accuracy. For example, a player may be able to complete all of the taught techniques individually, but may not be able to perform them effectively in a game. You need to come up with suggestions for improvement for each of the weaknesses described in P4. For example, a player may be able to perform a drop shot, but may be unable to disguise the shot or change its direction. A player may also be able to play an individual shot, but may not be able to link shots together because of their court coverage. An example of linking shots can be seen in a rally that includes a sequence of: high serve, clear, drop shot, clear, drop shot, smash.

D1 ▶ Analyse strengths and areas for improvement

You must justify each of the weaknesses in M3. In the example above, the player has a problem with disguise. Disguise can be played by deliberately slowing the action down at the last minute, or by changing the direction of the wrist and altering the racket head so that the shuttle comes off the racket at an angle. The shuttle can also be sliced making it tumble, and this can reduce the speed significantly.

? Did you know?

Badminton is possibly the second most popular participation sport in the world – beaten only by football.

💬 Discuss

Discuss your strengths and weaknesses with a coach and set yourself some clear targets for development.

🔍 Research

Research opportunities for you to play at a local club.

Assessment checklist

To achieve a pass grade, my portfolio of evidence must show that I can:

Assessment Criteria	Description	✓
P1	Describe skills, techniques and tactics required in two different individual sports.	☐
P2	Describe the rules and regulations of two different individual sports, and apply them to three different situations for each sport.	☐
P3	Demonstrate appropriate skills, techniques and tactics in two different individual sports.	☐
P4	Carry out a self-analysis using two different methods of assessment, identifying strengths and areas for improvement in two different individual sports.	☐
P5	Carry out a performance analysis using two different methods of assessment, identifying strengths and areas for improvement in the development of an individual in an individual sport.	☐

To achieve a merit grade, my portfolio of evidence must show that I can:

Assessment Criteria	Description	✓
M1	Explain skills, techniques and tactics required in two different individual sports.	☐
M2	Explain the application of the rules and regulations, of two different individual sports, in three different situations for each sport.	☐
M3	Explain identified strengths and areas for improvement in two different individual sports, and make suggestions relating to personal development.	☐
M4	Explain identified strengths and areas for improvement in the development of an individual in an individual sport, and make suggestions relating to development of an individual.	☐

To achieve a distinction grade, my portfolio of evidence must show that I can:

Assessment Criteria	Description	✓
D1	Analyse identified strengths and areas for improvement in two different individual sports, and justify suggestions made.	☐
D2	Analyse identified strengths and areas for improvement in the development of an individual in an individual sport, and justify suggestions made.	☐

11 | Sports nutrition

LO1 Know the concepts of nutrition and digestion

▶ Understanding the components of a good diet is important to sports performance. Balancing the components can improve your health and affect your energy levels.

▶ Understanding how the digestive system works is important so that the type of food and timing of intake can be planned in advance.

LO4 Be able to plan a diet appropriate for a selected sports activity

▶ You must develop a good understanding of what a healthy diet is.

▶ You will need to make changes to a balanced diet that take into account the exercise or sport that you take part in. The intensity and duration of an activity will affect how much you need to eat and drink.

▶ A nutritional strategy for a sport should be planned in advance, with small gradual changes that take into account an individual's goals, for example weight gain, weight loss or muscle gain.

LO2 Know energy intake and expenditure in sports performance

▶ An athlete requires a certain amount of energy, but each athlete is different. The energy they need depends on their size, shape, weight, gender and activity level.

▶ The amount of energy that you consume and use must be balanced. Weight loss and weight gain can be influenced by shifting the balance in a certain direction.

LO3 Know the relationship between hydration and sports performance

▶ Hydration and fluid is extremely important in sport. Dehydration of less than 5% can significantly affect your performance.

Nutrition for sport

Nutrition and hydration have become increasingly important. Sports people, from world champions to amateur players, are now focusing on nutrition to try to achieve extra improvements in their performance. Good dietary planning can increase the effects of training on the body, and can affect energy levels. Many athletes now focus on diet, including nutrition, before, during and after an event. They also try to achieve a balanced diet to gain associated health improvements.

P1 Nutrition

The body requires a number of nutrients to function. These can be divided into **macronutrients**, such as carbohydrate, protein and fat, and **micronutrients**, such as vitamins and minerals. The body also needs fibre and water. There are recommended guidelines produced by the NHS for each nutrient.

Carbohydrates

Carbohydrates provide immediate sources of energy. Each gram of carbohydrate provides 4**kcal.** There are two types of carbohydrate: simple and complex.

- *Simple carbohydrates* – these include glucose, fructose, lactose, and maltose and can be easily absorbed to provide a quick energy boost. The simplest form is sugar (glucose). Fructose is found in fruit and vegetables, lactose in milk and maltose in cereal.

- *Complex carbohydrates* – these are longer chains of simple sugar. They are important because they can provide a slow release of energy over longer periods of time. Complex carbohydrates are contained in rice, pasta, wholemeal bread, root vegetables and potatoes. These food sources should make up the largest percentage of your diet.

Carbohydrates can be stored in the body as glycogen. Regular strength or power training can increase these stores. Carbohydrate that cannot be converted to glycogen is stored as fat.

Carbohydrates should make up 50%–60% of an individual's daily calorie intake (or 250g). A higher intake may be needed for athletes involved in endurance events, or high intensity activities. The intake should be increased to 60%–70%.

Carbohydrate recommendations vary from 6g to 10g/kg body weight. The amount required depends on the athlete's total daily energy expenditure, type of sport, gender and size.

To maintain health, it is recommended that five portions of fruit and vegetables should be eaten every day. One portion is a medium-sized piece of fruit, 150ml of fruit juice or three heaped tablespoons of vegetables or pulses.

Protein

Protein is essential for good health, growth and repair. It can also be used for energy, providing 4kcal per gram. Protein allows the body to function. The body requires 20 proteins or amino acids. It can produce 12 amino acids itself, but needs to consume eight essential amino acids every day to remain healthy as it cannot produce these. There are two types of protein: complete and incomplete. Foods that contain all eight essential amino acids such as meat, poultry, fish, milk, eggs and cheese are complete. Foods that lack at least one essential amino acid such as bread, rice, pasta, pulses and lentils are incomplete. Protein cannot be stored and the excess is either converted to energy or stored as fat.

Protein should make up 12%–15% of an individual's daily energy intake. The UK RDA is 70g per day for women and 90g per day for men.

Most athletes eat more than enough protein and do not need to increase their intake. The amount of protein they require can be calculated from their activity type and body weight:

- sedentary (does not train) – 0.75g/kg

- aerobic endurance – 1.2g/kg

- anaerobic/strength/power – 1.5g/kg

Research

Research the quantity of carbohydrate contained in the following foods and drinks:

- *1 banana*

- *1 cereal bar*

- *1 can of coke*

- *1 pint of beer.*

Discuss

Discuss which food or drink from the list would be better to consume, and explain why.

Practical

Calculate your daily intake for carbohydrate and protein.

Discuss

Discuss your results and compare them with other people in your class.

Key terms

RDA: recommended daily allowance

P1 Nutrition *continued*

Fats

Fats are essential as they provide energy, protect and cushion organs and insulate the body. Animal fats are also a good source of vitamins K, A, D and E (1g of fat provides 9kcal.)

There are two forms of fats: saturated and unsaturated. All fats that you eat are a combination of the two. Fats that have higher concentrations of saturated fat such as butter are solid at room temperature. Fats that have higher concentrations of unsaturated fats such as olive oil are liquid at room temperature. Foods that have higher levels of fat are dairy products such as cheese and red meat. A low fat intake is recommended to reduce risks from coronary heart disease.

Fats should make up 20%–35% of an individual's daily energy intake. Fats are a source of energy, fat-soluble vitamins and essential fatty acids, and are important in the diets of athletes.

Vitamins

Small quantities of vitamins are essential for health and growth. They are important in regulating metabolic functions in the body and support the nervous and immune systems. They assist in the production of hormones and help release energy and prevent disease. Two vitamins can be produced naturally (vitamin D from sunlight and vitamin K from bacteria in the intestine). All other vitamins need to be consumed.

Specific vitamins have specific functions, for example vitamin K assists with blood clotting. Foods that contain vitamin K are green leafy vegetables, liver and cauliflower. Vitamin A maintains healthy eyes, skin and bones. It also assists with hormone synthesis. Foods that contain vitamin A are milk, cheese and dark orange fruit and vegetables.

Fat-soluble vitamins such as A, D, E and K are stored in the liver and fat cells. Water-soluble vitamins such as B and C cannot be stored and excess amounts are excreted via the kidneys.

The UK RDA of vitamin A is 0.7mg per day for men and 0.6mg per day for women. The UK RDA of vitamin B6 is 1.4mg for men and 1.2mg for women. Vitamin B6 is necessary for turning food into energy and making haemoglobin.

Your assessment criteria:

P1 Describe nutrition, including nutritional requirements using recommended guidelines from public health sources associated with nutrition

---

Q | Research

Research the amount of fat contained in the following foods:

- *1 sausage*
- *1 bag of chips*
- *1 bag of crisps*
- *1 pizza*
- *McDonald's quarter pounder cheeseburger*
- *Beef rump steak grilled.*

? | Did you know?

Most people have adequate vitamins and minerals by eating a varied diet. In most cases supplements are not necessary.

Minerals

Minerals are essential to health and are important for bone and connective tissue formation. They also assist in the production of enzymes and hormones, in muscle contraction and the function of nerves. They can be divided into macro and micro groups. Macro-minerals are those that the body needs large amounts of, such as calcium. Micro-minerals such as copper are required, but only in very small quantities.

Calcium is contained in dark green leafy vegetables, broccoli, milk products and salmon. It is essential for strong bones, muscle contraction and relaxation, blood clotting and nerve function. A deficiency can result in poor bone growth in children and bone loss in adults. Potassium is contained in meat, vegetables, bananas and milk. It assists in the transmission of nerves and helps lower blood pressure. A deficiency can cause muscle weakness, confusion and tiredness. Iron is found in red meat, egg yolk, green leafy vegetables and dried fruit. It helps produce haemoglobin. Deficiencies cause anaemia and fatigue.

The UK RDA of calcium is 700mg. The UK RDA of potassium is 3,500mg. The UK RDA for iron is 11–14mg.

Fibre

Fibre is important because it provides bulk to your diet and aids the movement of food through the intestine. It ensures that your intestine functions properly and helps prevent cancer, diabetes and irritable bowel syndrome. It also makes you feel full, so can assist in weight loss. Fibre is a complex carbohydrate. Foods that are high in fibre include wholegrain cereals, pulses, fruit and vegetables. The recommended intake of fibre for adults is 18g per day.

 Did you know?

The estimated average daily requirement for adults aged 19–49 is 2550kcal (males), and 1940kcal (females).

 Research

Research the role of vitamins and minerals in the body.

Discuss

Discuss your results and compare them with other people in your class.

Digestion

The stages of **digestion** determine how quickly nutrients can be absorbed. Sports performers need to plan the type of food they take in to maintain energy levels. The amount and frequency of consumption are important factors. For example, tennis players need to regularly maintain their fluid and energy levels during a competition which often lasts between two and four hours. They regularly drink a range of fluids and often eat small amounts of food to maintain their performance level. Not drinking enough will cause them to run out of energy and become dehydrated.

P2 | Structure of the digestive system

The digestive system includes: the buccal cavity; oesophagus; stomach; duodenum; pancreas; liver; gall bladder; small intestine; large intestine and kidneys.

Buccal cavity and oesophagus

Digestion begins in the buccal cavity. The teeth break up the food and saliva begins to digest the starch or carbohydrate. Swallowed food moves into the oesophagus. It is then squeezed down to the stomach by rhythmic muscular contractions (a process called peristalsis).

The stomach

The stomach is a sack of muscle. It can hold between 50ml and 1.5 litres and has the ability to stretch. The muscular walls of the stomach churn food around, mixing it with digestive juices. The stomach also contains hydrochloric acid which kills any bacteria, and an **enzyme** called pepsin that breaks down protein. Gastric juices in the stomach gradually break down food into a liquid known as chyme. Tiny amounts of this are gradually squirted through a sphincter muscle into the small intestine. Large particles of food remain in the stomach as the sphincter only opens a small amount. Carbohydrates pass quickly through the stomach, protein passes through more slowly, and fats take the longest.

Your assessment criteria:

P2 Describe the structure and function of the digestive system in terms of digestion, absorption and excretion

Key terms

Digestion: *the process of breaking down food, absorbing nutrients and excreting waste products*

? | Did you know?

We produce between one and three pints of saliva per day.

Key terms

Enzymes: *proteins that produce chemical changes*

Research

Research how much hydrochloric acid your stomach produces each day.

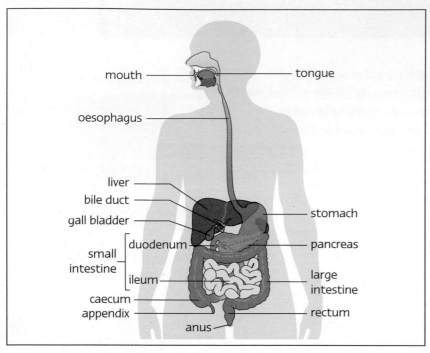

Figure 11.1 The digestive system

Small intestine

The small intestine is made up of three parts. The first part is the *duodenum* which absorbs iron and receives digestive juices from the liver, pancreas and gall bladder. These important organs play different roles in the digestive process:

- The pancreas produces bile that breaks down carbohydrate, fat and protein. Enzymes such as amylase break down starch into sugar, and lipase helps to break down fat.

- The liver secretes bile to the gall bladder and is important in carbohydrate, protein and fat metabolism. It also stores vitamins and glycogen.

- The gall bladder stores and concentrates bile which disperses fats into small globules, making them easier to break down.

The other two parts of the small intestine are the *jejunum* and the *ileum*. Water is absorbed throughout the small intestine. Villi (finger-like structures) increase the rate of absorption.

Large intestine

Finally, material is moved to the large intestine where more water is absorbed and bacteria produce vitamin K. The leftover material is excreted through the anus.

 Did you know?

The complete digestion process takes between 24 and 72 hours.

Discuss

Discuss the stages of digestion in which each of the following are absorbed: sugars; fats; carbohydrates; proteins; vitamins and minerals; water.

Research

Research the speed of absorption for types of carbohydrate.

Energy intake and expenditure

Energy intake and expenditure are important aspects of sports performance. They need to be balanced to maintain performance. An athlete will lose weight if energy is consumed and not replaced. Too high an intake of energy and insufficient exercise will cause an athlete to put weight on and possibly impair their performance.

P3 Describe energy intake

Measures

Energy is measured in **calories** or joules. It can also be expressed in 1000s. (See Figure 11.2.)

Sources

Energy comes from a variety of sources as previously mentioned:

- carbohydrates = 4kcal/gram
- protein = 4kcal/gram
- fats = 9kcal/gram.

Figure 11.2 Measures of energy

Calories and joules	Energy expressed in 1000s
• A calorie is the energy required to raise 1g of water by 1°C.	• A kilocalorie = 1000 calories.
• A joule is the energy required to move 1g (mass) at a velocity of 1m per second.	• A kilojoule = 1000 joules.
• 1 calorie = 4.2 joules.	

Energy intake is difficult to record and can take time to analyse. Keeping a food diary is the easiest way to monitor your intake. To do this, you will need to record everything that you eat and drink for each day.

Food labels are useful in providing information on the calories, carbohydrates, protein and fats contained in food. There are also a number of useful websites and nutritional texts that provide details of the calorific value of foods. Once you have collected your information and recorded it in a chart, you need to add all of the scores together to calculate your total daily energy intake.

Describe energy expenditure

Energy expenditure depends on a range of factors including gender, height, weight and physical activity level. It can also be affected by the amount of active muscle tissue that you have.

To calculate your daily energy expenditure, you need to work through the following equations:

Females: BMR = 655 + (9.6 x weight in kilos) + (1.8 x height in cm) – (4.7 x age in years)

Males BMR = 66 + (13.7 x weight in kilos) + (5 x height in cm) – (6.8 x age in years)

This calculates your basal metabolic rate.

You then need to multiply the score by your activity level below:

If you are sedentary	BMR x 1.2
If you do light exercise/sports 1–3 days a week	BMR x 1.375
If you do moderate exercise/sports 3–5 days a week	BMR x 1.55
If you do hard exercise/sports 6–7 days a week	BMR x 1.725
If you do very hard exercise/sports and a physical job or training twice a day	BMR x 1.9

Energy expenditure can also be calculated by direct or indirect calorimetry. Direct calorimetry measures the actual amount of heat the body produces. The heat measured can reveal the calorific expenditure. Heat produced by the subject warms water in an airtight room. The temperature difference reveals the calories used.

Indirect calorimetry estimates the amount of heat produced. This is done by measuring respiratory gases. The consumption of 1 litre of oxygen = 4.8kcal.

Key terms

Basal metabolic rate (BMR): the number of calories the body requires during its resting state to maintain normal body functions

Research

Research activity levels for a variety of sports.

M1 Explain energy intake and expenditure

Energy intake is dependent not only on the type of food and drinks that you consume, but also on the method of cooking. People can increase their calorific intake substantially by adding oil to recipes and dressings to salads, and by frying foods, and they often forget about the calories in alcohol and other drinks. There is typically 200kcal in a pint of beer and 130kcal in a medium glass of wine. A large milky coffee from a coffee shop can contain 102kcal.

Activities have different calorific expenditure rates. It depends on how hard and how long you exercise for.

Figure 11.3 Calorific expenditure rates for some popular activities

Activity	Intensity	Calories per hour
Aerobics	Light	240
Running	9km/h	640
Cycling	9km/h	240
Swimming	25m/min	330

Energy balance

P4 Describe energy balance

You have an energy balance when your intake matches your expenditure. This means that you will maintain your current weight. If your intake exceeds your expenditure, your weight will gradually increase. Eating an extra chocolate bar a day, or about 280 calories, can lead to an increase of 14 pounds of fat over six months.

If you expend more than you intake, your weight will decrease. An extra 60 minutes of moderate exercise per day can produce a weight loss of up to 14 pounds in six months.

Energy expenditure can first be determined using the equation on page 219.

Example: BMR calculation for a 40-year-old sedentary male, weighing 85kg and measuring 175cm:

Males

$$BMR = 66 + (13.7 \times weight\ in\ kilos) + (5 \times height\ in\ cm) - (6.8 \times age\ in\ years)$$

$$= 66 + (13.7 \times 85) + (5 \times 175) - (6.8 \times 40)$$

$$= 66 + 1164 + 875 - 272$$

$$= 1833$$

Total calorie expenditure for sedentary male = BMR x 1.2 = 2199.6

Changes in climate can cause an increase in BMR to maintain internal temperature. You tend to burn more calories when it is cold. Cold climates can increase BMR levels to nearly three times their normal rate. Hot climates can also increase energy expenditure. Sports undertaken in tropical climates can push internal temperatures up. Energy expenditure can increase by nearly 7% for an increase in core temperature of 0.5°C.

It is important to know your total energy requirements for your current weight. You can then compare this with the amount you consume and plan either to increase or decrease your weight as necessary.

Your assessment criteria:

P4 Describe energy balance and its importance in relation to sports performance

M2 Explain the importance of energy balance in relation to sports performance

D1 Analyse the effects of energy balance on sports performance

? Did you know?

Weight loss can be achieved by increasing your activity level.

An increase of less than 150mins per week produces minimal weight loss.

>150mins per week produces a modest 2–3kg weight loss.

>225–420mins per week produces 5–7.5kg weight loss.

🏃 Practical

1. *Calculate your total calorie requirements by working out your BMR and additional activity level calories.*

2. *Calculate your recommended weight for your sport based on your lean body mass and body fat percentage figures.*

M2 Explain energy balance

To determine the amount of weight loss or weight gain required, you need to be able to assess your body composition. How much fat you have will determine the amount you need to lose/gain. There are a range of tests that can be used to determine body composition. These are covered in Unit 7.

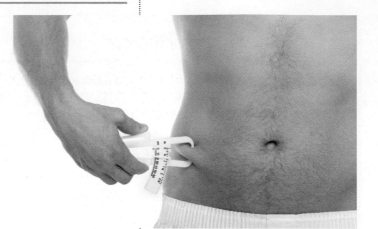

Percentage body fat can be checked and then a percentage reduction identified. The number of calories needed to achieve the new weight can then be calculated.

For example, a male with 15% body fat may want to reduce their percentage to 10%. If they weigh 85kg, they have 17.6kg of fat and 67.4kg of lean mass. To achieve 10% body fat, they need to reduce their weight by 10.2kg to 74.8kg.

D1 Analyse the effects of energy balance

To calculate the number of calories you should be consuming in a day, you need to determine your body fat percentage and the recommended body fat percentage for the sport that you play. For example, the recommended body fat level of a male tennis player is between 12% and 15%, and a female player between 16% and 24%. You then need to calculate the weight you should be by taking your existing lean body weight and adding on the extra weight for the desired body fat percentage level.

Using the example above, an 85kg male with 15% body fat has a lean mass of 67.4kg. He wants to reduce his body fat percentage to 10%. He will use the following equation:

Lean weight/(1 – required body fat percentage) = new ideal weight (NIW)

67.4kg/(1 – 10%) = NIW

67.4kg/(0.9) = NIW

NIW = 74.88kg

He then needs to recalculate his BMR using the new weight:

BMR = 66 + (13.7 x 74.88) + (5 x height in cm) – (6.8 x age in years).

Hydration and sports performance

P5 Hydration

Hydration and fluid intake is important in a number of sports to maintain and increase performance levels. Pre-event drinking can provide fluid and energy to ensure that performance is at its peak. During activity, sports performers sweat and lose water. This eventually leads to dehydration and a gradual decrease in performance, unless the fluid is replaced at regular intervals. When an activity has finished, athletes need to replace any fluid that has been lost to enable them to recover quickly.

Athletes can sweat over 1 litre of fluid in an hour. The sweat is lost to maintain body temperature. A loss of 2% of body weight impairs performance, 4% prevents the muscles from working properly and 5% can lead to heat exhaustion.

Signs and symptoms

The signs of dehydration are a lack of energy, feeling hot, a headache and flushed skin. Dehydration can be known as **hypohydration**.

Hyperhydration is where the body has too much fluid. Signs of this can be tiredness and confusion. Hyperhydration can cause a problem as it decreases the amount of sodium in your blood, and this is needed for muscle movement.

Superhydration is where large volumes of water are consumed. Some people think that this can help with weight loss, but there is little scientific evidence to support this belief.

Fluid intake

The recommended daily intake is between 2 and 2.5 litres of fluid. 60% of this should come from fluids that you drink. The rest comes from the food that you consume.

- *Pre-event:* athletes must ensure that they are hydrated before they start a competition. They should drink 300ml to 500ml of fluid 10 to 15 minutes before the activity so that it has time to be absorbed.

- *Inter-event:* the amount that you need to consume depends on the following factors: sweat rate, temperature, length of activity and intensity. General guidelines are to drink 150ml to 200ml of fluid every 15 minutes.

Key terms

Hyperhydration: too much fluid in the body

Hypohydration: the effects of dehydration

Superhydration: the consumption of large volumes of fluid prior to exercise

- *Post-event:* any lost fluid must be replaced. The easiest way to work out how much you require is to weigh yourself before and after an event. You need to drink at least 1 litre of fluid for each kilogram lost. Recommendations are to consume 1.5 times the amount required in the first two hours after activity.

Sources

Drinking water quenches thirst, but does not replace lost energy or minerals. Water contains no carbohydrate or electrolytes.

There are three types of drinks that can be used instead of water:

- *Isotonic drinks* – these contain fluid, electrolytes that replace minerals lost in sweat, and 6% to 8% carbohydrate. They quickly replace fluids lost and provide carbohydrate. This drink is the choice of most athletes, particularly middle and long-distance runners or athletes involved in team sports.

- *Hypotonic drinks* – these contain fluid, electrolytes and low levels of carbohydrate and are often used by athletes who need to replace fluid without extra energy, such as gymnasts and jockeys.

- *Hypertonic drinks* – these contain high levels of carbohydrate and are used in ultra-distance events. They provide additional carbohydrate on top of normal intake and are used after exercise to top up muscle glycogen stores. If they are used during exercise, they should be used with isotonic drinks to replace fluids. This is sometimes seen in a tennis match when players have a selection of drinks.

> **Q | Research**
>
> *Research types of sports drinks and the claims that they make.*

> **Practical**
>
> 1. *Find a recipe, and make your own sports drink.*
>
> 2. *Calculate the amount of fluid that you need to consume after an activity by taking part in a 60-minute practical and comparing your weight before and after.*

Case study

Arana has been chosen to represent her college in a regional badminton tournament. She has trained hard to improve her fitness and skill levels and is confident in her ability. However, she recognises that the last time she competed she started to run out of energy during the last games she had to play. She struggled to maintain her hydration levels and also found that she felt tired.

1. How much fluid should Arana drink before her tournament?

2. How much fluid should Arana drink during the event?

3. How much fluid does she need to drink after the event to help with recovery?

4. What type of drink would you recommend pre-event, inter-event and post-event?

Planning diets

P6 Balanced diet

Your assessment criteria:

P6 Describe the components of a balanced diet

M3 Explain the components of a balanced diet

A diet needs to be balanced so that the body can obtain everything it needs. Foods can be divided into five main groups:

1. fruit and vegetables,

2. starchy foods, such as rice, pasta, bread and potatoes

3. meat, fish, eggs and beans

4. milk and dairy foods

5. foods containing fat and sugar.

A **balanced diet** should contain five portions of fruit and vegetables a day. These help to lower your risk of heart disease, stroke and some cancers.

Starchy foods containing carbohydrate, such as bread, cereals, potatoes and pasta are also important. They provide energy and are the main source of a range of nutrients in our diet.

Meat is an excellent source of protein, vitamins and minerals, such as zinc, iron, and B vitamins. It also provides vitamin B12. However, red meat also contains saturated fat. Poultry is better as it has a lower fat content. Fish is also an excellent source of protein. It contains vitamins and minerals. Oily fish is particularly rich in omega-3 fatty acids.

 Key terms

Balanced diet: *a diet that provides all necessary nutrients without excess*

224

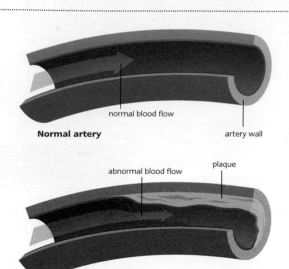

Figure 11.4 The effect of high cholesterol on the heart

Milk and dairy foods such as cheese and yoghurt also provide protein. They contain calcium, which helps to strengthen your bones. The problem with dairy products is that they tend to be high in saturated fat which can raise blood cholesterol levels and increase the risk of heart disease (see Figure 11.4). It is a good idea to drink semi-skimmed milk, skimmed milk or 1% fat milks, and eat lower-fat hard cheeses or cottage cheese, and lower-fat yoghurt to avoid this problem.

Fats and sugar provide energy, but they can also lead to obesity, which increases the risk of heart disease, type 2 diabetes and cancer. Saturated fat in pies, sausages, cheese, butter, cakes and biscuits can all cause problems. Unsaturated fats help to lower cholesterol and provide essential fatty acids needed to stay healthy. Oily fish, nuts and seeds, avocados, olive oils and vegetable oils are sources of unsaturated fat.

 Did you know?

A high level of cholesterol in the blood is a risk factor for coronary heart disease (CHD) and stroke.

The risk factors for high cholesterol include a fatty diet, lack of exercise, drinking alcohol to excess, inherited conditions, and getting older.

 Discuss

Discuss your diet with a partner and identify any problem areas in the balance of your diet. Are there any food groups missing?

Research

Research the food pyramid, and identify how many portions of each food group you should eat every day.

 Describe

Describe three targets that you could set to improve your own diet.

 M3 **Explain a balanced diet**

Athletes may need to supplement their carbohydrate foods with dried fruit or sports drinks to make sure that they consume enough. Their fat intake will need to be reduced as most people eat too much fat. Athletes tend to overcompensate with protein and eat too much. The recommended amount is 1.2–1.7g/kg body weight per day. 1.2g is sufficient for endurance sports athletes and 1.7g for strength or power athletes. Fluid should be consumed at the rate of 30–35ml/kg body weight per day. Fibre should be consumed at 18g per day. This is usually not a problem for athletes with a high carbohydrate diet. Vitamins and minerals tend not to be significantly affected by exercise.

P7 ▸ Plan a two-week diet plan

You need to plan an appropriate diet for a selected sports performer for a selected activity.

This involves initially collecting information about the sportsperson. You need to record some data including the sport they are involved in, their body fat percentage, weight, height, age, gender and activity level. From this information, you can calculate their energy expenditure and set clear targets for weight loss or gain. You should also record details of the training that they take part in. This information will give you an idea of how active they currently are.

You need to make an initial assessment of the sports performer's current diet. Asking an athlete to keep a food diary can provide useful data. However, some people record less than they actually eat and drink when using a food diary. Amending a diet is much easier and more realistic than creating a new diet. From your analysis of their food diary, you should be able to calculate the athlete's carbohydrate, fat and protein intake, and make an assessment on their total calorific intake.

You need to know the stage of training that they are in. During **pre-season** training an athlete's energy requirements may increase. During the mid-season, athletes try to maintain energy and fluid levels to maintain performance. During the post-season, athletes often relax some of their dietary requirements. Energy and fluids are targeted at recovery.

Modifications to an athlete's diet should also take into account the type of athlete they are.

Athletes that are involved in aerobic activities need to increase their carbohydrate stores two to three days before a competition by carbohydrate loading. The athlete depletes their carbohydrate stores six days before competition through training. The body compensates by trying to store more than it normally does.

Endurance athletes may need to increase their protein intake for recovery from intense endurance training from 1.2 to 1.4g/kg body weight.

Athletes involved in resistance training may need to increase their protein intake. Additional protein is needed along with sufficient energy to support muscle growth. A recommended protein intake for strength-trained athletes can be as much as 1.7g/kg body weight.

Your assessment criteria:

P7 Plan an appropriate two-week diet plan for a selected sports performer for a selected sports activity

M3 Explain the two-week diet plan for a selected sports performer for a selected sports activity

D2 Justify the two-week diet plan for a selected sports performer for a selected sports activity

 Key terms

Pre-season: a period just before the start of the competitive calendar in a sport

M3 › Explain a two-week diet plan

From your analysis of all of the information you have collected, you should be able to explain the amendments you have made to your sportsperson's diet. Weight loss goals should reduce calorific intake by no more than 5000 calories in a week (approximately 700 per day). Any greater loss can reduce strength and power levels. Weight gain involves similar increases in calories. The aim of weight gain will be to increase muscle, but not fat. Your explanations may include recommendations for the substitution of foods to decrease fat levels or increase protein or carbohydrate levels. Recommendations may also include methods of cooking, fluid intake and pre-event, inter-event and post-event advice.

D2 › Justify a two-week diet plan

Each of your recommendations must be justified and supported by evidence. Justifications for calorie decrease are based upon a variety of factors:

- your calculations of BMR and additional activity levels

- your calculation of body fat percentage

- research that clearly states the recommendations for fat levels in the relevant sport

- subsequent calculations to determine recommended body weight for the identified body fat percentage.

This information will provide the total recommended calories for each day. Additional research should support your justification for amendments to the athlete's diet for endurance or strength reasons.

Q | Research

1. Research the recommended body fat percentage in your sports performer's sport.

2. Research websites where you can find out food information, including carbohydrates, protein, fats and the number of calories contained in different foods.

🏃 | Practical

Organise a consultation and obtain information that you need to complete your analysis, including body fat percentage scores. You should also be prepared to explain the requirements of the analysis and the use of food diaries.

Assessment checklist

To achieve a pass grade, my portfolio of evidence must show that I can:

Assessment Criteria	Description	✓
P1	Describe nutrition, including nutritional requirements using recommended guidelines from public health sources associated with nutrition.	☐
P2	Describe the structure and function of the digestive system in in terms of digestion, absorption and excretion.	☐
P3	Describe energy intake and expenditure in sports performance.	☐
P4	Describe energy balance and its importance in relation to sports performance.	☐
P5	Describe hydration and its effects on sports performance.	☐
P6	Describe the components of a balanced diet.	☐
P7	Plan an appropriate two-week diet plan for a selected sports performer for a selected sports activity.	☐

To achieve a merit grade, my portfolio of evidence must show that I can:

Assessment Criteria	Description	✓
M1	Explain energy intake and expenditure in sports performance.	☐
M2	Explain the importance of energy balance in relation to sports performance.	☐
M3	Explain the components of a balanced diet.	☐
M4	Explain the two-week diet plan for a selected sports performer for a selected sports activity.	☐

To achieve a distinction grade, my portfolio of evidence must show that I can:

Assessment Criteria	Description	✓
D1	Analyse the effects of energy balance on sports performance.	☐
D2	Justify the two-week diet plan for a selected sports performer for a selected sports activity.	☐

14 | Exercise, health and lifestyle

LO1 Know the importance of lifestyle factors in the maintenance of health and wellbeing

▸ There are various lifestyle factors which are directly linked to physical activity.

▸ Making poor lifestyle choices has some serious risks associated with it.

▸ A healthy diet is of crucial importance in maintaining good health.

▸ There are several recommendations and guidelines which can help to maintain a healthy lifestyle.

LO2 Be able to assess the lifestyle of a selected individual

▶ Using accurate questionnaires are both valuable and important in making assessments.

▶ There are various personal choices which an individual has to consider.

▶ Different consultation methods are available for use.

▶ Carrying out consultations requires the use of some very specific skills.

LO3 Be able to provide advice on lifestyle improvement

▶ An individual's activity levels can be increased in a variety of different ways.

▶ There are many examples of good advice and guidelines which are available for use.

▶ There are several different ways of coping with both stress and tension.

▶ There are important nutrition guidelines which are linked to correct food preparation.

LO4 Be able to plan a health-related physical activity programme for a selected individual

▶ There are different ways of gathering information.

▶ Goal setting is very important and there are different ways of doing this.

▶ The principles of training are important factors which should be utilised in the final programme.

▶ It is possible for physical activities to be carried out with different intensities.

All individuals can choose to adopt a particular lifestyle, making specific lifestyle choices, so it is very important to be aware of what these choices are. To ensure good health and wellbeing, the choices need to be sensible and well informed.

P1 Lifestyle factors

Physical activity recommendations and guidelines

It is important that our bodies are kept active and that a sedentary lifestyle does not predominate. Scientific evidence has clearly shown that physical activity not only contributes to wellbeing, but is also essential for good health. People who are physically active, reduce their risk of developing major chronic diseases by up to 50 per cent, and the risk of premature death by 20–30 per cent.

A total of at least 30 minutes a day of at least moderate intensity physical activity on five or more days of the week reduces the risk of premature death from cardiovascular disease and some cancers, significantly reduces the risk of type 2 diabetes, and can also improve psychological wellbeing. These guidelines are adjusted according to age as it is considered that for adults at least 30 minutes of activity a day is for general health, but for many people 45–60 minutes of moderate intensity physical activity is needed to prevent obesity.

Children and young people require a total of at least 60 minutes a day of at least moderate intensity physical activity, and at least twice a week this should include activities to improve bone health (activities which produce high physical stresses on the bones), muscle strength and flexibility.

Benefits of physical activity

Regular physical activity has the following benefits:

- It reduces the risk of cardiovascular disease.
- It reduces the dangers of being overweight or suffering from obesity.
- It reduces the risk of diabetes.
- It improves musculoskeletal health.
- It improves psychological wellbeing and reduces mental illness.
- It reduces the possibility of contracting cancer.

Key terms

Cardiovascular disease: a disease of the heart or blood vessels

Obesity: an abnormal accumulation of body fat, usually 20 per cent or more above an individual's ideal body weight

Sedentary: accustomed to sitting and taking little exercise

Walking is one of the most effective ways of ensuring that you have a session of moderate intensity exercise.

Alcohol recommendations

Generally speaking, alcohol is not necessarily harmful, but there are recommendations and guidelines on drinking alcohol, as it can have both short-term and long-term harmful effects. The recommendations are linked to 'units' (or standard drinks). In the UK, a unit is 8g or 1cl of alcohol and the Government's recommendation for sensible drinking is three to four units per day for men and two to three units per day for women. However, this does not apply to young people who have not reached physical maturity, and people with conditions which may be affected by alcohol such as high blood pressure, those taking medication and pregnant women.

Risks associated with excessive drinking

Medical research has clearly shown that there are risks associated with excessive drinking, not only in the short-term, but also long-term, with serious medical conditions developing.

In the short term, a bout of excessive drinking can cause drunkenness which results in lack of co-ordination (one of the principal reasons for the drink–driving laws), vomiting and possible mood swings, including violent behaviour.

In the long term, excessive drinking is associated with the following health risks:

- strokes
- hypertension
- cirrhosis
- depression.

Smoking

This is clearly a poor lifestyle choice as by law every packet of cigarettes carries a government health warning pointing out the risks to health. Unlike drinking alcohol, there are no guidelines or recommendations, but only laws in place to prevent young people being able to buy cigarettes as well as smoking being banned in public places.

The health risks associated with smoking are:

- coronary heart disease
- cancer
- lung infections.

Stress

There are a great number of health risks associated with a high level of stress, including the following:

- hypertension
- angina
- strokes
- heart attack
- ulcers.

Did you know?

You can track alcohol consumption and use by using free 'trackers' which can be downloaded from the internet. These calculate the number of units in drinks and help an individual keep track of their drinking over a period of time. An example can be found at www.nhs.uk/tools/pages/nhsalcoholtracker.aspx

Key terms

Angina: chest pain due to an inadequate supply of blood to the heart muscle

Cirrhosis: a chronic disease of the liver

Heart attack: sudden interruption or insufficiency of the supply of blood to the heart

Hypertension: abnormally high blood pressure

Stress: a mentally or emotionally disruptive or upsetting condition which affects physical health

Stroke: the interruption of the blood supply to the brain which cuts off the supply of oxygen

P1 Lifestyle factors *continued*

Diet

There are a great many benefits of a healthy diet and this is clearly required to remain healthy.

A **balanced diet** is essential. It includes an intake of nutrients which are found in carbohydrates, fats, proteins, vitamins and minerals. The other vital ingredient of a healthy, balanced diet is water as this is essential for life.

Poor **nutrition** can result in illnesses such as obesity, or being undernourished which can make a person extremely weak and thin. A lack of vitamin C can cause scurvy, which can result in skin disorders and bleeding gums, and a lack of vitamin D can cause rickets which is a disease which affects bone development in young children.

The recommendations and guidelines for a healthy diet include the advice that everyone should have '5 A DAY' (that is five 80g portions of fruit and vegetables every day) as this is proven to lower the risk of serious health problems such as heart disease, stroke, obesity and type 2 diabetes.

The eatwell plate

Use the eatwell plate to help you get the balance right. It shows how much of what you eat should come from each food group.

FOOD STANDARD AGENCY
food.gov.uk

Figure 14.1 A balanced diet

M1 The effects of lifestyle factors on health

Every lifestyle factor has an effect on health, but some have a more dramatic effect than others.

Levels of physical activity

Although this is a factor of choice, it is clear that there are real benefits to be gained from taking part in regular physical activity which can have a positive effect on health. There are various factors relating to this which you need to take into account:

- The age of an individual – there are different guidelines for specific ages, so levels need to be matched to age.

> **Key terms**
>
> **Balanced diet:** a diet that provides all necessary nutrients without excess
>
> **Nutrition:** a source of nourishment, food

> **? Did you know?**
>
> *Dehydration can be a serious condition if you exercise for long periods of time. If you are exercising for 90 minutes or more, you will need to drink 200–300ml of liquid every 15–30 minutes.*

- Present activity levels – some individuals may already be leading a fairly active lifestyle, but for someone who is largely inactive, there would need to be quite a significant increase in levels.

- Occupation/time availability – this may well dictate how much time is available for physical activity. A school student or someone in a full-time job has most of their time accounted for, but an unemployed person might have more time available.

Alcohol consumption

This is a factor of personal choice. If an individual does not consume alcohol at all, then this factor does not need to be considered. However, anyone who does consume alcohol needs to be aware of the short- and long-term effects this can have on their health. Their levels of consumption need to be compared with the guidelines which are available.

Smoking

This is another factor of personal choice, but unlike alcohol consumption, there is no argument against the fact that smoking is harmful to health. There are no guidelines for safe levels, but there is a great deal of evidence available which shows the damaging effect of smoking on health.

Stress

This is believed to trigger 70 per cent of visits to doctors and 85 per cent of serious illnesses. In the UK, over 13 million working days are lost thorough stress every year, so it is clearly a very important lifestyle factor. Stress levels vary between individuals, and the health risks associated with stress need to be assessed and controlled.

Diet

Food is essential to all individuals, but it is the quantity and type which is important. It is also important to balance the amount of food and nutrients required for intake and output. Output is related to levels of activity. If these increase, then more calories are required through diet.

BMR can be worked out by using the following calculation and this can then be compared to Figure 14.2 which shows how many calories are used in some moderate activity exercises.

Women: BMR = 655 + (9.6 x weight in kilos) + (1.8 x height in cm) – (4.7 x age in years)

Men: BMR = 66 + (13.7 x weight in kilos) + (5 x height in cm) – (6.8 x age in years)

Did you know?

There are over 4,000 different chemicals in tobacco smoke, at least 50 are carcinogens (which cause cancer in humans) and many are poisonous. Cigarettes are one of the few products which can be sold legally despite the fact that they can harm and even kill over time if they are used as intended.

Figure 14.2 Calories used during moderate intensity exercise lasting 20 mins

Leisurely walk	80
Cycling	160
Running	90
Aerobics	140
Weights	140
Tennis	120
Swimming 25m/min	107
Swimming 50m/min	230
Rowing	200
Golf	45
Circuit training	260
Skipping	100

Key terms

BMR (basal metabolic rate): the number of calories the body requires during its resting state to maintain normal body functions

Calories: a measure of energy expenditure

Practical

Work out your own basal metabolic rate by using the calculation formula on the left.

Assessing the lifestyle of a selected individual

The most effective and efficient way to assess the lifestyle of an individual is to ask them to fill in a **questionnaire** which covers all the factors which need to be considered.

P2 Lifestyle questionnaire

This questionnaire is concerned primarily with lifestyle, so it is the factors related to this that are important. All information given must be correct and accurate.

General information

Firstly, it is necessary to obtain some important personal details from an individual. These include the individual's name, date of birth, gender, full address, telephone number, email address, weight and height. This purely factual information is easy to obtain, unlike some of the other information which needs to be collected and which may be related to opinions rather than actual facts.

Levels of physical activity

These have to be either described or listed factually. For instance, if an individual attends an aerobics class, they can state how long the class is and give an indication of how active the session is. Other physical activity might be more difficult to describe or rate accurately in terms of how active it is.

A good method is to use a diary approach, noting down everything an individual does in a period of a week and rating each of the things according to their level of activity. Being asleep or sitting still would be rated 1 (for no activity), and any activity of exercise could be marked up to a maximum of 5.

Alcohol consumption

This is something which can be checked and recorded quite easily. Alcohol is measured in units, and it is quite a simple process to record this on a daily basis.

Many people have high levels of physical activity through carrying out their normal jobs.

Key terms

Questionnaire: a form containing a set of questions

 Design

Design a diary/log covering a week-long period in which you can record levels of activity which have taken place during that period. Use some form of rating chart for the levels of activity.

Smoking

The number of cigarettes smoked each day simply needs to be noted and recorded.

Stress levels

This is not an easy factor to assess and measure as it can occur in many ways. There is no existing measure or guideline, so this has to be a matter of opinion for an individual. An exception is where an individual has been medically diagnosed as suffering from stress and is receiving medication.

Diet

This can easily be recorded by using a food diary as shown in Figure 14.3.

Research

Find some examples of lifestyle questionnaires which are already being used, either from some local clubs or gyms or through searching on the internet.

Figure 14.3 Nutritional intake diary

Time	Meal	Food and drink	Amount	Environment (e.g. home, meal out)	Feelings (e.g. hunger pangs, snacking)
7 a.m.	Breakfast	Orange juice	1 glass	Home	Hungry
11 a.m.	Snack	Packet of crisps	1 bag (small)	School	Snacking (not really hungry)

Time	Meal	Activity undertaken/type	Duration	Environment (e.g. school, club)	Intensity
1 p.m.	PE	Football	40 mins	School	Moderate
7 p.m.	Club	Badminton	1 hr 30 mins	Leisure Centre	Light

Consultation

As part of the process of assessing an individual's lifestyle, it is necessary to carry out a one-to-one **consultation** which is a confidential meeting with the person concerned, with particular emphasis on the following:

Communication

It is very important that the focus of the meeting is both clear and precise and this involves good communication skills. The interviewer must prepare in advance to ask appropriate questions.

Questioning

This must be very carefully planned in advance of the meeting, and it is likely that these questions will focus specifically on the content of the questionnaire.

Key terms

Consultation: a conference between two or more people to consider a particular question

P2 Consultation *continued*

Listening skills

It is important not to interrupt the individual being interviewed, and they must be given the opportunity to fully answer any question set. Careful listening to the responses given also helps to prepare the interviewer to ask further more detailed questions relating to answers already given.

Non-verbal communication

This refers to the ways in which someone's body language can influence someone else. For example, it is important to appear interested and attentive throughout an interview rather than distracted and uncaring.

Client confidentiality

A lot of personal questions are likely to be asked and some may be of a sensitive nature, such as the amount of alcohol regularly consumed. It is important that anything discussed is treated with complete confidentiality and not discussed with other people.

M2 Explain strengths and areas for improvement in lifestyle

This will depend on the particular 'lifestyle choices' which an individual has made. The strengths are likely to represent what can be seen as positive choices which will have a positive effect on health.

Increasing levels of physical activity are usually a strength, but this does have to be reasonable. Raising levels to a very high level could actually be damaging to someone who is either not used to it, or for whom it would be too much of a drastic step.

The physical activity levels and alcohol consumption should be compared with national guidelines, stress levels and smoking levels should be assessed, and diet should be assessed against guidelines.

 Case study

Rhiannon chose Sharon, one of her mother's work colleagues, to carry out her lifestyle questionnaire and consultation. After she carried it out, she found out that Sharon was a heavy smoker and would best be described as

Your assessment criteria:

P2 Design and use a lifestyle questionnaire to describe the strengths and areas for improvement in the lifestyle of a selected individual

M2 Explain the strengths and areas for improvement in the lifestyle of a selected individual

D1 Evaluate the lifestyle of a selected individual and prioritise areas for change

 Discuss

Test out some questions which might be used in a consultation session with other members of your group. Obtain some feedback on communication and listening skills as well as any comments on non-verbal communication.

having a 'drink problem'. Sharon is a receptionist, so she sits at her desk for most of the day, and she claims that she is, 'Too stressed out from work to even think about taking any form of exercise'. However, she is very keen on cooking which she considers to be her hobby as she is very aware of, and committed to, a healthy eating regime.

Rhiannon has to explain Sharon's strengths and areas for improvement as a result of her assessment.

1. What strengths would be apparent from Rhiannon's findings?

2. Which areas of improvement should be the main priority, and in what order should they be put?

3. What possible issues of confidentiality might Rhiannon have to deal with?

D1 Evaluate the lifestyle of an individual

This will depend on the findings after the questionnaire has been completed and the consultation has been carried out. This can only be considered once judgements have been made on the strengths and areas for improvement.

Case study

Leroy is carrying out his questionnaire and consultation with Aaron who is a fellow member of his BTEC teaching group. Aaron is a non-smoker and only drinks alcohol in moderation, well within the recommended guidelines. As well as taking part in all of the PE and sports programme which is provided within his school, Aaron is also a very keen basketball player, he trains twice a week with a local club and usually plays a competitive match at the weekends.

Due to his very busy and full lifestyle, Aaron does not consider his diet to be a priority, and he is not overweight or suffering from any nutritional deficiencies. He tends to snack a lot and likes 'fast food' which he finds to be both convenient and in his opinion, 'More than adequate for my needs!'

1. What overall judgement is Leroy likely to make regarding the strengths and areas for improvement in Aaron's lifestyle?

2. What is likely to be the highest priority as an area for change which Aaron might be recommended to make?

3. What recommendations is Leroy likely to suggest to Aaron?

Providing advice on lifestyle improvement

Lifestyle is a choice. There is always a possibility that poor choices might be made, but there are also many alternative choices and strategies which are available and possible. Many of these are neither expensive nor difficult to adopt. Being aware of the alternatives that are available is very important – especially if advice and guidance is to be given to another individual.

P3 Lifestyle improvement strategies

There are many of these, and they are clearly related to all of the factors listed on pages 232-235. Some of these just require a change of attitude with a commitment from the individual as they will be able to implement these changes on their own. Others require a greater commitment as they might involve working with other people, such as advisors or counsellors, or even joining a particular programme which might provide help.

Ways to increase physical activity levels

Physical activity levels can be increased relatively easily with some simple changes, such as:

- Walking more often and further – this might mean getting fewer lifts in cars or walking at least part of the journey. Getting off a bus several stops early or being dropped off by car before your destination are simple methods of achieving this.

- Stair climbing – using an escalator or lift is sometimes an alternative to using the stairs. Just as with the walking example, it may be possible to use a lift or escalator only partly and not wholly.

- Cycling – this is an alternative means of transport to walking and using buses or cars, and has the added advantage of being free!

Alcohol

Reducing, or controlling levels of alcohol consumption is obviously a positive factor. If consumption is above the recommended guidelines, then there clearly needs to be some action taken. This can include seeking alternative types and quantities of drinks, or counselling and therapy which can help to reduce a possible dependence on alcohol. It can be helpful to join a self-help group (such as Alcoholics Anonymous), or even investigate the possibility of alternative treatments and therapies such as hypnosis.

> **? Did you know?**
>
> *Two of the most popular aerobic type machines in gyms are the 'climbers' or 'steppers' and the exercise bikes. Gym providers always make sure that several of these machines are available for customers. These machines exactly reproduce the movements which a person makes by walking up stairs (the climbers/ steppers) or by riding a bicycle, which can be achieved without even going to the gym!*

Smoking

This ideally needs to be stopped altogether, but at least reduced. Smoking is addictive, so a regular smoker usually needs help to stop the habit. Help is available through various agencies including the NHS (National Health Service), but the first step is usually to contact an individual's doctor for help and advice.

Alternative treatments which may be recommended include acupuncture, hypnosis and nicotine replacement. Nicotine is the most addictive aspect of smoking, so the use of nicotine patches or nicotine gum helps to reduce the craving and addiction.

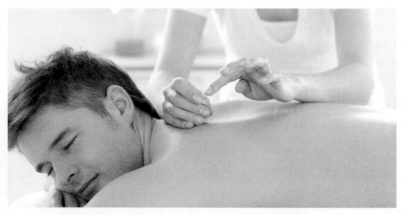

Acupuncture is an accepted form of alternative treatment.

Stress management techniques

Stress is not something which can be treated totally with medication, so management techniques are the most appropriate way of dealing with it:

- *Assertiveness* is recommended, as an individual will feel less pressured if they are able to stand up for themselves in stressful situations.

- *Goal setting* is important as it enables an individual to set and meet specific targets, and this makes the individual more organised.

- *Time-management* can also make an individual more organised, for example by using a diary to plan ahead.

- *Physical activity* is generally considered to help reduce stress levels as being physically tired can help an individual to relax more.

- *Positive self-talk* encourages an individual to reduce their negative thoughts and this can boost self-esteem, which in itself helps to reduce stress.

- *Relaxation techniques* are often combined with breathing control, and have a physiological effect to help slow down breathing and heart rate which can combat the negative effects of stress.

Key terms

Acupuncture: a traditional Chinese treatment where thin sharp needles are inserted in the body at specific points

Addictive: a compulsive physiological and psychological need for something which then becomes a habit

Discuss

1. *Discuss the levels of smoking in your peer group.*

2. *Discuss any measures which have been suggested or used to either cut down or stop smoking.*

Did you know?

You can find information about the NHS smoking helpline and NHS stop-smoking services at www.smokefree. nhs.uk

Yoga is an effective way of learning how to relax and use breathing techniques.

P3 ▸ Lifestyle improvement strategies *continued*

Diet

As well as ensuring that a diet is balanced, there are other factors associated with diet which can be adapted too:

- *Timing of food intake* – regular meals at regular times are recommended, as this helps to reduce 'snacking' where additional food is eaten at various times of the day, making food intake very difficult to control and monitor. Eating just before or after a bout of exercise is not advisable.

- *Eating more or less of certain foods* is a very simple strategy. Eating less unhealthy food and more of the recommended healthy food is an obvious positive step which can be taken.

- *Food preparation* is important as the ways in which food is prepared to be eaten can influence the effect it has, for example grilling food is healthier than frying it.

Behaviour change

This is the most crucial factor regarding a lifestyle improvement as behaviour is at the centre of this strategy.

Change does not happen immediately. There is a factor known as 'stages of change' which means that several gradual changes must be put in place before the final outcome is achieved. The first stage is that of being unaware, and there are then progressive stages of change, including preparing and trying, before the desired change finally takes place.

There are common barriers to behaviour change such as motivation. An individual lacking the motivation to change is unlikely to do so. For others, the barrier might be lack of time, more pressing commitments (such as work or home life) or even economic pressures.

Cognitive factors must be considered in relation to any behavioural strategies as the individual has to be aware of the changes which need to be made, as well as able to make sound judgements on how they might be achieved.

Key terms

Cognitive: the mental process of knowing, which includes aspects such as awareness, perception, reasoning and judgement

M3 Explain recommended lifestyle improvement strategies

If a lifestyle improvement is recommended for an individual, then it is important that it is fully explained in terms of its suitability and made relevant to their lifestyle. For example, the individual may be a manual worker who has a great deal of physical activity in their day-to-day life. This means that they are already attaining the recommended levels of physical activity, so this is not an area which needs to be prioritised. However, if the individual is a smoker and believes that smoking has not affected their fitness levels, they may need advice.

D2 Analyse lifestyle improvement strategies

It is unlikely that one particular strategy will be sufficient or solely responsible for achieving a significant lifestyle improvement. It is for this reason that you are required to analyse in detail the different strategies which are possible and available, and to consider the positive and negative aspects of each, together with the impact they are likely to make. For example, having three regular meals a day would not necessarily be an improvement and a benefit if the content of these meals did not match the recommended guidelines and endorse the '5 A DAY' suggestions.

? Did you know?

A Government scheme has been introduced known as 'Cyclescheme'. This scheme allows employers and employees to combine to provide a bike to be ridden to work. Brand new bikes are provided through a hire agreement as part of a cycle to work scheme, and the employees have the option to buy the bikes at the end of the hire period. There are incentives for tax savings for the employers too, which is why they are keen to be involved in the scheme.

Case study

Kris has chosen his Aunt Leanne as the individual he is going to advise on a lifestyle improvement. Kris has identified that his aunt has very low levels of physical activity as she has an office-based job and she uses her car for all of her personal transportation, even for short journeys to the shops. Kris feels that increasing physical activity levels is the most important strategy to advise his aunt on. He has made suggestions about walking more, and possibly buying a bicycle to use instead of her car.

1. What is likely to be the main positive impact of Leanne using a bicycle instead of a car?

2. What are the likely negative impacts which Leanne might experience in reducing her reliance on her car?

3. What other strategies relating to increasing levels of physical activity could Kris advise his aunt on?

Planning a health-related physical activity programme

One of the best ways to increase physical activity levels is to take part in some form of organised programme, and a six-week health-related programme would be an effective way of achieving this. Careful planning of this is important as there are some very specific guidelines which must be followed in order to make this both safe and effective.

P4 ▶ Plan a programme

Careful planning of a programme is essential if it is to achieve particular aims, and it is also important to have the correct content in place as well. The following factors should be considered.

Collecting information

This programme has to be planned for a particular individual, so it is very important to collect the specific information relating to the individual:

- *Personal goals* – these have to be considered and much of this will relate to the levels of physical activity which are already being undertaken. The whole focus of an individual programme must relate to the personal goals which the individual has identified, so it is not possible to repeat a previously planned and delivered one.

- *Lifestyle* – this has already been considered in some detail in this unit, so it is likely that quite a lot of lifestyle information has already been gathered.

- *Medical history* – this has to be considered very carefully as there may be underlying medical conditions which can affect how much exercise can be taken. Any form of injury or illness can prevent full participation and a condition such as asthma can limit activity levels.

- *Physical activity history* – this can have a significant impact as someone who is used to high levels of activity would not find it difficult to be set quite demanding targets in a new programme. However, for someone who has not experienced high levels before, it would be unwise to set levels too high.

- *Attitudes/motivation* – the attitudes and levels of motivation of the individual must be considered. A very positive attitude will help with setting some quite challenging goals, but if levels of motivation are low, then it is unlikely that an individual will fully take part or even complete the programme.

? **Did you know?**

Having a medical condition does not necessarily prevent you from taking part in quite strenuous physical activity. Marathon runner, Paula Radcliffe, Olympian swimmer, Rebecca Adlington, and footballer, Paul Scholes, are all high profile sports people who suffer from asthma, but still achieved sporting success!

Setting goals

There are three specific categories of goals – short-, medium- and long-term. In a six-week programme it might not be possible to achieve the long-term goals as there might not be enough time. The short-term goals would be the focus of the programme and it might be possible to link these to some medium-term ones as well. The overall plan should be to make some sustainable goals over a longer timescale than the six-week period, and these could be the identified long-term ones.

All goal setting needs to be matched to SMART targets:

- **S**pecific
- **M**easurable
- **A**chievable
- **R**ealistic
- **T**ime-bound.

Principles of training

There are some set principles of training which always apply when any form of programme is being devised.

Specificity

Any type of training must be suitable, or specific, to the identified need that is being trained for. This does not necessarily mean that one type of training needs to be chosen or that one particular aspect needs to be concentrated on. Due to individual differences, individuals may react differently to different methods, and combinations of different forms of training/exercise are often advisable.

Progression

Any training being undertaken must be increased gradually (progressively) so that the body can adjust to the increased demands being put on it. Staying at the same training level means there will be little or no improvement, and if too much is done too soon, then there is a danger of injury.

Abdominal curls or stomach crunches are good examples of specificity as they are specifically targeted at the stomach muscles.

P4 > Principles of training *continued*

Overload

This involves making the body work harder in order to improve fitness. Everyone has a capacity to train at comfortable levels, but in order to improve, that capacity must be extended by increasing the workload. This is achieved by using the FITT principle:

- Frequency – increasing the number of sessions being taken

- Intensity – increasing the degree of difficulty or working harder in each session

- Time – this is sometimes referred to as 'duration' as it means increasing the time allocated to particular aspects of the training

- Type – there are many different types of training available, and changing to a more demanding one can increase the workload.

Reversibility

Just as progression can lead to improvement, if training is either stopped or decreased, then effects which have been gained can be lost.

Variation

It is important to avoid the **tedium** of training as someone who is bored is likely to lack motivation. This can be achieved by varying training, for example changing the methods, the venue, the targets or even making use of training partners.

Appropriate activities

It is unlikely that the activities in a health-related physical activity programme will be of very high intensity, so basic options such as walking, cycling, hiking and swimming should be considered. It is possible to use machines in gyms, or even at home, for both walking (treadmills) and cycling (exercise bikes).

 Your assessment criteria:

P4 Plan a six-week health-related physical activity programme for a selected individual

? | **Did you know?**

Elite performers are well aware of the effects of reversibility as they know that if they have to stop training, possibly through injury or illness, then it takes three times as long to regain the levels which have been lost. A two-week break requires a six-week training period to reach previous levels.

Key terms

Tedium: a state of being weary, tired of something or bored

? | **Did you know?**

Principles of training are often referred to as the SPORT acronym which stands for:

- *Specificity*
- *Progression*
- *Overload*
- *Reversibility*
- *Tedium.*

Exercise intensity

This is a vital factor when planning a programme as the levels of intensity have to be matched and achieved in order to bring about the desired results.

Rating of perceived exertion

Known as RPE, this is a common method for determining exercise intensity levels. It is related to how hard someone feels they are working, which is a **subjective** judgement. There is a recognised scale, known as the Borg scale, which rates exertion on a scale of 1 to 20, where 1 is no exertion at all and 20 is maximum exertion. Various descriptions are included between these two such as 'somewhat hard' for level 13 and 'very hard' for level 17.

Maximum heart rate

This is the maximum level which the heart rate should be raised to. It can be calculated as follows: 220 minus age, so for a 16-year-old this would be 220 − 16 = 204. Being aware of this rate is important for setting targets for work rates.

Maximum heart rate reserve

This is the difference between the maximum heart rate and the resting rate. For example, a 16-year-old with a resting rate of 72 (the normal rate for an adult) would subtract this from 204 (the calculated maximum heart rate) to give a result of 132.

Talk test

This is used as a very simple gauge of exercise intensity. If a person is able to talk whilst exercising they are judged to be working at a low to moderate pace (level 4 on the RPE scale), but if they are breathless, then they would be working at a harder pace (around level 8/9).

> **Key terms**
>
> *Subjective: something based on an inner experience or opinion rather than fact*

Being able to both take and monitor the pulse rate is vital for calculating maximum heart rate.

> **Practical**
>
> *When you next take part in physical activity, use the 'rating of perceived exertion' to give you a better understanding of how this activity might be used when planning a physical activity programme for someone else.*

Assessment checklist

To achieve a pass grade, my portfolio of evidence must show that I can:

Assessment Criteria	Description	✓
P1	Describe lifestyle factors that have an effect on health.	☐
P2	Design and use a lifestyle questionnaire to describe the strengths and areas for improvement in the lifestyle of a selected individual.	☐
P3	Provide lifestyle improvement strategies for a selected individual.	☐
P4	Plan a six-week health-related physical activity programme for a selected individual.	☐

To achieve a merit grade, my portfolio of evidence must show that I can:

Assessment Criteria	Description	✓
M1	Explain the effects of identified lifestyle factors on health.	☐
M2	Explain the strengths and areas for improvement in the lifestyle of a selected individual.	☐
M3	Explain recommendations made regarding lifestyle improvement strategies.	☐

To achieve a distinction grade, my portfolio of evidence must show that I can:

Assessment Criteria	Description	✓
D1	Evaluate the lifestyle of a selected individual and prioritise areas for change.	☐
D2	Analyse a range of lifestyle improvement strategies.	☐

17 | Psychology for sports performance

LO1 Know the effect of personality and motivation on sports performance

▶ There are different types of personalities which can be identified.

▶ The type of personality an individual has can affect their performance.

▶ As sporting situations change, so can the different types of motivation experienced by performers.

▶ Motivation is an important factor which affects sporting performances.

LO2 Know the relationship between stress, anxiety, arousal and sports performance

▶ Stress has a major role in sports performance.

▶ Performances can be affected by stress in a variety of different ways.

▶ Anxiety can be caused by various factors, and there are ways in which it can be dealt with and controlled.

▶ Experiencing arousal is an important factor, and its effects can be dramatic.

LO4 Be able to plan a psychological skills training programme to enhance sports performance

▸ A starting point is to use a suitable method of assessment.

▸ A plan must have clear aims and objectives.

▸ The impact of psychological skills must be clearly understood in relation to enhancing performance.

▸ There are various techniques associated with psychological skills which need to be identified.

LO3 Know the role of group dynamics in team sports

▸ Group processes contribute greatly to team play.

▸ It is advantageous to develop cohesion within a group.

▸ Good leadership is an essential factor for successful performances.

▸ Leaders can adopt a variety of different leadership styles.

The effect of personality and motivation on sports performance

Just as physiological factors can affect a performance, so can psychological factors. The ways in which **personality** and levels of **motivation** can affect a performance should not be underestimated. Many top level sports performers, and certainly their coaches, are very aware of this and will pay particular attention to raising levels of motivation especially to improve a performance.

P1 Personality

A great deal of research has been carried out on different types of personalities and there are several theories related to the subject. There is little doubt that an individual's personality characteristics can have an effect on their performance levels in sport. However, it must be remembered that a theory is not based on fact, and that there is some overlap on certain aspects of the theories.

Theories

Marten's schematic view – this theory considers personality to be at three levels:

- The psychological core – also known as 'the real you' as this is what your values, beliefs and attitudes are. In most cases, these are considered to be stable, constant factors which a person retains.

- Typical responses – this is the usual way in which a person would be expected to respond in particular situations or circumstances.

- Role-related behaviour – this is where circumstances might change, possibly because of a role or situation someone finds themselves in.

A boxer expects to be making full physical contact and exchanging blows is a typical response.

Key terms

Motivation: an inducement or incentive coupled with a desire to do something

Personality: the distinctive qualities of a person in terms of their character and behaviour

? Did you know?

Many young people are encouraged to take up boxing because it allows aggression to be used in a very controlled manner. In common with martial arts sports, boxers are expected to adhere to a code of not using their fighting skills outside a sporting situation, and can be banned from their sport if they do so.

252

Psychodynamic theory – this theory considers there to be three components of personality, and it is often used when describing behaviour:

- the id, which is responsible for all needs and urges and which reflects your instincts

- the superego, which is responsible for morals and ideals, and could be your 'conscience'

- the ego, which moderates between the id, the superego and reality.

Trait theory – trait is considered to be a typical pattern of behaviour, usual thoughts and emotions, and they are generally thought to be inherited. A well known theorist, Eysenck, believed there are three major traits:

- Extroversion – being assertive, enjoying the company of others and seeking out excitement. The opposite is introversion when someone is more reserved, quite shy, less outgoing and less sociable.

- Neuroticism – experiencing negative emotional states where feelings of anxiety, anger and guilt can lead to feeling depressed. This trait often results in dealing badly with environmental stress (for example, a challenging sporting environment such as a potential heavy loss in a competitive game) by getting extremely frustrated and experiencing a feeling of hopelessness.

- Psychoticism – suffering from a personality disorder and not in touch with reality which can prevent a person from meeting the ordinary demands of life.

Situational approach – this theory considers the environmental situation (rather than a particular personality or traits) to be the main factor which determines a person's behaviour. This can be a combination of both the environment and circumstances, but it is accepted that some aspect of the personality is involved in the resulting behaviour.

Interactional approach – this theory considers the situation and the person as the causes of behaviour, so it includes personality and personality traits contributing to the choices being made which result in the final behaviour being demonstrated.

Arguing with an official is often role-related behaviour.

P1 ▶ Personality *continued*

Personality types

Another aspect of personality is type. There are two types of personalities:

- Type A tends to be competitive, impatient with a sense of urgency and has low tolerance levels towards others.

- Type B tends to be far more relaxed and easy-going, is often described as 'laid-back' and is more tolerant of others.

Effects on sports performance

There is no proven link between personality and sporting performance, but there is evidence that certain personality types are attracted to specific sports. There is no evidence, however, that this makes someone either a better or worse performer.

- *Athletes versus non-athletes* – physiological factors rather than psychological factors are more likely to determine whether someone is an athlete or a non-athlete. However, the personality type is likely to influence the type of activity they opt to take part in.

- *Individual versus team sports* – extroverts are more likely to get involved in team games where there is more of a social aspect, and sometimes a more competitive element. There is almost an expectation in many team games that the team will stay together after a match to socialise, and there is often an expectation that both competitive teams will meet at the conclusion of the game. In football, rugby and cricket there is often a meal served at the conclusion of the game and it is certainly 'socially acceptable' for players to join each other for a drink in the clubhouse at the end of a match. The tradition of the 'tea interval' between innings at cricket matches is an integral part of the match with the home team providing refreshments. Introverts, on the other hand, may wish to take part in more individual activities such as middle and long-distance running where they train and run on their own.

- *Elite versus non-elite athletes* – athletes performing at the elite level are more likely to be in the public spotlight and enjoy the high public profile, so this would indicate a more extrovert personality type. The influence and existence of the media means that it is just about impossible for any elite performer to avoid recognition in public, so performing at an elite level almost puts pressure on the performer to endorse an extrovert personality type. As introverts are generally quite shy people, they are likely to avoid competing at an elite level (even if they have the ability), or choose activities which do not have an elite or competitive element such as yoga, keep fit or aerobics. They are aware that public acclaim and recognition is something they will have to deal with in certain sports and activities, and this could be enough to put them off taking part in the first place.

- *Type A versus type B* – a type A personality is competitive so is likely to enjoy this aspect of sports involvement, and choose sporting activities such as team sports where this is an important element. However, there are individual activities such as tennis, squash and badminton which are extremely competitive with the same sense of impatience and urgency. Regular games (even daily) can be arranged, rather than having to wait for team mates and less frequent games or matches in team activities such as netball, hockey, rugby and football.

A type B personality may not be concerned about participating regularly or even competitively because of their more laid-back approach, and they are less likely to be too worried about which type of activity they take part in.

Introverts often prefer individual sports as opposed to team games.

Discuss

1. *Discuss which personality type each member of the group considers themselves to be in, and find out if the other members of the group agree.*

2. *Discuss whether the personality types match the types of sports involvement which would be expected.*

? Did you know?

The majority of elite performers employ sports psychologists to work with them and to advise them on aspects of their personality which could affect their performance. Many think that at the top level the mental barriers they face are sometimes more significant than the physical ones.

P2 Motivation

In sporting situations, motivation usually links to someone's desire to win and there are different views of what motivation is.

Views

There are three identified views relating to motivation:

- *Trait centred* – this is where behaviour is primarily related to an individual interest such as needs, interests, goals and personality.

- *Situation centred* – this is where the situation the performer finds themselves in provides the motivation, for example this can be as simple as having spectators watching, or being in a particularly challenging situation.

- *Interactional* – this is a combination of the two factors above and the result of the interaction between them.

Types

There are two identified types of motivation:

- *Intrinsic* – this is where someone is taking part for their personal satisfaction or enjoyment, or because they have an inner drive to achieve a goal or objective. This is also known as 'self-motivation'.

- *Extrinsic* – this is where external influences or people are the main incentive, and this can include rewards, social recognition or benefits. The possible rewards can range from medals and trophies to money.

Theories

There are various theories relating to motivation and these include:

- *Achievement motivation* – this leads individuals to set realistic but challenging goals, and there needs to be a balance between a desire to succeed and the fear of failure. A high achiever has a great desire to win, they are not put off by the fear of failure and they enjoy challenges.

- *Attribution theory* – this is where a person's own perceptions or attributions for success determine the amount of effort they will put into the activity in the future. The individual considers four factors which can contribute to this: ability (their own and possibly that of opponents in comparison); task difficulty (this is the level of challenge they are facing);

Your assessment criteria:

P2 Describe motivation and how it affects sports performance

? Did you know?

Tiger Woods regularly tops the 'chart' for being the highest earning sports performer and as 'rewards' are a form of extrinsic motivation, this may indicate a link to his success. In his last full year of playing, Woods' total earnings were $90.5 million which consisted of $20.5 million for winnings and salary and an additional $70 million for endorsements!

Tiger Woods showed mainly intrinsic motivation during his successful amateur career before moving on to extrinsic motivation in his professional one.

effort (perceived levels which they are prepared to make) and luck (their perception of what might be termed luck in terms of being 'good' or bad').

Effects on sports performance

As motivation clearly has an effect on a performance, it is considered to be a very important factor:

- Positive effects – someone who is positively motivated wants to do well and puts in as much effort as possible which is likely to result in an increased level of performance. The reasons behind the positive attitude are not relevant, as it is the fact that a positive approach has been adopted that results in this higher attainment level.

- Negative effects – low levels of motivation result in low level performances. The performer may show little indication of interest, and little or no desire to win or even compete. There can, however, be instances where a performer becomes overly motivated to succeed, and overtrains as part of their preparation. Fatigue then reduces their efficiency levels and their enjoyment levels too.

- Future expectations of success and failure – this links very closely to the attribution theory as a performer has to rationalise why they were either successful or unsuccessful and consider all of the factors which contributed to it. It is likely that levels of motivation will be one factor, but the other factors (in this case, ability, task difficulty, effort and luck) must be taken into account as well. If a performer experiences a higher proportion of positive effects which results in improvements in performance, then this is likely to continue. On the other hand, negative effects are likely to result in a downward spiral where performance levels continue to fall which in turn has the effect of reducing levels of motivation.

Players often attempt to motivate each other just before a game starts.

Developing a motivational climate

This refers to the sporting situations and environments which a performer finds themselves in, and it is clearly preferable for this to be a positive one rather than a negative one. It is important that performers receive some help with this, and coaches, advisors and even captains can play a role here. The positive attitudes and thoughts which the performer is able to establish (through a combination of intrinsic and extrinsic motivation) can be further reinforced by receiving support and encouragement from other people.

? | Did you know?

It is possible to take an online test to measure the various levels of an individual's motivation by visiting www.testcafe.com/mot

M1 Explain the effects of personality and motivation

The two factors of personality and motivation interlink and combine to have an effect on sports performance. It may be possible to explain some aspects of a performance by finding out more about a particular individual, and identifying characteristics of both personality and levels of motivation. This is easier to explain if some form of evidence has been gathered which gives more information about the individual. In order to achieve this, it might be necessary to interview an individual, as making a judgement about a personality type, or levels of motivation being experienced, is very difficult for someone who is only an observer.

Your assessment criteria:

M1 Explain the effects of personality and motivation on sports performance

D1 Evaluate the effects of personality and motivation on sports performance

It is difficult to judge how high levels of motivation are in a particular individual.

Case study

Ben is seen by his peers to be a very outgoing and confident personality type, and he took part in an online evaluation which suggested he strongly matches the type A personality category. Ben is a very keen and committed sportsperson, and is the captain of both the school and district rugby team. He is very proud of the medals and trophies he has won, and he has made it known that his goal is to become a professional rugby player. However, there is some resentment from the rest of the rugby team as they feel that Ben, in his role of captain, is harsh on them if they make mistakes in games, or give a poor performance.

1. Which trait type is Ben likely to be when considering trait theory?

2. Which particular type A personality characteristics does Ben most clearly show?

3. Would you consider Ben to be positively or negatively motivated?

4. Which type of motivation, extrinsic or intrinsic, seems to be most applicable to Ben?

D1 Evaluate the effects of personality and motivation

Being able to both describe and explain the effects of personality and motivation on sports performance are a starting point for this, but an evaluation requires a judgement to be made on what influence these two aspects might have had on a final performance.

Case study

Beth has been taking part in gymnastics for several years, and has been a club gymnast for ten years, ever since she was five years old. During that time, she decided not to take part in any competitions, although she was pleased to collect a large number of gymnastic awards for satisfying the national governing body award schemes. Beth finally gave in to pressure from the club coach to take part in a gymnastics competition and surprised herself by winning the floor routine competition. Following on from this success, Beth is now in full training to take part in a higher level competition, and is attending additional training sessions with the coach who first encouraged her.

Using the descriptions and explanations above, what judgements would you make on the following:

1. What personality type is Beth most likely to be, and what personality traits has she demonstrated most?

2. How would you apply both the achievement motivation and attribution theories to Beth's progress as a sports performer?

3. What is most likely to have motivated Beth to finally take part in a competition?

4. What is motivating Beth to take part in an even higher level competition?

? Did you know?

Gymnastics is considered to be one of the last truly amateur sports as there are no professional competitions. The motivation for performers in this sport has to come from the joy of taking part and wanting to win as there is no prize money available.

The relationship between stress, anxiety, arousal and sports performance

Stress, anxiety and arousal are experienced by all sports performers, but they can affect them in different ways. These psychological factors can have both negative and positive effects. It is important to be aware of the relationship between stress, anxiety, arousal and sports performance, and to be aware of appropriate strategies for dealing with the effects they may have in order to achieve a maximum level performance.

Your assessment criteria:

P3 Describe stress and anxiety, their causes, symptoms and effect on sports performance

P3 Stress

Stress often plays a positive role in sports performance. However, too much stress can have a very negative effect on performance.

Types

Stress falls into two distinct categories:

- *Eustress* – this is the 'good' type of stress that comes from the challenge of taking part in something you enjoy, but have to work hard for. A sports performer uses this to train harder and achieve higher levels, so it is effectively a factor of intrinsic motivation.

- *Distress* – this is the 'bad' type of stress as it is linked to reacting to negative demands such as anxiety, worry and apprehension.

Causes

There are many causes of stress and the most significant ones are:

- Internal – this includes low self-esteem, low expectations or even physical stresses such as illness, pain and lack of sleep. Mental stresses such as worry or anxiety are also in this category.

- External – this is linked to any environment which has to be coped with, and factors which are beyond individual control, e.g. bereavement, or life-changing situations, e.g. divorce.

- Personal – this is very individual and refers to any personal circumstances, e.g. lack of money and relationship difficulties (especially those involving family).

- Occupational – these are work-related factors for individuals who are in employment, and these can be quite severe as lifestyle factors are usually very closely linked to the jobs people have.

Key terms

Anxiety: a state of uneasiness and apprehension

Stress: a mentally or emotionally upsetting condition which occurs in response to adverse external influences and is capable of affecting physical health or wellbeing

Discuss

In a group, give examples of both eustress and stress that individuals can fully describe from personal experience. Discuss and identify the causes for both in these examples.

- Sports environments – these can be very challenging. These can vary from the climber who has to perform a difficult and dangerous climb, to any competitive sport where the opposition is considered to be stronger or superior, and therefore the pressure of competition is experienced.

Symptoms

Stress is a recognised clinical condition and it has clearly identified symptoms which include:

- Cognitive – these are symptoms linked to an individual's mental state and include worrying, poor concentration, poor attention to detail, indecisiveness, forgetfulness and feeling helpless.

- Somatic – these are symptoms linked to an individual's physical state and include fatigue, chest tightness, breathing difficulty, backaches and headaches.

- Behavioural – these include decreased levels of activity, increased levels of smoking and alcohol consumption, relationship conflicts and overeating with resultant weight gain.

Effects on sports performance

High levels of stress clearly affect any situation, but they can be serious in sporting situations.

Stress can affect two parts of the nervous system: the sympathetic nervous system which is responsible for stress responses such as 'flight or fright' (to either want to run away from the situation or to remain and face it head on), and the parasympathetic nervous system which prepares the body for rest and relaxation. Stress means that the sympathetic system keeps the body in a constant state of alert, not allowing the parasympathetic system to come into play at all.

Cognitive symptoms combine to create a negative mental state in the individual which is unhelpful in a sporting situation. Worrying about the opposition (possibly seeing them as stronger or superior) and feeling helpless (not good in match/game situations) are very likely to decrease performance levels.

Loss of self-confidence and poor concentration usually result in low performance levels as even simple skills can be difficult to accomplish. Golfers can experience the 'yips', a movement disorder associated with putting. When confidence is low, they miss simple putts which they would previously have holed.

Bernard Langer was a top flight golfer who suffered from the 'yips' when putting.

P3 ▶ Anxiety

Anxiety is a negative, emotional state which is caused by stress, and is evident in feelings of uneasiness and apprehension.

Types

Two types of anxiety have been identified:

- *State anxiety* – this is the anxiety the individual experiences when something causes them to feel appropriately and temporarily anxious, and this continues until normal feelings return. This is not always a negative factor as all performers expect to be slightly apprehensive at the start of their performance, and as long as this only lasts for a short period, then it is not likely to affect the overall performance.

- *Trait anxiety* – this is the 'pre-set' levels of anxiety experienced by an individual who has a tendency to be more anxious. If an individual has high levels of trait anxiety, they must try to learn to cope with them as though they are normal, otherwise they are likely to have a more damaging negative effect in the long-term.

Symptoms

Just as stress displays symptoms in the categories of cognitive, somatic and behavioural, so does anxiety.

- Cognitive – symptoms include inability to think clearly, poor concentration, being easily distracted, decreased problem-solving capability, negative thinking and mental fatigue. There are few, if any, sporting situations where these cognitive factors do not have a negative effect on the level of performance, especially in any individual activity or event. Even in a team competition, the individual is unlikely to be useful to the team if any of these symptoms are being experienced.

- Somatic – symptoms include excessive sweating, shaking, dizziness and blurred vision, breathlessness or shortness of breath, stomach upset, and neck and chest pain. These physical effects clearly have a negative effect on a sporting performance as they have physiological effects on the performer over and above the ones which they expect to have to deal with. Excessive sweating affects the grip on rackets in badminton, tennis and squash, dizziness affects balance, and blurred vision affects every aspect of a performance.

- Behavioural – symptoms include increased irritability, anger and suspicion, with fears of impending doom and even dying. Irritability and anger are likely to get any performer into confrontational situations

Your assessment criteria:

P3 Describe stress and anxiety, their causes, symptoms and effect on sports performance

🔍 Research

Research the effects of anxiety and 'choking' at www.collinseducation. com/sportspsychology.

❓ Did you know?

In the acting profession, these cognitive symptoms would be seen as 'stage fright', and this can happen to sporting competitors to the point where they are unable to function usefully in a sporting competition.

with team mates, opponents and the officials who are in charge, and these are emotions which are normally kept in check. Anyone experiencing high levels of behavioural symptoms is unlikely to be allowed to continue taking part as they are very likely to infringe both rules and accepted levels of etiquette.

Effects on sports performance

Anxiety affects sports performance in a similar way to stress.

Anxiety often results in loss of self-confidence which is very closely linked to the cognitive symptoms. Performers are constantly seeking to exploit weaknesses in opponents, and if they are able to identify low levels of confidence in an opponent, then this is a weakness which they may choose to exploit. Lack of concentration and being easily distracted result in an immediate reduction in performance levels and also have an impact on confidence levels. A football goalkeeper who is unable to concentrate is ineffective and likely to concede goals, and this inevitably leads to reduced self-confidence. It is also likely to lead to a high level of negative comments from team mates which will only make the situation worse!

Anxiety can result in decreased expectations of success. Loss of confidence creates a downward spiral as it creates a feeling that lower levels of performance are inevitable and this then perpetuates the low confidence levels. If a gymnast continuously fails to properly complete a particular move in their floor routine, they may decide to replace it with something easier or cut it out completely. By doing this, they will reduce the 'tariff level' (the degree of difficulty of moves which judges use as part of their marking criteria) of the routine which in turn is likely to result in lower marks being attained.

Many performers are so preoccupied with the fear of failure that they will have a negative, rather than positive approach. For example, a football team which fears failure will play very defensively in order not to lose, and this obviously reduces the chances of winning.

Divers have to choose the level of difficulty for the moves which they include in their dives in order to attain the highest marks.

P4 ▶ Arousal

Arousal is a state of heightened physiological activity which increases alertness. Arousal can be an important psychological factor in sports performance because it results in a change in the physiological state, such as an increase in muscle tension.

Theories

There are four arousal theories to consider:

- Drive theory – the more arousal and anxiety an individual experiences, the higher their performance will be.

- Inverted U hypothesis – this theory considers that there is a medium amount of arousal and anxiety which causes an individual to perform at a higher level, and that too little arousal and anxiety results in a decreased performance level.

- Catastrophe theory – as long as there is a low level of anxiety, then the individual performance is best at a medium level of arousal. If there is a high level of anxiety (e.g. extreme worry), performance is better at a medium level of arousal, but suddenly drops off and becomes very poor. A crisis point is reached when the performance level decreases dramatically.

- Individual zones of optimal functioning – this theory takes into account that individuals have different levels of arousal and anxiety which are unique to them. Some individuals perform best at low levels, some at medium and some at high as optimum levels are related to individual characteristics.

Home advantage is considered to be advantageous in sporting competitions because it helps to raise the arousal levels of the players.

Effects on sports performance

As long as a performer does not become over-aroused, performance levels are likely to increase, especially if the drive theory is realised. However, an additional theory, known as the reversal theory, states that arousal can be thought of in two ways. If it is seen as pleasant and exciting, then performance will improve, but if it is seen as unpleasant and anxious, then the performance levels will decrease.

As levels of arousal increase, an individual's attention focus tends to narrow. For a performer who can perform skills consistently, it is likely that the performance of these skills will continue at that level, but they will find more challenging tasks more difficult to perform. In any performance, there are a great number of aspects a performer needs to concentrate on (for example, their skill level and choices, the opposition, environment factors, crowd/spectator influence), so if the focus narrows, then overall performance is likely to decrease as well.

Arousal may lead to an increase in anxiety level, but this depends very much on the individual. For some individuals, being anxious is a positive factor and can spur them on to a better performance. For others, it is a totally negative factor which overrides others to result in a decreased performance level.

'Choking' is when an individual is unable to perform a skill they have previously mastered due to high anxiety levels, for example missing the target in a penalty kick, or constantly double-faulting in tennis.

 M2 **Explain arousal theories and the effect on performance**

The arousal theories described above clearly have an effect on performance, but it is important to be able to explain, with examples, how the theories have affected the final performance.

Jean Van de Velde playing in the 1999 Open Championship where he lost despite having a three-shot lead at the final hole

 Case study

Mandy regularly plays netball in a team of which she is captain. She also coaches and co-manages the team. She considers it her responsibility to get the team ready for all of their competitive matches, and she has no problems preparing herself psychologically for games. However, Mandy does not find all of her team as easy to prepare, and feels that in many games there is a lack of attention and loss of focus from some team members.

1. Which theory of arousal is Mandy most likely to have to consider in relation to the team she helps to manage?

2. Which theory of arousal is most likely to apply to Mandy in particular?

3. What is the effect on the performance of the factors which are linked to levels of arousal?

? Did you know?

One of the most famous examples of choking was when the golfer Jean Van de Velde had athree-shot lead going into the final hole of the 1999 Open Championship. He could afford to drop two shots and still win, but had a triple-bogey 7 (on a par 4 hole), having made some very poor shot choices, and this left him in a three-way play-off which he lost.

The role of group dynamics in team sports

All team sports involve a group of individuals working together. It is essential that the interaction between all the team members is positive, enabling the team to be as successful as possible.

Your assessment criteria:

P5 Identify four factors which influence group dynamics and performance in team sports

P5 Group processes

The factors which affect the interaction between individuals can be both positive and negative depending on how they are dealt with.

There is a distinction between a group and a team. A group does not necessarily have a common goal or identified 'group identity', whereas being part of a team offers unity and the sharing of common aims and objectives. Bruce Tuckman first identified the following stages of group development in 1965:

The six members of a volleyball team have to work together very closely to be successful.

- Forming – this is the first stage of team building when the team first start to get to know each other and exchange personal information. The team members act quite independently, but move towards setting some common goals.

- Storming – team members open up to each other with their different ideas, and conflict is a real possibility as a leadership model has to be agreed upon. Differences must be resolved, but if they are not, then the team will never move past this stage. This is an important stage, allowing the group to grow and develop.

- Norming – the team agrees just one goal and comes up with a mutual plan for the team. All the team members take up the responsibility and work together for the success of the team's goal.

- Performing – only some teams reach this final performing stage where they function as a unit to achieve goals smoothly and effectively as they are motivated and knowledgeable. Many established teams will go through the four stages many times as they react to changing circumstances.

Steiner's model of group effectiveness

Steiner's model suggests the following equation:

actual productivity = potential productivity – losses due to faulty group processes

In the context of a sporting group, the actual productivity relates to how the team performs, the potential productivity refers to the best possible

performance the team is capable of and the losses refer to any faults in the group or team performance which prevented them from performing to their full potential. These faults can be linked to levels of motivation, anxiety and similar psychological factors, and to physiological factors such as skill levels and effective teamwork.

Ringelmann effect

This is a situation where there is a decrease in average individual effort as a group size increases. Performers are effectively able to hide amongst a larger group in terms of the effort they put in. With eight individuals within the team pushing at a scrum, it is unlikely that all eight are exerting maximum effort at all times. This is also referred to as 'social loafing' where individuals make less effort to achieve a goal when they work in a group than they do when they work alone.

Interactive and coactive groups

Interactive groups require the team members to work directly with each other in order to achieve a successful performance. The whole performance relies on interaction and co-ordination between the members of the team for the performance to be successful.

Coactive groups require individuals to achieve success in their individual games, events or performances in order to achieve overall team success. The last day of the Ryder Cup in golf is a good example of this. There are twelve singles matches worth one point each which usually decide the outcome of the overall winners.

Within an American football team there is a defensive unit, an offensive unit and a special team, and they all have to perform as distinctly separate units.

Cohesion

This is a state of uniting or sticking together, especially in the pursuit of a common goal. Two main aspects of this have been identified:

- Task **cohesion** is how much a group or team members work together to achieve the common goals and objectives or tasks which they face. High levels of this should result in a more successful performance.

- Social cohesion is how well the group or team get on and enjoy each other's company in a social environment. An individual does not need to enjoy full social cohesion with a team mate to be able to successfully achieve task cohesion, and conversely, just because a group gets on socially, it does not necessarily mean they will be successful in a performing environment.

? | **Did you know?**

Physical fitness includes muscular endurance, speed, flexibility, strength, body composition and aerobic endurance, and skill-related fitness includes balance, co-ordination, reaction time, power and agility.

 Key terms

Cohesion: uniting or sticking together

P5 ▸ Cohesion *continued*

Your assessment criteria:

P5 Identify four factors which influence group dynamics and performance in team sports

Effective team climate

This refers to how well the entire team get on as a unit, and particularly the individual's perception of this within the group. External members of the group such as managers and coaches play an important role here as they are given an overall responsibility to create this effective team climate and ensure that it is maintained.

Factors affecting cohesion

There are many of these, but the following are the most significant:

- environmental – general factors which bind a player to a team, such as location, contracts or scholarships

- personal – the individual factors relating to the group members, such as levels of motivation, common skill levels and experience

- leadership – leaders linked with the team such as captains, managers and coaches and also leadership styles

- team factors – all of the group characteristics, such as the group size and make-up and the group stability.

Discuss

Discuss the four team cohesion factors and rank these from most important to least important as far as members of the group are concerned. Consider personal experiences as part of this discussion.

Relationship between cohesion and performance

The higher the level of cohesion which exists, the greater the likelihood of a successful performance. There are many examples where a lack of cohesion has caused very low performance levels, as was evident in the French football squad who attended the 2010 World Cup. One player, Nicolas Anelka, was expelled from the team for abusing the coach following very poor results, and the rest of the squad boycotted training in support of Anelka. France won the World Cup in 1998 and lost in the final in 2006, but was eliminated in the first round in 2010!

Leadership

Qualities

The most important aspect of leadership are the qualities which leaders display as these are what makes them stand out as

leaders. These qualities can vary according to people's perceptions, and also in different situations. For example, a leader in a sporting situation may have different leadership requirements than a leader in industry who is working with a workforce. General leadership qualities include integrity, flexibility, loyalty, confidence, preparedness and patience.

Behaviour

Leadership is important because it influences behaviour. A phrase which is often used is that a leader should 'lead by example'. This can include the way in which they play the game as well as the way in which they conduct themselves within it.

Prescribed versus emergent leaders

Two types of leader have been identified:

- *Prescribed leaders* – these are leaders who are appointed by any form of governing body or agency which is outside of the group.

- *Emergent leaders* – these come from within a group because of the skills and abilities which they display, or through some form of nomination or election.

Theories of leadership

There are four theories which should be considered:

- *Trait approach* – this is the idea that individuals are born with certain character traits which are particularly suited to good leadership.

- *Behavioural approach* – this is the idea that it is the behaviour of the leader which is important and there is a 'set' of universal behaviours which characterise good leaders. Therefore, this theory involves factors which can be learnt or taught as opposed to the trait theory which is inherent.

- *Interactional approach* – this is where effective leadership is determined by the interaction between the leader, the group members and the situation they find themselves in.

- *Multidimensional model* – the group performance and group member satisfaction depends on how well three types of leader behaviour (required, preferred and actual) link with the characteristics of the situation, the leader and the members. If a coach, or leader, uses behaviours well suited to the particular situation which are consistent with the preferred choices of the members, the result is an optimum performance and member satisfaction.

Paul Collingwood is an example of a prescribed leader as he was selected to lead the Twenty20 World Cup cricket team, although he was not captain of the test match team which was led by Andrew Strauss.

P5 Leadership *continued*

Styles

There are four distinct leadership styles:

- *Autocratic* – this is where an individual is the only decision maker and they tell performers what to do and when to do it.

- *Democratic* – this style allows the performer to contribute to the coaching and performing process by adding their own experiences to that of the leader.

- *Consultative* – this is where full use is made of the skills, experiences and ideas of others, but the leader still retains the power to make final decisions.

- *Group* – this is effectively a mixture of the democratic and consultative styles as it is the group input which is of overriding importance. This is especially important when the leader is not present, and the group has to make decisions in their absence.

Your assessment criteria:

P5 Identify four factors which influence group dynamics and performance in team sports

M3 Explain four factors which influence group dynamics and performance in team sports

D2 Analyse four factors which influence group dynamics and performance in team sports

Football managers use an autocratic leadership style where they make the decisions and tell their team what to do.

 M3 Explain factors influencing group dynamics and performance

Group processes, cohesion and leadership all contribute to overall group **dynamics**, and these in turn have an effect on the final, overall performance.

🔑 **Key terms**

Dynamics: the level of interaction in social groups

 Case study

Lesley is the captain of the school hockey team which is selected and coached by one of her PE teachers. The majority of the team are very keen to play, but just before every match Lesley often finds herself having to persuade at least two of the team members to turn up and play. Before matches, the PE teacher in charge of the team sets out very clear instructions regarding every player's position and responsibilities, and the particular tactics to be used. Lesley would prefer to be given more scope to make choices with the team at various stages of the game, particularly during the half-time break.

💬 **Discuss**

Discuss the four leadership styles. Consider which one would be the first choice for each member of the group if they were in a leadership situation. If anyone has been in a leadership role, they should explain to the group which style they used.

1. Considering the Ringelmann effect, what term could be best applied to the two 'reluctant' players?

2. What leadership style best describes the PE teacher in charge of the hockey team?

3. Which leadership style best describes Lesley's preferred approach to leading the team which she would like to use?

D2 Analyse factors influencing group dynamics and performance

Once the effects of group dynamics have been identified and explained, it is important to go on to analyse exactly how they have inevitably affected an overall performance. This can be either a negative or a positive effect.

 Discuss

1. *Discuss the most negative and positive group dynamics effects which the members of the group have personally experienced.*

2. *Discuss the overall effects which this had on either the individual or team performance.*

 ## Case study

Lesley and her hockey team are playing in a match which is not going according to the plan of the PE teacher who has decided the team selection tactics and strategies which should be used. At half-time when the team are 2–0 down, the PE teacher has to go home due to a personal matter, leaving another member of staff in charge who knows little about hockey.

During the half-time interval, Lesley leads the team talk and encourages all members of the team to express their views. Two of the team want to switch positions, and another volunteers to man-mark the opposition's most threatening player. Lesley makes the decision to substitute two players who appear to have little enthusiasm or motivation. The team go on to win the game 3–2!

1. Analyse the group processes which are highlighted in this example.

2. What factors of cohesion were addressed by Lesley and changed through the decisions she made?

3. To what would you attribute the change of circumstances which turned a losing situation into a winning one?

Psychological skills training programme to enhance sports performance

The majority of performers are well aware of the need to prepare themselves through various forms of physiological training, working on skill acquisition and fitness levels. However, being psychologically prepared is also very important if a performer is to achieve an optimum performance level.

Your assessment criteria:

P6 Assess the current psychological skills of a selected sports performer, identifying strengths and areas for improvement

? Did you know?

Many coaches, trainers and managers consider their players to be as fully developed as they can be in terms of their physical preparation. However, they see their players' levels of psychological preparation as the only barrier. This is particularly the case in professional tennis where psychological preparation is considered to be the main difference between the top 100 players on the professional circuit.

Andy Murray is the most successful British tennis player in a sport where successful psychological training and preparation can make the difference between winning and losing.

P6 Psychological skills

When planning a programme, it is essential to be aware of the psychological skills which must be taken into account, and to consider the ways in which these skills can be accurately assessed. The ways in which these factors can be utilised and assessed can vary.

Motivation

Being motivated is crucial for an effective performance, and the following aspects of motivation need to be considered:

- Goal-setting – it is important to have a particular target to aim for and SMART target setting can be used to achieve this. To maintain motivation, goals must be reset once they have been achieved so that there are always challenges for the performer.

- Performance profiling is carried out using five stages:

1. Identifying the qualities that are required to perform consistently well. These may include physical, technical, psychological, co-ordination, strategy and character aspects of performance. The profiler must identify these and they should be activity/sport-specific.

2. On a scale of 1–10 (1 = not at all, 10 = very much), rate where an individual would want a performance to be on each of the qualities identified.

3. On a scale of 1–10, rate the current ability on each quality.

4. Calculate the 'discrepancy score' on each quality (the mark from stage 2 minus the mark from stage 3).

5. The individual then identifies the strengths and areas for improvement. The higher the discrepancy score, the greater the improvement needed.

Arousal control

It is important to achieve a state of arousal, but over-arousal can lead to negative effects so it must be controlled using the following methods:

- Progressive muscular relaxation involves alternately tensing and relaxing the muscles. It should be carried out through the muscle groups of the legs, abdomen, chest, arms and face, tensing each group for 10 seconds and then releasing for 20 seconds before moving on to the next muscle group.

- Mind to muscle relaxation involves focusing on relaxing the mind which in turn relaxes the muscles and the body. This can be achieved through breathing control (slowing and regulating the breathing), and autogenic techniques (a daily practice of repeated sets of visualisations which induces relaxation in identified parts of the body – often considered to be a form of self-hypnosis).

- Psyching up techniques increase arousal and then increase the intensity of the performance. These can be achieved by intense breathing, moving the body to increase heart rate, high energy 'self-talk' (e.g. 'I can do this!'), high energy body language (e.g. pumping fists or thigh slapping), or playing/listening to high energy music.

? Did you know?

Top level performers are aware of the concept of 'plateauing'. This is where they achieve a particular level against a particular target, and then they stay at that level for some time. It is important that they identify and set targets which will take them beyond this temporary 'stalemate', and on to the next level of their development.

Key terms

Profiling: *the use of specific characteristics or qualities that identify a type or category of a person*

? Did you know?

Some rugby teams have been criticised for over arousing players in the changing rooms prior to taking the pitch! For some teams, this consisted of encouraging all their players to stamp their boots on the floor loudly whilst chanting in order to intimidate teams next door with the noise levels, as well as raising their heart and breathing rates!

The New Zealand rugby teams perform the Haka to psych themselves up before a game.

P6 ▶ Psychological skills *continued*

Your assessment criteria:

P6 ▶ Assess the current psychological skills of a selected sports performer, identifying strengths and areas for improvement

Imagery

This involves a performer imagining themselves in a specific environment or performing a specific activity. The following can be used:

- Mental rehearsal – this is also referred to as visualisation as it involves the performer creating a mental image or intention of what they want to happen or feel. This can include visual (images and pictures), kinaesthetic (how the body feels) or auditory (e.g. the roar of the crowd). Many golfers stand behind their ball in a particular position and visualise the flight it needs in order to get to the green, further down the fairway or even to the flag itself. This helps them to make the correct club selection as well as gauging the amount of power they need to put into the shot they are about to make.

- Controlling emotions – the two major ones are anxiety and anger, so using stored imagery of dealing with these well is important to ensure they are kept under control. It is useful to remember how a previous similar situation was successfully handled, without allowing these negative emotions to result in an undesirable outcome. Performers need to learn from mistakes made when anger or anxiety has resulted in a less than satisfactory result, such as being reprimanded by an official or even being excluded from a game or match. Reliving examples when this has not been the case and resulted in negative results may also be used.

- Concentration – this is crucial to a successful performance, and blocking out other influences (crowd noise, movements, etc.) by imagining the perfect result or conclusion will greatly help with this. There are many factors which can affect levels of concentration, and players often refer to being 'in the zone' when they are able to concentrate fully without being distracted by external factors.

- Relaxation – imagining feelings and emotions associated with relaxing helps with this process.

- Pre-performance routines – for many activities which have repeated skills such as serving at tennis or driving in golf, the performers imagine the whole skill in its entirety before going on to actually perform it. The majority of golfers carry out one or more practice swings before they actually hit the ball. They stand away from the ball to do this before moving towards the ball to play their shot.

Confidence building

A confident performer is more likely to be a successful performer than one who is lacking confidence, so this is an important psychological factor to consider:

- Self-talk – this involves the performer giving themselves positive messages about how well they can perform.

- Positive thinking – this involves the performer concentrating on previous good and successful performances and blanking out less successful ones.

- Changing self-image through self-imagery – positive self-imagery helps the performer to improve their own self-image which directly links to increased confidence.

Assessment

When planning a programme, the initial stage involves carrying out an accurate assessment. This initial assessment is important as it can then be used as a benchmark for any progress which is made.

The individual's strengths and weaknesses (areas for improvement) need to be identified, and the most effective way to do this is through performance profiling.

As the psychological demands of different sports vary, it is important to identify the demands of the individual's sport. It is more demanding to be the individual walking out to bat in a cricket game when the focus of attention is entirely upon that individual, than to be one member of a team of fifteen in a rugby match who is involved in various parts of the play and game.

It is, therefore, important that these particular demands are considered and identified in two aspects: the particular demands of the activity and the demands of the individual's role within it. For example, the goalkeeper's role in a game of football can be more demanding than an outfield player as any mistake made by the goalkeeper can result in a goal being scored, whereas the outfield player may only lose possession of the ball.

 Discuss

1. *What has been the most psychologically demanding sporting situation that individual members of the group have found themselves in?*

2. *Match this situation to any of the arousal control methods and suggest which might have been most appropriate to that particular situation.*

P7 Plan a psychological skills training programme

A six-week psychological skills training programme must be devised for a selected sports performer to **enhance** their performance. The plan needs to cover the following:

- Current situation – this information will be gained through the initial assessment to identify the strengths and weaknesses.

- Aims and objectives – these must be clearly set out as they are the focus of the programme. It is through these that strengths are consolidated and weaknesses are rectified.

- Action plan to address aims and objectives – this is the main body of the programme which addresses the issues which have been raised, and lays out the procedures and content of the plan.

- Daily and weekly content of the plan – this must cover the six-week period, and will include detailed information.

M4 Explain the design of the programme

There is no set format for a psychological skills training programme as it depends entirely upon the sports performer it is being prepared for. The factors which need to be considered are the initial assessment (and what this reveals), the particular psychological demands of the sportsperson's sport, and the ways in which the psychological skills are relevant to, and part of, that performer's usual performance levels.

Case study

Leo is designing a six-week psychological skills training programme for his friend Martin who is a very keen golfer. When Leo assesses Martin, he finds his main strength to be his belief in his own ability whenever he is practising shots, either in the driving range or on the practice areas. His main weakness is being able to play the same standard shots when he is on the golf course, particularly when he is playing against another player in a match situation. Martin is not particularly concerned about losing, and is more interested in being able to play shots well when practising.

Your assessment criteria:

P7 Plan a six-week psychological skills training programme to enhance performance for a selected sports performer

M4 Explain the design of the six-week psychological skills training programme for a selected sports performer

D3 Justify the design of a six-week psychological skills training programme for a selected sports performer, making suggestions for improvement

🔑 Key terms

Enhance: *to raise to a higher degree*

1. What is Leo likely to say to Martin about the importance of motivation in a match situation?

2. How might arousal control improve Martin's match performance?

3. What imagery considerations could Martin include in his programme to improve his match results?

D3 Justify the design of the programme

When justifying the design of a psychological training programme, it is important to consider the suggestions for improvement by including these particular elements within the programme. For example, if improved levels of concentration are required, it is important to be able to state exactly when within a performance these were identified as being lacking, rather than setting a general target for the whole performance. A selected sports performer needs to be convinced that they should take on board the advice and content which has been suggested, and that it would lead to an overall improvement. This is why particular elements in the programme should be linked to specific improvement targets.

Case study

Vicky is planning a programme for her cousin, Matt, who is a rugby player. She carries out a full performance profile, identifies Matt's strengths and weaknesses and researches the psychological demands of rugby as a specific sport. Vicky has included a few elements within Matt's suggested programme which he has expressed doubts about, and Vicky now has to justify what she has included in order to get Matt to try out the programme.

In the assessment, Matt came across as being quite introverted, and he does not get involved in the 'psyching up' process which the team uses prior to each game. Vicky has suggested that he uses autogenic techniques for arousal control and adopts a more positive thinking approach.

How is Vicky likely to be able to justify the following, and what improvements can she suggest that Matt makes by taking her advice?

- that Matt fully participates in the team's psyching up sessions

- that Matt carries out a daily autogenic technique session with specific content

- that Matt focuses on confidence building, using positive thinking in particular.

> **? Did you know?**
>
> *Olympic javelin thrower, Steve Backley, has written a book entitled* The Winning Mind *in which he describes how psychological strengths and weaknesses were the major factors in determining whether or not he performed at his best in competitions. He also states that psychological strategies were the key to helping him deal with competitive stress.*

Assessment checklist

To achieve a pass grade, my portfolio of evidence must show that I can:

Assessment Criteria	Description	✓
P1	Define personality and how it affects sports performance.	☐
P2	Describe motivation and how it affects sports performance.	☐
P3	Describe stress and anxiety, their causes, symptoms and effect on sports performance.	☐
P4	Describe three theories of arousal and the effect on sports performance.	☐
P5	Identify four factors which influence group dynamics and performance in team sports.	☐
P6	Assess the current psychological skills of a selected sports performer, identifying strengths and areas for improvement.	☐
P7	Plan a six-week psychological skills training programme to enhance performance for a selected sports performer.	☐

To achieve a merit grade, my portfolio of evidence must show that I can:

Assessment Criteria	Description	✓
M1	Explain the effects of personality and motivation on sports performance.	☐
M2	Explain three theories of arousal and the effect on sports performance.	☐
M3	Explain four factors which influence group dynamics and performance in team sports.	☐
M4	Explain the design of the six-week psychological skills training programme for a selected sports performer.	☐

To achieve a distinction grade, my portfolio of evidence must show that I can:

Assessment Criteria	Description	✓
D1	Evaluate the effects of personality and motivation on sports performers.	☐
D2	Analyse four factors which influence group dynamics and performance in team sports.	☐
D3	Justify the design of the six-week psychological skills training programme for a selected sports performer, making suggestions for improvement.	☐

18 | Sports injuries

LO2 Know about a range of sports injuries and their symptoms

▶ The body responds to injuries in a variety of ways to protect and repair the damage caused. The healing process for most injuries is very similar.

▶ Sports people can be psychologically affected by the injury that they have experienced. They can progress through a range of emotions. For some people injuries can lead to psychological problems such as depression.

LO1 Know how common sports injuries can be prevented by the correct identification of risk factors

▶ There are a number of extrinsic factors that may place a sportsperson at risk from injury when they actively participate.

▶ Sports people can also have intrinsic factors such as flexibility problems that may increase their risk of injury.

▶ All sports have a variety of measures, including protective equipment and specialised clothing that can help prevent or minimise an injury.

LO4 Be able to plan and construct treatment and rehabilitation programmes for two common sports injuries

▶ Every sports injury will require slightly different types of treatment. The treatment may include rest, maintenance of endurance and gradual development of strength, speed and co-ordination.

▶ Rehabilitation should be gradual. A step ladder approach, building on gradual improvements, is advisable.

▶ Programmes are very specific to individual injuries.

LO3 Know how to apply methods of treating sports injuries

▶ Sports injuries can occur to a wide range of body parts. Joints and limbs are particularly susceptible.

▶ Specific first aid treatment may be needed to deal with an injury.

▶ PRICED, SALTAPS, bandaging and hot/cold treatments are methods that are often used to deal with sports injuries.

Risk factors in sport

Sports injuries can cause pain, discomfort and emotional distress. Injuries can put a player out of action for long periods of time and cost professional players and clubs large amounts of money.

The assessment of sports injuries has expanded in recent years with the number of private sports injury and sports therapy clinics growing. Most sports people suffer from injuries from time to time. Sport includes elements of risk. The level of risk can be reduced, but cannot be totally removed because of the nature of most games and activities. Managing risk, ensuring that athletes are prepared for the sport that they are involved in and monitoring physical performance is important in reducing the number of injuries that occur in an activity.

P1 Extrinsic risk factors

Risk factors in sport fall into two categories, extrinsic and intrinsic. Identification of the risk, and planning and preparation for an activity can reduce the number of injuries that may occur. The following extrinsic factors may lead to sports injuries.

Coaching

Poor coaching can create a dangerous environment. A coach must be able to explain practices and techniques. Inadequate explanations and poor demonstrations may result in injury as a performer does not know what to do. A coach must be able to control a session. Poor behaviour and failure to adhere to the rules of a sport can lead to dangerous situations and conflict. A sport's rules have been developed partly to protect performers.

Incorrect technique

Incorrect technique can cause injuries either because the technique is dangerous or because it contains forces that can produce repetitive strain problems. For example, poor technique in somersaulting may produce spinal injuries. Poor performance in a tennis forehand shot may cause wrist strain.

Environmental factors

Weather can produce an increased risk of injury. Dry, hard ground can increase the risk of fractures, particularly in contact sports such as rugby.

Key terms

Extrinsic risk factors: problems that can occur outside of the body that may lead to an injury (for example, physical contact)

Intrinsic risk factors: physical problems present in an athlete that may lead to an injury (for example, flexibility)

? Did you know?

Poor coaching in a number of sports can result in spinal cord injuries. Rugby union, American (gridiron) football, and ice hockey are the most dangerous sports for this form of injury.

Wet ground can cause more collisions from slips. Cold temperatures may cause hypothermia and frostbite, and increase the injury risk from falls. Hot temperatures can leave players dehydrated and cause cramp.

Clothing and footwear

Each sport has clear guidelines for appropriate clothing and footwear. For example, in football, players can only compete if they wear shin pads. Specialised protective clothing should always be worn to reduce a person's risk of injury. A referee or coach should prevent inappropriately dressed athletes from competing in sports.

Safety hazards

There are a wide variety of safety hazards that can cause injury. Each sport and area that the sport is carried out in will have its own specific problems.

The area that the sport is played in should be checked prior to its use to make sure that it is safe. In a sports hall this may mean making sure the floor is dry and clean, and on a field checking the surface for dangerous objects.

Equipment can be a safety hazard. It should be set up in accordance with the manufacturer's guidelines and checked regularly for wear and tear. For example, it is important to carry out a visual safety check of a trampoline bed and springs before participants use it. Any modification to equipment can produce additional dangers and may make the person who has carried out the modification directly responsible for any accident that occurs.

Planning for first aid

Inadequate planning for first aid can produce safety hazards. A coach should make sure that they have a current first aid qualification so that they can deal quickly with an accident. A centre should have a first aid procedure that ensures that accidents are managed as safely as possible. All staff have a responsibility to make sure that they are aware of the first aid procedure.

 Discuss

1. *Discuss the safety hazards in a sport of your choice.*

2. *Rank the hazards that you identify.*

3. *Discuss strategies for reducing risk in your sport.*

4. *Discuss suitable clothing for your sport.*

P1 Intrinsic risk factors

Your assessment criteria:

P1 Describe extrinsic and intrinsic risk factors in relation to sports injuries

Training effects

Poor training can produce muscular and joint problems that lead to pain and injury. Training should be balanced as muscles work together. Training and strengthening one muscle only will create a problem in its partner. For example, hamstring strength should be at least 75 per cent of the strength of the quadriceps. Muscle pairs should not differ in strength by more than 10 per cent.

Poor training can lead to flexibility problems. Athletes should make sure they work through a full range of motion. Exercising through a restricted range of motion may decrease the flexibility of a muscle and joint.

Poor preparation can cause injuries. Athletes should warm up using activities that will prepare them for the sport that they are about to take part in. They should gradually increase the intensity of the warm-up. An inappropriate warm-up may cause muscle strains as athletes are not properly prepared.

A mistimed tackle caused by fatigue

Level of fitness can lead to injuries because a tired athlete may lose concentration and focus. This may be evident in a football match when players start to miss tackles, causing a greater number of accidental collisions.

Training can produce injuries from overuse. Training too hard or too frequently can produce injuries such as stress fractures and repetitive strain injuries (for example, tennis elbow). Sufficient rest is needed during training to make sure that the body has a chance to heal and recover.

Individual variables

Athletes have a variety of individual variables that may increase their level of risk. These can include age, gender, nutritional status, medical history and personality. As people get older, they tend to take longer to recover from exercise and longer to heal from an injury. They are also more prone to injury because strength decreases with age and bones become weaker. Females are more prone to problems such as osteoporosis (brittle bone disease). Their skeletal system is weaker than

males and more likely to suffer from fractures. A person with a poor diet may have a higher risk of injury especially if their calcium intake is too low, as this can cause bone problems (lack of bone strength).

Athletes also have very different personalities. Those that like to take risks are more likely to have a greater number of injuries because of the situations that they put themselves in.

Previous injuries are likely to cause problems in the future. The injury is often weaker and there is potential for it to recur when put under pressure.

Postural defects

Postural problems can increase a person's risk of injury. Posture can change for a variety of reasons. Inappropriate training, slouching, carrying a bag on one shoulder, poor sitting positions, joint problems and previous injuries are all factors in developing poor posture.

Postural problems occur through gradual muscle imbalance. This stress causes pain, can restrict movement and affects flexibility and strength. Postural problems can occur at any joint, such as the ankles, knees and spine. The spine can suffer from three types of postural problem.

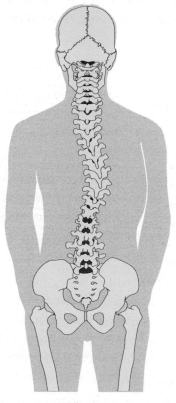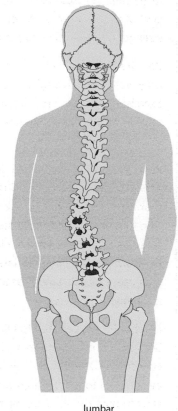

thoracic   lumbar

Figure 18.1 Scoliosis of the spine

Scoliosis – this can be caused by an imbalance of the muscles through participation in one-sided activities such as javelin or tennis, or by carrying a bag on one shoulder only. It results in a curving of the spine in an S or C shape.

Lordosis – this is a problem of the lower spine. It curves inwards more than it should. Stress occurs to other parts of the spine as the curve increases. Muscles around the hip and spine (trunk extensors and hip flexors) become tight and other muscles (abdominals and hip extensors) become weak and stretched.

Kyphosis – this is a problem of the upper back. The upper spine becomes rounded causing pain. In sports this can be caused through holding posture for long periods of time and is evident in cycling. Bodybuilders may also suffer from this problem as they overdevelop their chest and neglect to train their back muscles.

Discuss

1. *Discuss the intrinsic risk factors that a person in your class may have.*

2. *Rank the hazards.*

3. *Discuss possible methods of reducing the risks.*

P2 **Preventative measures**

There are a range of preventative measures that can be used to reduce both extrinsic and intrinsic risk. The measures can relate to the sport and the coach, including the role of the coach and the coach's knowledge and communication skills. Other measures can relate to the sportsperson, such as training and appropriate use of equipment.

Role of the coach

A coach is responsible for making sure that an activity is safe. They must make sure that their knowledge is up-to-date and that they only work within the sport that they are qualified in. The minimum standard for running a coaching session is a **full level 2** coaching qualification or an NVQ level 2 in Activity Leadership. Once a coach is qualified, they are then able to make an informed decision about safety.

Before an activity takes place, a coach should complete a risk assessment to identify potential problems. One of the first checks to be carried out is a visual inspection of the area. A coach must also make sure that a group is suitably dressed for the activity with appropriate safety equipment (for example, mouthguards and shin pads).

Equipment to be used during the session must be assessed for safety before the session starts. A coach should explain practices and demonstrate using clear instructions. When organising an activity, they should match participants for size and strength, particularly in contact sports. A coach should maintain control and discipline in practices and during games. Part of their role is to ensure that players understand the rules and regulations of the sport. A coach may need to change their teaching style according to the activity and group.

Equipment and environment

Equipment must be checked to make sure that it is safe. As previously mentioned, this should be completed in accordance with the manufacturer's guidelines. The check should include a visual assessment of whether there is sufficient space (including height) for the activity. For example, when setting up an area for trampolining, a coach should look at any structures that hang from the ceiling (and the height of ceiling) to make sure participants have enough space to jump.

Your assessment criteria:

P2 Describe preventative measures that can be taken in order to prevent sports injuries occurring

---

🔑 **Key terms**

Full level 2: a coaching qualification that allows you to coach unsupervised or run a club on your own

---

❓ **Did you know?**

Every year athletes are injured throwing the javelin. Even elite athletes have problems. In the Golden League meeting in Rome in 2007, French long jumper Salim Sdiri was injured when a javelin thrown by Finn Tero Pitkamaki left him with a 3cm wound in his side.

 Describe

1. Describe the equipment that is required in an activity of your choice.

2. Assess the equipment and determine whether you think it is safe to use.

Protective equipment can reduce the risk of injury. It is often specific to a sport. For example, boxers have their hands taped and wear gloves to spread the load and minimise damage to their hands and their opponent. Protective equipment may be something that a sportsperson wears, or it may also be something used in the sport, such as pads around a post in rugby, and matting in gymnastics and athletics. Protective equipment works in three ways:

- to deflect a force
- to reduce the force through some form of cushioning
- to spread the force over a wide area, thus reducing the injury caused.

Good examples of protective equipment in sport are in American football, ice hockey and cricket.

The use of equipment should be monitored. In the example above, boxers must be monitored by an official when they have their hands taped. There have been occasions in championship fights when a boxer has taped an object into their gloves (such as a piece of metal) to cause greater damage (this is against the rules).

A coach must ensure that an activity is supervised. For example, during javelin throwing, participants must be made aware of the dangers and take the activity seriously.

Boxer with taped hands

 Case study

Alex is a female rugby player. She has recently joined her local team and is looking forward to playing her first competitive game. She has trained for several weeks, but is still a little unfamiliar with her role as a prop. As she is new to the game, she has not yet bought a mouthguard or a pair of rugby boots. She has decided to use the boots that she has for football.

1. Should the referee allow Alex to play?

2. Should the referee change the rules because of Alex's lack of experience?

3. Do you think that rugby boots will reduce her risk of injury?

4. Is a mouthguard necessary for rugby?

 Research

Research protective equipment in a sport of your choice.

 Design

Design a poster identifying the protective aspects of the equipment you have researched.

M1 **Explain risk factors**

Risk assessment

A risk assessment is used to identify the severity of hazards in the activity taking place. It is a checklist that enables a coach to plan and put in place measures to reduce the risk. Each hazard is assessed and scored on likelihood, severity and frequency. When scores are combined, they provide a risk rating (low/medium/high). Any activity that is rated high, should be reviewed again to see if there is sufficient justification for it to take place and to look at the measures needed to make it as safe as possible.

Coaching style

Coaches who teach activities that have high elements of risk (such as somersaulting), or who work with participants of a low ability or a young age, will often use an autocratic style to maintain discipline and control. Their instructions are clear and specific. This enables a coach to take total control of a session. A democratic or laissez-faire approach can often be taken with low risk activities, with adult participants and athletes who have a good level of experience. Professional athletes already know the safety aspects of their sport. A coach can be more democratic and allow athletes to take more responsibility for their own development. Adults are more likely to be able to manage their behaviour and work within the rules and regulations of a game.

Coaching level

A level 2 coach is able to work up to a certain standard in the sport of their choice. For example, a level 2 coach in trampolining can teach progressions up to and including front and back somersaults. They are not allowed to deliver more difficult skills such as triple somersaults, because they have not been trained up to this level and therefore cannot provide safe advice and guidance.

Protective equipment

Protective equipment typically works in three ways. Shin pads protect the shins from kicks and blows. They prevent bone and soft tissue damage or reduce the injury caused. They have a hard outer layer (often some form of plastic) to deflect the force away from the leg so that the

 Your assessment criteria:

M1 Explain how risk factors can be minimised by utilisation of preventative measures

 Key terms

Autocratic: *one person has control over everything and makes all the decisions*

Democratic: *members of the group participate in the decisions made*

 Discuss

Discuss the coaching style that you used in a sport that you have coached. Reflect on the reasons for your choice of coaching style, and explain why you chose the style and whether it was effective.

 Research

Research protective equipment in mountain biking and rugby.

impact is reduced. Underneath the outer layer is a layer of material to cushion the force. This reduces the impact and spreads it over a wider area, thus minimising damage.

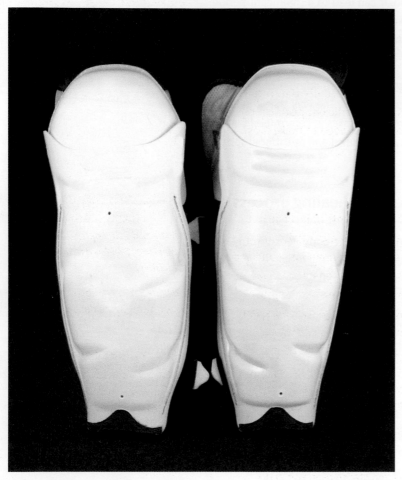

Shin pads protect the lower leg.

Monitoring

A coach explains and demonstrates techniques, emphasising any safety points. They must then carefully monitor a group to ensure that they adhere to the safety points in the activity. A coach may need to reinforce the safety points to any person who is not adhering to them. However, if they persist in dangerous activities, they may then have to be excluded from the activity for the safety of the whole group. A coach in javelin should explain how to carry the javelin, explain and demonstrate how to throw the javelin (including where people waiting to throw should stand), monitor a group throwing the javelin, and explain how to collect and give the javelin to a partner.

Discuss

1. Rugby has traditionally had very little personal protection equipment. However, manufacturers are starting to produce a wide range of products. Should rugby players wear more protection?

2. Cyclists are recommended to wear helmets. Do you think helmets in mountain biking lead to, or prevent injuries?

Research

1. Research risk assessment forms for a sport of your choice.

2. Using one of the forms, carry out a risk assessment and identify the risk level for the activity at your centre.

Injury can be catastrophic for a sportsperson. It can lead to a significant period of rest and recuperation and even permanent retirement from a sport. Injuries can also cause feelings of isolation, anger and depression because an athlete is unable to train and loses contact with their friends.

When a person is injured, they tend to progress through a number of stages. Each stage has both physical and psychological effects. The way that a person progresses, recovers and the time that the recovery takes is determined by a number of factors – personality, age, gender, fitness level and nutritional status.

> **Your assessment criteria:**
>
> **P3** Describe the physiological responses common to most sports injuries

P3 Physiological responses (the healing process)

There are a number of phases and responses that the body goes through when an injury occurs:

- **acute** inflammatory phase

- sub acute proliferation/repair and regeneration phase

- remodelling phase.

Inflammatory phase

When an injury occurs, tissue is damaged resulting in pain and a potential loss of function. The loss of function will depend on the severity of the injury. Injuries are often graded as first, second and third degree types. A first degree injury such as an overstretched muscle (strain) occurs when

> **Key terms**
>
> **Acute:** *a sudden injury, or the first stage of healing*

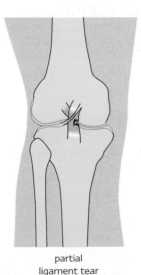 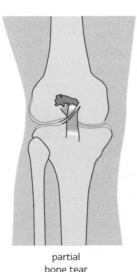 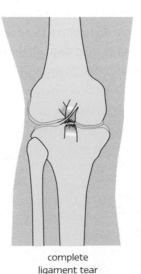 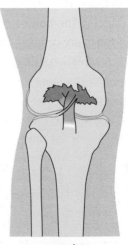

| partial ligament tear | partial bone tear | complete ligament tear | complete bone tear |

Figure 18.2 Types of ligament and bone damage

less than 5 per cent of the muscle fibres are damaged. There is no great loss of strength or function, but active movement will cause pain around the damaged area. A second degree injury involves a more significant tear. The muscle is painful when moved. A third degree injury is a complete rupture of the muscle. The muscle will not contract at all.

Ligament injuries (sprains) can be graded into partial or complete tears. A partial tear occurs when only a few fibres are damaged which may affect stability. A complete tear involves most or all of the ligaments, creating an unstable joint.

When a person sustains an injury, there is an immediate loss of blood to an area because of the damage from ruptured blood vessels. This results in the death of cells around the damaged area because they stop receiving oxygen. Ruptured blood vessels create inflammation. The signs of inflammation are pain, swelling, redness, bleeding, heat and loss of function.

When cells are damaged, they produce chemicals such as prostaglandin that increase vasodilation and the permeability of capillaries. Blood flow increases to the injured area. These chemicals also attract white blood cells. White blood cells move to the damaged area and remove harmful bacteria and dead cells. This usually takes up to 72 hours but may continue for several weeks. The main role of the inflammatory response is to fight against harmful substances, remove dead tissue and prepare for new tissue.

Proliferation/repair and regeneration phase

After approximately two days, fibroblasts begin to construct new collagen that acts as a mesh or frame for new cells. The area also grows new capillaries. Once blood flow has returned, cells can begin to grow. Cells replace those that have been previously damaged (muscle cells regrow in muscle). This phase lasts from 48 hours to three to six weeks. However, if the injury is severe (second or third degree), the regrowth may include granulation tissue. If this is not removed, it will form scar tissue which can lead to a decrease in function.

Remodelling phase

After approximately three weeks, new cells and fibres arrange themselves into a pattern that can take the stress placed on them. It is important to stretch the cells to make sure that they align in the correct direction and build strength. Collagen is laid down and fibres are strengthened. This process can take months or years to achieve.

Key terms

Collagen: *a fibrous protein*

Fibroblasts: *cells that produce connective tissue (collagen)*

Permeability: *a condition of the structure of the wall of a capillary that allows blood to pass through to tissue spaces*

Vasodilation: *the expansion of a blood vessel*

Discuss

Discuss recent injuries that have occurred in your class, and identify the healing stage of the sports people.

P4 Psychological responses

Sports injuries can cause significant psychological distress. Athletes often react to injury with a response similar to grief. They can become emotionally distressed by pain and the loss of function. This produces anxiety about the effect that the injury will have on the person's lifestyle. Some athletes may try to play through the pain of the injury. They use denial as a defence mechanism, pretending that everything is fine. This eventually turns to anger when an athlete can no longer ignore the injury and they often express negative thoughts such as 'Why me?' Most athletes are prepared to rest for a short time to allow recovery, but an athlete may sometimes become depressed when they realise the extent of the injury. Eventually they should accept the injury and the length of time needed to recover.

An athlete may also respond negatively to rehabilitation. They may try to bargain with a therapist to decrease the time in a rehabilitation programme. During a programme, any relapse can cause anxiety. The athlete feels frustrated if little progress is made. It is important to set an athlete clear targets and goals. These should be achievable in a realistic time frame. An athlete's motivation may vary depending on the improvements that they have made.

Your assessment criteria:

P4 Describe the psychological responses common to sports injuries

M2 Explain the physiological and psychological responses common to most sports injuries

 Research

Research professional athletes that have had psychological problems overcoming an injury.

Design

Relaxation and imagery can help to speed up the healing process by reducing anxiety. Design a relaxation and imagery rehearsal script that you could use to help reduce an athlete's stress levels.

M2 Explain the physiological responses (the healing process)

An injury is caused when tissue stretches or tears. Swelling and lack of oxygen result in cell damage and death within the first 24 hours. Phagocytosis then begins to rid the area of cell debris and oedema.

Proliferation/repair and regeneration phase

Fibroblasts begin to form scar tissue. They produce type III collagen in about four days. This is randomly organised. The growth of capillaries brings nutrition to the area, and collagen cross-linking begins. As the process continues, the number of fibroblasts decreases as more collagen is laid down. The injured area is gradually reconnected.

Remodelling phase

Cross-linking and shortening of the collagen fibres promotes the formation of a tight, strong scar. The muscle is not fully restored to its previous level, as fibrous scar tissue slows muscle healing.

Explain the psychological responses

The way a person responds may depend on their level of performance. Sport is a way of life for many athletes. It is often also their occupation. An injury to an athlete may mean the end of their career and the removal of many things in life that the athlete enjoys. Career-ending injuries can cause athletes to develop depression that may in some instances lead to suicide. An injury to a professional athlete may have a greater psychological impact than an injury to a recreational athlete. For example, an injury to a professional football player may mean that they no longer train and socialise with their team mates. This can lead to feelings of isolation. Many teams combat this by making players train in the gym together and encouraging attendance at all competitions even if a player cannot play. In this way, they maintain their social connections.

Psychological responses can depend on the severity of an injury. Spinal injuries and paralysis will be substantially more traumatic than a muscle strain. The injury will have much greater life-changing implications.

Taking part in sport and exercise may be a person's way of handling stress. An injury for that person can lead to a build-up of stress and frustration. The lack of activity can also lead to weight gain and a gradual loss of confidence and self-esteem. Therefore, it is important that an injured athlete can complete some form of physical activity.

Key terms

Phagocytosis: the ingestion of foreign bodies by phagocytes (white blood cells)

? Did you know?

Type III collagen is produced quickly by young fibroblasts. Stronger type I collagen is then synthesised to produce scar tissue.

? Did you know?

There are several signs that may indicate that an athlete is in psychological distress. These include:

- *displaying anger*
- *failing to take responsibility for their own rehabilitation*
- *reduced effort in physical therapy*
- *emotional mood swings.*

D1 Analyse the physiological responses (the healing process)

Scar tissue heals by reaching in the direction of the neighbouring muscle, thus attaching these tissues together. An athlete can strain a hamstring and the tear heals, but the scar tissue cannot connect to a neighbouring muscle sheath. This means that the hamstring muscle still functions, but the athlete complains of a dull ache or pain. The athlete's muscle functions and the limb moves, but the normal gliding that occurs between neighbouring tissues is lost. This causes a constant amount of low-level inflammation.

Scar tissue can cause a problem as it has a poor blood supply and is not as strong as the tissue it replaces. Injuries can repeatedly recur at an area of scar tissue.

Analyse the psychological responses

The way a person reacts to an injury will vary according to their psychological needs. An athlete needs the support of friends and family to help with rehabilitation. They may also need financial help to cope with any loss of earnings. Some athletes may require help with everyday tasks such as shopping or visiting a physiotherapist. They also need someone to listen to their problems. This will help to reduce their fear, anxiety and frustration.

An athlete needs to express their feelings during rehabilitation as this can help to identify problems with treatment. Long-term rehabilitation can become boring which may lead to frustration. A therapist should be able to provide alternative training methods to maintain commitment. If an athlete is not allowed to express their feelings, they are likely to drop out of the programme. An athlete may need the support of a rehabilitation partner to help motivate them through their training. The partner acts as a distraction to prevent the athlete from dwelling on their problem.

Education and knowledge during recovery is important. An athlete wants to know what is happening and why they are been asked to complete a range of exercises. They also need to develop mental strategies for returning to a sport and staying confident.

Your assessment criteria:

D1 Analyse the physiological and psychological responses common to most sports injuries

? | Did you know?

Coaches' attitudes can lead to an increased chance of their players developing an injury. Attitudes like 'no pain, no gain', and 'give 110 per cent' mean that players can often take unnecessary risks. Athletes need to be assertive and play as hard as possible, but they should play within safe limits.

Case study

Paul is an elite basketball player. During the last game, he landed awkwardly, damaging the end of his tibia and the ligaments in his ankle. He has had several scans and they reveal that he has a fracture of his tibia and a grade 3 injury to his lateral collateral ligaments (a complete tear). In a recent consultation to discuss the injury, Paul was informed that the injury would mean that he was unlikely to play for the rest of the season.

1. Discuss the psychological problems that Paul may have as a result of the injury.

2. Discuss exercises that may be useful to Paul's rehabilitation.

3. Identify three specific targets to help Paul gradually progress through his rehabilitation.

4. Suggest additional support that could be arranged to help motivate Paul during his recovery.

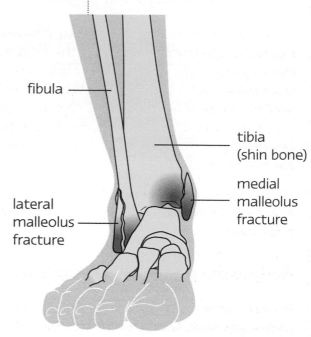

Figure 18.3 An ankle injury

Collision of two players caused by attentional focus

> **? Did you know?**
>
> *Injured athletes often feel that they lack emotional stability, they feel prone to stress and lack emotional self-control.*

> **? Did you know?**
>
> *Stress can be the cause of athletic injuries. The state of being stressed can lead to increased anxiety. This can alter the athlete's attentional focus and muscular tension. A narrrowing of an athlete's attentional focus may mean that they miss peripheral cues. A footballer may concentrate on the ball, but forget to withdraw from an unrealistic challenge.*

Types of sports injury

You must be aware of the common types of sports injuries and the first aid that can be used to treat them. As a professional working in sport, you will come across a wide range of injuries. The most common are **sprains** and **strains**, haematomas and fractures. Injuries are classified into two types: hard and soft tissue. However, an injury will often occur to both types. The type of sport that you play dictates the type of injuries that you will see, for example dislocated and fractured fingers often occur in basketball.

Soft tissue injuries

Strains

Strains are caused by overstretching or overloading a muscle and they often occur at the muscle–tendon junction. They frequently occur in explosive events such as sprinting and jumping. Strains can be graded as first, second and third degree as previously mentioned. An athlete may have a strain if they feel a stabbing pain, or if their muscle does not contract properly. They may feel that there is a defect in the muscle or the muscle may bunch up. After 24 hours, bruising may be seen below the injury site.

The injury is treated using PRICED (protect, rest, ice, compress, elevate and diagnose).

Haematoma

A blow or kick can cause bleeding in or around a muscle. Bleeding in a muscle is called an intramuscular haematoma. A rupture inside the muscle causes bleeding. This increases the pressure inside the muscle, causing pain. Swelling can last for two to three days and decreases the mobility of the muscle.

An intermuscular haematoma is an injury in which bleeding occurs between muscles. Initially there is an increase in pressure, then it falls rapidly as the blood spreads. This tends to last one to two days. Bruising may be seen below the injury site. The swelling is temporary because pressure only increases for a short time. Muscle function should return to normal quite quickly.

Your assessment criteria:

P5 Describe first aid and common treatments used for four different types of sports injury

🔑 Key terms

Sprain: *an injury to ligaments*

Strain: *an injury to a muscle or tendon*

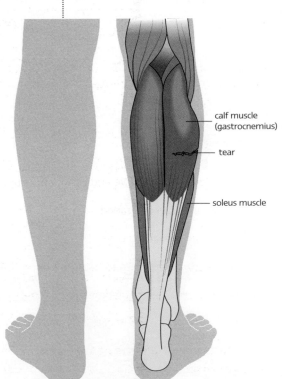

calf muscle (gastrocnemius)

tear

soleus muscle

Figure 18.4 Calf muscle strain

Treatment is PRICED. The injured area should be bandaged as soon as possible to provide compression to reduce blood flow and swelling. Ice should be applied to assist in the reduction of swelling and pain. After 72 hours, heat should be applied to promote blood flow and encourage healing.

Hard tissue injuries

Sprains

Ligaments provide stability at a joint. A partial tear involves only a few fibres. Only part of the ligament may be damaged. The ligament attachment may also be torn away with or without a piece of bone. A complete tear means that all of the ligaments are torn. The ends may be separated from each other, or one end totally detached from the bone.

A partial tear can be classified into two grades if it is stable: grade 1 (a few fibres) or grade 2 (less than half of the fibres).

A grade 3 injury is a complete rupture or tear. Fibres tear and bleeding occurs into the surrounding tissue. This is seen as bruising. The injury will cause pain when the limb is moved, and instability.

Treatment is PRICED with bandaging to support the injured joint.

Cartilage

Cartilage minimises the impact of forces on the skeleton. It reduces friction to minimise wear and tear. Damage can be gradual (chronic wearing away) or acute (sudden from a dislocation). Articular cartilage may be superficial or deep. Superficial cartilage injuries do not heal unless in weight-bearing areas. Full thickness cartilage injuries will gradually develop into osteoarthritis. Cartilage cannot heal by tissue repair as it lacks blood, nerve and lymphatic supplies.

Cartilage injuries can be graded:

• grade 1 – superficial damage

• grade 2 – several splits up to half the length of the cartilage

• grade 3 – cracks extending down to the bone

• grade 4 – complete loss of cartilage and exposure of bone.

Cartilage may break up creating loose, sharp bodies in the joint. Cartilage damage can produce swelling, pain, locking or catching and creaking of a joint.

The injury is treated using PRICED.

Discuss

Discuss sports in which muscle strains are likely to occur.

? Did you know?

There are several signs of a strained muscle. These include:

• *pain*

• *trouble moving the muscle*

• *muscle weakness*

• *muscle spasms*

• *cramping*

• *swelling.*

Discuss

Discuss with a partner or group injuries that you have experienced. Describe how your injuries occurred, the treatment you received and how long it took for you to recover.

Common treatments of sports injuries

There are a variety of methods that can be used to treat sports injuries. Some of the methods include initial assessments, while others can be used at a later stage in the healing process.

SALTAPS

This is a method of assessing sports injuries. It should be used for all injuries and is particularly useful in a practical setting. The acronym stands for:

- **S**top – look at the injury
- **A**sk – ask questions to find out where the injury is and how much discomfort the casualty is in
- **L**ook– for signs of redness and swelling
- **T**ouch – **palpate** the injured part to identify exactly where the pain comes from and to find out the extent of the swelling
- **A**ctive movement – ask the casualty to move the injured part carefully
- **P**assive movement – move the injured part gently through a full range of motion to help identify if the problem is related to a specific position
- **S**trength testing – ask the player to stand up and bear weight. Check if the player can continue.

PRICED

Acute injuries should be treated using PRICED. The acronym stands for:

- **P**rotect – the injured person
- **R**est – allows healing and recovery
- **I**ce – helps prevent pain and reduces swelling
- **C**ompression – bandaging acts as a support and provides pressure, preventing swelling
- **E**levation – reduces blood flow, minimising swelling and assisting with drainage
- **D**iagnosis – refer to a professional to determine the problem. Many injuries require scans to determine the extent of the problem.

Your assessment criteria:

P5 Describe first aid and common treatments used for four different types of sports injury

 Key terms

Diagnosis: *the identification of an injury*

Palpate: *to touch or feel*

 Practical

Working with a partner, practise using the treatment method SALTAPS as a means of identifying an injury. Your partner can determine the injury that they would like to role-play.

Cold treatments (cryotherapy)

Cold treatments are applied to reduce blood flow and provide local pain relief. Cryotherapy is applied for 15 to 20 minutes every hour for the first 24 to 72 hours after the injury. There are a number of methods that can be used to apply cold including ice massage, ice packs, gel and cooling sprays. The temperature must be below 57°F to achieve the benefits required. However, cold treatment must be carefully applied as frostbite occurs when temperatures fall below 32°F. Ice bags are useful as they conform to different shapes and are cheap. Cold packs can be reused. Ice massage is useful for a small area, but will not provide benefits from compression.

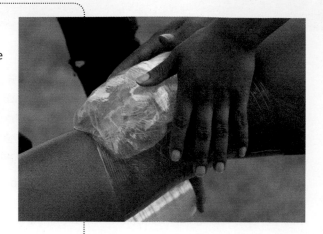

Heat treatments

Heat treatments can be applied at least 48 hours after an injury to encourage blood flow and promote the healing process. If heat is used before 48 hours, the clotting mechanism can be disrupted. Heat increases the elasticity of an area, allowing collagen fibres to respond better to rehabilitation. It increases the circulation and decreases muscle spasm. Heat should be applied for only a short time. For superficial effects, heat packs, infra red and whirlpool baths can be used. For deep effects, ultrasound is more beneficial. Ultrasound can produce heat 10cm into tissue and is especially good at treating tendon injuries.

 Case study

During a recent netball tournament, Jessica injured her gastrocnemius. She received first aid, but struggled to recover. Her first aid treatment lasted for 20 minutes. She was able to carry on working, but unable to play sport for two months. She felt frustrated that things were taking so long. Although she received first aid, she was unsure if there was anything that she could have done to speed up her healing process. She would like to know recommendations that she could use in the future if the same injury occurs.

1. When Jessica injured her muscle, which cold therapy would you have recommended to help reduce the risk of swelling?

2. How often should Jessica apply the cold therapy, and for how long?

3. When should Jessica start to use heat therapy?

4. Why should Jessica avoid having a bath for the first two days after her injury?

5. Which types of heat therapy would you recommend that Jessica uses?

 Research

Research products that are available for heat and cold treatment.

 Discuss

Discuss the claims made for each of the treatments, and how useful you think they are.

Planning a rehabilitation programme

Rehabilitation programmes must be objective and contain clear well-planned progressions so that an athlete can gradually improve. Each part of a rehabilitation programme should have specific aims. The progression through a programme will depend on a person's ability to complete the previous stage. If rehabilitation is rushed, it can produce a set-back in the recovery process and aggravate the injury.

Rehabilitation programmes often use three methods to determine exercise intensity: Borg's pain scale, Borg's RPE scale (rate of perceived exertion), 1 rep max per cent for loading (see Unit 4 Fitness training and programming).

Rehabilitation programmes can be divided between acute and **chronic** injuries. Acute injuries, such as a hamstring injury, progress through five phases of rehabilitation.

Your assessment criteria:

P6 Design a safe and appropriate treatment and rehabilitation programme for two common sports injuries, with tutor support

M3 Independently design a safe and appropriate treatment and rehabilitation programme for two common sports injuries

Key terms

Chronic: a persistent injury that lasts a long time, often occurring gradually

P6 ▶ M3 ▶ Hamstring rehabilitation programme

A hamstring strain is an acute injury caused from overloading or overstretching the hamstring. The injury often occurs in sports that have an explosive element such as sprinting or jumping. Here is an example of a hamstring rehabilitation programme:

1. Acute phase

Treatment includes PRICED.

2. Range of movement phase

To start this phase, a person needs to able to complete voluntary contractions of the hamstrings (Borg CR10 0–1). They also must be able to weight bear and perform a partial active stretch.

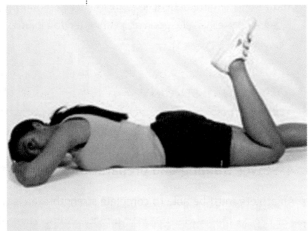

Prone knee bends

The main objective of this phase is to develop hamstring flexibility, maintain endurance, strength and hypertrophy of the muscle, help collagen stimulation and provide some resistance training for type I and IIa muscle fibres. Exercises in this phase include:

- Flexibility – lie on your back with your knee bent. Slowly straighten your knee until a stretch is felt. PNF stretches (partner assisted) can also be included. (See Unit 4 Fitness training and programming for PNF stretching.)

- Endurance – prone knee bends for 30 seconds to 5 minutes; low

impact step machine for 1–10 minutes (light pain); static cycling for 1–10 minutes; 400m walk, increasing every 100m to slow jog.

- Resistance training – use high reps to maintain muscle endurance and prevent atrophy; the exercise intensity is subjective light to weak pain Cr10 1–2; seated hamstring curl (inner middle section, 4–6 sets, 12–15 repetitions, 30 seconds' rest between sets, pace 3s push – 1s hold – 3s slowly lower, 1s rest); seated leg extension (inner middle section, 4–6 sets, 12–15 repetitions, 30 seconds' rest between sets, pace 3s push – 1s hold – 3s slowly lower, 1s rest).

3. Loading phase

A person must be able to complete a full range of pain-free hamstring stretches and be able to jog 400m. The main objective of this phase is to develop strength in the hamstring and co-ordination. Several exercises continue, but the emphasis is on strength training.

- Flexibility – active stretches against the wall (slow pendular movements/slow kicking actions).

- Endurance – rowing machine Borg RPE 11, 8–11 minutes.

- Strength – seated hamstring curl (full range, 6 sets, 8 repetitions, 45 seconds' rest between sets, RPE 14–16, pace 3s push – 1s hold – 3s slowly lower, 1s rest).

- Co-ordination drills – trampet; balance on each leg for as long as possible; balance on your damaged leg and pick an object off the floor; repeat the last two with your eyes closed; single leg dips on a box; hop while catching and throwing a ball against the wall.

 Discuss

Discuss alternative exercises that you could use to rehabilitate a hamstring.

4. Power training and preparation for team training phase

An athlete must be able to complete strength exercises to REP 17+. The main aim of this phase is to promote stimulation of type IIb fibres. Exercises include acceleration and deceleration patterns such as star runs, agility runs and sprint relays. Ball skills practices can be included and small controlled games.

5. Fitness testing phase

The injury should be assessed against pre-injury scores if possible, to see if the injury has completely healed. The athlete should use tests such as the sit and reach test and 30 sprint test to determine whether they are ready to return to competition.

P6 ▶ M3 ▶ Tennis elbow rehabilitation programme

Tennis elbow is a chronic injury that affects between 40 and 50 per cent of players. It is a repetitive strain injury caused by a number of factors, which tends to affect players over the age of 30. Technique, frequency of play, type of racket and quality of the balls are all contributing factors.

Vibrations along the tendon produce micro tears that lead to swelling and pain. Most players can still play with tennis elbow, but it is uncomfortable. Part of the rehabilitation programme will include advice to reduce the causes of the problem.

Technique faults can include leading with elbow, dropping the racket head and hitting the ball behind the body. These can be corrected by hitting the ball in front of the body, keeping a stiff wrist, and using the trunk to rotate when hitting the ball.

The racket should be examined. Using a racket with a larger head and a larger sweet spot reduces the vibration when the racket hits the ball. Having a larger grip reduces the pressure exerted on the tendon.

Balls should be changed at regular intervals to make sure that the impact on the racket is reduced. The fluff around the older balls gradually wears off, reducing the cushioning effect.

Here is an example of a tennis elbow rehabilitation programme:

1. Acute phase

Treatment includes PRICED.

2. Range of movement phase

The main objective is to improve flexibility, increase strength and endurance, increase functional activities and return to function.

- Flexibility – gently flex and extend the wrist and complete rotation exercises for 20–30 seconds, repeating five to ten times.

- Strength – with bent elbow and wrist supported, hold a 1kg weight with your palm facing downwards. Support the forearm on your knee so that only the hand can move. Raise and lower your hand slowly.

- Endurance – place a rubber band around all your fingers and thumb. Spread the fingers 20 times, repeating four times. To increase resistance, you can add a second rubber band.

- Functional activity – place a squash or tennis ball in the palm of your hand. Squeeze it 20 times, repeating four times.

Flexibility exercises for tennis elbow

All strengthening exercises should be pain free.

Massage with an ice cube can be used across the area of tenderness for about five minutes after exercise.

3. Loading phase

The main objective of this phase is to develop strength in the wrist. Exercises include:

- Strength – wrist curls working at 60% 1rm, 3 sets, 8–12 reps with 2 minutes' rest between sets.

- Endurance – increased finger extensions using stronger elastic bands. Both exercises should be performed at a set pace of 3s concentric contraction, 1s hold, 3s eccentric contraction, 1s rest.

4. Power training and preparation for team training phase

Continue previous exercises until there is no discomfort in the tendon.

5. Fitness testing phase

Gradually increase the level of playing activity with small progressions, for example:

- 15 minutes forehand
- 20 minutes forehand
- 25 minutes forehand and two-handed backhand
- 40 minutes forehand and backhand

- 40 minutes all strokes
- serve
- full play
- competitive play.

Strength activity for tendon strength

D2 Evaluate the rehabilitation programme

Rehabilitation begins with PRICED to allow healing to take place. After approximately two days, the athlete will move into phase 2. Fibroblasts start to construct collagen. Exercises can now take place, but activities have to remain low level as there is very little strength or endurance. Phase 3 can begin when the injury has healed enough to allow strength training to take place. Fibres need to align themselves in the direction of stress to build strength. It is important to work the fibres to encourage this to happen. Further collagen is laid down in phase 4 and fibres are strengthened. This encourages a tight strong scar. The strength of the scar needs to be tested in phase 5 to see if it has healed enough for normal training to resume.

 Research

Research alternative exercises that you could use in each stage of rehabilitation for tennis elbow.

 Discuss

Discuss your research findings.

Assessment checklist

To achieve a pass grade, my portfolio of evidence must show that I can:

Assessment Criteria	Description	✓
P1	Describe extrinsic and intrinsic risk factors in relation to sports injuries.	☐
P2	Describe preventative measures that can be taken in order to prevent sports injuries occurring.	☐
P3	Describe the physiological responses common to most sports injuries.	☐
P4	Describe the psychological responses common to sports injuries.	☐
P5	Describe first aid and common treatments used for four different types of sports injury.	☐
P6	Design a safe and appropriate treatment and rehabilitation programme for two common sports injuries, with tutor support.	☐

To achieve a merit grade, my portfolio of evidence must show that I can:

Assessment Criteria	Description	✓
M1	Explain how risk factors can be minimised by utilisation of preventative measures.	☐
M2	Explain the physiological and psychological responses common to most sports injuries.	☐
M3	Independently design a safe and appropriate treatment and rehabilitation programme for two common sports injuries.	☐

To achieve a distinction grade, my portfolio of evidence must show that I can:

Assessment Criteria	Description	✓
D1	Analyse the physiological and psychological responses common to most sports injuries.	☐
D2	Evaluate the treatment and rehabilitation programme designed, justifying the choices and suggesting alternatives where appropriate.	☐

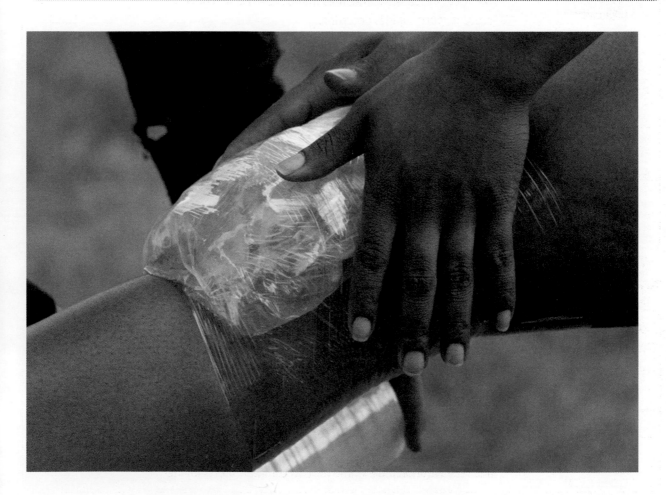

27 | Technical and tactical skills in sport

LO1 Understand the technical skills and tactics demanded by selected sports

- There are technical skills which are commonly used in sport.

- General skills can be used in a variety of different sports.

- Some skills are specific to a particular sport.

- There are a variety of different tactics which can be used effectively in sporting situations.

LO2 Be able to assess the technical and tactical ability of an elite sports performer

- ▶ A comprehensive checklist helps to correctly assess a performer.

- ▶ Performers must use both skills and tactics effectively.

- ▶ Elite performers have particular qualities which put them at this level.

- ▶ Assessment can be carried out in a variety of different ways.

LO3 Be able to assess your own technical and tactical ability

- ▶ An individual's own abilities can be assessed using different methods.

- ▶ It is important to consider strengths and areas for improvement when carrying out an assessment.

- ▶ A training log is an important assessment tool which should be used.

- ▶ A development plan is useful to plan for future improvement.

Technical skills and tactics demanded by selected sports

All sports have technical and tactical requirements, and performers must be aware of these in their selected sport. These will vary between sporting activities, but there will be many general ones which can be utilised in any sporting situation. The sport-specific ones have to be mastered and used appropriately.

Your assessment criteria:

P1 Explain the technical and tactical demands of three contrasting sports

P1 Technical skills and tactics

Knowing the **skills** and **tactics** that are required in a sport is very important for all performers. A performer will need to be proficient in all of the relevant skills, and they will have to be selective regarding the tactics they use and when they will use them. In a team sport these might be set by coaches, but in individual events the performer may select them themselves. In both cases, once the performance is underway, it is likely to be the individual who makes the tactical decisions.

🔑 Key terms

Skills: techniques that are automatic, learnt, fluid and that can be applied in game situations under pressure

Tactics: the choices made in the selection of a skill or method of play

Technical skills

There are three types of skills.

Continuous skills

As the name suggests, these are skills which are used continuously throughout a performance. These include walking, running, swimming, rowing and even cross-country skiing.

At least one of these continuous skills will be used in almost any sports performance. In some sports, the performance is based on these skills, for example:

- A marathon runner runs for the duration of a race.

- A rower rows continuously throughout a performance.

- A golfer walks around the golf course in order to complete their round. On some very uneven courses this can be quite demanding, especially when carrying a heavy golf bag.

- A tennis player runs at various speeds and over various distances throughout the duration of a tennis match.

- A water polo player swims continuously throughout a game of water polo.

Serial skills

These are made up of a combination of skills, and will usually require at least one of the continuous skills to be part of the sequence. Serial skills occur in the majority of sports. Here are some examples:

The high jump starts with an initial run (continuous skill) for the approach to the bar, followed by a take-off phase which involves some form of rotation over the bar. This phase includes a controlled flight as the body is in the air. The final phase is the controlled and safe landing. At least four serial skills are involved, and each one is a complex movement which must be performed with co-ordination.

The pole vault is another jumping event, but it has more complex phases than the high and long jump. An additional skill is the addition of the pole which has to be gripped, carried, used in the jump and then discarded. The performer also has to complete a fast, straight run-up and a very precise take-off involving the pole being inserted in the 'box' (a shaped metal or fibreglass box with a raised wall at the back which the pole has to be placed against) which aids the flight phase (often exceeding 6 metres as this is the elite level height often achieved) up to the bar. There must be controlled rotation over the bar with a complete change of direction, and then a controlled landing (from over 6 metres high) onto an inflatable landing area.

This is the fly-away phase of the pole vault serial skill.

Dribbling in football can be performed at a run or a walk (continuous skill), and requires the use of the inside or outside of the foot or boot (one or two as there is an option) and direction changes of the body. There could also be an obstacle which has to be dribbled around, such as another player or opponent.

In a 400-metre hurdle race, the runners use starting blocks, so at the start of the race they require the skill of mastering a piece of specialist equipment. They have to run at speed (this includes the skill of 'bend-running'), jump over ten 3 feet high (for men and 2 feet 6 inches for women) evenly spaced hurdles and then carry out a 40-metre sprint finish with a 'dip' for the line.

? | Did you know?

An elite pole vaulter would identify the phases of their jump as: the approach; the swing up; the chosen swing method (there are three of these they can choose); the extension; the turn; the fly-away and the landing.

💬 | Discuss

In a group, discuss some different examples of continuous and serial skills which are not described here. Each member of the group should try to give an example from their own experience of taking part in a sporting activity.

Technical skills *continued*

Discrete skills

These are the clearly identified skills which are needed in a specific sport, for example:

- A golf swing is not just one swing as it involves the use of several types of clubs which are different shapes, sizes and weights and which are designed for different distances and ground conditions. The driver is used for long distance shots and is the longest club (except for some specialist 'belly putters'). The iron is used for middle distance shots to the green. The sand wedge is used for shots out of bunkers. The putter is used for the final shot on the green, and involves a different swing as the club head is not raised as far. The swing is significantly different for each club and each shot.

- A snooker shot involves the use of a cue which can vary in length as players can add 'extensions' to make the cue longer for shots which are difficult to reach. The cue action varies in terms of pace, or if swerve, spin, stun or follow-through are required. The fact that snooker shots are played on an elevated table and not at ground level affects the body position as well.

- In board diving there are various heights and types of boards, including the springboard (where extra height can be gained from the 'spring' action), and the high boards where additional height (which allows for more moves) is gained by going up higher initially. The movements of the diver are similar to those used in gymnastics and trampoline, but involve a much longer sequence of twists, turns and rotations due to the amount of time the diver can be in the air, and there is the added skill of safely landing in the water at the end of the dive.

- As there are many rules to prevent a foul throw, a football throw-in has to be carried out in a very precise way with regards to feet placement, grip of the ball and initial preparation with the ball fully behind the head. This is a very distinctive technique which is specifically used in association football.

Tactics

Tactics are very specific to certain sports. This means that a tactic may be an option in one sport, but not in another. A tactic may be linked to a rule of the sport which has to be enforced, for example the 'offside trap'

Key terms

Invasion game: physical activities where teams have to get into their opponents' area in order to score

in football or 'man-to-man marking' in invasion games.

Tactics are appropriate to selected sports, but there are some aspects which apply in general:

- Positioning – this includes the positioning of an individual (e.g. where a player would stand in tennis), players' positions (e.g. defensive, attacking) and how players use the space in team activities. In netball, there are set positions and even rules regarding where each position can go on the court.

- Choice of strokes and shots – in any racket game, hockey, cricket, rounders or golf, the player has a choice of what strokes or shots to play. For example, in a game of rounders the batter may look for gaps in the field and decide to place the ball there, and a cricketer can choose the on or offside to play shots to.

- Variation – this can include many tactics. It can be the variation of spin and slice on a tennis ball, a bowler bowling faster (or slower), low or high deliveries, short pitched or good length deliveries (which will pass the batter at different heights), or even basketball teams varying from playing zone defence to man-to-man marking.

Playing to catch opposing forwards offside is a common tactic in football.

- Conditions – these vary a great deal, so players have to change their tactics accordingly. For example, an activity can be indoors or outdoors, and the weather may be wet or dry, windy or still, hot or cold, sunny or foggy. Other factors that can affect conditions include pressure from spectators, and the type of equipment being used, for example, a top tennis player has their rackets strung at a particular tension and if the tension is wrong, it can affect their play.

- Use of space – most sports have a designated space which the activity is played within (a pitch, court, hall or even a surface, e.g. table-tennis) and the performer can choose how to use that space. For example, a football team playing against a team who have a player sent off should be looking to exploit the additional space which is available.

? | Did you know?

Some tactics in sports are allowed to a certain extent, and after that are deemed to be breaking the rules. In cricket, a bowler is not allowed to constantly bowl 'bouncers' or follow through on the wicket in order to create 'rough' for spinners to bowl into from the other end. In both cases, the umpire will issue a warning at a certain point – the bowler can even be banned from bowling altogether.

M1 Compare and contrast technical skills and tactics

Technical skills and tactics can be compared between different sports. For example, in basketball and netball, the types of passes which are used (discrete skills in many cases) are almost identical, and the distance of the passes are also very similar. However, the tactic of zone marking would not be used in netball due to the movement restrictions on the positions, but in both sports man-to-man marking could be effectively used. Players are not allowed to move with the ball in netball, whereas in basketball all players are allowed to dribble the ball to move both themselves and the ball into different positions. This makes man-to-man marking easier in netball. Also, in netball players are only allowed in specific court areas.

Contrasting sports offer greater scope for comparison and contrast due to the different nature of the activity. For example, comparing a team game to an individual game means that team skills are used in one (for example, scrums and line-outs in rugby) whereas the other focuses on individual skills. However, it must be remembered that individual skills are also important in team games as rugby players, for example, have to develop the skills of passing to be able to involve the rest of their team in attacking moves. Also, indoor and outdoor activities can have 'conditions' factors which vary greatly. Badminton played in a sportshall is not affected by strong winds, whereas tennis on an outdoor court is.

Discuss

In a group, discuss some different examples in sports where specific individual skills contribute to the overall team skills (such as passing in rugby). These examples should be ones which members of the group have either experienced or developed when they have been involved in a team sport situation.

Using the examples of tennis and badminton, they are both racket games so they have many similar shots (the serve in tennis is the same action as the smash in badminton), and the courts they are played on are similar in size and shape. The main contrasts relate to the different rackets which are used, the fact that tennis uses tennis balls and badminton uses shuttlecocks, and the flight of these and types of shots which can be played are very different. There are also other comparisons and contrasts which can be made. For example, every shot in badminton is effectively a 'volley' as the shuttle is not allowed to land before it is hit. Tennis players have the option of allowing the ball to bounce once before they hit it, but they also have the option of playing a half-volley or volley by not letting the ball bounce.

? Did you know?

Badminton shuttlecocks are either made of feather and cork (16 individual goose or duck feathers attached to a 'semi-ellipse' cork base) or plastic. Top players never play with a plastic shuttlecock as the feather one has a more consistent flight and allows greater control of 'touch' shots so this has an effect on their technical skills. However, the feather shuttlecocks are very expensive and a shuttlecock is unlikely to last more than one game. This is why beginners and most club players use the plastic variety which lasts for hundreds of games!

 ## Case study

Helena has chosen to compare and contrast netball and trampoline as two of her selected sports. The netball she has been watching has been a televised major championship which was played in a large indoor arena in Australia, and she was able to record and watch the semi-finals and final of the event. Helena was able to go along to the national trampoline championships on an organised school trip and saw members of the national squad perform their competition sequences in the final of the event.

1. What are likely to be the main comparisons that Helena will make in her two chosen sports?

2. Which method of watching the sports is likely to be the most useful for her comparison, and why?

3. Which sport is likely to have the most serial skills to observe?

4. Is there an opportunity for use of tactics in both of these sports?

Assessing the technical and tactical ability of an elite sports performer

Using an elite performer gives a very good insight into the levels of technical and tactical ability which are required to compete at the very highest level. This will not only show the full range of options which are available in a particular sport, but also the correct timing and execution of those options in terms of skills and tactics used.

P2 Observation checklists

A checklist is essential to assess the performance levels of an individual. This should be compiled using a performance **profile** which uses the following headings:

Technical skills

These are the continuous, serial and discrete skills identified on pages 308–311.

Selection of skills

A major factor which makes an elite performer stand out is their ability to select skills from all of those at their disposal. A tennis player must know which shot to play, when to play it, where to direct it and the amount of pace, slice and spin to put on the shot.

Application of skills

Application of skills refers to the performer actually having the ability to perform the skills both correctly and effectively. Many performers can perform skills in isolation, in a practice situation, but it is the ability to perform them in a challenging match or game situation which allows them to succeed at the highest level.

Tactical awareness

This has two aspects in that the performer must be aware of the tactics which they are able to employ, and at the same time be aware of tactics which might be used against them. A tennis player who opts to play baseline rallies and stay at the back of the court, can be put off their stride if their opponent plays drop shots close to the net which makes them come to the front of the court. A serve and volley tactic might be useful for the player trying to combat the opponent who is content to play long, baseline rally points.

Key terms

Application: putting something to a special use or purpose, or putting something into operation

Profile: a formal summary or analysis of data, representing distinctive features or characteristics

Discuss

Choose a sporting activity or event and discuss the particular skills which a performer can select from. As part of this discussion, consider which of these skills are likely to be the most essential ones.

Application of tactics

Knowing tactics and being able to use them are two different things. If a tennis player decides to adopt a serve and volley tactic, they must be able to serve fast, hard and long in order to give themselves time to get into the net to play a volley off the service return. Application of tactics is largely dependent on the performer's skill levels. A low level skill player will have fewer options available to them.

Ability to defend

Adopting defensive tactics is often seen as a negative approach, but in some circumstances it is a necessity. In an invasion game there are occasions when the opposition are attacking, for example in netball when the alternate centre pass means that opponents are in an attacking position. In some sports, performers set out to have a defensive strategy overall, and then score on the counter-attack. This tactic is often used in football. The ability to defend is a necessity in all circumstances, but it would only be seen as negative if it were adopted as a strategy from the beginning of a match. This has occurred in some major football championships when teams have set out to defend from the very start and have gone all the way to a penalty shoot-out after extra time has been played. They consider this gives them the best chance of winning overall.

? | Did you know?

Most coaches and managers who are involved in sport consider organising and setting tactics for defending to be easier than attacking. This may explain why the most expensive professional footballers are always attacking players (many times more expensive than goalkeepers, for example) who are sought after to break down organised and efficient defences.

Netball teams are aware of the need for a good ability to defend when the opposition have possession.

P2 Observation checklists *continued*

Ability to attack

Making full use of attacking options is generally a very positive option and many performers choose it to gain the initiative over opponents. If a tennis player can win a match 6 – 0, 6 – 0 through attacking from the onset, then this is likely to be a better tactic than letting the match drag on for three sets by playing defensively and waiting for the opponent to make mistakes.

Shot selection

This only applies to sports or activities where it is possible for shots to be played (racket sports, cricket, football, rugby and hockey), and it is the appropriate selection of these shots which is important. Elite performers choose shots wisely and will even plan ahead, such as a badminton player playing a sequence of long deep shots to the back of the court to keep the opponent there before playing a short drop shot winner close to the net.

Good shot selection is very important to achieve success at badminton.

A finished observation checklist must be very sport-specific so that it includes all of the elements which might be present in a particular performance. Therefore, all of the sections outlined above have to be considered for inclusion, and within them there may be subdivisions. For example, if tennis were being considered, the selection of skills would need to consider serving, forehand shots (this could include topspin, slice, deep and short, smash shots and volleys) and backhand shots (all the variations for the forehand would be repeated) in the category of discrete skills. Any continuous skills would also need to be considered such as running.

Your assessment criteria:

P2 Produce an observation checklist that can be used to assess the technical and tactical ability of a performer in a selected sport

P3 Use an observation checklist to assess the technical and tactical ability of an elite performer, in a selected sport, identifying strengths and areas for improvement

? Did you know?

All elite performers would expect the equivalent of an observation checklist to be carried out on them for all performances. Many football clubs use a system called 'Prozone' which tracks all players throughout a game and records physical tactical and technical data relating to the players and the team. This is used by the managers and coaches and feedback is given to the performers. Examples of data which can be gathered include the actual distance each player runs, the number of passes and tackles made, and overall statistics regarding time of possession and areas of the pitch where play was focused.

P3 Elite performers

To assess the ability of an elite performer, it is important first to identify what makes a performer elite. They are considered to be in any of the following categories:

- professional athlete (or performer)
- national champion
- national representative
- international champion.

Not all professional performers are national representatives, and there are some sports such as football, rugby and cricket that have a relatively high number of professional performers in comparison to other less popular sports.

Assessment

A detailed observation checklist of various aspects which can be observed provides sufficient information to make judgements on levels of performance.

Observation checklists and performance profiles

These are devised to match a particular sport or sports performer, and give an overview of what is being assessed in terms of the specific aspects identified in P2.

Strengths

There are several categories which are likely to be identified:

- *Specific skills* – these link very closely to discrete skills.

- *Specific techniques* – an example is a spin pass in rugby where the technique is related to a specific skill. This technique is not used in any other sport due to the shape of the rugby ball which allows the technique to be used.

- *Tactical awareness* – this is being alert to opportunities to either use tactics or counteract ones being used by the opposition.

- *Fitness levels* – a performance may be dependent on this, especially any form of endurance event. For most other sporting activities, levels of fitness are a factor in whether a performer can sustain levels of performance. For example, an unfit rugby player is unlikely to be able to maintain a high level performance for the full 80-minute game.

- *Ability to read the game* – this is a commonly used term and it refers to the individual's ability to change their approach and adjust tactics. For example, if a hockey team are constantly attacking down one particular wing, it is important to realise this ('read' it) and adjust the defensive team formation to counteract it.

? Did you know?

'Elite' means 'the best or most skilled and gifted', and this term is applied to sports performers in particular. Each sport (especially through their national governing body) has a policy of identifying performers at this level, and ensuring that they are able to perform together either as individuals or in teams.

P3 Assessment *continued*

Areas for improvement

Areas for improvement might be difficult to predict because the purpose of the assessment is to identify them, but the likely areas are:

- *Attacking* – there are many alternative options which might be more successful. If attacking is proving to be unsuccessful or easily counteracted, then different approaches need to be made, e.g. changing formation or players' positions.

- *Defending* – no one defensive strategy or formation is guaranteed to be totally successful, so alternative options might be suggested if they are appropriate to the performer.

- *Specific skills* – it may be that some specific skills are not being used as effectively as possible, or even not being used at all.

- *Specific techniques* – it may be that some specific techniques are not being performed as well as they could be or used as often as possible.

- *Fitness* – this may include specific fitness (related particularly to the sport in question) and general fitness (the general levels required for the activity, e.g. endurance), and it is likely that both will need to be considered.

Your assessment criteria:

P3 Use an observation checklist to assess the technical and tactical ability of an elite performer, in a selected sport, identifying strengths and areas for improvement

This sprinter is pulling a parachute resistance bag in a training session.

Development

Further development is a crucial part of the assessment process, and there are particular aspects which will need to be addressed. These will relate to the areas for improvement identified in the process:

- *Training* – this relates to the specific aspects of the performance, and is likely to focus on skills, techniques and fitness as these can all be addressed in a specific training programme.

- *Competition* – varying the levels and even the regularity of competition can help a performer to improve. More challenging opponents are likely to bring out higher level performances, and they would be a greater test of any identified strengths.

- *Specific coaching/coaches* – particular identified areas for improvement can benefit from some expert or clearly focused coaching.

> **? Did you know?**
>
> *The demands of playing the full 80 minutes in a top level rugby union match are so high that the substitution rules have been adjusted to allow more permanent changes to be made. Up to seven of the original starting 15 can be substituted, so this means that nearly half of the team do not have to play the whole of the match. This allows for lower fitness levels among some of the players.*

- *Observational analysis* – this will focus on specific areas which were identified for improvement, and give ongoing feedback as to whether the suggestions are working. This is a method of recording number details such as how many shots were on target and how many off; how many passes were accurate and how many were intercepted. For example, in badminton you could record the percentage of smashes that were successful and the percentage of errors in completing the shot. Figure 27.1 is an example of observational analysis for a badminton match.

Figure 27.1 Observational analysis for a badminton match

	Front			Middle			Back		
	Effective	Ineffective	Normal	Effective	Ineffective	Normal	Effective	Ineffective	Normal
Drop Shot				1	1	1		2	2
Push		2	2	3	1	5		2	1
Block									
Smash	1			1				3	
Clear				1	1	5	1	2	4
Net		2	2						
Lift	1	3	1	2	2	4	1	2	4

- *Technical guidance* – whereas coaches assist with possible skills development, there might also be a need for 'technical' advice which can cover aspects such as using equipment or coping with particular conditions.

- *Nutritional guidance* – this is primarily concerned with dietary guidance of a general nature (proper preparation prior to performances), but may also be concerned with nutrition requirements during a performance.

- *Psychological guidance* – aspects of psychological factors are covered in Unit 17 Psychology for sports performance, and this is a very important area in relation to both success and failure in any sporting performance. The main factors are levels of motivation and anxiety.

- *Fitness guidance* – fitness levels are identified during the assessment process, and this is an area where there is always some scope for development.

Q | Research

For the sport you have chosen for the observation, research which of the technical and tactical factors identified are relevant to that sport and which are not. As part of this research, make sure that all skills, techniques and tactics are clearly identified.

M2 **Explain strengths and areas for improvement of the elite performer**

After identifying the particular strengths and areas for improvement which are evident from a performance, it is important to be able to explain these in some detail and then make specific suggestions for further development.

 Case study

Alisha chooses Beth Tweddle as the elite performer to carry out her observation checklist on, and she decides to focus on her successful asymmetric bars routine. As Beth performs at a very high level (she won the world championship in this event), Alisha finds it very easy to identify the Beth's strengths, but identifying areas for improvement is more challenging. Alisha performs gymnastics at club level, but does not perform an asymmetric routine. She is, however, aware of the tariff system of marking which considers the difficulty of each gymnastic movement performed.

1. What particular category of skills is Alisha most likely to have to explain in Beth's routine?

2. How might Alisha's knowledge of gymnastics as a performer herself help to assess Beth accurately?

3. How might the fact that there is a scoring tariff system in place in this particular event help Alisha in her assessment?

D1 ▶ Justify development suggestions

Once realistic areas for improvement have been identified and explained, they need to be justified in terms of how the developments in the specific areas for improvement could improve the overall performance and success of the elite athlete. It is the overall performance which needs to be considered, so factors such as levels of fitness or psychological factors might be more significant than some of the more skill-based ones.

 ## Case study

Sean chooses to carry out his observation on one of the players at his local championship league professional football club. Sean goes along to one of the recent home matches to carry out the observation, listens to radio commentaries on home matches and keeps press match reports.

The particular player Sean has been watching has been identified by the press as an 'exciting prospect' and 'star of the future', but some doubts have been expressed over his levels of fitness. In the match Sean watched, the player scored one goal and helped to set up another, but was substituted halfway through the second half when he was suffering from cramp and clearly showing signs of fatigue, but was still given the 'man of the match' award.

Jack Wilshere is a young, skilful footballer who plays for Arsenal and the England national team.

In his assessment, Sean particularly identifies the high discrete skill levels demonstrated by the player as his major strengths, and raising fitness levels as the main factor to improve overall performance.

1. How might Sean justify his view that his chosen player has high levels of discrete skills as major strengths?

2. How might Sean justify his view that his chosen player needs to improve his fitness levels as an area for development?

Assessing own technical and tactical ability

Understanding the demands of technical skills and tactics is important to all sports performers and this unit gives the opportunity to consider these demands at an elite level. It is equally important, however, for an individual performer at any level to take the opportunity to assess and develop them.

P4 ▶ Assessment

Competitive situation

As assessment needs to be carried out in a competitive situation, so this rules out a training session or non-competitive situation such as any form of conditioned or adapted game. The most effective way of achieving this is to record the performance on DVD/video so that it can be reviewed by the performer later.

Observation checklist or performance profiling

There is an option to use the most suitable of these methods, and this may well depend on the sport or activity being undertaken. For example, in a game of badminton set skills are used such as serving, forehand and backhand shots, and a specific number of games are played, so an observation checklist could be produced relating to this. However, for a game of football where involvement might be varied and there is no guarantee of all the discrete skills being used, performance profiling might be more appropriate. Whichever option is chosen, the following should be considered. These terms will be familiar as they are the same headings which were used when carrying out the observation on the elite performer:

- technical skills

- selection of skills

- application of skills

- application of tactics.

Strengths

Strengths must be identified, but the following are possible areas (also used when assessing the elite performer):

- *Specific skills* – these may be discrete skills which are particularly applicable to the sport or

? Did you know?

Physical fitness includes muscular endurance, speed, flexibility, strength, body composition and aerobic endurance. Skill-related fitness includes balance, co-ordination, reaction time, power and agility.

This phase for a sprinter involves the skill-related fitness factor of reaction time.

activity, or they may be specific skills which the individual performer has and which they particularly bring to the performance. For example, a football goalkeeper may be particularly skilful in the areas of agility and good reaction times, and these would clearly be strengths.

- *Specific techniques* – similarly, these may be techniques which are particularly suited to the sport, or ones which the individual can display.

- *Tactical awareness* – a full range of tactics should be available to be used, and also to be dealt with.

- *Fitness levels* – there are many factors of fitness which can be considered here including physical fitness and skill-related fitness.

- *Ability to read the game* – it is important to receive feedback on this as an independent observer is more likely to be accurate with this assessment. An individual involved in a game is not always aware of the options which might be available, and as a result may be less accurate.

Areas for improvement

The option areas here may well be similar, or the same, as the strengths options. Some skills may be identified as particular strengths, and others as areas for improvement. The main headings to consider are:

- *Attacking* – the whole aspect of attacking will need to be considered, such as how many players might be committed to an attacking role. However, it may be the case that the individual is primarily involved in a defensive role (goal defence in netball, or goalkeeper in football), so this area may not need to be addressed.

- *Defending* – the same comments may apply for defending as they do for attacking in certain activities. A goal shooter in netball is not allowed to defend, but a striker in football is expected to drop back to defend corners.

- *Specific skills* – it is unlikely that all specific (discrete) skills will have been fully mastered, so this is an aspect which may be in need of improvement.

- *Specific techniques* – once again, these are unlikely to all have been mastered, and therefore are likely to be identified.

- *Fitness* – it is important to consider all of the aspects of fitness. Once again, it is unlikely that none of these will be in need of any improvement.

A goal shooter is not allowed back into a defensive situation in a game of netball due to the rules.

323

M3 Explain own strengths and areas for improvement in a competitive situation

Once assessment has been carried out, it is important to be able to explain the identified strengths and areas for improvement. An explanation is required as to what impact these may have had on the competitive situation, and why certain aspects were identified as strengths and others as areas for improvement.

Your assessment criteria:

M3 Explain strengths and areas for improvement, in own technical and tactical ability in a competitive situation

P5 Complete a four-week log of own technical and tactical ability in a selected sport, identifying strengths and areas for improvement

Case study

Rachel plays netball for the school team and her specialist position within the team is that of goal shooter. She manages to get the whole of one of her recent school match performances videoed, and because of the restrictions of her position around the court, the camera is focused on her all the time. She then replays the video several times, and produces a performance portfolio where she lists all the specific skills required and her success ratio for each.

She receives 90 per cent of the passes made to her, evades her defending marker regularly, completes all of her passes to her goal attack team mate and has a 50 per cent success rate when shooting for goal.

1. What is Rachel likely to explain as her main strength in terms of specific skills?

2. What is Rachel likely to explain as her main strength in terms of her tactical ability?

3. What is Rachel likely to explain as her main area for improvement?

P5 Identify own strengths and areas for improvement in a four-week log

A four-week log of own technical and tactical ability must be completed, and the strengths and areas for improvement identified. The following information should be included in this log.

Diary of specific training sessions

Skills, techniques and tactics should be included in this diary. These need to be broken down, taking into account the three areas of skills which might be considered as well as specific techniques.

Planning tactics to be employed is an important aspect of any performance.

For example, the skill of passing might be identified, but the various techniques of chest pass, bounce pass and overhead pass could be outlined as well. Tactics covered would usually be in the categories of attacking and defensive.

Competition analysis

This should consider the particular strengths and weaknesses which are displayed in a competitive match, so there must be at least one of these within the four-week block. A coach analysis should also be included after competitions and training which would provide some feedback on how successful these have been.

Areas for improvement

These are linked to the previously identified areas, but there is additional feedback, especially from the coaches following the competition and training sessions, which might highlight any of the following areas:

- attacking
- defending
- specific skills
- specific techniques
- fitness
- specific practices that could improve performance.

Golfers make use of practice facilities to practise both skills and techniques.

? Did you know?

Elite performers plan training sessions to alternate fitness work and skill-based work. They would normally allow at least one day for their bodies to recover from a strenuous fitness training session before taking part in another one. However, specific skill-based work can be carried out more regularly as the more often practice takes place, the more likelihood there is of achieving an improvement.

M4 ▶ Explain own strengths and areas for improvement in a selected sport

Various elements of the four-week training programme will have been identified as areas of strength where progress was made in the technical and tactical areas, and these must be explained. The ability to critically analyse attainment is important as individuals must be able to give a realistic explanation. For example, having a good endurance level may be seen as a strength for a performer in an invasion game such as rugby where they will be required to keep playing throughout an 80-minute game. It is this ability to 'keep going' which is the strength rather than any particular contribution which is made to the game in terms of technical skill or selection of tactics.

Your assessment criteria:

M4 ▶ Explain identified strengths and areas for improvement of own technical and tactical ability in a selected sport

P6 Produce a development plan of own technical and tactical ability, based on identified strengths and areas for improvement

? Did you know?

A training programme must be carried out for at least a four-week period for the principle of progression (one of the principles of training) to apply. This refers to allowing the body time to adjust gradually and therefore improve as the training becomes progressively harder – there is no short cut to achieving this!

 ## Case study

Laurence plays in goal for the school football team and has also been selected for the county squad. He feels that he is achieving quite high levels of success, and that overall he has mastered most of the technical skills which he requires to be an effective goalkeeper. In his four-week programme, Laurence plans to have two general 'fitness' sessions per week on Mondays and Thursdays, and skills-based sessions on all of the days in between. In his fitness sessions, he chooses circuit training with a mixture of exercises and co-ordination practices, and in his skills sessions, he is focusing on agility and reaction time.

1. Explain why Laurence has chosen to have only two fitness sessions a week.

2. What explanation is Laurence likely to provide for including a mixture of exercises and co-ordination practices within his circuit training sessions? How are these likely to help him in his sport?

3. For what reasons would Laurence be focusing on agility and reaction time in his skills practices?

P6 Development plan

The development plan needs to be produced based on the strengths and areas for improvement which were identified in completing the four-week training programme. This can be achieved in the following way:

Setting SMART targets

This stands for:

- **S**pecific – the particular aspects to be worked on must be identified. It is not specific enough to simply state 'to be a better performer' as there needs to be clarity regarding any skills or tactical aspects of a performance which require improvement in order to make the overall performance better.

- **M**easurable – levels of performance need to be established at the completion of the programme in order to measure how much progress is made during the development process. It is important that skills and tactics which can be easily measured are chosen, and that these link to the specific factors already considered. For example, if 'accuracy of passing' is identified as a specific area for improvement, a record could be made of how many times an accurate pass is executed in a performance situation.

- **A**chievable – it is important not to be too ambitious regarding what is to be achieved as only a certain amount of progress can be made in specific time frames.

- **R**ealistic – this links closely to 'achievable' as it must be established that both the resources and the ability are present. This also links to the aspect of being measurable.

- **T**ime-bound – a daily, weekly or longer-term commitment must be made for this plan. It may even be ongoing over a quite extensive time period.

Specific targets

It is likely that these will revolve around identifying improvements of technical weaknesses, such as being able to complete skills effectively at the start of a performance, but having reduced levels of success as fatigue sets in towards the end. The other main area is likely to be tactical awareness, and looking for ways to improve this.

 Discuss

Choose two particular sports or sporting activities and consider what the main technical weaknesses are likely to be in those activities. These should be weaknesses which are most likely to result in a reduced level of success for the performers involved in them.

P6 Development plan *continued*

Resources

A commitment to a development plan involves taking part in specific practices, and the following factors must be considered:

- Human resources – other people are likely to be involved, including coaches, team mates and fellow competitors, and their needs and responsibilities must be considered. Other people's time availability may need to be factored in.

- Fiscal – there is likely to be a cost involved in any development plan. In order to progress and develop substantially, it may be necessary to attend specific courses (such as those organised by the national governing bodies) which have to be paid for. There may be a cost to secure the relevant coaching, and even entering competitions can involve paying an entry fee.

M5 Relate plan to own strengths and areas for improvement

Once the plan has been developed, it is important to be able to relate how completing the practices, undertaking any specific courses, working with coaches and taking part in competitions will improve an overall performance in a selected sport. This should have been carefully considered during the specific aspect of the SMART target setting.

Your assessment criteria:

P6 Produce a development plan of own technical and tactical ability, based on identified strengths and areas for improvement

M5 Relate development plan to identified strengths and areas for improvement in own technical and tactical ability

D2 Justify suggestions made in personal development plan

🔑 Key terms

Fiscal: *financial, relating to expenditure*

🔍 Research

Find out what particular coaching awards the national governing body for a chosen activity has available. Find out which one is likely to be most relevant to any of the factors identified for improvement in the development plan and the costs and commitment involved.

Case study

Sarah has based her assessment, training log and development plan on her chosen sport of football which she has been playing for five years. She does not play at a very high level, but would consider herself to be a competent football player. Sarah has identified quite a few areas for improvement in her technical skills, but her biggest concern is the targets she has set herself for improving her tactical awareness as she rarely gets the chance to play in a competitive team situation. She has enrolled on the Level One Award in Coaching Football course which is being run locally and has joined a local ladies football club. Sarah has also joined a local gym as she identified her levels of general fitness as another area for improvement.

In what ways is Sarah likely to be able to relate her following decisions to enhancing her performance?

• enrolling on the FA coaching award

• joining the local ladies football club

• joining the gym.

D2 ▸ Justify suggestions made in development plan

Once a plan has been developed, it is necessary to justify the suggestions which are made within it, and then give examples of how the suggestions in the plan can be met. This will focus very much on the realistic and attainable aspects of the SMART target setting.

Case study

Jason has used SMART targets to produce a plan for his chosen sport of basketball. He plays at a reasonable level for his school team, has attended trials to be a member of the regional squad, and is optimistic of becoming a squad member in the near future, despite failing to get in the previous year. His main targets are to improve his speed, endurance and dribbling skills, and he also feels he needs to work on the tactical side of his game as he finds some of the tactics the coaches suggest quite hard to follow and put into operation.

Jason spends some time on the time-bound aspect of his SMART target setting as he feels that to be both realistic and achievable, he needs to plan over a nine-month period to meet some of his desired outcomes.

1. How can Jason justify this quite long time-scale for achievement of his SMART targets?

2. What evidence can Jason provide to support his decisions?

3. Are all of Jason's overall aims likely to be attainable?

Assessment checklist

To achieve a pass grade, my portfolio of evidence must show that I can:

Assessment Criteria	Description	✓
P1	Explain the technical and tactical demands of three contrasting sports.	☑
P2	Produce an observation checklist that can be used to assess the technical and tactical ability of a performer in a selected sport.	☑
P3	Use an observation checklist to assess the technical and tactical ability of an elite performer, in a selected sport, identifying strengths and areas for improvement.	☑
P4	Use an observation checklist to assess own technical and tactical ability, in a competitive situation for a selected sport, identifying strengths and areas for improvement.	☑
P5	Complete a four-week log of own technical and tactical ability in a selected sport, identifying strengths and areas for improvement.	☑
P6	Produce a development plan of own technical and tactical ability, based on identified strengths and areas for improvement.	☑

To achieve a merit grade, my portfolio of evidence must show that I can:

Assessment Criteria	Description	✓
M1	Compare and contrast the technical and tactical demands of three contrasting sports.	☐
M2	Explain strengths and areas for improvement, in technical and tactical ability, of the selected elite sports performer, and make suggestions relating to development.	☐
M3	Explain strengths and areas for improvement, in own technical and tactical ability in a competitive situation.	☑
M4	Explain identified strengths and areas for improvement of own technical and tactical ability in a selected sport.	☑
M5	Relate development plan to identified strengths and areas for improvement in own technical and tactical ability.	☑

Financial

This factor can affect athletes at two extremes. A professional athlete might find that they have a fairly large income, and the way they handle this is important. At the other end of the scale, an amateur athlete may have no additional income and a shortage of money will be their main concern. The following aspects must be considered:

- Spending – this needs to be controlled in line with the athlete's income. If income is low, the athlete must decide on priorities for spending. There may be essential items such as travel, accommodation and equipment which have to be paid for, and this may leave little money for anything else.

- Saving and investing – very few athletes in any form of sport have a long career, and most retire from competitive sport in their forties at the latest. Few female gymnasts keep on competing into their twenties, and the average age for professional footballers is 35. Therefore, saving and investing for the future is very important, and one 'investment' might be to plan and prepare for a second career which will start when the athletic one ends.

- Sponsorship – for all performers, this is likely to be a substantial aspect of their financial income. For amateur athletes, this is the way in which they receive money or services (such as coaching, transport, food, accommodation) or equipment, and for professionals, sponsorship deals can double or treble their income. The level of sponsorship received is largely dependent on the level of success of the performer and to some extent the sport they are associated with.

- Tax – a top level athlete may have a very complex income profile and income tax must be paid on any income they receive. If they are self-employed, they are responsible for self-assessing and paying their own tax, and the majority of performers employ accountants to deal with tax matters for them.

- Insurance – the risk of injury, to themselves or others, is a constant worry for top athletes, and taking out insurance to cover such eventualities is a common and wise decision. The cost of this insurance is likely to be quite high because of the factors and pressures associated with their lifestyle.

 Discuss

1. In a group, discuss the amount of money each individual spends on their main sport in terms of equipment, fees and travel, etc.

2. Each group member should then come up with a 'wish list' of what they would be able to make use of if they had sufficient money or what they could obtain through lucrative sponsorship deals.

Puma refused to divulge details of Usain Bolt's sponsorship, but referred to it as 'the largest ever given to a track and field athlete'.

M1 ▶ Explain different lifestyle factors

You need to explain different lifestyle factors which particularly affect athletes, and the best way of doing this is through appropriate examples. For example, you could explain the pressures experienced through a young athlete living away from home.

Andy Murray had to leave home at an early age to further his tennis playing career.

Case study

Sean is 16 years old and has been signed as a junior by a premier league football club, but as his home is so far away the club have arranged for him to lodge with a family in the city. Sean is studying for his GCSEs and the club have arranged for him to attend a local school which several other junior players from the club also attend.

Sean is expected to train with the rest of the squad every weekday after he has finished his schooling, and the junior team which he is a member of, play in league matches every Saturday. The family which Sean is lodging with have two teenage sons, aged 17 and 19, and they are keen for Sean to socialise with them quite regularly – especially as he plays for the high profile, local football club.

1. What particular pressures is Sean most likely to have to deal with by living away from home?

2. How much leisure time is Sean likely to have, and what 'appropriate activities' would he be advised to take up?

3. Is Sean likely to be subjected to any particular peer pressure, and what form is this likely to take?

Your assessment criteria:

M1 Explain five different lifestyle factors that can affect athletes

D1 Analyse five different lifestyle factors that can affect athletes

? Did you know?

Tennis player, Andy Murray, was invited at the age of 15 to train with the Scottish football club Glasgow Rangers and to join their School of Excellence. Murray turned them down and opted for a tennis career instead. Instead of pursuing a football career (which his grandfather had done), Murray moved to Spain where he studied at the Schiller International School and trained on the clay tennis courts of the Sanchez-Casal Academy run by Emilio Sanchez, the former number one ranked doubles player. Murray describes this period of his life as having been a 'big sacrifice'.

D1 Analyse different lifestyle factors

Once you have identified and explained different lifestyle factors, you must analyse them. This can take the form of considering how the identified factors are related and the effect they are likely to have on performances. For example, clubs may encourage young players to move away from home and live nearer to the club, so that they have a greater influence upon them and are able to deliver and monitor training more effectively.

Nadia Comaneci was awarded a perfect 10 score for her performance.

? Did you know?

In the 1960s and 1970s, a Rumanian gymnastics coach, Bela Karolyi, pioneered the idea of centralised gymnastic training camps. Young gymnasts were selected for their 'athletic potential' and attended a boarding school where he worked. One of his early successes was Nadia Comaneci who was spotted and selected at the age of six! She then went on to become the first gymnast to achieve the perfect mark of 10 in an Olympic final in Montreal in 1976.

Many of the present Schools of Excellence took their lead from this model of training schools and camps.

 ### Case study

Think again about Sean, the young footballer who has moved away from home as part of his arrangement with the football club.

1. What level of specific training is Sean likely to receive from his club, and what impact is this likely to have on his performance?

2. What level of contact is Sean now likely to have with his team mates, and what effect is that likely to have on his performance?

3. Are there any factors which are likely to be negative ones relating to Sean moving away from home? If so, what effect are these likely to have on his performance levels?

Appropriate behaviour for athletes

Since top athletes are constantly in the spotlight with high levels of media scrutiny, it is important that they are aware of their responsibilities to behave appropriately. Their behaviour may be seen as an example for others – especially young people who look up to them for inspiration.

P2 Behaviour

There are many times and situations when a top athlete's behaviour is observed by others.

During competition and training

Competition is carried out publicly, and more and more access is being given to the public to observe top performers undertaking their training. This is particularly common with professional football clubs where the training grounds do not have the full security that the stadiums have which enables the players to be watched by both fans and the media.

Chelea Football Club's training ground in Cobham, Surrey has clear views open to the public.

In both competition and training, athletes must adhere to rules. In a competitive situation, not adhering to the rules may be considered to be cheating. All sports have disciplinary procedures, and footballers and rugby players can be sent off and even banned which sets a bad example. With the introduction of technology enabling all actions to be reviewed and checked by officials, there is little likelihood of any rule breaking going unpunished, and action can even be taken following a competition.

Athletes must show respect for peers and others. This includes demonstrating good etiquette and good sporting behaviour (often known as 'good sportsmanship') before, during and after both training

and competition. It is particularly important that athletes show respect for officials who might be in charge of competitive situations. Crowds and spectators are included in the 'others' category. It can be challenging for performers to be respectful to crowds who might be booing them or chanting unpleasantly, but this is a difficult aspect of an athlete's behaviour which must be considered and controlled.

Athletes must wear appropriate clothing. Most sporting activities have very specific rules about what clothing should be worn during competition, and there may be penalties imposed for ignoring these. The rules for training situations can be more relaxed, but a player choosing to not wear suitable protective clothing when training might be seen to be setting a bad example.

> **? Did you know?**
>
> *The Wimbledon tennis authorities insist that all players wear 'predominantly white' clothing during the two-week tournament, and this is the only major tennis tournament which still has this ruling. They have agreed to relax this ruling for the 2012 Olympic tournament which will take place there.*

Equal opportunities

The issue of equal opportunities is a legal one due to the various legislation which is in place. This puts an onus on all individuals to respect others and not to discriminate in any way against them in terms of race, religion, gender or sexual orientation. All athletes benefit from being treated equally in their careers, so they must ensure that they treat others equally too. There are more female officials in senior positions in major sports, notably football, and performers must be aware of the importance of treating them with respect.

P2 ▸ Behaviour *continued*

Appropriate role models

Successful sports performers find themselves as **role models** as a result of their status, so it is essential that they take this responsibility seriously. They should also consider role models they may have, for example Sports Ambassadors which is a 'Young Ambassadors' scheme set up in 2006 following the successful 2012 Olympic bid where young people aged 14–19 can work with the 5–19 age group due to their sporting talent. There are various sports ambassadors (ambassadors in sport for some activities) who are leading sports people in their own particular sport, and these are often individuals who have stopped competing but use their knowledge and experience to help others.

Many celebrities become role models because of their status, and many successful performers become celebrities due to their achievements and profile in sport. A good example of this is David Beckham who has enjoyed celebrity status throughout his playing career.

Enhancing the status of sport

Good conduct serves to raise the status of sport in the eyes of all the people who are either directly involved in it as participants or as spectators. Generally, sport enjoys the status it has, but as it is always in the public spotlight, it is the responsibility of all those involved to make sure that this status is enhanced rather than tainted.

Encouraging excellence

Young performers will be encouraged to reach excellence if they see examples of appropriate behaviour by top performers who have already achieved the top standards and levels.

Increasing participation for all

One of the main aims of sport in general is to increase levels of participation, and each individual sport aims to improve participation levels in that sport. They look to top level performers to set good examples of conduct and behaviour so that the next generation of performers are encouraged to get involved as well.

Your assessment criteria:

P2 Describe the importance of appropriate behaviour for athletes

M2 Explain the importance of appropriate behaviour for athletes

D2 Justify the importance of appropriate behaviour for athletes

🔑 Key terms

Role model: someone who people look up to, and who is seen as a good example for other people

David Beckham became a role model for many people and he also enjoys celebrity status.

M2 Explain the importance of appropriate behaviour

You must explain identified descriptions in detail, with examples to make your explanations clear. For example, showing appropriate behaviour by correctly adhering to rules can best be explained with an example of not adhering to rules.

 ## Case study

Becky plays rugby at junior international level, and she recently took part in a televised match which was broadcast on one of the satellite sports channels. All of Becky's team mates from her club attended the match, and the whole of the junior section of the club was invited along to the clubhouse for a live televised screening of the match.

Towards the end of the match, Becky was yellow-carded for what the referee deemed was serious foul play when she appeared to trip a player running through to score a try. Becky disagreed with the decision and argued with the referee, and the penalty was advanced by ten yards. The action replay, which was shown after the incident, clearly showed that Becky did trip her opponent and it appeared to be very deliberate. The commentator suggested she would be cited on the evidence of the video for possible further punishment.

What effects is Becky's behaviour in this match likely to have on the following?

- her peers and any 'others' who could be identified
- her status as an appropriate role model
- the status of women's rugby in general.

 D2

Justify the importance of appropriate behaviour

When you have identified and explained any example of inappropriate behaviour, you need to further research or investigate it to justify the reasons why it would be considered to be inappropriate, and the action which would have been taken as a result of it.

Q | Research

Research details of a recent incident involving a top level sports performer who has demonstrated inappropriate behaviour. Find out the following:

- *how and when the inappropriate behaviour was either demonstrated or identified*
- *the impact on, and sanctions taken against, the athlete involved*
- *the possible effect on the status of the particular sport involved.*

343

P3 Coping and management strategies

It might be useful for athletes to consider some specific coping and management strategies to ensure that their behaviour is appropriate.

A **mentor** or coach is likely to have had to cope with the same pressures, and would therefore be well placed to offer advice and guidance as the athlete tries to deal with situations which may affect their behaviour.

Other individuals may be in a similar situation, so peer support in group and one-to-one discussions might be useful. As long as the influences and support of these groups and individuals is positive, then they can be recommended.

A change of lifestyle might be necessary if any of the inappropriate factors identified are included in the present lifestyle. Being aware of the ways in which lifestyle can affect an athlete's performance should encourage them to make sensible lifestyle choices.

Some routines may not be helpful to certain situations (for example, not having any relaxation in available leisure time), so a simple change may be effective.

Situations

A top level performer is likely to find themselves in a variety of situations which are specifically linked to their status as a top athlete.

On and off the pitch

A Davis Cup tennis captain is allowed to coach their players during a match.

This is an expression used in game activities in particular and it refers to actual performance situations (on the pitch when performing) related to any others (off the pitch situations) which are not performance-related. The truth is that top performers are in the spotlight whenever and wherever they are.

The athlete's profile is at its highest when they are actually competing as this is when fans and spectators are watching all the action.

The media are often invited along to training sessions, and there may also be public access which means very few training sessions are carried out in private. In some cases, the athlete may even be sharing a facility with members of the public, for example swimmers who are permitted to use a 'training lane' in a swimming pool during early morning sessions.

Your assessment criteria:

P3 Describe strategies that can be used by athletes to help deal with three different situations that could influence their behaviour

 Key terms

Mentor: *a wise and trusted councillor or teacher*

Discuss

1. In a group, discuss any instances where individuals have received advice and guidance during a performance which has helped them to cope with the situation better.

2. Discuss instances where having this advice and guidance available might have greatly assisted a performance.

If travel to and from the sports pitch or area is by public transport, the athlete is again in the public eye. If they are driving, the athlete must make sure they do not get into any confrontational situations with any other drivers.

Dealing with the media

A top performer is likely to have to deal with various forms of the media, including:

- Television – this may be in the form of games, matches or performances being televised, but it might also involve being interviewed, or even being involved in a documentary or an instructional programme. Television is a visual media, so every aspect of how the individual looks, behaves and acts is seen.

- Radio – many games, matches and performances are broadcast on the radio, and as this is a cheaper service to provide than television, there are more radio broadcasts. Interviews are quite common, and although the performers cannot be seen, they are judged on how clearly they are able to respond to questions. A point to remember about radio is

All performers must be prepared for instant media interviews, especially at the end of a performance.

that although the performance is not actually seen by the audience, it is the commentator's job to describe everything in detail to the listeners, so all actions are likely to be commented upon.

- The press – this includes newspapers, magazines and periodicals, and top athletes have to interact with journalists who write for these. Every newspaper has a comprehensive sports section and reports on all major sporting events and contests. They also like to keep an eye on sports performers' private lives. It is a journalist's job to investigate news, so they are very likely to pick up on any inappropriate behaviour and report it.

Dealing with the public

Most dealings with the public are pleasant ones, and these might include signing autographs or posing for photographs – being spotted and recognised by the public is the price of fame! However, dealing with disruptive and aggressive fans can be a common problem. A great deal of sport is divisive with fans being encouraged to cheer on their own players and boo opposing ones, so this is a situation which a performer knows they are likely to have to deal with.

 Discuss

Set up a role-play situation where one member of the group is an identified high profile performer and the rest of the group take on the role of being the media interviewers. Think of some questions in advance for the 'performer' to answer, and also come up with some which they would not have prepared for.

345

P3 ▶ Situations *continued*

Dealing with others

A top level performer comes into contact with a variety of 'others' and these include the following:

* Employers – these are likely to be the people who pay the athlete's wages, so behaving appropriately with these is very important. In some sports, such as football, movement between clubs via transfers is quite common, so even in a fairly short career a top athlete can have quite a high number of employers.

* Match officials – all sports have officials in charge and behaviour towards them should be appropriate at all times, even when decisions go against the individual or team, or if they appear to be incorrect ones. Different sports have different rules for dealing with officials, for example in rugby it is only the captain who can talk to the officials about decisions, and players know that they are not allowed to argue with the referee or dispute any decision.

* Club/regional/national coaches – these are all trained personnel who have a particular role of helping players improve or develop, and they are likely to be influential in the decision to recommend athletes to progress to the next level. It is often the role of these coaches to be critical in order to bring out the best in players or initiate improvement, so some feedback received might be difficult to take on board, but it must be received positively by the performer.

* Agents – many top performers employ agents who deal with personal details, such as negotiating employment and transfer deals.

Your assessment criteria:

P3 ▶ Describe strategies that can be used by athletes to help deal with three different situations that could influence their behaviour

? | **Did you know?**

Goalkeeper, John Burridge, was transferred or loaned 28 times to 26 different clubs in a playing career which spanned 26 years. He was the oldest player to play in the premiership when he played for Manchester City aged 43 years and 162 days!

Match officials communicate between themselves to ensure decisions are correct.

Top agents seek out potential sports performers to represent, and a good image (clearly linked to appropriate behaviour) is an attribute they are looking for.

- Managers – these are the main people in charge of sporting clubs, and usually have the final say in who stays with the club and who goes. They are clearly very influential individuals and have high expectations of the behaviour of all their staff. They are the ones who may give out constant reminders of behaviour on and off the pitch.

- Sponsors – many top athletes find themselves involved in both personal sponsorship and team sponsorships, and these are often different sponsors. Sponsors are investing money and have high expectations of behaviour – poor or inappropriate behaviour often results in a sponsor withdrawing the sponsorship altogether.

- Other team colleagues – sports people are often dependent on their team mates for support, and continued high level performances and poor behaviour can result in players being alienated from the rest of the team and even being forced out.

? Did you know?

It is part of the laws of cricket that players should appeal to the umpire for a batter to be given out – the umpire should not make the decision unless asked to by the players. This is why the cry of 'howzat' is heard. The laws actually state that the umpire is not allowed to make an out decision unless the fielding team appeals!

in cricket matches, players must appeal to the umpires in order for a decision to be given.

? Did you know?

Tiger Woods was involved in a sex scandal in November 2009 and by the middle of the following year, Woods had personally lost a staggering $23–$30 million in sponsorship deals as sponsors withdrew their endorsements with him because of his behaviour. Woods had been the first sportsperson to earn more than $1 billion from sponsorship deals and endorsements, and the estimated losses to his total sponsorship due to the bad publicity of the scandal was estimated at $12 billion.

? Did you know?

England footballer, John Terry, cheated on his wife with the girlfriend of former team mate, Wayne Bridge, and lost the England captaincy as a result. Bridge refused to play with Terry and received huge support from many of his club team mates, and many fans and supporters abused Terry due to his actions.

Communicating with the media and significant others

Communicating and dealing with the media can be a regular, day-to-day occurrence for many top level sports performers and athletes, and it is common practice for the media to be granted access to them. In this way, performers retain their high profile which guarantees their popularity, and this in turn ensures that lucrative sponsorship and endorsement deals continue to flow in.

Your assessment criteria:

P4 Describe the factors to be considered when giving two different types of media interview

P4 Factors

These factors are the many skills which must be taken on board when dealing with the media.

Communicating accurately and clearly

The most common form of interaction with the media is verbal through some form of interview, but it might be necessary to use written communications as well. It is very important that any statements are well thought out and clear, but most importantly accurate as any points made are likely to be checked to make sure that they are true and correct.

After each Formula One race, the three 'podium' finishers have to be ready for post-race press conference interviews.

Preparation for communication

An athlete must be prepared for communication with the media, and should consider the following:

- Purpose and content – for most media meetings, guidelines are issued beforehand which make it clear what the meeting or interview is about. For example, it could be a post-match interview where the purpose is to get feedback on how the performance went, so the content would involve reflection upon that performance. Alternatively, it could be a meeting about plans for the forthcoming playing season, so this would focus on training plans and programmes, and goals for the future.

- Audience – the audience may be only one person with a microphone or a film crew, but it is important to remember that the intended audience is everyone who hears or sees the interview once it is broadcast. The actual final audience size can then vary – potentially millions for a TV broadcast, or just several hundred if it is a local radio station.

- Rehearsals – it is advisable to go over the content beforehand, and it can be helpful to carry out a 'mock' interview to practise responses to certain questions.

- Scripts and prompt sheets – these can be prepared beforehand and then referred to during the meeting or interview. These are often used 'off camera' when the camera is not actually focusing on the individual, and they can be used as memory aids. They are particularly useful for radio interviews as they cannot be seen.

- Research – an athlete may find it helpful to research specific aspects which are to be covered in the interview to make sure that their knowledge base is wide enough to answer all the questions. It is advisable to gather resources and information in advance to ensure that all this information is available and up-to-date.

Golfers have to get used to being interviewed on the course just as they finish their round.

Personal delivery

Each individual has their own particular style of delivery, but there are factors to bear in mind:

- Communication styles and body language – an athlete must appear to be relaxed and comfortable with the interview process – even if that is not how they actually feel! Body language, in particular, must be positive (for example, not looking bored, nervous or fidgety), and should support other positive aspects such as a strong clear voice and confident manner.

- Language – this needs to be very clear and correct. Using inappropriate language (such as swearing or offensive terms) is not acceptable and the audience must clearly understand what is being said. Even foreign languages have to be considered at times.

- Speech – everything that is spoken must be clear, so it is important to consider the pace at which it is spoken, making sure that it is not too fast and gabbled. Using clear intonation means that all the spoken words can be clearly heard and understood, and helps with the overall clarity. It is essential that technical vocabulary is used whenever possible and appropriate, for example a performer would be expected to talk about the effects of fatigue and not simply 'being tired'.

 Key terms

Intonation: the pattern or melody of speech, especially the pitch pattern

Vocabulary: the range and variety of words used (or known) by a particular individual

 Did you know?

David Beckham took voice coaching lessons to improve his communication skills in interviews. He particularly wanted to deepen his voice and improve his accent so that he could continue a career in television, or even films, when his playing career was over.

P4 ▶ Factors *continued*

Appearance

This will depend entirely upon the circumstances. It might be appropriate to be dressed in sports clothing, but if it is a studio interview, then formal clothing would be expected. A scruffy, unkempt look should be avoided as it does not reflect the image which the performer is expected to portray.

Timing

It is essential to be in the right place at the right time for any media work – being late is unacceptable as the media work to very tight time deadlines. The timing of responses to questions is important as these must be quickly given with very little thinking time allowed.

Requirements of different media types

Requirements for interview vary according to the type of media. For example, television usually expects the individual to go to their studio, although a sound and camera crew may be sent to interview during training or post matches. A radio broadcast may also involve a visit to the studios, but the press are more likely to go to the performer. Some media expect athletes to attend press conferences immediately after their performance. For example, in both tennis and golf the players are expected to be available for a 'round' of media interviews where they go to an area to be interviewed by different journalists in turn – this can take a considerable amount of time. If players refuse to do this, they can be fined by their governing bodies!

Types of media interview

The main types of media interview are as follows:

- Television – this will include both national and local television, and the potential audiences will reflect this. However, it is quite common for an interview to start off on a local station, and then be taken on to be broadcast by a national one. With the growth of specialist digital channels, such as Sky Sports, there is a high likelihood that an interview will end up being an international one which is broadcast all around the world.

- Radio – this can also be both local and national, but there are far more local radio stations than television stations,

Your assessment criteria:

P4 Describe the factors to be considered when giving two different types of media interview

P5 Describe the factors to be considered when communicating with significant others

? Did you know?

The premier league is in the process of introducing rules which will force team managers to give television interviews after games, or face a fine. Alex Ferguson has refused to talk to the BBC, in particular, since 2004 after a BBC documentary made allegations against his son. His club, Manchester United, has been fined as a result of this.

so this is likely to be a popular interview option. However, just as the television networks share interviews, so do radio networks, and any controversial comments made to a small local radio may well end up being nationally broadcast.

- Print media – this includes local newspapers, national newspapers (tabloids and broadsheets and Sunday editions which often have additional supplements), specialist magazines and even club magazines (such as match day programmes). Top sporting personalities can even find themselves being interviewed for non-sport specialist magazines such as *Hello!* if they have a particularly high profile nationally and internationally.

P5 Significant others

This category includes the other people, and groups of people, who athletes come into contact with as a result of their position and status.

Employers

Communicating effectively with employers is crucial as these are the people in charge who make the decisions about their workforce. They are the people with whom negotiations take place, possibly for increased pay or promotion (for a sports performer this could be promotion from the reserve squad to the first team), and who deal with any personal issues which might arise.

P5 Significant others *continued*

Match officials

There might be rules regarding whether an individual should communicate with match officials, but if it is permitted, clarity of communication and respect are important. Often there is no reason why an individual should not talk to the match officials who are in charge, and there are occasions when this would be encouraged. In cricket, for example, it is perfectly acceptable for a bowler to ask the umpire why a leg before wicket decision has not been awarded. When a batter first comes to the batting crease, they have to ask the umpire to help them 'take guard' by lining them up with the wickets, and they often ask how many balls are remaining in each over. Communications should not be confrontational, especially in terms of body language displayed.

Club/regional/national coaches

These are individuals or groups of people who help performers to improve, so it is important that a performer is able to clearly communicate what help or guidance they might require. This is where the use of technical vocabulary and sport-specific terms are particularly important as both the coach and the performer need to be clear and precise about what they are talking about. For example, in trampoline a performer and coach might talk about a 'barani in fliffis' (a flight and rotation movement) which would be meaningless to a non-trampolinist.

Your assessment criteria:

P5 Describe the factors to be considered when communicating with significant others

 Discuss

Choose three different sports activities and discuss the 'protocol' or agreed standards which exist for the performers to talk to the officials. This should reflect any personal experiences members of the group have had when taking part in sport.

Agent

The agent is responsible for looking after the performer's main interests in terms of employment, sponsorship deals and endorsements, so communications require a large degree of resource and information gathering. As the agent is a person who the performer is likely to be paying to represent them, and who is largely responsible for much of their income and career advancement, channels of communication with them are very important.

Manager

The performer is in day-to-day contact with their manager regarding their training and performing, so a good working relationship is very important. Accurate and clear communication must be a priority, and the use of technical vocabulary is important too. Managers are very similar to coaches in terms of their responsibilities, but the manager will often be in charge of both performance factors and many personal ones. It is often the manager who is an intermediary between the performer and the media, and many sports performers issue statements to the media via their manager rather than talking to them direct.

Sponsors

These are people who must be impressed as they are a potentially large source of income. This means that all communication skills are essential here – especially personal delivery and appearance! For many performers, sponsors are crucial in the development of their career, and for the most successful performers, there are a large number of sponsors involved. The performer must, therefore, be very well organised so that they are sure who they are dealing with on a day-to-day basis.

Other team colleagues

Clarity and accuracy of communication together with the use of technical vocabulary are essential here. If a performer is a member of a team of various nationalities (and languages), technical terms may be the only ones which count as a 'common language' for communication and which are clearly understood by all. Effectively communicating with team mates is likely to be the most significant communication a performer has to make!

? Did you know?

In January 2011 in the match between Blackburn and West Bromwich Albion, a record was set when the 27 players who appeared in the match were from 22 different countries! The continents represented were Europe (18 players), Africa (four), North America and the Caribbean (three) and South America (two). In all there were 15 different languages spoken by the various players!

Producing a career plan

An athlete's playing career is not likely to be particularly long, so they need to plan how to make it as successful and enduring as possible. At the same time, they should consider the options to take part in other activities and move on to a different, or complementary, career once performing has stopped. The potential length of the career is something which the performer must consider from the onset, and when considering the average career span for a particular sport, it is a good idea to look at other performers in the same sport.

Your assessment criteria:

P6 Produce a career plan covering an individual's career as an athlete and their career outside competitive sport

P6 Career plan

A career plan is ideally designed to cover a lifetime. There are many factors to consider when putting it together.

Goal setting

Setting goals is important. It is important to be able to consider goals in particular time frames.

Short-term goals must link to the situation that the individual is initially experiencing or currently experiencing. These goals, therefore, need to take stock of where the career is at any point in time. During the initial stages, goals might be set to get the career off the ground, so levels of performance must be maintained and initial contacts made with agents, sponsors and coaches who can help to 'shape' the career.

Medium-term goals are required during a period of consolidation within the career when levels of performance must be maintained, but further developments must be made in terms of establishing media relationships.

Long-term plans must be made for the period beyond the playing or performing career. An athlete has to consider a second career, putting plans in place for this, such as obtaining various coaching or other qualifications. It is quite common for the second career to involve more than one option. For example, many former international cricketers combine a broadcasting role (television or radio) with a journalistic one which involves writing for newspapers as specialist cricket columnists.

Self and needs analysis

The individual's particular needs must be considered before forward planning can take place.

> **? Did you know?**
>
> *Professional golfers often turn professional in their late teens and early twenties and play on well into their forties. Once they are 50, they can join the 'Senior Tour' where high prize money is still available, but they only have to play three rounds over three days instead of four rounds over four days as a concession to their age!*

Carrying out a SWOT analysis (stands for strengths, weaknesses, opportunities and threats) can be useful. For example, a young gymnast might identify their strengths as their current ability levels in terms of performing; weaknesses might be the difficulty in obtaining sufficient sponsors to continue performing; opportunities might be the possibility of developing a role as a commentator or analyst; and threats might be balancing training and performing against other interests and possible developments.

Short and long-term career goals will themselves have identified needs which must be met. For example, if a medium-term goal is to concentrate on training to improve performance levels, then this will leave little time for other things such as gaining additional qualifications and awards.

Technical and practical skills are a constant factor for all performers, so they must be included in all analysis stages. Whatever stage is reached, it is still necessary to either work on or improve these skills, and they may need to be prioritised. For example, many professional footballers convert to more defensive roles as they get older as this is physically less demanding than being a midfield player. This requires them to work on some different technical and practical skills more aligned to defensive play.

Key and basic skills are the 'core' skills which the individual requires for their particular sport (such as flexibility for gymnasts, and endurance for distance runners) so these are essential at all stages of planning.

Flexibility is a core skill for gymnasts to focus on.

Golf is a sport which can be played competitively up to and including senior level.

P6 Career plan *continued*

Athletic career

This encompasses the actual playing or performing period of the athlete, and must include all the factors which may occur or be influential during that period:

- Planning – this is initially the current expectations as an athlete, and is very closely linked to the short-term goals.

- Key review dates – these might be specific target dates, such as getting to the finals of certain events, qualifying for the final stages, victories over specific opponents or even achieving a tournament or competition win by a certain date.

- Transitions – this is when some form of significant change is made during any period within the career, and this can include changing a coach, moving or changing club or even achieving national or international status. These last two result in the athlete moving up to a higher level of performance, and are considered to be a real breakthrough in terms of levels of success.

- Contingencies – plans have to be put in place for anything which might go wrong and which could result in some form of setback. This may include illness (this could be as temporary as a couple of days, or a matter of weeks), accident (depending on the seriousness, this is difficult to put a time frame on) or a permanent injury which could mean the end of the performing career.

Second career planning

This is an essential part of any career plan.

It is highly likely that the athlete will have gained a high level of experience during their performing career, but this is not always matched by having the corresponding qualifications. If possible, the plan should include goals to gain these qualifications as their career progresses. This is particularly important if the athlete is aiming to link this second career to their chosen sport or activity.

There are career options outside professional sport. A sporting background may pave the way for a variety of linked occupations. These include: coaching (this is very common

Your assessment criteria:

P6 Produce a career plan covering an individual's career as an athlete and their career outside competitive sport

M3 Explain factors involved in career planning for an athlete

Key terms

Contingencies: *possibilities which must be planned for*

Transitions: *changes from one stage or state to another*

Jamie Redknapp's career was dogged by injuries and he was advised to retire at the age of 32 as a result of constant injury problems. He is now a football commentator and pundit, and writes a football column in the *The Daily Mail* newspaper.

in athletics in particular); teaching (a PE teacher is a logical step, but any subject can be considered); the media (this can include commentaries, expert adviser, pundit, presenter or interviewer); sports development (either in a general capacity, or specifically within the performer's specialist sport or activity); physiotherapy (this is clearly linked, but it requires degree level study, just as a teacher would) or sport science support.

Gary Lineker followed a successful international football career with an equally high profile media one.

M3 Explain factors in career planning

It is important to explain the factors which make up the career plan that you have produced. There should be particular emphasis on goal setting, self and needs analysis, athletic career planning and second career planning.

 ## Case study

Gary is an 18-year-old professional footballer who has been signed by a premier league football club. He has already played two games for them and is regularly in the first team squad. He has been attached to the club since he was a junior, and has only just moved out of the 'club home' where he lodged with a family for two years. Gary finished his education at a local school where he combined his education with his training, but he only continued to GCSE level as he focused on his football from the age of 17. Gary only thinks about playing football and becoming a regular member of the first team, but his team mates are recommending that he finds an agent.

1. What level of goal setting does Gary seem to be focusing on the most at present?

2. What contingency plans would you advise Gary to be most aware of in his chosen career as a professional footballer?

3. What second career options are most likely to be available to Gary, and what plans could he start to put in place?

Assessment checklist

To achieve a pass grade, my portfolio of evidence must show that I can:

Assessment Criteria	Description	✓
P1	Describe five different lifestyle factors that can affect athletes.	✓
P2	Describe the importance of appropriate behaviour for athletes.	✓
P3	Describe strategies that can be used by athletes to help deal with three different situations that could influence their behaviour.	✓
P4	Describe the factors to be considered when giving two different types of media interview.	✓
P5	Describe the factors to be considered when communicating with significant others.	✓
P6	Produce a career plan covering an individual's career as an athlete and their career outside competitive sport.	✓

To achieve a merit grade, my portfolio of evidence must show that I can:

Assessment Criteria	Description	✓
M1	Explain five different lifestyle factors that can affect athletes.	✓
M2	Explain the importance of appropriate behaviour for athletes.	✓
M3	Explain factors involved in career planning for an athlete.	✓

To achieve a distinction grade, my portfolio of evidence must show that I can:

Assessment Criteria	Description	✓
D1	Analyse five different lifestyle factors that can affect athletes.	☐
D2	Justify the importance of appropriate behaviour for athletes.	☐

Further reading

You may find the following publications and websites useful when carrying out research.

Books

Adams G M – *Exercise Physiology Laboratory Manual: Health and Human Performance* (McGraw Hill Higher Education, 2001)

Adams M et al – *BTEC Level 3 National Sport (Performance and Excellence) Student Book* (Pearson, 2010)

Burton D and Raedeke T D – *Sport Psychology for Coaches* (Human Kinetics, 2008)

Carling et al – *Performance Assessment for Field Sports: Physiological, Psychological and Match Notational Assessment in Practice* (Routledge, 2008)

Collins M – *Examining Sports Development* (Routledge, 2006)

Cox R – *Sport Psychology: Concepts and Applications 6th Edition* (McGraw-Hill, 2007)

Cross N – *The Coaching Process* (Butterworth-Heinemann, 1999)

Diagram Group – *Rules of the Game: The Complete Illustrated Encyclopedia of All the Sports of the World* (Saint Martin's Press Inc, 1995)

Dixon B – *Careers uncovered: Sport, Exercise and Fitness* (Trotman, 2007)

Elicksen D – *Positive Sports: Professional Athletes and Mentoring Youth* (Freelance Communications, 2003)

Hazeldine R – *Fitness for Sport* (The Crowood Press, 2000)

Health and Safety Executive – *Essentials of Health and Safety At Work* (HSE Books, 2006)

Heyward V H – *Advanced Fitness Assessment and Exercise Prescription* (Human Kinetics, 2006)

Hill et al – *In Pursuit of Excellence: A Student Guide to Elite Sports Development* (Routledge, 2007)

Hoeger W W K, Turner LW – *Wellness: Guidelines for a Healthy Lifestyle* (Thomson Brooks/Cole, 2006)

Jarvis M – *Sport Psychology: A Student's Handbook* (Psychology Press, 2006)

Knowles et al – *Animated Skill Drills for Soccer Coaching* (Tacklesport, 1999)

Mottram, D R – *Drugs in Sport* (Routledge, 2005)

O'Brien E, Moore R – *Healthy Lifestyles* (Gill and Macmillan, 2007)

Palastanga N – *Anatomy and Human Movement* (Butterworth-Heinemann, 2006)

Shamus E — *Sport Injury Rehabilitation* (McGraw-Hill Education, 2001)

Sharkey B and Gaskill E – *Fitness and Health* (Human Kinetics, 2006)

Tortora G J and Derrickson B H – *Principles of Anatomy and Physiology* (John Wiley and Sons, 2008)

Weinberg R S and Gould D – *Foundations of Sport and Exercise Psychology 4th Edition* (Human Kinetics, 2007)

Websites

American college of sports medicine http://www.acsm.org/

BBC www.bbc.co.uk/health

British Association of Sport and Exercise Sciences www.bases.org.uk

British Nutrition Foundation www.nutrition.org.uk

Human Kinetics www.humankinetics.com

Institute of Food Research www.ifrn.bbsrc.ac.uk

Sport England www.sportengland.co.uk

Top End Sports www.topendsports.com

Index

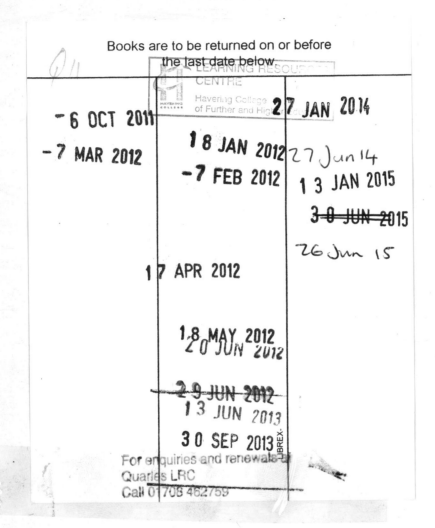

Books are to be returned on or before
the last date below.

‾6 OCT 2011

‾7 MAR 2012

27 JAN 2014

1 8 JAN 2012 27 Jun 14

‾7 FEB 2012 1 3 JAN 2015

3 0 JUN 2015

26 Jun 15

1 7 APR 2012

1 8 MAY 2012
2 0 JUN 2012

2 9 JUN 2012
1 3 JUN 2013

3 0 SEP 2013

For enquiries and renewals
Quarles LRC
Call 01708 462759

372

Published by Collins Education
An imprint of HarperCollins Publishers
77-85 Fulham Palace Rd
Hammersmith
London
W68JB

Browse the complete Collins Education catalogue at
www.collinseducation.com

ISBN 9780007418459

British Library Cataloguing in Publication Data.
A Catalogue record for this publication is available from the British Library.

Commissioned by Charlie Evans
Project Managed by Jo Kemp
Design and typesetting by Joerg Hartsmannsgruber and Thomson Digital
Cover design by Angela English
Printed and bound by L.E.G.O.S.p.a

Collins

BTEC NATIONAL

Sport
Level 3

Kirk Bizley and Simon Chalk

ACKNOWLEDGEMENTS

The author wishes to make the following acknowledgements to those who have assisted him directly, or otherwise facilitated the writing of this book:

Gabrielle Allen, whose diligent picture research surmounted difficult traditional obstacles; Cambridge Computers, who facilitated the use of the Z88 portable computer on which much of the notes and travel research were written and recorded, and who assisted in the interfacing with an Apple SE; Marjory Chapman at William Collins, who gave thoughtful encouragement; Thomas Charles-Edwards at Corpus Christi College, Oxford, for assistance in consideration of the social background to Irish *peregrinatio*; Jim Cochrane and Jeremy Cox of Genesis Productions, who conceived the idea in the first place and who gave unstinting and patient support; Ian Hill, for valiant efforts to secure safe passage from the Antrim coast to Iona; the historian Edward James at the University of York, who unselfishly gave access to his own work, and offered valuable suggestions; Christos Kondeatis and Jane Ewart, who designed the book; my agent Michael Shaw at Curtis Brown/John Farqhuarson; and Susan Collier, who shared much of the journey.

Thanks are also due to the following for permission to use quotations:

Jonathan Cape Ltd and the Estate of Cecil Day-Lewis for permission to quote from the translations of Virgil's *Eclogues*; John Montague for permission to quote from 'Colmcille' translated by John Montague; Miss Mary Margaret Martin of Kilmacrew House, Banbridge, County Down, Northern Ireland and Dame Felicitas Corrigan and the Community of Stanbrook Abbey, Worcester for permission to quote from the writings of Helen Waddell.

William Collins Sons & Co. Ltd
London · Glasgow · Sydney · Auckland
Toronto · Johannesburg

First published in Great Britain by
William Collins 1988
Copyright © Genesis Productions Limited 1988
Text copyright © Frank Delaney 1988

Designed and produced by
Genesis Productions Limited
30 Great Portland Street
London W1N 5AD

ISBN 0-00-217858-3

Design and original drawings by
Christos Kondeatis
Picture research by Gabrielle Allen

Printed in Great Britain at The Bath Press, Avon

CONTENTS

Iona

R. Tweed Lindisfarne

Armagh Whithorn Whitby

R. Boyne York

Dublin Lincoln

Durrow

Skellig Killarney Ely
Michael Cashel

London
Canterbury

Boulogne
Arras

English Channel St Quentin

R. Somme
Reims

Paris Toul
Nancy Strasbourg
Lake
Constance
Basel St Gallen

Atlantic Ocean

Bergamo Lake Co
Vere
R. Po

North Sea

R. Rhine

R. Marne

R. Rhône

Vosges

Al

Mediterranean Sea

| 0 | 100 | 200 | 400 | Kilometers |

| 0 | 50 | 100 | 200 | 300 | Miles |

THE ROUTE OF
THE LATTER-DAY
PILGRIM

No such accurate route maps as these existed in the seventh
century, and although the Romans measured in lengths rather than
days a traveller in the Dark Ages had few precise concepts
of distance. The pilgrim journey of this book both crossed and
followed trade routes of the times – those which were usually
taken for safety and expediency by migrants, soldiery,
international legations and other travellers. Pilgrims did not,
however, always adhere to their planned route, but might
take detours for reasons such as illness, religious worship, bad
weather, or to visit a shrine or a famous abbot.

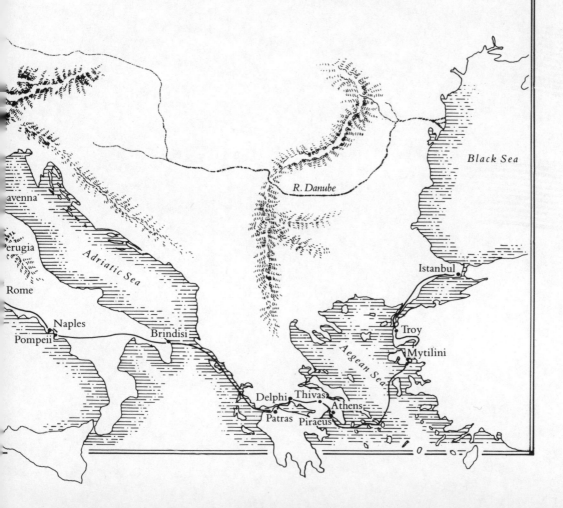

Black Sea

R. Danube

avenna

erugia

Adriatic Sea

Istanbul

Rome

Naples

Brindisi

Troy

Pompeii

Aegean Sea

Mytilini

Delphi   Thivas

Athens

Patras   Piraeus

PREFACE

TRAVEL THROUGH EUROPE has become a novelty of reducing value. The old enterprise attached to visiting Rome if you were a cleric, the fashionable *cachet* of taking the Grand Tour if you were socially eager, have disappeared. Few new journeys may be made, no new ground can be broken. The dimensions of distance, means of travel and geographical accessibility have all been brought under control. We have little left by way of adventure.

Except . . . except the elements of time and the imagination: we can make journeys which have to do with the past, hunting Medicis in Florence, visualizing what Guidobaldo's court at Urbino must have felt like, measuring in educated guesses the life of the people of Herculaneum.

The journey of this book, from the harsh rock of Skellig Michael to the – equally, but differently – harsh city of Istanbul, certainly had physical travel in it: every moment of the way was covered. It had, however, much more to do with time and the imagination than with travel in the intrepid sense. No dangers lay in my way greater than, at either extreme, wet socks or sunburn: beyond a few clerks, juggernauts and hotel managers, no beasts threatened my pathway. Yet the sense of adventure never dimmed, and it became a true voyage of discovery – not because I had never travelled such a route before; indeed I already knew many of the places thoroughly – but because the light in which I was seeing everything had changed.

One of the emblems of early European travel portrayed a monk, upright and hopeful, walking the long roads of Europe with staff and satchel – a pilgrim to a holy place, walking in the Dark Ages to Rome or Santiago de Compostela or Tours. He cut a necessarily puny, none the less interesting figure, a dot on the landscape, in his awkward robe with his unbecoming appearance, dishevelled, that curious haircut, a little wild perhaps, or unsettlingly saintly. He had his reasons for travelling – genuine prayer and preaching, or – one of the farther reaches of self-denial – self-imposed exile in the service of God, or penance. He had his place, too: the wandering monk, especially if he had learning – and whether he travelled alone or in a group of fellows, a mobile monastery in search of a site, like bees looking for a hive – contributed an as yet unmeasured wedge of culture to the shifting jigsaw that became Europe.

My travels sought to follow the seeker, to discover such a monk on his voyage of discovery. I would look at the sights he saw, try and view them as he viewed them, balance the impressions against the facts of my own existence. That, in theory, was my intention. The facts of the journey, however, often put me down on shores and hillsides which had not changed since the seventh century, and in truth, and many times quite rightly, I found myself as bewildered as he must have been, and with no option but to work out the implications – for myself as well as for this figure through whose eyes I had set out to look.

Even though I began by inventing such a man – to establish a physical presence, for the purposes of keeping an eye on him – the fiction of him, like the composite technique used by any novelist creating characters, came from fact. He therefore became real, and feasibly so, and although no traceable individual made this precise geographical journey, many hundreds, perhaps thousands, walked different stages of it and were known to have done so.

Since we do not necessarily know all there is to be known about the fictional, any more than the real, characters of our acquaintance, I have taken care not to state my monk's spiritual purpose. That must remain unknown, his business entirely. Maybe he merely wanted to pray, with a little evangelizing. Perhaps he had doubts about his faith, queries which pushed him towards Constantinople, to ask what lay behind this burning light called Islam. The factual men who went before him, and whose names – Columba, Gallus, Columbanus – remain enshrined in the ecclesiastical and secular history of the Dark Ages, usually intended to spread the word of the Christian God, while gaining their own salvation, as their faith instructed them to do. I did give the monk whose road I followed a purpose they could never have had (except unwittingly and much later as historians tracked them down). I made him my pathfinder on a purely personal – selfish, if you like – expedition whose greatest end was knowledge and discovery, whose lesser aim was the pleasure of travel, shifting on from town to town. By gazing at the sights and places he must have seen, and in many cases could not have avoided, my own learning, the permanent state of being educated, would be assisted. In my imagination I followed at a distance behind this decent and gentle man of the cloth, trying to see what he saw thirteen hundred years ago, and without the benefit of a historian's training, trying to survey and to judge the life and times of his world.

Although the year of his great journey, AD 687, was chosen for the obvious reason of being a straightforward thirteen centuries ago from the time I embarked, it had other factors to recommend it. By the seventh century the Church had established itself sufficiently to accommodate such a wandering monk, a man equipped with enough education and social experience of other such travellers to allow him to contemplate such a journey. He held some language in common to ease his task: he certainly had at least a slim knowledge of Latin, from his texts and from the written communications of Rome and the bishops. The Church to which he belonged had developed a clear and muscular identity, emerging as a world power with experience of all the divisions and schisms necessary to the growing process of any movement with an intellectual dimension. The continent of Europe stood at perhaps its most turbulent juncture politically, as the terms of reference of old empires and new invaders shifted and swung. Cultures collapsed, the vacuums they left began to fill again; laws changed, borders disappeared or were redrawn – all happening with what seems, in history's telescope, bewildering speed. Full record of the new had not, by a long chalk, begun to be kept, and at the same time the whitening relics of the old, the pagan and the classical, could still be seen and felt. It soon became apparent to me, an eager, amateur enquirer, that it must have been one of the most exciting periods Europe has ever known – and one of the most difficult to capture.

The terms of reference I gave myself – to regard, insofar as I could, the Europe that such a monk of the Dark Ages would have seen – proved impossible to keep. The record of the period too often proved too slim, and parameters of a century either side, or sometimes deeper consideration of the periods before him, frequently became necessary. The attraction of choosing as Dark an Age as possible also became the frustration. Time after time the longing to know just that little bit more – the wish that somebody, somewhere, in a house of Lombardy, or an office in Greece, had kept a journal – became almost unbearable. In the end I had to settle for the feel of the period above the minute facts, for the atmosphere and possibilities of the age above the specific documented moment – which did not, after all, exist, hence the term 'Dark' Ages. In fact this limitation enhanced, rather than crippled, the aspect of the journey most vital to me – the imaginative element.

The journey achieved its end – and merrily defeated it. As required, it opened out the era for me – and smartly told me how little it opened it out, thereby threatening to send me off on all sorts of future journeys, on further searches for the Merovingians and the Franks and their jewelled cicadas, for the musicians who wrote the hymn annotation at Delphi, for the fictional possibilities in Theodora, the whore who became Empress of Constantinople. It sent me searching, too, for the monk himself, to whom I so often stood so near, chagrined at myself for allowing what essentially began as a travel book to turn so riskily towards obsessive preoccupation, because it did, on another level, turn into a personal journey, out of darkness into light. I may have left him standing on a street in Constantinople, but I will go on wondering what is to become of him, which is not a fit occupation for any traveller, armchair or otherwise.

Essentially the result stays close to its planned original identity – a travel book whose intention was to make a journey of the imagination as well as of the body. Such voyages, made in an effort to refresh the variations of modern travelling through Europe, offer possibilities: why not trace a soldier in Napoleon's army, or a centurion in Caesar's, a manservant in a prince's entourage or a secretary in a merchant's wagon train? Time and our imagination have, after all, a large part to play in the difficult business of history, where point of view has as much importance as fact.

In the end it comes down to escape, and why should it not? Stalking, at a respectable distance, this monk in his robe as he went looking for a cave on a Scottish headland, or walking not far behind him through a lantern-lit fair in Lincoln, or across a hill in the Marne valley had the same quality of escape as a novel or a film. He became real, often, and almost dragged me off course once or twice, almost made me stay longer than I should have in places that he found important, and made me wonder on many occasions whose book it was. That was, of course, the whole idea – that I should follow him cheerfully, in a spirit of enquiry, and with a great deal more comfort than he had, and that the whole enterprise should result in a vicarious relationship of three tiers – monk, writer and reader. I can only render an account of the first two.

Frank Delaney
London
Summer 1988

I wish, O Son of the Living God, O ancient, eternal King,
For a little hidden hut in the wilderness that it may be my dwelling.

An all-grey little lake to be by its side
A clear pool to wash away sins through the grace of the Holy Spirit.

Quite near, a beautiful wood around it on every side,
To nurse many-voiced birds, hiding it with its shelter.

A southern aspect for warmth, a little brook across its floor,
A choice land with many gracious gifts such as to be good for every plant.

This is the husbandry I would take, I would choose, and will not hide it;
Fragrant leek, hens, speckled salmon, trout, bees.

Raiment and food enough for me from the King of fair fame,
And I to be sitting for a while praying God in every place.

'The Prayer of Mauchan'
from the Gaelic: early monastic,
between seventh and tenth century

CHAPTER ONE

HERE IS GOD, IF YOU LIKE

JUST AFTER DAWN on a summer morning in AD 687, a robed figure descended the side of an island rock out in the Atlantic. From the summit he trod down the steep irregular levels, moving resolutely, though wary of his foothold; a calm morning, no breeze, not a ripple on the ocean. If seen from the distance he could be picked out, a small moving figure, made conspicuous against the darker surroundings of the rock by his garment of rough off-white wool.

The descent took almost an hour. He stopped from time to time and gazed over the edges of the cliffs at the shelves of seabirds in their vertical tenements; they had just begun to clear their throats for the first huge chorus of the day. A gannet dived. As it hit the water its wings closed so fast he could not follow the movement. The bird completed the shallow underwater trajectory in the calm green sea and came up swallowing a fish.

Above, on the summit of the rock, the monks whose raw but devout community he was departing had already been in prayer for some hours, rising at two in the morning for the first of the many daily devotions. Through the oratory window the other rock came into view, handmaid in shape and respectful distance to this great monastery crag. The small Skellig whitened in the dawn with the flocks and flocks of birds.

He continued his descent to the lower reaches, carrying a small parcel of food, bread wrapped in cloth. As he reached the cove and the water's edge, he looked back up the pathway of his descent and saw another white-robed figure descending more rapidly than he had done – another monk, who would row him ashore.

From here the cliffs rose sheer and hard and black, straight above his head, with grass and green fronds glistening with damp. St Michael had promised that nobody who came on pilgrimage should fail to make the crossing from the mainland safely – but had he said anything about getting back again? The tribe of monks who stayed here all the year round aged rapidly, their faces gouged by the fasting and the weather, and calmed by their meditations.

In the distance the thin line of light marking out the coastline had brightened and the mainland could now be seen clearly. The two men lifted the skin coracle from the cranny which sheltered it in the boulders, carried it to the water, set it down and climbed in. Facing the bow, the rower picked up the wooden rowing staves, handed one to the monk behind him and began to work the other, bobbing about until they got the coracle under control. The small rock, soon coming up on their immediate left, had a population of seals sitting around the base, brownish and blackish, with interested, old, wise, pleasant faces, like monks themselves. Above them, the white birds and their guano covered the rest of the rock like snow.

In the noon sunshine the two men landed on a small beach. The rower held the boat steady until the parcel of food had been lifted clear, took a warm leave with many blessings, and then set off again, back to Skellig Michael. The monk sat down on the sand and began to eat his bread. From this excellent vantage point, the slight haze rendered the two rocks sailing out in the ocean even more mystic. The only noise came from the small waves and larksong; behind him, in the empty land, not a sight nor a soul.

I stood on the top of Skellig Michael on a summer afternoon, trying to visualize the departure from this rock of such a monk – and his life here, the weather, the hardship and the emotional pressures. I had gone to the

Skelligs from Valentia island, on Des Lavelle's boat. He descends from five generations of Valentia islanders, and three generations of lighthouse keepers.

'What is it, Des? About the Skelligs? Why does the place captivate people?'

Not a pick of flesh on him, rangy and tanned and reserved, with a natural exquisiteness of language.

'I don't know. I suppose it's the ... it's the ... the soul of the place.'

Searching for words. He has a shrewd face, without cunning or guile, and is possessed of instinctive courtesy and intelligence beyond the reaches of formal education.

'No other message that is written or spoken can convey the same message. To me at any rate. Here is God, if you like.'

His life revolves exactly and metaphorically around the Skelligs. In the winter he lectures across America on the phenomenal nature and presence of the two Skelligs rocks, catalogues his photographs, plans forthcoming private visits, wildlife vigils and diving journeys into the 250-foot depths, pursuing his obsession as the Skelligs' most sedulous recorder. In the summer he ferries boatloads of travellers, such as our motley pilgrim caravan, from Britain and Europe, from other parts of Ireland. We had a pair of priests, a young couple, six pupils with their teacher and two local folk who had lived within sight of the Skelligs all their lives but had never gone there.

Five boats sat anchored at the jetty of Portmagee, one a small French yacht, the others local lobster boats; Valentia once commanded the transatlantic cable to America. The Skelligs boatmen travel down a long sound, and by Bray Head they hit the ramp of the Atlantic swell. Sometimes the boatmen refuse to leave the pier, even though the sea and the morning seem perfectly calm. The foam and the tide on nearer stretches of the coastline can tell them whether an attempted landing on the rock will succeed. Skellig Michael has one, highly vulnerable landing place. Query their reluctance to sail and, full of experience and local precision, they will tell you that on 27 December 1955 a wave took out the Skelligs lighthouse, 175 five feet up.

'The volume of the place' – Des Lavelle stood in the wheelhouse, about to turn on the engine – 'the sheer magnificence of it, would strike everyone, it must do. Even people who have a preconceived idea of the place, who have read about it, may even have seen a slide programme or two, it still strikes them. This is bigger than humanity, if you like.'

The waves could hardly be calmer, no sea-legs required. They say you can see porpoises and the occasional school of whales in these waters, and the emperor butterfly borne over from the Americas in the jet slipstreams.

Skellig Michael from the air.

We trembled a little, no more than that, as the waters of the sound folded us over into the Atlantic.

Blind Man's Cove has been smoothed with concrete. Climbing from the boat none the less requires concentration; the slightest swell out there in the ocean would make the landing in this cove impossible. In the television series *Civilization*, Lord Clark argued that in the Dark Ages western European culture clung on by the fingernails at the Skellig, and in similar settlements, where the monks kept thought and art alive.

Des Lavelle pointed out above us the outlines of old steps, thought by some – and feasibly so – to be the route by which the early hermits ascended: dangerous now though, and officially ruled out of bounds. In any case we would have needed a long ladder to reach the first of them, so we took the broad tarred way to the lighthouse.

They lived here in all weathers, a tribe of fishers. The anchorites of the desert, whose tradition these monks pursued, selected locations where the force of their veneration was driven on by nature in the raw. 'To this spot', says the *Vitae Patrum*, an anthology of the words of the Desert Fathers, 'those who have had their first initiation and who desire to live a remoter life, stripped of all its trappings, withdraw themselves: for the desert is vast, and the cells are sundered from one another by so wide a space that none is in sight of his neighbour, nor can any voice be heard. One by one they abide in their cells, a mighty silence and a great quiet among them....' Here, on the Skellig, that early eastern tradition of the desert hermit, and the ensuing Christian tradition of the monk, merged. The remote Irishmen also lived in cells, but nearer to each other and with a closer sense of community.

By looking up, you can see how they first survived on Skellig Michael, sheltering in the lees of the great crags, and then moving upwards to slightly more benign terrain. They ate seabirds, whose meat a later visitor described as 'fishy and rank'. At Cross Cove, the roadway turns a hairpin into a cauldron of noise so loud you have to raise your voice to be heard. Over the low wall you can touch the nests of the guillemots and the fulmars and the kittiwakes, in their perilous niches, descending straight down the cliffs to the water's edge. The noise rises in a constant edgy surge, screeching and screaming, with 'kitti-wake, kitti-wake, kitti-wake' dominant. Feathers, and sometimes an egg, tumble down, way down, into the green waters. Further on, the ground cover teems with variety, mosses and lichens and small plants and little bright pink flowers, fed with dampness from fissures in the rocks, gathered rainwater, or mysterious springs.

Beyond the noisy, feathered, high density of Cross Cove, broad and considered steps lead up to the right; some of the slabs must weigh half a ton. People in Waterville, on the mainland coast, had said, 'Be sure and count the steps.' According to tradition, nobody knows the exact number of steps up to the monastery, and visitors, confused with the wonder and holiness of the place – 'Here is God, if you like' – never remember whether it was 593, or 538, or 584. Neither did I.

To the north-east behind us lay the long line of coast we had left. To the north-west lay those low islands, the clusters of rocks, towards which Ir, the son of Mil, rowed so hard that he collapsed and died within sight of landfall, and thus gave his name to the shore he never gained, 'Ir-land'; instead he found a rocky grave on the Skellig. To the south and west you will find nothing save sky and green ocean between here and the coast of Brazil. At Christ's Saddle, beneath the Needle's Eye, the rock's highest point, 714 feet above the sea, I turned right, climbing upwards on the last of the broad steps, out of breath.

Since boyhood, I have been tramping the ruins of abbeys; their skeletal cloisters have always drawn me in, regardless of their state of preservation. Some stood directly by the roadside, or far in the depths of fields, glimpsed through trees from small by-roads, the bicycle flung suddenly behind the ditch. Now on Skellig Michael, a farm of stones, I had never seen a monastery garden so small, and so unelaborate; no medieval choirs of nightingales here, yet the simple walls and their jagged edges immediately offered more peace than any other holy place of my acquaintance. Just ahead, through a short 'tunnel' to the terrace, camouflaged in the harvest of rocks, stood several tall igloos of stone.

These buildings have received generous care. The settlement has been restored to its six cells of dry stone, shaped like beehives. The floor of each cell has a roughly quadrangular shape; as the building rises, the walls curve gently inward to form the dome of the beehive. The stone smells a little musty, friendly, and the way in which the ascending stones softly overlap each other adds to the warmth.

As the courses of stones were laid from the ground upwards, each circle of walling advanced in upon the previous one, with each stone projecting a little further inward, overlapping the one on which it rested. This building system – known as 'corbelling', from the way in which the upper beak of the raven, the Latin *corvus*, the French *corbeau*, the Scots *corby*, overlaps the lower – progressed serenely upward until eventually, when all the courses had moved closer and closer to the centre of the circle, the remaining gap could be sealed with a single stone. No mortar was used, no plaster, no masonry; nothing but the grey-beige stones, dry with surface dust.

The cells have a roomy tranquillity, with walls almost six feet thick, and

– surprisingly, given how small they seem on the outside – no sense of cramp, or confined space. Some pegs for hanging clothes still project from the walls; you can still see the shelves and cupboards of the monks. Nobody has inhabited these for many, many centuries. Sunlight walks through the narrow doorway, and inside the hearts of the cell walls small birds have made their nests; they lie there and cheep drowsily. Emerging from the cells, every monk who ever lived here saw the full spectacle of the place, vastnesses of sky and ocean, every morning of his life.

A few steps away, past the well which dries up, they say, at the sound of blasphemy, the oratory window, oriented liturgically to the east, also happens to frame the small Skellig. This tiny chapel was built on the same corbelled principle, though rectangular rather than circular, and the finished effect resembles an upturned boat. The ancient builders picked out, with playgroup simplicity, one or two small quartz-flecked crosses in the stonework. Occasionally a priest from the mainland celebrates Mass here; the legend of St Michael says that the altar wine never runs out and never needs replenishing.

In the churchyard, among a small cluster of other ancient stones, all crude, some fallen, some leaning, one cross stood out. It had rays cut into it, radiating out from the centre as if in echo of ancient sun worship; it would not have surprised me to find it in a Mexican forest or a South American temple. Perhaps the pagan hermits carved it, before the Christian monks came, although it also suggested the familiar configuration of the later Celtic cross, the arms of the cruciform held within a circle, an image which has always conjured for me a holy man standing against the sun with his arms stretched out in prayer.

Occasional mares' tails of cloud drifted across the blue sky. During rough weather, though, the spray from the waves can drench the Needle's Eye far above the beehive huts. In various nooks and crannies around and about the monastery, runs of ground showed traces of reclamation from the bare rock, trenches made, filled with good clay brought from elsewhere and then fenced against the wind. Up here the wind can knock a man forward, the rain drives and drives into every pocket in the skin. The rock has unsafe cliff edges, boulders which slip and topple, and the ocean below completes the gang of dangers, clutching higher, ripping away. Countering these forces, total silence frequently falls. On a calm night, the only noise comes from the occasional shuffle of a puffin or the swish of a petrel.

I had received rare permission to stay overnight on the rock, sharing the sleeping quarters of the lighthouse men, ferried nowadays by helicopter. About ten o'clock, in darkness, I left the lighthouse and climbed the steps back up to the monastery walls. Nothing moved. I found myself reciting all the words I could think of in the English language to hold in suspense a

High Cross at Clonmacnoise, County Offaly.

quieter moment than I had experienced for years. All failed, none of them adequate.

I walked back down the pathway for mugs of tea and talk of shipwrecks. Mainland folklore claims that the Atlantic Ocean flows deepest round the Skelligs, and that the two rocks once formed part of Macgillicuddy's Reeks, Ireland's highest mountain range. In the lives of those who see it daily from the mainland, Skellig always had a presence. Easter came later to Skellig Michael, they said, than to the mainland; perhaps this echoed the liturgical disturbances of the seventh century, culminating in the Synod of Whitby in 664, where the Roman timing of Easter finally took precedence over the Celtic Church's interpretation.

I had set the alarm clock to wake me at four and catch the dawn. Instead, I woke naturally – the silence, I think – and as the dark began to lighten, climbed for the third time to the beehive cells. Again, not a puff of wind, not a noise, peacefully and utterly silent. I had a tape recorder with me, a Uher 4000, a professional machine. I turned it to 'Record'. Hardly a flicker showed on the needle; the machine displayed almost no sign of recording anything, as if no sound was taking place. When I played it back later I could hear no more than the mildest atmosphere. In a few moments this changed beautifully as a wren, perched on the sun cross just before me, opened up and sang hard for the next hour in the clement light.

The morning grew warm and the rock could be explored before the boat came back. On a far, high corner, a pilgrim pathway called the Stations of the Cross demands a rigorous nerve. It ends in a long, narrow stone overhang at the Needle's Eye, out along which the pilgrim must crawl, 700 feet above the foam, kiss the cross carved into the rock, and return.

I understand Des Lavelle's obsession with the place. He sees the Skelligs in the distance almost every day of his life, holy mirages, mountains of the local moon.

'Even on a calm day the potential is here for power. For destruction. The sea. And the wind of course, the gales. And another thing – these waters were the trade routes, even in the most ancient times. So we're sitting here at the crossroads of our roots. With all that power. I've been here in the winter. You should see a winter storm.'

On the last step downwards, the birds flocked around and about, the puffins looking tailored and inquisitive, and the white javelins of the gannets piercing the waters. We left in the early afternoon.

The monk whose fictitious, composite path I wanted to trace had set out only for Columba's Iona. Intending to follow in the footprints he would have made if he had left the Skellig rock and journeyed from shrine to shrine in search of wider enlightenment, I intended to fetch up in the city once called Constantinople, which was then, according to its emperors, 'the centre of the known world', confluence of East and West. By means of abbeys and ancient sites, my map references would be, wherever possible, seventh-century places which the monk would have stayed in or passed through.

Transfixing contrasts lay ahead – between origin and destination, beween the corbelled beehive cells of Skellig Michael and the minarets of Istanbul, between the empty rock of this retreat and the bright, busy waters of the Golden Horn. In 675, Bishop Arculf in Iona (on a pilgrimage in the opposite direction) gave the Abbot Adamnan a detailed description of the founding of Constantinople. The Emperor Constantine, after a dream, led a procession to mark out the boundary, and he walked and walked – much farther than his attendants had anticipated. Eventually, in answer to their enquiries, he replied, 'I shall still advance until He, the invisible guide who marches before me, thinks proper to stop.' The modern measurement of Skellig Michael suggests an area of forty-four acres, most of it inaccessible.

The boat, which doubles as a trawler or a lobster boat, pushed away from Blind Man's Cove. The spray came over the deck on the way back to Valentia. The crowded galleries of birds on the small Skellig stood shoulder to shoulder, no room for an extra feather. Soon, like hands over the ears, the sound leading to Portmagee closed in about us.

The unknown builders of those stone beehives, so generous with their peace and with the vision they bequeathed, could have been in the Andes, or on an Asian mountain, or in a dream. Hours later, from high up the pass on the Dingle peninsula, I looked back for a last view of the two rocks as their peaks drifted into a mist.

Out to the west the Blasket islands lay in sunlight, a secret world which until earlier this century still held the traces of a people both neolithic and imaginative, with stories probably current before Christ. On that Dingle shore, for instance, near the village of Ventry, Daragh Donn, the Brown Oak, who was King-of-all-the-World-except-Ireland, tried to subjugate the people, and he suffered a great defeat at the hands of the mighty Finn McCool. Ireland's monks built the beginnings of a literature on the back of such stories, founded upon a clear folk culture. The history of the land since the earliest times took the form of epic tales – of travel, faraway places, exotic names, part legend, part fancy, part fact. Early record and pseudo-history, such as *The Annals of Innisfallen*, fused mythological, biblical and Christian themes and told, for example, how the sons of Mil, a Scythian ruler who died in Spain, eventually arrived at the shores of Ireland, *en route* from Scythia.

[They were] three months at sea until they reached Pharaoh, king of Egypt. They remained seven years with Pharaoh in Egypt ... Scotta, Pharoah's daughter, married Mil, son of Bile, in the eighth year. Pharaoh was drowned subsequently with his host in the Red Sea .... They voyaged after that around Scythia to the entrance to the Caspian Sea. They anchored twenty-seven days in the Caspian Sea by reason of the singing of the mermaids until Caicher the Druid delivered them. Caicher the Druid said to them 'Until we reach Ireland we shall not halt.'

Other tales, current in these parts when Christianity washed over Ireland in the fifth century, told of Persians and tribes of Babylon, of Haman and Cyrus, son of Darius, and Abraham. When missionaries returned from monasteries in Britain and on the continent they supplemented the romance with exotic names, prayers and descriptions of faraway kingdoms. With this new information, added to the aeons of oral mythology, Ireland laid the foundations of a great early literature.

Through the mountain passes I headed for Killarney. Further up through Ireland, the land becomes less stony, more lush.

> The splendour falls on castle walls,
> And snowy summits old in story;
> The long light shakes across the lakes,
> And the wild cataract leaps in glory.

High above Ladies' View, the panorama for which people have wanted to buy Killarney, the rain came down across the mountains and blotted out the long light of Tennyson's lakes. My paternal ancestors belong near here, and lived through the Famine, the Great Hunger, of the nineteenth century. Only sparse living ever came from this earth: one blow of the spade, my father said, and the sparks flew off the rock beneath the clay. Yet the vegetation in the woods blooms huge and luxuriant, with great leaves, brilliant, strange flowers, and the damp plush of large mosses; the Gulf Stream comes right up the Kenmare River and encourages these growths.

From the coast I had left, home of St Fionan the Crooked from Derrynane, or St Fionan the Leper from Ballinskelligs, and all along this countryside, early holy men had found niches for themselves in crags and caves and hollows in the mountains, or clearings in the woods. They went on their solitary way before the monastic idea was well established, with neither scrip nor scrap, the principle of the arid desert. Let us not get carried away with the notion that all those who grew to monkish stature did so out of zeal and the love of God. Many fled life, for reasons of crime or eccentricity or madness or weakness or other unacceptability, or the liberty to practise psychologically doubtful rituals such as self-denial on a violent scale, or self-inflicted corporal punishment.

In truth, the legends often overwhelmed the fact – which may have been intentional, since much of their performance of sanctity had a bravura quality. Simeon of Antioch, in the fifth century, raised his platform from ten feet to sixty feet above the ground and prostrated himself 'ten dozen times a day'. He came down by ladder for ceremonial and political events; otherwise he communicated by means of a basket raised and lowered. He also offered to passers-by, in the course of his thirty-seven years on the perch, cures for infertility and impotence.

Some of these early religious – including the Irish – came from families who had no place for them, who cast them out, left them to wander and mutter. Others had gone on the run from their own temptations, like the fourth-century Jerome, in the desert.

Every day tears, every day sighing: and if in spite of my struggles sleep would tower over and sink upon me, my battered body ached on the naked earth. Of food and drink I say nothing, since even a sick monk uses only cold water, and to take anything cooked is wanton luxury. Yet that same I, who for fear of hell condemned myself to such a prison, I, the comrade of scorpions and wild beasts, was there, watching the maidens in their dances: my face haggard with fasting, my mind burned with desire in my frigid body . . . .

For those so tempted and for those cast out, the development of the anchorite tradition still came as an awkward kind of godsend – shelter, community of sorts, no responsibilities and a licence to be egregious. Anchorites were granted full permission to visit outrage upon their person, and eventually admiration of a kind – that such worship could be so intense – could only come to mean that they were actually chosen by God. The life in the stone cells which they scattered through these hills decreed hardship, privation, cold, damp and loneliness. I have been in these mountains at night, in rain, in fog; all notion of hospitality disappears. The black light of the night shines on the lakes and a wind comes down through the crags and takes the skin off your lips.

Beyond here, going north, the land improves. Kerry's tradition of poverty led Patrick to bless the county from its borders, evading the need to travel through. The place of my next signpost, Emly, fared much better – prosperous country, where, according to some sources, *The Annals of Innisfallen* were written in a monastery founded by St Ailbe. Five centuries after the death of Christ, the ancestors of this society received the evangelists bringing Latin and the faith which would pervade the island – first Palladius, sent by Pope Celestine to minister to 'the Irish who believe in Christ', and later the former slave from Britain, Patrick. They also brought with them Greco-Roman ideas and ethics – if not fully observed or put into practice, at least in sufficient presence to cause some impact. Early trade with France encouraged the monastic idea, seen in Tours and similar establishments. When it got well under way, in the sixth and seventh centuries, the monastic system offered much to Irish society: respectability, social stability, a consolidation of the local kingship – since many of the abbeys became extensions of the tribe – as well as a source of learning.

The young monks, who filled the monasteries to overflowing, were required to perform the many physical labours of the community – the tending of the animals, the sowing and harvesting – and in the *scriptorium* they made books, needed to further the education of the monks and to add to the worship. These contained sacred writings, scriptures and psalms, in Latin, as well as local and national genealogies and annals of the countryside. Some took the form of plain and direct entries, some became beautifully decorated.

One distinguished strand ran through their worship. The seeds of Christianity in Ireland had fallen into an earth fertilized by centuries of natural worship. The 'pagans' believed in tree gods and water goddesses, in mountains and animals and sunlight. When combined, the new faith and the old belief gave Irish Christianity a unique flavour.

Late that morning I drove into the Golden Vale, a broad fertile seam which runs across part of the counties of Cork, Limerick and Tipperary, the sparkling waistband of the province of Munster. Easy to see why the love of nature persisted and played as much a part in the worship of their God as the imported Latin rite. Rich land here, on the borders of Limerick and Tipperary, long valleys of loam and timber. Thirteen hundred years ago, woods of oak and box and myrtle crowned these hills, and large lakes flooded the countryside. In these ancient parishes neighbours of the Dark Ages arrived by boat.

As they wrote about 'many-voiced birds' and 'speckled salmon', the monks of the *scriptorium* also called upon nature for the practical end of their trade. They used quills made of badger hairs and the tail-brushes of squirrels, they made dyes and inks from vegetables and wild herbs. Their manuscripts included the figures from these small wild kingdoms.

The storytellers say that long before the Bible was written the giant, Finn McCool, hunted over this land and heard 'the music of what happens', which he described as 'the sweetest sound in all the world'. By the shoulder of the Galtee Mountains the signposts had enticing names – Anglesborough, Ballylanders and Galbally; in the distance squatted the small sloping range of hills known as Slieve na Muck, the Hill of the Pigs, where Patrick turned a horde of devils into swine, and I had approached from the south-east the village of Emly, the first actual foretaste of monkish Europe.

Emly, Gaelic name Imleach Iubhair, the city of St Ailbe, forms the other half of the archdiocese of Cashel and Emly, one of the four pillars of Irish Catholicism. Emly has been important, say its people, since 1900 BC (difficult to establish quite how they calculate that date). Ptolemy called Emly one of the three principal centres of Ireland. According to the earliest legends – preferred locally – Ailbe preceded those first evangelists, Palladius the Gaul in 431, and, in the following year, Patrick. Time was when any such suggestion would have come close to Irish heresy. None the less, part of Irish teaching now accepts that Patrick may only have been the most powerful evangelist, the most – dare one say it? – publicized.

The legend of Ailbe begins with the name: Imleach Iubhair means the 'land of yew trees bordering on the lake'. A few miles from here, where the lake began, in Knockainey ('the hill of Aine', a goddess of the moon), lived Olencus, a courtier at the local kingship of Cronan. According to the biographical documents of Ailbe in Salamanca, young Olencus fell in love with a woman of the household – an unsuitable match, older than him, not of the same class. The child she bore him was taken away and left under a rock to be discovered, raised and educated by a chieftain. Another translation of the word Ailbe is 'alive under a stone'.

Thus one of the most ancient motifs since man became literate attached itself to this small, innocuous place – the belief that great people have unconventional birth. It happened to Moses, it happened to Christ, it ran rife among the gods. By it, nations created a figurehead or leader or deity, whose associations and circumstances, from the very beginning, had an out-of-the-ordinary quality, a divine aura sustaining both worshippers and worshipped.

Sub-legends usually followed. In Ailbe's case he became a slave of the Britons, among whom he acquired Christianity. He travelled as far as Rome, where he received holy orders, preached the whole way back and landed in Belfast. He then evangelized his way down Ireland and finally met Patrick, who made him a bishop on condition that – ingenious hierarchical thought – Ailbe could perform no miracles without Patrick's permission. He established his monastery at Emly in the second half of the fifth century and built a holy centre there, renowned for learning, missionary work and the warm welcome it gave to wandering priests.

In such establishments the physical edifice of the church dominated, a rectangular building of strong planks, where possible of local oak, otherwise of wattle daubed together with mixed mud. The cells of the monks, made of wicker and thatch, clustered around the church, the size of which remained remarkably small; even when the community expanded they built other churches according to the demand, rather than always enlarging the existing one. Two other buildings had importance, the refectory and the guest house, and in the case of the larger and more important monasteries a school completed the compound, which was the nearest the pre-Viking Irish ever came to having towns.

Nothing of Ailbe's time remains to be seen in Emly, though; only the name survives, enshrined in a Pugin-Gothic Victorian church which sits on the hill, visible for miles around, typical of the nineteenth-century statement of Irish rural Catholic power. The original monastery, developed from the flimsier wattle-and-daub buildings, suffered heavily from Vikings in the ninth century, and even though it flourished for many centuries afterwards, the friends of Henry VIII finally finished it off.

No traces remain either of the influence this little village had, or the importance of Ailbe, but if a great early medieval document such as *The Annals of Innisfallen* had truly been written here it needed the support of a deep background in learning, thought and intellectual stability. Even now, the countryside displays how it must have been able to maintain an important monastery. Such good earth on either side of the road, tilled land, with beef cattle, and large old trees, and houses in excellent repair; the prosperity of the farmers has kept this countryside stable for a couple of thousand years.

Ten miles further east the town of Tipperary, where I went to school, has the typical long main street of many Irish and Scottish towns, though in this case several other streets radiate off to the left up the hill, and to the right down the hill, towards the foothills of the mountains. Revolutions flared here; land war leaders came in from the countryside, debated the intellectual principles of democracy and plannned the practical, often brutal, strikes against landlordism. In the town itself the workers formed one of the very early soviets and raised the red flag over the gasworks, while a creamery in the outlying countryside joined in with the slogan, 'Knocklong Soviet Creamery – We Make Butter, Not Profits.'

The road east, past the graveyard where my father and sister are buried, climbs a hill to further feasts – a wide plain with one, two, three, castles in the distance: Grantstown, Thomastown and the fabulous Rock of Cashel. This castle and church stand on top of a limestone crag and still command the countryside; the modern town only stands and waits. An important place, Cashel of the Kings, a rallying point for the eyes and the hearts of the people of these plains, a place of inspiration and romance. From the Rock

'The magic that takes you far, far out, of this time and this world',
wrote Shaw – Skellig Michael and the small Skellig, eight miles
out in the Atlantic, seen from the coast of Kerry.

Macgillicuddy's Reeks, Ireland's highest mountains. According to folklore, the Skelligs originally formed two further peaks of this range, which dominates the south-east of County Kerry.

Aerial view of the beehive huts constructed by the community of fisher monks on Skellig Michael (above), and (below) Gallarus Oratory in County Kerry, built on the same principle and in the same spiritual tradition as the huts of Skellig Michael.

Lion, representing St Mark the Evangelist, from one of the earliest
Irish manuscripts, the seventh/eighth-century *Book of Durrow*.

One of Irish art's earliest representations of the Crucifixion, this
hammered gilt bronze plaque from the late seventh or early eighth
century is believed to have decorated the cover of a religious book.

Seventh-century carved whalebone casket from Northumbria,
showing Frankish influences. Pagan and Christian traditions are
wedded: on the left is the Germanic mythological figure Wieland
the Smith; on the right the Magi march under a star.

The sands of Iona (above) owe their famous whiteness to deposits
of calcium carbonate from the sea-bed borne in shoals
across from the Hebrides.
'Cut off on the landward side by very deep water, and facing on
the other side the limitless ocean', as Bede described it, Lindisfarne
(below) lies a mile and a half off the shore of Northumbria.

King David playing the harp, from the eighth-century *Psalter of St Augustine*.

of Cashel, the spectacular view alerted the kings of Munster. In the centre of the horizon to the north sits the Devil's Bit mountain, a peak with a chunk taken out. Patrick chased Lucifer down these fields, and when the fleeing demon found a mountain in his way he took a bite and spat it out at Cashel.

In the entrance hall museum on this Rock they display a Hallstatt sword. The definition means not that it comes from that little village in the Austrian Alps, but – regardless of where it was manufactured – from the early period of Celtic culture, anywhere from 750 BC to·500 BC, descended from, or belonging to, a pattern of metalworking from eastern mainland Europe. (The man who discovered this sword in County Tipperary took it around in the boot of his car for a while, showing it to friends and neighbours, before sending it to the experts.) Another twenty or thirty miles to the north, gorgets turned up in the earth – semicircular configured neckbands, rich personal ornaments. Unique around here, and thought to have German origins, they were made of gold, hallmarks of wealth and comfort. Maybe the sword was owned by a farmer, for protection; equally likely, it belonged to a warrior. The gorgets, though, tell a clearer, firmer story.

The people of these parts who owned such goods had a society and economy of some depth, a long prehistory of cultivation, fought for and protected by the warrior class. By the time of Christ they knew their land well, had tamed it, worked it, legislated for it, through a thousand, perhaps fifteen hundred years. Their lives moved slowly; like many of their countrymen around Ireland, they had traded usefully with Europe. Even passing through, you can feel their depth still. Today, they continue to own comfortable farms and benefit from the wealth of their produce and the bonus of all the food they might need. The continental connection persists; many of these homes grew wealthy through European Community grants.

In the shadow of the Rock, I had no difficulty whatsoever imagining a monk walking through these fields thirteen centuries ago. His welcome was assured: 'respect for the cloth' prevails here, and for learning, and for the endeavours of holy pilgrims. Parish excursions leave for Knock, the Marian shrine in the west of Ireland, and flights are chartered to Lourdes.

Of all the territories through which he might pass, this place offered as much safety as the monk might meet; here the Dark Ages shone brightly enough. In any case he came from the same stock, with the same social and cultural and religious references. Life around here has changed little – the same landscape, farmed by the descendants of the same people that met Patrick, took in his word and followed his followers.

They spoke Gaelic, an Indo-European language, reshaped by time and nomads from the European Celtic – I learned it at school. They had been trained to be practical countryside dwellers, hewers of wood and drawers

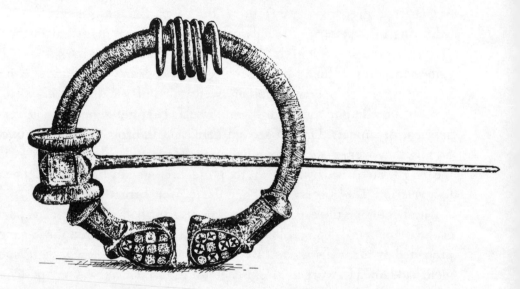

Enamelled bronze brooch from County Offaly.

of water, and to spend hour after hour upon their knees praying to God. This area supplied the many monasteries of the county with monks; in the local towns, the boys' schools enjoyed a reputation envied all across Munster for providing vocations to the priesthood.

So I stayed a night in Cashel of the Kings, a small town with a tiny population. It still prides itself on the royal antecedents, and the wide main street offers glimpses of the stunning Rock and the enchanted limestone complex on top of it. From any angle, in any light, at sunset or at dawn, or floodlit on a rainy night, it fulfils every visual and imaginative impression of the fairytale Celtic castle, a place of wishes and princes. Magic flutters around the place, in pre-Christian whispers. High on the wall squats a rowdy-faced sheelagh-na-gig, a randy fertility symbol. Put your arms around the trunk of the cross in the courtyard and you will be free of toothache forever. Then, the Christian powers: on certain solstices the angle of the architrave on Cormac's Chapel corresponds with the direction of the sun's rays. When Patrick arrived here, Natfraich, the King of Munster, according to one account, 'congratulated him'. On what? On sticking his crozier through the uncomplaining foot of Aengus, Natfraich's son, during the baptism ceremony until 'the blood flowed down the side of the rock'?

Looking back, from a few miles along the Dublin road, the Rock seemed to grow in enchantment through the morning showers and sunshine, a fortress where, typically, the secular and the sacred lived side by side. Twenty years ago the courtyard facing north had been dominated by a great Celtic cross, which commemorated a local nineteenth-century landlord, ' a bad pill' named Scully. When a storm broke the cross in two the people said, 'He had it coming to him.' Time will always have a very slow march here.

This main road joins the Republic's two largest cities, Dublin and Cork. More alluring signposts: Horse and Jockey, Boherlahan (meaning 'the wide road') and eventually my next ancient stage, Kildare; Cill Dara, 'the church of the oak tree'. I left Cashel early, aiming to reach Kildare mid-morning, on an empty road save for occasional tractors, some going to the peat bog at Littleton.

I stopped briefly in Durrow, again derived from the Gaelic/Celtic word for oak tree – *dara*. Here, before he left Ireland – amid political difficulty – for Iona, Columba was once believed to have written *The Book of Durrow*. This relatively small, very beautiful, illuminated manuscript of the Gospels, now in the care of Trinity College, Dublin, lights up the second half of the seventh century. The style of the decorated script belongs to the late mainstream of Celtic civilization. The craftsmen who pioneered western European ornamentation of this standard worked in the same tradition of whorls, leaf patterns, tendrils, spirals and interlacing now synonymous with the words 'Celtic Art'. They dropped capitals and designed introductions to each chapter by creating entire pages of illumination, carpeting the vellum with multitudinous patterns of the greatest intricacy.

The Book of Durrow has all the power not only of a single major work of art but of an entire movement, a school of endeavour. Although the volume was conceived as an act of worship, it has had secular reverberations far beyond that. The capacity for the fantastic would do a science fiction illustrator proud, and the presence of animals and beasts in the interiors of the drawings takes it and its themes out of the devotional arena and creates an earthiness and a menace which question the roots of the religion to which it subscribes.

Eagle illumination from *The Book of Durrow.*

Sadly for local pride, the essence and fame of Durrow was conceived elsewhere. It was kept in the monastery here, perhaps in memory of Columba, but its neatness of hand, elegance of accomplishment and evidence of the spread of influences – Anglo-Saxon and Coptic – all mark it down as Northumbrian in authorship.

Brigid of Kildare bids fair to be the most powerful female icon figure in western Europe. Boadicea, the warrior queen, rebelled because she had been unjustly treated. Queen Mab of the fairies may never have existed, or, if she did, had to share an identity with Queen Maeve of Connaught, the warlady of the mythologies. Brigid towered over them all, right alongside Patrick in Irish sainthood. Her name and some of her magic efficacy descended from the pagan goddess of many hues and places and benefactions, known in France and Britain – Brighid, or Bride, or Brigantia. The gift of woman's fertility had so much actual and emblematic importance that followers became eager to praise it further with other marvellous attributions.

She cured ailments of the eye and the head and the limbs. She hung her clothes to dry on the rays of the sun. She had two sisters of the same name and this fecund trinity was born of the Daghda, the greatest god in Celtic mythology, who had an insatiable appetite for both porridge and sexual intercourse (though in what order the myths never quite specified).

Brigid the saint founded a convent in Kildare by a stratagem. When she approached a local landowner for a gift of land to build a monastery, he told her contemptuously that she could have as many acres as her cloak would cover. Brigid laid her cloak on the ground, and it spread and spread. She gained enough land to found a famous establishment which she and her nuns shared with the monks of a nearby monastery – to whom they could only speak through an oaken screen. It did not prevent Brigid, they say, from proposing to Patrick who, sworn to celibacy, turned her down and also prevented women from ever proposing to men again, except once in four years, on the leap-year day of February.

The magic persisted. Brigid's convent of twenty nuns had among their tasks the guardianship of a perpetual fire, surrounded by a ring of shrubs, entry through which was absolutely forbidden to any man. Furthermore, Brigid herself had been born at sunrise on 1 February, one of the four great feasts in the pagan Celtic calendar, when the lambs drew milk from the ewes.

The monastery of Kildare, vanished now, stood at the spot where she had once spread her cloak. The graveyard and the church were completely deserted on that rainy morning when I visited them. A notice advertising the perpetual appeal for the restoration of the buildings had begun to yellow in the rain; Brigid is becoming more remote, supplanted by recent saints. The town outside stands at a crossroads of rich farms where the great horses of the flat racing world have been bred and trained for centuries; the grass, grown on strata of limestone, builds calcium and strong bones. On the edge of the town, at the National Stud, the mares are falsely induced into heat by a conducive atmosphere of artificial light and environment – so the fecundity of the goddess Brigid has an appealing modern application.

I drove north through the Curragh of Kildare. Ptolemy called Dublin Portus Eblanorum. The old name for the area was Eblana; the Vikings developed the site a long time afterwards. In the seventh century the entire area around the city was regarded as dangerous land; today the acres of poverty-stricken urban developments bleed with social pain – drugs and homelessness rather than wild boar or wolves. The only reason a Christian pilgrim of the seventh century would have had for visiting Dublin was to see for himself the place where Patrick is said to have landed and to have founded a church, now St Patrick's Cathedral, by a well which sprang up when he stabbed the ground with his crozier while seeking water to baptize his new converts.

Patrick's actual landing place has been disputed. One ancient source says he landed at Drogheda, a port some thirty miles north of Dublin; others argue for Wicklow, in the opposite direction; while a third says he landed in Dublin itself. The only benefit to be gained from a visit to Dublin in pursuit of a Dark Ages wanderer is that the museum illuminates the secular life of the period.

Ireland had a small population in a wooded country – deep, dense forests, some less impenetrable woodland and open birchwood; the large inland seas of Kildare, thirty miles to the south-west, had only recently (geologically speaking) dried up. The peasant society, self-governing by simple election, had recognizable strata and divisions based on skills, learning, warrior prowess and priesthood. The judges had laws to use, the poets had metrical structures, the families had alliances. When Patrick travelled through Ireland the kingship system prevailed, and the families with riches had slaves and glory. Two hundred years later, any holy pilgrim received a welcome from the same great families in their palaces.

Stature revealed itself by the usual European systems – forms of dress, ornamentation, quality of personal possession. The noblemen and women wore tunics of linen covered by outer cloaks of wool, many of them multi-coloured, with much gold and jewelled ornamentation. The more exalted the woman the more beautiful her costume, with exquisite brooches in leaf shapes; the men went into battle dressed for impressiveness, bearing shields with scalloped edges. Above all, land divided the classes: 'as much land as his eye could measure' defined a rich man; 'as much as his cloak could cover' befitted a poor one.

Around the central room of the huge thatched house extended cubicles, like bedrooms or ante-rooms, slept in by many members of the family on hides and animal skins. In lesser houses the sleepers took up positions by the walls, still within the light and heat of the fire, but not occupying the central eating and living place. Outside, in a large yard, domestic animals fed and slept, behind wooden fortifications reinforcing outer earthen ramparts. No Roman occupation had taken place, so no stone ruins could be cannibalized for building houses. Class related largely to agriculture; royalty and aristocrats came from those who farmed the largest ranches. Alongside them the priest, the monk, the abbot filled the role of honour always allotted in terms of intellectual prowess and spiritual integrity, even though the days of the Druids had long gone. Beneath this top stratum of society, smaller farmers, tenants and freemen gave to a king, a chieftain or an abbot their tribute in food or produce, such as wool, leather or precious metals. They ate meat, largely pork, some smoked or boiled fish, a little bread loosely and soggily baked with rough oats, and they drank wheaten beer sweetened with honey.

Other places further along had more relevance to my traveller. I took the Navan road out of Dublin to County Meath, wide, rich and royal, with the Hill of Tara still a touchstone for romantic legend and myth. Tara rises above the plain of the Boyne valley, and up to the eighth century had a powerful part to play in the national body and mind. Five provinces shared Ireland – Munster to the south, Leinster to the east, Ulster to the north, Connaught to the west and Tara, the governing province. Here the High Kings of Ireland were chosen on the most renowned, if not quite the most archaeologically valuable, Celtic hillfort.

The name Tara means a wide vista – the first line of defence consists in seeing the enemy approach. The excavations here revealed a passage grave dated to before 2000 BC, in which had been buried a boy wearing beads of Egyptian influence. At Tara the new king mated with the earth; on this mound a pair of stones parted to let the chariot of the rightful king drive through, and a stone phallus, still standing – Lia Fail, the Stone of Destiny

– screamed when touched by the man who would be king. Almost every facet of mythology and early history seems to have been represented at Tara – taboos, bonds, law enactment, the divine right of kings, heroic endeavour, curses, ritual, feasts, births and burials. Now the place has been graced with an unfortunate statue of Patrick which weather and vandals have damaged – but not nearly enough.

I followed the course of the Boyne from Tara. This valley has some of the most accessible antiquity in the world. Knowledge of the passage grave at Tara offered only an advertisement of what was to come. The Boyne, which rises in Carbury in County Kildare, several miles away, never becomes a broad or powerful river, never expands into no more than a wide and reasonably placid stream. People who live on the banks speak of the fact that by day the waters flow dark and at night they gleam brightly.

Beneath the ground, though, the Boyne valley exercises the greatest power. At the passage graves of Knowth, Dowth and Newgrange the deep, long corridors end at burial chambers. In the archaeological drawings, each tomb appears like an exaggerated version of the medical symbol for the female – a long, skinny neck culminating in a small cross.

Newgrange, the largest of them, whose name some have tried to translate as 'the cave of the sun', is reached by a series of small side roads, country lanes, past the entrances to quiet farms. The exterior resembles some enormous grass-covered amphitheatre, high and white, with a dome of grass and earth. The reconstruction returned Newgrange to the days of glory – long before the Pyramids or Stonehenge. Ancient bones rested in this place, the most holy ground of pagan Ireland, and any early Christian coming upon Newgrange had cause to shudder and pray to his new god.

At the entrance stands a large stone embossed with whorls which mirror the river looping through the trees down at the bottom of the hill. The passage, flanked by tall boulders etched with more designs, geometric, almost mechanical or astral, draws the soul far into the tomb to the stone dish where the burnt bones of the dead resided. Directly over the entrance to the tomb a slot appears in the roof, which the guide described as 'the light-box'. Newgrange disappeared for years under the hill, as the grass overgrew it and the earth piled up; eventually a seventeenth-century antiquarian rediscovered the great tomb and later excavations revealed this light-box. In such investigations archaeology and mathematical science can have common purpose, and the possibilities of Newgrange emerged. The light-box had a specific, ritual function.

On a clear morning of the winter solstice – frost makes ideal weather – the rising sun, as it comes over the far hill, filters slowly at first into this light-box, fingering its young eastern light up along the passage of the grave, turning the stones to light gold. When fully risen, the sun floods the stone dish deep in the heart of the chamber, as if bathing the dead with the only warmth available in winter. Then the light slips away again back down the passage and out into the fields, as the sun climbs higher into the winter morning sky.

❖

After Newgrange, I turned away from the main Dublin–Belfast road to look for the abbeys of Mellifont and Monasterboice. Unlike a wandering scholar I could have no shelter among them unless I bedded down among the stone ruins and ragwort at Monasterboice.

If I had been a wandering monk arriving at a monastery like these in 687 the monks would have welcomed me with open arms and questioned me for any political or ecclesiastical or monastic gossip. In a strict regime they had a benign and familial atmosphere. They spoke Gaelic, and they also had Latin; the extensive contact with the continent of Europe received boosts from visiting monks or returning missionaries, and this constant fertilization helped the Irish monasteries to establish their unique character. Lecturers at Trinity College, Dublin in the early part of this century made these observations:

Egypt furnished the original type and imparted the original tone. The Irish schools then developed themselves in accordance with their own genius. They had one pre-eminent quality, distinguishing them ... they pursued learning for its own sake. They did not require to be bribed by prizes and scholarships. They conceived and rightly conceived that learning was its own reward. The schools had moderate landed endowments, and their teaching was apparently free to all, or at any rate, imparted at a very low charge. Bede tells us that Irish professors were in the habit of receiving English pupils, educating, feeding, and supplying them with books without making any charge at all .... They lived under very simple conditions of society. They had no solid halls or buildings; a few wattled huts constituted their college. They lived an *al fresco* life. They taught and studied in the open air ... yet they had an organised system. They usually had a chief or senior lecturer. They had professors of law, of poetry, of history and other branches of education. They had an *oeconomus*, or steward, who managed the temporal affairs of the institution. They had special schools, too, some of which lasted till modern times. The union of law and history ... was not unknown there ....

I left Mellifont and headed across country, bypassing the town of Dundalk, and turning my face to the plains of glory. These small fields and hills of scrub and gorse suggest no grandeur, bear no trace of the huge and epic exploits that gave a people an entire prehistory, yet here the cycles of legend were spun.

The names give some clue – Ardee, the ford of Ferdia, boyhood friend and eventually mortal enemy of the great Cuchulainn. Who was the son of Lugh of the Long Arm, father and son each a Celtic Apollo. Who slew hundreds and thousands in bloody combat and turned the rivers of these plains red with blood. Who resisted the temptations and blandishments of witches and goddesses and shape shifters and lovers and Druids. Who campaigned and rampaged through aeons of fireside histories, and who created icons for rebels and children.

From here to Armagh, the fields are crammed with such ancient mysteries and memories. The three daughters of a wizard conjured the sounds of battle and the sights of phantom armies to make it seem as if the valley was afire with battle and therefore lure Cuchulainn forth. Cuchulainn's battle ardour stirred; in battle ardour his body gyrated within his skin, each hair on his head sprang out into a spark of flame and a burning aura surrounded his head. Torn with wounds and his life blood ebbing away, he lashed himself to a pillar so that he might stay upright and not fall before his enemies, and they, so fearful of his reputation, kept their distance and only knew he had died when a black bird, the raven goddess of death, came and perched upon the hero's shoulder.

I travelled on through Cuchulainn's warfields, north through Ravensdale and Faughart, where St Brigid is supposed to have been born, where the weathering of various stones has produced configurations that to this day are credited with having descended straight from the saint. Into the head stone, hollowed by rain and geological change, you put your head if you suffer from headaches. An eye stone collects rainwater in which you bathe your ailing eyes. Kneel in the knee stone for anguished joints. Ahead, over the hill by a cemetery, the Gap of the North opens out, and I am struck by how relevant the symbolism of mythology remains.

The cycles relating to Cuchulainn are full of tales of Ulster's sickness, Ulster's wasting, Ulster's capitulation to the forces which threatened its province. When called upon to defend themselves the Ulstermen refused, because for several days at a time they lay under a curse which made them

The death throes of Cuchulainn: statue in the General Post Office, Dublin.

more feeble than a woman giving birth. Three times in one morning I was stopped on the road by men with guns and uniforms. One patrol came from an army regiment, while the two other platoons brought me back to the legends. These, from the Ulster Defence Regiment, stopped me, with minimum civility, on a small road – ironic twist – near Armagh, and the road led me to the fort of Emhain Macha, without doubt still famous in the seventh century, perhaps still populated then, and still echoing with the stories which transferred across from the pagan to the Christian tradition.

This fortress, named for a goddess who could outrun a chariot, had almost as much power and importance as Tara, and here a great temple was built, with 'a rooftree a hundred feet high', a temple large enough 'to hold a thousand people'. The labour to build this temple lasted surely for several years and within these earthen ramparts – still there, still high and grassy – they erected hollow wooden walls which they filled with stones. Then one day, for no traceable reason, they burnt the temple to the ground. Nobody knows why; it may have been a sacrifice to the gods, it may have been an economic decision, but having built the equivalent of a great cathedral they razed it.

At this point the Christian tradition, as it so often did, commandeered the legend and the fact which prompted it, and in a later, suitably created myth suggested that the temple burning took place in an unconscious, synchronistic commemoration of the death of Jesus Christ, and that on the day now called Good Friday the earth of Emhain Macha shuddered and the king murmured, 'A god has died.'

Apple country, Armagh, where they play a curious game. It involves throwing a cast-iron ball along the road, judging nicely the camber of the tarmacadam to negotiate corners, and the person who covers a set distance in the least number of throws is the winner. They play the same game further south in west Cork, and some say it comes from the time of Cuchulainn; in Cork they call it bowls, which they pronounce 'bowels'; here, with even less fortunate connotations, they call it 'bullets'.

I intended to travel along the shores of Lough Neagh, home of Ireland's first settlers, and from there join a boat on the coast of Antrim which would take me in Columba's wake to Iona. I began to wish that the basalt stepping stones of the Giant's Causeway, specially provided for Finn McCool to walk across the sea, stretched north to the islands rather than east to mainland Scotland. I discovered why even a giant like Finn needed a causeway: boatman after boatman found the Atlantic too mighty. The journey takes more than a ferryman's wage and skill; these waters run high and deep.

I arranged to join Andy Seaton at the harbourmaster's office in Portrush and from his boat, the *Carole E*, I would clamber on to that same 'sloping westerly beach' kissed by Columba and his monks on 12 May 563. Andy, on the telephone, said the wind had moved to the north and the seas were running very high. No chance? No. If we were to try – how many more days should I wait? Impossible to say – this was Tuesday – it could be the weekend. And no chance of trying to catch the tide tomorrow just after noon? No.

I had wanted to retrace Columba's journey to the footstep, though that would have involved leaving his city of Derry (other sources say he left from Howth, the great hill that lies snouting like a pig across Dublin Bay), and furthermore I should have been bringing with me an uncle, two cousins and the son of a king in a party of twelve.

On some island I long to be,
a rocky promontory, looking on
the coiling surface of the sea.

To see the waves, crest on crest
of the great shining ocean, composing
a hymn to the creator, without rest.

To see without sadness the strand
lined with bright shells, and birds
lamenting overhead, a lonely sound.

To hear the whisper of small waves
against the rocks, that endless sea-
sound, like keening over graves.

COLUMBA
trans. John Montague

CHAPTER TWO

THE
WHISPER
OF SMALL
WAVES

THEY SET FORTH in a giant coracle made of cattle hides and willow basketwork. Under a cloud too. Columba is believed to have accepted an enforced exile after some political, legal and military business not compatible with the holy calling of a monk. Copyright law entered the issue, with accusations of copying a book, and a famous Irish judgement: 'To every cow her calf and to every book its copy'.

Columba on his stated mission to travel into exile for Christ – *pro Christo peregrinari volens* – had not intended Iona as his destination. He imposed upon himself a condition, that he could only disembark in a place from whose highest point he could never again see Ireland. First of all he stopped at Dunadd, the great fort in Argyll, where the Irish kings of Dalriada ruled the west of Scotland. Next he found that the high points of Jura and the islands of Islay, Oronsay and Colonsay still yielded glimpses of distant Ireland, so he settled for Iona, a small flitter on the edge of the west Highlands, a blip on the map of this ravishing archipelago.

I had no choice but to get there by long and mundane means, by ferry from Oban to Mull, then by road to Fionnphort, 'the white bay', for another ferry crossing across the short sound to Iona, over to this stub of land, a

liturgical powerbase which had fair claims to being called the Rome of the
North.

> On some island I long to be,
> a rocky promontory, looking on
> the coiling surface of the sea.
>
> To see the waves, crest on crest
> of the great shining ocean, composing
> a hymn to the creator, without rest.
>
> To see without sadness the strand
> lined with bright shells, and birds
> lamenting overhead, a lonely sound.
>
> To hear the whisper of small waves
> against the rocks, that endless sea-
> sound, like keening over graves.

Columba's poem confirms his desire for exile.

They call the little bay where he landed the Port of the Coracles, a small
sloping beach divided in two by an outcrop of rock that reaches out some
thirty feet into the sea. To edge into this otherwise very safe landing place
the boat would have had to negotiate several stiff bunches of rock further
out, and ease itself on to the sloping shingle – although the word 'shingle'
does small service to this deep tray of stones of all colours and smoothnesses.
A million stones lie here, forty million years old, and they twinkle with red
and silver, and have jewelled names too, like mica and marble and quartz
and gneiss and augite and silica and schist and tremolite and trachite and
glittering crystal and yellow epidote and green hornblende and feldspar the
colour of bleeding rouge. Uncomfortable underfoot, though, and as I
turned my back to this clean and historic water to my right I saw the Hill
of the Back of Ireland, where Columba at last assured himself that he could
no longer see the land of his birth.

He did flex a little; a dozen years after his establishment on Iona he
returned to Ireland for a conference of some political and ecclesiastical
importance, and in order that he could never be accused of breaking his
vows he remained blindfolded for the year of the conference's duration,

with high clods of turf from Iona bound to the soles of his feet. H'm.

It is true, though, that from the Hill of the Back of Ireland you cannot see the Irish coast from which I had hoped to sail. You can see other coasts and flat-topped outcrop islands and even a needle of lighthouse in the blue distance. My own monk must also have set forth across Iona to find the monastery. (If you are obliged to come by the ferry route I have already described you cannot miss the monastery, but that is another matter.)

From the rock where Columba could not see Ireland a sheep had fallen and died; a roughish walk only if your expectations are of an easy and green place, and on the crest of another hill a long narrow loch has pipes leading from it and spares lying about the ground – the loch feeds the freshwater needs of the village. Now a view opened to the north and more islands and coasts of wonder, little Atlantises, appeared far away. Which one is Ulva, and where is Staffa, where Mendelssohn was inspired to write *Fingal's Cave*? White sands fringe the green open common of Iona. The satellite photographs have apparently shown deposits of calcium carbonate, brilliant white moving across the sea like great white shoals and coming to rest on the beaches of the Western Isles.

Open ground again; tufted and comfortable after the rocky path descending from the loch. I opted for the farthest end to get to the highest point of the island, a rocky peaklet from which, according to the map, I would be able to see the entire place. I kept the sea on my left hand and walked across the broad turf, up into heights along the first of many misleading paths. They did seem as if they had been travelled daily by humans, these wide and sensible paths between the rocks, but time after time they petered out on tops of crags leaving only a sheer drop to a beach or rocky inlet 150 feet below. Then I realized that sheep care nothing for scenery, and sweet grasses can be found right up to the edges of the cliffs.

I turned insland and found myself in a small wild valley, not a human trace, nor an animal's, only a deep and slightly treacherous marshland. A struggling walk this country, not easy; to make my way up towards the high point I had to work hard. *En route* the square tower of the abbey building appeared.

The monastery proved useless to me; late medieval, and therefore irritating. Traces of Columba exist, though; nearby earthen ramparts, subjected to detailed excavation, located the site of the monastery more precisely – in the shelter of Iona's highest peak, the Dun I, and a little to the west of the existing buildings but underlapping them. In the graveyard a descent of kings is buried – Irish, Scottish, Scandinavian, before, contemporary with, and after Columba, including (again maddeningly outside my brief) Macbeth.

In the interrogation of Columban Iona two sources, archaeology and the biography of the saint, describe the settlement as it existed when Columba founded it and as it must have stayed, more or less, for the next two hundred years. He had precise dates: he arrived on the feast of Pentecost – how full of coincidences hagiography can be, since Columba means 'dove' and, according to some sources, Iona means 'dove' in Hebrew – and he died on 6 June 597, aged seventy-seven.

The monastery consisted of a large central cell, Columba's own, on higher ground and a little away from the others, in which he slept on a stone slab using a piece of rectangular granite for a pillow. Around this building, each monk had his own cell. They gathered during the day and night for community work and prayer in the monastery buildings, which included a church whose oak beams were sailed across from the mainland of Argyll or the isle of Mull half a mile away. By the fireplace in the refectory sat a stone vessel in which the feet of arriving pilgrims were washed, according to the rules of hospitality which transcended all other disciplines on the island.

Columba had his own writing place and the monastery had a *scriptorium; The Book of Kells*, early western Christianity's most elaborate ancient manuscript, is believed to have been created on Iona, and taken to Ireland to escape the ravages of marauders.

Barns, sheds and a refectory completed the large settlement which, at the highest point of Columba's reign, held 150 monks. Whispers of early lives came to light during excavations – a piece of red slipware from North Africa, a midden containing the bones of animals, domestic refuse, clay moulds for making glass beads, a tiny bell, traces of a kiln for drying corn – and they seem to corroborate, one way and another the biographical details included by a later abbot, Adamnan, who wrote *Vita Sancti Columbae*.

Iona held a clearly defined community, with known and agreed tasks, divided among seniors or elders, a middle stratum of workers and the juniors, novices and learner monks. Each Wednesday and Friday they fasted, each Saturday they rested, and each Saturday night and all day on Sunday they knelt or walked in prayer. Adamnan portrayed these hard-working men wearing white cowled tunics, leather sandals and a tonsure. No trace of them here now; the abbey, handed on by a series of trusts and gifts, is maintained in Christian fellowship, non-denominational, and the friendly hotel filled up with singing Christians from the north of England.

One of the symbols of the Evangelists from *The Book of Kells*.

Previous travellers have referred to the peace of Iona. Undeniably, it has a soothing, eye-bathing tranquillity. Equally unquestionably, the propaganda of Christianity attributed this quality to Columba and the sanctity of his settlement. But it may have occurred the other way round – Columba and his landing party may have found the combination of colours in the sea and on the beaches, and the undulating green ground, conducive to worship.

They arrived in May, remember, the time of the year when Iona may possibly look its most beautiful. Their first view, to the west, showed no other great or threatening lands, and the openness of the green plain they saw ahead of them still – deceptively – suggests fertility. The island has no harshness, at least nothing alarming, and even where the cliffs do have threatening faces they give way to exquisite sands. Peace, yes, from nature – therefore, in their terms, from God. Iona provided the perfect opportunity to offer prayer and sacrifice while staying in touch with a tangible slice of the natural world so beloved of Irish monks.

Columba evangelized forth from here, to the islands and the Highlands, to the Picts and the other peoples of Scotland. On his way to their souls he often performed miracles for their bodies. He cured a wife of her loveless distaste for her husband; he fought off the ancestors of the Loch Ness monster; he calmed unfavourable winds; he healed a mysterious illness in a wizard – by making him drink water in which he placed a pebble he had blessed; and he created a firm and influential input into the politics of Scotland and Ireland. Columba walked the corridors of power and became a grey eminence in the affairs of the people who were called Scotii, who came from Ireland and gave their name to Scotland.

The ferry from Iona to Fionnphort on Mull only takes a few minutes and the Christians, some of them, stood on deck praying with each other. Mull has stunning views. The road, single-tracked to test the coach drivers, sweeps by long lochs with red columns of mountain in the near distance. From Craignure the larger ferry sails to Oban several times a day, and from the top deck the views open down along long narrow sea lanes to isles, gorse-lit fjords and Sir Walter Scott castles on crags. Oban feels like a Norse town, overlooked by an eyeless, unfinished colosseum, a charitable man's folly, started by him to keep unemployed masons in work. When my monk crossed from Mull, Oban had long been in existence, a large Bronze Age settlement of hunters and fishermen who left ancient spoor in the caves nearby.

The road to Lochgilphead turned out to be one of the most beautiful roads I have ever travelled. I hope my monk saw the same views: he would have chanted aloud psalms to the glory of his God. From time to time, breaks in the trees and in the crags revealed small harbours with boats and cottages; mountains in the distance, Jura, and long waters. Off the narrow roads, lanes and byways invited and intrigued. It would have been quite possible never to reach the end of this journey. I had to make one essential stop, though, in the valley of the small River Add. I survived the temptation of some standing stones in a field to the right, and beyond Kilmichael, at the end of a long straight dusty lane, I climbed Dunadd.

It rises out of marshy land on a sudden rocky height, and the fortifications can still be seen in ascending interfacing walls, making the place impregnable. The entrance is gained through a short narrow pathway. A little defile hemmed in by stones, it could still be defended by one man. Winding around another old wall I reached a small open plateau and then, further up, through a larger 'gateway' of rock, the pathway bends to the right and eventually to the summit.

Shades of Cashel and Tara and Armagh: again I stood on a place which commanded great views of the countryside all around – a boy and a dog could be seen with clarity by the watchman. On the ground a small stone held rainwater in it, used in the consecration of kings here. Dunadd, one of the four Dalriada capital forts, had a powerful significance in the Irish government of early Scotland. Nearby, a footprint in the rock selected the king; if the foot fitted, the king had stepped into the royal shoes. On the rock beside the footprint careful tracing reveals a boar etched in stone, a Pictish symbol, they say, though the boar has rampaged across at least one Celtic legend – in the Fenian cycle, where Diarmuid, who has stolen Finn McCool's lover, Grainne, is gored to eventual death by a wild boar. Tremendous hospitality was available here too, especially for somebody bringing a letter – or some other identifying means of introduction – from the Abbot of Iona.

A sudden depression came in, not from the sea or the sky, but from the spirit. Perhaps those investigators of the paranormal have a point, that the smell of ancient bloodshed hangs in the air to haunt future generations. Dunadd must have seen a share of violence and intrigue. I have heard tales of people who wandered unwittingly on to old battlefields, such as bloody Culloden, and were overcome with deep melancholy and suicidal depressions, and who then returned to their hosts in bemused and sad frame of mind, and were not surprised at all to find that they had been traversing bloodstained ground. My mood changed the moment I climbed this rock. 'Be alone in a separate place near a chief city', said the Rule of Columba, 'if thy conscience is not prepared to be in common with the crowd.'

I was tempted to linger, to wander out to the islands and track down all the saints who lived out there in caves. I could have gone, for instance, to Holy Island, by Lochranza and Brodick on Arran, to the cave of Maol Iosa, St Maolaise, 'the chosen son of Jesus', one of Columba's disciples whose marks are still on the wall there. Instead, I headed for a point much farther south.

Rain hammered across Galloway, hard rain, the road hopped with it. Not much stands between these strong-housed farms and the sea; the wind prevails from the west. Again the landscape has not changed; no geological upheavals, no landslips or earthquakes. Centuries of rain and wind have caused small weathering, but not enough to change the horizon since the Dark Ages. The town of Whithorn, small, long and grey, which begins on a hill with a signpost to St Ninian's Cave and ends at the Black Hawk inn, scarcely possesses a single side street.

To the west of Whithorn, by the farms of Physgill in the area called Glasserton, a signpost advertises the car park for St Ninian's Cave. Callers at the end of this long winding private road are invited to place tenpence in the box, which in itself exhibits a Scottish cliché: the collection box for these tenpences consists of a huge safe, of the type usually found in old banks, some four feet high and two feet thick. A path leads through a private wood, down by a burn which develops a spate – headlong it pours, through birches and old beeches. The path breaks out into open ground after a short walk, and then falls down with the stream to the sea and ends in a small cove. In the cliffside a small cave opens, very high but not deep. As much as any place in Galilee, as much as any Aramaic retreat, as much as any closed and festered haunt of a Stylite, this shore represents the eastern tradition of the holy man who withdrew from society to fast, to pray, to mortify the body and invigorate the soul.

The waves ran high, leaving giant-sized saliva along the steep edges of the sloping shingle. On my left, at the entrance to the cave, some pilgrims had left a series of small crosses, sticks tied with thread or cord – on several different pilgrimages by the looks of them, since each cross seemed to have a distinctive personality. On the wall another series of crosses, very old, had been carved with care and emphasis, the simplest ones with T shapes on the extremities. Further in, through the steady trickle of water from the overhang, more pilgrim crosses lay on the ground, one tied with tinfoil, one made with wire and quite good wood, and many made of twigs tied with grasses. One had a note tied to it; no need to feel squeamish about prying into another person's votive hopes – the note, encased in clear plastic, had every intention of being read. 'To any pilgrim who reads this: Ninian the Great cured me I thank him and Almighty God.'

Immediate fascination: cured of what – the palsy, the dropsy, or other biblical ailment, or buboes from some strange Galloway plague? Or the effects of radiation – Galloway took an extra blast of Chernobyl's fallout, and the mutton remains unsafe. And 'To any pilgrim' assumed not just any but many pilgrims to Ninian's Cave. On the evidence of the little crosses, at least twenty people had worshipped or prayed here in the recent past. The view from the warm and sheltered interior of the cave gives only light and water: some divine architect, no doubt knowing of this place's potential as an anchorite retreat, had angled the mouth of the cave so that as little land as possible might be seen.

Freestanding crosses, taken from here for safety a century ago and now in the Whithorn museum, bear one exquisitely incised distinguishing pattern. This, the symbol of the Whithorn Trust which conducts the archaeological investigation of the ancient monastic site in the town, comes directly from the association with St Ninian. Called the marigold cross, it encases the arms of the simple T cross within a circle and compares with the shape of a flower. We are back again in attractive theological territory, where the old connection with nature still flourished and had not given away fully to the new religion.

The land undulates in tailored farms between here and Whithorn, and at the little bay which marks the isle of Whithorn, and with a ruined chapel named for, and probably descended from, an earlier building of St Ninian, a fishing trawler got ready to put out.

'In the year of our Lord 565,' wrote the Venerable Bede,

when Justin, the younger, the successor of Justinian, had the government of the Roman Empire, there came into Britain a famous priest and abbot, a monk by habit and life, whose name was Columba, to preach the word of God to the provinces of the northern Picts, who are separated from the southern parts by steep and rugged mountains; for the southern Picts, who dwell on this side of those mountains, had long before, it is reported, forsaken the errors of idolatry, and embraced the truth, by the preaching of Ninias, a most reverend bishop and holy man of the British nation.

Bede's statement has never needed much by way of gloss. This holy Welshman, Ninian, whose monastic training took place in Tours where French is said to be spoken at its most accentless perfect, built a monastery not of wattles or even oak, but of stone. (Whether he should have played down the Tours connection offers the possibility for some speculation. Martin of Tours, an unkempt little pleb, relinquished his commission in the Roman army and took up residence with a band of followers in the cliffs along the river at Marmoutier, whence he went forth to work miracles for the country folk and attack Roman shrines with a hatchet.)

In 1984 an archaeological dig began at Whithorn, and it intensified in 1986. The results proved enormously useful, both in terms of new knowledge and in confirmation of the history of the site as Scotland's earliest recorded Christian community. In the red shadow of the medieval priory they have assembled caravans and sheets of polythene, and in a dark building on the street outside, where the welcome is warm, students and archaeologists assemble the record from Ninian onwards.

The ground lies stripped open, cut in trenches. The archaeologists' minds refuse to be impressed by the sight of a skull, round and bone-white, peeping out of the cross-section, the cranium helplessly exposed. This constitutes no more than nuisance, as it comes from a later burial ground. More value has been derived from the slice they call Trench 4, with deposits dated to between the fifth and seventh centuries. These, according to the interim report, included 'a midden incorporating ironworking debris, bones and scraps of 5th/6th century glass imported from the continent .... This deposit was cut by a broad drain capped with flagstones. Two graves were subsequently excavated beside the drain. Both graves contained coffins made from split tree-trunks.'

Neat, convenient, ingenious – split a tree of sufficient girth down the middle, hollow the halves like the dugout of a canoe, two coffins provided. In Trench 2 they found paving, some shards of *amphorae* dated fifth to seventh century, as well as the foundations of timbers which may have been the 'corner and doorway of a rectilinear building'.

Most compelling of all came the information a few lines later on – and by now the rain whipping sourly over the grassy hills had begun to soak the roneo-ed pages of the report: 'Although the early Christian layers were not fully examined in the 1986 period, deep deposits were observed in the sides of later pits and graves. Finds included a broken arciform cross which had been re-used in a later building.' The report concluded that the same ground had been used over and over again for centuries. The Christian habitations seemed to extend beyond the ground later used by the Anglo-Saxon ecclesiastical authorities.

The Candida Casa at Whithorn, which Bede describes as 'generally called the White House' of Ninian, has disappeared despite the strong construction, 'a church of stone, which was not usual among the Britons'. Other investigations have located the site of the monastery, though the full extent of the settlement still remains in some doubt. It occupied the same grassy hill where the Trust polythene flutters, a little to the west of the long central street of Whithorn. None of the old stones from the original building is visible today, but descriptions have become available which explain the remarkable whiteness. Rough local stone, cut crudely into blocks, was set in clay foundations. Then they plastered it with a white or cream-coloured dressing, which made it stand out from the occasional other unplastered, dry-stone walls or buildings in the area.

From Galloway to the Farne islands on the coast of Northumberland, the journey cuts across some of the most remote inland terrain on the island of Britain. A pilgrim way from Wigtown to Lindisfarne – folklore picked up in Ireland – did not appear on any maps. Roads remain few, and had I followed the valleys of the rivers I came across, the Nith at Dumfries and, further on, the Annan and the Esk, I would have fetched up a long way off course.

I stayed on the main roads, Dumfries to Moffat to Selkirk, until it became safe to join a river, the Tweed, at Melrose. Appropriate, too – the first

Christian foundation at Melrose, many centuries before the Cistercians, housed famous men, notably Aidan, a monk of Iona, one of the leading lights in the Celtic Church. Kings befriended this controversial, saintly man, who became the subject and object of many miracles. His eventual successor and one-time student, Cuthbert, became one of the favourite sons of English Christianity.

The Melrose community – never as important as the parent house at Lindisfarne – originally sprang up on the riverbank some two miles east of Melrose Abbey, but in the driving rain and the drenching grass, the river in spate, I could find no trace of it. The walk did eventually reward me, though, with the first spectacular view through the trees of Dryburgh, where Sir Walter Scott is buried, and where the river has a useful crossing place and a hotel to stay for the night. I left Dryburgh mid-morning, and about a mile below the Abbey where a small weir fords the river I took the right-hand bank. When heavy floods come down it probably becomes impassable. Further on, the going gets easier on the far side, more level with long stretches of open parkland, and great houses and castles. The sun came out, my waterproofs became sticky inside. I had arranged to collect my car in Kelso, and then head for Holy Island.

Even in such weather, or maybe even because of it, the Tweed valley possesses amazing and varied beauty. An uncouth geological history threw the ground into many vigorous contortions; the dips and crags create a welter of ravines, combes and outcrops. Each turn of the terrain offers a new view. It includes the kind of great Gothic house which Scott or Stevenson would have been proud to describe, a tall gaunt building with, on one side, a tower or turret rising to a point, straight from the pages of *Lammermuir* or *Hermiston*. I know that somewhere ahead two rivers met, the Tweed and the Teviot, and I did not wish to be caught in their confluence and have to retrace my steps. On the fence, as I rejoined the road, farmers or stewards – the 'factors' of the landed gentry – had pegged the tiny bodies of moles, four on one strand of wire, ten dripping on the next, eight over there. The rain stopped and I moved out on to the road again. The Teviot came in behind me on my right-hand side, beneath high grassy banks, a fine brusque river.

Near the Teviot Bridge, just outside Kelso – a small town with a cobbled square – the rivers, if you face back the direction in which I had come, fork away from each other to right and left, and meet. The walk had taken four hours. I asked a man in Kelso the names of the rivers, just to hear him speak. The best way, he told me, to get to the coast is through Coldstream, which did not exist in the Dark Ages. I was glad to drive; along the journey – arduous to walk, since the land undulates tremendously – you see Holy Island far off, from the crest of a hill; to the south the rich ploughed fields of Northumbria, to the north the lowering skies of King Lear. In the distance the North Sea foams high, breakers of spume identifying the long low stretches of rock that mark the Farne islands.

The list of them reads like a schooner's log: Great Whin Sill, St Cuthbert's Gut, the Churn, the Brownsman, North and South Wamses, Clove Car, Roddam and Green, Nameless Rock, Staple Island, Gun Rock, Skeney Scar, Callers, Crumstone, Fang, Oxscar or South Goldstone, Glororum Shad, Megstone, Elbow, Swedman, Little and Big Scarcar, Wideopens, Northern Hares, Knivestone – to explore them would take a number of summers, because the journey to them risks life and boat, and the sea shoots up here in flows and scurries and there are no saints around to save foolish lives.

Lindisfarne is clearly defined by two citadels – a castle and an abbey. A highway must be crossed, the A1 to London, and a terrifying railway, by Beal, and then the causeway to Holy Island. 'Which place, as the tide ebbs and flows twice a day, is enclosed by the waves of the sea like an island; and again twice in the day, when the shore is left dry, becomes contiguous to the land.' Bede's description has been taken fully to heart by the local authorities. At the entrance to the causeway the Northumbria County Council has posted up the times of the tides, when it becomes possible safely to cross the mile and a half to the island.

Warnings heralded the way, stringent warnings, of the bridge's submerging, warnings that if the water reaches the causeway at this point one should turn back. I walked along the shore in the direction of Bamburgh in the distance, yet another Celtic fairytale castle, while waiting for the tide to let me through to Holy Island, and trying at the same time to get a better perspective of this flat, moody, long slip of land out in the northern seas. The forecasts of hazardous weather had their uses: the wind rose, to such a degree that it blew me flat forward, all fifteen stone of me, to my hands and knees on the sand.

On the causeway mats of green slime from the floating tide-borne seaweed spread across the metalled road, and the scrub dunes led off into creeks and shallows with waders, occasional grebes and an ethnic population of seabirds. No pilgrims at this time of year; the village had the air of a seaside resort closed down for the winter. The hotels were closed, tables piled in the windows, curtains inadequately drawn.

The Monymusk Reliquary, which contained relics of St Columba.

Iona led the way and Lindisfarne reinforced it, the way being the political power and statement of the Celtic Church, the monkish power of the Irish and Scots in western European Christianity during its early period. Columba emerges, whatever his saintliness or undoubted evangelical zeal, as a wheeler-dealer politician, as easy with temporal intrigues as with spiritual leadership. Aidan, who came from Iona, therefore understood such clout and in any case his appointment came about as a result of temporal conflict.

A Northumbrian prince, Oswald, had taken refuge on Iona while British and Saxon armies fought wars in his king's territory. Northumbria embraced the Roman, that is to say the English, that is to say the

Canterbury version of Christian liturgy, whereas Iona remained Irish and ancient.

Edwin reigned most gloriously seventeen years over the nations of the English and the Britons, ... Cadwalla, king of the Britons, rebelled against him, being supported by Penda, a most warlike man of the royal race of the Mercians, and who from that time governed that nation for twenty-two years with various success. A great battle being fought in the plain called Heathfield, Edwin was killed on 12 October, in the year of our Lord 633, being then forty-seven years of age, and all his army was either slain or dispersed.

Bede goes on to describe how 'a great slaughter was made in the church or nation of the Northumbrians; and the more so because one of the commanders, by whom it was made, was a pagan, and the other a barbarian, more cruel than a pagan; for Penda, with all the nation of the Mercians, was an idolater, and a stranger to the name of Christ.' In a few sentences, as the wind almost blew the book out of my hand, Bede thus sketched in the violent picture of Christianity in the days of the early Church in Britain.

After Oswald came out of Iona and defeated the 'impious' Cadwalla, he sent 'to the elders of the Scots' for a bishop. 'Nor were they slow in granting his request; but sent him Bishop Aidan, a man of singular meekness, piety and moderation; zealous in the cause of God, though not altogether according to knowledge; for he was wont to keep Easter Sunday according to the custom of his country. ... from the fourteenth to the twentieth moon.'

Whereby hung several tales. Not only did Aidan live here, and perform great deeds of charity, of chastening the rich, and of monastic commitment and self-denial, but 'he was wont to traverse both town and country on foot, never on horseback, unless compelled by some urgent necessity; and whenever in his way he saw any, either rich or poor, he invited them, if infidels, to embrace the mystery of the faith; or if they were believers, to strengthen them in the faith, and to stir them up by words and actions to alms and good works ....'

Role models: Aidan, Columba and the other famous abbots, priors and bishops provided figures worth emulating, a little below divinity but of feasibly attainable stature. The path to power lay in sanctity, and this interchange between political influence and holiness lay at the core of the Church's strength. Almost without exception every individual who gained power also had renowned capacity for devoutness. It became a benign circle: a man received power within the Church because of his appearance of immense holiness – and when he had power it became essential for the system to give him a reputation for sanctity, so that he could lead his community. The closer a monk grew to God the more powerful he grew – and vice versa.

The powers extended beyond the normal. Aidan performed miracles, not mere local cures and spells – though he received credit in the hagiographies for these too. Bede recounts how Aidan predicted a storm at sea and in advance provided the royal sailors with oil to pour on the troubled waters, which they did with the desired effect.

On the night of 31 August 651 Aidan died, leaning against a timber baulk in Bamburgh. (The village and the church where Aidan died were put to the fire by the warlord Penda; the wooden post upon which Aidan had leaned at the time of his death would not ignite.) On that same night, a young shepherd near Melrose saw 'a stream of light from the sky breaking in upon the darkness of the long night. In the midst of this, the choir of the heavenly host descended to the earth, and taking with them, without delay, a soul of exceeding brightness, returned to their heavenly home.' The youth, named Cuthbert, felt strongly moved, 'And in the morning, learning that Aidan, bishop of the church at Lindisfarne, a man of specially great virtue, had entered the Kingdom of Heaven at the very time when he had seen him taken from the body, Cuthbert forthwith delivered to their owners the sheep which he was tending and decided to seek a monastery.' Patrick, remember, had also begun herding animals, and archetypally ascended to eminence and sainthood.

Cuthbert, like Aidan, became the perfect role model – even in his chapter headings: 'How on a journey he foretold that provisions would be brought by an eagle'; 'How, while preaching to the people, he foresaw that the devil would send a phantom fire, and how he put it out'; 'How Cuthbert checked the flames of a house that was really on fire'; 'How he exorcised the wife of a sheriff even before he reached her'.

My wandering monk could have met him: Cuthbert reigned as Abbot from 685 to 687. 'So full was he of sorrow for sin, so much aflame with heavenly yearnings, that he could never finish Mass without shedding tears … he wore quite ordinary clothes, neither remarkably neat nor noticeably slovenly.' He removed himself to Farne island, which 'lies a few miles to the south-east of Lindisfarne, cut off on the landward side by very deep water and facing, on the other side, the limitless ocean'. Cuthbert routed the devils who dwelt there; according to another hagiography, the *Life of Bartholomew*, these devils were 'clad in cowls, and rode upon goats black in demeanour, short in stature, their visages most hideous, with long heads which gave the whole platoon a disgusting appearance'.

Past the walls of the later priory, I walked to the water's edge to see whether Aidan's view of Bamburgh could have informed him that the castle had had 'an immense quantity of planks, beams, wattles and thatch' piled up like a pyre beside it by the dread Penda. The wind was in my face now, tearing the water out of my eyes, and still blowing hard enough to make me watch my step – 'a touch freakish today,' a man in the village said. Lindisfarne, like so many islands off these coasts – hard Skellig Michael, treeless Iona – has little lushness except for the tuftedness of the long grass. Unfamiliar birds, with long bills and dark brown feathers, swoop and then wander. The flora could give a botanist a life's employment among the mosses borne in on the wind, unimpeded, from Scandinavia.

The name Holy Island came several centuries after Aidan and Cuthbert. The medieval monastery and the later parish pay lip and eye service to the glories of ancient Lindisfarne and to Cuthbert and Aidan. Taken together, as the great pillars of Lindisfarne, both men made the place a holy of holies and had a remarkable effect upon all of Christendom and its mythology in Britain.

The miracle stories attached to them, however improbable, have their uses. Between the lines, mainly due to the tales of miraculous cures, glimpses appear of the way people lived. The life of western Europe, whatever the improving communications, had not risen stratospherically above the primitive. Illness abounded – women with headaches, boys with ague, people with distressed limbs and internal pain, dysentery and plague. In the absence of medicines they needed all the saints they could get. The diet included bread and the meat of sheep and poultry. They gave gifts of food – a lump of pig's lard had prized status. They drank wine if they were rich – and sometimes a visiting prelate miraculously made the water they drank taste of wine – and they made their own beer. They suffered terribly from the elements, and lived in fear of fire consuming them and their dwellings; their wooden houses dried out easily in summer, and the fireplaces did not yet have the protection of stone.

They wore garments of linen and wool, and, if they were clergy involved in worship, vestments of silk, coloured and embroidered. They travelled by foot, sometimes on horseback, though a good horse suggested wealth or royalty. People also travelled on carts, makeshift or large with strong, iron-bound wheels. Ill people seeking cures were brought on such wains to Lindisfarne. The monks wore boots or shoes of leather and carried sticks, and they used rafts and boats to transport themselves and their materials, either for trade or for building along the rivers.

Hygiene had not quite taken hold; if the body truly grew to be 'the temple of the Holy Spirit', it needed sweeping out from time to time. Cuthbert, for instance, wore skin boots and, in Bede's account, 'care of his own body was so far from his thoughts that he kept his soft leather boots on his feet for months on end without ever removing them. If he put new boots on at Easter they would not come off until the next Easter and then only for the washing of the feet on Maundy Thursday. The monks found long thick callouses, where the boots had chafed his shins all through prayers and genuflexions.'

Any visiting monk, whether or not he knew the Rule followed by his hosts, participated in the regime. They greeted each other with the word of God, and in the community observed a demanding routine of prayer and work. They rose at half past one in the morning; at two o'clock celebrated Nocturns; at half past three Matins; at six o'clock Prime, to greet the sunrise; at eight o'clock Terce; at half past eleven Sext, at half past two in the afternoon None; at six o'clock in the evening Vespers; and at eight o'clock Compline, to accept the gathering dusk. In winter these times altered a little: they rose an hour later, at half past two in the morning, and retired at half past six in the evening. Diet and fasting constituted part of worship, except if rigorous work such as farming or building had to be done, when it became necessary for men's strength to be maintained.

Avenue at Château St Pois, northern France. Forests of beech and
oak covered many of the plains and hills of Dark Ages Europe.

Seventh-century Frankish stele or stone memorial with heroic
depiction, designed to stand upright. The stele was typically used as
a funeral or royal commemoration among the Franks and
contemporary European peoples.

Simeon Stylites of Antioch (390–459) on his pillar. One of the early
hermits, he squatted for thirty years on stylus platforms high above
the ground.

Late seventh/early eighth-century glass jar from the Seine-Rhine area. The pre-Christian Romans, who traded wine with non-Mediterranean peoples such as the Celts, introduced vessels with new shapes which influenced European craftsmen.

Seventh-century French baptistery. The western Church favoured relatively simple architectural expression, and employed less ornate decoration than the churches of Ravenna and Constantinople.

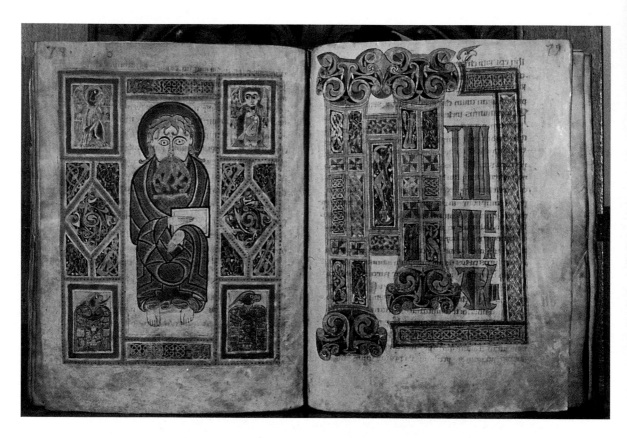

Beginning of St Mark's Gospel, in the seventh/eighth-century
illuminated Irish Evangeliarum from the Library at St Gallen.

Christ in Glory from the Gospel according to St Mark, from
the St Gallen Evangeliarum.

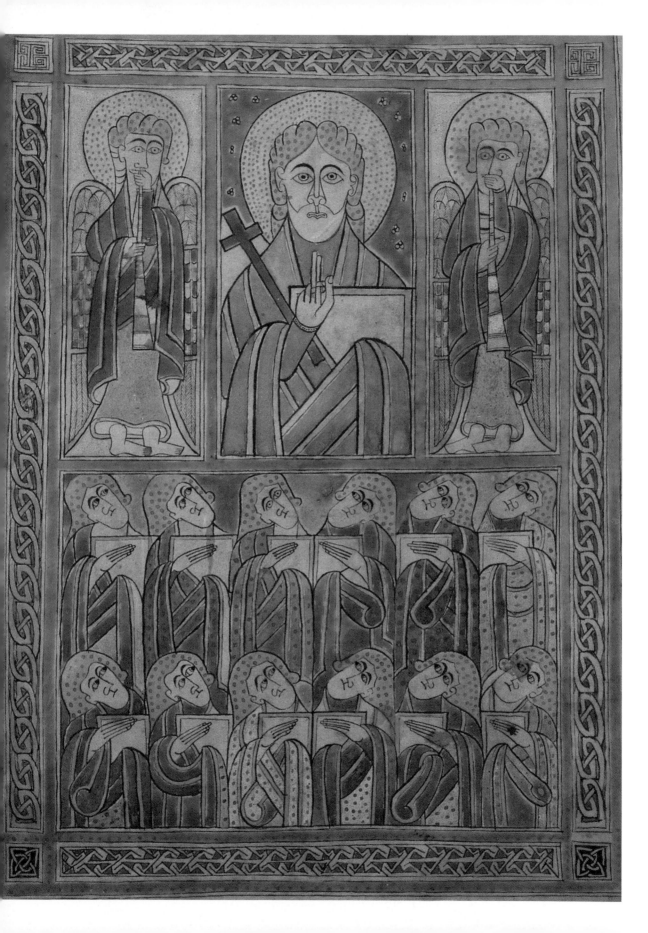

In 612 Columbanus led his party of monks over the rough terrain
of the Alps into northern Italy. At Bobbio he founded
another of the monasteries which made him so renowned among
early pilgrim monks.

As well as the famously holy monks, Lindisfarne produced one vivid, eloquent testament to the spirit of those Christian pioneers. A traveller arriving at Lindisfarne and sharing in the life of the community in the seventh century almost certainly had the opportunity to observe the *Lindisfarne Gospels* in the making. Some claim it to be the most glorious of all the illuminated manuscripts, a treasure trove of visual stimuli.

The book had four creators, all monks. Eadfrith, who became Bishop of Lindisfarne in 698, wrote the text; Ethelwald, who became Bishop in 721, bound it; Billfrith the Anchorite constructed the precious metal and jewelled casing; and some centuries later Aldred translated the text into Anglo-Saxon. The script seems certain to have been written by one hand alone, unusually in such works, and therefore it must have taken a number of years to complete, allowing for cold winter days, freezing hands, rheumatism or arthritic pains. It consisted of the four Gospels in Latin, followed by the translation into Anglo-Saxon, the earliest 'English' version of a translation of the Gospels. The book, intended for ceremonial use, was almost as important as a sacred vessel, occupying a place of distinction on the altar of the monastery, to be used on the feast days of favourite saints, to celebrate a visit by a dignitary, the remembrance of a death, the consecration of a bishop or the ordination of priests.

Eadfrith the scribe ruled his page and then wrote on it with wide-tipped nibs: strong letters, clear and flowing strokes, so excellently achieved that many wondered whether this style of script, brought to a high standard by the monks of Northumbria, had not been executed by Italians. In *Civilization* Lord Clark told a story which illustrated twentieth-century international cultural differences, a sad little tale of how much we have lost. A Japanese woman, he said, asked him when he met her, 'And what is the state of calligraphy in your country?' In the seventh century he would have been able to point with pride to the *Lindisfarne Gospels*.

These illuminations have a generosity and an obvious beauty, but put aside the emotional reaction and examine them for the state of man at the time. No morality appears: the primary purpose – the worship of God – has not been inhibited with visual or verbal opinion. Every intention seems clear and confident, and proceeds in a kind of muscular innocence towards the celebrations of God's word and wonderful world. Four of the major pages give firm attributions: '*imago hominis*', the representation of a man, begins the Gospel according to St Matthew; '*imago leonis*', a lion, marks the opening of Mark's Gospel; '*imago vituli*' shows a calf carrying a book and introduces the Gospel according to St Luke; and '*imago aquilae*', the image of an eagle, opens the Gospel according to St John.

Most of the other illuminations in the book are either abstracts, or portray the life of the natural world. All merge: plaits and eyes, legs and

St Matthew, from the *Lindisfarne Gospels*.

tails, whorls and dots – several thousand of them per page – and interlining and interlacing and spirals and trumpets and cross-hatching and fretting. If gazed at with intense concentration the illuminations effect hypnotic fascination, as the eye tries to follow and absorb each abstraction and thought suggested. When taken as an expression of worship, mild religious trance may have followed.

At this point the pathway of Europe not so much bifurcates as diverts, like God, in all directions and each one a kaleidoscope of possibilities. The famous plaiting and whorling has immediate Celtic associations, the interlacing which moves gracefully to a point and then returns to itself performing gentle arcs of pattern; the intricate mazes and arenas which overlap and counterpoint each other attach themselves surely in time and place to the far west of Europe, to the monks of Ireland and Northumbria who created – perhaps 'performed' has more accuracy – the illuminated manuscripts.

Until ... until you observe holy art from the east, from Ethiopia for instance, which, though an idiom unto itself, has the same 'Celtic' patterns in abundance and for good measure borrows from Byzantium too. Slowly the role of the monk in Europe, and the possibilities attaching to a wanderer such as the one I have in mind, widen attractively and excitingly, and the world, not Ireland or Europe, has become his oyster. The Coptic influence in the illuminations also confirms such far connections, apart from the known Egyptian role in the development of the monk – anchorite and monastic. The figure of the Dark Ages monk seems no longer merely provincial and insular, though thoughtful and devout, but a man who, whether in his wanderings or as a member of his community, made an important cultural contribution, widened the pool of artistic reference, and did so by means of choosing a life contrary to that of the way of the world.

Lindisfarne still removes itself from the mainland with the assistance of the tides twice a day. I walked a wobbly pathway along the highest dunes by the dishevelled lighthouse, past the flagpole with its triangular beacon emblem, the wind slamming in from the north-east. Some sheep grazed; there were a few fishing boats and one small trawler rested up on land. The crafts centre which advertised 'Lindisfarne Mead' had a sign which said 'Open at Easter' and a huge exclamation mark followed.

With the *Lindisfarne Gospels* in mind, it became possible while walking along the dunes to see the inspiration for many of the decorations. The sand swirls in the wind; the water shades from very dark to light and foamy; the seabirds, though less menacing than those in the *Gospels*, have, at close hand, an astonishing amount of colour in their plumage; and the mainland in the distance must surely vary in light and colour when the sun comes out. No sunshine while I walked there; Holy Island remained grey and still. The people had a silence about them, some sort of claim upon the past – or else they merely tire of the inquisitive face of the tourist.

The life of the monk or the anchorite in the Farne islands had much to offer emotionally. The weather and the low dull land and the wild sea, added to the thought, repeated prayer and occasional ecstasy of the religious life, took care of almost every aspect of emotional expression – from excess to withdrawal.

I drove along the coast by Bamburgh, whose castle confirms all the fairytale impressions from the distance, and then by Warkworth and Amble and Newbiggin-by-the-Sea, undistinguished and depressing places, except where the sea beats majestically. It had started to rain by Whitby. Through the gaps in the high-sided roads I caught glimpses of the cliffs which contain the famous local black jet. The harbour inside the bridge had been crammed with fishing trawlers, sheltering like children piled into a bed. The town has a resort's high boarding house quotient, but every place I approached either had no room at the inn or had ceased to trade. Eventually I found myself virtually the only guest at a big old house now becoming a hotel on the high outskirts of the town, run by a couple called Keith and Electra.

Now we must praise the Guardians of Heaven
The might and powerful intent of the Judge.
The deeds of the glorious father, as He
Eternal Lord established each marvellous thing.
First, the Holy Creator, the Guardian of Mankind
Raised up Heaven, as a roof for sons of men,
Then the Eternal God, the Lord Almighty,
Created the earth.

The words of Caedmon, the first author of sacred song in English: 'Whatever was interpreted to him out of Scripture,' wrote Bede, 'he soon after put the same into poetical expressions of much sweetness and humility in English, which was his native language.' By now Bede had grown into a most agreeable travelling companion – authoritative, involved, prejudiced, eventful, full of what newspapers used to call 'human drama'.

Caedmon had been a farmhand, ignorant, unlettered, and then he had a dream, that streams of poetry flowed to him. He conveyed this vision to Hilda, the great Abbess of Whitby, founder of Britain's most powerful, that is to say most holy, gynaeceum, who died in 680 and whose death her community mourned actively for ten years. Not only did Hilda encourage Caedmon to sing 'the creation of the world, the origin of man and all the history of Genesis', she constructed the most important settlement for women in the early British Church, 'and taught there the strict observance of justice, piety, chastity, and other virtues, and particularly of peace and charity; so that, after the example of the primitive church, no person there was rich, and none poor, all being in common to all, and none having any property'.

The ruins of the later monastery stand above the sea, visible from almost every quarter of Whitby, reached by climbing endless steps. The cemetery, in the grounds of the more recent parish church, consists of a forest of gravestones, all leaning in the same direction, clearly under pressure from the prevailing wind, all of the same colour, sand-brown tinged with black. The arched spars of the Abbey ruins stimulate the Gothic quarter of the imagination; Bram Stoker used Whitby prominently when recounting the life of Count Dracula.

Out to sea the waves ran higher and higher, and within lip-smacking of the monastery's rounded green lawns the waves hit the coast. Not another soul visited the place that afternoon. A curious light shone – the combination of bright sunlight and a biting wind which had suddenly whipped around to the east. Not a ship ploughed the sea, not even those low tankers which, for the last few days, had lain like long slugs on the horizon.

'At this time, a great and frequent controversy happened about the observance of Easter.' Bede enshrined Whitby's claim to fame – the difficult, if not very large Synod of 664. 'Those that came from Kent or France affirming that the Scots kept Easter Sunday contrary to the custom of the universal church.' Yes, but there was a woman in the case, Queen Eanfleda, who 'observed the same as she had seen practised in Kent' and this lay at the sting of the difficulty, because 'when the king having ended the time of fasting, kept his Easter, the queen and her followers were still fasting' – and, presumably, still abstaining.

It became a matter of moons, whether Peter's calculations at the moment of the Resurrection 'ought to be observed, so as always to stay till the rising of the moon on the fourteenth day of the first moon, in the evening' and, with various adjustments according to the day of the week on which the Sabbath fell, 'thus it came to pass that Easter Sunday was only kept from the fifteenth moon to the twenty-first'. But the Celtic delegation, including the Irish, Scots and Northumbrians, observed Easter on the Lord's Day any time between the fourteenth and the twentieth day of the moon, which sometimes led to them beginning the celebration of Easter on the evening of the thirteenth day of the moon, said to be earlier than the moment at which Jesus began the Passover.

They spoke harsh words in these Abbey grounds, an Irishman called Colman for the Celtic Church and the Englishman Wilfrid. Terms such as 'contemptible' and 'ignorant' and 'scandal' and 'prejudicial' batted back and forth in what diplomats call 'a tense exchange of views'. Bede's lengthy account makes wonderful reading, and from it emerges the impression that Wilfrid, being articulate and very well briefed, won the day over the more passionate and instinctive Irish monk, ironic enough in the light of the fact that what they all sought to achieve was an Easter which would be as close an emulation as possible of the first Eastertide.

'Colman, perceiving that his doctrine was rejected and his sect despised', returned to Scotland with his followers and liturgical history had been made. More than that, a point regarding evangelism had been proven: the rational, organized English would gain political control of the British Church even in the north, where it had been the fief of the less disciplined, though more fervent, Irish and Scots. It continued thus until the Reformation, which splintered them all.

Not difficult to imagine monks walking around the grounds at Whitby overlooking the sea, taking a break from the Synod and discussing with grave wags of their tonsured heads the spiritual and political implications of the argument between Colman and Wilfrid. With very little adjustment in language, and accurate costume, reconstruction would be credible. More dificult to survey and to judge emotional differences between a man of that period, exactly my own contemporary in years, and myself.

An afternoon of wind and rain on the heights of Whitby promoted a desire for comfort. Dinner at the dim hotel, and the birthday party which half a dozen girls from the town were having at the next table, with many balloons and ribald talks of husbands and hoots of 'birthday treats', took me down with abrupt candour to the real world, and the eventless journey in the morning over the moors to York.

Wilfrid, who out-argued the Irish monks at Whitby and about whom therefore my suspicions had now been aroused, restored the church at York while bishop there. His epitaph at Ripon, as well as including the observation 'He likewise brought the time of Easter right', goes on to give a glimpse of the life of a man for whom the title 'turbulent priest' might have been coined, who,

> In lapse of years, by many dangers tossed;
> At home by discords, and in foreign realms,
> Having sat bishop five and forty years

eventually received a saint's burial and reputation.

Unquestionably Wilfrid dominated Church rumour and gossip in Britain during the last quarter of the seventh century. His king in Northumbria expelled him, and again a woman in the case caused the trouble. The queen became jealous because Wilfrid's monasteries threatened to outshine the grandeur of her husband's royal trappings and buildings. His biographer, Eddius Stephanus, found his 'poor mind quite at a loss' to describe the church Wilfrid built at Hexham, 'the great depth of the foundations, the crypts of beautifully dressed stone, the vast structure supported by columns of various styles, and with numerous side-aisles, the walls of remarkable height and length, the many winding passages and spiral staircases leading up and down'.

Enough indeed to tempt envy, and hilariously the biography goes on to describe how the tempter, 'like a roaring lion' worked against Wilfrid. 'In this skirmish he [the tempter] chose his usual weapon, one by which he has often spread defilement throughout the whole world – woman ... she corrupted the king's heart with poisonous tales about Wilfrid, imitating Jezebel....' Great stuff, and it unhorsed Wilfrid and threw him out of York in 678.

Wilfrid's York has disappeared beneath the usual march of masonry, but one of his successes at Whitby has fuelled the popular image of the monk ever since (and further scratched at my irritating notion of times unchanging). Colman had been Bishop of York before Whitby, and he was, says Wilfrid's biographer, 'told that if out of respect for his own country's customs, he should reject the Roman tonsure and the method of calculating Easter, he was to resign his see in favour of another and better candidate' – Wilfrid, as it transpired. He, as a young monk, 'had an ardent desire to receive St Peter's, that is the Roman, form of tonsure, which goes round the head in the shape of Christ's own crown of thorns'.

The monks of Iona, and therefore most of the monks in the Celtic Church, retained a different type of haircut, one associated by their rivals with Simon Magus, whose magic had opposed Christianity in the first century AD. 'Upon the forehead,' wrote the Abbot of Jarrow to the King of the Picts,

it does seem indeed to resemble a crown; but when you come to the neck, you will find the crown you thought you had seen so perfect cut short; so that you may be satisfied such a distinction belongs properly not to Christians but to Simoniacs, such as were indeed in this life thought worthy of a perpetual crown of glory by erring men; but in that life which is to follow this, are not only deprived of all hopes of a crown, but are moreover condemned to eternal punishment.

The tonsure question had been causing trouble since the days of the anchorites in the eastern deserts, some of whom wore a long forelock so that God could haul them up to Heaven. For such presumption they eventually received the same abuse as Simon and his Magicians. In a paper on the subject the York historian Edward James makes the point that the old tonsure favoured by the Celtic monks found further disfavour since it may have originated with the Druids, who also used magic to counter Patrick's evangelism.

Dr James discusses the connection between hair and ritual. 'The offering of shorn hair to God or the gods seems to be known throughout the ancient world. Pliny reported a tree in Rome called the Hair Tree on which the vestal virgins used to hang offerings of hair; according to Pausanius the statue of Hygeia at Sikyon was covered with the offerings of women's hair

. . . . The rite of baptism in the Greek church included the offerings of the first hairs.' Paulinus of Nola dedicated the shavings of his beard to his heavenly patron, St Felix; a century later the pilgrim Antony described how on Mount Sinai, 'many people on account of their devotion shave off their hair and beard. I took off my beard at this place.'

The monkish tonsure offered public proof of the wearer's commitment: it echoed the crown of thorns in the passion of Christ and it marked out the wearer as a humble man, without vanity or interest in his own appearance. An Irish monk passing through York at the end of the seventh century would almost certainly, if not already prevailed upon, have agreed to have his hairstyle changed and would thereby have assured himself of an easier welcome at the holy places still ahead of him in Britain – the Lincoln of Paulinus, the Ely of Ethelreda and the Canterbury of Augustine.

If we accept the term Dark Ages as an accurate description, meaning that period after the Romans and before other literacy, after the brilliance of the Greeks, after the European world had learned how to express itself – and then almost forgot, as the barbarians had their day – then the darkest of the ages occurred in the fifth, sixth and seventh centuries, although by then the learning of the monks had, in places, begun to make the skies bright again. Earlier, the Romans had left considerable record of their world; the Greeks had founded the civilizing process called democracy and had laid down principles of thought and encouraged debate upon them. The advance of Christianity often seems like a response to a changing world – as if a spiritual power vacuum had arisen to match the temporal one the Romans had left in western Europe when they retreated to their (no longer everlasting) city.

In Britain, the local client kings and the Anglo-Saxon overlords contested the post-Roman power – to begin with in a rather haphazard way, and then in more formalized, regional structures, taking and creating kingdoms. Bede's *Ecclesiastical History of the English Nation* describes the country which the Irish wandering monks undoubtedly found. 'Britain excels for grain and trees, and it is well adapted for feeding cattle and beasts of burden.' My journey after York had to take into account the state of Christian Britain at the time, in terms of safe passage and refuge, and alongside such practical requirements, a logical direction. Given what Whitby had been discussing and Lindisfarne had been regretting, the destination became obvious: Canterbury now dictated the liturgy the travelling Irish monk would have to observe.

En route Lincoln, a Roman city, had been an established diocese, therefore an assured welcome on the road south could be obtained there. Always a priestly town, in fact: the Romans contributed to the cult of emperor worship in Lindum Colonia. Lincoln suffered some, though not all, of the ghost town indignity of other Roman cities in Britain, where the marble statues had either been decapitated and dismembered, or ignored in the general overgrowing. The Anglo-Saxons bypassed most of the cities and villas of the Romans, and the tiles and walls had been cannibalized in a relaxed fashion to build anew. In Lincoln the River Witham assisted the decay caused by neglect; as the trading posts moved away from the Roman centre, the walls went unrepaired and fell victim to the floods and the creeping silt.

I rounded a corner of the Cathedral in Lincoln on a foggy evening as a great fair thronged the cobbled closes. Pedlars and sideshows and entertainers maintained the long continuity of the marketplace's atmosphere. People with lanterns and brown accents bought food and clothing. Country people, largely, who had climbed the hill for the fair. The city conducts its affairs on two physical levels. On top of the hill, by the Cathedral (I had already begun to long for one cathedral built in or before the seventh century), little heavy trading takes place except at fairs. The commerce begins further down, supported by a large indigenous population of farmers, and the city itself now includes in its population the new commuters who travel a journey every day to London which, in the time under my consideration, would have been allotted the greater part of a week.

Travel on: Ely, the ship of the fens, did not then have the great Cathedral which now sails across the evening sky, but Ethelreda's sanctity had already inspired and invited pilgrims. Wilfrid's grey eminence had a part – delicately indirect – to play in Ely's foundation. Ethelreda, daughter of an East Anglian king, retired to Ely in 655 when the husband of her unconsummated marriage died. Five years later she made a political marriage to a teenage king of Northumbria who, much her junior, eventually chafed against her desire to continue with her virginity. Ethelreda consulted Wilfrid, who advised her to adhere to her holy wishes; her husband left her, and Ethelreda became a nun and founded the great establishment of Ely in 673. 'She preserved the glory of perfect virginity, as I was informed by Bishop Wilfrid, of blessed memory,' wrote Bede, 'of whom I enquired, because some questioned the truth thereof; and he told me that he was an undoubted witness of her virginity.'

Such purity nominated Ethelreda's body as a candidate for miraculous preservation. She died in 679, of a tumour on her neck, because as a girl she 'bore there the needless weight of jewels'. Several years after her death her grave was opened and the late Ethelreda 'being brought into sight, was found as free from corruption as if she had died and been buried on that very day'. The ubiquitous Wilfrid, still cleverly associating with matters of immense holiness, testified again – he had witnessed the exhumation. Ethelreda's virtues extended beyond virginity. In Bede's words, 'It is reported of her, that from the time of her entering into the monastery, she never wore any linen but woollen garments, and would rarely wash in a hot bath, unless just before any of the great festivals, as Easter, Whitsuntide, and the Epiphany.'

Is it my imagination, or does the Cathedral at Ely have a femininity absent in York and Lincoln? It came much later than Ethelreda, though her mixed monastery of nuns and monks must find some small echo in the pupils at the school in the Cathedral grounds. The light falling across the Cathedral, seen from miles off, has a different quality, a bright soft light, stoked by the gases off the fens.

The choice lay ahead – London, or Canterbury direct. Undoubtedly such a traveller as mine went to London, probably entered by one of the Roman roads, the one which became Aldersgate Street, and sought shelter in any one of a dozen religious refuges, houses or small local monasteries in the city at the time. The Christian Church had an uncertain existence in the seventh century. Not all of Britain had been converted, and Anglo-Saxon warlords did not necessarily respect the cloth of God that the priests wore. Throughout England, though unevenly, priests, priors, monks, bishops and abbots died violently, were embattled, evicted, banished, imprisoned or robbed. The uncertain state of the countryside, where a traveller could be laid waste by a wolf or a bandit or a plague, mirrored itself in the Church,

Illumination from the *Psalter of St Augustine*.

which had no divine writ across the entire country. Christianity had gained a strong foothold, no more than that yet. In 616 the Bishop of London, Mellitus, who had sufficient stature to confer with Pope Boniface and thereafter become a senior figure in the conduct of Church affairs in Britain, had to flee to Canterbury and then to France. A new king, Eadbald, 'proved very prejudicial to the new church; for he not only refused to embrace the faith of Christ, but was also defiled with a sort of fornication not heard of even among the Gentiles – for he kept his father's wife'.

But I live in London, and the place will little serve my journey's purpose, which had begun to unfold further. I had set out feeling somewhat at one with the idea of the hermit monk, 'the despiser of the world'. The contemplation of the man, and then, in my imagination, pitching him into the landscapes I had visited, where he must surely have walked, and into the monasteries I had seen, where he must surely have been a guest, mellowed me.

The fascination with his life and times grew – indeed it often had to be kept under control. Did he negotiate this hill in a cart on which he had hitched a lift? Did he sit by that river, washing his feet or his face out in the green open air? Did he meet, as in one of Tennyson's lines, 'an abbot on an ambling pad'? I had already encountered some of his difficulties, such as the contrary winds while trying to cross the sea to Iona. Even our diets had some similarities. As ever, though, urbanization provided the obstacles. Easy enough to stand on a windy hill in Kent, look in a direction where no roof could be seen (still occasionally possible) and presume that it may have looked very much the same in 687 , but where towns and cities intruded I lost him.

At the entrance to Canterbury Cathedral a plaque on the wall reads, 'On this spot Christian worship has been offered for 1350 years continuously. The Cathedral is built on the site of an older church which was used by British Christians of the fourth century.' Social observers say that immigrants congregate in those areas nearest their ports of arrival – which could make a case for Canterbury's eminence as the capital of the Church in Britain. Kent first saw most of Britain's invaders, good and bad – 'the landing place for nearly all the ships from Gaul', Julius Caesar called it – and the inhabitants had benefited from such close contact with the mainland of Europe. 'By far the most civilized inhabitants are those living in Kent,' Caesar continued, 'whose way of life differs little from that of the Gauls. Most of the tribes in the interior do not grow corn but live on milk and meat and wear skins.'

Six centuries after Caesar wrote those words, Kent received a visitor whose presence also penetrated and influenced the land of the Britons. Augustine, with forty followers, and interpreters from France, landed on the isle of Thanet, eventually received the permission of the King, Ethelbert, and from the house granted to him in Canterbury – the King had a Christian wife – began to evangelize with great success; in one day he baptized ten thousand people on a riverbank.

Organization guaranteed Augustine's success. He had been chosen for the British mission by that most efficient administrator, Pope Gregory I, 'the Great'; Augustine had been a Benedictine prior in a Roman monastery. Gregory, famously, had seen fair-skinned boys in a slave market, made a play on the word 'Angles', called them 'angels' and, having sent Augustine to convert their native land to Christianity, had several of the young men purchased for the priesthood. Augustine became a bishop, and cleared his lines of authority by putting a series of questions to Gregory, cunningly making the Pope responsible for defining how Britain's Church and faithful were to be governed, though along thoughts put in his head by Augustine. The issues he raised included how the gifts of the worshippers should be divided among the clergy, 'whether a bishop may be ordained with other bishops present', and 'How are we to deal with the bishops of France and Britain?'

Essentially Augustine set up a system of administration geared to retaining the evangelical fruits he gained. He created bishops along the lines of the guidance he had wrung from the Pope; Canterbury, where these prelates were created, became their reference point – the Pope copper-fastened its stature. 'But to you, my brother', Gregory wrote to Augutine, 'shall, by the authority of our God, and Lord Jesus Christ, be subject not only those bishops you shall ordain, and those that shall be ordained by the bishop of York, but also all the priests in Britain; to the end that from the mouth and life of your holiness, they may learn the rule of believing rightly and living well and fulfilling their office in faith and good manners ....

Canterbury Cathedral's more luridly famous associations blot out the patient work of Augustine. The shrine of Thomas à Becket has drawn pilgrims since his assassination two days before the new year of 1171. The building, on three levels, rises above an undercroft, whose whitening stones feel as if they have some relevance appropriate to my purposes. Regrettably not; this building was begun in the eleventh century, which explains why Canterbury, Cantwaraburg, the town of the people of Kent, leaves me unmoved by comparison with Iona or Lindisfarne or even Whitby. I suspect some nationalism in myself, or admiration for those who held out for a long time against the general rule of Rome, and who chose to make their own interpretation of the Scriptures. Another, sadder thought: Canterbury represents the first centralization in these islands of a religion which also had centralization at its core. The monotheism of Christianity had replaced all the gods in the trees and the rivers and the mountains. It may have been more organized intellectually, but the spirit of man surely lost something fundamental when the word 'paganism' became a derogatory term.

My monk has come to the end of his British walk. In Canterbury he has found that he has merely reached another stage. He has learned that Iona and Lindisfarne no longer have the power to which they were formerly accustomed and for which Ireland looked to them, that it now resided in Canterbury. And having reached Canterbury, the power, he discovered, resided elsewhere, in Rome, and even then Rome had to observe other considerations, especially those coming from the East. He has had a history lesson, as well as religious instruction; he has seen places and people he has found unfamiliar, but perhaps has not felt a stranger ... yet.

O God, that art the only hope of the world
The only refuge for unhappy men,
Abiding in the faithfulness of heaven,
Give me strong succour in this testing place.
O King, protect Thy man from utter ruin
Lest the weak faith surrender to the tyrant
Facing innumerable blows alone.
Remember I am dust, and wind, and shadow,
And life as fleeting as the flower of grass.

THE VENERABLE BEDE
trans. Helen Waddell

CHAPTER THREE

DUST
AND WIND
AND
SHADOW

OR A TIME, in the seventh and early eighth centuries, the figure of the Irish monk in Europe acquired a status near to that of a living saint, with his prayerbook in his satchel and his mind on his destination, visibly engaged upon *peregrinatio*. Stepping from a boat at any of the harbours of the period, from Etaples up to the borders of Frisia, such a monk set out across the countryside now facing me as I came ashore at Boulogne – more wooded then, beautiful and wide with rolling farms now. Today it offers few traces of the life of 687, and the local history of much of the landscape ahead has either not been uncovered in great detail yet, or has never been written down.

Although historians increasingly dislike the term 'Dark Ages' – since their profession is rightly invested in brightening them, letting in more and more light from the texts and the invaluable law-book sources of the period – the phrase acts as a useful shorthand. By comparison with the largely ameliorated society of the twentieth century, darkness prevailed – not just lack of information, but the darkness of ambiguity and uncertainty. Dark deeds abounded, executed by men whom we would now presume to rise above such things. Moral expectations had not been clarified – bishops, though men of God, went to war. Priests kept concubines, despite repeated threats of excommunication, and in some cases they attempted to circumvent Church objections and laws by adopting the concubines or making them nuns. The Irish monk's near-contemporary, Boniface, complained that many priests kept four or five concubines, and that, worse, this fact did not impede their chances of promotion – some became bishops. Even the taboos necessary to the establishment of clean genetics in a growing civilization still needed to be enforced by law: the declarations against incest had to be restated repeatedly.

The political and social super-ego of the time, in the country of Gaul-becoming-Francia, on whose shores the Irish monk had now landed, contained many familiar strands. In Ireland, the Celtic inheritance had given him an awareness of aristocracy, which protected itself by enshrining principles of kindred, honour and bonding, to be upheld if necessary through waging blood feuds and local war. The society from which he came resembled this one whose land he now set out to cross; it had grown along lines which in our eyes have by now become historically archetypal – family ruled by chosen leader, retaining territory, forming alliances, avenging slights which undermined the family's status, declaring laws which ensured continuity of ownership. Developments under the Romans had introduced a further concept, that of public service, the official as functionary of the administration. From the time of Constantine onwards those functions had increasingly passed into the hands of Christian bishops.

Therefore a society had evolved which had institutionalized power based on a ruling class of kindred, and it had retained and spread that power in its own extended families. Religion added a further dimension to society, in the emergence of the powerful churchman, abbot or bishop, part of the kindred or an outsider with a reputation for sanctity, quite prepared to accumulate wealth, quite prepared to defend it and his spiritual position bloodily.

I travelled from the coast eastwards to Arras, intending to get on to a good route through the kingdoms of the Franks and into areas which contained whatever little relevant history these Dark Ages had reluctantly yielded up. Curious place, Arras – the people, who seem flat in personality, with little trace of enthusiasm, maintain a town of lovely buildings, a town of squares and colonnades. The vans had begun to rig for a fair in one of the squares; the church, like so many others, proved too new for my purposes and despite the noon sunshine the temperature in the shade of the lane leading to the church dropped considerably.

After Arras I found a river, the Somme, and locked on to it, as an earlier traveller would have done. The same feeling of unease that I felt at Dunadd, that others have recounted from Culloden, multiplies along the Somme. The air overhead seems filled with the silent screams from the bloody ridges, a memorial on each one, from Picardy where the blood flowed through the orchards. Somewhere near here stands a hill which, as the archive photographs show, has grown appreciably in size in the twentieth century – not through accumulation of soil, but from the bodies of dead soldiers buried inside it.

I lunched in the Hostellerie des Remparts in the walled town of Péronne; local pâté, rough and open, *magret de canard*, some beans, a strong chèvre, a light local rosé, excellent. In Péronne, familiar names and feelings became available to the wandering monk. To begin with, the monastery, called Peronna Scotorum, had almost exclusively Irish associations (the name Scotii still attached to them), and the place acted as a rest and a staging post for the many monks on their way through – peregrinating outwards or homewards. In 650, thirty-seven years earlier than the date that my mythical monk was making his journey, the Irish monk Fursey, or Fursa, had died here and his cult flourished energetically.

Fursey had joined the ranks of these many 'pilgrims for Christ' and when he left Ireland, with his brothers Foillan and Ultan, fetched up eventually in Suffolk, in Burgh Castle, near Great Yarmouth. The terrifying Penda, a name from the Northumbrian lore, brought about another abrupt change in the political structure, and Fursey's patron, King Sigebert, was killed. Fursey fled the monastery he had founded at Burgh – 'pleasantly situated in the woods, and with the sea not far off', according to Bede – and upon landing in France moved eastwards, as I did, from the coast, though further south than my route.

From the fifth to the eighth century this region evolved from Gaul, to the kingdoms of the Franks, whose kings founded the Merovingian dynasty, to Francia. Fursey arrived in Neustria, the western third of the domain (though not embracing the Bretons). Burgundy and, in the east, Austrasia completed the *tria regna* of the Merovingian kings. He was welcomed by Erchinoald, the mayor, that is to say chief duke, of Neustria, who could just as easily have slaughtered Fursey, as he almost did with a local bishop – of Noyon – who tried to stop the people dancing and holding traditional local games. On this occasion, too, Erchinoald's better nature prevailed. 'He was a gentle, good-natured man,' wrote Fredegar, the Franks' historian, 'in brief both patient and canny, very humble and kindly towards the bishops, ready with a civil answer to all questioners and quite without pride or greed. So long as he lived he sought peace, as is well-pleasing to God. He was certainly clever, but open and straightforward about it; he lined his own pockets to be sure, but quite moderately, and everyone was very fond of him.' Erchinoald gave Fursey land to establish another monastery, at Lagny-sur-Marne.

Like Columba, Fursey built a reputation for extraordinary sanctity, promoted by, among others, Bede: 'Quitting his body from the evening till the cock crew, he was found worthy to behold the choirs of angels and to hear the praises that are sung in heaven.' Furthermore, Fursey was taken on an excursion by the angels, a sort of mystery tour of the cosmos. When they instructed him to look back he saw the four fires that would consume the world – falsehood, covetousness, discord and iniquity. 'These fires, increasing by degrees, extended so as to meet one another, and being joined, became an immense flame. When it drew near, Fursey, fearing for himself, said to the angel, "Behold the fire draws near me", and the angel answered, "That which you did not kindle will not burn you" ....'

Nevertheless, Fursey did not escape fully: he recognized one of the damned souls, whose clothes Fursey had been bequeathed, and since while on earth the man had acquired all he owned by way of ill-gotten gains, Fursey shared in the blame, that is to say the fire – which licked out and scorched him. 'Throughout the whole course of his life he bore the mark of the fire which he had felt in his soul, visible to all men on his shoulder and jaw; and the flesh showed publicly, in a wonderful manner, what the soul had suffered in private.'

In 650 Erchinoald took advantage of these legends when Fursey died on his territory. A shrine had tremendous uses – it drew people, motivated commerce, conveyed the sanctity of a kingdom; a cult made a region holy by association. Some nobles even created the cult of a man they had just martyred, on the grounds that they had been present when the soul was raised to Heaven. Twenty-seven days after Fursey's death, the mayor took the body and laid it in the porch of a church he was building at Péronne, until the church could be formally dedicated. When Erchinoald died, and Fursey's body was – predictably enough – found to be preserved from decay, Eloi, or Eligius, the same Bishop of Noyon whom Erchinoald had wanted to assassinate on account of his killjoy interference, saw the value of the cult of Fursey and squabbled with another local luminary who also wished to exploit the dead monk's santity. Eligius won, and in 654 set up a shrine in the shape of a small house at which the body of the monk was venerated for centuries. Fursey's peregrinations to East Anglia and then these wooded, watered valleys of northern France make him an ideal component in the composite make-up of the monk from Skellig Michael.

I followed the Somme to Ham, north of Eligius's see of Noyon, then turned north-east upstream with the river, to St Quentin. The history of early France is as difficult to unravel as an old path through these woods: to quote the historian Edward James: 'It has been said of France that governing a country with three hundred and twenty-five varieties of cheese is an impossibility, so, arguably, is writing its history.' My concern – discovering the past rather than writing about it – had to be contained at the modest level of any events or developments, or their relevant antecedents, that I could trace which could have had a bearing on my monk's journey; hence my route via St Quentin.

In the post-Roman, that is to say Gallo-Roman, structure of Gaul – where, even though the Western Empire had technically returned to Rome and been disbanded, much Roman political influence remained, and helped actively to govern – the invading Germanic tribes, Visigoths, Burgundians and Franks, dominated. The Visigoths had come into southern Gaul in 413 and established wide domination, with, eventually, royal palaces in Bordeaux and Toulouse. The Burgundians, under kings with names such as Gundioc and, later, Gundobad had, after invading Roman Gaul, reached agreements with Rome and in time established a capital at Lyon. The name 'Franks', as applied to the people in these parts of northern Gaul, no longer meant that they belonged to the Germanic tribe which had invaded by way of the Rhine. The term described the people living in the north of the country, who ruled territory other than that of the Alemanni in the east and the Bretons in the west. The Franks, a smallish group of families living along and at the mouth of the Rhine, eventually moved into a region of Gaul north-east of the main Roman military and civil supply road from Boulogne down to Cologne. The regime which came to be called Merovingian,

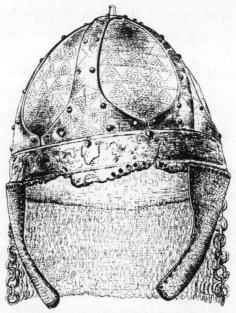

Seventh-century Frankish warrior's helmet.

through which the monk of 687 passed, began in the middle to late fifth century with the son of Merovech, Childeric, the first ruler who could with some authority be called 'King of the Franks'.

In the town of Soissons, through which I intended to drive after St Quentin, a Roman officer, Aegidius, had established his own state; Childeric assisted him in defeating the Visigoths in 463, and helped his successor in another successful battle against the Visigoths in 469. Both exercises meant that the Franks under Childeric not only had visible power, they also had the political wisdom to establish alliances with the Roman presence in Gaul, and Childeric's enterprise laid the foundations for the expansion of Frankish power.

Childeric emerges colourfully. According to Gregory of Tours, the sixth-century bishop and historian,

Childeric, King of the Franks, whose private life was one long debauch, began to seduce the daughters of his subjects. They were so incensed about this that they forced him to give up his throne. He discovered that they intended to assassinate him and he fled to Thuringia. He left behind a close friend of his who was able to soothe the minds of his angry subjects with his honeyed words. Childeric entrusted to him a token which should indicate when he might return to his homeland. They broke a gold coin into two equal halves. Childeric took one half with him and the friend kept the other half.

In due course Childeric did return, and married the queen of his royal Thuringian host who left her husband. She said to Childeric, 'I know that you are a strong man and I recognize ability when I see it', reports Gregory of Tours. 'You can be sure that if I knew anyone else, even far across the sea, who was more capable than you, I should have sought him out and gone to live with him instead.' She gave birth to Clovis, who acceded to the throne when Childeric died in 481, and whom some historians describe as the real founder of the Merovingian dynasty. With the same vigorous aggression as his father, Clovis continued to press the ascendancy of this collection of modest but determined Frankish tribes. He marched on Soissons in 486, an event described by Gregory of Tours.

'In the fifth year of his [Clovis's] reign Syagrius, the King of the Romans and the son of Aegidius, was living in the city of Soissons, where Aegidius himself used to have his residence. Clovis marched against him ... and challenged him to come out to fight. Syagrius did not hesitate to do so, for he was not afraid of Clovis. They fought each other and the army of Syagrius was annihilated.' Rapidly, Clovis imposed his will across the countryside and effectively created a Frankish dynasty. He eliminated all rivals to the throne and displayed himself imperially, using a combination of public show and deliberate cruelty to consolidate his power. He married a woman called Clotild, a Burgundian princess, who had been drive into exile during internecine power struggles. She, a Christian, ridiculed the gods whom Clovis worshipped, accusing Jupiter of bisexuality and incest. 'You ought to worship,' Clotild told Clovis, 'Him who created at a word and out of nothing, heaven, and earth, the sea and all that therein is, who made the sun to shine, who lit the sky with stars, who peopled the water with fish, the earth with beasts, the sky with flying creatures; at whose nod the fields became fair with fruits, the trees with apples, the vines with grapes, by whose hand the race of man was made ....'

Clotild then bore a son, whom she had baptized; then the child died, proving, it seemed to Clovis, that his wife's God was less powerful than his gods. She bore a second son who also began to ail, but according to Gregory of Tours, 'Clotild prayed to the Lord and at His command the baby recovered.' Clovis did not hold out very much longer against Christianity. In a battle against the Alemanni,

he was forced by necessity to accept what he had refused of his own free will. It so turned out that when the two armies met on the battlefield there was great slaughter and the troops of Clovis were rapidly being annihilated. He raised his eyes to heaven when he saw this, felt compunction in his heart and was moved to tears. 'Jesus Christ,' he said, 'you who Clotild maintains to be the Son of the Living God ... if you will give me victory over my enemies, and if I may have evidence of that miraculous power which the people dedicated to your name say that they have experienced, then I will believe in you and be baptized in your name.'

When the king converted, he renounced both his pagan ways and his aggression towards the Christians, and he began to 'adore that which he had once burned, and burn that which he had previously adored'.

The baptism of Clovis and his peoples, who also renounced their pagan deities, took place in Reims, at the hand of St Remigius or Rémy, who had welcomed Clovis on his father's death and written advising him on how to be a king.

The public squares were draped with coloured cloths, the churches adorned with white hangings, the baptistery was prepared, sticks of incense gave off clouds of perfume, sweet-smelling candles gleamed bright and the holy place of baptism was filled with divine fragrance. God filled the hearts of all present with such grace that they imagined themselves to have been transported to some perfumed paradise. King Clovis asked that he might be baptized first by the Bishop. Like some new Constantine he stepped forward to the baptismal pool, ready to wash away the sores of his old leprosy and be cleansed in flowing water from the sordid stains which he had borne so long.

The three-hundred-year line of descent from Childeric through Clovis, who died in 511, by then in command of all the territory between the Somme and the Pyrenees, led to two four-way divisions of the kingdom within 150 years. The second of these quadripartite divisions, Neustria, included a king called Theuderic III, the reason for my journey through St Quentin. At this point re-enter Erchinoald, who was kind to Fursey – or rather Erchinoald's son, Leudesius.

A brother of Theuderic III, another Childeric, had been made King of the Franks in the east, in Austrasia; his king-makers deposed Theuderic and exiled him along with the mayor of Neustria, a schemer named Ebroin, Erchinoald's successor. Ebroin's place of exile was the monastery at Luxeuil. The Austrasians then installed Childeric in Theuderic's place. St Léger, the Bishop of Autun, fell out with Childeric and was exiled to Luxeuil, where he found himself sharing a cell with his enemy, Ebroin.

When Childeric was murdered – along with his pregnant wife – for ruling too harshly, St Léger and Ebroin left Luxeuil and raced each other back to Neustria. St Léger got there first and set up in power with Leudesius, the mayor and son of Erchinoald. (In unravelling all this, Edward James's comment about writing the history of a country 'with three hundred and twenty-five varieties of cheese' strikes home with force.)

Ebroin gathered an army of followers, and, having agreed a treaty with Leudesius – who was godfather to his son – ambushed and killed him. Ebroin also captured St Léger, blinded him during torture, amputated his lips and dragged him, stripped, through the streets. Two years later he decapitated him. Ebroin thereby regained the mayoralty of Neustria and Theuderic was restored to its throne.

Then Ebroin was assassinated at night and his murderer, Ermenfred, prevailed upon a Duke of Austrasia, Pippin, to take an interest in Neustria, which had several changes of mayor after Ebroin's death. Pippin attempted negotiations and alliances with the Neustrians but eventually marched from the east across the countryside, into these parts through which I now travelled; be defeated Theuderic's forces at Tertry-sur-Omignon, a hamlet just off the Péronne–St Quentin road, about twelve miles due west of St Quentin. The battle took place in 687, the year in which my monk walked through. He could hardly have encountered a more significant conjunction of timing and location. The battle at Tertry became one of the most important moments in the emergence of the country we call France – ultimately it led to the eastern portion, Austrasia, having power over all the Franks, it sealed the eclipse of the Burgundians and the Neustrians, and it paved the way for the Carolingian empire of Charlemagne.

The prosperity here is tangible. St Quentin, though small, has an extremely busy air along its sloping main thoroughfare. The town possesses a river frontage where some boats had drawn up when I arrived, large flat barges with unmarked cargo, barrels and containers. The countryside has wide farms with mixed disciplines – cattle and tillage, and extensive drainage patterns, land worth warring over. The memorials on the hillsides, from two wars in this century alone, confirm the impression, though with different, international emphasis. All across this countryside the Franks fought their battles and carried on their ferocious feuds, against family members bidding for supremacy and against outside enemies. The power struggle did not distinguish between secular rulers and churchmen, many of whom, in the opinions of their later critics, merely used the garb of holy men as a dissembling stratagem, to create an impression of goodness. Then, when killed in the quest or manipulation of this power, they became holy martyrs, and their venerated shrines acted as assets in the aspirations of those continuing with the struggle.

The monk travelling towards Reims in 687 found himself in a civilization which had wide divisions – especially between those of royal birth and association, and those at the other end of the scale. The Frankish kings lived amid storybook colour and drama, as well as squalor and barbarism. At Tournai in the seventeenth century the fifth-century tomb of that first king, Childeric, was discovered. It contained enormous riches – a mounted crystal ball, a hundred gold coins in a purse, a hundred silver coins, gold buckles and bracelets, two heavily jewelled gold-inlaid swords, the king's battle axe and the head of his horse, and his signet ring bearing his face and motto – *Childerici Regis*. He was laid out in a brocade cloak, to which three hundred gold cicadas had been sewn, and their wings had been decorated with garnets. These were mistakenly interpreted as honey bees, and became so emblematic of France's early glory that Napoleon had them copied for his ritual decoration; some vineyards adopted the same emblem for wine bottle labels. Childeric's burial took place presumably when the king died in 481, or if it took some months to prepare – not unusually for such funerals, which sometimes took on the aura of local festivals – in 482.

Nearly a century later another royal person was buried at St Denis. Aged about forty and female, the body, discovered in a stone coffin during church excavations, had been laid out in a cloak of bright red, dressed in linen and silk, with stockings and garters. The clothing was decorated with two

Seventh-century brooch with niello, garnets and gold filigree.

circular gold brooches inlaid with garnets, two gold pins fixed her veil to her long fair hair, and she wore ear-rings and a ring with the word 'Regine'. A large belt buckle, ornamented with garnets and gold, had been laid in the coffin. Her burial date has been put at around 570.

Other graves – of Gallo-Roman notables, of Frankish chieftains and their children – contained sceptres, javelins and throwing axes (one etymological derivation suggests that 'Frank' derived from a Saxon word for their favourite tribal weapon, the throwing axe), silver spoons and other decorated cutlery, swords and scabbards with jewelled inlays, and hoards of coins. Long before the monk's arrival, immense wealth existed in the ruling classes, who relied upon a treasury-based economy: each family with power accumulated wealth in the form of money, after the Roman fashion, or precious metals, or jewels. (Interestingly, from the point of view of Christianity, which sought to change pagan ways, old traditions of burial persisted. One of the spiritual roots of the lavish style of burial with grave goods lay in the belief that the deceased had not died but had embarked upon a journey.)

Such opulence gives an impression of gilded halls, with languid courtiers playing lutes, while outside, in a land of poplars and doves, the royal subjects strolled, the peasants happy in their ruddy-faced work in the fields, the monks singing in tune with the choirs of angels, peace and prosperity reigning. The laws of a slightly later period give a different picture; where they address, for instance, such matters as compensation, they supply a vivid picture of the past. For example, a financial award could be made to a woman of no means who had been raped; in instances of multiple rape all the rapists, if found and convicted, each paid their victim an amount equal to the total fine. The gouging out of an eye required financial compensation, as did the severing of either or both ears – whether hearing had been affected or not – and likewise the slitting of nostrils, the tearing of beards, the crunching of testicles, the amputating of fingers, limbs or tongues were judged by the courts to be worthy of substantial compensation. The criminal law applied financial compensation to murder, too. A scale of values had been determined, assessing the amount of the fine according to the level in society of the murdered person. It included large fines for killing children under twelve and women of breeding age, smaller fines for freemen and smaller still for slaves, both trained and untrained.

Trials of suspects were conducted in the towns and villages at regular intervals, such as every forty days: witnesses testified before important local people who acted as magistrates, advised by members of the populace who knew the law. A suspect could take an oath, supported by witnesses testifying to his innocence, or he could undergo trial by ordeal. If a fire did not burn him, nor boiling water nor oil scald him, his innocence became obvious. If a suspect or a witness committed perjury, they fell upon the ground and fractured their skulls upon the church floor, or they remained transfixed, as if turned to stone, where they stood. Conversely, the law itself contributed to the everyday cycle of violence by handing down sentences which required barbarism – court officers sliced across major muscles and tendons, cut hamstrings and cartilages, branded foreheads with irons, burnt the sexual organs of men and women by smearing them with pitch and briefly setting fire to them. In the name of justice they castrated and mutilated, and usually, as from time immemorial, it was the poorest who suffered most from the law.

The poor abounded, too – in smallholdings, in slavery, in twilit lives, no fixed abode nor employment. For every garnet, pearl, bead and jewelled inlay found in a royal coffin, as many beggars could be found in the streets outside. Some took the guise of pilgrims, wearing chains on their scabbed and half-naked bodies, claiming they had been condemned to wander in penance for some hideous crime, usually against some authority so far away that the facts could not be checked, or begging for alms so that they could continue their journey to the shrine of some saint, or to some distant reliquary, in order to cure an obvious ailment like a hunchback, or a twisted leg, or a fat goitre, or blindness.

Thieves and rogues lurked in this huge sub-life which thronged the streets and the roads and which, supplicating, shuffling and wailing, blocked the gates of towns and cities. Fifty years after our monk passed through these regions, Boniface, the Englishman who became 'the Apostle of Germany', complained ferociously that the brothels of Europe had filled up with women who once had been holy pilgrims. Most of those brothels predictably located themselves where trade might be briskest – cheek-by-jowl with the walls of the large monasteries. At the gates of a city such as Reims, long established as a centre of politics and administration, these motley crowds milled, accosting those arriving and leaving.

The contrast with the life on Skellig Michael, or in the rich plains of Munster, must have struck the Irish monk with considerable force. The stories he heard in the monasteries had to do with sexual and political intrigue, adultery and fornication, drunkenness and treachery, all across society, both lay and religious. Exactly a century before, in 587, Gregory of Tours had described how

there appeared in Tours a man called Desiderius, who gave it out that he was a very important person, pretending that he was able to work miracles. He boasted that messengers journeyed to and fro between himself and the Apostles Peter and Paul ... the country folk flocked to him in crowds, bringing with them the blind and the infirm. He set out to deceive them by necromancy, rather than to cure them by God's grace.

This outrageous charlatan 'wore a tunic and a hood of goat's hair, and when anyone was present he was most sparing in his food and drink. When he was in private and had come to his lodging, he would stuff so much into his mouth that his servant could not keep pace with his demands ....'

Another such 'impostor' approached Gregory 'dressed in a short-sleeved tunic, with a mantle of fine muslin on top, and he carried a cross from which hung a number of phials, containing, or so people said, holy oils'. He went to Paris where a bishop at whom he swore had him locked up. 'His stock in trade was examined. He carried with him a big bag, filled with the roots of various plants; in it, too, were moles' teeth, the bones of mice, bear's claws and bear's fat.' In chains, he escaped from his prison and made his way to the church of St Julian, where Gregory went to pray. The impostor had, he recorded,

collapsed on the stone floor on the exact spot where I was due to stand. Exhausted and sodden with wine, he fell asleep where he lay. In the middle of the night I got up to say my prayers to God, quite unaware of what had happened. There I found him sleeping. He smelt so foul that compared with the stench which rose from him the noisome fetor of lavatories and sewers quite pales into insignificance. I was quite unable to step into the church for this odour. One of the junior clergy ventured forward holding his nose and tried to rouse the man. He was unable to do so, for the poor wretch was completely drunk. Four other priests went up to him, lifted him up in their hands, and threw him into a corner of the church which they then fumigated with 'sweet-smelling herbs'.

After St Quentin I went due south, picked up the Canal de St Quentin and followed it to Fargniers, Tergnier and Chauny. Near the hamlet of Abbecourt another canal, the Canal de l'Oise à l'Aisne, cuts off across country past Anizy (superb food in the village *relais* – similar culinary standards hallmark the villages of Suzy, Danizy and Lizy not far away) and, skirting the forest of St Gobain, I reached the Aisne somewhere near another little farming village, Bourg-et-Comin. I could have gone with the Aisne as far east as Berry-au-Bac to join the canal which links the Aisne to the Marne – since I intended to travel down the Marne valley anyway. The river, though, had begun to turn an unhealthy white from some chemical effluent dumped upstream, a most disagreeable sight and smell, and time had run against me – too much lingering on the wooded hillsides, too much exploring the village churches, not one of which I found bore any relevance

Baptistery of St Jean, Poitiers, begun in the fifth century and altered in the seventh.

to the period in which I was interested. With some regret I succumbed to the autoroute for the last few miles to Reims.

The Remii, a large tribe whose name survives in their chief city, sided with Caesar and in effect betrayed their neighbours, the Senones and Carnutes, who had made a tribal alliance against the Romans. Caesar called Reims Durocortorum, 'where he convened a Gallic council and held an inquiry into the conspiracy of the Senones and Carnutes. Acco, the instigator of the plot, was condemned to death and executed in the Roman manner' – meaning he was whipped with scourges and had his head cut off. The Roman influence in the city can be seen in some ruins not far from the champagne suburbs where the signs on the walls of their cellars – Lanson, Heidsieck, Dom Pérignon, Perrier Jouet – read like some litany of social extravagance. Monks, according to folklore, invented – or discovered – champagne, and immediately turned it to the praise of God saying he had permitted them to 'drink the stars'.

Reims had been a centre of Belgic administration. Clovis (a corruption of whose name gave rise to the esteemed regal name Louis) had elevated the status of the city by being baptized under the hand of St Rémy himself in 498, and one of his sons established a palace here. Before that, Christian bishops had established a diocesan basis at Reims as early as the third century. The oil of chrism with which Rémy anointed Clovis during the ceremony came (naturally enough) straight from the Dove of the Holy Spirit, and reposed in the Shrine of the Holy *Ampullae* until the French Revolution. Both Clovis and Rémy are commemorated in the carvings which festoon the Cathedral's exterior. That baptism of the Dark Ages made a direct bequest to Reims: generations of kings of France were crowned at Reims right up to the middle of the nineteenth century. Rémy's successors, the bishops of Reims, became powerful among the prelates of France and ruled over several diocesan fiefs in a wide rural radius.

On my journey into Reims, where from afar the Cathedral dominates the eye, I had none of the encounters of Gregory of Tours in 587. 'There was a serious epidemic of dysentery in the town of Metz. As I was hurrying off to have an audience with the King, I met on the road near Reims, a citizen of Poitiers called Wiliulf, who was in a high fever and suffering with this disease. He was already seriously ill when he set out, accompanied by his wife's son.' Wiliulf died, and his wife married again, 'Duke Bepolen's son. It is common knowledge that he had already deserted two wives who were still living. He was loose in his habits and libidinous. Whenever his desire for intercourse drove him to it he would leave his wife and go to bed with the servant-girls.'

A few years before the Irish monk came through here Wilfrid of York, who behaved like an intellectual fascist at Whitby and who had made many enemies in Britain, set out on a journey to Rome. Effectively he felt obliged to – his power and wealth had made him suspect among his fellows and he had many enemies. The Archbishop of Canterbury, Theodore, from

From the basilica of Sant' Apollinare Nuovo, Ravenna: a mosaic
depicting Theodoric's Palace, showing the typical architecture of
the Byzantine Empire.

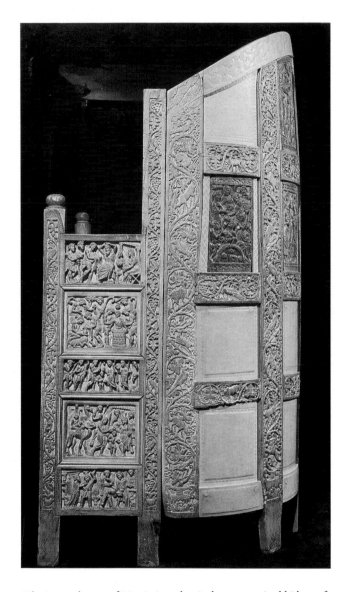

The ivory throne of Maximian, the sixth-century Archbishop of
Ravenna who consecrated San Vitale. The exquisitely carved
panels depict biblical scenes, such as the distribution of the loaves
and fishes, as well as motifs from the natural world.

From the basilica of San Vitale in Ravenna, consecrated by Bishop
Maximian in 548: the Emperor Justinian walks frowning to his
place of worship (above) and his wife, the 'actress' Theodora
(below), leads a procession of women to a portal under a raised curtain.

Mosaic depicting ships in the port of Classe, near Ravenna, from
Sant' Apollinare Nuovo.

Christ the Ruler, depicted in a sixth-century wall painting in the
Byzantine style: from the catacomb in Rome of St Calixtus, born a
slave, died pope and martyr.

Rome: the Forum. In the sixth century, St Benedict prophesied that
'Rome will never be depopulated by the barbarians but will be
reduced by the natural disasters of storms, earthquakes and
lightning, and will decline of her own accord.'

The church of San Lorenzo in Rome, built by the Emperor
Constantine.

...INVS · TENEBRAS · VT · LVCE · CREATA ... PRAESVLE · PELAGIO ... MARTYR · LAV...
...LATEBRIS · SIC · MODO · FVLGOR · INEST · TEMPLA · SIBI · STATVIT · TAM...
...VS · VENERABILE · CORP/VS · HABEBAT ... MIRA · FIDES · GLADIOS · HOSTILES...
...POPVLVM · LONGIOR · AVLA · CAPIT ... PONTIFICEM · MERITIS · HAEC · CE...
...ES · PATVIT · S/VB · MONTE · RECISA ... TV MODO · SANCTORVM · CVI · CRESCERE ...
...A · CRAVI · MOLE · RVINA · MINAX ... FAC · SVB · PACE · COLI · TECTA

SCS LAVRENTIVS · SCS PETRVS · SCS PAVLVS · SCS STEPHANVS · SCS YPPOLITVS

PELAGIVS · EPISC

...M LEVVITA SVBIST. IP IVRE TVIS TEMPLEIS...

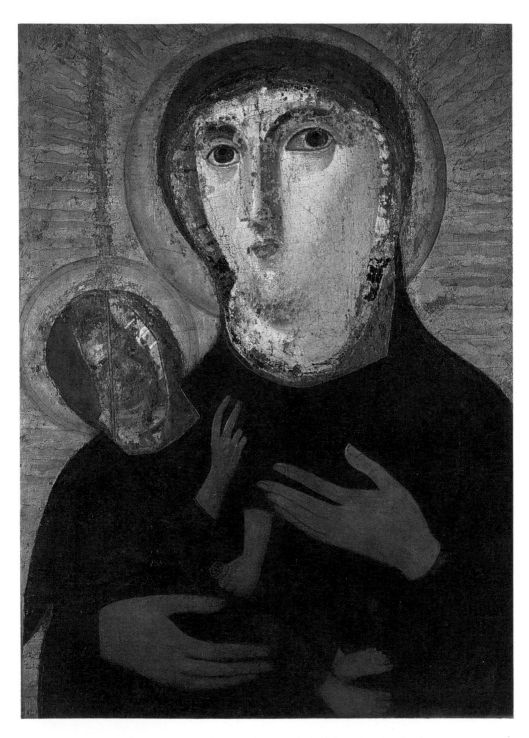

Sixth-century icon of the Madonna and Child from the church of
Santa Francesca Romana in Rome. The Byzantine influences are
characterized by the gold ground on which such pictures were painted.

Tarsus, ordained in 668, had set out for Britain on 27 May with the colleague who had nominated him, Hadrian, an African prelate. They sailed from Rome to Marseille, and journeying up through France came into the power of Ebroin, the powerful Neustrian mayor. He allowed Theodore to proceed but detained Hadrian, suspecting him of spying – such was Ebroin's power. (One German historian has suggested that Hadrian was detained because he was black.) In 674 Theodore deposed Wilfrid, who then set out for Rome in an attempt to go over Theodore's head and plead his case with the Pope himself. Eddius Stephanus, Wilfrid's hagiographer, who claimed that Theodore was bribed to depose Wilfrid, describes a sticky case of mistaken identity by which Wilfrid managed to continue with his journey through Europe, eight years before the Irish monk came through.

Wilfrid's enemies, finding more scope for their malice in the supposition that he was bound for Etaples and thence by the direct route to Rome, sent off envoys with bribes to Theodoric, king of the Franks, and the wicked Duke Ebroin. They were either to exile him for good or kill his friends and take all his possessions. The Lord freed him from his enemies as though from the hands of Herod himself, for just then Bishop Winfrid, who had been driven out of Lichfield, happened to be on the selfsame route. He fell into their hands and may as well have fallen into the lion's jaws, for they seized him, took all his money, killed many of his friends, and inflicted the extremes of misery on him by leaving him naked. Luckily for our bishop they had mistaken the first syllable of Winfrid's name.

Wilfrid fared better. Several years before, a young prince, Dagobert, with rights to an Austrasian Frankish title, had been exiled to Ireland. In the power struggles of the Franks, when Ebroin seemed to be gaining the upper hand after Childeric's death in 675, the Austrasians, in the territory between the Rhineland and Reims, remembered this boy. According to Eddius Stephanus,

His friends and relatives learnt from travellers that he was alive, flourishing and in the prime of manhood, and sent to Wilfrid to ask him to invite Dagobert across from Scotland or Ireland and then to send him over to them as their king. This our holy bishop did; he made him welcome on his arrival from Ireland and sent him back in great state with a troop of his companions to support him. The king did not forget such kindness. He now begged Wilfrid to accept the chief bishopric of the realm, Strasbourg, and when Wilfrid declined he sent him on his way with lavish presents.

Unfortunately for Wilfrid, his return journey proved less agreeable. While he argued his case in Rome,

His faithful friend King Dagobert had been assassinated by some treacherous dukes and (Heaven defend us!) with the bishops' consent. One of these prelates rode out to meet Wilfrid at the head of a mighty army, intending, had not God intervened, to rob the whole company, reduce them to serfdom or sell them into slavery, or to kill any who resisted. Our holy bishop was to suffer the anguish of being imprisoned and reserved for Duke Ebroin's judgement.

Wilfrid talked his way out of it: 'I raised him [Dagobert] up not to your harm but for your good, sending him to build up your cities, to put spirit into your citizens, to counsel your senate and, as he promised in the Lord's name, to defend the Church.'

Outside Reims, on a hill going to the south-east, some entrepreneur has taken a World War I fort and turned it into a tourist attraction. In the car park beneath, juggernauts and their drivers sleep, beside a caravan which sells *frites* and sends thick black fumes into the air. The melancholy fort does not merit a visit, unless to reflect on the lives of the men who fought and were terrified in these filthy trenches; otherwise the exhibit has little visual, military or historical value. From the hillside, though, the land stretches out in a fine vista, and opens the way through the Marne valley. For the long haul that would eventually take me to St Gallen in Switzerland I joined the Marne near Epernay, due south of Reims, beyond the Forêt de la Montagne de Reims, a high and pretty wooded area with the smell of sawmills.

'A force of Burgundians and Austrasians set out on instructions from Brunechildis and Sigebert, son of Theuderic, to meet Chlotar. When Sigebert had advanced into Champagne to the river Aisne, in the territory of Châlons-sur-Marne, Chlotar came to intercept him. ...' The slivers of Frankish history, from Gregory and Fredegar, give slim glimpses of sixth- and seventh-century life in the Marne valley – battles and forced marches and ecclesiastical provinces, powerful local churchmen, abbots and bishops vying with the landed gentry for power over the people. In any house of these parts, where a wandering monk sought hospitality, the talk was of rivalry and kingship and Rome and Paris and bishops.

From Châlons-sur-Marne, where they have a museum devoted to

Goethe and Schiller, I followed the Marne through heavy farming country and many flooded fields to Vitry-le-François. Not far from the town, still travelling south-east, a roadside sign advertised a very old rustic church, though the century was not listed. Taking a chance that it might be old enough for my purposes, I climbed the hill off the thoroughfare to a village as closed and suspicious as only French hamlets can feel. The French must be losing their sense of *la gloire*: time was when a twelfth-century church would not have been classified as *ancien*.

From Vitry-le-François the River Ornain winds north-east; at the village of Revigny I asked a man who spoke perfect English whether any local people took in guests, passing strangers, for the night and gave them bed and breakfast. He looked extremely doubtful, and called his neighbour, the wife of a council official who worked in Châlons. She said, no, hotels were best, that round there the people had become much too wealthy to do that sort of thing any more. I stayed in a small hotel in Bar-le-Duc, where I could join the Canal de la Marne au Rhin, which led me to the town of Void – by name and by nature – and then to Toul.

The land journeys of my monk's day were somewhat facilitated by the continued existence – unmaintained but still marked by the wear and tear of travel – of the Roman roads. The legends of natural disasters, repeatedly told to travellers, heightened anxiety. A hundred and twenty years earlier a landslide had occured on the banks of the Rhône. 'Here a curious bellowing sound was heard for more than sixty days: then the whole hillside was split open and separated from the mountain nearest to it, and it fell into the river, carrying with it men, churches, property, houses. The banks of the river were blocked and the water flowed backwards.'

Long after this and long after the Irish monk, travellers were warning each other of the dangers of these roads thronged with slave merchants and their numerous stock, outlaws in the woods and groves, bandits in the hills. 'We advise you to use the most vigilant precaution in choosing a road,' wrote Lupus of Ferrières in the ninth century, 'for, in the wake of troubles which have erupted, brigandage is committed in the realm of King Charles with impunity, and there is nothing surer or more constant than violence and rapine [this, in the legally aware reign of Charlemagne's son]. Therefore, seek out travelling companions whose numbers and courage will enable you to avoid groups of brigands, and if necessary, to repel them with force.' Above all of these, the threat of illness hung most menacingly. 'When the plague finally began to rage,' wrote Gregory of Tours,

so many people were killed off throughout the whole region and the dead bodies were so numerous that it was not even possible to count them. There was such a shortage of coffins and tombstones that ten or more bodies were buried in the same grave .... Death came very quickly. An open sore like a snake's bite appeared in the groin or armpit, and the man who had it soon died of its poison, breathing his last on the second or third day ....

The landscape ahead of me now had a different feel to it from the Somme valley, a drier lushness, even though you would never have thought so, so widely did the floods spread. The dangers of the landscape in the Dark Ages are difficult to exaggerate. In the forests of beech and oak which covered all these plains and hills only an occasional settlement had been cleared, with a terrace of vines and land for some grain and pasture. Wolves abounded – local rulers offered bounties for wolves and their cubs. Villages grew up around palaces or monasteries, which had been located at river crossings or at high vantage points, such as the hillforts once occupied by the earlier tribes who fought the Romans. (All over Europe, many of these heights have had continuous fortified life – for instance, the Hohenasperg outside Stuttgart still has the traces of the fortifications Hitler built.) Travellers who had to sleep in the countryside, who did not get to a village or a house before nightfall, cut or tore swatches of briar from the thick thorn hedges and surrounded their pallets or makeshift shelters to keep out the boar and wild dogs and bison, as well as the wolves.

Bridges suffered constant wrecking from heavy flooding, especially in areas like the Marne valley where the land lies low, or further east towards the Vosges where the spring thaws of the snows pelted torrentially down the mountain. Some bridges could be replaced temporarily – as Caesar had done – by stringing boats together, but if this remedy did not work travellers either had to go miles further, usually upstream as the river narrowed, to find a ford or a working bridge, or wait for weeks until the spates abated. The greatest dangers came from brigands, bands of outlaws who lived wild and rough in the tremendous shelter of the forests and who slaughtered whole trains of travellers. Pilgrims, especially the entourages of churchmen, caried reliquaries, sacred vessels, gifts for their episcopal or monastic hosts ahead. Many of these had been richly adorned, made of gold or silver or both, as jewelled as the grave goods of the Merovingian kings.

The town of Toul had a benign air from the moment I entered the walls, at about half past three on a sunny afternoon. It has the status of a city, even with a population of about fifteen thousand. It grew up in the Dark Ages – it had a sixth-century bishopric – some fifteen miles west of Nancy. The Marne-Rhine Canal, the Moselle and the Meuse all flow in, near or around Toul, and the town gets its pleasing aura of light from this watered land; the countryside is strutted with little bridges. The narrow streets have old houses and small closes, chapels with turrets, gorgeous doorways preserved from Gothic and Renaissance times, occasional fountains, an old gaol and cobbled walks. 'Eight or nine previous edifices', they will tell you, 'were built on the site of the Cathedral.' Toul has serviced a rich farming hinterland with sheep and cattle markets for a thousand years, and trades vigorously in the produce of its agriculture – leather, cheese, woollen cloth. In the year 612 the city and the open country nearby saw great Frankish strife between rival kings.

Museums in small French towns have a special appeal – so often deserted or dusty, and the descriptions of the exhibits may have been written in pen and ink, in a hand which can only have come from the local school. And they do not hesitate in their chauvinism; the artefacts bequeathed by or commemorating a local dignitary will also bear testimony to his great virtue. (A museum I visited in the Vendée some years ago displayed a pair of epaulettes which had belonged to one of the many military sons of the area – except that this one had 'the courage of a lion, the strength of a bear and the demeanour of an angel'.)

Nothing so boastful appeared on the highly professionally displayed exhibits in the Toul museum, but the museum guard, a tall young man with an imperial moustache to supplement his navy blue uniform, followed me around, pausing at every exhibit, perhaps offering a word or two, studying me, and when I exclaimed or showed some pleased expression, nodding in agreement. He had an air of confidentiality, and frequently looked around to see whether we were being followed. I did not understand much of what he said, but he made it perfectly clear that part of his duty, as he saw it, lay in ensuring that I admired the museum and approved of it.

Who could not? A short catalogue of the finds on display reads like the monk's bag of souvenirs (or the impostor's bag of tricks): remains of elephant, bear, hyena, all found in these fields; a bronze comb from the La Tène period of Celtic art; a whisper of Byzantium in '*monnaie de Constantin portant le symbole du Christ*'; a medallion bearing the perfect image of a faun; coins with Merovingian effigies; river transport in the shape of what looked like a prehistoric catamaran, two long Indian-type canoes, with outriggers; fingers of Egypt – in fragments, masks and shards of Isis and Rameses; the pottery and bronze proceeds of the *Temple Gallo-Romain de la côte Chatel*, excavated between 1966 and 1973; drinking glasses and bowls of the sixth and seventh centuries, simple but lovely, with patterns and ridges embossed like slipware along the blue glass.

Then came a moment of sharp excitement: in one exhibit, not claiming any special status or advantage, sat a cross with the same T extremities as the crosses on the shore by St Ninian's Cave in Galloway. It had not been enclosed in an arciform, but it had undeniably the same feeling, the same mood as those in Whithorn. Of course it could have come from a European archetype, or it could have been a cross whose form had been beloved of pilgrims, or a design standard among the early Christians, or it could have developed in the morphogenetic forces which dictate that unconnected people across the world behave in conventionally inexplicable similar ways from time to time. Whatever its origins it closed a gap for me, between the heartlands of eastern France and the west coast of Scotland.

The museum in Nancy – a city otherwise inadequate to my Dark Ages enquiries – occupies part of the Ducal Palace of Lorraine, and you require a map to travel through its many halls. Large it may be, but Toul could give it lessons in charm and archaeological clarity. In a corner of the museum an antique frame contains a picture of a wandering saint with an Irish name. Fiacre settled in Meaux, an Irish pilgrim, hermit and misogynist – he banned women from coming anywhere near his establishment and encouraged other monks to pray for the damnation of women. He possesses a most interesting set of efficacies. Born in Ireland around the turn of the seventh century and dying in France in 671, Fiacre is the patron saint of gardeners, taxi drivers – whose vehicles were called *fiacre*, after those which formed a rank outside the Hôtel St Fiacre in Paris – and sufferers from venereal disease and haemorrhoids.

Outside Lunéville, where from a terracotta house blue bed-sheets hung out of the top floor windows, the emptiness of the French countryside gleamed, with a glimpse of an occasional shiny-slated château turret through the trees. The Canal de la Marne au Rhin led me a pleasant run, on lanes and byways, then back to the main road to Sarrebourg, a smallish market town, with some industry on the outskirts, though not the typical *zone industrielle*.

I parked the car in a central parking zone in the middle of a main street on two levels and went to a closed market in the Place du Marché. Here only two stalls were operating, selling eggs and cheese – large drums of waxy Emmenthal. Sarrebourg heralds the first taste of great mountains – any European traveller of the day heard warnings of their 'snowy fields and glacial roads'. Snow lingered on the peaks despite the warmth, and the rivers poured in full spate with the melting which had begun. The bridge at Sarrebourg looks down on a calm flat weir; the island in the middle has a mild municipal decoration of some small box bushes. The legend on the wall of the Place du Marché says that Sarrebourg's history began in the third century – and little more. The landscape around becomes interesting where it begins to be mountainous. Convoys of army lorries shook the little shrines of local saints; through the trees peeped exciting hints of onion domes on village churches. As I looked up through the wooded slopes, my blood chilled slightly at the sight of swathes of trees snapped off during last year's avalanche.

❖

If Wilfrid had accepted the see of Strasbourg from Dagobert, would the debates in the European Parliament here have the urgency and abuse of Whitby? The members of the Parliament, highly paid, travel briskly between Luxembourg, Brussels and Strasbourg, according to where the Parliament sits. Few try their patience by attempting to hurry legislation through. 'We may not have terrific teeth but we can do a lot of damage with our gums,' said an MEP. The architecture of the parliament building at Strasbourg has a vaguely post-Albert Speer, Art Deco mood; busts of Adenauer and Churchill feature around the circular walls. Time, and the attitude to it, reflect the essential paradox of this unwieldy institution in search of an importance. Every speaker, except perhaps a *rapporteur* or a Commissioner, is limited to three minutes on a clock which lights up with huge red digital nipples, and when the three minutes are up a bunch of

Tombstone or panel from a choir screen, seventh century.

irritated asterisks begins to flash. It may then take nine years for any notice whatsoever to be taken of what those three minutes contained.

Despite many murmurs from the floor, we had no clear recommendation of when Summer Time should be standardized. Innovation centres, latter-day follies, would increase employment in the poorer regions of the EEC – but when? The size of aircraft that may be used between regional European capitals became the subject of a debate in which the Irish wanted 120-seaters but the British lobbied for their objection. When the time came for the vote, the Irish adjusted to the English demands, as they had at the

Synod of Whitby, though it seemed likely that the decision would take longer to implement.

Strasbourg, the birthplace of Gutenberg, inventor of movable type, has a perfect set of museums, one of which contains the history of the men who hunted mammals when this town was a thorn hedge. Another, the Musée d'Alsace, which has gathered together the life of the hill farmers, has an unrivalled collection of faience ceramics; when the town was called Argentoratum it had a Roman ceramics factory – archaeologists have found a tile from it, bearing the name of one of the earliest bishops. Otherwise, the most powerful reason for my monk's journey to Strasbourg was the means of getting out of the place – via the Rhine.

The foremost man among the Helvetii, in rank and wealth, was Orgetorix. In the consulship of Marcus Messala and Marcus Piso, he was encouraged by the hope of obtaining power to organize a conspiracy of aristocrats, and persuaded his countrymen to emigrate in a flock, telling them that they were the best fighters in Gaul and could very easily possess the whole country. They listened very readily to his proposal because their territory is completely inhibited by natural defences – on one side by the Rhine, that deep and very wide river, which is the frontier of Germany ....

When Caesar, in his writings, praised an enemy, it usually heralded their swingeing rout a few pages on.

Basel, a dull place, has some remains of his much-quoted Romans versus Helvetii. Somewhere up above Basel, in Granval, one of the high valleys, Germanus became a martyr just a few years before the Skelligs monk came up the Rhine. From an old Gallo-Roman family of Trier, Germanus embraced the new monasticism of Columbanus; when he came into this region he found a valley with very steep scree walls, a fast-flowing river and lots of pools, a place which, even though it already had some inhabitants, seemed ideally remote for the foundation of a monastery. He widened the passes at the northern and southern ends and came into conflict with the local overlords who wanted to possess the valley in order to expand their own Alsatian territories. Germanus resisted all encouragements, whether hostile or friendly, to leave the valley. A band of hired mercenaries from the Alemanni swept down from the southern pass, the rampaging warlord came in from the northern pass, and Germanus became a martyr, though he had been just as secularly involved in the battle for the valley as his enemies.

Sleeping and waking, I lost count of the number of stoppages on the Rhine between Strasbourg and Basel, just as I lost count of the steps to the monastery at Skellig Michael – though for different reasons. The journey took a long time, too long. Other waters promised richer rewards, notably the 'high inland lake', Constance, across which two distinguished Irish monks travelled on a famous *peregrinatio* – Gall, or Gallus, and remarkable Columbanus, who conducted his men up the Rhine with a rowing song:

> The driving keel, cut from the forest – look – travels the current
> of the twin-horned Rhine, and slides over the water like oil.
> Together, men! Let the sounding echo return our cry.
>
> The winds raise their breath, the harsh rain hurts us,
> but men's proper strength prevails and drives off the storm.
> Together, men! Let the sounding echo return our cry.

To the refrain, chanted in Latin – *Heia viri, nostrum reboans echo sonet heia* – this big-spirited, crotchety, fearless disciplinarian entered Switzerland, conquered the Alpine passes and the river rapids, just a part of the monkish swathe he cut across Europe in the early seventh century.

Columbanus was routed from the monastery he had founded at Luxeuil, a deserted Roman spa in Burgundy, capacious enough for his six hundred monks. 'By the fourteenth year [609] of Theuderic's reign,' wrote Fredegar in his chronicles of Frankish history,

the reputation of blessed Columbanus was increasing everywhere in the cities and provinces of Gaul and Germany. So generally reputed was he, and so venerated by all, that King Theuderic used often to visit him at Luxeuil humbly to beg the favour of his prayers, and as often the man of God would rebuke him and ask why he chose to surrender to mistresses rather than enjoy the blessings of lawful wedlock; for the royal stock should be seen to issue from an honourable queen, not from prostitutes.

Columbanus further offended the royal household by refusing their blandishments and gifts, 'but he thrust them away with a curse, saying "It is written, the Almighty reproves the gifts of the impious. It is unbecoming that the lips of God's servants should be polluted with that man's dainties ...."'

Theuderic's grandmother, the legendary Brunhild, a formidable and lascivious woman who was Queen Regent of the court of Burgundy, held the throne in trust for her grandson, and from that position of power she dissuaded all serious contenders for the young King's hand in marriage. She encouraged concubines, who bore children, and when Columbanus so energetically condemned these bastards the Burgundians expelled him. They hustled him across France, from the Vosges to the port of Nantes, and put him on a boat for Ireland. Contrary winds grounded the vessel on a sandbank at the mouth of the Loire, and Columbanus took this as a sign from God that his mission to convert the Europeans had not ended.

He found refuge at another court, out of reach of his former enemies, and told them off as well for their immorality and hedonism. Eventually he took to the Rhine and led the monks on their prodigious coracle journey, singing upstream from Koblenz right into Lake Constance, which he and Gallus crossed and came to the town that now bears Gallus's name. Columbanus's forthrightness and messianic insistence on attacking pagan shrines and smashing their icons had created a furore behind him. He alienated the Christian authorities as well, establishing monasteries – such as Luxueil, and many others – without reference to, or regard for, the wishes of the local bishops. He had a personality which flowed over the reaches of his task, and therefore made enemies of the calibre of Brunhild.

Gallus and Columbanus epitomize one breed of the Irish wandering monks in the Dark Ages. They both entered the holy life through a typical Irish route – born of good families, off fat land, from the cleared and populated provinces, they became novices at a typical Irish monastery of the late sixth century. Both men had come from the same community, that of Comgall in Bangor, County Down, on the north-eastern shores of Ireland. The young Columbanus encountered repeated sexual temptation from the local women: 'The old foe raised before him the desires of lewd girls and young women, of a sort whose voluptuous bodies and superficial beauty stir mad lusts in the minds of weak men.' Columbanus ran, literally. He left home and entered a monastery in the west of Ireland, and in time progressed east to Bangor and thence, in his mid-forties, to Gaul. Like Columba on his passage to Iona, Columbanus took the archetypal, messianic twelve followers, including Gallus, and went into exile.

He had the good fortune to gain the attentions of a biographer called Jonas of Bobbio. The hagiography, a common literary form of the era, the life of a saint, local or national, expressed in radiant terms, constituted one of the few vehicles for intellectual expression. The intention may have been a contribution to the sanctification process, and perhaps for the personal gain of the hagiographer – none the less, as a genre it has served a useful purpose in unveiling the otherwise very Dark record of these Ages. The writer typically began with a denunciation of his own equipment for the task, protesting that he was rural, perhaps, and certainly ignorant. As he warmed to it, the tools of the hagiographer – adjectives and adverbs of uninhibited praise, extravagant subjectivity, vitriolic denunciation of all his subject's enemies – assisted him greatly. No compliment remained in its closet, no praise seemed too excessive, fact and opinion became as one. Even though flickers of the light of the times shine through between the lines, the hagiographies must be regarded as somewhat untrustworthy in almost all but the reconstruction of atmosphere. Columbanus's chroniclers exceeded the customary pious applause and told, among other things, of the (inevitable) miraculously attended birth. About to give birth, his mother dreamed that the sun rose from her breasts in a brilliant light, signifying that the forthcoming child would illuminate nations.

In the fields which reach high up above the railway track from Zurich to St Gallen the early summer harvesting had begun. The mountainside acres, which might not be expected to yield much, held little bubbles of stacks in a closed circle, not so much hay as high grass. From time to time in the trees above the track large houses appeared, some with immensely tall flagpoles rising from the front lawn, bearing the Swiss flag, the white cross on a red ground waving in the wind.

Cattle the colour of grey malt grazed in fields that had no right being as lush on such high foothills; every slope was an incline; every incline a steep gradient. Occasionally a village church with a dome hinting at the onion-shaped churches of the Balkans, like those on the edge of the Vosges, emerged from the trees. Deep in heavily wooded ravines, clear rivers, sometimes torrents, appeared, and the windows of the tall shingled houses, beneath the manicured edges of the woods, seemed unnaturally high from the ground – of sufficient altitude, perhaps, to stand above the deep snows. Tall, high, deep, these were the words that kept time to the rhythm of the train. In the fields, occasional sheds made of wood contained neat stacks of firewood, or hay for the cattle to browse through should they need a change of flavour from the green, juicy grass.

In the Dark Ages a pathway such as this, which ran like a natural fault, a winding terrace, along the hill, held substantial perils – timber wolves, alpine cats and bears. Columbanus, walking in similar terrain, reached the mouth of a cave whose inhabitant, a brown bear, menaced him. Columbanus told him off, saying he wanted the cave to meditate in and worship God.

The railway station shone as clean as the legends of modern Switzerland. In the Altstadt, by the Cathedral, I came to the Gallus-Strasse and the collection of large buildings which stand at the heart and soul of St Gallen – the Stiftsbibliothek, the Abbey Library, a relict of the old Benedictine monastery and now protected by Church and State alike. An usher took my arm and led me back to the corridor outside the Library room where, ranged in rows along the floor by the wall, like quiet stalls of small furry animals, lay large slippers, galoshes made of felt, in grey and beige. Patiently he assisted me to slip a pair on over my shoes.

The Library at St Gallen has great beauty, on a par with, say, the Queen's College in Oxford. The surprisingly small room gives an immediate impression of brown chocolate-and-gilt baroque, in simple rounded designs, bookcases and bulging stacks, all pleasingly harmonized in a honey light, the floor now highly polished by the generations of felt clogs. The only manuscript on view whose work was remotely contemporary with 687 sat in a case in the middle of the floor, catalogued as 'Irisches Evangeliarum – geschrieben und gemalt von Iren um 750' – Irish Gospels written and illuminated by Irishmen about 750. It had the same faces that peeped out of the *Lindisfarne Gospels*, and the same perspective appeared in the figures – the impossibly long fingers, the cunning animal entrapped in long spars of design, more dots travelling down the length of the long designs, within the controlling lines and the foreshortened views.

The whorling and skeining along the margins might have come from the Northumbrian illuminations and, as with all the great books of the era, the colour bathed the prayers, gentle, lit with rich pigments made from plant dyes and drawn carefully by a loving hand with no long tradition of handwriting or painting. Where the tourists shuffled around in the big felt overshoes, the gilt and brown bow-fronted cabinets and cases contained lives, biographies – usually hagiographies – of Gallus and his successor Otmar, as well as copies of the Rule of Columbanus and Benedict. The Library relates generally to a much later period, when the incunabulae preserved here were created in the middle of the high period of European Christian manuscript illumination.

Gallus should have gone on into Italy over the Alps with the curmudgeonly Columbanus, but his age and a fever prevented him and he became a hermit, partly in response to Columbanus's admonition of him – despite his great age and sickness – for his tardiness, his not being able to walk over the mountains. 'Equal your equals' became a motto with Columbanus, and when monks did not work hard enough he condemned them to a year's illness: 'No man shall sleep until he has tired himself enough to sleep on his feet.' Gallus's punishment for being old and infirm specified that he could never celebrate Mass again during Columbanus's lifetime. He did, however, create enough of a reputation for sanctity in his cell near the town that now bears his name to draw many visitors, and to cause a Benedictine monastery to be established after his death.

Gallus refused all offers from local potentates of bishoprics or abbacies; a hermit he became and a hermit he stayed, discomfited by the punishment of Columbanus. A big and awkward man, he sometimes left his hermit's cell and walked, preaching, through eastern Switzerland. He outlived Columbanus by fifteen years, and when Columbanus died in Bobbio in 615 his monks sent Gallus the pastoral staff, a wooden crozier, which Columbanus had carried, as a sign that Gallus had now been released from Columbanus's censure.

Gallus lived gently in his hermitage. His legends also ran true to the traditional hagiographical form: he banished the demon of the waters who formed an alliance with the demon of the mountains to drive him out. He built his hut by the River Steinach because he stumbled and fell in the undergrowth, and the fall revealed to him a small, secluded and welcoming clearing on the riverbank. A bear roared into this woodland oasis; Gallus bade him put a log on the fire and rewarded the bear with bread (the legend appears on some versions of the town crest). Where Columbanus used aggressive denunciation and insistence upon rote and the most emphatic interpretations of the word of God, Gallus used persuasion and diplomacy and made friends, not enemies, of the ruling classes.

His quieter stature drew many to the place he lived in, and the numbers of pilgrims increased after his death as his reputation grew. His town keeps an awareness of him alive; hymns and songs composed in his honour after his death are displayed in the Library. His place in the canon of Irish monks who evangelized in Europe stands perhaps second to that of Columbanus, and above that of the many others: Colman, who went to Austria; Deicola, who dropped out of Columbanus's band when the great man was arrested and went to live in a hut in the forest that also grew to a monastery; Fiacre, whom I encountered in the museum at Nancy; Fridolin of Glarus; Fridian, who established his monastery in Tuscany at Lucca and became known as San Frediano; Fursey, whose memory is venerated in Péronne; Kilian, who also travelled along the Rhine and met a violent death in Franconia. The list grew so long that their presence in Europe in the sixth and seventh centuries can be counted as a cultural and religious invasion. Many of them still retain a place in the liturgical calendars of France, Italy, Switzerland and Germany as well as their native Ireland. They held on for as long as they could to the liturgy of the Celtic Church in matters such as the timing of Easter and the tonsure, and their influence in the monasteries continued, with reinforcements, for several centuries.

Downward the various goddess took her flight
And drew a thousand colours from the light.

VIRGIL *Aeneid*
trans. John Dryden

CHAPTER FOUR

THE MANY COLOURS OF THE LIGHT

IN DUE COURSE Columbanus had to leave Switzerland. Attacks made upon him and his followers had escalated intolerably, and he lost produce, animals, buildings and followers in burning, slaughtering raids by neighbours whom he had offended. He left with a bad grace: 'We found a golden egg, but it contained serpents,' he said as he hiked with his party – without Gallus – over the mountains into Lombardy and founded his last monastery at Bobbio.

The Library at St Gallen contains a ninth-century copy of Columbanus's Rule, the austere regime which he laid down for his monks. Those innumerable holy peregrinators who travelled routes like mine, even those who never made it to sainthood – the *Liber Memoriales* in Reichenau contains lists of pilgrims' names like a visitors' book – were expected to fall in with the regimen while accepting a monastery's hospitality. It seems inconceivable that a martinet such as Columbanus would permit anyone to stay under his roof who would not attempt to harmonize with his rigorous theme. Privation took precedence, a belief that stringency led to spiritual improvement, the only goal. He insisted on maintaining a heightened awareness of death, that the brief mortal span had been allotted only to enhance the glory of the Creator, and that to this end human beings while on earth had only the tenancy of a guest: 'Think about death. Then will pleasure and amusement, desire and luxury fall silent; then will the body lie rotting in the earth.'

The Rule stipulated a complete rejection of sensuality in all but the most unavoidable forms of sensations – such as a fine morning, or a succulent fruit – all of which in any case had to be turned to the praise of God. Columbanan monks had to eschew every personal possession: the Rule demanded asceticism in diet, alternating between plain food and fasting: 'The food of monks will be plain – cabbage, vegetables, flour mixed with water unto a biscuit, all to be consumed in the evening.' Work guided prayer and vice versa: his disciplines resembled those of earlier Irish monastic rules: 'The wise man's work is in his mouth; the unlearned work with their hands.' He also demanded utter obedience: 'Do not disagree, even in your mind, do not speak as you please, do not go anywhere with total freedom.' Punishment was the custodian of obedience and it played a leading role. 'Love the good men,' Columbanus proclaimed, 'but treat the dishonest harshly.' A monk who spoke at table received six strokes of a cane, as did a monk caught laughing at prayers. The man who did not sing as well as he should, even though 'through a cough', also received six strokes, and for gossip or lies or contradicting superiors the number of strokes went up to fifty. Penitential in stated intent, he therefore imposed upon all wills their contrary tendency: 'The talkative person is to be sentenced to silence, the disturber to gentleness, the sleepy fellow to watchfulness.'

The typical legends of miracles and sanctity grew up around Columbanus. He had a particular efficacy in the animal kingdom. As well as subduing the bear in the cave, he won a psychological victory over a pack of wolves who nuzzled his robe and departed; the squirrels warmed themselves on his breast, and he scarcely needed to sew the nets he and Gallus fished with in Lake Constance, since the fish leaped to his outstretched hand on the bank of the lake. He dominated his communities in the monasteries he founded at Annegray on the lower slopes of the Vosges, on the Burgundy–Austrasia border, at Luxeuil ten miles away and finally at Bobbio in Italy, on a tributary of the Po. His followers multiplied and, taking inspiration from his harsh but powerful style, spread his Rule on both sides of the Alps in France and northern Italy. Estimates compiled from his own works, from those of his biographers, from contemporary sources and from historians suggest that by the end of the seventh century up to sixty monasteries had been founded across France and Switzerland by Columbanan-trained religious. Two centuries later a writer, Adso of Montier, still humming with wonder at Columbanus's achievements, observed, 'And now what place, what city, does not rejoice in having for its ruler a bishop or an abbot trained in the discipline of that holy man? For it is certain that by virtue of his authority, almost the whole land of the Franks has been for the first time properly furnished with regular institutions.'

Columbanus wrote Latin verse, some of it in a light vein, and it was he who brought to the continent the Irish version of Easter and the Irish tonsure, both of which were later conceded at Whitby. His image survives powerfully – tall and aggressive, an impression of brute endurance traversing France not once but twice, exhorting his monks to row hard and rhythmically against the mighty current of the Rhine and finally stalking determinedly through the Alpine passes until he emerged into the sunlit plains of Lombardy in 612. For every monkish missionary of the Dark Ages and for many since then – even for modern pilgrims – the image of Columbanus remained inspirational, with his 'pastoral' staff (to ward off attackers); his holy book, one he was either writing or reading, borne in a leather bag that had been steeped in wax to make it waterproof; perhaps assorted relics either brought from Ireland or gleaned from shrines along the way; consecrated hosts in special small wallets for Last Rites or in the event of being only able to celebrate Communion; and, where exceptionally fortunate, a spare pair of shoes or sandals.

As I followed in my own monk's footsteps, obvious temptations threatened to divert me – to visit all the shrines of the Irish *peregrinii* in northern Italy: Lucca of San Frediano, Aosta where the 'man of wondrous power', Orso, became a bishop in the late sixth century, and Columbanus's Bobbio. But in the event the light coming from the East offered newer wonders, and I set my sights on Ravenna. I made careful enquiries about the possibility of walking through the Alps to St Moritz and down into Italy, aiming for Como and then Brescia. My admiration for Columbanus grew further: in his day only the fearless, the desperate or the mad braved the Alps – in summer the brigands made up for any of the dangers that had been alleviated by improved weather.

If it had been Columbanus's intention to found yet another monastery in line with the ambition stated in his own works – 'The salvation of many souls and a solitary spot of my own' – then he must have had a team of bearers, probably the monks themselves, and whatever his obsession with

Bronze gilt plaque, probably Lombard, *c.* 600.

the denial of possessions they required some luggage, which made for difficult hauling over the rocky passes. Yes, said a precise Swiss Alpine guide, ancient walking paths did exist in the Alps, very old, many centuries. Thirteen centuries? He said that if I was asking him had these been missionary paths, he did not know, since he was not a historian. Yes, it would have been possible, he said, to walk these mountains in those days. I asked him how long I should allow to make such a walk and he said, pursing his lips, 'To Brescia – or Como?' and looking at my clothes added, 'No insult, please, but you are not dressed well.' I took it that he meant not dressed appropriately for the mountains. 'With boots and pack it would take – for you – one month allowing for safety and resting.' Therefore in 612, in who knows what kind of weather, in robes and sandals, praying and chanting psalms along the path, Columbanus's journey shakes the imagination: he was in his early seventies.

From St Gallen, by a series of small trains and buses I joined the Rhine where it came out of Lake Constance, and stayed with it as far as Chur; more public transport, another of the long high trains, and down to Lugano, to a hectically busy station full of schoolchildren and university students on their way home for the weekend, and then a half-hour train journey to spend Friday night in Como amid a spectacular lightning storm. The banks of Lake Como range in terraces up to high bushy hills which are sprinkled heavily with white and ochre villas owning boats at the water's edge. Hitler wanted Como for his own toy when his conquest of Europe had been completed, just as he wanted Oxford as his capital of Britain. The Romans got to Como first and gave it an important regional position. The silk trade flourished here, and now the town's hotels had filled with textile and furniture people attending a fair in Milan. In the seventh century it sat on the edge of an area of turmoil, where the Lombards ruled.

'They shaved the neck, and left it bare up to the back of the head, having their hair hanging down on the face as far as the mouth and parting it on either side by a part in the forehead.' Paul the Deacon, born during the Skelligs' monk's lifetime, though thirty years after he passed through Lombardy, wrote *Historia Langobardum*, the widely influential history of the Lombards. 'Their garments were mostly loose and linen, such as the Anglo-Saxons are wont to wear [historians have claimed this as the first appearance of the term "Anglo-Saxon" in print], ornamented with broad borders woven in various colours. Their shoes, indeed, were open almost to the tip of the great toe, and were held on by shoe latchets interlacing alternately. But later they began to wear trousers over which they put leggings of shaggy woollen cloth when they rode.'

Paul, of vague birth date, somewhere between 720 and 730, was descended from an oppressed family of Lombard aristocrats, and wrote his great work at the end of the eighth century largely while living in the southern Italian monastery of Monte Cassino. He already had a reputation as a historian, as a man of good character beloved of his fellow monks – 'he had every good quality at one and the same time' – and with pronounced, and for the time revolutionary, ideas about the raising of young people. 'Act with moderation and do not birch them, or they will return to their beastliness after correction. A master who in his anger reprimands a child beyond measure should be pacified and corrected. Strong-arm methods may render a child naughtier than ever.' He also suggested that 'to make the children strong and satisfy their natural requirements of relaxation and high

Gilded copper relief, part of a Lombard helmet decoration.

spirits they should, at the discretion of their teachers, be sent each week or month into a park or some open field where they can play for one hour, under the watchful eye of their teachers.' On closer examination the suggestion does not seem at such odds with the kind of regime required in Paul's monastic environment: parents seeking prestige willingly gave up their children to God – and from very young ages, from four onwards. The acceptance of the child in the monastery school may have required a donation from the parents to the abbot, and in rich, successful foundations a visiting monk would have met whole groups of small children.

Paul's history of the Lombards refers to ancient historical sources such as Pliny in order to place the Lombards geographically, which he does as coming from the place he calls 'Scadinavia' (*sic*), but which in reality probably meant northern Germany, and indeed he does lump the Lombards together with Goths, Vandals 'and also other fierce and barbarous nations [that] have come from Germany'.

They migrated under the tribal name of Winnili, meaning 'the people from the meadowlands', or, in another attribution, 'those eager for war', and their name changed as they came south. 'It is certain, however, that the Langobards were afterwards so called on account of the length of their beards untouched by the knife, whereas they had first been called Winnili; for according to their language "lang" means "long" and "bart" means "beard".' After generations of depredating migrations, including ravages towards the east of Europe into the Hungarian Plain, they came in 568 into the valley of the River Po under their hero-king Alboin, who married the daughter of Chlothar, the King of the Franks. After she died Alboin married Rosemund, daughter of the slain king of another Germanic tribe, the Gepidae, in whose conquest Alboin had his finest hour – and it led to his last.

'After this king had ruled in Italy three years and six months, he was slain by the treachery of his wife, and the cause of the murder was this', according to Paulus Deaconus.

While he sat in merriment at a banquet at Verona longer than was proper, with the drinking-cup he had made of the skull of his slaughtered father-in-law, he ordered it to be given to the queen, Rosemund, to drink wine from it, and he invited her merrily to drink with her father. Lest this should seem impossible to anyone, I speak the truth in Christ. I saw King Ratchis [at whose court Paul was educated] holding this cup in his hand on a certain festal day to show it to his guests. Then Rosemund, when she heard the thing, conceived in her heart deep anguish that she could not restrain, and straightway she burned to revenge the death of her father by the murder of her husband.

Rosemund impersonated her own dressing-maid with whom the strong man of the court, Peredeo, 'was accustomed to have intercourse, and then Peredeo, coming in ignorance, lay with the queen. And when the wicked act was already accomplished and she asked him who he thought her to be', Rosemund revealed herself, thereby blackmailing Peredeo. 'Then Rosemund, while Alboin had given himself up to a noon-day sleep, ordered that there should be a great silence in the palace, and taking away all other arms, she bound his sword tightly to the head of the bed so it could not be taken away or unsheathed, and according to Peredeo [by now the adviser rather than the executioner in the matter] she, more cruel than any beast, let in Helemechis the murderer.' Against the man whom Rosemund had chosen to commit the actual deed Alboin defended himself with a footstool, 'but unfortunately alas! this most warlike and very brave man being helpless against his enemy, was slain as if he were one of no account, and he who was most famous in war through the overthrow of so many enemies, perished by the scheme of one little woman'.

The lives of the Lombards were daubed with blood: the least developed of the Germanic barbarian invaders, they pillaged and slaughtered to gain their conquests and then persisted likewise among themselves. If the term 'Dark Ages' means the darkness of slaughter, the darkness of the uncivilized, then the Lombards define it. Rosemund married her co-murderer Helmechis, who tried with her to usurp the kingdom, and when this failed they fled to Ravenna.

Then the prefect Longinus began to urge Rosemund to kill Helmechis and join him, Longinus, in wedlock. As she was ready for every kind of wickedness and as she desired to become mistress of the people of Ravenna, she gave her consent to the accomplishment of this great crime, and while Helmechis was bathing himself, she offered him, as he came out of the bath, a cup of poison which she said was for his health. But when he felt that he had drunk the cup of death, he compelled Rosemund, having drawn his sword upon her, to drink what was left, and thus these most wicked murderers perished at one moment by the judgement of God Almighty.

These ages darken further in terms of the information available. The picture of the Lombard period remains hard to grasp, especially in the flashing darts in which Paul, whose opinions and capacity for factual innovation not infrequently overthrow the historian in him, illuminates the landscape. He begins long passages of early, necessary but obscure history where legend and fact seemed indistinguishable with sentences worthy of a novelist rather than a historian: 'At this time a certain prostitute had brought forth seven little boys at a birth, and the mother, more cruel than all wild beasts, threw them into a fish-pond to be drowned....' Several chapters begin with tantalizing environmental snapshots: 'At this time there was a deluge of water in the territory of Venetia and Liguria, and in other regions of Italy such as is believed not to have existed since the time of Noah. Ruins were made of estates and country seats, and at the same time a great destruction of men and animals....'

Behaviour under pressure also casts fresh, if oblique, light on these untrammelled people. When the Avars over-ran the Lombards in a sharp and vicious war in the region of Venice about a hundred miles due east ahead of me, they impaled the rebellious Lombard queen – Paul calls her 'abominable harlot' – on a stake in the middle of a field. Her daughters, 'striving from love of chastity not to be contaminated by the barbarians ... put the flesh of raw chickens under the band between their breasts, and this, when putrified by the heat, gave out an evil smell. And the Avars, when they wanted to touch them, could not endure the stench that they thought was natural to them, but moved far away from them with cursing, saying that all the Langobard women had a bad smell.' Paul recommends this stratagem to all women eager for chastity in such circumstances.

Irritating road from Como to Bergamo, especially in the rain. These villages and small towns will soon be joined together as one continuous stringy suburb, peppered with ugly light industry and scabby, straggling smallholdings – unlike the precise farms and manicured allotments with their minuscule wood huts along the railway lines of Switzerland. The thunderstorm in Como last night came straight out of Wagner: long flashes along the lake right upon the huge peals which, as every child knows, means that the storm is raging right overhead. It seemed to travel up and down the lake at will, never leaving and taking off to where it belonged, in the hills and wooded mountains. Beyond Bergamo the hard decision again forced itself upon me – to leave the small roads of the people and take the motorways of the impersonal. It turned out to be the right decision. Only from the *autostrada* could I begin to see the prettiness of the distant villages, the walled small towns which had been obscured by their own local outcrops of buildings as I drove through them.

I stopped for lunch at Desenzano, a village on Lake Garda, twenty miles or so west of Verona. 'Verona further seems than India, Lake Garda is remote as the Red Sea', wrote the fourth-century poet Claudian Claudianus, and so it must have seemed from his beloved, triumphal Rome. Digressions in multiple choices now came dangerously close to irresistibility. For instance, the map reveals a famous and familiar name just off this eastwards route; is it the same place whose name graces the tables of the restaurants even in faraway Rome? In the legends another Irish pilgrim died of thirst on his road to Rome, and where he fell there rose by his head a great inexhaustible mineral spring – which in veneration they called San Pellegrino.

Only six others ate in the restaurant at Desenzano, all Americans, a party of four and an ancient couple who apologized that they could not eat their salad as the waitress had given them too much food. The water lapped hard and direct beneath the window, and the view changed as the mist on the lake came and went with the hydrofoil. When a new corner of the far distance appeared, picked out by a tranche of sun which managed to shaft through the midday gloom, the scene turned into an Edwardian engraving – crags appeared and the village on the far shore, with a small campanile and cream houses, looked like a miniature Venice. Now the light moved to another part of the lake and in a tint of mist and ochre revealed another group of houses much farther away. Hilaire Belloc on his *Path to Rome* observed, 'If one wanted to give a rich child a perfect model or toy, one could not give him anything better than an Italian lake.' The light changed again over the poplars on the little peninsula on the far side and the hydrofoil returned, disturbing the water. The wind had risen further and old people clutched at their summer hats along the *lungo di lago*. My thin green pasta had been heavily infiltrated by garlic; the local wine had the colour of nutty blood. The sun came out again for the umpteenth time revealing distant cypresses and houses behind tall walls, a brusque and confident contrast to the hard-edged, muddy survival, the bad-toothed, ill-clad ekeing endured by the citizens of the Dark Ages.

The light distracts so, even from the exquisite poetry of a local – the Mantuan, Publius Vergilius Maro. A poet's poet: to Cecil Day-Lewis, who translated him, he became 'that divine poet'; Pope called his *Eclogues* 'the sweetest poems in all the world'; Tennyson, 'at the request of the Mantuans for the nineteenth century of Virgil's death', wrote an ode which called him 'lord of language' and described him as the 'light among the vanished ages'. The Irish writer Helen Waddell, who in her own undoubted commitment to Christianity still applauded 'the pagan learning that flows like a sunk river through the mediaeval centruries', summarized Virgil's importance: 'the beacon to guide ages to come, the voice not only of Rome, but of all mankind, the pattern of history, and perhaps the pattern of eternity, translated into time'. Dryden called the *Georgics*, Virgil's four-volume poetic essay, written between 37 and 30 BC during the poet's thirties, 'the best poem of the best poet – he licked his verses into shape as a she-bear her cubs'. His poems praise the countryside, urge the reader to enjoy the fruits of these small hills where he was born:

Here spring is everlasting, and the summer extends into months not its own: the cattle bring forth their young twice a year, the apple tree produces fruit twice. There are no ravening tigers, or fierce brood of lions, no deadly nightshade deceives the unwary pickers, no scaly snakes writhe in immense spirals or coil in mighty sweeps over the ground. Think too of our many lovely cities, the toil of men's efforts, all those towns we have built heaped high on their sheer cliffs and the rivers gliding beneath their ancient walls.

Virgil achieved superstar recognition in his own lifetime, lionized by both plebs and patricians; his verses were found scratched on the walls of Pompeii. He left these parts early, went to Rome and then Campania. His connection with the land continued to fuel him, and even though the heroic/historiographic *Aeneid* became his monument, the boyhood spent on the farm near Mantua permanently illuminated his vision. This road, heading towards Verona and Ferrara and his own Mantua, is still his landscape: the sun flooded it as I drove through, hoping that the monk from the Skelligs had picked up even a snatch of Virgil, perhaps the *Aeneid*.

By 687, though, any traveller would have been much more concerned with the political situation, since his safety depended upon it. At least among the Franks sides had already been taken, and intelligence would have been available as to which kingdom or mayoralty would receive such a traveller favourably. (Wilfrid, for instance, was assured of an uncertain welcome, to say the least, among the Austrasians in eastern Francia, especially having been offered the see of Strasbourg by their upstart, the returning carpetbagger Dagobert.) Here, in these hills and plains, uncertainty rather than unity reigned. The Exarchs of the Eastern Roman Empire, Constantinople's lieutenants, still administered Ravenna – but the Lombards lived nearby. They too lived a little nervously. Shortly after my monk's time a Lombard king promulgated a law requiring all travellers from north of the Alps to carry a passport. The Lombards lived in terror of invasion by the Franks – justifiable terror, as it eventually turned out.

In 687, 119 years had elapsed since Alboin led the Lombards with their luggage into the Po valley. They entered a land which had just experienced a period of enormous and troubled flux. While Rome had been building its Empire, tribal movement downwards from Scandinavia, to escape a climate changing from temperate to harsh, had taken place continuously for five centuries – before, and for a time after, the birth of Christ – and the wanderers settled in eastern Germany. The Goths among them continued to travel, and along the Black Sea in the second century AD they split into roughly two groups, Ostrogoths and Visigoths. From further east came a barbarian people of Mongol derivation, the Huns, who first of all routed the Ostrogoths, and then put pressure on all the peoples who had settled in Germany. Those of western Germany, Angles, Saxons and Franks, migrated westwards, and since they had come of settled, farming stock tended largely to conform to their tribal model. Those of eastern Germany, Burgundians (who became part of emerging Francia), Gepids and those who defeated them, the Lombards, Goths and Vandals, continued, like their herdsmen ancestors, to roam.

All – in due course – exerted pressure on the Roman Empire. In order to escape the Huns the Visigoths crossed the Danube in 376, at first with the agreement of the Emperor Valens, whom they had petitioned; then they defeated him at the battle of Adrianople in 378. 'By the care of his attendants', wrote Edward Gibbon,

Valens was removed from the field of battle to a neighbouring cottage, where they attempted to dress his wound and to provide for his future safety. But this humble retreat was instantly surrounded by the enemy; they tried to force the door; they were provoked by a discharge of arrows from the roof; till at length, impatient of delay, they set fire to a pile of dry faggots, and consumed the cottage with the Roman emperor and his train.

Adrianople was the most crushing defeat the Romans had suffered in almost six hundred years. It taught them that the old Roman infantry legions were obsolete – from now on Germanic cavalry were to dominate the army – and led increasingly to the policy of buying off the barbarian invaders that was eventually to procure the downfall of the Western Empire.

In 410 Alaric the Goth – whose earlier invasion from the east had so shaken the Empire that 'even the legion which had been stationed to guard the wall of Britain against the Caledonians of the North was hastily recalled' – actually besieged and brought to her knees 'the queen of the world', the brilliant city of Rome itself. 'Many thousands of the inhabitants of Rome expired in their houses, or in the streets, for want of sustenance; and as the public sepulchres without the walls were in the power of the enemy' – how Gibbon enjoyed lurid moments – 'the stench which arose from so many putrid and unburied carcasses infected the air; and the miseries of famine were succeeded and aggravated by the contagion of a pestilential disease.'

These two events, Adrianople and Alaric's onslaught on Rome, stand out like giant markers on the downward path of the Empire, which the invaders began to dismantle. Increasingly throughout the fifth century, and especially after the death of Attila in 453, those Germanic tribes who had been under constant pressure from Attila's Huns emerged as forces in their own right. Since they no longer had to fight Attila they could now afford to flex their muscles in other directions of their own choosing. The Angles and Saxons began to expand forcibly in Britain. The Franks took control of northern Gaul, with the Burgundians a considerable presence in Alpine and Rhône territories. The Vandals crossed the Rhine in 406 and went on to rupture the Empire's demeanour in North Africa. By 455 they commanded the North African shore of the western Mediterranean and sailed up the Tiber with their well-fed fleet to attack Rome. The Visigoths had penetrated as far as south-west France and had established considerable power in Spain.

The Empire which they were all attacking had substantially changed its complexion from the traditional Rome-based institution of the early Caesars. Rome still remained an emblem, and attacks upon it still constituted havoc, but the administration was conducted from elsewhere. In 325, nineteen years after his soldiers had hailed him 'Caesar' at York, Constantine embarked upon becoming 'the Great'. He assessed his wide Empire shrewdly, reasoned that Rome's effectiveness as a central post of command had diminished. It was no longer a swift, convenient supply and power base to defend borders as far-flung and diverse as Persia, the Rivers Danube and Rhine, Gaul, Britain, Spain, Syria and Africa. The Empire needed two imperial centres, East and West. In the East he chose a fishing town called Byzantium. In the West – though Rome still played a part – Milan evolved as the Empire's headquarters. When Alaric attacked Milan, the Western Emperor Honorius, young and fearful, moved his headquarters in 403. According to Gibbon,

The recent danger to which the person of the emperor had been exposed in the defenceless palace of Milan urged him to seek a retreat in some inaccessible fortress of Italy where he might securely remain, while the open country was covered by a deluge of barbarians. On the coast of the Hadriatic, about ten or twelve miles from the most southern of the seven mouths of the Po, the Thessalians had founded the ancient colony of Ravenna, which they afterwards resigned to the natives of Umbria. The adjacent country, to the distance of many miles, was a deep and impassable morass; and the artificial causeway which connected Ravenna with the continent might be easily guarded or destroyed on the approach of an hostile army.

It was in Ravenna that Caesar had prepared his troops for the crossing of the Rubicon, four and a half centuries before.

For seven years Honorius had the powerful assistance of his mentor, the general Flavius Stilicho, himself a Vandal, who contained Alaric and even defeated him when he tried to take Verona. As a result of what Gibbon calls 'the obscure intrigues of the palace of Ravenna' – it was whispered that he was too soft on his fellow Vandals – Stilicho fell from favour with the Emperor: 'the respectful attachment of Honorius was converted into fear, suspicion and hatred', and Stilicho was beheaded in Ravenna in 408. Honorius, ever more beleaguered, unable to rule effectively without the strength of his trusted senior adviser, died of dropsy in 423.

In 476 Odovacar or Odoacer, a German officer of barbarian descent, raised an army which deposed the Western Emperor, Romulus – at which point Odovacar suggested to the senate that the Western Empire did not now require an emperor. He therefore chose to rule himself, and the moment of his assumption is pointed to in history's shorthand as the moment at which the Western Roman Empire ceased to exist. 'Odoacer', says Gibbon, 'was the first barbarian who reigned in Italy, over a people who had once asserted their just superiority above the rest of mankind. The disgrace of the Romans still excites our respectful compassion, and we fondly sympathise with the imaginary grief and indignation of their degenerate posterity.'

Odovacar did not rule well: during his reign 'the country was exhausted by the irretrievable losses of war, famine and pestilence.... After a reign of fourteen years Odoacer was oppressed by the superior genius of Theodoric, king of the Ostrogoths; a hero alike excellent in the arts of war and of government, who restored an age of peace and prosperity, and whose name still excites and deserves the attention of mankind' – and whose presence can still be felt, I am told, in the gleaming town ahead of me, Ravenna.

On a sunlit Saturday afternoon, past those distant brown villages which threaten to spill down the side of their hills, I arrived in the only town I have ever wanted to steal, the beautiful cobbled place that claims Virgil. I prefer the town's Italian name, Mantova. Round a bend in the road a dome appeared, some spires, that terracotta again, cinnamon impressions, then a bridge, then a lagoon from which the light rose brightly.

Until this point in his journey the Dark Ages traveller from Ireland had seen little enough in stone, and then not well-built: the White House of Ninian in Galloway, occasional Roman ruins across Britain, a monastery or two in Ireland or England, overgrown villas of Gallo-Roman luminaries in France, a Merovingian palace rising above the wood and wattle houses of Reims, but nothing which prepared him for the extent and richness of the architecture of the south, of the Adriatic and then the Mediterranean. Mantova began to fill that void.

The Cathedral in Mantova has a self-possessed air which it has had for several centuries, due to a relic entrusted into its care. When Jesus Christ died on the cross a Roman officer ascertained death with a spear, causing one of the famous wounds of the stigmata, the condition which some devout people believe they may have inherited. In their bodies appear the replications of the wounds of Christ – the hands, the feet and the long wound in the side caused by the spear of Longinus.

Not long after Good Friday the centurion converted to Christianity, so moved did he feel by the events of the Crucifixion, and he had within his possession the blood he had gathered at that consummate moment on Calvary. Longinus took his place in the general hagiographical development of Christianity within the first six centuries or so; he became 'the good Roman'. The blood he collected, which also entered the Holy Grail legends, came to Mantova, was enshrined within what became the Cathedral and annually forms the centre of religious veneration.

The Cathedral at Mantova has been undergoing restoration, and despite the beautiful and monumental coolness does not offer the same opportunities for contemplation as it otherwise might. Outside, the colonnades of the palaces and their courtyards do not urbanize the place so much that you forget the rhythms of the surrounding countryside, the small hills, the light off much water. In the streets, grass sprouts from the less busy cobbles, and a canal, with fronds and moss at the water's edge, slips between the terracotta alleyways, beneath the sloping roofs with their crazy gingerbread tilts. Those who built this exquisite town and who commissioned the wall paintings and large frescoes with a cast of local people – heavy faces, brooding and watchful, swarthy-lidded eyes, rich fabrics in gold and red and black, modest but wealthy head-dresses on the gentlewomen of the court – gave their gift to the world long after 687. However, the power of towns such as Mantova derives from the political upheavals of that time, when the history of Italy changed yet again within a century or so, and the foundations of a disunited state were laid by the Lombards a century after Theodoric the Ostrogoth.

Theodoric, son of an Ostrogothic king settled in the Danube valley, was enabled to overthrow Odovacar because the Emperor Zeno in Constantinople both hated Odovacar's domination in Italy and feared Theodoric's growing military power, which could be turned against Constantinople. Zeno achieved the by now typical Roman compromise – he turned both his greatest threats inwards upon each other. He promised that if Odovacar could be defeated Theodoric could rule Italy. In 493, after a campaign which lasted almost five years, Theodoric won, and at a treacherous banquet in Ravenna murdered Odovacar. Theodoric then governed Italy, outwardly in the name of the Roman Emperor, though when he had coins struck bearing the Emperor's head he had his own likeness or initials placed on the obverse. Although he gave himself the title of *Rex* – taking care not to stipulate the precise jurisdiction of his kingdom – and although he wore the purple robes exclusive to an emperor, Theodoric did not publicly overstep the imperial boundaries in a way that the Emperor in Constantinople would have found provocative or intolerable. He attempted to rule well, in a more civilized fashion than might have been expected from a 'barbarian' – he had after all been educated for a decade in Constantinople and was a Christian, though of the Arian heresy, like most of the Goths.

In the beginning his reign achieved widespread popularity by harnessing Roman thought and skill to the energy and drive of the Goths. He embarked upon a building programme to restore the towns and morale of Italy, both of which had been crumbling, and he attempted remarkable legal unification – 'one law and equal discipline' for Romans and Goths. He shrewdly had in his entourage Flavius Magnus Aurelius Cassiodorus, a Calabrian whom he appointed as his secretary and mouthpiece. Cassiodorus was able to promulgate the thoughts of his master in an enhancing way. 'Understand', Cassiodorus reported Theodoric as declaring, 'that men progress not so much by bodily violence as by reason, and that those who deserve the greatest praise are those who excel others in justice.' Such statements – particularly in a culture which had, in its 'barbarian' incarnation, glorified violent action and disconsidered intellect – amounted to revolution. It meant that by the late seventh century, when the Irish monk walked through, at least one barbarian kingdom had some experience of trying to apply the mind instead of the sword, an uncommon experiment among those tribes which had invaded from Germany.

In fact, the level of thought which Theodoric tried to bring to bear upon the governance of Italy – he attempted, initially at least, to create a one-nation, post-barbarian state – would seem remarkable even if it had not been established in the brutal and turbulent context of the times. As well as Cassiodorus, he had another great official who made an equally powerful contribution to his social and policy ambitions – Anicius Manlius Torquatus Severinus Boethius, who had spent eighteen years in the academies of Athens attempting, as Gibbon suggests, 'to reconcile the strong and subtle sense of Aristotle with the devout contemplation and sublime fancy of Plato'.

Boethius had contemplated 'the geometry of Euclid, the music of Pythagoras, the arithmetic of Nichomachus, the mechanics of Archimedes, the astronomy of Ptolemy and the logic of Aristotle ... and he alone was esteemed capable of describing the wonders of art, a sundial, a water-clock, or a sphere which represented the motions of the planets'. He then devoted himself to public service, in which his fine mind and eloquent voice were 'uniformly exerted in the cause of innocence and humanity'. He became a consul in 510, but times had not become so civilized that he did not fall foul of his king. He was condemned for alleged treason and 'magic', wrote in gaol five volumes *On the Consolation of Philosophy*, was tortured – a cord was tied around his head 'and forcibly tightened till his eyes almost started from their sockets' – and was beaten to death in 524. Later he was canonized as St Severinus and his Latin paraphrases of the Greek philosophers became the sole source of Greek thought in the Middle Ages. Cassiodorus (perhaps through prudence) fared more fortunately and retired to a monastery which he founded.

Theodoric's reign, more ambitious than successful, created divisions and eventually became riven with typical suspicions. Boethius and Cassiodorus had tried to persuade their master to introduce laws which moved government continually towards the principle of equality. He did not, however, succeed in uniting Romans and Goths: complex legal divisions remained in which both factions obeyed laws held in common but administered by separate Roman and Gothic judiciaries. The army was exclusively Gothic, and Romans were forbidden to bear arms. Religious division played a part too. Those Goths who had been Christianized had embraced Arianism, a belief originated by an Egyptian priest called Arius who, in the fourth century, argued that since Christ was the Son of God he was therefore junior to God and therefore less than God. Furthermore, since Christ had a stated birth he did not possess the necessary quality of eternity, as the whole True God had no beginning and no end. The matter appeared to be resolved at the Council called by Constantine at Nicea in 325, which declared Christ, in the Nicene Creed, 'God from God, Light from Light, True God from True God, begotten not made' – therefore to true Christians 'one in substance with the Father'. In theory that declaration settled the question: in practice entire peoples, such as Theodoric's Ostrogoths, retained the Arian beliefs. Theodoric, though he did not contest the Catholicism of the Romans, built churches in which to worship in the Arian creed, further emphasizing the divisions he had hoped to heal.

Finally, after some years of considerable unease between Theodoric and the papacy, and between Theodoric and Constantinople, where the Emperor was persecuting those who remained Arians, Theodoric ordered, on 30 August 526, that all Catholic churches in Italy should be assigned to the Arians. He died, though, on the very day he made the decree.

From Mantova I took the road to Ferrara, a different town altogether, more fortified, more self-conscious, higher and not as humble. The road between the two wanders contiguous to the Po. Across the meadows beyond Ferrara, standing by the river, the warm terracotta towers of village churches appear, like local jewellery – satellites to the place which has been called 'the most interesting town in Italy', some say 'in Europe'. Ravenna overwhelms, overstimulates, and the pleasure redoubled for me in the certain knowledge that the glories on display certainly bathed the eye of any seventh-century travelling monk – the basilica of San Vitale had, after all, been consecrated on 17 May 548.

Honorius abandoned Milan for Ravenna in 403 – I have placed the monk from the Skelligs on the streets of Ravenna in 687. In those two and three-quarter centuries, the fortunes of the city swung from Roman to Gothic and back again. Theodoric, in Gibbon's words, 'preferred the residence of Ravenna, where he cultivated an orchard with his own hands'. His tomb there is one of the treasures of the place. During the years that followed his death, years in which Ravenna was still in the power of Theodoric's successors, Justinian (of whom more later) began his huge campaign to recover the lost ground of the old Roman Empire. In 539 Belisarius, Justinian's brilliant general, captured Ravenna and accepted the Goths' surrender. Justinian, and after him successive emperors in Constantinople, appointed exarchs to rule Ravenna, and while the Byzantine Empire retained its swathe across Italy Ravenna remained a keystone city, though

The Basilica of San Vitale, Ravenna.

hemmed in north and south, if not westward. The exarchs were in office, therefore, in 687, with directions to answer unambiguously to the Emperor in Constantinople. This remained the position – despite some local insurrection – until the Lombards under King Liutprand captured the city in 727, marking the beginning of the end of Ravenna's Byzantine commitment.

The glories to be seen in Ravenna today were created over a long period – from the earliest days before Honorius to the high point of Justinian's triumphal Empire. As you look up from street corners, the high skies give a hint of the broad lakelands and the Adriatic. Within walking distance of the Piazza del Popolo the compact town holds great treasures – churches, tombs, baptisteries, of which at least five or six stand as greater or smaller wonders of the world, a status attributable wholly to Ravenna's mosaicists. It is wondrous that so much technical expertise and colour could have been available as early as the fifth and sixth centuries: marvellous, too, that patrons existed with sufficient perception to commission the work, even if vanity may have been one of their motives.

Honorius's death in 410 placed his sister, Augusta Galla Placidia, in eventual command. Captured when the Goths sacked Rome and forced into marriage with a Gothic chieftain, she was restored to her stature in Italy in 416. Now widowed, she fled Ravenna to escape an incestuously inclined, dropsical brother. Her uncle in Constantinople, Theodosius, the Emperor of the East, gave her shelter and then restored her to Ravenna. Here she acted as a protector for a quarter of a century, and during this period the mosaic artists flourished in this ancient town. One of the earliest buildings in Ravenna commemorates the name and memory of Galla Placidia. She died in 450, in Rome it is thought, but in her lifetime a mausoleum was built in Ravenna which followed that spiritual theme of the ideal relationship between the body and the soul – a plain building outside, with the interior most beautifully decorated, in this case with mosaics.

Not a large building – not quite forty-two feet long, and thirty-three and a half feet wide; twenty people would fill it beyond comfort, though the arched roof offers breathing space. Two hundred lire in the meter outside give light, and the mosaics are revealed. The cupola of the mausoleum has been schemed as a starry sky, the floor of Heaven. A quartet of figures commands the base of the dome – a man, an ox, a lion and an eagle, the symbols of Matthew, Luke, Mark and John, each resting upon, or rising from, a whisper of red and white cloud. The roof of the entrance to this cruciform building has the traditional shape of a barrel, and it consists of one continuous mass of gold and white flower-stars, crystal-snowflaked on a background of the blue sky of early night. Not a square inch has been left unadorned. The mosaicists covered all the surfaces in a profusion of reds and blues and yellows and greens and browns and whites – primary colours and rainbows and many, many shades and hues, brilliant as well as subtle.

The Good Shepherd in gold robe with blue stripe sits among his sheep, wearing thonged sandals, on a small outcrop of gold-tinged rock, with fern and palm: the sheep have fat tails. Bronze deer lower their antlers through friendly undergrowth, pairs of doves drink from bowls or contemplate a small fountain. Peter and Paul, the Lamb of God, flowers, fruits, birds, crosses, shrubs and abstract forms greet every turn of the head. One continuous basket of flowers arches right across the barrel shape where the entrance becomes the centre of the building, while another arch of a long, geometric frieze reaches the same distance – and all in colours that might have been mixed yesterday.

Some stone sarcophagi stand on the floor. Even though the mausoleum has been named after Augusta Galla Placidia, the folklore and the history agree that she may have been buried in Rome. This building immortalizes her protectorate and her patronage, and the brilliant interior has the same smell as the beehive huts on Skellig Michael, a dusty smell of stone. Not many other comparisons have validity – even though the mosaics in the mausoleum also honour the Christian tradition, with no hint of the Eastern influence that was to come from Byzantium. Skellig Michael did not, it would appear, get a monastery for at least a century after these buildings were consecrated. The two places shared the same tradition, of a Christian imagery and canon, the leadership of Peter, the intellect of Paul, the iconography of the Lamb of God and the Good Shepherd, the doves, the fountains, the scriptures and the echoes of the natural world. So that if a wandering scholar from Ireland marvelled at these images he none the less connected with them and received them, regardless of Arianism or Whitby or any of the other intellectual difficulties which shivered through the early Church.

Across the courtyard from the mausoleum stands Ravenna's showpiece, the basilica of San Vitale. Built a century after the mausoleum, it bore the name of a gentleman of Bologna, Vitale, who took instruction in Christianity from his slave – both received the honour of martyrdom. To an even greater degree it commemorates Justinian, then at the height of his success. The basilica, made of thin russet bricks on layers of lime mortar, has an air of strength and calm, bulking large and multi-layered, on levels of fat, short towers, angled roofs of curved tiles. At the core rises a high octagonal central building, and a bell-tower stands a little away and higher than the rest. The arched windows harmonize in shape with the main door, and the stepped levels give an impression of bulky security whose peaceful mood comes from the colours of the brick and the lime mortar. Work began in 527 and finished in 548. The mosaics of the interior were designed to be included as part of the architecture.

Such range and accomplishment, technical and thematic: Moses receiving the Ten Commandments on Mount Sinai, with the angels announcing

Carved stone capital from San Vitale, Ravenna.

the birth of Isaac to Abraham, while Sarah stands by the door, smiling, a finger held to her lips in a shushing surprise for her husband; wreaths of flowers, leaves and fruit, pears, apples, soft fruits, with the fantails of the quartet of peacocks symbolizing the Resurrection; the bread and wine sacrifice of Melchizedek and, opposite him, across the white-and-gold-clothed altar, Abel, holding a lamb aloft in offering; Moses approaching the burning trees; Abraham preparing to sacrifice his beloved son Isaac; St Vitale receiving the crown of martyrdom; the Emperor Justinian walking with a frown to his place of worship, accompanied by equally concerned priests and alert soldiers bearing shields and spears.

Under billowing canopies of blue and red, along a green lawn, the Empress Theodora leads a stunning procession of women, all of whom have aware expressions, and by a fountain they prepare to enter a portal under a raised curtain; they wear jewels and robes falling in folds, and their faces have seen pleasure. Angels surround and support Christ, hawks and ravens strive to keep their balance, trees grow tall and bushy and green beside the walls of Bethlehem and Jerusalem, which have been studded with green jewels. The birds of the air and the beasts of the field, heron, ibis, dove, tortoise, lamb, terrifying lion, confident ox – all appear, composed and immortalized in these tiny squares, *tesserae*, of stone, glass, serpentine, marble. The dull red brooch which the Emperor Justinian wears to fasten his cloak on the right shoulder is in fact a large, fashioned chip of cornelian.

In small dark corners, beneath the breathing of the eight high arches and their noble columns, the treasures continue, and in the broad weaves of the mosaics each glance divulges something new, some fresh detail, with a gasp of charm, some small nudge of sheer joy – like the tortoise slogging his way towards the legs of the stork, or the anger on the face of the lion or the smile of Abraham's wife. San Vitale amounts to a gift – of a different world, created by highly skilled workmen, who worked long hot hours, exempt from taxes, and all paid for by a sixth-century banker who lived nearby and who called every day to see how his munificence progressed. Virgil, in book four of the *Aeneid*, recalls Iris, the unsleeping goddess whose persona dwelt in the rainbow, down which she glided with her messages from Zeus: in the context of the mosaics the description fits Ravenna, the last capital that the Roman and Byzantine Empires had in the West:

Downward the various goddess took her flight
And drew a thousand colours from the light.

Blinking in the sunlight outside the basilica, but still within the embrace of San Vitale, you will see the Museo Nazionale, which, housed in a wing of the former Benedictine monastery, has a vast display. Even by taking account only of those exhibits which, in terms of their period, fit the purposes of my (that is to say, the monk's) journey, it would still be impossible to consider all within a week – or, with any thought, a year.

Begin with finds consistent with Celtic burial rites, Iron Age weapons, bronze clasps and fasteners – they could have come from the museum in Dublin or the one on the Rock of Cashel, with the Hallstatt sword and the gorgets. A monastery might have found them and kept them either as curios or in its own small collection, gathered out of antiquarian interest for the wonder and education of the monks, for the visual benefit of the *scriptorium*.

Progress to the Hermaphrodite Room: among many fifth- and sixth-century images it contains the sculpture of Hercules capturing the Hind of Ceryneia, a year-long Labour to bring back this wonderful creature with her hooves of bronze and horns of gold. Other rooms display textiles and tunics from the seventh century, which the Irish monk would have seen on the people in the streets and markets of Ravenna (some walking along with eucalyptus leaves held to their noses to abate odours); lead pipes bearing the Emperor's name, still in use then – one of Theodoric's reforms aimed to restore the water supplies in towns where the pipes had become dilapidated or overgrown; the carved covers of books, secular and religious, in use in Ravenna during the seventh century – a visiting monk, a guest or assistant at worship, could have handled these; a green wine jug, or a violet one, a cloudy drinking cup with a rim of raised indigo glass as a grip running lazily around the circumference; gold coins, used as payment to the artists who decorated San Vitale.

A corner of the museum belongs to the early Benedictine cloister. The shaded rooms off the cloister contain the shards and jigsawed restorations of *amphorae* and terracotta vessels. Where the grass in the cloister square grows long, burnt and untended various monumental fragments line the walls of the paved walks. They include stones bearing Roman inscriptions; representations of the Lamb of God; chunks of sarcophagi; wistful images of children taken from first-century tombs; a carpenter's gravestone which shows him using an adze. One tall stone the colour of oatmeal has an image which recurred on this journey and in circumstances far away from that hot dusty morning by the salt-marshes of the Adriatic – the cross with extremities like the letter T carved in the rock at Ninian's Cave on the west coast of Scotland, and which appeared again in a glass-fronted museum showcase in Toul.

The other treasures of Ravenna take days to inspect. The basilica of Sant'

Apollinare Nuovo, whose high, cylindrical bell-tower led some scholars to believe that the architecture of Ravenna had caused or influenced the Irish Round Towers, has long marching friezes of mosaics as brilliant as those of San Vitale. Magi, a procession of virgins, apostles, a series of miracles – including the raising of Lazarus, portrayed as a white mummy staggering from the tomb – angels, Pilate washing his hands and the Last Supper, martyrs, harbour walls made of wide bricks, square-rigged ships in the port,

Sant' Apollinare Nuovo, Ravenna.

doves, stars and ferns – all gleam on a gold background. They run the length of this peaceful, three-naved, colonnaded building with twelve columns on either side of the main nave. The octagonal Arian Baptistery shows a naked Christ, standing waist-high in transparent water, being baptized by John the Baptist. The image recurs in the Neonian Baptistery, behind the Cathedral by the Piazza del Duomo; this building, also octagonal, erected around 380, predates both San Vitale and the Mausoleum of Galla Placidia. The mosaics here have, if anything, a greater intensity than in the other buildings, as if the artists crammed in everything they thought of, lest they might never have such good ideas again – swirling festoons of acanthus leaves, bordered with broad stripes of red and green, inhabited by apostles in gold or white tunics, altars, peacocks, icons and crosses.

The fifth-century basilica of St John the Evangelist, built by Augusta Galla Placidia in thanksgiving for being saved from shipwreck on her return to Ravenna, has no elaborate mosaics of the period: a later abbot removed them all in the fashionable interests of renewed austerity. The fifth-century basilica of St Francis has a flooded crypt through whose clear waters tantalizing fragments of mosaic appear. The sixth-century church of St Agatha, small, pretty, often overlooked, has mosaics of leaves and roundels, broken and dispersed in earthquakes and wars.

At the edge of the town Theodoric's Mausoleum, a powerhouse of cut stone, has the same T cross of Whithorn, this time housed in a circle, unlike that in the museum cloister and therefore more reminiscent of Ninian's marigold cross, though not as free and arciform. The tomb was built on the orders of the King in 520. They roofed it with a single vaulted block of stone, 108 feet in circumference and weighing 300 tons, quarried on the Istrian peninsula across the gulf of Venice and brought south-westwards on a specially built raft to Ravenna. A split in the stone prompts the legend of Theodoric's sudden death. Lightning struck him while he stood within the mausoleum – revenge, they said, for his ordering the surrender of all the Catholic churches in Italy, that very day, to his own Arian co-religionists. Variations on the legend say he fell off his horse during a thunderstorm, was swallowed by a volcano on whose crater's rim he stood, or died of a seizure after he cut open a fish he was about to eat and found the head of an enemy within. His 'palace' stands on the Via di Roma, a much-altered and later building, constructed, it is suggested, on the site of the earlier imperial residence where Theodoric grew his orchard.

The energy which Ravenna once had may still be seen. It lies within the long marching friezes of apostles, virgins, martyrs, lords and ladies on the immediacy of that gold background, and the peacocks and the doves by the little fountains. It parades among the geometric borders in red, green, blue, gold and indigo. It inhabits the animals and the sacrifices and the jewelled walls of Bethlehem, and that extraordinary fan-splay of colour in blue, gold, red and yellow by a window opening in San Vitale, so savagely uncompromising in its execution, so restful in its achievement.

Ravenna confirmed an observation made by Samuel Butler in *Erewhon*:
'Time walks beside us and flings back shutters as we advance; but the light
thus given often dazzles us, and deepens the darkness which is in front.'
Theodoric has been blamed by some historians for ushering in the Dark
Ages in Italy by attempting to implement a cultural reformation which he
misunderstood and finally misplaced, thereby causing confusion and
eventual regression where he wished for progress. Whether or not the
allegation seems unfair, the truth of the Ages' Darkness lay ahead of me.
Between Ravenna and Rome lay many beautiful places, lands strewn with
walled towns in terrain to which many travellers have lost their hearts.
Useless to me, though – their eminence did not bud until long after the
seventh century. The road ahead coiled unflinchingly towards Rome, then to
the south and finally to Constantinople – irresistible to a traveller who had
seen Ravenna and therefore had tasted Byzantium.

The early medieval history of the regions between Ravenna and Rome
remains largely obscure. The pleasures of drifting through Tuscany again –
the hot days and warm nights, and the vines and the sun on the honey-
coloured rocks, the lizards and the cypresses and the fragments of Roman
ruins in the long grass off the main roads – did not include a detailed record
of how the people lived. The local history of the period never, so far as seems
known, got written down, and the national record did not fare much better.

During the sixth century Justinian's desire that all Italy should be
liberated from Gothic rule had clearly been misfounded. The 'barbarians'
from whom he sought to 'release' Roman citizens formed an integral – and
integrated – part of the society, politics and administration of Justinian's
Empire, both East and West. Theodoric's efforts to unite the peoples of
Italy had not been entirely without effect, and had clear practical
developments. Generations of Germanic soldiers had served and went on
serving in the Roman Empire and in its Byzantine continuation. This fact
involved Germanic officers and men in the regaining of lost imperial
provinces – but from Germanic tribes. In other words two lots of German-
descended armies fought each other, one to retain, the other to regain slices
of the Roman Empire.

For example, when Justinian's successful general, the Armenian eunuch
Narses, campaigned against the Goths, he raised an army of 5200 soldiers

from among a Germanic tribe, the Lombards (he also had 3000 Huns and several thousand Persians.) On 15 June 552, Narses left Ravenna and after a short and unstoppable sortie south along the coast marched south-west along one of the major Roman roads, the Via Flaminia which ended at Rimini. After raising some local soldiery he set out to engage with Totila, the rampagingly successful Gothic king. In the battle which followed at Tagina, near the modern town of Nocera, just east of Perugia and Assisi,

The Mausoleum of Theodoric, Ravenna.

Totila was killed – despite his display of chased gold armour, purple banner and lance-slinging comparable to that of a drum major. In victory the Lombards behaved savagely. They raped the women and girls, often on the altars of the churches, and had to be sent home – whither they marched in triumph – not so much for their atrocious behaviour as for the fact that they had emerged as a force to be feared and Narses wanted to be rid of them.

Fourteen years later, in 566, large areas of Italy, especially in the north, suffered what Paul the Deacon calls 'a very great pestilence . . . there began to appear in the groins of men and other rather delicate places a swelling of the glands, after the manner of a nut or a date, presently followed by an unbearable fever, so that upon the third day the man died'. It cleared the landscape, as people fled from it or died where they stood. It emptied the villas and the towns; corpses lay where they fell, their relatives so weak that the effort and infection of any funeral rites proved fatal. 'You might see the world brought back to its ancient silence', wrote Paul, 'no voice in the field, no whistling of shepherds, no lying in wait of wild beasts among the cattle, no harm to domestic fowls. The crops, outliving the time of the harvest, awaited the reaper untouched; the vineyard with its fallen leaves and its shining grapes remained undisturbed while winter came on.' In its disturbed imagination the surviving fragmentary populace heard the muffled blaze of ghostly trumpets and the tramp of thousands of marching feet, as if a phantom army was marching across these very fields I now saw being sprayed by huge machines to keep the crops green and the earth moist. Every village that stood here then became its own mausoleum.

On the night of 14 November 565, Justinian died at the age of eighty-three; the old man's last words appointed his nephew Justin as his successor, and in the morning the new Emperor of Constantinople and his wife Sophia received the applause of the people. The eunuch Narses, who had eclipsed the Goths' power in Italy, had lost his great admirer, and in the next couple of years the envious took over. They whispered against him, pointed to the size of the treasury he had accumulated, noted how well he had done out of his victories. The jealous words reached the ambitious Empress Sophia, who let Narses know that she felt he should be in the palace, in a eunuch's rightful place, carding the thread for the handmaidens' sewing. The piqued Narses has been accused by history of then inviting the Lombards, whose ferocity he had remembered from the battle against Totila, to leave the Hungarian Plain and come to Italy – hence Alboin's arrival in 568 with a huge auxiliary force of Saxon allies. On the heights of Monte Maggiore or Matajur, fifteen miles north of the modern town of Cividale, directly inland from the Gulf of Trieste, the Lombards stood and gazed down into wealthy Italy. Here, the animals grew so large that fifteen men could lie on the hide of one wild ox. The Gothic wars, the plague and resultant famine had debilitated the people. The Lombards, with their long, plaited hair and their pale complexions now red with sunburn and their total lack of niceties, met little enough resistance, and any spirit shown by the Italians was crushed with speed.

The Lombards became a major influence in Italy. They ranged as far as Sicily and even though they never – due to their own disunity – established a single Lombard jurisdiction over the entire country, they commanded large tracts, especially in the north where they first arrived. Later they created individual duchies, such as Spoleto and Beneventum, which became powerfully independent of that original, establishing Lombard kingship. In the year 600, the Lombards ruled all of Italy from the Gulf of Trieste right around the southern edges of the Alps to the Mediterranean and almost as far as Rome. Ravenna, Perugia and Rome stayed in the hands of the exarchs of the Eastern Empire, a thick tranche weaving from the Adriatic to the Mediterranean and sandwiched on the southern side by the Lombard dukes of Spoleto and Beneventum, while Naples and the heel and toe of Italy remained imperial.

The monk's route took him down through the middle of the lands governed by the Exarch of Ravenna. To the north and south lay Lombard dominions. I travelled likewise diagonally across the vertebrae of Italy. In the forest at Caprese, 'the place of the goats', they have restored the house of Michelangelo's birth. (An accidental occurrence: his mother's carriage overturned in a lightning storm and the young Buonarroti arrived a little early.) These areas through which I passed, which came to their full stature in the Renaissance period – towns like Sansepolcro, Anghiari, Città di Castello, which was once levelled by Totila – had in their seventh-century antecedents monks who also acted as local government officials and made returns to Ravenna for the greater government of the Empire. The Church in those days had begun to play an increasing role in the affairs of state: Justinian's Pragmatic Sanction of 554 and his great commissioned Corpus of Civil Law restructured the administration and involved local bishops in the appointments of magistrates and other officials, as well as passing responsibility for such civic details as weights and measures to local priests.

I lost count of the number of times I crossed the Tiber. Maps give a poor impression of how seductive the river becomes as it wanders by Perugia in Umbria and snakes fatly down to Rome. Perugia's domination of the countryside persists: it was taken by Totila, and the later Perugians dug catacombs into the rock beneath their town and used them as siege bases in the many wars against their neighbours. Now the Italians have installed startlingly congruous escalators in these honeycombs to take visitors up into the part of the town where cars are not allowed.

The nights were hot down here, full of mosquitoes from the banks of the

Tiber, assisted by another fly, long-legged and buzzing. In me they found a banquet and feasted night after night. The owner of one small hotel in Narni raised a sympathetic eyebrow when I asked for a mosquito net. He suggested that the bedroom's metal shutters should be kept closed – which seemed illogical, since he advertises the wonderful view down into the old town from the high points along the river, and in any case the heat of the night required wide-open windows. Did they not drain the swamps around here in the early Middle Ages because the mosquitoes killed off appreciably large segments of the local population?

The smallholders still use oxen to pull the plough here. The river appeared again – in the fields off the main roads, through the single streets of dusty yellowed villages that do not even appear on the map, in the acres of tillage divided by raised pipes running like cords across the country. Whether at that moment the stream deserved to be called the Tiber did not matter – it became broader, capable of being followed vaguely down to the outskirts of Rome.

The sacred killing grounds of the Christians, the bloody theatres of the gladiators, the *ad limina* visiting place of the bishops, the consistories of the cardinals, the black smoke, the white smoke, the cry of '*Habemus Papam*', the seminaries of the Irish, the city as Fellini's raddled landscape, the mother-whore of Moravia's writings – a quarter of a million books have been written concerning Rome. When Rome falls the world will end, said Byron: in the 1920s, James Joyce said Rome reminded him of a man 'who lives by exhibiting to travellers his grandmother's corpse'. By 687 Rome had fallen a long way down: even by then it was a city of ruins.

In the fifth and early sixth centuries, while Theodoric ruled, enough of Rome's Caesarean grandeur remained to justify the description of a city, having twenty-four Catholic (as distinct from Arian) churches dedicated to the apostles, two basilicas, over three hundred streets, two Capitols, eighty golden and sixty-four ivory statues of gods, bakeries, reservoirs of clean water, food supply depots, theatres, baths, brothels, a full infrastructure of maintenance, police and tax officials, servicing over 46,000 'ordinary'

The shrine at Delphi: the pillars formed part of the massive temple,
outside which stood a statue of Apollo seventy feet high.

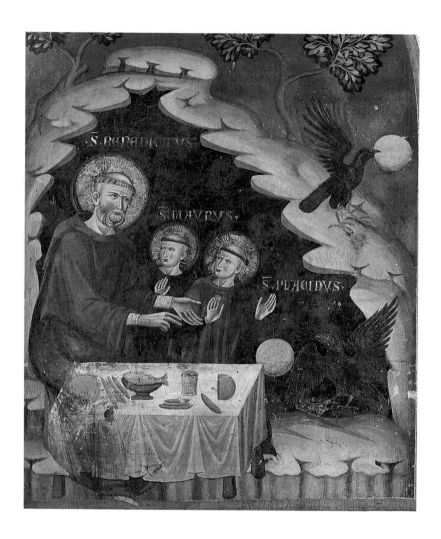

St Benedict: a thirteenth-century representation of the sixth-century powerhouse who reformed monasticism and created universal principles of religious community life.

Mohammed taming a lion: a sixteenth-century depiction. Such miraculous control over wild beasts was also ascribed to Christian holy men such as Columbanus and Gallus. The prophet is shown veiled, a convention preferred by many artists.

In the seventh century tribal invaders from the north, Bulgars, Avars and Slavs, added to Islamic pressures on the Byzantine Empire from the east. Eleventh-century depictions of events from these turbulent times.

ορμευατο φυγην μετα τουτρακων και μακεδονων κατατοδεξιον μεροσ τ' ρονιζομενον κρα
τ ηρτουσ χθεσ' ων και πολιφορου εργα ζεσθαι τουσ σαρακηνων. κατα τα' τευμβε τονπροκο
πιον ητα ρ ομενον μετατων σκλαβηνων και δυτικων. υποτων εναντι ασπε ζεσθαι ω
πεμφ θεισ οδε ςαρατον στρατηγου πολιτειαν τουσ προσωπη σ διατην προτιμη σαμενην φιλονεικι
αν. εκλινε προσ προτην τοκατατον προκοπιον μεροσ. καιαυτοσ εκεινοσαπε σφαγη ρ ρωι
κοσ εσφαγη σαμενοσ. και καιταντον τονοχυρω ματεσσω

ό πρόκοπιος   αγαρκηνοι

δε αισων, τελευτικαι επρονα τερ γασασθαι λαμπρον. και το εκ τησ σεριοσ συσκιασαι συνιπαρα
τ' υχμα. το οικειον στρατευμα λαβων. και τουτ' αστευ τ' ευτασ εκ τησ προ τουσ πολιν τα τομενων
ι τον τον προκο πιον συνεπαραλαβων. το ταρ αυτοσ καιφρονετι ταρα το ρα αρη ρων καπε χυ
μερον εξ επολιορκησε. και πανταντα τον εναντι λαω εξ ηνυδρα τ' οσ δι οσατο

ΕΓΝΟΥΣΔΕΠΙΛΑΤΟΣΟΤΙΕΚΤΗΣΕΞΟΥΣΙΑΣΗΡΩΔΟΥΕΣΤΙΝΑΝΕΠΕΜΨΕΝΑΥΤΟ
ΠΡΟΣΗΡΩΔΗΝΟΝΤΑΚΑΙΑΥΤΟΝΕΝΙΕΡΟΣΟΛΥΜΟΙΣΕΝΤΑΥΤΑΙΣΤΑΙΣΗΜΕΡΑΙΣ

ΤΟΤΕΛΕΓΕΙΑΥΤΩΟΠΙΛΑΤΟΣΟΥΚΑΚΟΥΕΙΣΠΟΣΑΣΟΥΚΑΤΑΜΑΡΤΥΡΟΥΣΙΝ
ΚΑΙΟΥΚΑΠΕΚΡΙΘΗΑΥΤΩΠΡΟΣΟΥΔΕΕΝΡΗΜΑΩΣΤΕΘΑΥΜΑΖΕΙΝΤΟΝΗΓΕΜΟΝΑΛΙΑΝ

ΒΑΡΑΒ
ΒΑΣ

Troy, described by Byron as 'High barrows without marble or a
name, a vast untilled, and mountain-skirted plain'; today only
earthen mounds, scraps of wall and a jarring replica of the
Wooden Horse attempt to summon Hector's glory.

The Rossano Codex: a sixth-century illumination, depicting
Pontius Pilate offering the crowds a choice of Christ or Barabbas.

Istanbul: the mosque of Haghia Sophia and the city at night seen
from the harbour. 'Stamboul, peerless of cities, thou jewel beyond
compare,/Seated astride upon two seas, with dazzling light aflare!'
in the words of Ahmet Nedim (1681–1730).

residences and 1800 aristocratic villas. The fifth century also produced sieges and attacks – Alaric in 410 – riots, uncertainty, plague and, in 498, rival popes. The contest between Lawrence and Symacchus brought violence to the streets. As Symacchus, accused of adultery, fled to a refuge outside the city walls, Lawrence's supporters, including senators, went on a murderous rant. They killed anyone suspected of being against their man, they cleared the convents of all nuns and novices, they stripped and publicly whipped women in the streets, and they slaughtered clergy. A legate sent by Theodoric settled the matter: Symacchus became the recognized Pope, Lawrence was given a bishopric.

In the sixth century Rome was captured, liberated, captured again, liberated again. In 536 Belisarius, Justinian's other great general, had freed it in celebratory style – with the agreement of the small Gothic garrison. The Gothic King Vitiges, however, raised an army of 150,000 men and returned to besiege the city for a year and nine days. The siege was lifted by reinforcements sent in by Justinian, and Belisarius set about rebuilding the city and restoring strong defences along the 'twelve miles and three hundred and forty-five paces' of walls. In 546 Totila the Ostrogoth, showing great military skill, besieged the city, using among other devices a fireship floated along the Tiber. Totila was eventually admitted to the city by treacherous sentries, who found the place virtually empty of troops and the people reduced by starvation. When Narses defeated Totila at Tagina, he marched on Rome and freed it once more. During Justinian's reign Rome had experienced five violent changes of fortune – in 536, when Belisarius claimed it for the Empire; in 546, when Totila's Ostrogoths threatened to level it; the following year, when Belisarius recaptured it; in 549, when it was again taken by Totila; and in 552, when Narses rode in after his defeat of Totila. The debilitation had mounted; the city had been riven with famine and mayhem little more than a century before the Skelligs monk walked in. The great St Benedict had taken part in a conversation during the siege of 546, in which a bishop from Constantinople had gloomily forecast that Rome would be so destroyed as to become uninhabited. Benedict contradicted him, saying that, 'Rome will never be depopulated by the barbarians but will be reduced by the natural disasters of storms, earthquakes and lightning, and will decline of her own accord.'

Whatever the ruins the pilgrim monk found – and the city, its aqueducts clogged with weeds and debris, had at one time shrunk to a population of not much more than thirty or forty thousand people from, at its height, a million – one building in Rome, the Pantheon, stood strong, its dignity and firmness still unimpaired to this day. The height of the building has majesty. That quiet massive portico, with its curious air of modesty, those granite columns, have retained more meaning than the embrasures of the Colosseum, as if the gods knew their own worth and on this site at least needed no exaggerating splurge. Up through the centre of the dome the *oculus*, in sunlight, looks like a circle of blue. No glass, no man-made interference – the roof had been kept open so that the sun came straight in and illuminated the statues of the gods in their niches. The disc of golden sunlight on the floor, beamed down from the *oculus*, travels across the paving of the interior as the sun traverses the skies.

Enter a monk of the Dark Ages, come to visit the See of Peter: '*Tu es Petrus.*' In 687 any priest, abbot or bishop travelling the roads of Europe understood that, Arianism notwithstanding, all roads led to Rome. The rock on which the Church had been built may have been quivering, but to the wandering pilgrim, with his beggar's wooden staff and his strong leather shoes, replaced or refurbished along the way, the visible Head of his Church, his Christ's representative on earth, dwelt in the Eternal City. The impression, shaken at times by ambivalent rulers such as Theodoric, or by nervous emperors in Constantinople who feared the influence of the Church in secular matters, had been reinforced massively by the figure of Gregory the Great, who dominated Rome and the Papacy, not only from 590 to 604 but for centuries afterwards.

Gregory was born into a Roman senatorial household, one of those families where authority and the obligation to govern had been almost a matter of genetics: a forefather had been Pope in the previous century. He entered the public service, and at the age of thirty-three he was appointed by the Emperor to the senior civil post in the city's administration, that of *Praetor*, the prefect of Rome. He knew fully the extent of his city's degradation, and wrote,

She that had once been the mistress of the world [has been] shattered by everything that she has suffered from immense and manifold misfortunes – the desolation of her inhabitants and the menace of her enemies. Ruins on ruins, without senate, without people and for that which survives nothing but sorrows and moanings increasing daily. Rome is deserted and burning, and we can only stand by and watch as her buildings collapse of their own accord . . . .

Gregory resigned from his secular duties, became a monk, founded a chain of monasteries inspired by his great contemporary Benedict of Monte Cassino, and entered one which he established in his father's house in Rome. In 579 the resident Pope, Pelagius II, made Gregory his legate to Constantinople, with a specific brief to solicit help from the Emperor in the defence of Rome: the Exarch of Ravenna had refused, saying that he could barely defend his own walls. The Emperor paid no attention to Gregory, but in 590, five years after he returned from Constantinople, Gregory was elected Pope. He immediately broke new intellectual ground within the Church by calling himself 'the servant of the servants of God', and turned the Papacy into an unprecedented institution of charity: Gregory believed, that as an abbot takes responsibility for the spiritual and physical care of his monks, so the Papacy should protect the people.

Bede called Gregory 'a man renowned for learning and behaviour', an opinion with which history unhesitatingly concurs, though it flatters Gregory's own view of himself. He suffered from gout, poor digestion and malaria, which he quelled with quantities of retsina. A slight man, average height, bald with a brown fringe – his biographer studied the family portraits – he had brown eyes and supercilious eyebrows, and a high colour. Self-conscious about his appearance, he believed himself to be feeble, said he was 'an ape obliged to act like a lion' and had superb qualities as an administrator. His impact upon the Church reached far, wide and deep. As well as sending Augustine to Canterbury, he attempted the abolition of slavery, reformed the liturgy, clarified the rubrics and procedures for public ceremonials, reinforced the idea of music as part of worship, stressed the glories of chanted office, and established in the Church an administration that laid the foundations of its later considerable power. His governance of the Church's missions might have been a new Roman Empire: like some spiritual Caesar he looked to the farther world as the generals of old Rome had sought colonies. He administered the Church's treasuries and estates to guarantee funding for the maintenance and blunt evangelical spread of the Roman version of Christianity. (He also believed that the pain of childbirth made women pay for the pleasure of sexual intercourse, and he suggested that all men should 'love women as if their sisters and flee them as if their enemies'.)

During Gregory's reign the Lombards continued their unbridled campaigns. He negotiated with them, especially with Agilulf, the Duke of Spoleto, even while referring to him as 'unspeakable'. Gregory's duty, as he saw it, lay in ensuring that the right climate existed for the spread of the Catholic faith and for the military and political protection of his flock in his capacity as Bishop of Rome. In 592 Agilulf embarked upon a campaign which took him as far as Naples; he captured towns such as Perugia, thus cutting off the direct route between Rome and the exarchate in Ravenna. Gregory succeeded in arranging a treaty with Agilulf, whose wife, Theudelinda, had been a confidante of his, and he then wrote the Queen a letter of thanks for her part in the peace negotiations: 'Nor was it to be expected otherwise from your Christianity but that you would show to all your labour and your goodness in the cause of peace.' To her husband, the unruly Lombard, Gregory wrote: 'Wherefore we strongly praise the prudence and goodness of your Excellency, because in loving peace you show that you love God who is its author. If it had not been made, which God forbid! what could have happened but that the blood of the wretched peasants, whose labour helps us both, would be shed to the sin and ruin of both parties.' This immensely skilled diplomat left hardly a possibility of his office untouched, and he embarked on many initiatives avoided by his predecessors: indeed, his peace treaty with Spoleto angered the Emperor and the Exarch, who understood quite clearly the political and secular precedent that Gregory had set on behalf of the Papacy. All of this happened less than a hundred years before my monk arrived in Rome. The brilliance of Gregory's papal reign still informed the seventh-century Church: in Gregorian chant, in the role that religious played in the life of the Papacy, in the formalized recognition and general tightening of the structures of monasticism.

The Irish monk walked into a Rome where occasionally an ancient, once brilliant building fell into a street without warning. Thieves stole such metal pipes and bronze statues as remained; residents or newcomers building houses carried away chunks of marble and stone from monuments, public buildings and uninhabited villas. Services had broken down substantially, leading to black markets in food and domestic essentials. Water shortages created health hazards – few of the original aqueducts had been restored to anything like their former efficiency. Rows upon rows of houses were empty, though some had been squatted in or simply taken over by the descendants of refugees of earlier wars. Fevers started like lightning, without warning, and ran like wildfire through the city: mortality ran as high as poverty. In 664 the depredations of the Emperor Constans II, a petulant, vicious and hated ruler, had ruinous effects. He took whatever metal he could find, the statues, the railings, the roofs, the props and ties of the great monumental walls, and melted them down to make weaponry. He drowned in his bath, clubbed on the head by a vase in a servant's hand, and the weather carried on with the erosion of the Eternal City.

By the end of the seventh century, a most arresting contrast had grown up between the ragged life of this decaying city and the pomp of any rituals which included the Pope. The Church ceremonies had developed a flavour which spoke of more exotic fashions in worship, a feeling of the Eastern Church. In 687 a new pope took the throne, again amid a dispute. Pope Conon died, and two prelates, the archdeacon Paschal and the archpriest Theodore, offered themselves. Stubbornness prevailed and the deadlock was broken only with the introduction of a third candidate, a Syrian priest living in Naples called Sergius. Despite Paschal's attempt to bribe the Emperor's representative in an effort to prevent the ratification of the election, Sergius's consecration went ahead. He augmented the procedures which had begun with earlier popes anxious to lend the papal court some of the pomp of imperial ceremonial at Constantinople. In Sergius's reign music took on an even greater significance: he had been educated as a cantor. The prelates assisting the new Pope capitalized on his Eastern sense of ceremony. A papal trip to a church other than St Peter's – such as the basilica of Santa Maria Maggiore – became a major event, staged and stage-managed, with different grades of vestments and a series of impressive protocols which further aggrandized the Papacy.

The Pantheon and Santa Maria Maggiore served me as twin outposts – one ancient and pagan, one relatively new and Christian – of a city and an empire which had brought to bear upon the world two immeasurable influences, one secular, one spiritual. I know no other city that can repay the walker so handsomely: I walked from the Pantheon to the great railway station, crossing first of all the Corso. My route took me under the shadows of the Quirinale Palace, with the high flights of steps and, in the alleyways, the old, unexpected fountains that characterize Rome. Old women wearing ancient black sat in their doorways, just looking. The men on the streets had the faces of senators, and the shops, even here, a few paces off one of the most glamorous and lauded streets in the world, sold, like villages, salami and tin openers. Between the Via XX Settembre and the Via Nazionale high, dated bureaucratic offices, closing for the afternoon, stuck handwritten notices, usually cancellations, on the windows. The civil servants of Rome work here, in the Telecommunications Ministry, the Quirinale itself, the Interior Ministry, the Agriculture and Forestry Ministry, the Finance and Defence Ministries, managing the country, while politicians exchange government.

The basilica of Santa Maria Maggiore represented in Rome one of the first examples of the kind of decorative power which Ravenna made famous. Regrettably, the mosaics, higher and farther away than those of Ravenna, cannot be seen as distinctly. The interior has the same high coolness and wide architecture of the contemporary San Vitale in Ravenna. Many claim that this church, rather than San Giovanni in Laterano, should be Rome's cathedral. The basilica has had many internal alterations since the first construction, though the edifice which materializes hugely past the corner of the Via Cavour into the Piazza Esquilino belongs in principle to the fifth century. Santa Maria Maggiore was built by Pope Sixtus III, who blessed Patrick's mission to Ireland in 432, and had to survive arraignment on charges of seducing nuns – his defence quoted Christ (speaking in rather different circumstances): 'Let him who is without sin cast the first stone.'

The night before, as Rome steamed, I had walked from my small *pensione* near the Justice Ministry across the Ponte Sisto to Trastevere to see an even older church. Santa Maria in Trastevere has a more solemn and reclusive air. It is earlier than Maggiore by either one or two centuries, according to differing versions, and it also claims to have initiated church dedication, in

Rome at least, to the Virgin Mary. Mustier and smaller than Maggiore, the original has suffered many superimpositions, amounting to an almost complete rebuilding at various stages down through the centuries. Notwithstanding that, in the church's gloom there shines a Byzantine influence which may not even have been included in the original designs – the gold background and mosaic illuminations come from a much later period.

Pope Sergius I ascended the throne in the year 687 and ruled until 701. His name rarely appears in any high profile among the history of the Papacy, yet the Church owes him a debt for an action which, if he had not taken it, could have changed the entire course of Catholicism. Despite considerable pressure, including the sending of troops, Sergius held out against the demands of the Emperor Justinian II who wanted Constantinople to have equal status in the Church with Rome. The army marching upon Sergius mutinied: the officer in charge of the mission fled for his life and hid – under Sergius's bed.

In Rome by the end of the seventh century successive popes had given themselves a viable Church. By then it had consolidated, turning into a powerful institution, a new European influence, which had created and defended its own credibility. Rocky and scandalous times lay ahead but it had already survived political, military and doctrinal turbulence, even though the means of such survival had often included unthinkable immorality. With each further phase of survival the committed priests and faithful became more assured that the Lord's will protected them. The city even now, especially viewed in the precincts of St Peter's, has the air of a liturgical Washington. Power, even in the service of God, has the same seekers: lofty spiritual ideals do not conceal the wish to influence great numbers of people all over the world. The Church which serves the poor and the needy and the sick and the maimed and the underprivileged has at the centre of operations a sense of power as absolutely sought as in any governed secular society, a legacy directly traceable to Gregory the Great. A Roman Empire still exists, with the same interest in colonization, however different its currency may be.

This child shall enter into the life of the gods, behold them
Walking with antique heroes, and himself be seen of them.
And rule a world made peaceful by his father's virtuous acts.
Child, your first birthday presents will come from nature's wild –
Small presents: earth will shower you with romping ivy, foxgloves,
Bouquets of gypsy lilies, and sweetly-smiling acanthus.
Goats shall walk home, their udders taut with milk, and nobody
Herding them: the ox will have no fear of the lion:
Silk-soft blossom will grow from your very cradle to lap you.

VIRGIL *Eclogues*
trans. Cecil Day-Lewis

CHAPTER FIVE

WALKING
WITH
ANTIQUE
HEROES

O N THE LAST STRETCH of his *peregrinatio* the monk had to find a Roman road, to take him where he wanted to go. In Rome, despite its grassy ruins and gap-toothed monuments, the pope enjoyed an emperor's kind of status; the worship of God smacked of the East. To a humble pilgrim who had completed his quiet examination of Peter's Rock, Rome governed the Church and Constantinople governed Rome. So, *quo vadis*? The question applied intellectually as well as geographically: difficult for an intelligent man not to enquire further into his faith, given what he had now seen and heard since Ireland.

The history alone of the development of the Church's teachings had immense attractions for the questioning mind. The centuries after Peter had bred controversy after controversy. Those that failed, however well founded intellectually, or well argued theologically, became heresies; these habitually arose in places remote from Rome – North African Christians, for example, stirred several volatile discussions. The Church, centralizing in Rome, with the imperial assistance of Constantinople, reinforced itself spiritually, intellectually and sometimes physically: Pope Sixtus III built Santa Maria Maggiore as a response to the decisions of the Council of

Ephesus in 431, one of the many convocations at which the early Church laid down the principles by which it still governs itself.

The scriptures, containing the biography of Jesus Christ and the history of his times, had become holy writ, accepted, transcribed into illuminated manuscripts, memorized, analysed and discussed. The life of Christ, and his miracles and his teachings, had become a broad strand in the Church's literature. The dominant discussion during the third and fourth centuries after Christ's death dwelt on his nature as Man and God, the human and the divine, and, if both, in what sequence or proportion. Donatists and Montanists and Docetists and Monarchianists and Sabelianists argued – and were often massacred for it – along multifarious lines, a typical example being the thought that, as God, Jesus Christ did not suffer the agony of the Passion, since he had a divine being, or, if he did not suffer, he did not have a divine being, he therefore was not God. These divisions, denounced by the Church as heretical, multiplied; many were promulgated by those who lived outside society – extreme sects, fugitives, refugees. In the late fourth century Filastrius, Bishop of Brescia, stated that as a result of his researches he could identify 156 such dissenting voices existing within Christianity.

The question asked by Arius of Alexandria – whether Christ, having had a beginning in birth, therefore did not have the necessary attribute of God 'in whom there is no beginning and no end' – stimulated the Council of Nicea in 325. Constantine the Great, as well as convening Nicea, further helped the Roman Catholic view by stamping out any examples he found of polytheism, its oracles and auguries. In 394 on the calendar employed by Bede, Pelagius, a Briton, thought to be a Welshman otherwise called Morgan, 'spread far and near the infection of his perfidious doctrine against the assistance of Divine Grace ... St Augustine, and the other orthodox fathers, quoted many authorities against them, yet they would not correct their madness.' Pelagius, though his views on human perfectibility seem developmental and humanistic, got short and abusive shrift from the old men of the Church. Bede wrote:

> A scribbler vile, inflamed with hellish spite
> Against the great Augustine dared to write
> Presumptuous serpent! from what midnight den
> Darest thou crawl on earth and look at men?

Ephesus, in 410, the third ecumenical council (from *oecumenicus*, or *oikoumenikos*, meaning the whole, inhabited earth) became the battlefield in another long schismatizing war. It broke down into two essential schools of thought – those, supported by Rome, who believed that within Christ had existed the perfect union of God and Man, the human and the divine, against those led by Nestorius, Bishop of Constantinople, who, by contrast, emphasized the human manhood of Christ. This view would have denied Mary (who, legendarily, had been buried at Ephesus) the accolade of having borne God. The Roman Church, which crudely routed the Nestorian view, then affirmed its devotion to the cult of Mary the mother of God – hence the building of Santa Maria Maggiore. Rome banished Nestorius, but his thesis evolved into a separate and widely divisive strand of belief, which long prospered in Syria, Persia and Iraq, and whose adherents even took Christianity to India and China.

Certain circumstances of the Council of Ephesus were repugnant. The opponents of Nestorius dismayed those who believed that churchmen should set exemplary standards. They bribed the local clergy and hierarchy, reviled and threatened those who advocated the beliefs of the much-respected Nestorius, lobbied the gathering prelates shamelessly, and brought forward the convening of the Council in an attempt to force the issue before Nestorius's allies arrived from the East. The caring spirit, as exemplified later by Gregory, put in no appearance in these early matters of the primitive Church. When Nestorius eventually died a rival said, 'The living on earth rejoice; the dead regret his death, fearing that they may have to endure association with him. Let those who bury him lay him beneath a large gravestone, lest his deceitful spirit rise again. May he take his teachings to Hell, where he will doubtless entertain the damned from morning to night.'

The faith adhered to by the monks of western Europe followed, therefore, the simple rules laid down by Rome – that Jesus Christ, born of Mary, was the Son of God sent to earth to redeem humanity, and that he was sacrificed by God in this cause, that he ascended to Heaven and that Peter, his fisherman, created the Church to carry on the work of salvation. The Gospels of the Four Evangelists made this understanding available to humanity, and the Rome of the popes carried it forward as uncomplicatedly as possible. Nevertheless, the monk from the Skelligs wanted to find out more, wanted to see the East, hear other voices, see the colours of other vestments – already in Rome much more vivid even than those in France – wanted to view further the spirit he had found in Ravenna and naturally expected to find an enlargement of it at Constantinople. On the way he could survey what fragments he found of the Greek classical world.

Ivory panel, possibly carved by craftsmen in Rome, showing the
Hippodrome in Constantinople.

The journey, first to Brindisi, then onwards eastwards, filled up with mixed fortunes. The territory below Rome, scarcely recorded during the Dark Ages when it lay under the control of the Lombard dukes of Spoleto and Beneventum, contained some, but not much, relevant history – whereas yet again those periods which proved irrelevant had immense fascination. The first – obvious – destination, Monte Cassino, provided an immediate overshadow of later events. The early view of the monastery, seen from many miles away, way up on the heights, brings back the memories of all those post-war grainy black-and-white photographs of the Allied bombardment in 1944, when it was believed to be a German redoubt. As pounded as Dresden, the building now offers no visual rewards at all. Neither does the interior, and the place has no hint of ancient thrill befitting the fountainhead of such a powerful cultural development. I shall most remember the arid din of the cicadas, deafening on the hard climb, reaching unpleasant crescendoes on each turn of the road. Skellig Michael contained far more natural piety in its wild stones than the corridors and innumerable windows of Monte Cassino.

The war must have done this. Before the bombardments an atmosphere of ancient devotion must, surely, have been available here? The disappointing shallowness resonated so forcibly that when I did see a monk crossing the concourse I momentarily took him for a visitor too. The war memorial on the hill contained more spiritual intensity than the entire monastery, and the view across the valley, clear and without haze on a brilliant morning, also offered more to the spirit – the white cemeteries said more than the chants of the monks inside, even though they still follow in the footsteps of the man who endowed the world with his sensible and impressive *Regula Monachorum* in this place in 515.

On the way up to the monastery, the town beneath had a more hostile and closed atmosphere than any Italian town I have ever visited. Perhaps the citizens have long memories, in which case they have good reason for gathering their folds surlily about them – who knows what ruin from the air strangers may bring? A breakfast of coffee and chocolate turned out to be a matter of silence and brooding. Within a few hundred yards of the town's pine-straggled edge, the silence grew official in the rows of white crosses of the many cemeteries. Those ordered acres yielded multitudes of Irish names, Ruane, MacCarthy, O'Brien; if any truth lies in my recurring impression that places of turbulence retain their violence, this place, by virtue of the antiseptic decency in which they have dressed it, had an unencompassable awfulness.

Benedict, who founded Christianity's most influential monastery, came from Norcia, one of those mosquito-happy hill villages near Spoleto in Umbria, and as a teenage boy chose mortification by living in a cave near Subiaco beyond Rome. The reputation of such piety gave him the customary stature among clerics; he advanced in the ranks of the Church and at the behest of the local hierarchy became an abbot. 'And when he had come here,' wrote Paul the Deacon, 'that is to the citadel of Cassinum, he always restrained himself in great abstinence, but especially at the time of Lent he remained shut up and removed from the noise of the world.' Benedict had ambition, and he fulfilled it by expressing disapproval for the unruliness of contemporary monastic orders. European monks still followed Coptic and even earlier traditions, and, despite substantial leaps forward in the definition of dogma, much of the structure of monastic life, both practical and spiritual, lacked clarification. Benedict adopted a position which, viewed now, has the hallmarks of that early, developing Christianity, and can even be seen to mirror the new statement on the nature of Christ – that is to say, he insisted upon a wedding of the spiritual and the physical, as if to echo the human and divine in Christ. If the object of the monastic life were to be devotion, Benedict believed, then practical arrangements must permit that devotion to be observed.

One of his major themes ordained that 'Idleness is the enemy of the soul.' With this one moral stroke he transformed the lives of men who followed God, lifted the monastic life out of the rough and elevated it to a kind of spiritual art form, in which every gesture had a creative motive – creative, that is, in the love and service of God. To establish this new and revolutionary monasticism – a break with, and vast improvement upon, the more haphazard rule of the past – he took followers from his abbacy and began with the discipline of time. Every house of what would become the Benedictine Order had to observe a timetable, a full roster of prayer and practical duty. He applied the good sense of an executive to ensure that if the monks could be kept occupied when not at prayer, the quality of their communal life – often, hitherto, not far above the habits of the wild – would improve. At the same time, he ordained that silence – what he termed *taciturnitas*, a general disposition towards the condition of eschewing talk – should be observed as widely as practicably possible: a shrewd thought, it promoted contemplativeness and proved helpful in the preservation of harmony in such enclosed communities.

The basic ingredients of Benedict's Rule could be applied to any group of people desirous of a disciplined, thoughtful life, in any surroundings, in any culture. Benedict took a few fundamental requirements necessary to the maintenance of human survival and supportive of personal dignity, and with them he gave monks permission to live safely, without unnecessary eccentricity, savage denial or any other pietistic extravagance. In other words, he took simple human conditions for community life and elevated them to a Rule. For instance, he encouraged monks towards sensible and regularized clothing, with changes of shift, tunic, cowl, stockings and shoes. Each man had the right to take care of himself without running the risk of being called materialistic, or self-aggrandizing; a man could keep his clothes neat and clean and tidy and not be charged with lacking the gift of self-mortification. No private property could be held: the clothing and the bedding, though used individually, belonged in common, along with the utensils of the monastery, the pen in the *scriptorium*, the hoe in the field.

Food had to be of a good and standard quality, not elaborate, yet nutritious, the victuals of the local countryside and people. The cooking of the food took on a new importance: the monks grew and boiled their own vegetables, and with fruit and their own bread they supplemented this largely vegetarian diet, which sometimes included fish and poultry, but rarely red meat. The monks devised diets and medicines for those who ailed, and it became a privilege of almost holy dimensions to serve a sick brother or sister. The stringent self-mortifications of the anchorites fell quietly out of favour, as it transpired that health and energy contributed to a more vigorous worship of God. Severe discipline prevailed, with corporal punishments for such serious offences as attempting to have any form of personal possession – members of the community had to submit to searches.

The central control of this life revolved around the rota. A time to rise, a time to pray and a time to meditate, a time to work and a time to eat, a time to study and a time to fast, a time to recreate and a time to retire – the Rule of Benedict became, effectively, an innovative strand of civilization which he designed in a way that permitted the human capacity for worship to be maximized. It adapted widely and connected with the growing common sense of civilized man, which understood that to pursue the spirit successfully the body had to be put in order. The Rule stood up under investigation, with its sensible mix of prayer and work. It could be criticized neither for severity nor for laxity. It applied – to the great relief of those who embraced it anew, coming from other directions, with previous experience – boundaries to human conduct which did not test them to unbearable levels, and yet permitted them to be devout. For the sake of accessibility it had been written in vernacular Latin.

The Church, once it understood the principles, embraced Benedict and his Rule, gave this new monasticism its enthusiastic blessing and protected Benedictines when they came under fire. Gregory led the enthusiasm. When the Lombards attacked Monte Cassino in the late sixth century, one of the documents which the fleeing monks remembered to save was Benedict's Rule. When it came into the hands of Gregory it answered his need for a standardized monastic policy within the Church. Benedict had died in 547, excellent timing for a biographical work consistent with the widespread principle of hagiography, and Gregory undertook this: the book became famous and popular for many centuries. He also advanced energetically the cause of Benedictinism, urging it upon the various – particularly the Western – provinces of the Church. Any late seventh-century Irish monk on his *peregrinatio*, if not already converted to Benedictinism, would have been giving Benedict's Rule the most serious consideration. It had begun to spread in the sees that such a monk passed through, in the monasteries where he had stayed, through France and Germany, and he could compare it with two other great rules he had encountered, those of Columba in Iona and of Columbanus, still remembered at St Gallen. A survey of the Benedictine way of life, and in Cassino itself – though the monastery had suffered enough hostility from marauding princes to disrupt its occupation – would provoke in a *peregrinus* a re-examination of the monkish life.

The south, where as in Umbria I longed to linger again, has a different quality. Robert Browning called it 'the land of lands' and dreamed of houses where

> ... for ever crumbles
> Some fragment of the frescoed walls,
> From blisters where a scorpion sprawls.
> A girl bare-footed brings, and tumbles
> Down on the pavement, green-flesh melons ...

In the monk's time Virgil's poems still had currency and distinction, especially in the courts of Naples, where he had lived, and in the minds of religious scholars pondering the eclogue he wrote forecasting the birth of a child who would inaugurate a new Golden Age.

> This boy will be accepted into the life of the gods, will view them
> Walking with antique heroes, and himself be seen as one of them
> And will rule a world pacified by the virtues of his father.

The Messianic Eclogue provoked wide discussion among Church scholars. Did Virgil appear to prophesy the birth of Christ? Even in the Middle Ages mystical qualities were still being attributed to Virgil, and those lines contained much comfortable room for Christian interpretation, no matter how otherwise pagan Virgil's era seemed.

The names of these regions of the south, however obscure their Dark Ages history may be, echo ancient events. Ancient Capua (now called Santa Maria in Capua Vetere) has a Roman amphitheatre which preserves the mood of the circus. Satellite X-ray photographs might reveal early patterns of land division just beneath the surface of the earth. Three hundred years before Christ Rome began a system of colonization here, by allotting plots of land to over two thousand families. Capua had the status of second city and, though established by the Etruscans, became coveted by Rome for its strategic position, twelve miles from the sea, and for its fertility. In later centuries a beleaguered and besieged Rome often commandeered the harvests of Capua and Campania.

Outside the town, my frustration set in once more: regrettably, the Italians do not always flag the sites of their early battles. I could not trace the spot where, in 554, Narses the eunuch won a famous victory along these riverbanks over Bucellinus, one of two barbarian brothers who raided Italy with an army of 75,000 German warriors. On the banks of the Volturno Narses laid a trap into which marched the barbarians in a wedge of fighting men, mainly infantry, carrying throwing-axes and javelins, for hand-to-hand combat. In a circle on their flanks rode the Roman archers, fully armoured, out of reach, deadly and, in the brilliantly engineered circumstances, invincible.

Naples in the Dark Ages received a battering as severe as Rome, if not more catastrophic. It commanded a position of crucial usefulness, a port where reinforcements from other parts of the Empire could land. It suffered heavily during Justinian's attempts to remove the Gothic influence from the government of Italy. In 536 Belisarius, after a campaign in Africa, returned to southern Italy across the Straits of Messina. Those towns in Gothic hands surrendered until he came to Naples, where the citizens explained their dilemma: their mixed Gothic and Roman population had grown so integrated that any attack by Belisarius upon the city would throw it into confusions of loyalty. They argued that he should ignore the city, which, if he took Rome, would automatically become part of the Empire. But Belisarius reasoned that the strategic importance of Naples as a garrison and a port warranted the confirmation of the city as part of Justinian's restored Empire. He laid siege, eventually got through along a water channel, breached the gates and sacked the city. In 542 Totila in his turn levelled its walls. Naples remained a prize, a fact which ensured continuous aggression, which sometimes led to the city being divided equally between Gothic and imperial interests, as well as being cut off from both Rome and Ravenna. From here, his detractors alleged, Narses sent for the Lombards when he fell out of favour with the new Byzantine Empress. From here in 664 Constans, frustrated at his impotence against the Lombards of Beneventum, set out for Rome on his mission to strip the city of its remaining valuables. What is true of Naples is true of Italy as a whole in these centuries. Byzantium's attempts to bring it back within the imperial fold, and the bloody campaigns that accompanied them, in the end fragmented and then eroded Roman culture in the peninsula.

Records kept in Naples attempt to trace every known murmur of Vesuvius. The eruption in 685 amounted to no more than a cough, a short paroxysm, with little of the force of previous eruptions, such as the one in 472 whose ash had been borne on the west wind as far to the east as Constantinople itself – and certainly none of the lava flow that four centuries earlier eclipsed Pompeii and Herculaneum. By 687 Pompeii, along with Herculaneum, constituted not much more than a race memory, with both towns stratified under solidified volcanic rock which would not be excavated with any organized concentration for another eleven hundred years. The lore of Vesuvius, however, could easily have formed part of the conversation of the monasteries. The farmers – monks among them – knew when the mountain stirred: the animals whinged and shifted, the birds flew away from the area, gaseous and unpleasant smells filled the air, the sun darkened and the earth trembled: dreadfully comforting portents for a man of faith who had read of the momentous events which marked Calvary. The pagan stories also thrilled: for days before the great eruptions the people could see huge men walking about high up on the rim of the crater, or flying through the air and alighting on the mountain's saucer peak, and then wandering and clambering gigantically through the rocks and the scrub. These gigantic, unreal figures later populated the black smoke that poured up out of the mountain; to the sound of terrible trumpets they swirled about within the smoke, gods and dervishes at once, as the awful rivers of rock and mud raced down the slopes.

I knew full well that the monk could not have seen any of Pompeii – all he saw was black landscape, overgrown where the grass found it possible, where a stunted shrub got a foothold – yet I could not resist digressing there. At seven o'clock in the morning the workmen, with the aid of some lire, proved obliging. In a deserted little street, which has yet to receive the full attentions of twentieth-century archaeology and restoration, the deep chariot ruts in the paving stones whistled up at once the *frisson* of Pompeii.

Away from these small artisan areas, the great villas had decorations of a standard according to the family's wealth and cultural awareness. Extensive use of colour, with an Egyptian red prominent, and the employment of *trompe l'oeil* and animal and erotic images gave Pompeii an early sophistication and distinction. The statuary, the painting and the general quality of work such as the famous ithyphallic tripod – three satyrs in an exaggeratedly happy state holding up a bronze bowl, now in the Museo Nationale on the Piazza Cavour in Naples – portray Pompeii as a rich and relaxed town, full of money and education, with a confident economy and a stable, middle-class society from which many inhibitions had been expelled. By 687, throughout Italy, such societies had been swept away as thoroughly as if they too had been in the shadow of Vesuvius.

Along the platform in the great arched railway station at Naples, hawkers sold food in small baskets – half bottles of wine, fat rounds of bread, some fruit, some ham, cheese. They handed the baskets up to carriage doors several steps above them. The bread proved too hard to eat, the wine too warm and thin to drink, the *prosciutto* too leathery, the fruit too old. The crowded train had severe old women in the inevitable black, grinning soldiers, some nuns and children. These Italian trains, more pronouncedly in the south, leave the station with a degree of ceremony and like departing guests have the good manners not to put on any momentum until they have attained a respectable distance from the terminus. The train jerked past signposts to Eboli where Christ stopped unpityingly, thus rendering the region poorer than the poor, and at Potenza I changed to a small, two-carriage train.

The train journey, long, diverse and awkwardly slow, offered little opportunity for anything but reflection. The road of this Dark Ages pilgrim had for the first time veered towards the improbable: in Britain and France and Switzerland and Italy as far as Rome, records existed to confirm such pathways – the pilgrims who trod this land south of Rome had been travelling in the opposite direction: to, not from, the Eternal City. This raised questions about the nature of the *peregrinus*, or rather about the social tempo which observed him, encouraged him and celebrated him.

To begin with, he came from a tradition which ensured that he stood apart, in some cases spectacularly so; holy men included those who had visibly conquered the demands of the body by achieving triumphant feats of self-denial, such as Simeon Stylites or Jerome or the motley desert fathers. Their performance of their chosen lives had entered the race memory of both Christianity at large and that of the monastic life. The Irish monk of the period was describing a curious full circle which connected him to the asceticism by which the holy man of Byzantine times had gained his reputation. The famed demonstrativeness of the hermits in the Syrian desert was replicated, though in less heat and with fewer spectators, by those who lived on Skellig Michael or in the beehive huts of Kerry, or like St Cuthbert who took to an isle off Lindisfarne. From the available accounts, the western hermits did not seem to behave as flamboyantly as, say, Simeon on his stylus, or the anchorite with his pet lion whom Jewish travellers met and reported to Theodoret, the historian Bishop of Cyrrhus. On the extreme edges of the Byzantine Empire, however, traditions existed of severe religious expression on the parts of individual monks who had then banded themselves into groups, either in monasteries such as Skellig Michael, or roaming bands who frequently, out of hunger or wilfulness, smeared themselves across Syrian landscapes. The Benedictine Rule did not begin to take marked effect in western Europe until the ninth century, before which the Irish followed an independent tradition which had sprung from an Egyptian prototype. In the seventh century, a form called *regula mixta* frequently obtained, which combined the practical elements of the Benedictines' monastic persuasion with the purity of the Irish.

By the seventh century, the irregularities which had characterized the earliest holy men had in any case calmed down. The holy man had long come to be regarded for his special powers, such as efficaciousness in illness, both before and after his death, a figure who could bring order out of chaos: Aidan of Lindisfarne controlled vicious human beings as well as unspeakable demons. The holy man could, as Columbanus did when taking on the arduous career of evangelist, draw great numbers of followers, both kings and slaves: this was a new power, comparatively speaking, and a mystical one, beholden to no temporal principles. On the contrary, it gave the holy man the right to interfere, sometimes dramatically, in affairs of state at the highest level – remember how fearlessly Columbanus chided the whoring Theuderic. In all circumstances the monk, religious, monastic or hermit, eventually had a special place, one which he frequently turned to political advantage as in the reign of the Merovingian kings, or as in Gregory's Papacy, when priests became the pope's provincial governors and the lines between religious and secular grew blurred.

On and beyond the western extremities of the Roman Empire, from the beginning, perhaps due to the fixed and accepted position of the Druid in pre-Christian society, an expectation existed, and therefore the emergent figure of the Christian holy man seemed not too egregious. The efficiency with which the early evangelists, such as Palladius and Patrick, organized their missions must have contributed. In small, relatively compact societies a man who chose ascetically and demonstratively to follow the word of

Part of a sixth-century ivory diptych depicting the circus, with an audience in the top corners.

God, which the local king had just accepted, received respect – unlike the less fortunate Eastern figures who were often blamed for making local girls pregnant, or causing crops to fail, or disturbing the weather. In the East, the hermit or anchorite frequently seemed to act as a fantasy *alter ego* which expressed or drew off the shadowy in people's natures; in western Europe he acted as a lightning conductor of the gods-become-God, an agent of efficacy, a conduit of supplication and salvation.

The Irish, and other monks of the Celtic Church, brought a further special dimension to the status of the holy man turned pilgrim. By choice he was often an exile – not a traveller, not a tourist, not a banished person;

his exile had within it a glory and a distinguished tradition, a white, as distinct from a bloody red martyrdom. Such exile – and they used the word calculatedly – originated deliberately. Nobody instructed them or conscripted them; they did not represent their monasteries, nor were they necessarily expected to return. If they gave reasons for their departure it was explained simply as the feeling of having received a divine instruction. 'O, Father,' prayed Boethius, Theodoric's ill-fated philosopher, 'give the spirit power to climb to the fountain of all light and be purified.... Thou carriest us, and Thou doest go before, Thou art the journey and the journey's end.'

At source, the Irish form of *peregrinatio* had a number of forms. These embraced the holy man who wished to make such a journey, like Gallus, for Christ, but whose flesh, through age or infirmity, did not permit. Another category of pilgrim never left the shores of Ireland, but travelled internally, visiting Irish shrines and monasteries. Others travelled to Scotland, to Ninian in Galloway, to Columba on Iona, or to Britain, to the Lindisfarne of Aidan and Cuthbert, perhaps to David in Wales. The elite, if one may use the term, travelled to Europe. Sometimes they carried on missionary work, sometimes not; perhaps, like Egbert, they exiled themselves, temporarily or permanently, as a form of penance, supplication or worship. In 664 Egbert, ailing to the point where he feared death, as the Venerable Bede describes,

went out of his chamber where the sick lay, and sitting alone in a convenient place, began seriously to reflect upon his past actions, and being full of compunction at the remembrance of his sins, bedewed his face with tears, and prayed fervently to God tht he might not die yet, before he could make amends for the offences which he had committed in his infancy and younger years, or might further exercise himself in good works. He also made a vow that he would, for the sake of God, live in a strange place, so as never to return to the island of Britain where he was born....

Not all travellers came from the religious life. Sometimes a *peregrinatio* resulted from a punishment and it applied to several offences – as in the case of the man who visited Columba on Iona, a man who had been accused of committing incest with his mother and murdering a relative. Columba sentenced him to wander until God forgave his sins, because such a man should not, under law, have been allowed to pollute the shores of Iona. An Irish monk wandering the roads of Europe in the seventh century could also have been pursuing enforced exile, banished for a period of penance for intercepting and helping himself, in part or in total, to the gifts intended for his bishop or abbot.

If, for whatever aspect of godliness, the Irish monk of 687 had chosen to travel through these lands to atone for past sins, he must have felt his penance lift the guilt from him. Life runs hard in the south, whatever the sun and the clear sky. Many of the farms remain small, many of the regions are classified close to Third World status by the EEC. Looking out of the window of the hard, two-carriage train, I tried to visualize what the monk saw as he came across these hills, perhaps on horseback, and for his sake I hoped that he had the company of a large wagon train of merchants and their protectors. He travelled through dangerous anarchic lands, though wealthier then than the north – the reverse situation, which today maintains an economic gulf between the poor south and the now much wealthier north of Italy, did not come about until the Norman invasions several centuries later. The countryside, initially comfortable, seemed to me to grow more inhospitable by the mile, even though much farming territory has been won back from the scrubland and, in parts, from the volcanic seashore. By 687 the south of Italy had experienced large and regular influxes of Greek refugees from Islam and the Slavs, including prelates making significant contributions to the affairs of the Church, for instance Pope Sergius I and Theodore of Tarsus, who became Archbishop of Canterbury. My destination, Brindisi, the great port of Brundisium, which today feels as if it could be a Greek as well as an Italian town, has a past which, when scanned chronologically, sums up the history through which the monk walked – with many fleets embarking on brave departures, many hostile landings, many invasions, many returning heroes, many conflicts, even a significant treaty signed in the city.

Two and a half centuries before the birth of Christ, Rome built a colony which capitalized upon Brundisium's geography as a fine natural harbour.

Twin arms of land curved out in a wide embrace, creating a port large enough to contain an effective fleet, with which the Roman generals intended to prevent Carthaginian ships using the Adriatic. It also acted as a launching pad for assaults across the Adriatic, into the land of Illyria, corresponding with modern Yugoslavia and Albania, and into Greece. Forty years before, in 280 BC, King Pyrrhus had ventured out from the north-west of Greece and taken Sicily and the south of Italy. The Illyrians also had to be contained, and when they reacted against the Roman establishment in Brundisium by killing merchants and legates, the Romans attacked the Illyrian queen with considerable success.

On the night of 10 January 49 BC, Julius Caesar changed Roman history by crossing the Rubicon – a physically insignificant, symbolically unforgettable river in north-eastern Italy – and executed an act of civil war. He had only a small army, which he split, and led one half down along the coast to Rimini. His declared opponent, Pompey, had also been his son-in-law (Caesar's daughter, Julia, Pompey's wife, had died five years earlier). Caesar, vastly experienced, pursued the less effective, lazier Pompey down to these parts until Pompey slipped the blockade intended for him in Brundisium.

Virgil, having taken a fever in Athens, died in Brundisium on 21 September 19 BC. He had lived through a most vivid period of Roman history, largely of civil war, and, as a favourite at the courts of the aristocrats, had heard the gossip, the intrigues and the manoeuvres of Caesar and Pompey, Brutus and Cassius, Mark Antony and Cleopatra. Pompey was assassinated when he landed, on the run, in Egypt in 48 BC; Caesar suffered the same fate on the Ides of March 44 BC; and Antony and Cleopatra lost to Octavian in 31 BC.

In the later history of Italy, Brundisium shared many of the destinies of the fluctuating empires, Roman and Byzantine, the raids of the foreign tribes, the establishments of small rulerships, and through the descending centuries it retained the constant state of importance due to such a vital harbour. Long after the monk reached it the Crusaders made it a naval base. In the seventh century it flourished as a valve of trade between Italy and the East, a point of contact, often tumultuous, between the Lombard dukedoms of the south and Byzantium. For four hundred years before the monk arrived in Brundisium Byzantium's brilliant civilization had kept this port busy with trade. For four hundred years before that Rome itself had dominated this sea, and for a further four hundred years before that the Hellenistic civilization, cultural and political, metaphysical and military, exercised its powerful influence throughout much of the Adriatic and eastern Mediterranean.

Brundisium marked a point of marvellous departure for a conservative traveller out of western Europe. Behind him lay a turbulent continent, with a history which he had by now encountered, admittedly in snatches and lore, in glimpses of the life at the courts and in the monasteries and in the streets and farms. Before him, on the last leg of the journey, lay a synthesis, a fusion, of past and future. He had the opportunity to sample the pagan glory of ancient Greece, whose flavour he had tasted in the writings and language of his education – albeit confusedly and well salted with Christianity – and in his conversations with other travellers. The ancient, thrilling past could be surveyed at Delphi, shrine, home and breeding ground of antique heroes, a magnet for travellers and pilgrims since the sixth century before Christ, reached by a long sea crossing from Italy to Greece, from Brindisi to Patras.

Brindisi still has a powerful port and has lost none of its deepwater capacity for large shipping. I arrived late on a Thursday afternoon, when the wind from the sea – how surprisingly threatening the Adriatic looks – kept the town cool. Scaffolding surrounded one of the twin columns which marked the end of the Via Appia, and across the water of the harbour the huge monument to Mussolini, an enormously tall, half-curved, half-flat slab of concrete, looked like the inverted comb of some mad fighting giant bird. Nobody sat in the Piazza del Popolo. Everybody, locals and tourists, had congregated in the street which leads down to the harbour and is lined with agencies selling ferry tickets. Corfu, Patras, Piraeus – the names read like the travelogue of a Homeric adventure, and I embarked with three hundred other foot travellers, mostly backpacking American students.

We left at a few minutes before midnight, two hours late and nobody caring. For an hour I could see the lights behind us, especially the bright glow on top of the Mussolini column. No wonder this harbour had such value to the Roman and then the Byzantine Empire: no fleet could get in here without being seen hours in advance. Ships passed us; the tug, padded with tyres, which chugged by lest we needed guidance and assistance, turned like a unicyclist and belted back to the dockside. Huge ferries, vast bulks, lay at anchor, motionless and lit up inside, light pouring out through their vast embarkation doors and tiny men, toys, standing by.

On deck the American students teemed everywhere – without them the passenger list would have amounted to no more than twenty, a sad-eyed old man, a crisply spoken English businessman who drank hugely for several hours, an Italian honeymoon couple, two couples in cars with Scandinavian registrations, three Italian families travelling together, one Greek priest and a young man from Dublin who had left the seminary because he had decided that he could not take the religious life (his mother had accepted his decision much better than he had ever expected). The Americans partied on the top deck, laughed like urban hyenas and danced to the flashing disco lights. I had to go as far for'ard as the ship's regulations would permit to catch any glimpse of the stars. The night bore on hot and noisy: by morning, when I could not sleep in the hard metal cabin, the Americans had subsided into largely drunken slumbers. In the dawn haze an island appeared in the ferry's sights – Corfu, where many disembarked and walked away into the small town. The ship left the port and headed out again, deeper into the spotlessly clean Ionian Sea. The sun came out, turned as pitiless as the Ancient Mariner's.

At four o'clock in a roasting afternoon we landed at Patras, where Byron first encountered Greece. After Christ's death St Andrew, the second of the apostles, Peter's brother, preached along this coast and in AD 61 was crucified diagonally. His successor as Bishop of Patras, St Regulus, also known as Rule, was told by an angel in a dream that he must end the constant squabbling over the relics of Andrew, take them away and find them a new home. He became a pilgrim traveller, sailed through the Mediterranean and got shipwrecked off the coast of Scotland as part, apparently, of the angel's plan. He founded St Andrews in Scotland – hence the white diagonal cross of Andrew's crucifixion as Scotland's (much later) national flag. So the Scots said, though they are suspected of having tried to compete with the elitism of an English cult of St Peter himself, in whose initiation Bede played a large part. Nor did Rule's journey settle the differences over Andrew's relics. A busy mythology sprang up around the saint, which had his head in one place, his limbs and cross in others, and gave him the credit for founding Contantinople. It also resulted in a rather ugly neo-Byzantine church in Patras called Agios Andreas, where a gold casket is said to hold Andrew's head.

I waited for a local bus to Rio, and a ferry took me on the shorter route to Delphi. A handful of people, with children, stood on the brown wooden deck. The few cars included a van taking across what seemed like the entire fitments of somebody's new bathroom. When the van's wheels stuck in the metal cleats of the ferry after the short crossing everybody, myself included, pushed until it snorted up the ramp where a boy waited, with an old-fashioned barrow on which was mounted a large perspex box from which he sold rings of hard bread studded with sesame seeds.

The road to Delphi wound by the sea, seen through outbreaks of olive and azalea, with islands and lagoons shimmering in the wooded distance. Very early the following morning, from the hills above Delphi, on the side of Parnassus's long harsh escarpment, I walked down through scrubland and olive groves and chickens and early old men with hats and moustaches, down the edge of the mountain to the shrine of Apollo, the navel of the world.

It must be possible that the monk saw this scene more or less as I now did. Delphi had been dismissed, desecrated and closed down, had even suffered enormous depredation, by the late seventh century, but none the less the ruins bulked too large to have disappeared by the time he got there. In later centuries the land covered the shrine almost completely, people built houses on the earth above it, and the site remained largely forgotten and concealed until serious excavations began in the late nineteenth century. In any case, as well as the physical details, which took time and energy to absorb, the religious and historical implications of Delphi could not have been lost on an educated traveller of the seventh century. Whatever his – or anyone else's – spiritual leanings, Delphi's force could never, and still cannot, be ignored.

Delphi existed as a shrine in the time of the Myceneans, from the fourteenth to the tenth century BC. In common with civilizations as geographically far apart as the Mesopotamians and proto-Celts, Delphi then worshipped the goddess of the earth and made offerings to her, in the form of statues made in her – and the supplicant's – likeness. In due course she gave way to Apollo, the sun-god. This beautiful young man, with the classical slim-hipped, broad-chested physique, was born on the island of Delos. He had the conception and birth of a god: sired by Zeus, sharing a womb with Artemis, the goddess of fertility, he sprang forth into the light from the loins of Leto, Zeus's mistress. She had fled to escape the anger of Hera, Zeus's wife – who cursed the pregnant Leto, swearing that she could only bear the children in a place where the sun's rays could not penetrate. Poseidon, god of the seas, raised a canopy of waves over the island, all the Immortals attended and the goddesses gave Apollo a girdle of gold, while feeding him with ambrosia and nectar.

When the child was four days old, he strode off down the slopes of Olympus to establish his shrine. At Parnassus he was attacked by a malevolent female in the form of a serpent, but Apollo killed the dragon and cried aloud, as he watched it writhe to death, 'Rot where you lie.' The serpent rotted, and from the Greek word meaning 'to rot' the name Pytho was given to this rocky grove at the foot of a cascade under the brooding lip of Parnassus. Now that he had a shrine, Apollo needed priests to form his cult. On the sea he saw a ship bound for Corinth from Crete. He assumed the shape of a dolphin, pursued the ship and obliged the crew to forsake their old lives and become the priests and guardians of his temple, and since they first encountered him in the shape of a dolphin they gave the place the name of Delphi.

Apollo became multi-efficacious, capable of calming the seas or vanquishing giants, of making the beasts of the forests dance to his music or single-handedly banishing hostile armies to Hades, of laying the foundations of great new cities and removing the clouds from the sun. His attributes grew – Apollo the omnipotent as well as the beautiful, the peaceful as well as the warrior, replete with grace, strength and eternal youth, with whom the goddesses fell in love. His life, his efficacies, his adventures and his loves embraced almost all the mythological archetypes – he bore one lover away in a golden chariot, children borne by another received protection from the wolves when abandoned in the forest; he sired the father of medicine, Asclepius, gave Cassandra the gift of prophecy and fell in love with Hyacinthus whose blood, from a fatal forehead wound caused by a discus Apollo had thrown in sport but which got misdirected by jealous gods, spurted to the ground and from it sprang the hyacinth flower.

Whenever it was that Apollo selected Delphi as the place for his shrine, his sanctuary was completed in the sixth century BC, and thereafter, for several centuries – until AD 392 when the Emperor Theodosius the Great closed it down – drew enormous numbers of pilgrims. Apollo had chosen the site, nearly two thousand feet above sea level, because Parnassus was exceeded in height only by Mount Olympus itself, and because the place already had a reputation for the purest of air, which came forth directly from a cleft in the earth. Those who breathed in these airs gained the gift of superhuman clairvoyance. Apollo moderated – in the spiritual and political sense – Greek existence and morality by creating greater peace, first of all within the individual, then between neighbouring cities. As an expression of these achievements, and as a means of relaxation and reflection after them, he demonstrated the gentle munificence of the arts by playing the lyre and singing, by becoming the god of poetry and by making close friends of the Nine Muses.

At the shrine oracles were pronounced by the woman of Delphi, the Pythia, who sat in immaculate contemplation and handed down Apollo's prophecies. Suppliants washed in the nearby cascade, paid a varying amount of money, and brought an unblemished beast, a lamb or kid goat, for sacrifice on the altar. Water from the cascade was then poured on the animal before the sacrifice: if the creature shivered (not unlikely given cold water in such heat), the omens were good. The Pythia drank water from a sacred stream over which the temple had been built, chewed the leaves of a laurel, then climbed upon the sacred tripod, laid her hand upon the *omphalos*, the stone which marked the navel of the earth, and chanted her prophecy. The *omphalos* stood at the point where the clairvoyance-giving airs were believed to emanate from the earth. The entire ritual took place on this glorious height, with the sea in the glistening distance.

Heat, even so early in the morning, made the shade of the olive groves essential and blessed. Of Italy the light is what you remember, in Greece, the smell – oregano, olive, dusty myrtle trees, giving off a spicy, dry must. Sweat pouring from my forehead pooled inside the dark lenses of my spectacles. On my left I passed a beautiful small temple, the reconstructed Treasury of the Athenians. Tall columns stood ahead in a ruined row, a giant's rubble lay strewn around, fragments of columns with fluted cores and elegant pediments. More columns made of enormous roundels, thick biscuits of white-gold stone, stood inside the high sloping ramp which opened the way into the ancient temple: did they come afresh with the reconstructed temple of 330 BC, or from the one built in 510 BC and ruined in an earthquake in 373? The first temple, they say, had been made of laurel, the next of beeswax and feathers, the third of bronze and the fourth of this local stone in 650 BC. Inside, carved inscriptions, such as the famous 'Know Thyself' and 'Nothing to Excess', stimulated reflection.

The entrance hall of the museum has a replica of the *omphalos*; it resembles a huge stone thimble, across whose surface has been criss-crossed like an embossed lattice woollen weave. Friezes and shields, depicting quarrels and heroics, battles and chases, fill other rooms. Zeus raping Europa, gods meeting on Olympus, Apollo threatening Heracles – these works, from the five or six centuries before Christ, make this museum an album of classical mythology. The stone Sphinx of Naxos, perched on her column, her wings flying, possesses a dauntless magic. The silver bull, the horse's leg, anatomically perfect, the impertinent, patronizing head of a goddess in gold and ivory, the beaten gold griffin – they have a quality, a particular unity in their demeanour which must come from their common purpose, the worship of Apollo. Along one wall stands an extraordinary series of polished stones marked with hundreds and hundreds of small hieroglyphic engravings. These are now believed to be musical notations of hymns to Apollo – Greek sheet music, as it were, carved on stone, dated to several centuries before Christ.

The entire museum has been oriented to lead the visitor to one final point, the room of the Charioteer. This bronze statue, damaged and buried in the earthquake of 373 BC, has long been regarded as one of the world's great artistic masterpieces. It depicts a young charioteer, not more than twenty years old and about six feet tall, wearing a robe flowing in folds above and below a belt, holding in his hands the reins of four horses. It formed part of a large sculptured group commissioned by the winner of the chariot races at Delphi in 478 or 474 BC. His curly hair clings to his perspiring temples, round which he wears the slender headband awarded to the winner, and his eyes, made of white enamel and brown stone, transfix whatever he sees. He would be recognized if he walked into a room today, a tough and brilliant young aristocrat, with strong hands and arms and an athlete's balance.

I stayed that night in the worst hotel in Piraeus, the port which services the anticlimactic city of Athens. Delphi proved exhausting, spiritually and physically, with the heat around 110 degrees Fahrenheit. The police advised people to stay indoors: old people, they told me, had died out on the islands in the last heat wave. Like animals feeding, and just as numerous, the ferries lined up at the port in Piraeus. I had travelled across corn-filled hills through Thivas, site of Thebes: rustic wooden signs advertised the pathway to the birthplace of Oedipus. That such insignificant places should have had such monuments, such immortalization.

The decline of the great Hellenistic period which lit the Eastern world politically and intellectually for several centuries before Christ began at the same time as the reduction of Delphi's political influence, when jurisdiction over the shrine came into the hands of the Romans. In the second century BC, as the Empire expanded, the Romans had divided the defeated Macedonian territories into four independent republics and tried unsuccessfully to introduce the 'client kingdom' principle they practised elsewhere, in which conquered countries had 'freedom' but remained dependent on Rome and were obliged to supply the Empire. (When a similar relationship in Britain came adrift on broken promises, it provoked Boadicea's rebellion.) The Greeks mistook the client relationship for a greater liberty than the Romans had intended. Brutally, the Romans then annexed Greece completely, built a Roman road into Macedonia and to cement the subjection destroyed the old southern symbolic citadel of Corinth in 146 BC.

The fourth-century Haghia Eirene, Aya Irini Kilisesi, the church of
Divine Peace. Built on the site of a temple of Aphrodite, now on
the edge of the Topkapi Palace, Haghia Eirene has become a
museum and is also used as a concert hall.

Ivory relief from the late fifth century, showing an unidentified
emperor of Constantinople, possibly Anastasius.

The Archangel Michael: this sixth-century ivory panel shows him
holding a sceptre or staff, and an orb, as a sign of his regard for the
emperor. The inscription reads: 'Receive These Gifts.' The facial
characteristics of the emperor were sometimes given to the
subjects of such cult worship.

Sixth-century mosaic of a Gothic chieftain defeated by the
Byzantine emperor. Justinian's two superb generals, Belisarius and
Narses, reclaimed those western and African territories which the
Roman Empire had lost, including Ravenna from the Goths.

Mosaic from the Imperial Palace in Istanbul, depicting a woman
with a pitcher, *c.* sixth century.

Sixth-century ivory relief of a procession taking a reliquary
to a church.

The columns at Haghia Sophia, Ayasofia, the Great Church of the
Holy or Divine Wisdom. Justinian commissioned two architects
and mathematicians to build a church which would harmonize the
symbolic and physical powers of God and the Empire.

Interior of Haghia Sophia, lit by forty windows in the massive dome. The high-ceilinged gallery traditionally belonged to the women.

The Romans were already aware of Delphi: as early as the fifth century BC a Roman leader had paid tribute at the shrine in thanksgiving for a military victory. The importance of Delphi's symbolism to the Greeks could not be mistaken, and it acted as as challenge to those who wished to conquer Delphi in a local war, or Greece itself. Celts had attacked the shrine in 279 BC, but Apollo had poured rain and snow down on them, a move which greatly assisted the Aetolians who defended Delphi. A series of wars between 600 and 339 BC, during some of which the shrine's treasures were plundered to meet expenses, had shaken Delphi but none the less enhanced the lustrous reputation of the place. When the Romans took command the oracles no longer influenced the affairs of Greece with pronouncements of political importance. In 86 BC Lucius Cornelius Sulla, a Roman general besieging Athens (and in the process laying waste Piraeus) took from Delphi any valuable metals the shrine had retained in order to pay for his campaign. Three years later raiders quenched the eternal flame and caused damage to the temple. A hundred and fifty years on Nero, while professing to respect the shrine of Apollo, coveted the statues and took several hundred of them back to Rome. By the second century AD Christianity had begun to spread widely, with a consequent loss of devotion to Apollo, and though various Roman emperors acknowledged the former glory of the place, attending games and ceremonials there, and in some cases ordering restoration works on the temple, Delphi's great era had ended.

Constantine, though he had been honoured at the shrine, enhanced his new city in the East with some of Delphi's masterpieces. In 360 the Emperor Julian the Apostate, Constantine's half-brother, declared himself a pagan and attempted to restore the stature of Delphi. Finally, in 392, the devout but savage Emperor Theodosius ordered Delphi to be closed and the temple to be silenced. At the same time Greece was fully annexed into the Eastern Empire and played a substantial part in the affairs of Constantinople.

Throughout the fifth and sixth centuries the shrine of Apollo became a place of Christian worship, a bishopric, where the Christians built churches out of the stones and ancient monuments. By the end of the seventh century Delphi constituted a metaphor for Greece's fate – in ruins, overgrown, trampled upon, colonized, made to worship new gods, unimportant in the scheme of things, a yardstick of how the old pagan classical civilization had collapsed. Greece in the Dark Ages generally experienced enormous upheaval. Mass evacuation took place: the entire population of Patras may have moved across the Adriatic. Greek settlements were numerous in southern Italy, and the presence of Greeks in a community already mixed with Romans, other Italians, Goths, Jews, caused considerable problems. Greece's identity, even within the Byzantine Empire, had been eroded by

The Golden Gate, Istanbul, erected by the Emperor Theodosius.

invasions of tribespeople from the north, Slavs, Bulgars, Avars: the Empire only had effective control of the eastern shoreline of Greece down to the Peloponnese. The country did not regain any political Hellenistic *persona* of its own until the Byzantine recovery of the ninth century, and even then it had much Slavonic content.

I set out from Piraeus on a Sunday morning to reach, eventually, Istanbul. The route I had intended would take me on another long ferry journey up through the islands to Lesbos, and from there to Turkey. I walked to the harbour at half past seven down the narrow street, past the white marble steps leading up to the open door of an Orthodox church. People had begun to gather – very few, mostly old women and a child or two. Beyond the wide rows of golden icons the bearded priest chanted and was answered by a middle-aged man in a grey summer shirt who sat behind a high lectern. Though more exotic (partly because of the language) than the ceremonies of my childhood, the elements in common could be seen – the raising of the priest above the level of the worshippers, the drawing of the eye towards the light of the candles, the hypnotic calling of the prayers, the soothing yet anxious atmosphere of the icons and decorations. The notice board outside listed several services for the morning.

The boat from Piraeus to Mytilini in Lesbos was certainly bigger than the large wooden boats, like galleys or Egyptian dhows, in which travellers of the seventh century left Greece for the East. The islands that drifted in and out of this dreadfully hot noon haze must have looked exactly the same to the monk as they did to me. Pirates infested the busy seas then, greater dangers existed, he had more difficulties. I tried to work out, on this virtually empty ferry, how long the journey from Ireland would have taken him. Allow for rest periods, for times of new instruction in monasteries, for weeks or months of bad weather, for helping in a community short of workers at harvest-time, for assisting in the creation of a new manuscript, for the copying of a gospel book, for the celebration of a saint or the consecration of a bishop, for the withstanding of, or clearing up after, a raid. Allow time for ill health, or ministering to the sick after a swingeing local epidemic, or a wide diversion following the collapse of a bridge over an unfordable river, or the avoidance of a region currently known to contain especially fierce wolves or bears or brigands. His journey could have been completed in between fifteen and eighteen months, on foot, on horseback, on a cart in a convoy, on water.

He did not have time to dwell everywhere for long enough – in this he had my complete sympathy – nor could he consider everything to his full or even reasonable satisfaction, and he too must have arrived at this golden bowl of the world, the land of islands, with his head full of a wild and varied kaleidoscope to which were now added the colours of Lesbos. Sappho lived in this 'pleasant grove of apple trees, and altars fragrant with frankincense; there, cold water babbles among apple branches, all the place is shaded with roses, sleep comes down from the trembling leaves. There is a meadow for

horses, blossoming with spring flowers, and gentle breezes blow ... .'
Sappho hung her lyre upon the temple of Apollo and jumped from a cliff,
supposedly to her death, but on the way down she was changed into a swan
and flew away over the Aegean: 'I love delicacy, and the bright and
beautiful belong for me to the desire of the sunlight.'

Birthplace of Aesop of the Fables, setting for *Daphnis and Chloe*, Lesbos
has wooded roads, olives and myrtle and big grey birds. It also has a
typically long, typically chequered history. Thucydides, the Athenian
historian of the Peloponnese Wars, told how the inhabitants of Lesbos
turned their coats and reneged upon the Athenians in favour of the
Spartans. A galley, bearing death-dealing soldiers, sailed for the island
under instructions to execute each and every islander citizen, but another
galley, also from Athens, performing one of the greatest feats of rowing,
brought news of a reprieve just as the announcement of the carnage-to-be
was being promulgated. In Mytilini people were quick to point out that
Turkey lay only just across the way. Ancient enemies, ancient fears that the
Turks might one day again cast eyes of desire upon Lesbos, island of the
petrified forest and the richest greenery in the archipelago, 'where the
nightingales sing more sweetly than anywhere else', and where the women,
according to Homer, 'won the chief renown for beauty from their whole
fair sex'.

Say Istanbul and a seagull comes to mind
Half silver and half foam, half fish and half bird.
Say Istanbul and a fable comes to mind
The old wives' tale that we have all heard.

Say Istanbul and mottled grapes come to mind
With three candles burning bright on the basket –
Suddenly along comes a girl so ruthlessly female

So lovely to look at that you gasp,
Her lips ripe with grape honey,
A girl luscious and lustful from top to toe –
Southern wind, willow branch, the dance of joy ... .

Thus wrote the poet Bedri Rahmi Eynboglu in 'The Sign of Istanbul'.

Begin with the name, and the name began with Byzantium, after Byzas son of Poseidon and grandson of Zeus. His grandmother, Io, another mistress of Zeus, had, like Apollo's mother, to flee the jealous anger of Hera, Zeus's wife, who turned Io into a heifer and let loose upon her a stinging fly. Io plunged into the waters, which since then have been called Bosphorus, the ford of the cow. More practically, but with some mythical input, the city was founded on the geographical instruction of the oracle at Delphi, who told Greek colonists from near Corinth where to build. This happened in 658 BC, and three centuries later the symbol with which the city is most synonymous, the crescent moon, became the immortal emblem of this eastern region, and eventually of Islam. Philip the Macedonian attacked Byzantium in a surprise midnight raid. The Byzantines prayed to the goddess of the moon and she took away her light, leaving only a sliver, not enough by which to mount a successful attack. Afterwards they promised to remember the goddess forever in their banners.

Exhausted, I arrived at night, filthy, with several days' growth of salt-and-pepper beard. The hotel queried, then discouraged, my reservation, made several weeks before – almost the only advance booking I had made anywhere on this journey; the receptionist, otherwise pleasant, asked me for proof of identity, then to confirm my payment. When the air conditioning of the lift hit me my clothes adhered all over. The word 'manky', forgotten since schooldays, returned; I stank, high – clothes 'manky' with sweat stains. On days of temperatures just above the hundred mark I had spent too many hours in buses from beyond Izmir, travelling ovens, at a steady forty miles an hour. In Mytilini, the midnight temperature still skulked in the eighties and the unthinkable happened in front of my eyes – elderly Greek women, come out to dine with their families, actually took off their woollen cardigans.

The morning light over the Golden Horn seemed to reveal the curve of the earth, an illusion caused by the way in which, through the slightly bending glass of the window, the heat haze of the distance, a kind of grey-purple, cut off the view across the crowded hills. Roofs everywhere, in ragged plateaus; the colours of the tiles, many in disrepair, ranged from cinnamon and deeper terracotta to bright red; one long eave had been patched with a wide stripe of brilliant blue plastic, and from the shadows of the houses at street level occasional doors of turquoise or green or white perked up the rickety neighbourhood. Through the other window the Bosphorus became as busy as the life of a pond, ferries and pilot boats and tugs, ushering and shoving, back and forth.

My face lifted with the peeling skin, and the breeze rushing into the room stung my forehead. I will remember every hot, abusive inch of the Dardanelles for the rest of my life – and the grubbiness of Athens and the

Greek fire, the secret weapon of the Byzantine navy.

crestfallen disappointment in Troy. It now consists of no more than some badly restored walls, a hideous replica of the Wooden Horse, and some unremarkable earthen mounds, slopes of browned grass, which lack the force of the hillforts in Ireland or Argyll. I discovered one thing with clarity: the introspection experienced while travelling, especially during great heat, has a different quality from that of the everyday kind, and more frequently – or perhaps I mean more rapidly – the introspection becomes depression, becomes despair. Followed by that sneak thief, that con man, elation.

A smell of coffee niggled in from somewhere – not the cliché of the Turkish bazaar, this coffee was being brewed nearby, in some service room of the hotel. Such a jostling place, Istanbul. The formal lustre of Byzantium has given way to the shabby hustle of the grey city. The notion of those immediate golden backgrounds on which the icons and mosaics were painted, those dignified and brilliant images, was straightaway overwhelmed by traffic and German industry and fumes, heavy fumes, enough to make you cough, from too many engines. Istanbul has not yet travelled far enough around its own circle to be able to afford to burnish the past that was Byzantium and Constantinople. The entrances to the museums and castles had the shabbiness of such barely necessary amenities in all poor cities – other requirements, more urgent than history, must take precedence.

The heat of the morning continued to enter through the open window. No breeze, no pasha's fan turning overhead. My arms were sore, my neck and my forehead raw. When the citizens here had to defend their city against the Arabs in a four-year siege during the seventh century, they made use of an old Greek invention, a Byzantine cocktail called Greek Fire, a mixture of lime, sulphur, perhaps a little mustard and saltpetre, and some liquid with the properties of paraffin or petrol. When hurled, even on water, it burst into flames. Some of it must still be hanging about the place, if my face offers anything to go by. I supposed it could well be raining now on Skellig Michael.

Out in the air a chanting to prayer dinned across, above the roofs. I had never heard it before, a sound both cranky and arrogant, and it brought with it another disappointment – the minarets had posies of loudspeakers clustered to them, the sound had a metallic quality. Perhaps they use recordings, like poor parishes of the Church of England. 'And the silken girls bringing sherbet' – I remembered fragments from Eliot's 'The Journey of the Magi' as I walked down the street to the hotel. The road I came in along had cobbles for miles, perhaps the only cobbled motorway in the world.

> And the cities hostile and the towns unfriendly,
> And the villages dirty and charging high prices.

Byzantium; Constantinople; Stamboul; Istanbul. 'O City, Chief of all Cities, City Centre of all Parts of the World! O City! City, the glory of

Christians, and confusion of barbarians! O City, City second Paradise planted in the West with every tree abundant in its spiritual fruits! Paradise where is your beauty? Where is that copious outpouring of graces so salutary for body and soul?' Few cities in the world have been so assaulted, few cities have been so worth assaulting, few cities have been so dramatically lamented by their historians, such as – in this case – Michael Ducas. To the western colonists, Byzantium's location seemed like the door of a treasure-house called the East and vice versa, and thus the battles raged, for a thousand years since Byzas's foundation until Constantine, on 11 May, AD 330, formally inaugurated the New Rome, Constantinople.

Constantine had come from the Roman patrician classes who saw Christianity as no more than a creed followed by artisans, plebs, foreigners and slaves – yet he had been converted. On an October day in 312, as he prepared for a final battle against Maxentius, a rival contender for the position of emperor after the abdication and retirement of Diocletian, a cross of sunlight appeared in the sky, bearing the instruction, 'In this Sign Conquer'. He put the sign of the cross on his banners and did conquer, and took control, an impulsive man of great energy and self-confidence, a man in whom the civil administrator and military commander combined to create the empire builder. He had travelled throughout the Empire and had often lived outside Rome – it was at York, remember, that his soldiers acclaimed him Emperor – and he decided that the frontiers of the Empire, both in the Rhine and Danube valleys, and, to the east, along the Euphrates could better be supervised from a more strategically placed city than Rome. He measured the extent of his New Rome by walking: Edward Gibbon, in his *Decline and Fall of the Roman Empire*, describes Constantine's dream the night before (or rather, how later writers interpreted what Constantine might have seen):

The tutelar genius of the city, a venerable matron sinking under the weight of years and infirmities, was suddenly transformed into a blooming maid, whom his own hands adorned with all the symbols of Imperial greatness. The monarch awoke, interpreted the auspicious omen, and obeyed, without hesitation, the will of Heaven . . . . On foot, with a lance in his hand, the emperor himself led the solemn procession, and directed the line which was traced as the boundary of the destined capital, till the growing circumference was observed with astonishment by the assistants who, at length, ventured to observe that he had already exceeded the most ample measure of a great city.

At which point Constantine made it plain to his companions that the initial survey of the site lay in the hands of another – 'HE, the invisible guide who marches before me . . . .'

With intense industry, the Emperor then built a city of memorable style. 'A particular description,' wrote Gibbon,

composed a century after its foundation, enumerates a capitol or school of learning, a circus, two theatres, eight public and one hundred and fifty-three private baths, fifty-two porticoes, five granaries, eight aqueducts or reservoirs of water, four spacious halls for the meetings of the senate or courts of justice, fourteen churches, fourteen palaces, and four thousand, three hundred and eighty-eight houses which, for their size or beauty, deserved to be distinguished from the multitude of plebeian habitations.

This, the New or Second Rome, became a byword both for splendour and for efficient administration. The man who presided over it was described by Gibbon:

His stature was lofty, his countenance majestic, his deportment graceful; his strength and activity were displayed in every manly exercise, and, from his earliest youth to a very advanced season of life, he preserved the vigour of his constitution by a strict adherence to the domestic virtues of chastity and temperance. He delighted in the social intercourse of familiar conversation; and though he might sometimes indulge his disposition to raillery with less reserve than was required by the severe dignity of his station, the courtesy and liberality of his manners gained the hearts of all who approached him.

He also had his own son, Crispus, of whom he was jealous, executed. Constantine died in 337 at the age of sixty-four, at Nicomedia, appropriately at the noontide of Pentecost. His body was drawn slowly to his city in a gold coffin and his name stayed as his monument until the city fell to the Ottoman Empire, who even then called it Konstantinye, and eventually Stamboul, Istanbul.

Two centuries after Constantine died, when Justinian became Emperor, the city's population stood at about three-quarters of a cosmopolitan million. Constantinople represented a confluence of East and West. Under Justinian Germanic cavalry had honour in the ranks of the Empire's soldiery, part of the military and social fabric, here as in Italy. Copts from Egypt, people from Illyria and various tribal regions along the east coast of the Adriatic, Hittites and Armenians and Jews and Syrians and Italians and Greeks and Goths – they teemed in a city that could be a tinder box when it came to civil disagreement, a city notorious for major riots, quelled with equally notorious ferocity. A high level of employment existed, due principally to the bureaucratic infrastructure of the administration, where, confusingly, Latin prevailed. The support industries throve too, with accountants, jewellers, weavers, carpenters and a host of other trades. The tradesmen belonged to guilds, which regulated prices and apprenticeships – admissions to trades came under strict scrutiny.

The diet consisted of meat, often pork, fish, beans, barley, bread, wine, shellfish. Wheat became scarce after the granaries of Egypt were lost to Islam. The control of the food supply became one of the most important public functions. Most citizens received a measure of free food, principally bread – not out of altruism, but because in an environment where the supply of raw materials could be volatile hunger caused riots quicker than politics did. Beggars slept in the alleyways in the interstices of the houses; fires broke out frequently and destroyed entire streets. The wealthy travelled on horseback or in closed carriages, always protected against robbers. The common people walked everywhere – even nowadays the streets and lanes and bridges of Istanbul become so crowded that pushing through them feels like being part of a permanent football crowd. And still the street vendors try to lure you into their booths, to buy handmade leather which they tool before your eyes, and still they sell to all on the street food from instant stalls which unfold from bicycles, or kittens or small goats which they carry inside their jackets, or little donkey foals, or jewellery.

Justinian waited in the wings until his uncle, the elderly Justin, died in 527. While being patient he cultivated cliques of support, including a section of the populace known as the Blues, whose membership was led by wealthy conservatives and whose rivals, the Greens, hooting at them in the Hippodrome or at the games, or in the street riots, consisted of merchants and tradesmen. Justinian used his power to excess, and brutally, in favour of the Blues, who carried on rackets of blackmail, robbery and murder. In their company he met the woman who joined in his fame as he set out to establish a reputation as the brilliant ruler and entrepreneur of an Empire which once again, though briefly, became as dazzling as Rome had ever been.

The Byzantine historian Procopius, who was Belisarius's secretary, had a waspish and bitter demeanour in his writing. He also vacillated – across three sets of works his opinions of the Emperor and the Empress varied. In his *Historiae* – of Justinian's Gothic, Vandal and Persian wars – he adopted a neutral, factual position. In *De Aedificiis*, his discussion of the public buildings of the Empire, he became complimentary. He wrote a third book, however, *Historia Arcana*, the Secret History, in which he said he put facts unsuited to the disciplines of his other works: in short, he wrote a scandalous account of the lives and times of his Emperor and Empress.

He described Justinian's Empress, Theodora, the 'actress' daughter of a bear-keeper, in the following terms:

Before Theodora remained developed to the point where she could please a man in bed, or enjoy full womanly sexual activity, she acted like a young male prostitute, attracting clients of a very low sort, even slaves .... When she was old enough, though, she became a full-blooded courtesan ... and sold her total bodily pleasures to all and sundry. She did not possess even the smallest jot of modesty, and responded eagerly to the most lascivious requests ... quite capable of throwing off all her clothes and showing off those parts of her, before and behind, which common decency requires to be concealed from men's eyes .... She used to tease her clients, she made them wait, and then experimented with new methods of making love ... she went to parties with ten companions, copulated with each one, and then with their servants, often more than thirty in a night .... In the theatre she took off all her clothes except the compulsory girdle and lay face upward, her legs spread wide apart. Her servant then sprinkled barley grains upon her intimate parts and geese, trained specially, picked the grains off one by one.

Justinian married her in his early forties, and he had to change the laws of the Empire – which decreed that no member of the ruling body could marry somebody who appeared on the stage – in order to make Theodora his Empress. They married in the huge church of Haghia Sophia, where large black and gold discs bearing symbols of Islam now hang over the central concourse in the greatest basilica of the Byzantine world, originated by Constantine two hundred years before, and then rebuilt by Justinian.

Justinian's two superb generals, Belisarius and Narses, reclaimed for a time those Italian and African territories which the Roman Empire had lost to the Goths and Vandals. With his learned advisers Justinian drafted and redrafted laws for all citizens of the Empire, terrorized the Pope and pronounced on matters of Church as well as State. His lady wife Theodora, who had once reproached nature for not giving her a further orifice at her breast – 'to accommodate', as Gibbon put it, 'another dart, she wished for a fourth altar on which to pour her libations of love' – continued to lead a licentious existence in the palace surrounded by eunuchs and friends, while in his public statements her husband raised her to the level of living sainthood.

Justinian and Theodora both appear as semi-divine in the mosaics at Ravenna. During their reign, Halley's Comet passed across the skies and earthquakes shook Constantinople, in one instance for forty successive days. A plague came in from Syria and Persia, obviously of the kind that, as described by Paul the Deacon, had infected Lombard northern Italy in 566 and, according to Gregory of Tours, parts of France in 580. Gibbon describes similar symptoms: 'The infection was sometimes announced by the visions of a distempered fancy, and the victim despaired as soon as he had heard the menace and felt the stroke of an invisible spectre.' Eventually, as the illness progressed, 'The fever was often accompanied with lethargy or delirium; the bodies of the sick were covered with black pustules or carbuncles, the symptoms of immediate death.' Five to ten thousand people a day died in Constantinople, a savage toll, in that plague. Gibbon, perhaps too harshly, sums up Justinian's reign, the one whose imprint remained the most vivid in the time of our monk, as follows: 'The triple scourge of war, pestilence and famine afflicted the subjects of Justinian, and his reign is disgraced by a visible decrease of the human species which has never been repaired in some of the fairest countries of the globe.'

Theodora died on 28 June 548. Her husband died seventeen years later on 14 November 565. Some would say that at this point the Fall of Constantinople, not completed until 1453, had begun. By 687 the city had increasingly come under extreme pressure from internecine revolt and external threat. Two years before the monk arrived, in 685, Justinian II had ascended the throne, an ill man. By that time all the gains Justinian had made 160 years earlier had been lost. A period of long dynastic rulerships had, however, followed Justinian I, in which the remarkable Heraclius almost outshone both Constantine and Justinian.

With various hiccups, four emperors succeeded Justinian before Heraclius – Justin II, then Tiberius 578–82, Maurice 582–602 and Phocas 602–10 – an appalling, drunken, red-haired despot who had his predecessor assassinated. Heraclius, son of the Exarch of Carthage, was sent for by the patricians of Constantinople. The Frankish historian Fredegar described him as 'striking in appearance, for he was handsome, tall, braver than others and a great fighter. He would often kill lions in the arena and many a wild boar in unfrequented places. Being well read he practised astrology by

Coin of the reign of Justinian II.

which art he discovered, God helping him, that his empire would be laid waste by circumcised races' – an omen which led him to sanction a massacre of Jews in 629, unaware that the equally circumcised Arabs were to be the real downfall of the Empire. Heraclius invaded Constantinople with a fleet, tortured and decapitated Phocas and, upon becoming Emperor, immediately had to deal with the Persians in a war that had begun four years earlier in 606 and was to last until 628. In the end Heraclius defeated the Persians and recovered the lost territories of Syria and Egypt. But since the Empire had been debilitated by the length and ferocity of the Persian wars it lay feeble before the ominously emerging Arab powers that captured Damascus in 635, only three years after the death of Islam's founder, Mohammed.

This new force, fast, lethal and inspired, rocketing like a phenomenon out of the desert, impinged hugely upon the life of Constantinople in 687–8. The march of the Arab world brought Mohammed's followers into north-west Africa by the middle of the century, poised for southern Europe. After conquering Syria and laying siege unsuccessfully to Constantinople from 674 to 678 they came back in 717 and were repelled once more. And so it was to go on, a long, lingering death, with brief periods of remission, until the end came in 1453.

Once it held the title of Second Paradise and was called Mistress of the World, a strategic connotation. Istanbul offers not an end to a journey, but a starting point: you need to live here, not visit. The population stands at nearly seven million, many of them piled high in apartments, or in shanty towns behind great streets. The taxi driver took me up narrow streets to meet his friends, hectic alleys where the people had no visible means of support. Winding untarred lanes, some quite wide, lined with tilting houses of old wooden construction shored up with galvanized iron, contained dark-eyed children and men who stood on the street and talked, and women who sat. The city seemed unbalanced, toppled over by the poor, a city of small traders and old cars with rattling exhausts.

The Column of Constantine, the ruins of which still stand near the old bazaar, once housed in its base a time capsule chosen from the best of the Old and the New Testaments – the axe with which Noah built the Ark, the stone from which Moses drew water when he struck it with his staff, the loaves of bread from the Wedding at Cana where Christ turned the water into wine (though some said they came from the Miracle of the Loaves and Fishes, where a lot had been left over), and the alabaster ointment box which Mary Magdalene used when bathing the feet of Christ.

Haghia Sophia, the Great Church of the Holy Wisdom, stands out clear and calm among the mosques and minarets on the hill across the Golden

Horn. By the time my Irish pilgrim arrived here the Christianity of western Europe had just launched its Golden Age, while at the very gates of Constantinople Islam had begun to preside over its ruthless decline in the East. The Christian territories beyond Constantinople, once the most devout of all the regions of Christianity, when conquered by Islam were never regained.

'Now above these arches is raised a circular building of a curved form through which the light of day first shines, for the building which I imagine overtops the whole country, has small openings left on purpose, so that the places where these intervals occur may serve for the light to come through. Thus far I imagine the building is not capable of being described, even by a weak and feeble tongue.' Procopius had difficulty in grasping and then conveying in mere language the generous austerity of Haghia Sophia. The warm walls with pillars rise far to Heaven; the mosaics and decoration, where they can still be seen, and the general traces of Justinian's Empire and Constantine's intent have exhausted the efforts of centuries of writers and invaders. The difficulty in perceiving the building today lies in the fact that, though granted the status of a museum, it none the less feels like a temple in which the gods are confused. It may once have seen the coronations of emperors, and was raised in order to sing the glory of the Christian God, and then echoed to the wailed glories of Allah and dignified submission to Him embodied in the word Islam – but it fell to invaders in circumstances throughout which political and territorial considerations received a spiritual dimension. The spiritual connection which the building's architecture was intended to make has therefore been deflected, and, though gorgeous to inspect, the mix of religion and politics promoted unease in me. At least in Ayasofia (as it is now called) this discomfort can, presumably, be overcome by a concentration upon the architectural details.

The light pours in through forty windows in the massive dome which measures 101 feet in diameter and 180 feet in height; the church, 345 feet long, has two smaller domes east and west. The gallery, high-ceilinged and spacious, traditionally belonged to the women – except for one section reserved for the imperial household and for religious and theological councils. Eight of the huge marble columns which stalk the nave had been taken from an early Constantinople building – the materials for others were quarried on an island in the Sea of Marmara. In the vestibule, protected by enormous doors of bronze reminiscent of the Pantheon's doors, though lighter in tone and structure, the tenth-century mosaics need much light to be inspected fully. When revealed they show an idealized Mother and Christ flanked by Constantine offering a model of Constantinople and an unusually humble Justinian offering a model of Haghia Sophia; he wears the crossed vestments of a priest, has a halo and strapped sandals. The motif of a prelate or secular dignitary offering the building or city over which they had jurisdiction recurs throughout the imagery of the Byzantines – creating both an impression of the power held by the incumbent and the greater power of God and His Mother which the temporal leader acknowledges, as well as the semi-divine stature of the ruler.

On a more accessible scale Haghia Eirene, Aya Irini Kilisesi, the Church of Divine Peace, built in 300, on the site of a temple to Aphrodite, now on the edge of the Topkapi Palace, has become a museum and is also used as a concert hall. It has a sweetness in its nature and size, and in the Byzantine-ness of its scale and humour – smaller though in the same harmonies as Haghia Sophia, pillars and arches walking towards an altar in the distance, a domed peace with a gallery and dry walls, and dry air. Although it has experienced many rebuildings – as a result of earthquakes and fires – and the oldest visible parts date to the sixth century, it echoes the compact and organized round, domed buildings of classical Byzantine architecture as portrayed in the mosaics at Ravenna. The interior, quiet, cool and lofty, has three aisles with colannades and large columns supporting the central dome.

Resisting the blandishments of the rug sellers and the jewellers became an exhausting matter; on the one occasion on which I succumbed, certain that what I had agreed to would turn out to be spurious, I received a brilliant surprise. Unlike the larger museums around the Topkapi which possess many Babylonian artefacts, and boast a bust of Alexander as well as his sarcophagus, the Mosaic Museum does not seem like a building that has official saction. Down a modernized arcade, where the windows offer hookahs and the ineluctable Turkish carpets, the museum advertises itself with a brass plaque and very little authority. Inside, though unattractively laid out, in a loose collection of rooms, fragments of mosaic, many from the Great Palace, bid to become the most vivid I have yet seen, Ravenna notwithstanding. Stronger, more muscularly built and decorated, their colours do not gleam so lustrously as those at Ravenna or Haghia Sophia, yet – probably because they were designed as pavements for everyday use rather than precious exhibitions of spiritual high-mindedness and worship – they oddly open a pathway into a more tangible world.

The pictures include animals slaughtering and being slaughtered, heroes

Mosaic from the Great Palace of Constantinople.

in fights against villains or beasts, foliage, wooded environments, scenes from mythology. The combination of artist and artisan emerges strongly; these mosaicists built their work to last despite extensive use, and their tesserae were made of hard minerals. In Ravenna and in other civilizations, mosaicists included chips of gold, silver and more delicate substances such as the scales of reptiles and glass paste which they coloured as required. On these Byzantine pavements, dated to the fourth and fifth centuries, they used onyx, marble, green serpentine, mother of pearl, quartz, and rocks coloured with natural minerals, all beautiful and beautifully distributed, but above all durable. The mosaicists had substantial artistic talent; the anatomical accuracy and the life drawing of the animals and humans is exciting and universal: seen fifteen centuries later, their creations maintain total continuity – the figures, whether animal or human, and the flora are immediately recognizable.

Outside, not far away, a tiny shop in a busy street was crammed from top to bottom, in every corner and open piece of space, whether floor or counter, with spices – in sticks, powders, seeds, lumps, in boxes, jars and old brown paper bags of a kind which disappeared from western Europe twenty years ago. The proprietor sold vanilla pods, seed pods of cardamom, and saffron taken from the stamens of the orange-gold crocus. He and the other clichés of Istanbul and Turkey that I had seen and bewilderedly tried to encompass in a few days hammered home a point that Edward Gibbon made in his notes to the second edition of his *Decline and Fall of the Roman Empire*: 'The distinction of North and South is real and intelligible; the difference between East and West is arbitrary and shifts around the globe.' Not for a moment did I feel easy in Istanbul – I suspect that I should have found the seventh-century city easier to adjust to and comprehend. My head filled with staccato reverberations: too many people, the fervour of the devout at the mosques, too overstated for me, like the Christians praying aloud on the ferry back from Iona – and then the contrasts: the elegant linen coat worn by well-to-do gentlemen and called a Stamboul or a Stambouline, the endless supplications of peddlers and beggars, the beautifully gowned wives and the maimed. The city denies, crowds out the thinking function; only the sensation function can be made to work. I felt guilty about leaving my monk standing here, even in his time, fearing foolishly that he must have been as uneasy at the gates of the East of his day as I now felt. Still, if he discovered nothing else, he realized that the small island patch from which he had come did not constitute the centre of the universe, did not command the high moral ground of the world, did not hold the key to mankind's spirit. And he collided with a profound irony, since the word 'Islam' means 'resignation', or 'submission' – that is to say, submission to the will of God, and in the late seventh century Christianity and the cities which had constituted its most holy tabernacles outside of

Rome seemed about to submit, not to the will of God, but to submission itself, to Islam.

He stood on the edge of his past, in the Empire commanding the deserts of the anchorite fathers. South of the Mareotic Lake, round which the sages spake, in Nitria at the edge of deserts which stretched to Ethiopia, they had lived as he did on the Skelligs, in huts of stone, with a reed mat for a bed, a reed stool which at night became a pillow, drinking only water, eating their rough bread. There was God, if you like. 'Remember,' said Bede, 'I am but dust and wind and shadow and life as fleeting as the flowers of grass. But may the eternal mercy which hath shone from time of old rescue Thy servant from the jaws of the lion.'

The full circle of time and the imagination: I had set out to travel in the footsteps of such a man, not to make a comparative study of Europe then and now – too vast a subject, and already catered for excellently elsewhere. I had wanted to make a long journey which would link for me the pastoral ease and rich oral heritage of Ireland with the excitement and complexity of those civilizations of the Mediterranean and the Near East. The man who travelled from Skellig Michael to the gates of the East made a brief and illuminating passage out of some kind of darkness and into some kind of light. He wandered away from the traps of parochial and insular experience into a wider world, out of the residual darkness of childhood into a time of learning – and as with all such processes there was no digestion as yet of what he had learned.

I still had Bede in my bag, the *Ecclesiastical History of the English Nation*, and read him with kebabs and crumbling cheese in a huge restaurant, surrounded by more poor people than I had ever seen in one room. In the early seventh century Bishop Paulinus of York, whom Bede described as 'a tall man, a little stooping, with black hair, a meagre visage and a slender aquiline nose, with a presence venerable and awe-inspiring', preached to Edwin, the King of Northumbria, and his assembled soldiers. As he rose to full evangelical powers, a bird flew through the hall. One of Edwin's 'chief men' observed,

The present life of man, O King, seems to me, in comparison of that time which is unknown to us, like to the swift flight of a sparrow through the room where you sit at supper in winter, with your commanders and ministers, and a good fire in the midst, whilst the storms of rain and snow prevail abroad; the sparrow, I say, flying in at one door, and immediately out at another, whilst he is within, is safe from the wintry storm; but after that short space of fair weather, he immediately vanishes out of sight, out into the dark weather from which he had emerged. So, the life of man appears for a short space. But of what went before, or what is to follow, we are utterly ignorant.

His words could have applied to all the *peregrinii*, hardbitten or dying by the way, turning their faces back to home or permanently exiled.

SELECT BIBLIOGRAPHY

BEDE, ed. J. A. Giles: *Ecclesiastical History of the English Nation*. George Bell, London, 1900.

BROWN, PETER: *Society and the Holy in Late Antiquity*. Faber, London, 1982.

BROWNING, ROBERT: *Justinian and Theodora*. Weidenfeld and Nicolson, London, 1971.

BRUNDAGE, JAMES A.: *Law, Sex and Christian Society in Medieval Europe*. University of Chicago Press, Chicago and London, 1987.

CAMPBELL, JOSEPH: *Papers from the Eranos Yearbooks*, Bollingen Series XXX. Pantheon Books and Bollingen Foundation, New York, 1955.

FINLEY, M. I.: *Economy and Society in Ancient Greece*. Chatto and Windus, London, 1971.

FREDEGAR, trans. J. M. Wallace-Hadrill, *The Fourth Book of the Chronicle of Fredegar*. Thomas Nelson and Sons, London, 1960.

DUCAS, MICHAEL, *The History of the Emperors John Manuel, John and Constantine Paleologus*, Bucharest, 1948.

GIBBON, EDWARD: *The History of the Decline and Fall of the Roman Empire*. The Folio Society, London, 1984-7.

GREGORY OF TOURS, trans. Lewis Thorpe: *The History of the Franks*. Penguin, London, 1986.

JAMES, EDWARD: *The Origins of France*. Macmillan, London, 1982.

JOHNSON, PAUL: *A History of Christianity*. Weidenfeld and Nicolson, London, 1976.

JOHNSON, PAUL: *A History of the Jews*. Weidenfeld and Nicolson, London, 1987.

LEVI, PETER: *The Frontiers of Paradise*. Collins Harvill, London, 1987.

LLEWELLYN, PETER: *Rome in the Dark Ages*. Faber, London, 1971.

MACAIRT, SEAN, ed.: *The Annals of Innisfallen*. Dublin Institute for Advanced Studies, 1951.

MCNEILL, WILLIAM: *Plagues and Peoples*. Blackwell, Oxford, 1977.

MOORHOUSE, GEOFFREY: *Against All Reason*. Weidenfeld and Nicolson, London, 1969.

NEILL, STEPHEN: *A History of Christian Missions*. Pelican, London, 1986.

PARKE, H. W.: *Festivals of the Athenians*. Thames and Hudson, London, 1977.

PAULUS DEACONUS, trans. William Dudley Foulke: *History of the Langobards*. University of Pennsylvania, Philadelphia, and Longmans, London, 1907.

PAUSANIUS, trans. Peter Levi: *Guide to Greece*. Penguin Books, London, 1971.

RICHE, PIERRE, trans. Jo Ann McNamara: *Daily Life in the World of Charlemagne*. Liverpool University Press, 1978.

SARTON, GEORGE: *Ancient and Modern Civilisation*. Edward Arnold, London, and Nebraska University Press, 1954.

STOKES, GEORGE T. and Hugh Jackson Lawlor: *Ireland and the Celtic Church*. Macmillan, London, 1928.

THOMAS, CHARLES: *Christianity in Roman Britain to AD 500*. Batsford, London, 1981.

THOMAS, CHARLES: *Celtic Britain*. Thames and Hudson, London, 1986.

WADDELL, HELEN: *Songs of the Wandering Scholars*. The Folio Society, London, 1982.

WADDELL, HELEN: *The Desert Fathers*. Constable, London, 1936 and 1987.

WEBB, J. F., ed.: *The Age of Bede*. Penguin, London, 1986.

PHOTOGRAPHIC
ACKNOWLEDGEMENTS

COLOUR INSERT ONE

Page 33, Des Lavelle; 34 *above*, Des Lavelle; 34 *below*, Ancient Monuments Section, Board of Works, Dublin; 35, Bord Failte Eireann; 36, The Board of Trinity College Dublin; 37, National Museum of Ireland; 38 *above*, David Paterson; 38 *below*, Ted Spiegel/Susan Griggs Agency; 39, Michael Holford; 40, The British Library.

COLOUR INSERT TWO

Page 73, Charlie Waite/Landscape Only; 74, Ronald Sheridan's Photo Library; 75, Ronald Sheridan's Photo Library; 76, Ronald Sheridan's Photo Library; 77, Bridgeman Art Library; 78, Stiftsbibliothek, St Gallen; 79, Stiftsbibliothek, St Gallen; 80, Horst Munzig/Susan Griggs Agency.

COLOUR INSERT THREE

Page 113, Scala, Florence; 114, *above*, Giraudon, Paris; 114 *below*, Giraudon, Paris; 115, Scala, Florence; 116, Scala, Florence; 117, Erich Lessing/John Hillelson Agency; 118, Sonia Halliday Photographs; 119, Michael Holford; 120, Scala, Florence.

COLOUR INSERT FOUR

Page 169, Erich Lessing/John Hillelson Agency; 170, Scala, Florence; 171, Sonia Halliday Photographs; 172, Werner Forman Archive; 173, Werner Forman Archive; 174, Scala, Florence; 175, Erich Lessing/John Hillelson Agency; 176, Landscape Only.

COLOUR INSERT FIVE

Page 209, Sonia Halliday Photographs; 210, Ronald Sheridan's Photo Library; 211, Michael Holford; 212, Sonia Halliday Photographs; 213, Sonia Halliday Photographs; 214, Ronald Sheridan's Photo Library; 215, Michael Holford; 216, Giraudon, Paris.

INDEX

THE INSIDE STORY OF THE
LIONS IN SOUTH AFRICA
2009 # Pride
Restored

MICK CLEARY

WITH COMMENTS FROM
Ian McGeechan

OPINION QUOTES COMPILED BY
Terry Cooper

EDITED BY
Ian Robertson

PHOTOGRAPHS BY
Getty Images
and Matthew Impey

CORINTHIAN BOOKS

Published in the UK in 2009 by
Corinthian Books, an imprint of
Icon Books Ltd, Omnibus Business Centre,
39–41 North Road, London N7 9DP
email: info@iconbooks.co.uk
www.iconbooks.co.uk

Sold in the UK, Europe, South Africa and Asia
by Faber & Faber Ltd, Bloomsbury House,
74–77 Great Russell Street, London WC1B 3DA

Distributed in the UK, Europe, South Africa and Asia
by TBS Ltd, TBS Distribution Centre, Colchester Road,
Frating Green, Colchester CO7 7DW

This edition published in Australia in 2009
by Allen & Unwin Pty Ltd,
PO Box 8500, 83 Alexander Street,
Crows Nest, NSW 2065

Distributed in Canada by
Penguin Books Canada,
90 Eglinton Avenue East, Suite 700,
Toronto, Ontario M4P 2YE

ISBN: 978-190685-009-8

Produced by Lennard Books
A division of Lennard Associates Ltd
Mackerye End, Harpenden, Herts AL5 5DR

Production editor: Chris Marshall
Text and cover design: Paul Cooper
The editor is also grateful to Vivian Cooper and Clare Robertson
for their contribution to the development of this book

Printed and bound in the UK
by Butler Tanner and Dennis

■ Contents ■

883,839 players. 57,000 teams. 9,810 clubs. 4 nations. Behind one shirt.

www.lionsrugby.com/hsbc

■ Forewords ■

The X-Calibur Group are proud to support this book. We are a small group of companies but like rugby we are rapidly expanding worldwide. Even in these difficult times it is extremely important that companies however big or small continue to support sport and rugby in particular.

I attended the last two Tests and experienced the frustration and disappointment at Loftus and the jubilation and pride at Ellis Park. The Lions roared, they dug deep and the triumphant result at 28 – 9 was true testament to the quality of the team. They may have lost the series but for many including myself they won the tour. I must also recognize the Lions supporters; I understand that over 30,000 of them travelled to South Africa to support the Lions. The support was stunning: the Sea of Red was everywhere and they refused to let the first two results overwhelm them. Their dedication was rewarded not only with a win in the third Test but with a score that proved conclusively who was the better team that day.

Finally I would like to thank Ian McGeechan and his squad for their courage, determination and tenacity in making this British & Irish Lions Tour one for the history books. They made the people of the United Kingdom and Ireland proud and have earned our respect. ■

Brian Davies, Chairman, X-Calibur Group Limited and XQ International Limited

On behalf of everyone at Intrinsic Financial Services, I would like to express my appreciation for the phenomenal commitment and effort shown by the Lions during this summer's tour of South Africa. Every person involved in the Lions set-up, whether behind the scenes or on the pitch, should feel incredibly proud of their achievements. The players have produced some breathtaking rugby, pushing the world champions to the limit in a series that will live long in the memory.

What has been particularly evident is the immense pride with which the players have worn the Lions shirt. That pride was the basis around which a genuine team spirit was built; a spirit that resulted in a magnificent tour that has done so much to re-assert the true values of the British & Irish Lions. Congratulations to Ian McGeechan, his staff and players – and here's to Australia in 2013! ■

Lord Sandy Leitch, Chairman, Intrinsic Financial Services

The very fact that the British & Irish Lions only tour South Africa once every 12 years makes such a trip very special. Following the last series win in 1997 the Lions enjoyed a fantastic but ultimately unsuccessful tour to Australia in 2001 and in 2005 they were totally out-played by a fantastically motivated All Blacks side. Against the Springboks this year the support from 20,000+ travelling from the UK was phenomenal at each of the three Test grounds, and whilst the series was lost 2-1 the way the team recovered well to win the final game in Johannesburg showed immense character.

Greene King are delighted once again to sponsor this Lions Book; rugby and great cask ale go very well together. Greene King IPA has for the past three years been the official beer of England Rugby and we supply over 500 rugby clubs in England alone. We are also sponsors of Quins for a second year and have recently extended our club involvement with our support of Sale. Finally, let's raise a glass to the fantastic efforts of the squad in South Africa and look forward to visiting Australia in 2013. ■

David Elliott, Greene King Pub Partners

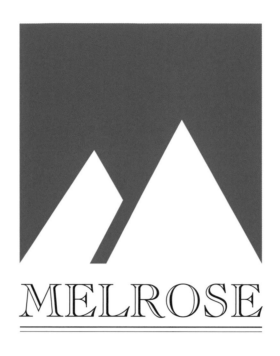

MELROSE

making acquisitions
driving performance
realising value

www.melroseplc.net

  MarelliMotori

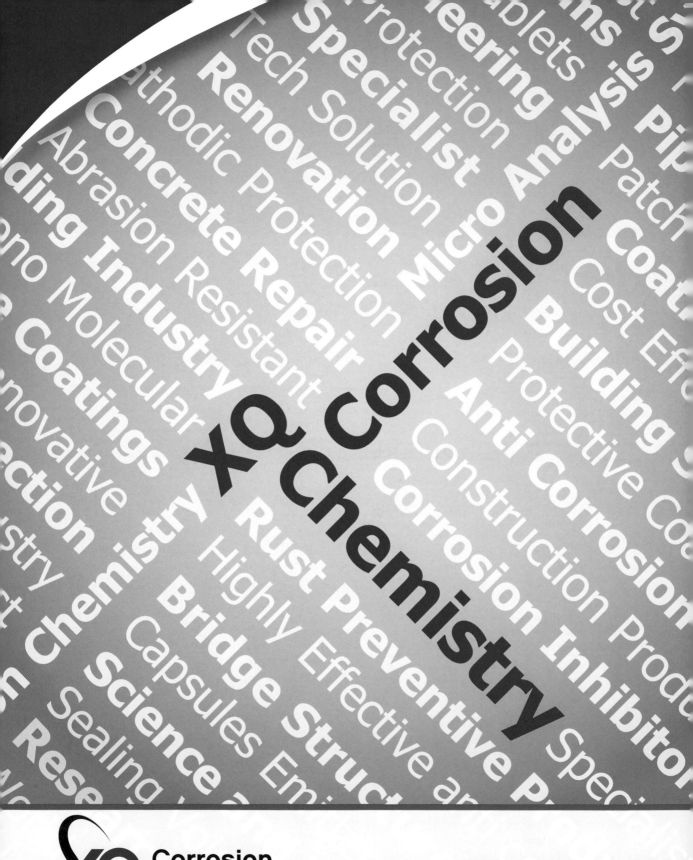

XQ Corrosion
XQ Chemistry

Corrosion
Chemistry

www.xqglobal.com

1
Ins and Outs

■ Do you want to know what it means to be a Lion? Well, don't bother asking the merry gaggle of blokes at the Lions pre-tour training camp at Pennyhill Park in Bagshot one bright mid-May morning. The mood there resembled the first day of a new school term: some older kids who knew what it was all about greeting old mates like long-lost brothers, while the fresh-faced mob smiled at everything and everyone, even the media. ■

You'd get all the usual jolly guff, sincere and meaningful in its way, about how this was the greatest challenge for a rugby player, about bonding and coming together, about tradition and folklore. All very proper and cheery and, let's face it, correct. For these men, and for those of us on the outside looking in, the Lions is exciting and different and unique.

Yes, as is always the case, it really was a nice place to be on that first morning in camp, with hope in every heart and horizons stretching out in front of everyone, possibilities still to be fulfilled, narratives to be written. You'd want to be there to drink it all in – to hear Ian McGeechan, once again in the chair, holding forth about what it means to be a Lion; to

listen to new head boy Paul O'Connell of Munster speak about the need to fill the jersey. Gerald Davies, dapper as ever, poetic and charming, making the hairs tingle every time he opened his mouth as once he used to do every time he got the ball, with that familiar white collar on red shirt starchily erect, ready to pounce. You knew the sidestep was coming, just as these days you know the bon mot is taking shape, and the heart skips a little beat.

It was an evocative backdrop, one that told you so much about the Lions. And Tom Shanklin wasn't there either to witness it or, more tellingly, to be part of it. If you truly want to know what it meant to be a Lion in 2009, to really understand the enduring appeal, the mystique, the grip it exerts on a broad spectrum of people, then ask Shanklin.

For starters, take a look at the snapshot of him being led along the touch line of the Arms Park a couple of weeks earlier, his shoulder immobilised, dislocation yet to be confirmed but already with the grim reality beginning to sink into his every pore and fibre. He was out. The dream was over before it had begun. No tour. No trip of a lifetime. No chance to express himself as one of the classiest outside centres in the British and Irish Isles, to put pressure on Brian O'Driscoll every step of the way, to push himself to his limits and O'Driscoll to his, all for the common good.

Shanklin would be denied all these opportunities. But do you know what he would miss the most? 'I was really up for it, really looking forward to giving of my best on the field, and then getting to know other players,' said Shanklin. 'We just don't do that any more. You fly in, you play, you fly out, and you rarely have as much as a beer together. For me, that is the special bit about the Lions. It's a throwback, it's different. To miss out at such a late stage is horrible.'

All the more so given that Shanklin's experience of the Lions in 2005 was brief and blighted. A knee injury after just three matches meant that he was one of the early casualties. He barely played again that season. At least in 2005 Shanklin got an inkling of what it was like. In 2009, he was already a footnote, an asterisk for future generations, a man denied.

You can easily forget in an era of slick PR and platitude-laden press conferences that these blokes are the self-same types that embarked for South Africa in 1974, or for New Zealand in 1950, or on any single one of the Lions tours to have left these shores. The players may be more remote these days, more single-minded in what they do and in what they are, less known as people and better known as celebrities – but in truth they haven't changed that much. Rugby blokes are rugby blokes, and a Lions tour does us all the great service of reminding us of that simple essence.

McGeechan knows that better than anyone. As he said during his opening remarks on that first day: '1997 was the first professional Lions tour and a lot of people at the time thought it would be the last.' Too many other competing interests. Too many games to play, too much money to be earned elsewhere first. McGeechan never doubted the worth of the Lions. Others did, and still do.

Professionalism has spawned many good things: better athletes, a broader-based interest in the game, tribal followings at club level, less stuffiness, bigger crowds, more noise and colour in grounds. But when money is involved, self-interest can take root. There are many factions who object to the great chunk of time taken up by a Lions tour. As if you could condense it into a fortnight and have done with it. As if it were rugby's Twenty20. Perish the thought.

In fact, there was a little spat to mar the beginning of this trip, when Scotland prop Euan Murray was withheld from attending the first day's gathering by his club, Northampton. There was a sense of grievance in the air that Monday morning, the Lions visibly annoyed that their symbolic coming-together for a few hours, before those playing in the European finals headed back to their respective teams, had been scuppered. Northampton were playing Bourgoin that Friday in the final of the European Challenge Cup at the Twickenham Stoop. Leinster and Leicester were contesting the Heineken Cup final the following day at Murrayfield. The five players involved in that little set-to (four from Leinster and Harry Ellis of Leicester; Tom Croft had not yet been called up) were all at Pennyhill Park. Murray was not.

The Lions stressed that the four unions had been fully apprised of their wishes the previous autumn. Northampton claimed that there had been a misunderstanding and that they knew nothing of that original request. Even so, what they did know was that Murray himself would have felt dreadfully compromised. Of course, the Challenge Cup final was a mightily important game. Of course, the tight-head prop is a key part of any training session. You do wonder, mind, how many training sessions a side needs in a nine-month season before it gets it right.

Northampton also invoked a ruling by the clubs' umbrella organisation, Premier Rugby, to back its decision not to release a player outside the designated windows outlined in IRB Regulation 9.

So much for procedure.

In real terms, of course, the only person really affected by Murray's absence was Murray himself. But the incident highlighted many of the underlying

■ FACING PAGE No replica this. Scotland hooker Ross Ford gets his hands on something far more valuable – a genuine Lions shirt as he is called up to replace the unfortunate Jerry Flannery.

strains. For the Lions to exist, to survive and, now, to thrive has been a monumental battle against various forces. Some clubs and some unions at times would be happy if they didn't have the quadrennial problem of how to shoehorn them into the schedule.

At this point, it's worth doffing the hat to those who have seen off these seditious types, who have fought the fight on behalf of the Lions and ensured that they are stronger today than they have ever been. And that is you, dear reader, and your many thousands of chums in Great Britain, Ireland and beyond. For the warmth of the welcome extended to the Lions spreads from all corners of the globe. The Lions are box office in South Africa, New Zealand, Australia and even beyond. Rugby fans of whatever persuasion love them. McGeechan had an adjunct to his one-time fear that the Lions might be under threat: 'And yet, here we are in 2009, and they are more popular than ever.'

The Lions shirt is one of the most lucrative bits of merchandising kit in world sport. In 2005, sales outstripped those of Real Madrid in the build-up to the tour of New Zealand, with 750,000 units sold. In 2009, the clamour for a piece of the Lions was as intense as it had ever been. Small wonder that the authorities could afford to make the 2009 tourists the best-remunerated Lions ever, with a basic fee of £38,000 and a £10,000 bonus for a winning series. Clubs would also benefit to the tune of £42,500 for each of their players selected for the tour. The coffers were full. Each union would make their quid and everyone should have been happy.

But they weren't. Not wholly and totally. There was a tingle of apprehension in the air as the tour made ready to depart. Not really within the party, although there was the usual sportsman's sense of nervous anticipation for what lay ahead. No, the questioning came primarily from outside, from the

sceptics as well as, it has to be said, from those who cherish these tours as the last great rugby adventure. So much of the modern touring experience is a soulless occupation. As Shanklin said so plaintively: fly in, fly out. Hang around hotel, utter a few clichés, invariably get beaten if you're a northern hemisphere side playing somewhere south of the equator and beetle back to Blighty and surroundings as quickly as possible. You can detect a weary tone in the mouth of every Super 14 player as they contemplate another season on the road.

The Lions offers the possibility of touring within a country and not just to a country. There are midweek matches, new combinations to sort and gel, mucking in with new mates and helping to create a mood – all these elements that were once the norm now only exist on a Lions tour. But what if the Lions were to get panned again, as they had been in New Zealand in 2005? There was huge hype, too, surrounding that trip, a sense of relish about what was to come. And it all went 'pop', so horribly flat.

The fact that thousands were emptying bank accounts to fly down to South Africa suggested that the disenchantment was short-lived. Some 40,000 people were supposedly on the move. The Lions beat the credit crunch! Spirits had been re-energised and

The physical contest is still the nub of rugby in South Africa. If you don't front up, then you're doomed. If you show the merest hint of doubt, you're finished. If you don't look the part, never mind play the part, then it's all over. The Lions body language had to scream defiance, their posture had to bristle with intent. And so their frontman had to be exactly that – a leader.

Central casting would have had no issues with giving the nod to O'Connell. He's a big bloke, and in the land of the Springbok that counts for something. But a Lions skipper also had to be able to cut it when the going got tough. In this regard, O'Connell had had to learn the hard way. The Munster way. He'd been schooled in hard knocks.

In New Zealand in 2005 O'Connell had started all three Tests. Yet he didn't step up to the mark. He was expected to take on a Martin Johnson-type role. As things turned out, he didn't even perform a Paul O'Connell role. He had grown enormously in stature since then, as shown by the manner in which he had helped take Munster to two Heineken Cup triumphs.

O'Connell now had to lead for McGeechan and the Lions. He had to be passionate, loyal and unrelenting. He had to set the tone. He had to take something from the McBrides and Johnsons. But above all he had to be himself. He realised that. He's a smart bloke as well as an ultra-committed one. A talented schoolboy swimmer and golfer, O'Connell is a top-notch professional athlete. He was aware, too, of the legacy of 2005, both in terms of his own form as well as the pall that hung over that trip. 'We've got to do justice to the Lions jersey and we didn't do that in 2005,' said O'Connell. 'A lot of us didn't bring our best form on tour back then. For us, it's not about sending out messages to the South Africans. It's about filling the jersey, doing the tradition proud. It's about us as a squad, as a team.'

The backbone of the Munster side that had dominated Europe in recent years, O'Connell was also the fulcrum of the Ireland team that had finally nailed down the Grand Slam in March. For all those achievements, though, there was simply no doubting where he would place a successful Lions series. 'It would top everything,' said O'Connell.

And who was he to lead into battle? The squad was revealed at a press conference at Heathrow Airport on 21 April. McGeechan named 37 players, figuring that he might need an extra body or two for the opening week: if Munster and Cardiff Blues got through to the Heineken Cup final, he'd be without 14 players for the first week's training pre-departure, then several very battered players would be clambering on to an airplane just 24 hours after contesting a European final.

And so to the unveiling, always a landmark moment. Gerald Davies read through the names in theatrical fashion. All round the four unions, the players themselves heard the news, good or bad, at the same time as the rest of the world. It was that special. It was that brutal. Joy for one lot, heartache for the others. Even so, there was a clear sense of logic about the selection.

Three national captains were missing: Ryan Jones of Wales, Scotland's Mike Blair and England skipper Steve Borthwick. Poor Ryan Jones had really tumbled down the rankings. As the Ospreys floundered in Europe, so did Jones's prospects wane. Blair was eventually to get the trip, a call-up for the stricken Tomás O'Leary, who was ruled out of the tour just three days after getting the nod. Cruel. Too cruel.

One team, one philosophy, one jersey. That Lions ethos was put to an immediate test when Warren Gatland was asked if he'd buried the hatchet with O'Connell, the man who'd publicly rebuked the Wales head coach only a few weeks earlier for his lack of grace in and around the Grand Slam game in Cardiff. 'We're all on the same side now,' said Gatland. Quite right.

They all knew that far sterner challenges lay ahead, a brutal, forensic, unremitting examination of their very being. That was why veteran Munster hard man Alan Quinlan had been chosen ahead of England's bright young thing Tom Croft. Quinlan was there to keep the midweek side honest, to bring his selfless character to the fore, to set the tone for the Test team. It's all about creating the right mood: a merciless, unforgiving environment on the field, a fun, one-for-all feel away from it. If there was one selection that summed up the Lions attitude, that was it. Croft was the fall guy, sacrificed for the greater good.

How quickly all that changed, Quinlan letting himself down and copping a 12-week ban for reckless play around the eye area of Leinster captain Leo Cullen in a dramatic Heineken Cup semi-final. You could pillory Quinlan for being a daft pillock, a rogue trader. You could. But you shouldn't. This will live with him for the rest of his days.

There were others who more rightly could be considered unlucky: England full back Delon Armitage, lively and reliable, missed the cut. Cardiff Blues wing Leigh Halfpenny profited from his club's recent surge. Halfpenny could kick goals and play full back, but Armitage, too, was versatile and a kicker. Again, how quickly all that changed, Halfpenny, the youngest of the tourists at 20, being held back after a thigh injury was found to be more serious than first thought.

Head coach Ian McGeechan was true to his word and opted for those in prime form. There were some subtleties in McGeechan's selection – Munster 'bolter' Keith Earls – but not many. There was heftiness up front, big bruising hulks such as locks Simon Shaw and Nathan Hines, the naturalised Scot from Wagga Wagga in Australia. Props Andrew Sheridan and Euan Murray, back-row forwards Joe Worsley, Stephen Ferris and Quinlan – bangers all, with a bit of nifty footwork there, too, to be fair. No team wins in South Africa by tiptoeing across the whitewash. Small wonder scrum coach Graham Rowntree referred purringly to the 'beasts' he was charged with knocking into shape. Gatland spoke of the need for players 'to fight in the trenches'. But did the Lions originally sacrifice their line-out potential by opting for Quinlan over Croft? 'I do accept that there are some limitations,' said forwards coach Warren Gatland in a bold admission of liability.

No wonder that the Lions management were arguing the toss until as late as the morning of announcement day. It's a fine-line business. Wales wing Shane Williams only sneaked home.

There were concerns elsewhere, notably at fly half. There was no out-and-out back-up to Stephen Jones and Ronan O'Gara, although Riki Flutey could switch across. The cupboard was bare. 'We wanted to go with three No. 10s but the third one didn't put his hand up,' said backs coach Rob Howley in an honest admission.

There were other borderline selections, such as England hooker Lee Mears over Rory Best of Ireland.

Wales No. 8 Andy Powell, who made such an impressive start to his international career the previous autumn only for his barnstorming approach to appear one-dimensional come more recent times, could consider himself fortunate.

The balance reflected relative fortunes. Sure, there might have been more Englishmen, but the Munster esprit de corps had swayed hearts and minds. By the time of departure, though, Munster numbers had dropped from eight to five. First O'Leary and Quinlan disappeared; now hooker Jerry Flannery was nursing his sorrows as well as a damaged elbow with his mates back home.

It would be interesting to see how the Wales coaching hierarchy dealt with the omission of their captain, Ryan Jones, when they reconvened the following autumn. Certainly the 2001 Lions head coach, Graham Henry, struggled when he returned to domestic duty in Wales. Thirteen Welshmen to South Africa in 2009, yet no captain.

There was a sense that the Lions were long on character and heart, short on glitter and go-to players. Where were the game-breakers? Where were the stars? The Robinsons, the Wilkinsons, the Guscotts? Would sweat and toil and team spirit be enough? Surely it would take more than mere grunt?

The names were known. Passports were being dusted down. Fingers were being crossed. The 2009 Lions looked to be in decent shape. They may have lacked rock 'n' roll status, star turns tuning up for another award-winning gig overseas. They knew that they had it all to do. They knew that their numbers had been drawn from a moderate Six Nations Championship, that they were perceived as toilers and workhorses, that they would have much to do to convince the outside world that the result would be anything other than a 3-0 whitewash. The only people that mattered were those who believed that it wouldn't be. The management were giving off all the right vibes, talking of unity and adventure. All they needed now was some luck. But luck for the 2009 Lions appeared to be in short supply.

■ FACING PAGE BA's 'Air Force Scrum' prepares to fly the 2009 British & Irish Lions tour party to South Africa on 24 May. Leigh Halfpenny, recovering from a thigh injury, joined the squad in South Africa in early June.

INTRINSIC

Our financial strength provides you with advice you can trust

At Intrinsic, we offer financial advice you can trust from a partner you can rely on.

Our national network of over 1,600 financial advisers provide expert advice and financial solutions based on each client's unique needs and aspirations. Intrinsic has the backing of leading organisations in the financial services industry and all Intrinsic services are endorsed by the Intrinsic Customer Promise – that we'll always be fair, open and honest with you.

www.intrinsicfs.com

For financial advice you can trust contact us today on 01793 647400 or visit www.intrinsicfs.com to find your local Intrinsic Adviser

- SAVINGS
- RETIREMENT PLANNING
- PROTECTION
- MORTGAGES
- ESTATE PLANNING

Proud to be associated with the 2009 British & Irish Lions

Intrinsic, Wakefield House, Aspect Park, Pipers Way, Swindon SN3 1SA

Your home may be repossessed if you do not keep up repayments on your mortgage

2

Up and at 'Em

■ The jigsaw. That's what it's all about. Making it fit. Making the picture complete. Unlike the normal box set from the High Street, the pieces spread out before Ian McGeechan kept changing. One day, it all seemed to make sense, with neat symmetrical edges, the next it was all of a jumble. It was an ever-changing scene, clear and distinct in the middle, fuzzy and confused round the edges as the great selector in the sky kept interfering. ■

Y ou can make all the detailed plans you like, try to cover every contingency, but fate will invariably trip you up. McGeechan and his management team had put a lot of thought and effort into the 37 men they would take to South Africa, even increasing the numbers by one when they realised there was a likelihood that they might have as many as 14 players involved in the Heineken Cup final on the day prior to departure. As it turned out, neither Munster nor Cardiff Blues made it through, leaving the Lions with a welcome extra few bodies at training.

But there was still a need to shuffle plans. As the Lions gathered to attend their gala farewell dinner at London's Natural History Museum, Ian McGeechan

and Gerald Davies were obliged to stand on the steps of the museum and announce yet more changes, further shifts in direction. And even as they gave the news to the media that Leicester's Tom Croft would indeed replace Alan Quinlan, whose appeal against the 12-week ban for foul play had failed, they were also aware that Munster hooker Jerry Flannery was getting the dreaded news that the elbow he'd pranged in a robust training session at Pennyhill Park that afternoon was indeed cracked and strained. His tour was over before it had begun. Munster's record-equalling contingent of eight players had shrunk to five. No wonder fly half Ronan O'Gara gave a rueful smile and looked around for the nearest piece of wood to touch when chatting about it all midway through the dinner. If the Lions hadn't been superstitious when they got together, it would have been no surprise to see them sidestepping every black cat in the land by the time they headed to their

'Air Force Scrum' flight to Johannesburg. Or were black cats supposed to be lucky? You see, no matter what you do, there's always a twist.

Five players had been lost from the original roster by the time of departure: scrum half Tomás O'Leary, centre Tom Shanklin, Flannery, Quinlan and Cardiff Blues wing Leigh Halfpenny, whose thigh injury proved to be more serious than first thought; he was despatched back to barracks in Wales for intensive rehab. The youngest player in the squad must have been alarmed by such a development, fearing the worst if things didn't go well. Thankfully, they did go well, and Halfpenny was able to rejoin the squad in Johannesburg only eight days into the trip. Phew!

Croft got the nod, as did Scotland duo scrum half Mike Blair and hooker Ross Ford, doubling the tartan contingent. There was now another call-up to think about as cover for Halfpenny in case that should all go wrong. The Lions realised that they could be light in the goal-kicking department. They made enquiries

about Danny Cipriani, whose fortunes with England had plummeted to the extent that he had been demoted to the Saxons squad for the summer tour to America, rather than picked for the senior squad that would play the Barbarians prior to a two-Test series with Argentina. That shunted the Wasps fly half down to six in the England pecking order.

Cipriani was effectively being sent to boot camp in Colorado with England's second string, having fallen foul of Martin Johnson. The England manager

was distinctly unimpressed with Cipriani's attitude, feeling that he was sulky and unco-operative. There were reports of a training-ground bust-up with one of the coaches at England's warm-weather camp in Portugal, as well as a sense that Cipriani did not like having to do tackle-bag duty if he was not required at the front line.

Whatever the precise truth of the situation, the evidence was clear. Cipriani was out of favour with England. McGeechan, though, saw it differently, and why wouldn't he? He knew Cipriani better than anyone from his Wasps days. McGeechan knew the talent was there within, and even though he might have had reservations on certain fronts, he knew too that Cipriani would bring something to the party. He might have been wary of the celebrity circus that has grown up round Cipriani, who was dating glam actress Kelly Brook, but as it turned out those issues never got a chance to surface. Cipriani had rolled an ankle in training, a minor ailment, but it would have prevented him from taking part immediately. Given that McGeechan had been strict with Halfpenny, insisting that the Lions flew south with a fully fit contingent primed for action in the first game, he could hardly make an exception for Cipriani.

James Hook it was, then. Hook had his backers within the management, too, notably those who knew him best, Warren Gatland and Rob Howley. Hook was contacted late on Friday night while he was dining out with his girlfriend and family at a restaurant in Mumbles, near Swansea. Hooks stepped outside to take the call. The whoops of delight must have echoed round the bay.

Hook had had a mixed season, with Stephen Jones the preferred choice for Wales at fly half. Hook has had his flaky moments, but at his best he brings guile and subtlety to the midfield. His defence would have to be more rigorous and his decision-making more precise, but there was little doubt that his inventiveness added something.

There was still a tense weekend of European action to negotiate, but the seven players involved from Northampton (who won a rough-house Challenge

■ LEFT Gerald Davies, Ian McGeechan and Paul O'Connell face the media. The 2009 management sought to balance winning with a return to the traditional touring ethos of the Lions.

Cup final), Leicester and Leinster all came through unscathed, even if Croft and Harry Ellis arrived in camp in slightly different mood from the still-celebrating Brian O'Driscoll and his Leinster pals.

The die was cast. The Lions were ready. On a beautifully sunny Sunday afternoon they mingled with their families and media in the Arcadian surrounds of Pennyhill Park, all manicured lawns and gentle pastures rolling away into the distance, a far cry from what awaited them on South Africa's stark Highveld.

South Africa is a wonderful place to tour. True, the country suffers from an image problem, with its crime rate and its poverty. It would be tempting to refer also to its political instability, but given that the expenses scandal brought the entire UK parliamentary system close to collapse while the Lions were away – not to mention the fact that the government unravelled – it would be unwise to throw stones. Similarly the crime in South Africa has attracted a fearsome reputation, with horror stories of car-jackings and muggings and shootings. Yet the incidence of crime is probably not that much different from any inner-city stats you could peddle

from the UK – you wouldn't fancy your chances much on any given Friday or Saturday night in lager-lout England.

The Lions had plenty of security advice to take on board, and were properly tooled-up in that regard. There were to be no curfews on players. They were trusted to be sensible. There was always a police presence outside the hotel, and the players would be taken here and there in organised combi-van convoys. There had been a terrible tragedy earlier in the year when the Brumbies' Shawn Mackay died after being knocked down in Durban following a night out with his team-mates.

McGeechan was mindful of all these things. Mindful, too, that players need space. They need time away from each other as well as from the intensity of the whole experience. The previous two Lions tours had been marred by different things. In 2001 the players had been flogged from dawn to dusk in training, prompting Matt Dawson's cri de coeur. In 2005, the entire set-up was inflated and top-heavy. The Lions lost sight of the essence of the trip: that you bring together a bunch of blokes to play some top-level rugby. That it is arduous and

exacting is all part of its appeal. For it all to come together, the environment has to be spot on: professional but sympathetic.

In 2005 the Lions hotel in Wellington had security railings erected along the street, causing locals no end of bother. It was a completely over-the-top arrangement, one that didn't reflect well on either the Lions or the hotel. In South Africa, McGeechan and Gerald Davies decided that they did not want to have that stuffy, imposing atmosphere. They were going back to basics, and if that meant sharing the hotel with the media, then so be it. It was a real throwback. Shock! Horror! Adults behaving like adults, each given their own space, pleasantries and chit-chat exchanged; then when it came to the serious press conference stuff, pointed

■ FACING PAGE **Rugby ambassador. Nathan Hines meets students at St David's School, Sandton, where the Lions trained ahead of their early games on the tour.**
■ RIGHT AND BELOW **Bonding with team-mates is also a key part of touring, and what better way to do it than by pushing a fellow threequarter into a cold swimming pool? An unsuspecting Luke Fitzgerald gets the treatment from Jamie Roberts.**

formal occasions. Davies and McGeechan were on the same wavelength. You sensed that not only were they intent on winning a series, they were also intent on winning back hearts and minds. They believed in the Lions, and they wanted others to believe, too.

Getting to grips with one another was one thing for the Lions. Getting to grips with South Africa was quite another. It has always been an experience. The long, rambling trail round South Africa may be a thing of the past. So, too, the elemental violence that used to be such a feature of matches in South Africa. They breed 'em tough out in South Africa, and the locals didn't mind showing the pasty-faced tourists what it meant to play rugby in the land of the Springbok.

The punch-ups might have vanished into sepia tint – and, boy, did we get some re-runs of the '99' escapades from the 1974 trip in the build-up to the tour – but confrontation remains at the heart of South African rugby. The South Africans even fight among themselves – politically, that is – as they probe for the slightest weakness in an opponent. They test the body first to see if the mind is willing. It's up front and in your face. First to blink, loses.

The players knew that. They were to get a rude introduction, too, to the effects of altitude. Their first three games were all at height, in Rustenburg, Johannesburg and then Bloemfontein. The Lions had intended to do some pre-tour altitude training at Granada in Spain, but the logistical difficulties of getting player release put paid to that well-intentioned plan. Instead, they practised with masks and oxygen at Pennyhill Park, but nothing can prepare you for the dry throats, scorched lungs, dizzy heads and empty legs that invariably result. You only had to see the first half of the opening tour game against the Royal XV to appreciate that. The boys were out on their feet. 'I was like a zombie,' said Joe Worsley. 'Robots and imbeciles' was Ronan O'Gara's assessment. Welcome to South Africa.

It was always going to be a rare old test. South Africa were in terrific shape. They were world champions – and also picked up the IRB Sevens title

questions were asked in a grown-up fashion before normal life ensued.

That mindset was crucial to the Lions. They bonded very quickly, which is not always a given on Lions tours. Much of that was due to the mood created by the management. Davies was key to it all. The man exuded class. Shaun Edwards referred to him as Mr Davies. But not for long. The air of urbane authority masks a genial inner. He could play hardball, too, if required, but his first instinct was to trust in the goodness of human nature. Davies commanded instant respect. He was no token figurehead, a meeter and greeter at official functions, a walking handshake, a dignitary wheeled out for as the Lions tour got under way – and had a whole host of experienced players available to them, all of whom had stayed on in South Africa rather than accept lucrative posts overseas just so that they could have a crack at the Lions.

If wearing the Lions jersey meant so much to Paul O'Connell and his men, it meant just as much, if not more, to face it. Springbok captain John Smit, all-consuming locks Victor Matfield and Bakkies Botha, wing Bryan Habana – you could go on. They all desperately wanted a slice of the action.

There was a tangible sense, too, that the South African people wanted to embrace the Lions. 'There is unbelievable interest here in the Lions,' said former Springbok captain Francois Pienaar, the man whose World Cup-winning podium embrace with Nelson Mandela in 1995 encapsulated the dreams of the rainbow nation. 'A World Cup is very significant, for sure, and there's a similar appeal with a Lions tour in that there's a contest to be won. But there are big differences, too. A World Cup is more cut-throat. You get two cracks in a series. But for me the Lions is a really special thing. It's a celebration of rugby, a festival. And, for us, it only happens once every 12 years. That's why everyone here is so, so excited.'

Pienaar never did get to play against the Lions – 'a great regret', as he puts it. He was in the Kings Park stands in Durban in 1997 when Jeremy Guscott swung the leg that dropped the goal that won the series. Pienaar was sitting alongside Saracens chairman Nigel Wray, the man who, eight months earlier, had lured one of South Africa's most famous sons overseas. 'What struck me that day, apart from, yes, the fact that South Africa had chances to win and didn't take them, was just how humble the Lions players were afterwards,' said Pienaar. 'They weren't boastful and arrogant. They mingled, sang songs and there was just this great spirit of rugby present That's why we love them. We want to beat them, of course we do, but above all we want them to continue.'

The Lions were soon to become aware of those levels of interest. They garnered no end of column inches on arrival and were top billing on a range of TV sports shows. There was another show in town, mind, the Super 14 final. True, it was up the road from Jo'burg in Pretoria, home of the Blue Bulls. It was a great shame in one sense that the Super 14 final clashed with the opening Lions game. There is little doubt that it had a massive impact on the gate, with only 12,352 present at the great bowl of the Royal Bafokeng Sports Palace in Phokeng on the outskirts of Rustenburg. It was a low-key, echoey backdrop to what ought to have been a tumultuous occasion.

The missing thousands were 80 kilometres up the freeway at Loftus Versfeld, watching their beloved Bulls smash the living daylights out of the Waikato Chiefs, taking the Super 14 title for the second time, by the record margin of 61-17. Impressive stuff. Pace, power, ruthlessness – all the elements were there. But as Warren Gatland was to say, the Bulls, rather like Auckland in their heyday, would beat most any side in the world, international or provincial.

The Lions didn't need reminding that South African rugby was in rude health. The display by the Bulls merely confirmed it. The Lions had other things on their minds that weekend. They were desperate to get the tour off to a winning start. And they so nearly did not.

There had been a slight prick to their status dished out by Springbok coach Peter de Villiers, who asserted that this generation bore no comparison to the 'legends' of 1974. The Lions took that in their stride, as well they should have. So far they were all promise and no substance. 'It's not appropriate to look over our shoulder [at 1974],' said Gerald Davies. 'The past is the past, and let it rest there. The future is what matters, Saturday is what matters, not the reputation of those from over 30 years ago.'

The Royal XV, the Lions' opponents in the opening game, didn't sound much on paper and weren't that highly regarded within South Africa. They were based largely around the Griquas, who provided 11 players. To face them, the Lions picked a heavyweight pack of forwards. Wales No. 8 Andy Powell was on the original team sheet, although he was forced to withdraw with a hand injury on the morning of the match. But Joe Worsley could look after himself, as could the second-row pairing of Simon Shaw and O'Connell. If that went well, it could become the template for a Test partnership, now that the maul had been restored to its full glory.

O'Connell also swatted away the remarks by de Villiers. 'This is all about ourselves,' said the Lions skipper. 'It's not a question of having to win people over. 1974 is what made those players. That's what we're here to do. If you win a Lions series, that's what makes legends. And that, of course, is our goal.'

Worsley had had a burgeoning season. Initially overlooked by England, he had come through

■ BELOW Alarm bells ring for the Lions in game one. Hooker Rayno Barnes raises his arms aloft as his front-row partner Bees Roux makes it 25-13 to the Royal XV.

■ FACING PAGE Full back Lee Byrne, who had a storming match against the Royals, finishes off a chip-and-chase individual try to help drag the score back to 25-20 with about 13 minutes to run. The Lions then scored two further tries to win 37-25.

strongly. 'Joe had one of his best international campaigns,' said McGeechan, formerly his coach at Wasps. 'He's a very strong defender and it's been obvious from training that he's very keen to develop his game.'

McGeechan picked a middle line between using tried combinations and throwing people together to see what they were made of. The back three – full back Lee Byrne and wings Shane Williams and Tommy Bowe – all came from the Ospreys, while the midfield pairing of Munster's Keith Earls and Cardiff Blues' Jamie Roberts was completely untried.

Earls, 21, was one of the surprise picks for the tour. He had a chance to become one of its stars, or

to disappear off the radar if it all went horribly wrong. Performing cameo roles for a province is one thing. Stepping up to this level quite another. McGeechan had a hunch and went with it. O'Connell certainly rated Earls: 'He has something special, with great pace, a fend and step, and a good head to go with it,' he said.

Mike Blair was to get an immediate chance to impress at scrum half, while Ronan O'Gara would be expected to keep the scoreboard ticking over. Andrew Sheridan was first into the loose-head shirt, and while most observers felt that Gethin Jenkins was in the box seat regarding selection for that position after a fine championship for Wales, there was great interest in seeing whether Sheridan could rouse himself to give the South Africans the sort of going-over in the tight scrummage that he had meted out to one or two Aussies down the years.

The Lions decamped to their base at the evocatively named Wigwam resort, a few kilometres outside Rustenburg. The roads around Johannesburg are clogged these days, what with the huge expansion of business in the area, the lack of a public transport infrastructure which forces everyone into cars and the large-scale rebuilding work going on for the 2010 FIFA World Cup.

Still, the Lions would have enjoyed the respite from their five-star shopping mall experience of Sandton in the opulent northern suburbs of Johannesburg. All very upmarket, all very sterile. The stark, engaging landscape at Wigwam, on the other hand, was very South African, with 'blou' monkeys swinging through the trees. There was an army of insects on the move, too, with 20 players being treated for bites at various times. The Lions were forced to shuffle their hand once again, Stephen Ferris joining Powell in withdrawing on the morning of the game. The Lions were stretched in the back row, anxious to give Jamie Heaslip and Tom Croft time to recover from their Heineken Cup exertions. David Wallace filled in at No. 8, with Heaslip moving on to the bench.

All to play for. So much expectation. So little delivery. The Lions wilted, struggling with the hot conditions and with the fact that several of them had not played for four weeks. The Royals took full advantage, spurred by the intelligent, energetic play of scrum half Sarel Pretorius and the clever support work of No. 8 Jonathan Mokuena, a Sevens specialist.

Poor young Keith Earls. He had a shocker. Ball after ball was spilled. When the fourth one went down with only 16 minutes played, the Munster centre just belted the ball high into the stand in embarrassment and frustration. It was a very public crisis of confidence. His more experienced pals weren't faring much better. When Royals hooker Rayno Barnes trotted over from a poorly defended line-out maul to make the score 18-3 in the 25th minute, thoughts of a calamity for the Lions began to take shape. Such notions were deeply rooted by the time prop Bees Roux touched down in the 66th

■ FACING PAGE Flanker Cobus Grobbelaar encounters in-form Lions centre Jamie Roberts during the tourists' demolition of the Golden Lions, in which the impressive Roberts scored twice.

minute. The Lions sent on the cavalry, a five-man posse comprising Mike Phillips, Phil Vickery, Riki Flutey, Alun-Wyn Jones and Heaslip. Sound the bugle to advance! Three tries in 13 minutes from the splendid Lee Byrne, Alun-Wyn Jones and O'Gara to spare blushes. O'Gara bagged 22 points in the 37-25 win. Close, too close for comfort.

The Lions didn't attempt to disown their failings. 'If they didn't know it before, the players really know now that they're in South Africa,' said Howley. 'They are very despondent. Let's now see what the Lions badge of 2009 means to them.'

Small wonder that Phil Vickery was warning of the perils that might lie ahead. 'We've got to be a hell of a lot better or we'll be in a lot of trouble,' said Vickery. 'That was a good kick up the backside for us, a reality check for everyone. The pressure is on.'

And so it was. Back to Johannesburg, where Super 14 side the Golden Lions awaited. Almost an entire new cast was chosen, with 2005 captain Brian O'Driscoll asked to lead the side in what would be his first appearance in a Lions shirt since the spear-tackling misery of Christchurch. Three players, Bowe, Roberts and Wallace, had to do duty again – nothing that they couldn't handle, as McGeechan pointed out. 'When you're a Lion, you're asked to do things you're never asked to do in any other situation,' said the head coach. 'The players know that and if we're to come together as a group, then the ones who will grow the quickest are those who just get on and do it.'

And did they do it! None more so than Jamie Roberts. If there was an excess of gloom and misery after the flat anticlimax of Rustenburg, then there was a surfeit of *Gloria in excelsis* after the 74-10 demolition number on the Golden Lions. Shaun Edwards had spoken of the need to 'put down a marker', and the Lions certainly did that. They were back in business. Big time.

It's easy to get lulled into seeing the Lions as you might any old international side. So when they struggle to put away modest opposition, you reach for the sharpened barb straightaway. That's the wrong criterion to use, which is not to say criticism is forbidden. But context has to have its place, too. If the 2009 Lions were no better after six weeks together, then fine, put the metaphorical boot in.

The key thing to look out for was evidence of growth. Between the opening Saturday and the midweek game at Ellis Park, the Lions emerged from the chrysalis and sprouted wings, if that's not to mix the animal metaphors too much. They took on an identity, gave a sense of themselves and suggested, thrillingly, that there might be great things to come.

Again, best not to get too carried away, for the shifts in a Lions narrative are many and varied. There is no such thing as a smooth progression. But already the Golden Lions performance had the air of being a landmark moment. Certainly the squad saw it in those terms, although no sooner had they reached for the superlatives than they were applying the brake on expectations. These Lions had no intention of worshipping false idols. Hubris was banned from the premises.

Out in Africa, though, something was stirring. The Lions, listless and muted in Rustenburg, roared back to life in Johannesburg with a vibrant performance, washing away the blues from the downbeat opening weekend. There was an entirely different feel to nearly everything they did. Brisk in attack, resilient for the most part in defence, the Lions looked the part, scoring ten tries and posting the half-century before the hour mark. They never once managed to be this commanding, this impressive, four years ago in New Zealand.

In the city of gold, the Lions unearthed some treasures of their own. There was already a sense of Test pairings taking shape, with Roberts putting in an all-consuming man-of-the-match display to push him clear in the race to partner Brian O'Driscoll in midfield. Roberts scored two tries and was a menace all evening before taking a well-earned break after 53 minutes. And to think this was his second game in five days. England and Harlequins wing Ugo Monye also looked dangerous, scoring two good tries. Monye was busy and bothersome. Flanker Tom Croft, who owed his presence on the tour to the wandering fingers of suspended Munster back-row forward Alan Quinlan, did his cause no harm. No. 8

■ RIGHT **Ospreys and Ireland wing Tommy Bowe, another Lion to strike a vein of form early on, breaks free of the Golden Lions defence at Ellis Park. Having scored in the tour opener against the Royal XV, Bowe added another brace to his account here.**

Jamie Heaslip also showed well, as did wing Tommy Bowe, who bagged a couple.

The Lions were desperate for the uplift of victory, the succour of feeling good about themselves. On such a short trip, momentum is everything. With it, anything is possible, even victory over the world champions. Without it, doubt is a constant companion. Touring parties can unravel quicker than New Labour if results go awry.

The Lions were bristling with intent as they put the ball through the hands and popped it out of the tackle. It was a high-tempo, high-risk strategy, but the Lions were up for it. Defence had been an issue, the Lions getting a roasting from coach Shaun Edwards for their failings. They conceded a try just before half-time when they got dog-legged in the middle, but that apart they were generally sound.

The Golden Lions were supposed to be a step up in quality from the previous weekend's opponents. In truth, they were a shower, noticeably at odds with each other and the occasion, a legacy of internal wrangles that had led to coach Eugene Eloff being sacked. They sprinted out on to the field as if they were contesting the Olympic 100m final, but they were all show and nothing else. Posturing doesn't get you anywhere at this level. The Golden Lions simply could not cope with the greater power and verve of their opponents.

Once the early wobbles were out of the way, the Lions began to shred the opposition. They were three tries to the good within 21 minutes, O'Driscoll putting Roberts over with a neat inside pass for the opening score. O'Driscoll himself touched down moments later after fine approach work from Roberts. A couple of penalties from Stephen Jones kept the scoreboard ticking. The Lions were having fun, eager to show what they had to offer. Croft surged through a couple of tackles for his try, while a tap penalty on the stroke of half-time yielded a second try for Roberts.

It was time to share around the goodies. After the break, it was the turn of wing Tommy Bowe to get in on the action, the Irishman benefiting from lovely soft hands from O'Driscoll and Stephen Jones for his first try. A loose pass from Walter Venter then enabled him to race in from 55 metres for an interception score. A burst of substitutions ensued, before Monye raced in for the eighth try – having already crossed once in the first half – and James Hook, on from the bench, added a ninth. The Lions made it look easy, opting to play out the last eight minutes with 14 men after Monye went off to rest his hamstring. Stephen Ferris rounded it all off with a 70-metre romp to the line in the final minute.

The job was done. The tour was very much back on track. 'Hopefully, that's the start of things to come,' said O'Driscoll, who had given out to McGeechan about substituting him on the hour mark. McGeechan would have liked that response. He wants his men to want to play. Few heard O'Driscoll's caveat: 'But we don't want to get too far ahead of ourselves.'

The South Africans would certainly have taken notice. Pity more of them weren't there to take notice on the night itself. The attendance was 22,218. True, this was double the normal gate for Super 14 games there. But even so. Much had been made of how special the Lions concept was to South Africa. Maybe the union should instruct its national team to get behind the idea, for, as happened in 1997, few, if any, of the Springboks were to be released to play for their provinces. No wonder spectators had mixed feelings, put off too by the inflated costs. Ticket prices were at least double the normal rate, a ploy intended perhaps to make cash out of the influx of visitors. It backfired, and was a disturbing trend. People want tours, not the simple fare of Test rugby and nothing else.

The Lions left Johannesburg in good heart and headed deep into prime rugby country in the Free State. There was a gathering sense of a tour taking shape, of a caravan on the road, of everyone mucking in and getting on with things. There could be no disguising the uplift achieved by Wednesday's victory: part relief, part euphoria. The importance of victory cannot be underestimated.

Now the others wanted a slice of the action, none more so than the three players making their tour debuts, lock Donncha O'Callaghan, wing Luke Fitzgerald and Leigh Halfpenny, the 20-year-old now charged with lugging the lion mascots around South Africa as the youngest member of the party. Nine players in total were getting their first starts of the tour as McGeechan stayed true to his intention of

Lions Stephen Ferris and James Hook bring down Cheetahs centre Meyer Bosman. Flanker Ferris once again showed a fine turn of speed at Bloemfontein to get on the scoresheet for the second time in two outings, while fly half Hook kicked 16 points to enable the tourists to pull through 26-24.

giving everyone a fair crack. There was another newcomer, Leinster centre Gordon D'Arcy, who, in true surfer dude fashion, was halfway round the world en route to a holiday blow-out in San Francisco with some mates when the call came through. About turn.

D'Arcy, summoned as cover in a back division beset by injury worries, was named on the bench for the Cheetahs game, getting into action barely 24 hours after landing in South Africa, following numerous changes of plane along the way. D'Arcy had been on the 2005 Lions tour. It had not ended

happily, the Lions suggesting that he had cited fatigue as his reason for not making himself available for selection for the third Test. 'It was Sir Clive who said it and I nearly fell over when I heard that,' said D'Arcy. 'I can't tell you what was going through his head. But I can tell you that I have never pulled out of a game in my life and I have never asked to. I was very cross at the way it was handled.'

The Lions put their faith in a gargantuan pack and a nimble back line. It was one of the heaviest ever sets of forwards fielded by the Lions, and one of the youngest sets of backs. Fingers were crossed in some quarters that the Cheetahs would not swat them aside. 'Pound for pound, our backs are very powerful,' said head coach Ian McGeechan.

The Cheetahs ended up bottom of the Super 14, two places below the Golden Lions. Yet they had finished the competition in good order, with home victories over the Sharks and Crusaders towards the end of the campaign. The Cheetahs were missing only two Springboks, back-row Juan Smith and wing Jongi Nokwe. Flanker Heinrich Brussow was unlucky to miss out on selection for the Boks. He was expected to be a real live wire.

The macho pride of South African rugby had taken a dent in Johannesburg. The Cheetahs intended to right that wrong. 'We will get in their face for 80 minutes,' said head coach Naka Drotske. 'We feel it is important for the Springboks that the provincial teams do not give the Lions an easy ride. They should not be allowed to build momentum. We want to do the Boks a favour.'

They almost did just that. As the ball left the boot of Louis Strydom and headed towards the posts in virtually the last minute of the match, the pulse rate of the watching Lions management soared. The ball soared, too, onwards and upwards, the 45-metre dropped goal looking as if it had the legs to go all the way. Well, it had the distance but not quite the accuracy, the ball hooking to the right at the last minute. 26-24 it was.

The Lions were still unbeaten: three matches, three wins. But, boy, was it close. And how they would have kicked themselves if they had indeed let this one slip. They were 20 points to the good within the opening quarter, looking for all the world as if they would do to the Cheetahs just what they had done to the Golden Lions in Johannesburg. There wasn't quite the same accuracy and fluency in their play, but the Lions had scored two good tries.

The first, from flanker Stephen Ferris, was an opportunist bit of work, the Ulsterman spotting the ball bobbing out from the side of a ruck and pouncing with telling effect to stride in unopposed from 30 metres. The second Lions try was better crafted and superbly finished. Fly half James Hook, as he is wont to do, drew the defensive line on to

him, then chipped a neat kick in behind them. Keith Earls read it well, raced on to the ball, swerved and sidestepped and was on his way to the try line, banishing the blues of the previous week as he did so. It was a lovely moment for the 21-year-old from Munster, who'd had to deal with an embarrassing setback in Rustenburg, gather his thoughts and shore up his confidence and also get over a worrying chest injury. The Lions experience is often about getting back to your feet after a knock-down. Earls managed that in Bloemfontein.

With Hook in fine form with the boot (he finished with 16 points from an unblemished goal-kicking performance), the Lions were cruising at 20-0. Then it all went horribly wrong. Ferris was sin-binned for blocking release – a marginal call, but it did occur in the red zone of the Lions 22. Fair enough. And disappearing with him went the tourists' composure and structure. They struggled to hold it together in his absence, the Cheetahs scoring 14 points through tries from their dangerous dreadlocked wing, Danwel Demas, and prop Wian du Preez.

The Lions were on their uppers. In many ways, their current troubles would stand them in good stead, by forcing them to cope with adversity and find a way through. They were dreadfully fallible at the breakdown, cleaned out by Brussow and his back-row mates. They were also careless with ball in hand, conceding 19 turnovers in all.

Once again, they could feel pleased with their set piece, the scrummage in particular. If only English referee Wayne Barnes had let them take full advantage of their superiority. Andrew Sheridan destroyed his opposite number, Kobus Calldo, but the scrum was rarely stable. Barnes also let much go at the breakdown, much to the annoyance of the Lions. Sheridan was only one of a few to enhance his reputation that afternoon. Hook showed well, as did Ferris, his yellow card apart.

The Lions had a dilemma, of a good sort, on the loose head. Who to pick: Sheridan or Gethin Jenkins? Cheetahs coach Drotske, a former Springbok hooker, had no doubt as to who should get the shirt. He'd have gone for Sheridan as a means of exploiting the fault line in the South African scrummage that runs through their captain,

■ FACING PAGE Andrew Sheridan prepares to pack down for the Lions against the Cheetahs in Bloemfontein. Cheetahs coach Naka Drotske emerged as a big fan of the Sale prop, indicating that he would pick him at loose-head against the Springboks.

converted hooker and now tight-head John Smit. 'When Sheridan is good, he's really good, and can destroy any tight-head,' said Drotske. 'I rate Sheridan above the others. If I were a Lion, that's definitely where I would attack South Africa. There is concern that there is no recognised tight-head in the Springbok squad. It's too much pressure on Smit to ask him to play tight-head. I hope I'm proved wrong but I am worried, definitely.'

Sheridan was competing for a spot with the highly regarded Jenkins, a more all-court player and outstanding in the Six Nations Championship. However, he was not considered to be as destructive in the tight scrummage as Sheridan, although he was more productive in the key phase of the breakdown, an area in which South Africa excel.

It already looked as if the Lions were intent on moving the Springboks around the field as their prime means of attack. They figured that they could make the heavy-duty South African front five blow hard if they kept them on the move. The Lions were looking to hit 38-40 minutes of ball-in-play time, stretching play from touch line to touch line. That would suit Jenkins more than Sheridan. Nice dilemma to have.

The ball-in-play return from the Cheetahs match was only 29 minutes. Too many errors, too stop-start. The Lions were too one-dimensional in their play at times, Wales No. 8 Andy Powell showing that he may well be a strong brute, but he is a front-on runner, rarely coming off-line to trouble the defence.

Hook, meanwhile, didn't miss a thing, which is more than could be said for the Cheetahs. If they'd kicked their goals, they would probably have won. As it was, they missed three penalties. Strydom did convert Corne Uys's 75-metre breakaway try in the 73rd minute, which closed the scores to 24-26, but the Cheetahs could not close out what would have been a famous victory.

Uys had been set up for that score by a rash pass from Shane Williams, who was trying to force the play moving right in a bid to find James Hook.

■ RIGHT **Putting it all to rights. Keith Earls, having endured a nervy debut at Phokeng and an injury-induced wait for his next game, shows what he can do by blazing to the line to score the second Lions try against the Cheetahs.**

Williams was desperate to make a mark, fully aware that Ugo Monye had created quite an impression at Ellis Park. Williams was still playing catch-up.

The Lions' focus was on honing a game that would cause the Springboks problems. Victory in the provincial games was not absolutely essential to that end. But it still tasted sweet. The Lions were in good heart as they headed south to Durban that Saturday night. Stage one over. Mission under way.

Ian McGeechan in conversation with Ian Robertson

In 1997 you produced a brilliant brand of rugby to win the Test series. Have you got a plan to win the series in 2009 and how satisfied are you with the first two weeks of the tour?

■ *'I'm really satisfied with the progress after the first two weeks in South Africa. I have been planning for the Test series for 12 months and after analysing the Springbok Test team since their triumph in the 2007 World Cup and especially in the last 12 months, I felt there was one style which the Lions could develop which would give us a reasonable chance of winning the series.*

'I have known all along it would not be easy. They are the world champions and have kept together most of their outstanding team which proved to be the best in the world in 2007 and they are still incredibly difficult to beat at home. They have a world-class pack and some world-class backs. My conclusion has been that our best chance has to be to take them on physically up front in the set pieces where they are at their strongest, but then to move their forwards all over the pitch to stretch them in the open. We know they have a formidable front row supported by the best second-row partnership in world rugby in Victor Matfield and Bakkies Botha and arguably the best back row in Schalk Burger, Pierre Spies and Juan Smith.

'My plan and my hope is to match them in the set pieces and outplay them in the loose. It is a huge ask and a big mountain to climb, but I really believe it is our best chance of winning the Test series. It will come down to our ability to win a ruck, drive forward to set up and win another ruck and perhaps win six or seven rucks or even 10 or 12 in succession all over the pitch before releasing our backs. I have every confidence that we will produce the better back division and we will play the best attacking back play throughout the whole tour but we have to raise our game to match their forwards. Also of course our tactical kicking game has to be ruthlessly efficient and even inspired.'

How pleased are you with the results and performances after the first three matches?

■ *'Having determined the basic style and pattern of our play, it has been very important that all 36 players buy in to it. It is good to report that they have – and the building blocks have been put in place. Each team for the first six matches will play the same pattern so the players will be interchangeable. They are all part of a six-week exercise to win the Test series.*

'For all six matches before the first Test each team will feature important combinations of players but at no point will the probable Test team play because I won't pick that Test team until three days before the Test. Every single player will start in at least two games before the Test so every player has a real chance to nail down a Test place. With that in mind, we picked an interesting team for the opening match against the Royal XV in Rustenburg. This was always going to be a very difficult game because we were playing 6000 feet above sea level and on that particular afternoon the temperature was in the mid-20s.

'The general guidelines suggest players need a minimum of eight days at altitude before playing 80 minutes of rugby. We had five days to prepare and a very hot day for that opening match. We trailed 25-13 midway through the second half. But then following up Tommy Bowe's try in the first half, Lee Byrne, Alun-Wyn Jones and Ronan O'Gara scored tries in the second half. When you consider the lack of preparation time and the fact that on a very hot day we were still trying to adapt to life at 6000 feet I was very pleased with our effort.

'We made 12 changes for the second match against the Golden Lions and tried several new combinations. We won 74-10 and perhaps we should not have read too much into the scoreline. But I was very pleased with our new centre combination of Brian O'Driscoll and Jamie Roberts and the established Welsh international half-back partnership of Stephen Jones and Mike Phillips. It was by any standards a very good performance.

'The third match of the tour gave me the chance to give nine more players a first start. This included a new half-back pairing of James Hook and Harry Ellis and a first start for Stephen Ferris in the back row. We fielded an inexperienced threequarter line which was a calculated risk, but we led 23-14 at half-time. A late try by the Cheetahs gave the Lions a fright but we hung on to win 26-24.

'The first three results were good – played three, won three. The combinations were beginning to work and I was pleased with our progress.'

LAAGER
LAGER
IS ALSO
KNOWN
AS
'RHINO
HORN'
FOR ITS
SUPPOSED
APHRODISIAC
QUALITIES.
**ONE OF
THE NEW
DESIGNER**
BEERS POPULAR
AMONGST THE
COGNISCENTI
OF CAPE TOWN
AND THE
EARLS COURT RD
SERVED
IN A FAUX
CROCODILE
SKIN
BOTTLE.

The pint with nothing to prove

OFFICIAL SPONSOR

A SURGE OF GENIUS

PROUD SPONSORS OF THE 2009 BRITISH & IRISH LIONS

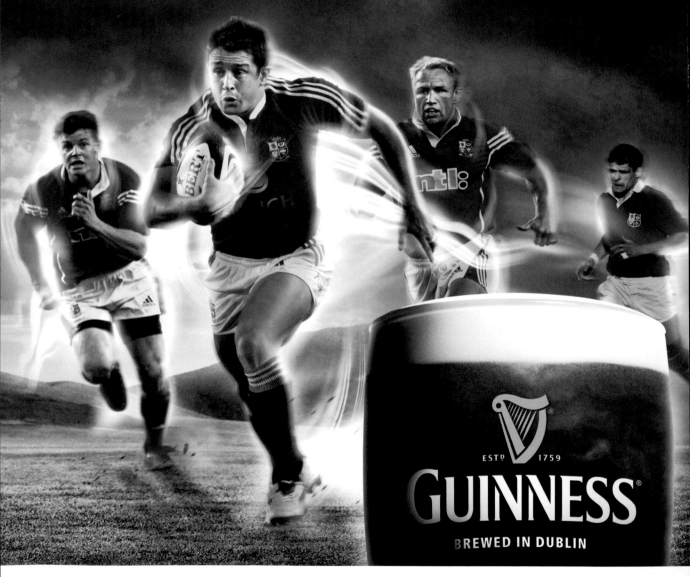

GUINNESS®

BREWED IN DUBLIN

3
Narrowing the Focus

■ It was quiet, too quiet. As Dr James Robson briefed the media at the Beverley Hills Hotel in Umhlanga Rocks just outside Durban, Ian McGeechan reached across and touched wood. It was Sunday afternoon, the day after the retreat from the Highveld. The Lions were in good mood and great shape, the unusually overcast skies notwithstanding. ■

As McGeechan was to say later, 'If you were to tell me that after three matches we'd be unbeaten, that every player had made a start and that we'd only have one player unavailable for Monday training [Martyn Williams with a shoulder injury] I'd have bitten your hand off.' Geech was listening as Robson went through his medical bulletin. A week earlier in Jo'burg, the good doctor had spent so much time listing the squad's various injuries it was as if he were narrating a three-volume novel. He was crocked, he was ailing, he needed to rest, he couldn't take contact – on and on he went. This particular Sunday was different. Robson even apologised for dragging us over to Umhlanga for not much news. We didn't mind. No news – is news.

There was no disguising the relief on the head coach's face. All the planning, all those months and months of scheming and plotting, had got them this far. The Lions had had a down day, with several players heading to Durban to dive into a shark tank at uShaka Marine World, others hitting the golf course and some just chilling after the exertions of the previous weeks.

Robson and his team had no such slack in their schedule. They were always on call. And they were fundamental to the success or otherwise of the Lions. McGeechan did not hesitate to point out that the biggest single difference between his two tours as coach to South Africa – the 1997 experience and this trip – lay in the enhanced medical and conditioning teams. Robson was common to both tours. He and McGeechan went back a long way. Their relationship was crucial to the holistic wellbeing of the squad. Geech had to trust Robson's judgment wholly and utterly. Robson, for his part, had to be acutely aware of the needs of the moment. In fact, he admitted that if Wednesday's game against the Sharks had been a Test match, then Williams, who had pranged his shoulder, would have been able to play. Those are the sort of judgment calls that McGeechan needed. He wouldn't question Robson, just ask for information. It made for harmonious interaction.

Robson, 51, was on his fifth Lions tour. He had first come into McGeechan's orbit as team physio on the Scotland tour to Canada in 1991. He was now head of medical services and national team doctor for the Scottish RU. He had some very good men alongside him, including Dr Gary O'Driscoll, son of former Ireland full back Barry. He had been with the Lions four years earlier in New Zealand and had just taken up a post with Arsenal. The physio and massage team was also impressive and included Prav Mathema, who worked for McGeechan at Wasps after a long stint at Queens Park Rangers, and Phil Pask, the hard-nut former Northampton flanker who had come to McGeechan's attention when he was fitness coach at Saints and had since done sterling service as England physio. Bob Stewart (physio) and Richard Wegrzyk (masseur) completed the team.

And so they'd got to this point, where Robson was able to declare that he'd never known anything like it. 'I can't remember any tour where at this stage I'd only had one player not available for training.' Clang. Not even the superstitious lunge for the

nearest piece of wood by McGeechan could stave off the gods of cruel fate. Within 24 hours, Robson was having to break the news to Ulster flanker Stephen Ferris that his tour was likely to be over. A scan the following morning confirmed the worst fears. Ferris had a grade two tear to his medial collateral ligament and would be sidelined for up to six weeks. Tour finished, dreams in tatters. Ferris had been in pole position for the Test blind-side slot, although Tom Croft had a chance to close that gap against the Sharks at Kings Park.

One man's misery is another man's opportunity. Wales captain Ryan Jones, who had taken his original omission with customary manliness and good grace, was summoned. Déjà vu for Jones, who'd had a similar call four years earlier from Clive Woodward and had made such a splendid fist of things that he played in all three Tests. Clang. Within 24 hours of arriving in South Africa, Jones was packing his bags to return home, the head injury he'd sustained in the Test against the USA five days earlier causing problems when put under the scrutiny of a neurosurgeon. It was an embarrassing episode and did not reflect well on anyone.

The downturn in fortunes was still not upon the Lions. That Sunday, Robson was able to reflect that two players, Keith Earls and Riki Flutey, might well have been despatched home on previous tours such was the severity of their injuries. Earls, who'd had such a traumatic debut, had sustained a nasty blow to the chest, one that Robson likened to being in a car crash. No wonder he'd looked so out of sorts against the Royal XV. Pask had nursed him back to health. Flutey, too, had come very close to being declared forfeit. Robson thought he'd be the first to be sent back to Blighty but praised the commitment of the Wasps midfielder, who had been woken every two hours through the night for intensive ice treatment. Flutey, who'd strained his knee when coming on as a sub in Rustenburg, was back on the roster and was on the bench for the Sharks match.

There were concerns about Leigh Halfpenny in the lead-up to that game. The roller-coaster ride was continuing for the youngest member of the squad. He'd only just joined up with the tour and had spoken of his despair at having to stay behind when the party left for South Africa after a thigh injury

■ ABOVE Stephen Ferris signs autographs at Simondium School, Paarl, at the unveiling of rugby facilities provided by winemakers FirstCape as part of the FirstCape Lions Legacy project. Sadly, the flanker's tour as a player had already been ended by injury.
■ FACING PAGE Chief medic Dr James Robson ushers Tom Croft off the field and into the Lions pitchside nerve centre at Ellis Park as the physio team go about their work.

proved to be more serious than first thought. He was delighted to be in South Africa, so when he felt his thigh stretch once again after extra kicking practice at Northwood School in Durban on Monday afternoon, his spirits must have plummeted through the floor. Not again! The life of a professional sportsman may appear a bed of roses. But beware – roses have thorns. Halfpenny had been scheduled for bench duty against the Sharks. He was withdrawn and replaced by James Hook.

McGeechan was putting out a strong line-up, even though he refused to contemplate identifying a

Test team at this stage. He had been adamant all along that he was going to give everyone a fair crack. 'There are to be no separate teams, no way that I'm saying to players at this stage that they're not involved in the Test match,' said McGeechan. 'I'm not prepared to do that. The Test XV is unlikely to play as a XV before the Test [on 20 June]. There are some risks, I'm aware of that. But the strength we get out of it as a squad far outweighs anything else.'

The head coach had chosen certain putative Test combinations as the Lions looked to maintain their unbeaten record on the tour against the depleted Super 14 outfit. There were some significant partnerships, the athletic Wales lock Alun-Wyn Jones joining forces with captain Paul O'Connell, who was playing his second game in five days, even though they would both be considered middle jumpers. Highly regarded full back Lee Byrne was also required to back up, immediately after being on duty at the weekend, primarily as a means of giving him, a Test certainty to most observers, a chance to work with another Test combo, centres Brian O'Driscoll and Jamie Roberts. McGeechan had also compiled a back-row trio of Tom Croft, Jamie Heaslip and David Wallace. That had a ring of a Test line-up, too.

Heaslip believed that McGeechan's philosophy had had an uplifting effect, to the extent that No. 8 felt that even the captain's place was not assured. 'There are no untouchables, not even Paulie [O'Connell],' said Heaslip. 'No one has got that Test slot guaranteed. It means that we're all pushing each other all the time. The competitiveness that Geech wants to create on the field as well as the camaraderie he wants to create off the field, has made for a great mix. It's brought the best out of us.'

The Sharks had finished sixth in the Super 14 but were without nine Springboks. Sharks coach John Plumtree felt that their absence devalued the whole concept of Lions tours. 'It is a pity,' said Plumtree. 'This tour should be a celebration of rugby. There should be less emphasis on just winning the series, and more on appreciating what is great about rugby.'

■ FACING PAGE Alun-Wyn Jones in line-out action against the Golden Lions. Against the Sharks, Jones was paired in the second row with skipper Paul O'Connell – a possible Test combination?

Well said.

Plumtree's concerns were well founded. There were just 21,530 populating the cavernous stands of Kings Park. There's no point blaming the locals. Why would they turn out? Ticket prices had doubled, to R250 (about £20), while the quality of the home side had halved. That's not favourable mathematics in anyone's eyes.

There's a bigger picture to consider here, too. The Lions touring concept has to be upheld. They have to have meaningful competition and they have to have at least six warm-up games. If the build-up is to be a perfunctory exercise, then pretty soon the whole project will wither. You had to wonder, too, how the South African players felt about it all. Those that didn't make the Springbok match-day 22 might never get to face the Lions. How daft is that?!

The Lions had plenty to ponder. Wing Shane Williams was desperate to show that he still had the class, the devilry, the self-assurance to make things happen. He had struggled for form, and after his howler at the weekend, when he had thrown a rash pass that was intercepted for a late try, the Lions had decided to put him straight back on the horse with instructions to be bold. 'Shane can't be scared,' said Shaun Edwards. 'He's got to play in the face of the defence as he's always done, continue to force himself on the play.'

By the end of the game, the Lions' feel-good vibe was still beating loud after their fourth victory of the trip, the tourists racking up 32 unanswered points in the second half to run out comfortable 39-3 winners. There were glitches still to be ironed out, though, routines to be sharpened. The Lions managed to post a record score in the fixture without ever quite hitting their stride.

The fluency of the previous week was missing, that ease on the ball and with each other. There was a lot of promise in the approach work but nowhere near enough accuracy in delivery. Chance after chance went begging. There were a whole host of handling errors. There was a definite air of the Lions going through their patterns in order to get their game in good shape. Even so, the management would have been concerned by the wastefulness.

There was solace in some stand-out performances, notably loose-head Gethin Jenkins, whose work rate

was phenomenal. Jenkins, though, got on the wrong side of referee Jonathan Kaplan at the scrummage, a strange state of affairs. Kaplan, a Durban man, did the Lions no favours.

Hooker Lee Mears threw in well to the line out and Ireland No. 8 Jamie Heaslip was robust and bothersome. Scrum half Mike Phillips, meanwhile, served notice that the Test shirt would be his. He was commanding around the field and scored a superb solo try right at the start of the second half to set his side on the way to victory. It was an X-factor moment, just the sort of uplift the Lions needed, Phillips spotting the gap, haring through, rounding one man and throwing an outrageous dummy to befuddle another. Classy stuff.

There was a lot riding on the second-row pairing of Alun-Wyn Jones and Paul O'Connell. The captain needed a big game. He was more prominent, leading the drives and being a nuisance at the restarts. Jamie Roberts once again showed what a threat he is in midfield, smashing through his opposite number, Riaan Swanepoel. There was a worrying moment for Lions fans when Roberts needed lengthy treatment

on his right shoulder. As for Shane Williams, he struggled to get into the game, chasing hard but finding neither space nor the ball.

Chances, chances – the Lions had to execute with more precision. The build-up was purposeful, the end product slipshod. The Lions kept their own line intact, which was a huge boon. That might keep Shaun Edwards happy. Well, it might. The only nagging concern was whether the Lions were being really tested. Were they getting a stiff enough work-out prior to taking on the world champions?

Finally the try came, bringing relief for the Lions after the early anxiety. The Lions drove from a line out in the 23rd minute, O'Connell peeled off, scrum half Mike Phillips had a dart, Jamie Heaslip took it on before hooker Lee Mears was able to pick up and dive over. Ronan O'Gara converted.

■ FACING PAGE Jamie Roberts evades Luzoko Vulindlu of the Sharks. The Lions centre had been a constant menace in midfield throughout the tour to date.
■ BELOW Hooker Lee Mears dives over to score the first Lions try against the Sharks.

There were several baffling calls from referee Kaplan. He gave two penalties against Gethin Jenkins for not binding, one of which led to a successful penalty kick by Sharks scrum half Rory Kockott. There were three scrum offences against the Lions in the first half alone.

The Lions were rarely troubled in the second half, Phillips setting the tone from the outset with his try. O'Gara kicked a couple of goals to stretch the lead before the Lions struck hard with two tries within six minutes midway through the half. Slick hands featuring Tom Croft, Lee Byrne and Brian O'Driscoll sent Luke Fitzgerald on his way to the try line for the first. Byrne then had an easy run-in from halfway. Vickery was yellow-carded near the end for reckless use of the boot. He was fortunate it wasn't red. Silly. Jamie Heaslip then tapped and flopped over for a try in the last minute. The Lions were still unbeaten and in good order.

The boys were giving it their all, which is all they could do. They were earning a quid for it (38,000 of them to be precise), but their financial returns for six weeks of sweat and toil were put into perspective by the news breaking as they left Durban for Cape Town. Manchester United's Cristiano Ronaldo had finally put pen to paper and signed for Real Madrid for £80 million. That's a cool stash in anyone's terms.

How long before rugby delivers routine million-pound transfers? It's getting there, with the likes of All Black fly half Dan Carter, who had his lucrative stint at Perpignan truncated by injury, and Toulon-bound Jonny Wilkinson fetching top dollar. It's hard to imagine rugby coming anywhere near reaching out to the same sort of market as football. Even cricketers have leapfrogged the muddied oafs, thanks to the riches on offer in Twenty20.

Rugby players aren't moaning, nor are they the grasping sort. They want to be respected, and that should be reflected in a proper pay packet. It matters not a damn that some narrow-minded fools might say that they ought to be grateful to be on a Lions tour, never mind getting paid for it. That sort of hokum went out with the ark.

■ RIGHT Shades of Matt Dawson? 'More Gareth Edwards,' according to Lions scrum half Mike Phillips, as he leaves the Sharks cover for dead to score at the start of the second half.

The 2009 Lions were magnificent ambassadors – hard-working and approachable. They had not been cocooned away, were having to dutifully queue for their breakfast alongside other hotel guests, even on match days. Normal blokes going about their work. There aren't many front-line sportsmen who do that. You can't see a Wayne Rooney or a Roger Federer getting up close and personal in front of the fried egg a few hours before stepping out at Wembley or Wimbledon. The rugby lads were the better for it. The vast majority, if not all of them, do not want to be prima donnas. That is not the nature of the sport. And if Ian McGeechan had achieved one thing on this trip – no matter what happened in the Test series – it was that. Back to basics, and all the better for it.

What had been fuzzy outlines a few weeks earlier were now acquiring a clearer edge. Fittingly, the Lions arrived at Newlands, the scene of one of the most outrageous dummies ever thrown, confident that they had found in Mike Phillips a scrum half as capable as Matt Dawson was 12 years ago of winning a Test match through an act of individual brilliance. Dawson's show-and-go try at the ground in 1997 was the X-factor moment that triggered that against-the-odds series victory. Against the Sharks, Phillips had shown that he was back to his best after a faltering season, scoring a solo try, complete with dummy, to ensure that not only would he be wearing the Test No. 9 shirt at the same venue in ten days' time but that the Lions would have a player on top of his game in a key position. Think Dawson, think Gareth Edwards, think Robert Jones – the great Lions teams have all had a pivot with nerve, perception, cheekiness and, of course, sound basics.

Phillips, 26, had battled back from a serious knee injury, seeing off notable rivals in the Wales camp, Dwayne Peel and Gareth Cooper, to make the tour. Even then it was felt that he was not as sharp as he

used to be, not as slick or as self-assured. So much is channelled through the scrum half that any glimmer of doubt or hesitation is ruthlessly exposed. Phillips exudes confidence, brashness even, no mean attribute for the territory he occupies. He's a cocky bugger, in an impish way. He was asked that Wednesday night just what had been said at half-time with the Lions struggling to get points on the board despite a glut of possession. 'Get it to Mike Phillips,' said the man in question, who set off on his 45-metre run to glory within 60 seconds of the restart. It was also pointed out that the try had shades of Dawson in it. 'More Gareth Edwards,' said Phillips, with another laugh.

He's a big, imposing specimen, as befits a former back-row forward. But size is only an asset if it is allied to speed and intelligence. The Lions are all too aware of the ferocity of South Africa's game at the breakdown. They would need every hand to the pump to cope with Juan Smith and his back-row chums. Phillips was perfectly capable of playing the role of auxiliary bouncer if need be.

There is a downside to being a bit of a bruiser, and that, too, was in evidence on Wednesday night at Kings Park. Phillips can get too involved, too wrapped up in the niggle and nudge, too concerned about being the macho man. He used to have a short fuse. It was telling that forwards coach Warren Gatland should highlight Phillips' occasional shortcomings. 'Mike was on the ground too much,' said Gatland bluntly, aware that if his forward pack had worked their nuts off to secure good ball, then he didn't want a scrum half wasting it by getting dragged into the argy-bargy that can occur around the fringes. The Lions wanted Phillips to be strong and bothersome, but above all else they wanted him to get the ball on the move.

Phillips' form, though, was a real plus for the Lions. Scrum halves can make all the difference. Dawson certainly did. And that might have spooked more than a few South Africans as the Lions flew into Cape Town for their first match at Newlands since Dawson did them like a kipper down the blind side.

Cape Town is one of the great cities of the world, with its dramatic Table Mountain backdrop and its resonant history offshore on Robben Island. Newlands, too, is a fabulous setting for rugby, with the back of the mountain towering above it and the suburbs stretching down the slopes and off as far as the eye can see. The players even had a little down time, with those not involved on Saturday heading out to the FirstCape winery at Simondium near Paarl to help open a local village facility and then enjoy a glass or two themselves.

Back at base, meanwhile, things were more serious, emotional too, all encapsulated in the formidable shape of Phil Vickery, who was rapidly becoming one of the seminal figures on tour: for his honesty, his integrity, his sense of perspective and, of course, for his play. Vickery had been asked to captain the side against Western Province and there could have been no finer man for the job. He knew that the tour had suddenly acquired a keener edge. There were Test places on the line, with players tilting furiously for a spot. And the fans had started to pour into Cape Town. 'I'll be telling the boys just before we run out that they are carrying the dreams and aspirations of millions back home,' said Vickery

on the eve of the game. 'When you're banged up in your hotel room, with the locals not liking you very much, you can forget that a hell of a lot of people are actually right behind you.'

If the Lions were to overcome significant odds in seven days' time and beat the world champion Springboks, then they could do no better than replicate the courage, the nerve and the sheer

bloody-mindedness of the man who was to lead them down the tunnel for their last major run-out before the Test series began. Three years earlier, Vickery had been told by Gloucester that his rugby career was over because of chronic neck problems. Ian McGeechan, then director of rugby at Wasps, thought differently. He signed him up. 'But it was a huge risk,' said McGeechan. 'Phil has a great buzz about him, and is one of those really pulling things together on this trip.'

Vickery was twitchy that Friday, emotional, too, when he realised the responsibility on his shoulders. 'You think it's fantastic to get the captaincy and then two seconds later, you think, crikey, this is a big deal,' said Vickery. 'This is a very dangerous time of the tour. All eyes are on the Test and the Red Army is on its way. It's a worrying thing for me. It could all fall apart over the next four days if we don't realise that we've still got games of rugby to win. I certainly don't want to be part of a Lions team that loses on tour, and especially not to be the captain of a losing Lions team. If I were the opposition tomorrow, I'd be wondering if the Lions were really going to go hell for leather for it seven days out from a Test match.'

Vickery was one of those with an eye on a Test shirt. Wings Tommy Bowe and Ugo Monye and fly half Stephen Jones, all on parade at Newlands, had good reason to imagine that they might be trotting out at Kings Park in Durban the following week, while lock Nathan Hines and prop Andrew Sheridan could have caused McGeechan some soul-searching.

Flanker Martyn Williams, who had been hampered by a shoulder injury that had allowed David Wallace to cement his claim, likened the last pre-Test Saturday experience to a 'final trial', and it certainly had that feel. To that end, McGeechan had paired two grafting locks, Scot Nathan Hines and Ireland's Donncha O'Callaghan. Paul O'Connell's partner in the Test second row had yet to be settled, and Hines in particular, as well as Simon Shaw off the bench, could yet create a stir.

In the back line, Riki Flutey was making his first start after a knee injury and had ground to make up.

■ LEFT The impressive Tommy Bowe takes the Western Province last line of defence over with him as he registers the first Lions try of the match at Newlands.

■ ABOVE **Willem de Waal swings his trusty left boot to notch a 19th-minute dropped goal for Western Province.**
■ FACING PAGE **Lions No. 8 Andy Powell runs into heavy traffic on Route One in Cape Town.**

Time was running out, and the tension was being ratcheted upwards. 'There is always a lot more pressure and stress leading towards a Test,' said McGeechan.

Too true.

The clear skies of Friday gave way to filthy, lumpy clouds on Saturday. It was a brute of a day, with the wind howling and the blackened skies dumping great loads of water on to the pitch. It made for a limited spectacle, with both sides having to use the boot for field position, Western Province in particular.

The Lions, mind, did manage to play some rugby in spurts, and fine rugby it was too. If there had been any doubts about Tommy Bowe being one of the Test wings, they were well and truly banished by the end

of that soggy Saturday. The 25-year-old Ulsterman was the star turn of a wild afternoon, the stormy conditions causing most of those on view merely to cling on for dear life as the winds buffeted all and sundry, reducing the game to a hard-hitting close-quarters slugging match. It was no less engaging for that, perfect preparation for what lay ahead. Guts and gumption take you a long way. With the scores level at 23-23 with four minutes to go, the Lions went on to retain their unbeaten record through a mixture of their grit, their togetherness and their all-important sense of themselves, allied to James Hook's match-winning boot and Bowe's potency. These Lions were not always the flashiest, or the most commanding. They weren't again at Newlands. But they were winning. Self-belief was no longer an abstract concept. That 26-23 scoreline would look just dandy in the record books.

Hook stepped up to the mark in the 76th minute and nailed the winner from 50 metres. 'It was one of the most important strikes of my career,' said Hook, who was becoming more and more impressive with each appearance. 'A draw would have felt like a loss.'

As for Bowe, the Ospreys wing was the leading try scorer on tour with four touchdowns in three matches. Not only was he crossing the line, his clever angles, his lust for action and his deft technical control were putting others in position to score as well. Ugo Monye's try in the 34th minute owed everything to Bowe's finely timed intervention from the right wing. Monye, who himself was in fine form and the likely Test partner for Bowe, did the necessary by sliding home. Six minutes earlier Bowe had done what he had been doing all season, finishing with aplomb after a fine build-up. Bowe's name was already on the lips of the Red Army.

There were only a handful of genuine Test contenders on view at Newlands: the wings and captain for the day Vickery, with flanker Martyn Williams and loose-head Andrew Sheridan also looking to impress. Williams, in his first game since recovering from that shoulder injury, was his usual grafting, shrewd self, providing a key link in Bowe's try and plunging through a thicket of bodies to score himself in the 56th minute. Williams continued to push David Wallace all the way.

In the line out, lock Nathan Hines was bypassed, the Lions throwing everything short to Donncha O'Callaghan. Hines, though, was one of those vying for the spot alongside Paul O'Connell. For his part, Stephen Jones would have been considered to be in the box seat at fly half, but at Newlands, admittedly on a difficult day, his game control was wayward. Head coach Ian McGeechan admitted as much afterwards, lamenting his side's tactical kicking. It was rare for McGeechan to criticise in public.

Western Province made the Lions work harder than any other side, especially in their defensive work, despite the three tries they conceded. The Lions had to come up with something for those scores. That the tourists' blitz defence was breached for Joe Pietersen's score will concern them, although full back Rob Kearney was hors de combat at the time with a dead leg. 'That was a major flaw,' said Bowe. There were few flaws in Bowe's game. The Ulsterman was turning into one of the key players: sharp, eager and brimful of confidence. He was a certainty for the Test team.

The mood in camp often changes at this point in a Lions tour. The Test match was now imminent. The phoney war was coming to an end. Focus had to narrow, decisions had to be made, the dirt-trackers

■ ABOVE James Hook strokes home the winning penalty against WP to keep the tourists' 100 per cent record intact.

■ FACING PAGE Lions captain for the day Donncha O'Callaghan leads his side out against the Southern Kings in Port Elizabeth.

had to take their medicine, pledge allegiance to the cause and be good tourists. There was every indication that they would do just that. McGeechan had created the right vibe over the previous four weeks. Now was the time when it would be tested. It had been all froth and talk up to this moment. The right thing said almost for the sake of saying it. Now we would find out if the squad really did believe in the mantra of one team, one philosophy, one jersey.

The Lions were facing their most difficult match of the tour. Not in terms of the quality of the opposition, obdurate and nasty as they turned out to be, but in the timing of the fixture, four days before the Test match. In theory, everyone was still in with a shout for the Test team. In reality, only a few places remained up for grabs. Those still in contention must have been dreading this game. To come so close and perhaps have it all snatched away through injury.

Such thoughts must have been going through Ugo Monye's mind after he was promoted from the bench to take the starting place of Shane Williams, who had checked in for the team charter flight to Port Elizabeth on Monday afternoon, only to pull out moments later after being stricken with a vomiting virus. Manager Gerald Davies also cried off the trip. The pair were isolated for fear of the virus spreading. Two years earlier, England's squad had been decimated by illness during a Test tour to South Africa. Williams eventually flew up on Tuesday morning and took his place on the bench. Tommy Bowe had been put on stand-by, another case of a player reaching out for wood.

The pretence could not be kept up much longer. McGeechan had to reveal his hand. And the selection for the Southern Kings match did just that.

Andrew Sheridan was asked to play his second game in four days, effectively teeing up Gethin Jenkins for the loose-head spot, while the presence of Nathan Hines, Simon Shaw and captain for the day Donncha O'Callaghan would point to Alun-Wyn Jones being in pole position to partner Paul O'Connell.

But McGeechan was steadfast, upholding the credo that the selectors might yet be swayed. As with all good preachers, his congregation had the faith, and why wouldn't they when the head coach could cite the example of Irish lock Jeremy Davidson as one who came with a late, late run in 1997 to claim a shirt for the first Test despite playing on the Tuesday prior to the match?

And no wonder Shaw continued to believe in McGeechan's mantra, for it was he who lost out 12 years ago, the England lock having been expected to pack down alongside Martin Johnson. He partnered the 1997 captain in all the lead-in Saturday matches, only for Davidson to trump him at the last. The fact that for the first and only time on the 2009 trip the party split, with the front-runners for the Test side heading straight to Durban, meant that McGeechan had to offer solace as well as hope.

There was no scepticism in Shaw's mind. 'Yes, I do believe in what they're saying, 100 per cent,' said Shaw, the oldest member of the party at 35. He's no mug, though, recognising that he was tilting for a place in the match-day 22 rather than in the run-on XV. Even so, if he were to get the nod after missing out entirely in 1997, then it would top any of his achievements, including playing in the 2007 World Cup final. 'I'm probably looking at bench cover as best option but knowing the coaches, a huge performance could still change minds. If so, it would be more special than anything else. You learn to appreciate these things more as you get older, to savour the experience.'

Shaw had improved markedly after a stuttering opening. Forwards coach Warren Gatland told him what he thought of it: '[He said it was] crap,' said Shaw. 'The frankness of the coaches is a positive.'

Shaw had been hampered since then in only getting game time from the bench, doing terrifically well against the Sharks in Durban when replacing O'Connell for the last quarter. On Saturday, though, he felt under so much pressure to impress that he

took one of the most ill-advised of quick throw-ins, which resulted in Ugo Monye getting flattened inside the Lions 22. 'Yes, you can end up doing things you don't normally do,' said Shaw, who drew parallels between the current state of the 2009 touring party and their victorious predecessors in South Africa 12 years ago. 'The same sort of

togetherness is there and that ability to grind out wins when not playing well.'

Shaw's partner in the second row, Donncha O'Callaghan, was visibly moved when told that he was to lead out the Lions. 'I was taken aback,' said O'Callaghan, a Test Lion in 2005, who made light of the demands of turning out so soon after Saturday's hard-fought encounter at Newlands. 'It's old school stuff and great for that. It takes you out of your comfort zone. I'm sure that when the Test team is known that you won't have guys sulking and throwing their toys out of the pram.'

The match was to be played at the brand new Nelson Mandela Bay Stadium, a purpose-built 48,000-capacity Parc des Princes-style arena, one of six venues specifically constructed for the 2010 FIFA World Cup. It was a splendid setting, the sandy pitch notwithstanding. It was just about playable, and the biggest crowd of the tour, 35,883, gathered to witness events.

Port Elizabeth has staged some rare old games in its time. An England game at the Boet Erasmus in 1994 had erupted into sustained violence, with Tim Rodber eventually being sent off. Rodber famously lost his cool that day, which was completely out of character, and lashed out in frustration at the prolonged provocation.

It was a case of new stadium, old school rough-house tactics, as the locals set out to soften up the tourists ahead of the Test series. It was brutal and unedifying, cheap, late hits raining down on the Lions in a ferocious first half in particular. This newly formed South African franchise, who were looking to be part of an expanded Super 14, took their name from the Xhosa monarchs who fought the frontier wars against the British settlers in the early 19th century. The 21st-century Southern Kings certainly seemed intent on repelling the invader by any means. It was shameful.

Small wonder that Lions centre Gordon D'Arcy swatted away the handshake of his opposite number, Harlequins centre De Wet Barry, one of a trio of tough-nut midfielders imported for the occasion. Former Bath centre Frikkie Welsh was on a head-hunting mission, as was former Leicester fly half Jaco van der Westhuyzen. Ex-Northampton wing Wylie Human made no attempt to live up to his name.

The Lions, for the most part, turned the other cheek. They lacked presence on the field, real leaders who might at least have got in the ear of referee Nigel Owens. The Welshman did sin-bin van der Westhuyzen for a late, high and dangerous tackle on Riki Flutey. The Kings lost another man, lock Ross Skeate, for a technical offence, but Owens ought to have got to grips with the simmering violence, which did not abate until the final whistle. It was an unseemly spectacle.

This was the first dirt-trackers line-up of the tour, and it showed. There was a lack of communication in much of what they did, balls spewing out of contact and passes being sprayed around. It took time for the Lions to gather themselves, scrum half Mike Blair enduring a torrid opening.

The Lions fielded arguably their heaviest ever pack of forwards, and while they smashed the bully-boy Kings in the scrummage and were adept and bothersome in the line out, they lacked pace around the field. Time and again they lost ball on the floor, time and again they were counter-rucked as the opposition got more bodies there more quickly. The powerful scrummaging unit, with Andrew Sheridan to the fore, got their due return with a penalty try for a series of collapsed scrums in the 69th minute.

Somehow, without retaliating, without getting dragged into a slug-fest, the Lions persevered. It was a desperately fragile situation for a Lion, aware that if he let the red mist descend, his tour could be over. The home side knew that, and goaded the tourists all the more. Simon Shaw once again put in a prodigious amount of work, an incredible achievement given his age and the fact that this was his second outing within four days, the Wasps lock having played the last quarter on Saturday against Western Province, replacing Nathan Hines.

No. 8 Andy Powell did as he had done all tour and smashed his way forward. Even though the Welshman needed to bring more guile to his game, the full-frontal style suited the occasion. Joe Worsley drifted in the early stages but grew in stature, one clawback tackle on van der Westhuyzen in the 71st

■ FACING PAGE **Perhaps a little high, that one. Jaco van der Westhuyzen of the Southern Kings clatters a bemused Joe Worsley in a torrid game at Nelson Mandela Bay Stadium.**

■ ABOVE Lions centre Riki Flutey puts in a heavy hit on Harlequin-turned-Southern King De Wet Barry.
■ FACING PAGE Ugo Monye and Matthew Turner vie for the bobbling ball. Monye pounced first to score for the Lions.

minute keeping the Lions try line intact. Sadly it was not for long, irrepressible Southern Kings flanker Mphio Mbiyozo thrusting through weak defence from Nathan Hines to score just two minutes later.

Gordon D'Arcy also put himself about, one of a few to really take the game back to the Southern Kings. Keith Earls, at full back for the first time, showed a clean pair of heels on a couple of occasions, weaving upfield. Ugo Monye, only drafted that morning after Shane Williams was forced to drop to the bench, looked in Test form, one knock-on apart. He was perhaps fortunate to get the verdict from television match official Johan

Meuwesen after scrambling to collect and touch down a cross-field chip from Ronan O'Gara ten minutes into the second half. That score eased anxieties. The Lions then had to survive intact until the final whistle. They did – just.

The Lions were seething about the spiteful, bone-headed approach of the Southern Kings. McGeechan chose to keep his counsel, not wanting to be drawn into a slanging match which might prove a distraction. However, one or two of his players didn't feel the need to be so charitable. 'There were more cheap shots in the game than in the entire tour put together,' said O'Gara.

The Lions lost two players, fly half James Hook, who took a wild bang to the head, and prop Euan Murray, who badly sprained an ankle. Hook was out of the first Test; Murray was off the tour. He was replaced by Munster and Ireland prop John Hayes.

D'Arcy had been particularly incensed by what had gone on. 'We knew there was going be some rough stuff on this tour and it came today,' said D'Arcy afterwards. 'There would be things I wouldn't be happy with. Late hits, high hits, stuff like that.

They talked about how they were going to rough us up ahead of the first Test and they did that. You live and learn, and I'm still walking.'

Former Ulster and Northampton coach Alan Solomons, now in charge of the Southern Kings, made no attempt to hide the fact that his side had set out to knock the Lions out of their stride. 'The Lions made it clear that they were looking for physical intensity and we didn't want to disappoint them,' said Solomons. 'There was nothing untoward as far as I'm concerned.'

The Lions dashed straight to the airport for their charter flight north to Durban. They were relieved to have lost only two players. The unbeaten record was still intact coming up to the first Test, for the first time since the Lions tour to Australia in 1989.

The rest of the squad had been watching on TV at their beachfront hotel in Durban. If the Southern Kings thought that their reckless tactics would soften up the Lions, then they had got it badly wrong. It had the opposite effect. The Lions were drawn together by the experience. They were ready to take on the Springboks.

Ian McGeechan in conversation with Ian Robertson

How satisfied were you with the victory against Natal Sharks in Durban? Only 7-3 up at half-time – 39-3 in the end.

■ *'This was a very good performance, make no mistake about that. We spent the first half an hour producing a host of driving rucks and mauls moving their pack all over Kings Park and breaking their resolve and draining their energy. In the second half, the Natal Sharks pack found it harder and harder to contain the Lions forwards and with more possession and more room to play expansive rugby we ran in four more tries in a tremendous second-half display. What we wanted to do and what we achieved was to keep the opposition accumulatively under intense physical pressure. We were very patient and didn't panic in the first half and then we ran them off their feet in the second half. Our overall plan is to put the squeeze on for the first 50 minutes of a match so that most of our points may well come in the last 20 or 30 minutes of each game.*

'What I was pleased with was the momentum was being maintained. We were improving with every match and this was a good victory over the best of the four teams we have met so far. Perhaps the best news of all was the fantastic power, pace, thrust and angles of running of Jamie Roberts. He was the man of the match and he and Brian O'Driscoll had now forged a really great centre partnership. They were developing into a tremendous strength for the Lions and at this stage I was looking for combinations for the first Test.

'At this stage I knew I could rely on Roberts and O'Driscoll and also the long-established Welsh half backs Stephen Jones and Mike Phillips. For the next game against Western Province in Cape Town I had another chance to look at different combinations.'

This match against WP proved the toughest of the pre-Test games. Was it a big relief to win with almost the last kick and did it help you to ink in one or two names for the Test team?

■ *'This was a difficult game in difficult conditions and I thought we played well, particularly when you look at the tactics of the Western Province team. They fronted up against our forwards, but they didn't take too many risks in their back play and concentrated a little more on defence than on attack.*

'Again we stuck to our game plan and showed great patience in the build-up to our tries. Again, at the end of this win as I was trying to sort more combinations, I felt comfortable in looking for my back three who play as a unit. Bowe and Monye had stepped to the mark and raised the bar and it was going to take a very good display to displace either of them.

'[In this game] our problem was the referee gave several penalties against us which kept them in the game and I would have been very disappointed indeed if we hadn't won because we were really the only side trying to play rugby. Fortunately, we did not panic. We regrouped and kept control up front and won the match with James Hook showing great composure to kick the crucial penalty right at the end.

'With just one week to the Test, several players put their hands up to be included in the Test squad and with the pieces beginning to fall in place, I was looking forward to selecting the final midweek side before the moment of truth back in Durban on Saturday June 20th.'

The players knew the match against the Southern Kings was their last chance to stake a claim for a Test squad place but would you agree the match turned out to be a bit disappointing?

■ *'It was a disappointing game because the opposition seemed happy to mount a damage limitation exercise and there were too many off-the-ball incidents which smacked a little of a cynical approach. There were quite a lot of late tackles and a bit of offside which made it tricky to play the sort of rugby we wanted to play and in retrospect I just wonder if the referee and the two touch judges might have been a bit firmer in the opening 20 minutes and that might have made for a better contest.*

'It was a very scrappy first half and with one penalty for each team the scoreline of 3-3 summed up the first 40 minutes. We took more control in the second half and deserved our two tries. They scored a late try but by then we had won the game with a bit to spare. Our defence was outstanding throughout the match but it was not the easiest occasion for players to force their way into the Test team. In fairness to the whole touring party, we waited 24 hours before picking the Test team and selection was a lengthy process.'

Investec
Specialist Bank

Don't side step opportunity

We accept the challenge. We understand that success stems from a combination of commitment, teamwork and innovative flair. We thrive on working together with our clients offering a range of specialist banking products and services. For more information, call **+44 20 7597 4000** or visit **www.investec.com**

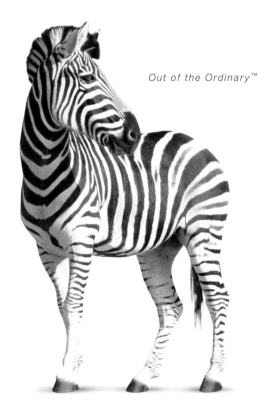

Out of the Ordinary™

award winning security solutions

At VSG we have invested in the development of market leading services that include the provision of high quality security personel, security systems and remote montoriing to blue chip clients across the UK.

Our success has been built on a foundation of bespoke service delivery giving customers a solution that delivers value, efficiency and trust.

VSG. The name behind your future security.

Northampton | London | Belfast | Dublin

Winners of the Security Guarding Company of the Year
Security Excellence Awards 2008

4
First Test

■ The waiting game. The guessing game. The side for the first Test was supposedly still in the melting pot. Places up for grabs. Combinations to be settled. The opposition strategy to be detected. Plans to be made accordingly. A fair crack to be given to all. We'd taken Ian McGeechan at his word when he said that it was an open book, that every player was in with a shout, that it was important that each individual believed that. ■

To be fair, the Lions played as if that were the case. They were a tightknit bunch, a group bonded by a common goal. The same side had not been put out in successive matches. There was no clear-cut divide between the traditional Saturday and midweek team. If anything, it was the dirt-trackers who had turned in the most impressive performances, while the Saturday team had laboured for their victories.

And yet to most observers a Test XV was taking shape. It was obvious to many that Jamie Roberts and Brian O'Driscoll should be the centre pairing, that Lee Byrne and Tommy Bowe would fill two of the back-three positions, that Mike Phillips would be at scrum half and Jamie Heaslip at No. 8. Gethin

■ ABOVE **Bakkies Botha arrives in the nick of time to dislodge the ball from hand of the stretching Mike Phillips just as he is about to touch down. No try.**

Jenkins had done quite enough to nail down the loose-head slot, while Lee Mears was the frontrunner in the hooking stakes.

If we knew all this, then the players did, too. They were no mugs. They would listen to McGeechan in good faith and be grateful for the chances that were coming their way, but they were not fools. This was not to be a selection that started from scratch. Nor should it be. The players had been given an even break. But to paraphrase George Orwell, some were more equal than others. There is nothing wrong in this. Players accept that natural divide as long as the process has been fair. And it had been fair. There was no denying that.

Inevitably the Lions were trimming and reshaping plans as they went along. There was to be more adjustment that Wednesday morning in Durban. The team had flown straight there by charter from Port Elizabeth. You didn't have to be

Dr Finlay to figure out that with a boot encasing his ankle and his leg raised throughout the one-hour flight, prop Euan Murray didn't look too clever. So it proved, his damaged ankle not only ruling him out of consideration for the Test match but for the entire tour. Little did we know, but Andrew Sheridan was also struggling with a back problem, an ailment that removed him from selection, albeit he would not have made the cut. Murray was eventually to be replaced by John Hayes, while Sheridan's difficulties led to a call-up for Tim Payne of Wasps.

There was another worry. Fly half James Hook had taken a bang to the head and was suffering from concussion. 'Losing James is a blow in that he can cover fly half, centre and full back,' said attack coach Rob Howley on that Wednesday. 'A player of that quality you're going to miss.'

There had been no formal citings from the match against the Southern Kings, although the Lions' displeasure was clear even 24 hours later. 'There was a cynical mark on the match and a lot of off-the-ball incidents that were not picked up,' said Howley.

The Lions did not want to get involved in a slanging match, aware that it might prove a distraction. Privately, though, they were fuming. They had been given no protection and had been left to fend for themselves. A few years earlier such a game would have resulted in a mass brawl. The Lions had lost two players to injuries, one of which – Hook's – was the result of the Kings' brutal approach. If the Lions had got stuck into the opposition, been goaded into retaliating, their resources might have been even more depleted. Red cards are as ruinous to a team's chances as a bang to the head.

The Lions had plenty to ponder about their own game despite going into a Test series unbeaten for the first time since the 1989 tour to Australia. As Howley conceded that Wednesday, the Lions had to get everything spot on if they were to have a chance. 'I wouldn't disagree with that view, no,' said Howley. 'But we will be battle-hardened going in while there is maybe rustiness in the South African camp.'

The Springboks had already revealed their hand. It was as expected, with the squat open-side Heinrich Brussow, who had caused the Lions so much grief in Bloemfontein, drafted for his first Test start in place of the injured Schalk Burger. Different men, different approach; Brussow was the snuffler while Burger was the all-enveloping banger.

The Lions had had their issues in and around the contact area. 'The breakdown is an area of concern for us,' Howley conceded. 'The first tackler is now allowed to stay in there a bit longer and we have to deal with that threat. We could deal with it much better than we have done and that will be our focus over the next couple of days going into the first Test. We've been getting isolated there, and going to ground too early. We need to stay on our feet longer as well as get our support systems in place a second or two earlier. Brussow was very efficient and turned over a lot of ball on the Cheetahs' behalf. We gave him easy targets. He's totally different to Burger, a fetcher as opposed to a ball carrier. When we haven't played with a fetcher, we've struggled so his presence will have an influence on selection.'

To that end, the Lions had to weigh up the merits of going with two open-sides, David Wallace and Martyn Williams, rather than opting for the athletic line-out specialist Tom Croft on the blind-side with either of the other two flankers at No. 7. Wallace, however, had had no game time at No. 6 on the trip, while the Lions' best showing in the six matches had been at Kings Park, when they defeated the Sharks 39-3 with a back row made up of Croft, Wallace and Jamie Heaslip. 'We showed against the Sharks how efficient we could be in that tackle area and if we can take that into the weekend, we'll be much the better for it,' said Howley.

Demoting Croft would have weakened the line out significantly, a potential failing made all the more acute if the Lions were to plump for Alun-Wyn Jones in the second row alongside O'Connell, both of whom are middle jumpers by inclination. That was the smart thinking. And so it proved when McGeechan did reveal his hand on Thursday after a two-hour selection meeting that Wednesday morning.

Meanwhile, in the South African camp, things panned out as expected. Morne Steyn, the stand-out fly half from the Super 14, was the only uncapped player included in the 22, but he lost out to Ruan

■ FACING PAGE **Assisted by physio Phil Pask, Euan Murray hobbles off the field at Port Elizabeth, and off the tour, after picking up an ankle injury against the Southern Kings.**

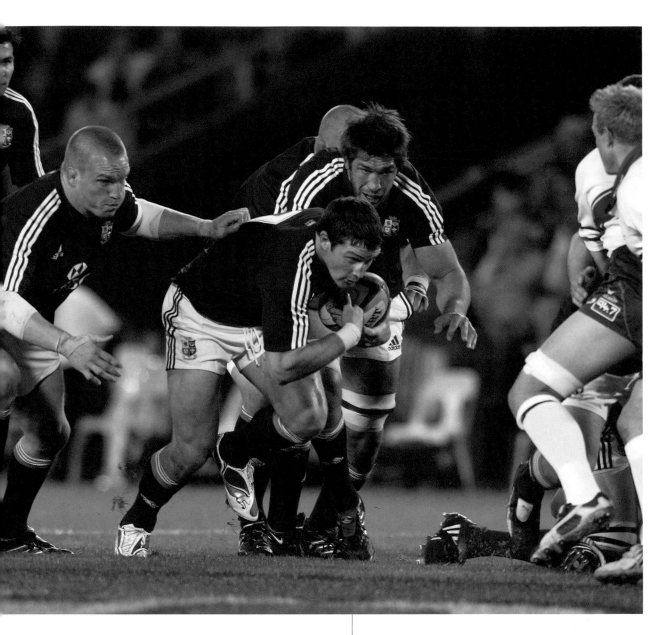

Pienaar for the starting No. 10 jersey. The other contested position, full back, went to Frans Steyn in a line-up packed with experience. Sixteen players in the Springbok match 22 had been in the squad for South Africa's previous Test, against England at Twickenham in November.

Assistant coach Dick Muir had no doubt that the Springboks would overcome any concerns about their lack of match practice. 'We have a team that can take the Lions on at forward and run at them behind,' said Muir. 'We have been together as a squad for a number of years. The players have won the World Cup and the Bulls lifted the Super 14. There is a confidence throughout the squad that will carry us through. We have not played together as a side for seven months but we will be ready for the Lions. We have had practice sessions against the Emerging Springboks in training and while we are

■ FACING PAGE David Wallace on the charge against the Golden Lions. McGeechan resisted the temptation to go into the first Test with two open-sides, pairing Wallace with Tom Croft.

■ RIGHT With Tommy Bowe and Ugo Monye in the tries, there was no Test place for Welsh wizard Shane Williams.

aware that the Lions have had more in the way of match preparation than us, there is an up and a down side to that because they have picked up injuries along the way.'

Muir was not expecting anything unexpected in the Lions selection. 'We have analysed the Lions minutely, not just this tour, but looking at the Six Nations and the clubs their coaches have been involved in. We know exactly how they are going to play and what their management team is all about. We do not expect any surprises in their team. We are not too concerned about what will be thrown at us.'

McGeechan let the players know the selection on the Wednesday evening before the formal squad announcement was made the following lunchtime. There had been no training that day. The players wandered about the hotel or strolled along the Durban North Beach front, where there was growing evidence of an influx of British and Irish supporters.

The head coach stood before the squad in their team room at the Elangeni Hotel and read out the names of the chosen ones. It was the way the players had wanted to hear the news: up front and personal. Immediately afterwards the entire Lions party – players, management, support staff et al – decamped to a nearby restaurant and spent the evening together. Handshakes were exchanged, commiserations and congratulations dispensed in equal measure.

Now was the time we would discover if that famed team spirit was that strong, if it was that deep-rooted and genuine. Handshakes for public consumption are one thing; holding tackle bags and urging the Test starter to give it all he's got for the greater good, quite another. But the facade was not false. That much was evident from time in the players' company.

As expected, McGeechan opted for specialist, in-form players, giving Ireland open-side David Wallace the nod over Wales's Martyn Williams and putting his faith in Leicester flanker Tom Croft, who won a Test spot despite not being included in the original 37-man squad. Stephen Jones beat Ronan O'Gara to the No. 10 slot, while Harlequins wing Ugo Monye won a coveted Lions shirt just 12 months after not being considered good enough for a starting place in England's second-string side in America, and only

two years after he was obliged to be fed through a straw by a friend after a career-threatening bulging disc problem reduced him to lying flat on his back. IRB World Player of the Year Shane Williams missed out as a result.

McGeechan made clear the enormity of the challenge: the side was destined for an examination of their sporting being. 'Nothing can prepare you for it,' said McGeechan. 'The players are in for something they have never experienced before.'

There was confidence bubbling in the camp, though. 'We've got enough shots in the locker, absolutely,' said captain Paul O'Connell. 'It'll be an emotional changing room on Saturday. We're all proud of where we come from, of the clubs and countries we play for. But for all of us, the Lions shirt is the greatest jersey you can put on. It's a different mindset now the side is known. We're only really starting out.'

O'Connell would need all his on-field lieutenants to front up. He was not the most demonstrative leader, either on or off the field. He was so much part of the fabric at Munster, so much a son of its soil, that he felt he had no need to be anything other than himself there. The Lions was different. Of course, the idea was not for O'Connell to contrive a false persona, but he had to be strong and firm for others, set some sort of lead. The next fortnight was going to define him as a player and in character.

He had good men alongside him, one of whom, Brian O'Driscoll, believed that the prospects for the 2009 side were better than those of the team he had captained four years earlier in New Zealand. Partly it was the upbeat mood among mates, but more especially it was the firm sense that this lot knew what they were about and what they were trying to do that caused O'Driscoll to feel that this squad was better placed to cause the opposition some bother.

'Yes, we can from the point of view that the team is more together and that we have more idea about what we need to do,' said O'Driscoll. 'We all want to be part of a team that creates history.'

O'Driscoll's partnership with Jamie Roberts, at 22 the same age as O'Driscoll had been when he enraptured the Gabba eight years earlier, would be crucial to the well-being of the Lions. Roberts was rapidly turning into one of the star turns of the trip: modest, affable, intelligent and dynamic – not bad qualities in anybody's book. Roberts had been a professional rugby player for only two years and was still studying to be a doctor. He was due to take exams at the end of August (and, no, he hadn't taken his books with him) and complete the remaining two years of his medical degree over four years, all the while honing his considerable rugby skills.

The Cardiff Blues centre was the epitome of what McGeechan wanted on a Lions tour – a player who thrived in the environment, one who was stimulated and not overawed by the experience. Surrounded by players such as O'Driscoll, Roberts found something within himself that had not been evident before. He had been shifted around the back line during the season but had found his true position here in South Africa. He was showing that he was not just a lump of crash-ball muscle. He was running good angles, the perfect foil to O'Driscoll.

■ FACING PAGE Matfield the magnificent. The towering Victor Matfield secures line-out ball for the Springboks at Kings Park.
■ BELOW South Africa's captain, hooker-turned-tight-head John Smit, powers through the Lions defence to score his side's first try in the fifth minute.

Any sense of the Lions coming to South Africa to beat up the Boks with their heavyweight sluggers had proved to be hokum. The Lions had opted for a mobile, big-tackling front row, one that was able to chop down the Springbok runners and also compete with ferocity at the breakdown. The work rate of Gethin Jenkins, Lee Mears and Phil Vickery had counted for more than mere grunt and muscle. How the Lions might come to reflect on that decision!

Once the Lions settled on Alun-Wyn Jones to partner Paul O'Connell in the second row, thus choosing players who are both normally middle jumpers, they had to bring in Croft for his dexterity at the line out. The Springbok line out was the most efficient and productive in world rugby, and the Lions needed to produce a trump card of their own. Croft was that card. How he was to live up to that billing! Another in the Roberts mould.

McGeechan acknowledged that he had given consideration to pairing two open-sides, David Wallace and Martyn Williams, but had rejected the idea on very sensible grounds. 'You need players used to playing in their number one position,' said McGeechan. There was some concern that the Lions might now be underpowered. It was a surprise that they had gone for Donncha O'Callaghan on the bench ahead of a more heavy-duty warrior such as Simon Shaw or Nathan Hines. That decision, too, was to come back to haunt them.

There were some tell-tale indicators on the eve of battle as to how events might unfold. Take the comments of forwards coach Warren Gatland. 'We've got to play some rugby really,' said Gatland. 'I think if we get involved in a set-piece battle and get into the physical one-on-one confrontation game, then that's something the South Africans are very good at. We've gone for some mobility. We've got to move their pack about a bit, go through some phases and ask some questions of their tight five. But we are expecting them to come out and be very physical.'

And how! This was the moment the Springboks had been waiting for. 'The 2007 World Cup was

■ RIGHT **Phil Vickery pops out of a scrum under pressure from Tendai 'the Beast' Mtawarira (No. 1). The verdict was split on whether the Zimbabwean was scrummaging legally. Nevertheless, the end result was a string of penalties against the Lions.**

phenomenal and a lot of the guys will have another crack or two at the World Cup, but we won't have another chance at the Lions,' said Springbok captain John Smit. 'It will be amazing to wake up and realise that it's finally here. The team has been buzzing for the last two weeks because of the importance of what is coming. There is so much at stake and we won't have another chance. The rarity of the occasion means the hype has been much bigger than any other Test match and that is saying something because there have been some huge matches over the last 12 years. A Lions tour is unique, it is the last link with the old school. What makes this series so important is that it is part of more than 100 years of history. Players who won the World Cup have stayed in South Africa to play against the Lions. What we have in the next couple of weeks will not come around again. There is pressure on us, but not in a negative sense. It is wonderful to have pressure like this because it shows how meaningful this series is.'

The atmosphere in Durban was building. Hordes of Lions fans were being disgorged from aircraft and making their way to the beachfront. What had once been a quiet backdrop – early morning joggers trotting along as the surf crashed on to the shore – now became a seething mass of red-clad humanity. The players, as ever, were obliging as they posed for autographs and photographs. Saturday dawned bright and warm. Temperatures were forecast to hit 27 degrees. The mercury was rising on all fronts.

Kings Park is a wonderful venue, its surrounding fields packed from the early hours with huge pick-up trucks and cars stashed full of food and booze, everyone and everything primed for a long day round the braai.

Yet again, though, there was disquiet about the price of tickets. Astonishingly, there were still some available, agencies being forced to put these high-end tickets out on to the open market, the rugby public shying away from prices in excess of R1000 (around £75-80). With an attendance of 47,800, later rounded up to 49,055, the 52,000-seat stadium was not full, and the empty seats did not reflect well on the tour. The Lions were moved to make their own comment on the matter a few days later.

'The South African Rugby Union and its provincial Unions had sole responsibility for the setting of ticket prices for the British & Irish Lions tour and the Lions management had no input whatsoever into any of this,' said Lions chief executive John Feehan. 'The Lions did appoint official overseas travel agencies to service the requirements of travelling British & Irish Lions supporters. However, the tickets for this programme were purchased at full price from the South African Rugby Union by the British & Irish Lions. It is true to say we are very surprised at the level of the attending crowds. The Lions only visit South Africa every 12 years and it is therefore disappointing that the stadiums have been far from full.'

So much for peripheral issues. The match itself was what it was all about. The time of reckoning was upon the Lions, the time when all the planning and scheming and finger-crossing would find an outlet. The setting was splendid, with the massed tiers of Lions fans disappearing up towards the clear KwaZulu-Natal skyline; the locals, too, all bedecked in their colours and in good voice.

And then it all went horribly askew for the Lions. All that could go wrong for them in that opening 50 minutes did go wrong. The scrum buckled, reducing one of the most noble warriors in sport, Phil Vickery, to an impotent, head-shaking wreck. The line out

■ LEFT **Ugo Monye dives in at the corner, only for Jean de Villiers (left) to stop him touching down, thereby preventing an immediate Lions riposte to John Smit's opening try.**

■ ABOVE Springbok fly half Ruan Pienaar about to strike one of his three first-half penalties.

■ FACING PAGE Frans Steyn is wrapped up by Lions Jamie Roberts and Tommy Bowe.

wobbled, with at least three throws missing their man – a black mark against Lee Mears, who had been picked for his accuracy alongside his athleticism. The Lions were being bossed up front, were vulnerable in the maul and on the back foot in the set piece.

It was their weak scrum that was to be their undoing. The scrum had been dominant all trip, but when it came to the big moment the Lions were found wanting. They never believed that the Springboks would be able to get after them in that regard. But get after them they did, notably through the presence of Tendai 'the Beast' Mtawarira.

The Zimbabwean is not a noted scrummager, despite his monicker. He had not looked too comfortable the previous autumn when up against Scotland's Euan Murray in Edinburgh. However, he had done his graft in the gym and his homework on the analysis DVDs. The Boks targeted Vickery once they knew that the Lions had forsaken their own beasts of burden.

Mtawarira didn't look too legal, driving up and through Vickery time and again. The Lions got a raw deal from New Zealand referee Bryce Lawrence. It was a supreme irony for the Lions that they had been pleading for referees to reward the dominant scrum all tour, and when it came to the Test match, what happened? The side putting on the pressure was rewarded.

The Lions were fuming but could do nothing to influence Lawrence. Some would question Lions captain O'Connell's role in this, wondering why he didn't manage to get into the ear of Lawrence the way that a Johnson or Dallaglio might have. Well, he tried but to no avail. Lawrence was not for swaying, the Lions were in big trouble and their woes continued throughout the half.

The Lions got nothing from Lawrence. Every 50-50 call went in favour of the Springboks. Of course, the Lions contributed hugely to their own downfall.

Vickery himself gave away nine points through penalties conceded. What was particularly galling for the coaches, though, was the slipshod manner of the Lions finishing. Chance after chance went begging.

After conceding a ludicrously soft try to Smit in the fifth minute, the Springbok captain crashing through some misshapen defence, the Lions could have hit back immediately. From a midfield scrum, Phillips set off one way on a dummy run, leaving

The Lions maul creaks and groans as the South Africans rumble purposefully, inevitably, towards the try line near the start of the second half. Moments later the Boks look pretty pleased with themselves after their forward effort results in a try for Heinrich Brussow (centre in white scrum cap).

Jamie Heaslip to pick up and go left. On to Stephen Jones and Brian O'Driscoll, before the ball found its way to Ugo Monye. The Harlequins wing was checked slightly in his stride by O'Driscoll's pass, but even so he still had a clear path to the line.

Monye was joint top scorer on the trip with four tries and needed no second bidding. Off he set. He dived and looked to have scored, only for Springbok centre Jean de Villiers to scramble across and somehow get an arm underneath him. The decision went to television match official Christophe Berdos. The verdict took an age to come. No try.

It was a good call, as it had been a bad call by Monye to have the ball in his right hand as he dived to the line, leaving himself open on that side to de Villiers. Left hand and he would have scored. Left hand and the scores might have been levelled immediately. Left hand and we might have had an entirely different scenario unfolding.

The same was to be true of much of the rest of the game. The Boks were structured and organised but limited. The Lions were edgy and febrile in their set piece, losing three of their own throws at the line out, conceding a host of penalties and being bullied in the scrum. Yet they were playing the rugby but getting no return, partly through their own profligacy, partly through unsympathetic refereeing.

Credit to South Africa. They had gone into the match seemingly undercooked, yet played with fixed purpose in that first half and just beyond to give themselves what looked to be an unassailable lead, 26-7, by the 47th minute. Ruan Pienaar and Frans Steyn had kicked their goals to give the Springboks a half-time lead of 19-7. Shortly thereafter, the tourists' sense of machismo was further dented when the Boks churned the Lions back over their try line from a line out, their close defence simply steamrollered, allowing Brussow to touch down.

The Lions had had their own moment of glory, and what a finely constructed moment it was.

Roberts and O'Driscoll yet again combined to splendid effect to shred the defence, leaving O'Driscoll to pop the ball up to Tom Croft for a straightforward finish in the 23rd minute. Even so, up in the stands the anguished looks on the faces of the Lions fans told their own story. It couldn't be happening, could it? All this way, all that money, all those hopes and dreams built up over four years, and the boys were being humiliated. This could get very messy. This could be a rout.

Except that it wasn't. All those qualities that McGeechan had been espousing came to the fore. All those hours spent in each other's company, on the field and off the field, came into play. The Lions did not fold. The Lions did not cash in their chips and head for the exit. They continued to play. They continued to back each other. They did not whinge and grumble and point fingers.

Significantly, the tourists made a couple of key substitutions. On went Adam Jones for Phil Vickery. Shortly afterwards, on went hooker Matthew Rees

for Lee Mears. Where there had been instability and fretfulness, now there was steadiness and self-assurance. The Lions set piece became what it ought to have been all along – a reliable source of possession.

Of course the Lions were helped in their quest by the changes made from the other bench. South Africa coach Peter de Villiers made six substitutions in nine minutes. Off went the Beast. Off went Smit. Off went Bakkies Botha. If there were three players that the Lions wanted to see the back of, it was this trio. The momentum began to shift. It was the turn of the Springboks to wilt. A glorious comeback was under way. Up in the stands, the mood changed. Spirits lifted and with it the volume.

In the 68th minute, the Lions struck, Croft winning a line out and then being on hand once again to take a pass from O'Driscoll and cross for a try. 26-14. The clock was ticking. Could it happen? Could the Lions really come back from beyond the grave? They could.

Rob Kearney began to show well, both with the downfield boot and the upfield run. In the 72nd minute, an improbable outcome began to take vivid shape. A tap penalty saw the ball eventually reach Monye, who stepped inside one defender and looked to touch down. Monye seemed too upright in his stance, though, and the ball once again appeared to be tucked under the wrong arm. In came Morne Steyn, out went the ball and another glorious chance had gone begging.

Still heads did not drop. Still the Lions pressed. Still the Springboks scrambled desperately. Like Monye, Mike Phillips had come within a whisker of scoring earlier in the half, only for the ball to be dislodged from his grasp as he stretched for the line. In the 75th minute, though, he did get the ball down, scooting over after fine build-up work involving Roberts among others.

Stephen Jones's conversion brought the Lions to within five points at 26-21. How fortunes had changed. There was still time left on the clock and the Lions did not relent. A lobbed pass from Jamie Roberts intended for Tommy Bowe was only just snatched out of the air by Jaque Fourie. There was bedlam in the stadium. One last line out on the

■ FACING PAGE Not for the faint-hearted. Paul O'Connell prepares to ram Springbok replacement lock Andries Bekker.
■ BELOW It's that man Croft again. The blind-side flanker turns up on Brian O'Driscoll's shoulder to cross for his second try of the match. The tide was turning.

Springbok 22. The Lions, though, for all their effort and guts, could not make it happen. Miracles would have to wait for another day. This was a failure, but, in the end, a glorious one.

Disappointment and frustration hung in the air, enormously so. Had the Lions just blown their best chance of victory? Never mind this being the first Test, the Springboks being rusty and the Lions catching them cold. Quite simply, the Lions had had more try-scoring chances in the game than they might have expected to have in the entire series. Monye had fluffed a couple, Phillips had been just short, Tommy Bowe had been called back after a crossing episode in the move – and so on. Ifs, buts and maybes count for nothing in the history books. The Lions knew that. It hurt and it rankled.

Monye was soon quizzed and soon reaching for the mea culpa. A decent man, and usually a reliable scorer, he knew that he'd let himself down. 'If I had my time again, it would be a case of tucking it in the left and diving over,' conceded Monye. 'I thought it was try time straightaway which is why I didn't feel the need to change hands. Of course, I'm upset by it. We've lost a game and I had an opportunity where I might have been able to influence that.'

Correct. There were other issues. Scrummaging. Scrum coach Graham Rowntree was not about to duck the obvious. His area of speciality had been, in the short term, a disaster. There had to be consequences. There had to be accountability.

Rowntree gave his views the following morning, pained but resolute and up front. 'Changes will be made,' said Rowntree. 'We failed to keep a lid on the Beast at engagement time and he got under us. We didn't dominate that engagement well enough and they had an incredibly powerful pack. Phil Vickery is a very honest guy and by his own admission he struggled. He is upset. He is sore this morning physically and mentally. It is not about hanging individuals out to dry. It is a collective thing and that is where I come in. I have to look at what went wrong.

'There were eight scrum occasions in that first half, three of which we were penalised. That put us

■ RIGHT Mike Phillips celebrates after touching down in the 75th minute. Stephen Jones's subsequent conversion put the Lions just five points behind South Africa.

■ ABOVE Out of time. The final whistle ends the Lions' heroic fightback at Kings Park. But could they carry their strong finish with them into the second Test in Pretoria?

nine points down. We will be looking very hard at those scrums where we looked so vulnerable. The changes we made sorted it out. I was delighted with the impact Matthew Rees and Adam Jones had in that set piece. The changes made the scrum better and we got some good playable possession. The referee was rewarding the dominant scrum as we had asked him to do. They won that engagement, they were going forward then their movement was upwards. It was legal. We were just under a lot of pressure and we have to take that on the chin.

Hooker Bismarck du Plessis is very strong and with the Beast they were able to get stuck into Vicks. It is not about one man. The guys next to him and behind him have to help him. There was one particularly uncomfortable scrum on nine minutes when we got lifted off the floor. If I was their scrum coach watching that I would have retired to Panama with a cigar.'

Instead Rowntree and his coaching pals would retire to their war room to plot their next moves. For all the gloom that Sunday morning, their glass was half-full. They had finished the Test the stronger side, they had taken the game to South Africa, who had been given a real fright. The series was very much alive.

IAN MCGEECHAN

Lions head coach Ian McGeechan was in the mood to cry foul after tight-head prop Phil Vickery had all but been penalised out of the Test:

■ *'We will try to get an explanation from the officials. It comes down to interpretation. The penalty count in the first half killed us.'*

McGeechan also rued the missed opportunities:

■ *'To leave five scoring opportunities unfinished will cost you in an away Test. Not scoring from those and giving away soft penalties meant that we had created a mountain to climb by half-time.'*

PAUL O'CONNELL

The Lions skipper was also bemused by the penalty count:

■ *'The referee was constantly warning Phil about "going in", but it was hard to see from just behind him. Phil is a very experienced prop and had been playing top rugby for a long time. How he would make the same mistake five times in a row is beyond me. It has never been a problem before. It seems as if he was refereeing us and not them. We conceded penalties, territory and points.'*

Nevertheless, the captain expressed satisfaction at the Lions' general play:

■ *'We played how we wanted. If we had not played well, it would be really hard.'*

BRIAN O'DRISCOLL

The Lions centre commented:

■ *'We were afraid of ourselves in the opening half.'*

GETHIN JENKINS

And the loose-head seemed to concur:

■ *'We needed to play a bit more in the first half. We went out and didn't play enough rugby and the Springboks got too far in front. Even though we finished very strongly it was too much of a gap. Decisions went against us on the right hand of the scrum – I'm not too sure what was happening because I had my head down on the other side. They didn't play much rugby, they just kicked the ball. We believed we were fitter than them and we believed we could put them to the sword in the last 20 minutes – that was the case.'*

TOM CROFT

The two-try flanker commented:

■ *'When we came in at half-time we knew we had a lot in the tank. We've played provincial games up to the 80th minute so we knew we could last. We played exceptionally well in the second half and we took the game to them. Add on a couple of minutes to the end of that second half and it could have been a different story. We are a dangerous team and we can create holes in defences.'*

STEPHEN JONES

The fly half praised his midfield colleagues:

■ *'I thought the centres played particularly well and created a lot of problems. Our pattern worked and our fitness levels were fine.'*

■ RIGHT Springbok No. 8 Pierre Spies is stopped in his tracks by Brian O'Driscoll and friend at Kings Park.

Heavy weights.
Linklaters

For further information please contact our mining experts.

Charlie Jacobs
charlie.jacobs@linklaters.com

Andrew Jones
andrew.jones@linklaters.com

Chris Kelly
christopher.kelly@linklaters.com

linklaters.com

PETER DE VILLIERS

The Springboks also adopted attitudes of self-criticism and internal blame. Their head coach confessed:

■ *'I made too many changes too soon.'*

He was, however, full of praise for Frans Steyn's display at full back:

■ *'What a brilliant player. Look at how he adapted to the position. We all know he was born for the job.'*

FRANS STEYN

Steyn himself was not so sure:

■ *'I don't know about full back being my position for the future. It will be a while before I am convinced that I was born to be there after three years without having the chance. There were some kicks that I was pleased with – but many really bad ones.'*

JOHN SMIT

His captain, meanwhile, said:

■ *'We took our foot off the gas and our kicking game went down the toilet. 'The Beast' played a really big role and our control flowed from his dominance. Our rolling mauls were in exactly the right parts of the pitch. I was quite happy to be taken off, but with four minutes left I went back on with the ship needing to be steadied and the ball kept secure to save our lead. But the substitutions accounted for our poor second-half performance. There was some rustiness and lapses in concentration.'*

TENDAI MTAWARIRA

For his part, 'the Beast' spread the credit:

■ *'No loose-head can manage what I did without the boys behind him.'*

VICTOR MATFIELD

South Africa's masterly lock observed:

■ *'It was all about individuals making mistakes. I think we can fix that. We had the chance to put the Lions away and we didn't exploit that option. We need to be hard on ourselves. I don't think it is for me to say whether all the substitutions were a mistake, but the whole 22 must take the responsibility for such a close call. We were very happy with what we achieved in the line outs. It was the first game back for us under the new laws and there is obvious work to do. It felt really*

■ ABOVE Springbok skipper John Smit and his front-row partner Tendai Mtawarira, aka 'the Beast', after the match.

good to score that try after a 30-metre drive and that really gave us the upper hand. The Lions had just conceded two penalties and we figured that they would not want to give away another. That gave us the chance to set up our successful maul.'

JEAN DE VILLIERS

The Springbok centre and backs leader had praise for his midfield adversaries:

■ *'The way Jamie Roberts and Brian O'Driscoll ran at us caused us defensive problems and once or twice they cut us up in midfield. In an even tougher game that could cost us the result. We certainly didn't produce an all-round consistent clinical performance.'*

■ COACH'S VIEW First Test ■

Ian McGeechan in conversation with Ian Robertson

How long did it take to pick the first Test team?

■ 'The selection took 2½ hours on the Wednesday in Durban. We discussed every single position and every combination of players, and whilst some were relatively straightforward several were very close calls. A lot of players had put their hands up during the six-match build-up and there were detailed discussions about the make-up of the front row and the back row in particular.

'We had a lot going for us. The team spirit was tremendous and every player had had a chance of showing he was worthy of a Test place. We had played some great rugby and scored some great tries in those first six games and we were not short of confidence.

'Furthermore the Springboks had not played a major Test since November 2008, so there was every chance that they would not be totally wound up and would be either a bit undercooked for this Test or at least a little rusty. I looked at their team, I looked at our team and I concluded we had a real chance of beating the current world champions just as we did in 1997.'

Do you accept that the first-half performance, especially the scrummaging and to a lesser extent the line-out play, was extremely disappointing?

■ 'It was quite a shock to see our scrum driven back several times in the first 20 minutes as South Africa produced huge physical eight-man shoves and we were not fully prepared for it. We had worked hard on our scrum throughout the build-up but we were taken by surprise by the way that they really disrupted our scrummaging. It was definitely not entirely the fault of Phil Vickery and Lee Mears because they rely on strong scrummaging from the other six forwards and the bottom line is that the Springboks disrupted our front row and reduced the potency of our set-piece play right through the first half. Not only did we lose quality possession, we conceded a lot of penalties which cost us a lot of points and made a mockery of our tactical approach.

'We were also driven back a few times in rolling mauls, and although we got our act together in the second half we found ourselves 19-7 down at the interval because we had given away four penalties which Ruan Pienaar and Francois Steyn kicked and had leaked a very soft try. We had scored a good try through Tom Croft but had not had enough possession to make a significant impact.'

What did you say at half-time and how did the team react?

■ 'Oddly enough at half-time I wasn't unduly worried. I knew we had to sort out the scrum but that apart I told the players not to panic, to keep the ball in play, to find or create space and to stop giving away penalties as that could cost us the game. It was a real blow when we gave away another pretty soft try right at the start of the second half, but then I made two changes in the front row and with all the forwards working flat out at every scrum for the last 30 minutes we had no problems at the set piece and suddenly we were able to begin our fightback.

'What followed was quite dramatic. I would argue that in the final 25 minutes of the first Test we produced as good a performance as any that I can remember from any of the seven tours I have been part of. The forwards were on top and our backs played all the rugby in the second half. We made six clean breaks, we scored two excellent tries and came within a whisker of scoring three more. Throw into the mix the fact that Stephen Jones narrowly missed two penalties which he would usually get and you can see how we could so easily have won the Test by 10 or 12 points rather than losing it by five. What pleased me was that we kept playing even, or especially, when we trailed 26-7 and we kept the ball in play and created several try-scoring opportunities. Every member of the squad knows that this was a game that we should and indeed could have won.

'For the second Test we have to start all over again. We will have a different team, a different mountain to climb as well as the claustrophobic intense pressure to succeed engulfing us. On all six previous Lions tours that I have been on there comes a point of no return. On Saturday morning in Pretoria that point of no return will be upon us. At Loftus Versfeld we will confront the 2009 Lions' moment of truth. It won't be easy, I know, but it is this sort of ultimate challenge that comes around so rarely and is so special. I have full confidence that the Lions will front up in the second Test.'

TEAMWORK · PASSION · COMMITMENT

...and then there's the rugby.

- 60 offices in 42 countries
- Third largest independent oil trader in the world
- Over 1.5 million barrels of crude and oil products traded daily
- Second largest nonferrous trading company in the world
- Over 8 million tons of metals and raw materials traded per annum.

www.trafigura.com

Official Sponsor

C/M/S/

Law . Tax

and prop Adam Jones. There was also a sense that Ugo Monye would pay the price for his blemishes. Luke Fitzgerald got the nod. There were to be two other changes, making it five in all. Lee Byrne had been struggling with a foot injury and then also damaged his thumb. Ireland's Rob Kearney had looked lively when he had come on in Durban, and even though Byrne was to be ruled out on fitness issues, the view from inside was that Kearney would have started in any case.

There was one significant call-up in the pack. After 17 appearances in a Lions jersey, dating back to 1997, the ever popular, ever reliable Wasps lock Simon Shaw finally got the Test shirt. The pack needed ballast in scrum and maul. Shaw was the perfect man for the job.

The Lions had sent for the cavalry. At 35, Shaw was the oldest Lions Test debutant. Lazarus had finally got the call. No other player had waited so long for a Test slot. On the 18th occasion of pulling the Lions jersey over his head, Shaw was to trot down the tunnel for a Test match, primed for some serious hand-to-hand combat in the close exchanges. The Lions had no intention of being the patsies they were in the scrum and at the driving maul the previous week. They wanted to play an all-court game in a bid to run the legs off the Springboks. But they couldn't do that if their forward platform was unstable. So they had had to rein back on ambition and insert some pragmatism. Muscular chess was the name of the game.

Shaw had proved a grandmaster in that regard, his huge frame belying soft hands and speed around the field. Shaw had suffered more knock-backs in his career than most. He had a World Cup winner's medal from England's 2003 campaign which he had tossed into a drawer as he didn't play a game. This was his third Lions tour, and he'd have been a man of colossal self-regard if he hadn't begun to doubt himself.

■ FACING PAGE Luke Fitzgerald makes a break against the Emerging Springboks. Both Lions wings that evening, Fitzgerald and Shane Williams, were vying for a Test start. In the end Fitzgerald got the nod, while Williams got a place on the bench.
■ RIGHT Before Morne Steyn went one better at Loftus Versfeld, Willem de Waal had squared a match against the Lions with a last-gasp place-kick for the Emerging Boks in Cape Town.

'You've got to keep yourself going no matter what,' said Shaw, who had seemed destined to partner Martin Johnson in the successful 1997 Lions Test team only to be trumped by Ireland's Jeremy Davidson four days before the first Test. 'Friends and family are supportive, but ultimately it ends up being your own head that makes you believe you can

■ RIGHT J.P. Pietersen cannot stop Rob Kearney from sliding in to score for the Lions in the eighth minute.
■ BELOW Springbok flanker Schalk Burger serves his time in the sin-bin after being yellow-carded in the first minute for an act of villainy around Luke Fitzgerald's eyes.
■ PAGES 98-99 The Red Army. British & Irish Lions fans lap up the atmosphere at Loftus Versfeld.

still do it. It's now not just about my first cap and the shirt, it's about winning. And if we should, then it would be my greatest ever achievement.'

Shaw had battled to contain his joy when the team was revealed to the players on Wednesday night, all the more so given that he was rooming with Scotland lock Nathan Hines, who had been ruled out of consideration himself that very day after picking up a one-week ban for a dangerous tackle. 'You can't be smug,' said Shaw. 'I've been there on the other side too often myself.'

Shaw's presence alone would not ensure anything. The Lions would have to improve significantly if they were to overturn history and win back-to-back Tests at altitude. South Africa would be looking to pummel them, goading them if necessary into mistakes. Scrum half Mike Phillips revealed that Springbok lock Bakkies 'the Enforcer' Botha had been sledging him with taunts about his 'sexy blue eyes'.

Whatever it takes is the Springbok mantra. Adam Jones insisted that he had no qualms about pitting himself against Tendai 'the Beast' Mtawarira, the man who so ruthlessly dismantled Phil Vickery. 'If you go out there bricking yourself, then you'll get drilled into the ground,' said Jones, who had coped well with Mtawarira at the Millennium Stadium in November. 'I'll be pulling all the tricks out of the bag to stop me going backwards.'

Ian McGeechan's Lions in 1989 (Australia) and 1993 (New Zealand) had both come back after losing the opening Test. The man himself had never lost a second Test either as player or coach. The Lions needed everything in their favour.

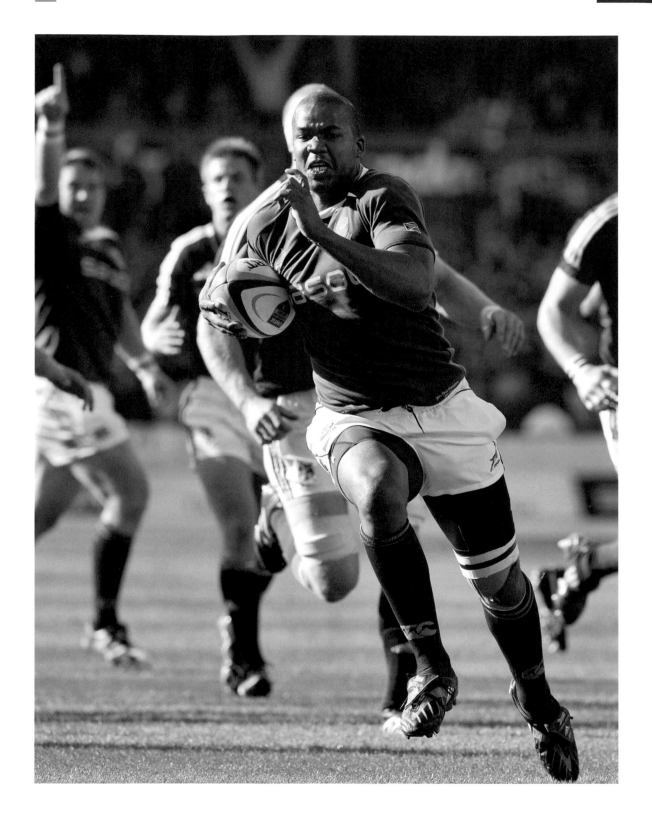

They left Cape Town on Friday afternoon. The airport resembled the last exit from Saigon. There were thousands of Lions fans heading north, all on edge themselves, all excited about what lay ahead.

There was a different mood in the Lions camp, a sense that they'd allowed the Boks to take liberties the previous week. It's not that they'd given way or been soft or not durable enough. No, a Lion is none of these things. But the Springbok forwards had been allowed to dictate tempo and, moreover, to throw their weight around with impunity. Not only had they gone after Phil Vickery in the scrum, they'd also tossed him around like a rag doll in and around the breakdown. This was their turf and they made damn sure that the Lions knew that.

It was time for some old-school reaction. It was time to get physical. That was certainly the message sent out by Warren Gatland prior to departure. The Lions forwards coach has a lot of the old ways about him. There are times when science and strategy and tactics will take you only so far. This was one of those times.

The Lions needed to be brutal and ferocious, for they had been simply too placid and deferential the previous week in Durban. Too often they had turned the other cheek. In short, they had to get nasty. It looked like they might. 'South Africans have a bullying mentality and you've got to get in their faces,' said Gatland.

The beasts of burden would hold the key. For it was they who would set the tone, they who would shape the game. So much rested on Simon Shaw. He was the cement that was needed to repair the fault line. If that held, improbable dreams had a rightful place in anyone's thoughts.

There are times when you invest a lot of faith and hope in a Test match, only to be badly let down by the reality. Anticlimax lurks inside the first peep of a referee's whistle.

Loftus Versfeld was hopping that Saturday afternoon, one entire side bedecked in red, while the rest of the ground was crammed with the Bokke faithful. It was a wonderfully clear afternoon, just right for a humdinger. And, boy, was it a humdinger. From first to last, the second Test did not disappoint. It not only lived up to expectations, it exceeded them, and will go down as one of the greatest Lions Tests ever played. It had edge and bite, energy and passion, huge skill, riveting twists and no end of contentious moments. That it was settled with the very last kick, and from beyond the halfway line, was quite fitting.

The Lions sank to the turf as if Morne Steyn had placed his boot in their solar plexus. The ball rose from his boot and soared into the Pretoria sky to exultant acclaim from various parts of the ground. Down on the pitch, Rob Kearney watched it go over and then slumped to the turf. He was followed by several team-mates, all of them stunned, all of them exhausted and all of them wretched inside.

To have given so much and to have come so close was agonising. Ian McGeechan made a valiant effort to speak rationally about what had just gone before, but it was to little avail. It had been an emotional roller-coaster ride.

There was a look of disbelief in the eyes of many Lions. For they knew once again that they had had the winning of the match. Fate, though, was not on their side. Nor was simple luck. If touch judge Bryce Lawrence had actually seen Springbok flanker Schalk Burger eye-gouge Luke Fitzgerald in the very first minute of the game, then what might have been? As it was, Lawrence reported that he had seen a hand over face and that it was 'a minimum yellow card'. French referee Christophe Berdos had not seen the incident at all and so could do little but go along with Lawrence's recommendation.

In any case, it made for a pretty explosive start, the Boks being reduced to 14 men and the Lions taking full advantage. Stephen Jones kicked the resultant penalty, and within eight minutes Rob Kearney had exploited the opposition's depleted ranks to zip down the blind side after a deft pass from Stephen Jones. 10-0 to the Lions, who were playing with real bounce and enthusiasm.

It was already apparent that the forward pack was in better shape, that the ambition first in evidence at Kings Park was still intact and that the Lions had every intention of carrying on from where they had left off. As expected, there was crackle and niggle,

■ FACING PAGE J.P. Pietersen is through and on his way to the try line. Ruan Pienaar could not manage the conversion, and the score was 10-5 to the Lions after 12 minutes.

too. Burger's sin-binning did not calm things down. Within a couple of minutes, punches were being thrown between Victor Matfield and Brian O'Driscoll, sparking a mini free-for-all. Things did settle, and the Boks did gather themselves. How much different it might have been. The gouging incident was to dominate the headlines not just that night but throughout the week. It was to become a cause célèbre.

At the time the Lions simply had to get on with it. They were in the driving seat but were rudely evicted from it with a snappy try from South Africa wing J.P. Pietersen. The Lions fell for a sucker punch, the Springboks attacking from a routine line out on the 22, scrum half Fourie du Preez arcing out and putting Pietersen into the hold. Fitzgerald had

tracked infield but simply failed to make contact with the Springbok wing. Simple score.

It was thrilling stuff. The roars swept round Loftus Versfeld as first one side then the other made their plays. Jones kicked another goal as Springbok back-row forward Pierre Spies was caught loitering. 13-5. Back came the Boks through Fourie du Preez and Pietersen. Danger within the Lions 22. Scrum five. This was a perilous position. But the Lions showed that they had learned from their mistakes

■ FACING PAGE **First to blink loses. Tom Croft mixes it with Springbok hard man Bakkies Botha as things get physical.**
■ BELOW **Lions lock Simon Shaw runs at Juan Smith. The 35-year-old Shaw put in a towering performance on his Lions Test debut, winning the man of the match award.**

■ FACING PAGE Brian O'Driscoll and Gethin Jenkins put in a tackle on South Africa's Bryan Habana. The collision resulted in a tour-ending cheekbone injury for Jenkins.
■ RIGHT Master of the skies. Rob Kearney was rock solid under the high ball, and here he swallows up yet another, despite competition from J.P. Pietersen.

and had corrected their scrummaging frailties. The Lions drove hard, up went the Springbok front row in a complete reversal of what had happened in Durban. Penalty to the Lions. Not only was the pressure relieved, but there was a huge upsurge in confidence as the entire back line rushed to congratulate the forward pack. The Lions had certainly stiffened their sinews.

But so too had South Africa. Jamie Roberts was not getting anything like the same purchase in midfield as the Springboks gang-tangled him every time the ball came near him. The Lions were having to really battle for every yard gained this week.

With that in mind, it was vital that they took every opportunity, which they did, Jones dropping a goal shortly before half-time after an attack was repelled. At 16-5 with the interval approaching, the Lions looked to be in good shape. But then, on the stroke of half-time, they called a loop in midfield, Roberts was pinged for obstruction and Francois Steyn stepped up to land a penalty attempt from inside his own half. 16-8. Would that late blemish prove significant?

The match turned in the opening moments of the second half. The Lions were struck with a double-whammy injury blow, losing both props. Gethin Jenkins sustained a fractured cheekbone after a crunching collision as he tackled Bryan Habana, while Adam Jones, who had been proving such a rock in the scrum, dislocated his shoulder after being cleared out at a ruck by Bakkies Botha, an incident for which the Springbok lock was to be subsequently cited and banned for two weeks.

Calamity for the Lions. They were obliged to go to uncontested scrums. A central part of their strategy was that they wanted to drain the energy from the South African pack so that they could then strike late in the game. The scrum had been far more effective and was not just holding its own but was taking a toll on the opposition. Uncontested scrums also scar a

game, alter its shape and feel. Players become hesitant and uncertain in defence as they are not used to being passive at the set piece. South Africa, of course, were also affected and would not have willingly chosen to go to uncontested scrums. As it happened, the change suited them more than the Lions.

It didn't end there. There was to be further ill-luck for the Lions, both centres being crocked

■ ABOVE Stephen Jones lines up a kick. The fly half booted 20 points in the match – including a nerve-jangling penalty to bring the Lions back to parity near the end – as well as providing the deft offload that brought about the Lions try.

■ FACING PAGE Bryan Habana is over, and Morne Steyn's conversion puts South Africa just four points behind at 19-15.

midway through the half. First Brian O'Driscoll smashed into substitute back-row forward Danie Rossouw in a collision that drew gasps from the crowd and reduced Rossouw to a Bambi-esque, wobble-legged wreck. He had to be taken from the field on a motorised ambulance cart, clearly dazed and out of sorts. O'Driscoll rose to go again, but it was obvious that he too was not himself as he was to later reveal. 'I was a little the worse for wear,' said O'Driscoll. 'I didn't have any emotions for the remaining ten minutes or so which was weird, like not having emotion whether we won or lost.'

South Africa took full advantage shortly thereafter, Habana scooting inside O'Driscoll to race to the try line in the 63rd minute. It was a set move from an inert scrum, Habana coming on a wide arc and hitting the afterburners. The Lions defence was caught off-guard, but it was a brilliantly executed piece of work. Jones had earlier kicked another goal for the Lions, but the Habana try and subsequent conversion from Morne Steyn closed the score to 19-15.

Morne Steyn had taken the field to thunderous applause in the 60th minute. Steyn was a Blue Bulls hero, and the locals had been clamouring for his entrance since early in the half. Morne was the man.

You could just sense the smallest shift in momentum. O'Driscoll bowed to the inevitable and gave way to Shane Williams in the 64th minute. Two minutes later Stephen Jones, who had been so accurate, missed a straightforward penalty kick to touch. The Boks ran the ball back, Francois Steyn chipped over the defence, Roberts went down to gather, was hit hard, held on, was penalised and re-

emerged from a pile of bodies clutching his wrist. Morne Steyn kicked the goal, and Roberts headed to the sidelines, his wrist clearly not right. Double disaster. The Loftus crowd sensed that things were turning in their favour.

Stephen Jones kept the hounds at bay with another penalty goal in the 70th minute, but three minutes later the stands erupted as substitute Jaque

■ ABOVE Jaque Fourie about to touch down in the corner as Tommy Bowe and Mike Phillips (hidden) try to drive him into touch. 25-22 to South Africa with five minutes remaining.
■ FACING PAGE Following up his own kick, Ronan O'Gara bumps Fourie du Preez in the air, conceding the fateful penalty.

Fourie piled through an attempted tackle by Ronan O'Gara down the short side and launched himself at the try line as Mike Phillips and Tommy Bowe closed in for the tackle.

The decision was referred to television match official Stuart Dickinson. The verdict took an age – try to South Africa. 25-22 to the Springboks. The Lions were not finished, though. Another penalty came their way, wide out and about 40 metres from goal. It was a difficult kick in any circumstances, but Jones's aim was true, the fly half getting a hug from tee-holding kicking coach Neil Jenkins as the ball sailed through the posts. 25-25.

A draw meant that the series would go to the final Test. A draw meant that excellence was to be rewarded on both sides. A draw was a fair share of the spoils on a dramatic afternoon. But the drama was not over. There was more to come.

The ball was belted deep into Lions territory as the game clock showed that there was no time left.

O'Gara, head swathed in a bandage following a heavy tackle, ran back to field. He could have cleared to touch and secured the draw. He could have cleared to touch because it was too risky to run the ball back. He opted instead for the medium-risk option of returning the ball to the middle of the field, trying to keep play alive and forcing South Africa themselves to make a decision. O'Gara was to be unfairly criticised for this decision. He was not to know that the game clock had run dead, for the clocks were sited low down at Loftus. It would also have been cowardly to simply accept the draw.

There was nothing wrong, therefore, with his decision to go for the return kick. There was everything wrong with his mid-air challenge on Fourie du Preez. The Springbok scrum half jumped high, while O'Gara, eyes on the ball, merely turned his shoulder into the advancing, leaping Springbok. Du Preez fell to earth, Berdos' whistle blew, O'Gara looked on in disbelief and Morne Steyn stepped up to win the Test match for South Africa with the very last kick. It was cruel, no doubt of that. But it was also sporting theatre beyond compare. The Lions were stunned, crestfallen, disbelieving. That was it. All over.

You could twist reality all you liked, curse misfortune, rue ill-luck, but you couldn't rewrite history. No matter how aggrieved the Lions were about Schalk Burger's despicable act of gouging, no matter how much they felt that a dismissal would have turned the game inexorably in their favour, and no matter how frustrated they were by the mass exodus of key players through injury in the second half, the record books will show for ever and a day that they lost the series. There was to be no comeback, no mitigation, no right of appeal. 2-0 to the Springboks. Game, set and match.

Few people remember that the Lions were comprehensively outplayed in the 1997 series in South Africa. Jeremy Guscott's winning dropped goal has acquired legendary status in much the same manner that Morne Steyn's 53-metre soul-destroyer will resonate down the years for South Africans.

■ RIGHT Unbelievable sporting theatre. Local, and now national, hero Morne Steyn is mobbed by his Springbok team-mates after converting the last-gasp penalty that brought South Africa a Test and series victory at Loftus Versfeld.

Were the Springboks that much better than the Lions? No, they were not. However, they had proven significantly superior in one key area – finishing. Over the course of the two Tests, the Lions had the greater number of opportunities. Yet South Africa had the killer instinct when it came to putting away what was created. They most certainly did at Loftus. Fine lines,

indeed, but they are what count. The Lions came up short in that regard. Yes, they were unfortunate; yes, they were noble and courageous as well as inventive and clever. But they didn't make the absolute most of what they had, particularly in the first Test.

It was scant consolation to them that they had participated in one of the greatest ever Test matches.

It was a game of noble stature, one that revealed, and in some cases exposed, character, one that soared to dramatic heights in the manner in which it unfolded; and in the play of Simon Shaw, Rob Kearney and Brian O'Driscoll in particular, it delivered performances of Wagnerian dimensions. Springbok scrum half Fourie de Preez and, for his

coup de grâce, Morne Steyn have claim to that standing as well.

Ian McGeechan, though, even in defeat, had achieved something of note: he had restored the credibility of the Lions. They needed to show that they could compete on the field with the southern hemisphere giants. These matches, and especially the second Test, would take rightful place in the annals. The Lions had meaning and significance once again.

■ BELOW The other side of the coin. As the Boks celebrate, Lions full back Rob Kearney sums up how it feels to lose such a close, hard-fought and important Test match.

IAN MCGEECHAN

The Lions head coach gave his take on the series defeat:

■ *'I told the players I was proud of them, and that they didn't deserve to be 2-0 down. They put in a fantastic effort, and today was a tremendous performance.*

'It was disappointing that we have given South Africa an opportunity they should have been denied. We haven't had the rub of the green in some of the decisions last week or this time. We could be sat here with two wins under our belts, or one win each.

'A lot of people thought we wouldn't be competitive, but we have been more than that. We have been winners in a lot of areas. Until the injuries we played some very good rugby.'

Regarding the Burger incident, McGeechan said at first:

■ *'That's for the referee, touch judge and citing officer to sort out.'*

After Springbok coach Peter de Villiers instantly played down the incident (see below), McGeechan responded:

■ *'I am very disappointed he said that. It certainly won't be part of the game I want to be associated with. I could never condone actions like that. I would hate to see that sort of thing happen again. It should automatically be a red card.'*

As for the incident's bearing on the result, McGeechan opined:

■ *'The reason we lost the second Test was not because Burger was not sent off.'*

PAUL O'CONNELL

The Lions captain gave his view of his team's performance:

■ *'We conceded a try that should never have been scored and then to give away the penalty at the end it's just very disappointing. During the run of injuries Brian O'Driscoll went off, and he's a linchpin of the team. It was tough, but we just didn't play enough rugby in the second half.*

'When we played rugby in the first half we were all over them and even when they came back I thought we'd done enough to get the draw and keep the series alive. Before we came on tour I believed we could do that. We needed to do it for 80 minutes though. We did it for the second 40 last week and we did it for the first 40 this week. That was

a big opportunity lost. It is a big challenge for the Lions to come together as a team, and the more professional the game gets, the harder creating a team becomes. We have been unlucky and probably made a few crucial mistakes.'*

STEPHEN JONES

The Lions fly half and kicker said:

■ *'It was the most physical match I have ever played in. The collisions were massive.'*

SIMON SHAW

The veteran lock and Lions Test debutant had this to say:

■ *'The feelings afterwards were the same that I had after the World Cup final in 2007. I am just absolutely gutted. I can't describe how bad it feels.*

'I just wanted to do myself and my selection justice. I was the most nervous I have ever felt before a Test. Two days before I couldn't sleep. Usually, I don't get that.

'Before kick-off I felt very confident what I could bring to the game. I would rather have played poorly and won. We have earned a bit of respect, but losing those two games you will always look back and wonder what could have been or what should have been, given our massive edge over them in the scrum this week.'

MIKE PHILLIPS

Lions scrum half Phillips was seething:

■ *'There were a couple of dodgy decisions by the ref in the second half that cost us. They seemed to be able to get away with a lot of punching and gouging. We are the straight guys and we came out second best. It cost us the game. You can't do things like that. You can't go swinging punches off the ball. There were punches going on off the ball throughout the game. All you can do is play by the rules. You can be a tough man on the pitch and stay within the rules. It is not nice if you are professional and you work hard all week for the big occasion. You work your socks off and when things like that happen, it really bugs you and hacks you off. You have just got to leave it to the referee. Referees are paid to do a job and we are paid to try to entertain. Pulling hands across the eyes is just not sport. It is not the gentlemanly thing to do.'*

FRESH GOLDEN BEER
GREENE KING

At the heart of the medieval market town of Bury St Edmunds
lies the Greene King Brewery where award winning beers
have been brewed since 1799.

Crafted for modern tastes using traditional brewing methods

LUKE FITZGERALD

The Lions wing, and victim of the eye-gouging incident, said:

■ '*I was surprised Burger only received a yellow card when his hand made contact with my eye: I had a bit of double vision and it is not part of the game. It was a strange thing for a fellow professional to do, especially one of his quality and experience. It is something that should be dealt with severely. Luckily there was no real damage done to me.*'

Referring to the incident, he also said:

■ '*It was a potentially career-threatening act.*'

PETER DE VILLIERS

The Springbok coach had a clear opinion on the gouging, believing that Burger did not deserve even a yellow card:

■ '*I don't believe it was a card at all. In the first minute already there had been a lot of needle and if you watch the whole game you will see how many yellow cards the Lions were let off. This is sport, this is great, this is what it's about. If things were clear-cut then we shouldn't even bother preparing for a game.*'

Forty-eight hours later, he was still defending his man, who had by then been banned for eight weeks:

■ '*He did not do it on purpose. He is a man of honour and would never eye-gouge. That offence, butting and spear-tackling have no part in our game, which we are trying hard to promote.*'

As for the series win:

■ '*The Lions have enjoyed their 1997 win, when Jerry Guscott dropped that goal, for 12 years. Now we will enjoy our last-kick triumph for the next 12 years.*'

JOHN SMIT

Springbok captain Smit remarked:

■ '*I can't remember a worse start in a Test. There were stern words at half-time because we had not brought much to the party. The comeback was colossal and makes everything worthwhile. It was a proper Test match and we're quite happy to take the win any way we can. We were quite sloppy before the fightback.*'

And regarding the winning kick:

■ '*I thought I wouldn't be able to look, but I saw that Morne's body language was good and when he cracked*

■ ABOVE South Africa's coach Peter de Villiers in jovial mood at a press conference two days after the second Test.

that ball I was pretty happy. At times like that I am glad my job is in the scrum and not the goal-kicker. To achieve that sort of kick in his second Test is simply massive.

'*But this team keeps amazing me and finding victories from dark rooms. The time is right to enjoy this win.*

'*The Lions must have taken heart from how poor we were in the final 20 minutes last week and they came with everything they have.*'

MORNE STEYN

South Africa's kicking hero explained:

■ '*I'm the kicker in the team and it is something I have been doing all my life. So it is expected of me to land those kicks. It was one of my best strikes ever. The moment I struck the ball I knew it was over. It was wonderful that I could influence the series triumph.*'

■ COACH'S VIEW Second Test ■

Ian McGeechan in conversation with Ian Robertson

The second Test ended in heartbreak, but at half-time you must have been delighted with an exceptional Lions performance.

■ *'Apart from one mistake which left a glaring gap for J.P. Pietersen to burst through and score the only Springbok try of the half, we played 40 minutes of the best rugby I can ever remember from any Lions side I have ever been associated with. That includes the unbeaten 1974 side to South Africa as a player and also the 1977 side to New Zealand and then my five Lions tours as a coach. I really believe our half-time lead of 16-8 was the reward for some unrelenting rugby of the highest order against the current world champions who remain the best team in the world.*

'That performance has to be put in perspective. Just imagine how hard it is to take 36 players from four different countries who have four different strengths in rugby and try to find firstly the best 15 and secondly blend them into a cohesive Test team in just four weeks. Our players achieved something very special in Pretoria.

'They played a tactical game that was full of quality and variety, confidence and decision-making. The lines of running were absolutely spot on and so were the angles of attack. The defence was outstanding with the exception of the missed tackle on J.P. Pietersen. Every part of our forward play was incredibly good. The scrum not only recovered from the problems in the first half of the first Test, we actually controlled and had the edge at the scrummage in the second Test. Our basic line out was good and our variation at the line out was very effective. Above all, our play at the breakdown was the best of the whole tour so far.'

The highlight of the first half was surely the try scored by Rob Kearney. Just how important was that for the team?

■ *'It was a fantastic try and it involved every single player in the side. We had talked at length about being patient in the build-up to try-scoring opportunities. We need to be accurate and precise enough in our play to create and win six rucks in a row or even eight or ten or even 15. And oddly enough for the Kearney try we did indeed set up and win 15 rucks in a row. That was phenomenal rugby and it was wrapped up with Kearney's surge to the line.'*

The Lions were leading 19-8 with only 17 minutes left and were still in control, so what went wrong?

■ *'The answer is very straightforward. We suffered bad injuries to four of our star players and we had to bring on four replacements. We lost both our prop forwards. As we only had the usual one replacement prop, Andrew Sheridan, the match went to uncontested scrums. This was certainly not to our advantage. We had a definite edge in the scrums and did not want the scrums to be uncontested.*

'Just as disastrous midway through the half, we lost both our centres who had played so brilliantly as a partnership in the first two Tests. [Brian] O'Driscoll unfortunately stayed on initially with concussion and it was no surprise that he wasn't right on top of the situation when Bryan Habana sliced through to score the Springboks' second try.'

Were you still confident with South Africa a point behind with 12 minutes to play?

■ *'I certainly was really hopeful two minutes later when Stephen Jones put us 22-18 ahead with a penalty and only ten minutes left. All the changes meant we lost some of our momentum and a little of our defensive organisation with several players playing out of position. I suppose it was almost inevitable we might make a mistake and that is what happened. We missed a crucial tackle as the Springboks attacked on the right. Jaque Fourie charged towards the try line on the right touch line and he just squeezed in at the corner flag. It was heartbreaking just 25 seconds from the final whistle to watch Ronan O'Gara follow up his own kick and give away a penalty as he hit Fourie du Preez while he was in the air catching the ball.*

'The kick by Steyn from inside his own half gave victory in the Test and victory in the series to South Africa. It was one of the very worst moments of my rugby career. It was a shattering disappointment and I felt so sorry for the players who had produced such fantastic performances in both Test matches.

'The one big consolation that Saturday night in Pretoria was a significant one – the 2009 Lions had at least succeeded in restoring the credibility of the Lions.'

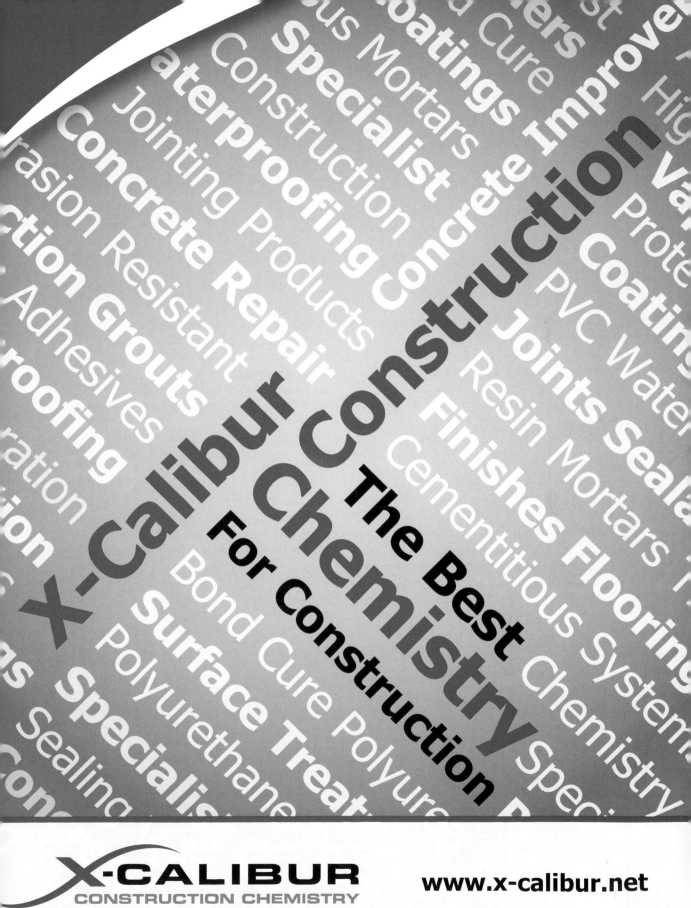

X-CALIBUR
CONSTRUCTION CHEMISTRY

www.x-calibur.net

6
Third Test

■ The fallout from the second Test was loud and prolonged. Just as the game itself had been characterised by its ferocity and drama, so was the post-match experience. So often these games give us routine sequences of play on the field and platitudes thereafter. But no, we were to be given the full-bore treatment, beginning with Peter de Villiers' assertion that he did not think Schalk Burger's offence merited a yellow card. ■

In effect, de Villiers implied that gouging was one of those things that sometimes happened in a tough man's game. 'I don't believe it was a card at all…. This is sport, this is great, this is what it's about,' said de Villiers.

It was explosive stuff. And utterly wrong. It's all very well defending your man, highlighting his previous good character. It's quite another to appear to sanction one of the most heinous acts in the book. De Villiers didn't see it like that. Others did. Ian McGeechan was the first to express his dismay. 'I am very disappointed he said that,' said McGeechan.

It took fully 48 hours before de Villiers was forced into some sort of belated apology. Even then his arm had to be twisted by a combination of public outrage

■ ABOVE Redemption. Ugo Monye and Phil Vickery leave their Durban demons far behind as they enjoy the Lions' success at Ellis Park. Both had a big hand in a rare Boks defeat in Jo'burg.

and pressure from behind the scenes at the International Rugby Board.

The disciplinary hearing took place on Sunday. Even that event was not without its controversy. The initial hearing in Pretoria was adjourned and relocated to Johannesburg. Taking everything into account, the whole process took 13 hours, the announcement of the eight-week suspension handed down to Burger coming at 0115 on the Monday morning. Earlier, Bakkies Botha had been given a two-week ban for a dangerous charge on Lions prop Adam Jones.

By Monday lunchtime, de Villiers was back in front of the media. The press conference opened with a formal notification that there would be no further comment made until the official transcript of the judgment had been received. De Villiers then proceeded to give comment on all manner of subjects for the next half an hour.

De Villiers launched his madcap defence of Schalk Burger by inviting those who might object to head 'to the ballet shop for some nice tutus'. De Villiers denied that there had been any wrongdoing and stated that if the Springboks had any need to gouge lions, then 'we would go to the Bushveld and eye-gouge lions there'. There were also references to Nelson Mandela, F.W. de Klerk as well as a contemptuous dismissal of the media. The Burger incident was referred to as one of those 'little small things'.

De Villiers' performance was bizarre and riveting but wholly inappropriate. The evidence against Burger was clear-cut. After explaining that he didn't believe the flanker had eye-gouged Fitzgerald, at least not deliberately, the Springbok coach went on: 'Rugby is a contact sport, so is dancing,' said de Villiers. 'So if some guys can't take it, make the decision. There are so many incidents that we can say we want to cite this guy for maliciously jumping into this guy's face with his shoulder but we didn't do it because we know that it's just a game. Sometimes you get away with things. Look, if you're going to win games in the boardroom or in front of television cameras, then, look, do we really respect the game we know or should we go to the ballet shop for some nice tutus and get a great dancing show going? And then there will be no gouging, no tackling, no nothing. In our game, there will be collisions and the guy who wins the collisions, he's the hardest and this is the guy we will always select.'

De Villiers also took exception to the notion that the Springbok victory had been overshadowed by the incident and that they had been lucky to beat the Lions. 'We would love people to stand up and take it on the chin, and say well done South Africa. But these little small things like Sunday night's judicial [hearing] cannot take away our joy. Nelson Mandela and F.W. de Klerk won the Nobel Prize for Peace whatever wrongs they did in their lives. But nobody can take away the fact they won that prize. And no one can take away that we are joyous to have won a series. It was not lucky. Luck is when someone swings a punch in a bar and misses. We showed character, not luck.'

■ LEFT **Peter de Villiers, here at a Springbok training session, whipped up quite a storm with his views on the Burger incident.**

■ ABOVE Schalk Burger, Bakkies Botha and Andries Bekker (left to right) enjoy the series win after the Pretoria match. Bans would prevent Burger and Botha from playing in the third Test.

De Villiers cared not a jot for his image. 'I am a God-given talent, and am the best that ever I can be,' he said. 'I know what I am and I don't give a damn. If I am supposed to be the weakest link [in the Springbok set-up], then we are bloody strong.'

Later that night came the PR-wrapped apology. 'We would like to apologise to the rugby community for the erroneous impression that acts of foul play are condoned by South African rugby,' said union president Oregan Hoskins.

Too late. The cannon was loose and functioning. The matter simply would not go away. By Tuesday, news had come that Brian O'Driscoll had concussion after crunching Springbok substitute forward Danie

Rossouw and was off the tour. He would fly home on Wednesday. O'Driscoll's parting shot was to fire a broadside into de Villiers for his comments, which the Ireland captain believed had 'brought the game into disrepute'.

O'Driscoll is no shrinking violet, either on or off the field. If something was on his mind, it was going to be said. 'When I heard those comments I wondered how someone could get away with something like that,' said O'Driscoll. 'Irrespective of any apology I find it an absolute disgrace that a coach of a national team can make comments as he did about gouging being part of the game. Parents watching an interview like that questioning whether they should have their kid play rugby or soccer, that's their decision made right there. To hear a national coach saying in any shape or form, gouging is acceptable is despicable. I find that mind-boggling. Essentially it brought the game into disrepute.'

De Villiers had not yet condemned Burger for the specific incident that led to an eight-week ban, albeit he had eventually expressed his disapproval of gouging. The beleaguered coach tried to claim that he had been taken out of context. 'It was a misunderstanding,' said de Villiers. 'Some journalists made mischief. The International Rugby Board was upset with what had been said.'

O'Driscoll's enforced absence looked as if it might leave a sizeable hole in the Lions midfield and a comparably hollow feeling inside the man himself as he completed a third tour of duty without a series victory. Prior to the trip he had been adamant that he was there only for victory, not for the ride. That perspective had changed. Intriguingly he did not quite close the door on the possibility of still being around in four years' time for the tour to Australia, although he would be 34 by then. O'Driscoll was a star turn of the 2001 trip to Australia and was captain four years later in New Zealand, only to have that tour cut short after being spear-tackled within 50 seconds of the start of the first Test. O'Driscoll had responded to the management style of Ian McGeechan. 'I always felt that this would be my last Lions tour but you see [35-year-old] Simon Shaw and think, "Well, there's hope",' said O'Driscoll, who would have won his 100th Test cap for country and Lions the following Saturday. 'Even having lost the

series, it's been an incredibly enjoyable tour, way more than the other two. There's been more to it than the previous tours. I've enjoyed the other factors that maybe I didn't enjoy in the first two.'

South Africa, meanwhile, were to appeal against the two-week ban handed out to lock Bakkies Botha for the cleaning-out action that caused Lions prop Adam Jones to dislocate his shoulder. 'We have concerns that Bakkies is being discriminated against,' said Springbok assistant coach Dick Muir.

So much for the furore. The Lions had to lick their wounds, tend to the injured and somehow get themselves back up for the third Test. It would be no easy matter. Their dressing room resembled a battlefield hospital, with players stretched out on makeshift beds. Later in the week, Phil Vickery was to explain the bizarre scene even during the game. 'I went in to comfort the props,' said Vickery, who had been on twenty-third-man duty that day. 'Adam [Jones] was lying there and in so much agony with his dislocated shoulder while Gethin [Jenkins] was on the other bed with his face caved in. He'd already had some stitches earlier in the game so could hardly speak. I was holding Adam's arm as they tried to get his shoulder back in but they couldn't manage it.' Meanwhile, O'Driscoll was concussed, while Jamie Roberts had a wrist sprain. Tommy Bowe was also being treated for an extended elbow. It was a mess.

The Lions' morale had taken a battering, too. There were some stark truths to confront. Some of the squad headed off to a game reserve to find some fresh perspective, while others chilled out at the hotel with friends and family. The squad needed time and space, a respite from each other as much as from rugby. It was to be Wednesday before they got back together and headed out on to the practice field. They had their own issues to sort out, plenty of them.

Even so, the Burger–de Villiers affair was to dominate the rugby agenda. The match officials had not escaped censure, some feeling that they had erred in not sending off Burger. The manager of international referees, Paddy O'Brien, defended their actions. 'It was a very good piece of touch-judging by Bryce Lawrence,' said O'Brien. 'He saw a hand on face but not the gouging. He has to be accurate. He can't go on gut feeling. He has to go on fact. You can't red card if you're not absolutely sure. And, no,

they didn't bottle it just because it happened in the first 30 seconds. That's nonsense. Bryce would not back down on that one. Any referee, Bryce included, who had seen it would have definitely given a red.'

The Lions kept their counsel for a couple of days on the pantomime that was being played out in the Springbok camp. Then O'Driscoll let rip; after that it was the turn of scrummaging coach Graham Rowntree to speak out about de Villiers' remarks on gouging. 'They were crass comments, completely out of order, pathetic really,' said Rowntree. 'It's ridiculous, it really is, for a national coach to say that. Yes, we're upset by it. There's just no room for that in the game. How a player thinks that he can get away with it is beyond me.'

Rowntree considered Burger's eight-week ban to be too lenient. The former Leicester and England prop, who stated that he had never gouged anyone during his lengthy career, felt that the regard in which Burger was held had been diminished. 'Yes, it probably has,' said Rowntree, who also took issue with de Villiers' support for the player. If a similar situation were to occur in the Lions or England camp, then was there any possibility of Rowntree backing the culprit as de Villiers had done? 'No, I wouldn't, it's indefensible,' said Rowntree.

The pressure was mounting on de Villiers from all quarters. It had been a bizarre few days, but there is

■ FACING PAGE Adam Jones is led from the Loftus Versfeld pitch after suffering a dislocated shoulder in the second Test.
■ BELOW Martyn Williams on the attack against Western Province, supported by Joe Worsley. Both would start in the Lions back row in the third Test.

■ ABOVE **Lions hooker Matthew Rees stretches every sinew to reel in Springbok wing Odwa Ndungane.**
■ FACING PAGE **Jamie Heaslip slips the net and is about to give the scoring pass to Shane Williams for the first Lions try.**

little doubt that not only were his critics within South Africa gunning for him but so too were International Board officials, who were moved to issue a statement condemning the 'heinous' act of gouging and announce that they were to investigate the whole matter of sanctions concerning such cases.

It was time to get back to rugby. Both sides announced their sides that Thursday and both made wholesale changes. There were 18 in all. The eight alterations to the Lions side included one positional change, Tommy Bowe moving infield to take on O'Driscoll's role at outside centre. There were first

Lions Test caps for centre Riki Flutey and flanker Joe Worsley, as well as first Test starts for prop Andrew Sheridan and open-side Martyn Williams, who was finally getting the chance on his third trip.

Shane Williams and the recalled Ugo Monye formed the wing combination. The latter was looking to redeem himself after those first Test bloopers with the try line in his sights. 'Sport can take you to the greatest peaks and drag you to the deepest troughs,' said Monye. 'It was quite a tough pill to swallow but you can't go feeling sorry for yourself. You've got to pick yourself up and dust yourself down. My faith is a huge part of what I am and that helps my belief. Of course, it went through my mind that I might never get another chance.'

Monye was asked what he might do differently this time around. 'I'll score tries,' he replied bluntly.

'Probably my biggest asset is my instinct for scoring tries. This is the last time we'll ever play as a Lions team so there's a lot at stake for us. We're all desperate to return home with our heads held high.' That had to be the spur to performance for everyone. A dead-rubber third Test is particularly difficult for a touring side. Change can stimulate but not if it is at the expense of quality.

The Lions were looking to stiffen their defence with Worsley, a knee-chopping tackler, in the pack. Twenty-one-year-old Ireland wing Luke Fitzgerald had the indignity of being dropped altogether to add to the pain of being gouged by Schalk Burger. Fitzgerald had been at fault for the Springboks' first try in Pretoria. Meanwhile, Jamie Roberts had almost passed muster, but the wrist sprain had not quite come good. Flutey and Bowe had a lot to live up to.

Vickery was nursing a throat infection and sat out Thursday training. He was determined not to miss the game itself. Vickery had his own act of atonement to prepare for, a rematch with Tendai 'the Beast' Mtawarira, the Springbok prop who had mangled the pride of England a fortnight earlier in Durban. Vickery didn't need to see TV footage to be reminded of just how bad an experience it had been at Kings Park. 'When your mom, your missus and your sister all text straight through to say that they still love you, you know things haven't gone too well,' said Vickery, a stoic to the end. 'People say you wouldn't have wanted your Lions career to end in Durban. Well, that's life. I'm still the same bloke, still trying hard. But now I've got this chance and I'm looking forward to it more than to any other game I've ever played. It is my last in a Lions jersey and I want to make sure I go out on a high.'

There was every indication that Vickery himself was in the mood to repair a damaged reputation. 'It's nothing new, nothing different, to go out again

against an opponent,' said Vickery. 'I've been doing it all my life. What you've done in the past doesn't count for anything. It's a clean sheet. I'm confident in my own ability. Maybe I was too nervous a fortnight ago. I've just got to make sure that I'm right up there emotionally.'

The Boks had opted for widespread changes as they looked to get a sighter on the upcoming Tri-Nations. Highly regarded Bulls full back Zane Kirchner was to make his debut, while the midfield pairing of Wynand Olivier and Jaque Fourie looked threatening. Even the perverse Peter de Villiers did not dare drop Morne Steyn after his heroics of the previous week. The wings were Odwa Ndungane and Jongi Nokwe. Almost the entire back line had been reconstituted, with scrum half Fourie du Preez the only surviving starter from the Pretoria match. In the pack, the Boks were without the suspended Burger and Botha. In came lock Johann Muller, while Ryan Kankowski was drafted into the back row.

Ellis Park is a forbidding place, and not just because it is located in one of the most dangerous parts of Johannesburg. Even in the days when nearby Hillbrow was a bohemian hang-out for Jo'burg trendies and not the drug-infested hellhole it is today, the Boks did not cede their turf lightly, if at all. It had been eight years since they had lost a Test match there, France the last visiting winners in 2001. South Africa had never been beaten there by a double-figure margin.

And yet a patched-up Lions side ripped them apart, 28-9, and would have posted a record margin of victory were it not for the ball toppling off the kicking tee as Stephen Jones prepared to take the straightforward, in-front-of-the-posts conversion of Shane Williams' first try.

It was a terrific display from the Lions, full of guts and character, one that showed that all that had been spoken about for so many weeks was, in fact, true. They were as one and they did play as a team, backing each other, trusting in each other's instincts and still playing rugby come what may.

The Springboks demeaned the fixture in two ways: first, by making ten changes, indicating that

■ RIGHT **Man on a mission. Phil Vickery prepares to pack down against his Durban nemesis, Tendai 'the Beast' Mtawarira.**

■ RIGHT AND FACING PAGE The second Lions try at Ellis Park. Riki Flutey chips past Odwa Ndungane with Shane Williams in support. The centre reached the ball first, batting it inside to Williams, who beat Jaque Fourie to the line.

shuffling resources ahead of the Tri-Nations was a more important consideration than finishing off the series in style. Furthermore, the Boks chose to wear armbands proclaiming their support for banned lock Bakkies Botha. The white bands were worn by players and management. 'Justice 4', they read.

Well, at least there was justice of sorts, with the Lions coming home with a thoroughly deserved Test victory to their name. In a country that has seen so much pain and trouble and institutionalised injustice, the protest was distasteful and out of place. It was an affront to the country, its people and to their opponents.

Springbok captain John Smit had played a blinder on this tour: smart and durable out in the middle, intelligent and balanced in public. He got this one badly wrong. He'd had his say the previous day, using the eve-of-Test press conference to articulate his concerns. And they were legitimate worries, centring on fears that the International Board might emasculate the game. At the very least the IRB were sending out confusing messages to players and officials alike. 'We are deeply saddened, and probably more angry than anything else with regards to the Bakkies Botha outcome,' Smit had said that Friday. 'I think we have to hope and pray that it is purely just victimisation of Bakkies, and not the way the game is going. A ruling like this could change this wonderful game we have for good. It is a great concern. The players are not happy, and we will stand together in this regard and make a point. We haven't had sanity prevail with his appeal.'

That's as may be. The armband gesture was petulant and beyond the pale. The International Board were quick to react and launch an investigation. The Springboks would have had cause to look into their own performance. They were beaten at every turn, suggesting that de Villiers' selection was pompously misguided and that the supposed strength in depth of South African rugby was a mirage.

The Lions were not to be denied. There was a monumental display from No. 8 Jamie Heaslip, some

defiant defence from outside centre Tommy Bowe and hooker Matthew Rees, another all-enveloping showing from scrum half Mike Phillips (if only he could get rid of that one step before passing) and genuine spark from Rob Kearney (a fluffed penalty clearance to touch apart) as well as from Shane Williams and Riki Flutey. Those midfield giants, O'Driscoll and Roberts, were not missed, and that is some compliment.

Flutey and Williams combined brilliantly for the latter's second try in the 35th minute, Flutey chipping, chasing hard before flipping the ball inside as he collided with Zane Kirchner. It was daringly crafted and thrillingly executed. Williams had earlier shown that he had rediscovered his scoring instincts when tracking Heaslip's spirited churn forward to be on hand for the decisive pass.

The Lions survived Simon Shaw's sin-binning for a knee in the back of Fourie de Preez just before half-time, conceding only three points. Shaw was later cited and banned for two weeks.

Ugo Monye, who'd had an eventful tour, was able to round things off on a high, pouncing on a loose pass intended for Kirchner to race in from 75 metres in the 54th minute. Monye was almost overcome. 'I saw all our supporters up there in the stands and I wanted to break down and cry.'

■ BELOW Stuart Dickinson explains to Simon Shaw that he is about to yellow-card him for use of the knee.
■ FACING PAGE Not this time, Victor. Lions skipper Paul O'Connell outreaches Victor Matfield in the line out at Ellis Park.

Stephen Jones rattled off a couple of penalty goals before a diving tackle by Bowe prevented a try by Odwa Ndungane. The decision was referred to video ref Bryce Lawrence. It was a tight call, but the right one, rather like the entire series.

It was an emotional finale to what had been a special series. The afternoon had begun with a stirring presentation of shirts by Warren Gatland. 'He held up the jersey and told us that it was only right that we play for those who would be wearing it for the last time,' said Monye. 'I looked around and

■ ABOVE **True to his word. Ugo Monye picks off a wayward Springbok pass and heads for the line from 75 metres out.**

there were tears in the eyes of the guys. That really rammed it home to me.'

Vickery was one of those to whom Gatland was referring. The old slugger was moist-eyed himself. Captain Paul O'Connell revealed that it had been Vickery's own words in the pre-match huddle that had had such an impact. 'It's been very emotional, for me personally after what happened in the first Test, and for the guys as a whole,' said Vickery, who made up for his Durban sins by popping the Springbok front row in the very first scrum. 'I was

quite tearful before the game. I've never been on a tour with so many good men. It's been hard, so hard and that's what makes everything so special and victory all the sweeter.'

There were tumultuous scenes at the final whistle, with both sides setting off on laps of honour. So mindful were the Lions of not being seen to disrespect the opposition that they had raced back from one corner of the ground where they were saluting the massed ranks of red to stand dutifully as the Springboks were awarded the official trophy for their series victory.

Despite the niggle and off-field shenanigans, the series had been played in a commendable spirit. It had not always been edifying, but the players had given their all from first to last. It had been hard and unremitting. There was a tangible sense that they had all participated in something of rare significance. At the post-match gala dinner, there was genuine camaraderie on show as the bitter rivals sought each other out for a beer.

The players' instincts were not wrong. This was a memorable Test series. The early games had been uneventful, lacking in punch and true drama. All three Tests, by contrast, were epic. McGeechan would find no dissenters when he proclaimed that this had been 'the greatest three-Test series' in which he'd ever been involved.

So much of what happens at international level somehow seemed hesitant and monochrome by comparison. There had been vivid colour, enough twists and turns to keep Charles Dickens happy, noble spirit, nerve and courage, raw tension and the occasional bit of knuckle. It made for a perfect script, one to be retold for many a year. It would need no embellishment.

It had been a watershed trip in many regards. It had rekindled faith in a favoured sporting entity and restored credibility. It had also shown that it is possible to have fun while playing professional sport. Too much of what happens on rugby's Test circuit is uptight and po-faced. It shows in the play, which is invariably limited and one-dimensional. Too many players exist within straitjackets fitted by coaches. McGeechan had dared to liberate his players, both on and off the field.

Not for them any of the grumbles that had tainted the previous two tours. They had set out with high hopes and they had all been met. Several players had grown through the experience, men such as Jamie Roberts and Rob Kearney, Mike Phillips, too. They returned as better players, that's for sure. The same might be said of a host of others: Jamie Heaslip, Tom Croft, Tommy Bowe and even Keith Earls, the youngster whose tour had got off to such a calamitous beginning in Rustenburg. But Earls kept the faith, and the Lions kept faith in him.

■ RIGHT After the might-have-beens of Kings Park, Ugo Monye holds his arms aloft in joy after he touches down for his interception try in the third Test in Johannesburg.

Australia in 2013 will be a trip too far for McGeechan, who declared that this had been his last tour of duty. What a wimp, calling it a day after a mere 36 years in the saddle as player and coach!

Geech was without doubt the real hero of the 2009 Lions tour. That there were many others who might have claim to that billing was actually due to the man himself. He had set the tone and the

■ ABOVE Lions Player of the Series Jamie Roberts celebrates victory with Joe Worsley and Rob Kearney.
■ FACING PAGE Head coach Ian McGeechan congratulates his captain, Paul O'Connell.
■ PAGE 140 One last hurrah. Ian McGeechan salutes the crowd at the end of the final match of the 2009 Lions tour.

parameters. He had not been afraid to reinvoke some old-school principles in getting players to share rooms and have a few beers. Most coaches would have been afraid to do that, fearing objections from pampered modern-day stars or even criticism from the media for late-night carousing. But, no, McGeechan was so confident that this was the way it had to be that the media were invited to share hotels as well, a practice unknown these days. Grown-ups on rugby tour trusting each other. It's a novel concept.

There is much still to do to ensure the wellbeing of the Lions. The schedule is unforgiving and the respective powers have to do something about that. Yet McGeechan had almost managed to pull it off with one hand tied behind his back. The build-up time was scandalously short, with several players still wet from taking their Heineken Cup final showers as they were bundled on a plane to South Africa. Also the fixture schedule was stacked against them and the principle of playing on a level playing field completely ignored.

The Lions were betrayed by administrators in South Africa and at home. It's no use to anyone if the Lions become uncompetitive: not to the host country nor to the game at large. There is no finer marque in rugby than the Lions. The players treasure it, the fans flock to it (ignore the sub-par attendances which were due to lack of money not to lack of interest) and the outside football-sated world sits up and takes notice. The Lions need a longer lead-in time. They need meaningful opposition, which is why the Lions should insist on Australia fielding their best players in the provincial games in 2013.

All that is for another day. This day ended with a great mass of humanity packing the foyer of the Lions' hotel in Johannesburg. Songs were sung, tall tales were told and a great tour was rounded off in style. The series had been lost, and that fact must

never be downgraded or disappear in the uplifting swirl that enveloped the tourists as they finished up with a win. They had come so far but still they had fallen short. If only, eh?

But hearts and minds had been won over. The Lions were back in business. They were to post record profits in excess of £4 million. But more than mere money, more than mere feel-good vibes, the Lions had shown that they were a force to be reckoned with. It's tough enough in any circumstances for a scratch side to mount a credible challenge. But the 2009 Lions had done that quite splendidly.

■ OPINION Third Test ■

PHIL VICKERY

The veteran prop's rehabilitation summed up the Lions' superb comeback in the third Test. Having been mauled by 'the Beast' in Durban, he dominated his rival this time:

■ *'There was a huge amount of pressure on me after Durban. It was nice to come out the other end being satisfied with your day's work. That first scrum was fantastic.*

'It was gratifying to come off feeling very proud of my own performance, and doubly so because of the team's display.

'We have been a fantastic group of people. You always remember your colleagues and I've played alongside some superstars on this trip. Someone said it was going to be my last Lions cap. I won on my first in 2001, and thought wouldn't it be brilliant if I could win the last one

■ BELOW Job done. Recalled Lions prop Phil Vickery trots away from a set piece, the tourists having gained a penalty through a display of strong scrummaging.

and also get the fiftieth Test success of my career. Nothing beats wearing the Lions jersey. It's the ultimate.

'South Africa thoroughly deserved their series win, and I take nothing away from them, but I felt we deserved something out of the tour.'

UGO MONYE

The wing felt a range of emotions as he scored his try:

■ *'I thought I was going to pull my hamstring, then I thought I was going to break down and cry when I scored. We didn't deserve what we got last week and we got what we deserved today.'*

SHANE WILLIAMS

Monye's two-try partner commented:

■ *'The defence won the game and I'm proud to be part of it on top of the tries. Two-nil down was unjust and we were determined to prove that point. I knew this would be my last appearance for the Lions. I was determined to get involved. I'm really glad that I've enjoyed myself.'*

250
Remarkable Years

SOUTH AFRICA 2009
GUINNESS
ESTD 1759
OFFICIAL SPONSOR

A SURGE OF GENIUS
PROUD SPONSORS OF THE 2009 BRITISH & IRISH LIONS

ESTD 1759
GUINNESS®
BREWED IN DUBLIN

RIKI FLUTEY

The centre was delighted that his emergency midfield pairing with Tommy Bowe worked so well:

■ 'No tries against. We put our bodies in front of them all day and by the end they seemed scared. We walked our talk. In the dressing room I looked into the players' eyes and I knew we were going to win.'

PAUL O'CONNELL

The skipper was thoroughly proud:

■ 'It was a very tough week mentally for everyone, knowing you are out of the series. Especially as it could have been an exciting build-up with the series still alive. We could have endured a tough summer, thinking "what if?" all the time. We dug deep. Some guys produced some serious form resulting in great scores. I hope people don't misconstrue our lap of honour. We're under no illusions that we lost the series, but a lot of people paid a lot of money to come out here and we wanted to thank them.

'We've probably never had our backs to the wall as much, with centres Jamie Roberts and Brian O'Driscoll out. They have probably been our best two players. Props Adam Jones and Gethin Jenkins were also missing, so it was going to be very tough for us. Everyone stood up and we backed each other and came up with the performance.

'We could have won the first Test. We should have won the second. We were eager that the memory of those close games wouldn't be upset by a poor performance today because we were down 2-0 and throwing in the towel. Vicks was outstanding. He spoke and galvanised the squad before the game and I will be plagiarising what he said for Munster and Ireland next season.

'The team that wins is better. Sure, people have been patting us on the backs for our performances, but for some guys here it was the first win in the southern hemisphere, and that's important.'

IAN MCGEECHAN

The coach had a grin as wide as Africa at the final whistle at the probable end of 35-plus years of dejection and delight with the Lions. He remarked:

■ 'They picked themselves up well. I mean the dressing room last week was one I never wanted to be in, so to come this week, play like that, shows they're an outstanding group of players. I was worried that they

■ ABOVE Shane Williams, scorer of two tries in the match, and Stephen Jones, who kicked 13 points, soak up the buzz on the Lions' lap of honour at Ellis Park.

wouldn't play or might go into their shells a bit but we didn't and we scored some very good tries. So it's a satisfaction but a secondary satisfaction because we came here only to win the series.

'Paul has epitomised what a Lions captain should be. You pull players together, tell it how it is. The fact we played so well with so many changes shows how well they have integrated into the environment they have created and Paul has led that.

'We got a couple of 50-50s in terms of decisions and bounce of the ball that we hadn't been getting. Despite our big margin in this Test, all the games could have gone either way, but we didn't have the breaks before. We could have come here 2-0 up, that's how tight it's been. It's been all little edges, hasn't it? We were very accurate this time, very intense, and we kept it tactically the way we wanted to play. It's a very pleasant victory to go home with – it lasts for four years. There are no regrets. This is international sport and international rugby, which is played on the edge.

'I must say congratulations to the Springboks. They won the series we both wanted. But what these players have achieved in just six weeks should not be underestimated. They have played the world champions in their own backyard and given as good as they have got for three Tests. There was just a total of eight points' difference in the first two Tests. We thought it might be the same in this one but the players came with a real intent and focus and it showed. Players that buy into that often find something. Shane was great. Tommy and Riki stepped in. They had a really good game – and the pack was immense.'

PETER DE VILLIERS

The Springbok coach observed:

■ 'We're grateful for having won the series, and have achieved our goal for the first part of this year. The fact we lost here hasn't taken any gloss off the series win – these things happen in international rugby. We will rejoice tonight.'

JOHN SMIT

His captain, John Smit, stated:

■ 'The Lions were better than we were. They showed more intensity and had more rhythm. This defeat makes us appreciate the series win so much more. We knew we were up against a top Lions side. We were poor and they were good. I have mixed emotions because we won the series, but they were all over us on the day. It has been a wonderful series. It would have been nice to win 3-0 and create history. Our boys are disappointed we didn't rack up today – our frame of mind wasn't there. They wanted to get a victory and they did.

'A lot of our guys put a huge amount of effort into it and we will remember this series for the rest of our lives and talk about the great series of 2009.'

JAQUE FOURIE

Meanwhile, the centre's view was:

■ 'It just didn't happen for us. They were really strong defensively especially in the inside channel. We weren't allowed to put any phases together and the few chances we got we never took. We tried a few different things out there that didn't work for us.'

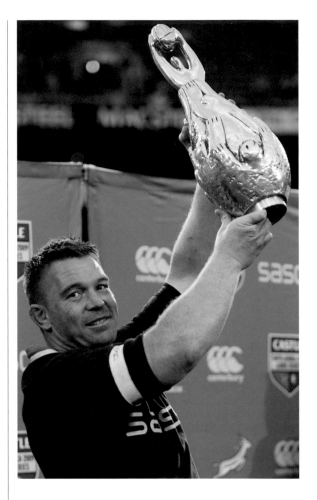

■ ABOVE **The Lions won the third Test, but let's not forget that South Africa won the series. Victorious Springbok skipper John Smit shows off the trophy.**

HEINRICH BRUSSOW

The South Africa open-side thought:

■ 'We didn't use our opportunities. They played rugby by securing their ball well.'

JOHANN MULLER

The Springbok lock said:

■ 'It was certainly not the kind of comeback I had expected. They were better than us at the breakdowns and they turned over quite a lot of ball as well. We arrived at the breakdowns too late and it cost us. We're not happy with the loss, but we're still celebrating a series win.'

Ian McGeechan in conversation with Ian Robertson

With eight changes to your team for the third Test were you still confident of victory?

■ *'Curiously enough I was confident. To lose four of our very best players through bad injuries was a real blow but because we had basically played one style of rugby right the way through the tour for all nine matches it meant the four players coming into the team would know exactly what was expected of them. Of course I would have liked to have selected Brian and Jamie but they were unavailable and I felt really comfortable with Riki Flutey and Tommy Bowe as their replacements. As for the props, I knew that Andrew Sheridan would cope with John Smit and I was totally confident that Phil Vickery would show what a great prop he is by containing the threat of the Springboks front row.*

'I also knew how much the fiercely physical battle of the first two Tests had drained our forwards both physically and emotionally. I had to pick two new props and I was happy to keep Matthew Rees at hooker as he had only played one and a bit Tests. Paul O'Connell stayed to captain and it was obvious to stick with Simon Shaw who had only played one Test and he did that brilliantly. I decided I wanted fresh legs in the back row and though Tom Croft and David Wallace had performed admirably I opted to put them both on the bench and instead chose Martyn Williams and Joe Worsley to start.'

■ BELOW **New Lions centre pairing Tommy Bowe and Riki Flutey put debutant Springbok full back Zane Kirchner under pressure during the third Test.**

How intense were your preparations for the third Test?

■ *'Surprisingly they were remarkably relaxed. I gave the players the whole of Sunday, Monday and Tuesday off. The squad went off to a game park for two days and on Sunday night they had a barbecue and some beer. We reconvened on the Wednesday. In the morning we only spent 45 minutes on a unit skills session and then had a team run-out for 50 minutes in the afternoon. They were both short but hugely intensive sessions. Like all our sessions throughout the tour we went for quality not quantity.*

'On Thursday we had just one 35-minute team session of great intensity and on Friday we did our final training session which lasted just 50 minutes but was of the very highest quality. It was after this session that I felt that we had a truly great chance of winning the third Test.'

How difficult was it to choose the two wingers for this Test?

■ *'Relatively easy. Shane Williams is a world-class player who relishes the big stage and his form had improved throughout the tour, to the extent that it was the right time to pick him. Ugo Monye was surprised when I told him that I had picked him for the Test and I told him he had my full permission to carry the ball under his right arm all match. He looked surprised as that had cost him two tries in the first Test when he was on the left wing. I pointed out that I had picked him on the right wing for this Test and he just smiled at me.'*

The first half could hardly have gone better so you must have been pleased to be leading 15-6?

■ *'It was very nearly a perfect 40 minutes. The only blips were Stephen Jones missing a conversion in front of the posts when the ball fell off the kicking tee, Simon Shaw getting a yellow card for a dangerous tackle and Rob Kearney missing touch with a penalty in injury time at the end of the half. South Africa counterattacked and were awarded a penalty which Morne Steyn kicked.*

'On the positive side the scrum was solid and gave us a good attacking base, the line out went well and we had a definite edge at the breakdown. Our backs were in superb form. The angles of running and ability to create space were much sharper than the Springboks' and we created two brilliant tries. Stephen Jones missed an early penalty but he did kick one after seven minutes and we deserved to be well up at half-time because we had played some outstanding rugby. Shane Williams scored both tries and completely justified his selection.'

Were there any moments of concern in the second half?

■ *'Only the first six minutes because we were down to 14 players with Simon Shaw in the sin-bin. I told the players that we didn't want any scrum against us and we still wanted to keep the ball in play as much as possible. The players reacted positively and once Simon came back on I felt that, barring injuries, we were always going to win. For that six minutes we played some absolutely superb tactical rugby.'*

What were the highlights for you in the second half?

■ *'It was mainly the fantastic accuracy and focus of our play which we maintained throughout the whole match. We put intense pressure on them and they cracked. They didn't match the speed and continuity of our play as we tried to keep the ball in play as much as was humanly possible. The interpassing between the backs and forwards was once again very special and some of the support play was breathtaking. We stretched the Springbok defence to the limit over and over again and eventually the gaps appeared and their cover defence disappeared.'*

All three tries were out of the very top drawer, weren't they?

■ *'They were all different but all very dramatic. The first was begun with a powerful run by Jamie Heaslip which breached the first line of defence, and Shane Williams burst through in support after reading the situation perfectly. The second was a great chip by Riki Flutey over their back line but short of their full back, and Flutey then produced the most magnificent flick pass to Shane Williams, who raced through to score by the posts.*

'In the second half Ugo Monye got the third with a brilliant interception as South Africa launched a dangerous attack with a two-man overlap. Ugo reacted very quickly and caught the ball with one hand before sprinting 70 metres to score.'

If the attacking play was so razor-sharp, you and Shaun Edwards must also have been delighted with the defensive effort.

■ *'Our defensive organisation and unbelievable commitment was as good as any I can remember at international level. I can't recall missing a single first-up tackle in the match and so many of the hits were massive. We didn't concede a line break in 80 minutes, and only once in the whole game did we look like having*

a try scored against us, and on that occasion a fantastic crashing tackle from Tommy Bowe smashed Ndungane into the corner flag and his right boot hit the touch line. The only Springbok points came from three penalties.'

Last week with defeat in the second Test you had one of your most disappointing days ever as a rugby coach. Do you consider the huge win in the third Test was one of your best days?

■ *'Definitely. I was so proud of the team for making the supreme effort to win that Test, and at the same time play some of the most exciting, adventurous and superbly skilful rugby I have ever seen from a Lions team.*

'All 15 played out of their skins and it was a truly unforgettable effort. The skill level was astonishing. It would be wrong if I didn't single out a handful of players. First and foremost has to be Phil Vickery. He suffered in the first Test – he was heroic in the third Test. I was so pleased for him. And for Martyn Williams, who made a huge contribution to the cause in his first start for the Lions in a Test. The same applies to Joe Worsley and to both centres, Tommy Bowe and Riki Flutey.

■ ABOVE **Open-side Martyn Williams, in his first Lions Test start, ships the ball out, under pressure from Heinrich Brussow.**

'Of course this match was not about a few individuals. It was about a truly great team performance and perhaps even more than that. It was a great performance by a squad of 36 players from four countries who, in the space of six weeks, became a team capable of beating the world champions in their own backyard at Ellis Park in Johannesburg at 6000 feet above sea level. I salute the 2009 party for restoring the image of the Lions and rounding off a magnificent three-Test series with one of the greatest performances by any Lions side in the 35 years that I have been associated with the Lions.

'On that Saturday night I felt full of pride and satisfaction for our pride of Lions. If that game is to be my last for the Lions I could not be going out on a better note. When the next coach takes the Lions to Australia in 2013, he will have the satisfaction of knowing that he will arrive on the back of a win in the last Test of the 2009 series.'

Peter de Villiers in conversation with Alastair Eykyn

What did you think of the Lions performance today?

■ *'I think they moved the ball about very well with the backs and forwards interpassing and they made very few mistakes throughout the match. I give them credit for playing very good rugby and also for outstanding tackling in defence.'*

Where does this series victory rank for you? You weren't part of the World Cup-winning coaching team so for you this must be the biggest prize of your coaching career.

■ *'It was a very big prize for me. I was very proud of our performance. The whole country can rejoice in our series win and the whole country can be proud of our team and we can celebrate for the next 12 years to the next Lions tour to South Africa, unlike the previous 12 years back to 1997, when the Lions won the Test series against us.'*

Do you feel the achievement of winning the Lions series is just as good as winning the World Cup?

■ *'It was great for me to win this Lions series, just as it was great for South Africa to win the World Cup two years ago. A Lions series is right up there just like the World Cup, every four years, but it is also great to win big matches in the Tri-Nations. For example winning a Test against the Lions is very special but it was also very special to beat New Zealand in Dunedin in the Tri-Nations and also winning any Tri-Nations match in South Africa.'*

How good do you think this Lions team was?

■ *'This was a very good Lions team who played well right through the tour and played very well in all three Test matches. They were well prepared and well organised and were a difficult team to beat, and I was very pleased that South Africa won the first two Tests even though both results were very close. Once we had won the series it was more difficult to motivate our team for the third Test – it was more difficult to psychologically build them up for the challenge of this Test match when we had already won the series.'*

Do you have any regrets about what you said last weekend following the Schalk Burger eye-gouging incident? You said

this is rugby, this is what it's all about and you defended Schalk Burger's actions.

■ *'I have no regrets. I repeat what I said before that I know Burger really well, I know everything about him and I know he would not commit deliberate acts of foul play. I do not agree that it was a deliberate act of eye-gouging but he received a ban and that's that.'*

How would you describe relations between South Africa and the Lions?

■ *'The relations between the two sides were very good. After the third Test, I went to the Lions dressing room to* *congratulate Ian McGeechan on winning the third Test. They were the better side on the day and they played the better rugby. They scored three tries and they deserved to win.*

'I congratulated Ian McGeechan on his victory in the third Test, which is all part of the sportsmanship which you get in rugby. There is no doubt it was a great three-Test series.'

■ BELOW The South African squad and management celebrate a Lions series victory after the third Test.
■ PAGE 149 Peter de Villiers and Ian McGeechan shake at the end of a monumental contest between the Lions and Springboks.

HSBC Rugby Festivals are uniting over 60,000 children across England, Ireland, Scotland, Wales and South Africa. If you'd like to know more on how HSBC is helping the Lions of the future to become even greater together, visit www.lionsrugby.com/hsbc

EVEN GREATER TOGETHER

HSBC

PRINCIPAL PARTNER

Investing in youth rugby for the future of the Lions.

Saturday 30 May Royal Bafokeng Sports Palace, Phokeng

Royal XV 25 British & Irish Lions 37
(HALF TIME 18-10)

■ **Royal XV:** R Jeacocks; E Seconds, D van Rensburg, H Coetzee, B Basson; N Olivier, S Pretorius; A Buckle, R Barnes, B Roux; R Mathee, J Lombaard; W Koch (c), D Raubenheimer, J Mokuena
REPLACEMENTS: P van der Westhuizen for Barnes 69, S Roberts for Buckle 60, R Landman for Lombaard 56, R Kember for Raubenheimer 71, J Coetzee for Pretorius 68, R Viljoen for Olivier 58, J Bowles
SCORERS: Tries – Koch, Barnes, Roux; Conversions – Olivier, Viljoen; Penalties – Olivier (2)

■ **British & Irish Lions:** L Byrne; T Bowe, K Earls, J Roberts, S Williams; R O'Gara, M Blair; A Sheridan, M Rees, AR Jones; S Shaw, P O'Connell (c); J Worsley, M Williams, D Wallace
REPLACEMENTS: L Mears for Rees 69, P Vickery for AR Jones 66, A-W Jones for Shaw 66, J Heaslip for Wallace 66, M Phillips for Blair 66, S Jones, R Flutey for Earls 69
SCORERS: Tries – Bowe, Byrne, A-W Jones, O'Gara; Conversions – O'Gara (4); Penalties – O'Gara (3)

REFEREE Marius Jonker (South Africa)
ATTENDANCE 12,352

Wednesday 3 June Ellis Park, Johannesburg

Golden Lions 10 British & Irish Lions 74
(HALF TIME 10-39)

■ **Golden Lions:** L Ludik; M Killian, J Boshoff, D la Grange, D Noble; A Pretorius, J Vermaak; L Sephaka, W Wepener, G Muller; B Mockford, W Stoltz; C Grobbelaar (c), F van der Merwe, W Alberts
REPLACEMENTS: E Reynecke for Wepener 57, J van Rensburg for Sephaka 50, E Joubert for Stoltz 4-11 (blood), 57, T Clever for Mockford 40, C Jonck for Vermaak 66, W Venter for Boshoff 50, S Frolick for Ludik 6
SCORERS: Try – Frolick; Conversion – Pretorius; Penalty – Pretorius

■ **British & Irish Lions:** R Kearney; T Bowe, B O'Driscoll (c), J Roberts, U Monye; S Jones, M Phillips; G Jenkins, L Mears, P Vickery; N Hines, A-W Jones; T Croft, D Wallace, J Heaslip
REPLACEMENTS: R Ford for Mears 66, E Murray for Vickery 66, S Ferris for Wallace 49, A Powell for Croft 66, H Ellis for S Jones 62, J Hook for Roberts 53, S Williams for O'Driscoll 61
SCORERS: Tries – Roberts (2), O'Driscoll, Monye (2), Croft, Bowe (2), Hook, Ferris; Conversions – S Jones (6), Hook (3); Penalties – S Jones (2)

REFEREE Craig Joubert (South Africa)
ATTENDANCE 22,218

Saturday 6 June Free State Stadium, Bloemfontein

Cheetahs 24 British & Irish Lions 26
(HALF TIME 14-23)

■ **Cheetahs:** H Daniller; JW Jonker, C Uys, M Bosman, D Demas; J-L Potgieter, T de Bruyn; W du Preez, A Strauss, K Calldo; N Breedt, D de Villiers; H Brussow, F Uys, H Scholtz (c)
REPLACEMENTS: R Strauss for A Strauss 50, WP Nel for Calldo 46, F Viljoen for Breedt 46, K Floors for Scholtz 64, G Odendaal for de Bruyn 44, L Strydom for Potgieter 60, F Juries
SCORERS: Tries – Demas, du Preez, C Uys; Conversions – Potgieter (2), Strydom; Penalty – Potgieter

■ **British & Irish Lions:** L Byrne; L Halfpenny, K Earls, L Fitzgerald, S Williams; J Hook, H Ellis; A Sheridan, R Ford, E Murray; D O'Callaghan, P O'Connell (c); S Ferris, J Worsley, A Powell
REPLACEMENTS: M Rees for Ford 62, AR Jones for Murray 62, S Shaw, N Hines for Worsley 67, M Blair, R O'Gara, G D'Arcy for Fitzgerald 75
SCORERS: Tries – Ferris, Earls; Conversions – Hook (2); Penalties – Hook (4)

YELLOW CARD Ferris (Lions) 22
REFEREE Wayne Barnes (England)
ATTENDANCE 23,710

Wednesday 10 June Kings Park Stadium, Durban

Sharks 3 British & Irish Lions 39
(HALF TIME 3-7)

■ **Sharks:** S Terblanche; C Jordaan, A Strauss, R Swanepoel, L Vulindlu; M Dumond, R Kockott; D Carstens, S Badenhorst, J du Plessis; S Sykes, J Muller (c); J Botes, J Deysel, K Daniel
REPLACEMENTS: C Burden for Badenhorst 26-35 (blood), 53, P Cilliers for Carstens 55, A van den Berg for Sykes 56, M Rhodes for Botes 70, C McLeod for Kockott 70, G Cronje for Jordaan 62, L Mvovo for Swanepoel 17, (Carstens for du Plessis 77)
SCORERS: Penalty – Kockott

■ **British & Irish Lions:** L Byrne; S Williams, B O'Driscoll, J Roberts, L Fitzgerald; R O'Gara, M Phillips; G Jenkins, L Mears, AR Jones; A-W Jones, P O'Connell (c); T Croft, D Wallace, J Heaslip
REPLACEMENTS: M Rees for Mears 69, P Vickery for AR Jones 69, S Shaw for O'Connell 64, J Worsley, M Blair for Phillips 71, J Hook for O'Gara 78, R Flutey for Roberts 64
SCORERS: Tries – Mears, Phillips, Fitzgerald, Byrne, Heaslip; Conversions – O'Gara (3), Hook; Penalties – O'Gara (2)

YELLOW CARDS Vickery (Lions) 76, Daniel (Sharks) 78
REFEREE Jonathan Kaplan (South Africa)
ATTENDANCE 21,530

Saturday 13 June Newlands Stadium, Cape Town

Western Province 23 British & Irish Lions 26
(HALF TIME 12-18)

■ **Western Province:** J Pietersen; T Chavhanga, M Newman, P Grant, G Bobo; W de Waal, D Duvenage; W Blaauw, T Liebenberg, B Harris; M Muller, A van Zyl; P Louw, D Vermeulen, L Watson (c)
REPLACEMENTS: H Shimange, JD Moller for Blaauw 75, DK Steenkamp for Muller 66, Z Jordaan for Louw 73, C Hoffmann, JJ Engelbrecht, G Aplon for Chavhanga 37
SCORERS: Try – Pietersen; Penalties – de Waal (4); Dropped goals – de Waal, Pietersen

■ **British & Irish Lions:** R Kearney; T Bowe, K Earls, R Flutey, U Monye; S Jones, H Ellis; A Sheridan, M Rees, P Vickery (c); D O'Callaghan, N Hines; J Worsley, M Williams, A Powell
REPLACEMENTS: R Ford for Rees 56, E Murray for Vickery 60, S Shaw for Hines 56, T Croft for Worsley 69, S Williams, J Hook for Kearney 66, G D'Arcy
SCORERS: Tries – Bowe, Monye, M Williams; Conversion – Jones; Penalties – Jones (2), Hook

REFEREE Mark Lawrence (South Africa)
ATTENDANCE 34,176

Tuesday 16 June Nelson Mandela Bay Stadium, Port Elizabeth

Southern Kings 8 British & Irish Lions 20
(HALF TIME 3-3)

■ **Southern Kings:** T Mangweni; W Human, F Welsh, DW Barry, M Turner; J van der Westhuyzen, F Hougaard; J Engels, D Kuun (c), R Vermeulen; R Skeate, M Wentzel; S Tyibilika, M Mbiyozo, D Nell
REPLACEMENTS: D du Preez for Engels 42-51 (blood), D Greyling for Vermeulen 10, L Payi, D van Schalkwyk for Tyibilika 64, J Fowles for Hougaard 42, B Fortuin for Welsh 8-14 (blood), M Stick for Human 55
SCORERS: Try – Mbiyozo; Penalty – van der Westhuyzen

■ **British & Irish Lions:** K Earls; U Monye, R Flutey, G D'Arcy, L Fitzgerald; J Hook, M Blair; A Sheridan, R Ford, E Murray; S Shaw, D O'Callaghan (c); N Hines, J Worsley, A Powell
REPLACEMENTS: M Rees for Ford 64, AR Jones for Murray 7, T Croft, D Wallace, H Ellis, R O'Gara for Hook 12, S Williams for Monye 64
SCORERS: Tries – Monye, penalty try; Conversions – O'Gara (2); Penalties – O'Gara (2)

YELLOW CARDS van der Westhuyzen (Southern Kings) 18, Skeate (Southern Kings) 63
REFEREE Nigel Owens (Wales)
ATTENDANCE 35,883

■ Tour summary ■

Appearances

Name	All matches	Tests	Name	All matches	Tests
Mike Blair	2+1		Lee Mears	3+2	1
Tommy Bowe	6	3	Ugo Monye	5+1	2
Lee Byrne	4		Euan Murray	2+2	
Tom Croft	4+2	2+1	Donncha O'Callaghan	4+1	0+1
Gordon D'Arcy	2+1		Paul O'Connell	6	3
Keith Earls	5		Brian O'Driscoll	4	2
Harry Ellis	3+2	0+1	Ronan O'Gara	3+2	0+1
Stephen Ferris	1+1		Tim Payne	1	
Luke Fitzgerald	5	1	Mike Phillips	5+1	3
Riki Flutey	4+2	1	Andy Powell	4+1	
Ross Ford	3+3	0+1	Matthew Rees	4+4	2+1
Leigh Halfpenny	1		Jamie Roberts	5	2
John Hayes	1+1	0+1	Simon Shaw	4+3	2
Jamie Heaslip	5+1	3	Andrew Sheridan	5+1	1+1
Nathan Hines	4+1		Phil Vickery	4+3	2
James Hook	2+4		David Wallace	5+2	2+1
Gethin Jenkins	4	2	Martyn Williams	4+2	1+1
Adam Jones	3+3	1+1	Shane Williams	5+3	1+1
Alun-Wyn Jones	3+3	1+2	Joe Worsley	6	1
Stephen Jones	5	3			
Rob Kearney	4+1	3			

(STARTS + REPLACEMENT APPEARANCES)

Tries

5 U Monye

4 T Bowe

3 T Croft

2 L Byrne, K Earls, S Ferris, M Phillips, J Roberts, S Williams

1 L Fitzgerald, J Heaslip, J Hook, A-W Jones, R Kearney, L Mears, B O'Driscoll, R O'Gara, M Williams

Kickers

	Pen	Con	DG	Pts
S Jones	12	13	1	65
R O'Gara	8	10		44
J Hook	6	6		30

■ FACING PAGE Stephen Jones successfully converts another penalty and Ugo Monye (below) celebrates his fifth try of the tour at Ellis Park.